The Sexual Abuse of Children: Clinical Issues
Volume 2

The Sexual Abuse of Children: Clinical Issues
Volume 2

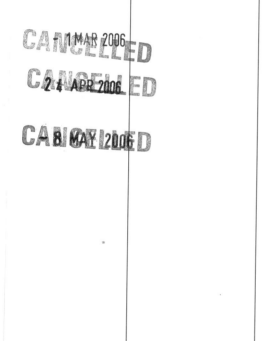
LAWRENCE ERLBAUM ASSOCIATES, PUBLISHERS

1992   Hillsdale, New Jersey   Hove and London

Lawrence Erlbaum Associates, Inc., Publishers
365 Broadway
Hillsdale, New Jersey 07642

Library of Congress Cataloging-in-Publication Data
The Sexual abuse of children : clinical issues / edited by William
O'Donohue, James H. Geer.
     p.   cm.
   Companion v. to: The Sexual abuse of children : theory and research /
edited by William O'Donohue, James H. Geer. 1991.
   Includes bibliographical references and index.
   ISBN 0-8058-0954-6 (cloth). — ISBN 0-8058-0955-4 (paper)
   1. Child molesting.   2. Sexually abused children.   I. O'Donohue,
William   II. Geer, James.   III. Sexual abuse children, clinical
issues.
   [DNLM: 1. Child Abuse, Sexual.   WA 320 S5175]
RJ506.C48S49 1991
616.85'83 — dc20
DNLM/DLC
for Library of Congress   91-16127
                                                     CIP

Printed in the United States of America
10   9   8   7   6   5   4   3   2

Contents

Preface

In the last few decades, there has been a dramatic increase in public attention and professional activity in the area of child sexual abuse. It is difficult to tell whether this heightened awareness has been caused by an increased incidence of abuse, by an increased sensitivity to the plight of these children, or by a combination of these and other factors. However, what is clear is that children are victimized and suffer, and that various professionals have been engaged in attempts to alleviate and prevent the myriad of problems associated with child sexual abuse. These two volumes were conceived as an attempt to aid these efforts by providing a scholarly, multidisciplinary compendium of the major issues involved in child sexual abuse.

Child sexual abuse is a complex problem that gives rise to other complex problems. This, to a large degree, explains the length of these two volumes. What is child sexual abuse? What is its moral status? What is its history? What happens in other cultures? What is its epidemiology? What causes it? What therapy is effective for the children and for the offenders? These are just some of the major questions addressed in these volumes. We believe that the efforts of the professional in this area will be aided by a thorough knowledge of the questions particular to his or her own field, and also by a comprehensive knowledge of other fields. For example, legal professionals must know the nature and effectiveness of current therapies in order to properly sentence, defend, or legislate; and conversely, therapists need to know relevant law and legal procedures in order to competently advise and prepare their clients (particularly children) for the psychological aspects of legal proceedings.

We asked the chapter contributors to both provide a basic introduction to their topic and a scholarly, rigorous treatment of its current status. We have asked them to be critical of past work, not to give rise to pessimism, but rather so that future work can be better informed and have more of an impact on the reduction of suffering associated with this problem. Unfortunately, knowledge in many areas is still in its infancy and many barriers exist to the growth of knowledge.

We are indebted to many individuals. We of course owe a great deal of gratitude to the chapter authors for their efforts and patience. Without all of their countless hours of hard work, this project would not have been possible. We also would like to thank Professors David Finkelhor and Noretta Koertge for their helpful suggestions regarding possible contributors at the outset of this project. We would also like to thank our editor at Lawrence Erlbaum, Judith Amsel, for her professional attention and patience with this project. We are also indebted to Marian Perry, Kathleen McAuliffe, and Shelley Ketchum for their help with diverse aspects of the manuscript.

Finally, we have a deep sense of gratitude to our families, Jane, Katherine, Jean, John, and David for their support and patience.

William O'Donohue, Ph.D.
James Geer, Ph.D.

I

DIAGNOSIS AND ASSESSMENT

Agency and Professional Roles and Responsibilities: The Need for Cooperation

Sue Righthand
Maine State Forensic Service
Sandra Hodge
Child Protective Services, Maine Department of Human Services

The passage of the federal Child Abuse and Neglect Prevention and Treatment Act (Child Abuse, 1974) provided monetary incentives to states for the development or expansion of statutes requiring a broad range of professionals to report suspected incidences of child abuse and neglect. The act also authorized the use of federal funds for technical assistance in providing professional training and increasing public awareness about the nature and seriousness of child abuse and neglect in our country. As a result of these activities, a steady, and in some states, a dramatic increase in referrals of suspected abuse and neglect occurred. Many states were not prepared to respond adequately. Information from such national organizations as the American Humane Association's report by Suski (1987) and the National Committee for the Prevention of Child Abuse and Neglect (1987), as well as individual state reports from New Jersey, Pennsylvania, and Virginia (Commonwealth of Pennsylvania, 1987; Commonwealth of Virginia, 1987; New Jersey, 1987), revealed that in less than 5 years the number of child sexual abuse cases reported to state agencies designated to receive reports of child abuse and neglect increased from 100% to 600% across states.

In spite of the fact that victims, perpetrators, and other family members frequently have found themselves involved with two or more agencies, protocols for interagency cooperation on these complex cases were inadequate or nonexistent. Many localities, regions, and states can point to cases that were handled poorly, leaving victims unprotected, and recidivistic offenders on the street. Failure in some of these cases, as some have pointed out (e.g., Cramer, 1987; Toth & Whalen, 1987), was due to lack of communication, poor coordination, and unclear roles and responsibilities. Sadly, it often took painful failures that resulted in repeated victimizations before the need for an intra-agency, multidisciplinary response to reports of child sexual abuse was recognized. This recognition has led to changes in how professionals work together. New and innovative programs designed to protect victims, assure appropriate intervention, and provide treatment resources to victims, offenders, and other family members are developing.

While most of these approaches and programs are relatively new (see Cramer, 1987; Toth & Whalen, 1987), there does appear to be a consensus developing among professional groups and agencies that address aspects of the problem of child sexual abuse that an intra-agency, multidisciplinary approach is the most effective way to intervene in these situations. Effective is defined here as an approach that: (1) provides the best possible protection and emotional support for the victim; (2) establishes the most protection possible for the community; (3) makes available a specialized continuum of treatment services; (4) results in successful prosecutions that minimize retraumatizing the victim; and (5) provides aftercare programs for offenders that have victim and community safety as priorities.

Unfortunately, as mentioned, "effective" programs are only just developing and are few in number. It is hoped that through increased agency cooperation, the 1990s will see a more effective response to child sex abuse—one that includes preventive as well as reactive measures.

Disclosures of sexual abuse made by children can be purposeful or accidental. Purposeful disclosures usually include the message, stated or unstated, that the victim wants the abusive behavior to stop and wants help in making this happen. Accidental and inadvertent disclosures come about when: (1) Children describe an interaction with an adult that is clearly sexually abusive, but the child doesn't view it as such, due to age or conditioning; and (2) Children who are experiencing intense emotions, such as anger or fear, disclose sexual activity between themselves and adults.

School personnel receive a large number of child sexual abuse disclosures yearly, as noted in the national reports published by the American Humane Association (1988). Educational professionals and school systems have struggled to develop appropriate responses to these disclosures that will protect the child, fulfill their mandatory reporting requirements, and minimize disruption in the school routine. In spite of data indicating that relatively few children falsely report sex abuse experiences (Jones, 1987), some teachers and school systems still tend to doubt children's reports of sexual abuse. Sometimes parents, including the alleged perpetrator, are notified as soon as a disclosure is made. This practice can put the child's safety in jeopardy.

Immediate and extended family members receive many disclosures of sexual abuse. In most states, they are not mandated to report, though many do. Mothers of victims' best friends receive a significant percentage of disclosures. As Herman and Herchman (1977) observed, the reason that many victims of intrafamilial sex abuse disclosed the incidents to people outside their family may be because the nonabusing spouse, most typically the mother, is often perceived as not available or emotionally accessible to the victim.

An increasing number of disclosures occur when child protective services workers are intervening in cases in which sexual abuse is not the presenting problem. It is the authors' experience that most mental health professionals who work with children now ask about sexual abuse no matter what the presenting problem was. The increased rate of disclosures reported to these and other professionals highlights the importance of asking clients about sexual abuse.

Infrequently, disclosures are made by perpetrators. For example, Abel et al. (1987) reported that out of 521 offenders in a clinical sample, 5.2% were self-referred. Offenders may not disclose their abusive behavior initially, but may present for mental health treatment with a variety of problems and concerns.

In all 50 states and the District of Columbia, a broad range of professionals (e.g., physicians, mental health professionals, school personnel, social workers, day-care providers, nurses), serving children and their families are required to report suspected abuse and neglect to the state-mandated child protective services agency (some states, e.g. California, also require reporting to law enforcement). Specifics of these reporting laws often vary from state to state. For example, in Maryland and California, mandated reporters are only those professionals who learn of suspected abuse of children through their work with children. In these states, professionals who suspect abuse from their work with adults who may be perpetrators would be violating client/therapist confidentiality and thus violating the law and professional ethics if they were to report their suspicions. The importance of knowing the laws in one's state is obvious. In spite of the nationwide legal requirement to report suspected abuse and neglect, a recent study by the National Center on Child Abuse and Neglect (1988) showed that many incidents that come to the attention of mandated reporters may go unreported. There are complex reasons why professionals may fail to report.

First of all, in spite of national statistics cited in the National Study of the Incidence and Severity of Child Abuse and Neglect (U. S. Department of Health and Human Services, 1988) indicating that as many as one out of three girls and one out of seven boys have been sexually abused, widespread acceptance of the pervasiveness of child sexual abuse does not exist, even among professionals required to report. This disbelief of sex abuse allegations has appeared to the authors even more prevalent when disclosures occur in a middle-class or upper-class family or involve a prominent community member. Other reasons for not reporting include (1) the professional's belief that he or she can handle the problem alone; (2) a promise to disclosing victims that this information will not be shared; and (3) prior negative experiences with reporting that left the clinician feeling the situation was not dealt with in a way that was helpful to the child or the family, and/or was not what the reporter wanted to happen.

Controversy regarding mandatory reporting laws continues to exist among mental health practitioners. Some clinicians maintain that exceptions to confidentiality in psychotherapy situations compromise the therapeutic relationship and its effectiveness. Others hold that without the therapist's ability to communicate with the criminal justice and child protective systems, as well as with the victim's therapist and family members, they cannot be effective in helping the offenders stop their victimizing behavior. The disclosure serves to break the secrecy that allowed the abuse to occur. If the offender and his or her family are well motivated to end the abuse, and if there is good interagency communication and cooperation, the reporting of the disclosure may serve not only to protect current or imminent victims, but may facilitate the therapeutic process.

Failure to report child sexual abuse to child protective services agencies, or law enforcement leaves a child unprotected and makes it unlikely the victims and their families will receive the services that they need to ameliorate the causes of the abuse. Mandated reporters who fail to report are also breaking the law and may be subjected to a variety of civil penalties, including fines. In some states (e.g., Maine), licensed professionals may also be subjected to licensing actions including conditional licenses and license revocations. According to Canfield and Horowitz (1987), failure to report can leave professionals liable for damages on behalf of a child in an action brought by a noncustodial parent or other guardian of a child injured or killed subsequent to failure to report.

The list of individuals and/or agencies that may intervene in child sexual abuse cases may include: (1) law enforcement (police); (2) child protective services (caseworkers, attorneys representing the mandated agency); (3) prosecutors, district attorneys, state's attorneys, county prosecutors); (4) defense attorneys; (5) court system (civil and criminal courts); (6) victim witness advocates; (7) guardians ad litem (including court-appointed special advocates); (8) mental health professionals or agencies; (9) physicians; (10) correctional agencies (e.g., correctional officers, treatment providers, and probation officers); (11) community service providers (e.g., day-care centers and day-care homes, homemaker services, self-help groups, shelters for battered women and children).

With such disparate disciplines, the barriers to establishing a team or cooperative approach are many. One barrier is that for many years the sexual abuse of children, although a crime in all states, was viewed as a family problem to be dealt with in the home. Sex abuse was often viewed as one of many symptoms of a family's dysfunction system and amenable to traditional treatment. At the same time, the law enforcement system was considered punitive and lacking in sensitivity to the victim and family. According to Berliner (1987), outdated views such as these have diminished.

Other barriers include: (1) Lack of a shared knowledge base about child sexual abuse indicators, dynamics, intervention, and treatment; (2) Lack of specialized training and experience concerning sex abuse as it relates to one's own discipline (e.g., knowledge of medical indicators, behavioral symptoms), (3) Professional chauvinism; and (4) Reluctance to change familiar relationships and responsibilities. The American Bar Association's (1987) publication reflecting the discussion at the policy conference on legal reforms noted that many of these barriers can be overcome when people work together for the benefit of victims and the community. These benefits include: (1) Decrease in the number of interviews of child victims, which can lessen the trauma of the intervention; (2) More appropriate and effective prosecutions resulting from more skilled interventions; (3) Less duplication of effort and more assured follow-up on each case; and (4) Fewer retractions by victims as a result of the strength of the support for the victim after disclosure.

In most states, child protective services and law enforcement agencies are responsible for the initial response to allegations of child sexual abuse investigation. The parameters of those responsibilities and how those responsibilities are carried out, vary greatly from state to state and locality to locality.

In policy and practice, decision-making authority in child protective services agencies can rest with a state office or a county office. It is important for professionals working with sexual abuse victims and their families to know where that authority lies when undertaking the development of a cooperative, multidisciplinary approach to sexual abuse. The resources that a child protective services agency has to intervene in sexual abuse cases will vary from county to county, depending on individual county budgets. States with a state-run system usually make attempts to equalize their internal resources.

The protective service investigative process involves gathering, synthesizing, and analyzing facts that help caseworkers reach decisions about the following issues: (1) did the abuse occur; (2) is the child safe; (3) what level of intervention is necessary to assure the child's safety; (4) what are the factors in a child and family's environment that contributed to the abuse; and (5) what are the strengths and weaknesses in the family that impact on the family's ability to ameliorate factors contributing to the abuse.

Protective service agencies in some states are only involved in cases of intrafamilial sex abuse (e.g., Oklahoma, Oregon, Vermont, Connecticut, and others). In cases of out-of-home perpetrators, law enforcement would have the primary investigatory responsibility. As most state laws include in their definition of child sexual abuse that the abuse is perpetrated by someone responsible for the child, many states interpret those statutes to limit the authority of protective services to intervene only in family sex abuse cases. The disadvantage to this approach in many states (e.g., Maine, New Hampshire) is that this effectively prohibits the victim abused outside of the home and his or her family from obtaining necessary support services.

The fact-gathering process employed by child protective services involves: (1) interviewing all relevant parties, such as victim(s), siblings, parents, relatives, involved professionals; (2) observations of family interactions; (3) review of past records; and (4) review of current reports, psychological evaluations, and medical records. After gathering this information, it must be analyzed and dispositional decisions must be made. If an allegation of sexual abuse is not substantiated, the case will be closed for protective services and the family will be referred to appropriate community resources, such as mental health providers, if they seem to require such services. If a case is substantiated (in most states "substantiated" means that credible evidence exists that abuse occurred), a decision is made as to what will be done to assure the victim's safety. Most protective services agencies have policies and practice standards that require at least a temporary separation of the victim and the offender. This is done to minimize possible coercion of the victim by the offender following a disclosure and to give the victim a sense of safety. Removing the offender from the home voluntarily, or by a court order if necessary, is preferred to taking the child victim out of his or her home. If the nonoffending parent is not supportive of the victim, and is primarily concerned with the well-being of the offender, the child protective service agency may seek to place the child outside the home. This is avoided wherever possible because it tends to confirm the victim's worst fears about disclosing (e.g., that he or she has done something wrong and is bad), and as such, has the result of punishing the victim for the behavior of the offender. Whether the child or the offender leaves the home, services are provided to all family members.

It is important that child protective services professionals conduct their interviews in a manner that is consistent with the standards of admissible evidence in court proceedings. As Jan Hindman (1987) noted, it is not always possible for caseworkers to be able to evaluate a young child's safety and abide by the standards. For example, mildly leading questions may have to be used to begin an interview with a young child. However, the standards must be kept in mind because court proceedings may be necessary for assuring the child's safety over time.

If the child protective services agency is unable to assure the safety of a child by providing in-home services and supervision, a Child Protection Order may be sought. The resulting court proceeding at which the agency, the parents, and the child are represented, can have several different results. The court can find that the protective service agency has not proved that a child is in circumstances of jeopardy (or whatever standard a particular state uses), and that the case would then be dismissed. If the court does find that the protective service agency has shown that a child is in jeopardy and in need of protection, a variety of court orders can be issued. Most states' statutes specify what dispositions are available to the judge in these situations. Commonly, these dispositions include a variety of court-ordered evaluations and services.

Most of the state laws that mandate public agencies to receive and investigate reports of sexual abuse also mandate that services to abused children and their families be provided. Conforming with the seemingly conflicting roles of an investigator and helper is one reason that child protective services are often seen as being child-centered and family focused. The authority of the state is considered necessary to protect children from the more powerful adults who have harmed them, but the state also has an interest in enabling parents to care for and protect their children. The dual role of the child protective services caseworker has resulted in a modification of traditional social work practice so that casework is more directive and authoritative, such as by using the authority of the court, and is also used to modify abusive behaviors and environments.

The two major national child welfare organizations, the Child Welfare League of America (in press) and the National Association of Public Welfare Administrators (1988), issued new standards for the investigation and provision of services in child abuse and neglect cases. These standards reflect considerable changes in how child protective services are provided. Both groups reaffirmed the effectiveness and appropriateness of this dual role of child protective services. Moreover, the impact of the volume and complexity of child sexual abuse cases was addressed. The standards cited the need for specialized training; increased cooperative working relationships with law enforcement; the need to develop and fund a continuum of specialized services for victims and their families; and the importance of using the considerable experience and expertise of child protective services' caseworkers in building a comprehensive response to management of child sex abuse cases. Both the Child Welfare League of America and the National Association of Public Welfare Administrators emphasize the leadership role that mandated child protective services agencies should play in program development efforts. In many states (e.g., Maine, Virginia, South Carolina), it was a protective service agency that acted as a catalyst for significant changes in the state response to sexual abuse.

Law enforcement investigation of child sexual abuse allegations assists in providing the basis for (1) assessing the believability of a child's sexual abuse; (2) determining whether evidence exists that corroborates the allegation; (3) evaluating whether evidence justifies the filing of criminal charges; and (4) whether the evidence can justify conviction in court. It is generally recognized that child sexual abuse cases require specialized skills on the part of investigating officers and accommodations to the unique status of child crime victims. Unlike most other criminal investigations, child sexual abuse cases involve considerable time and collaboration with other agencies, especially child protective services. Unfortunately, many localities do not have the resources to allow investigators to specialize. Criminal investigations vary considerably from state to state and locality to locality. In some states, all investigations are carried out by special units of the state police while in others investigations are carried out by the county sheriff's offices. In most states, there exist a patchwork of responsible law enforcement agencies that encompasses state and municipal police, and sheriff's departments. Which agency investigates the allegation depends on the geographical area of the state in which the alleged child sexual abuse crime occurs. Some states (e.g., Maine, Massachusetts), in an attempt to bring order to what is often multijurisdictional chaos, assigned overall investigative responsibility to District or State's Attorney's Offices. This allows this official to ensure that a sound investigative process is followed by the most competent officers in the area, regardless of traditionally defined jurisdiction.

In the last several years, specialized handbooks, curricula, and audiovisual training materials have been developed to train law enforcement personnel in investigating child sex abuse cases. The American Prosecutors Research Institute National Center for the Prosecution of Child Abuse published a comprehensive manual edited by Toth and Whalen (1987) and entitled *Investigation and Prosecution Child Abuse*. This manual details state-of-the-art methods of investigation as well as provides supporting theoretical information necessary for effectively carrying out investigative processes. Some of the areas covered are the dynamics and effects of abuse, developmental considerations when interviewing children of certain ages, and common reactions of offenders to disclosure. In addition, the National Sheriff's Association (Laszlo & Romano, 1988) and the National Center for Missing and Exploited Children (Spaulding, 1987) have also developed specialized material for law enforcement personnel, including specialized materials on out-of-home abuse investigations and sexual exploitation and child pornography investigation. This new literature, combined with the increased volume and complexity of child sexual abuse cases dealt with by law enforcement, has resulted in changes in the traditional methods of conducting these criminal investigations and has also placed severe strain on police agencies' capacities to respond adequately and appropriately to child sexual abuse cases. These cases are time consuming, complex, and as previously stated, require an unusual amount of coordination with other agencies. Experience indicates that staffing difficulties are often reported.

Prosecutors are the decision makers regarding whether prosecution occurs as a result of law enforcement child sexual abuse investigations. This decision will depend on state statutes, individual jurisdictional procedures, and the information provided by law enforcement. Furthermore, a prosecutor may decide not to prosecute a case due to inadequate evidence, insufficient admissible evidence, or because the age and/or condition of the victim witness makes the child a poor witness. Victims and families, as well as other professionals involved in a case, need to be informed of the reasons for not prosecuting cases so that the well-being of the child can be assured.

As can be seen from the descriptions of the roles of child protective services and law enforcement in the investigation of child sexual abuse, there are several commonalities. Both systems were confronted in the late 1970s and early 1980s with a tremendous increase in the volume of cases; both fields found the respective traditional approaches to victim protection inadequate; both have statutory mandates to investigate, and there was a rapidly developing literature from both fields as well as from mental health, corrections, and medicine that made a re-examination of policies, practices, and their underlying knowledge base a necessity. These pressures made, at least, talking about collaboration inevitable. Child protective services found that many victims of child sexual abuse could not be protected without the involvement of the criminal justice system. Law enforcement found that without the assistance of child protective services (e.g., placement resources, interviewing expertise), their investigations were inadequate or not sufficiently complete for the pursuit of prosecution. Effective joint investigations depend on clear and mutually understood roles and responsibilities.

Both child protective services and law enforcement need to gather facts, but the purposes of the fact-gathering activity are different—the child's safety vs. criminal prosecution. Both investigations are necessary. Role clarification between these agencies can be enhanced by joint training activities, written working agreements, pre-investigation conferences, and case disbriefings. While joint investigations are becoming commonplace, barriers still exist. Examples of such impediments include: remnants of professional chauvinism, lack of sufficient staff, lack of adequately trained staff, unresolved turf and power issues, and in some states (e.g., Pennsylvania), statutory prohibitions to information sharing between child protective services and law enforcement.

Laws governing sex offenses have changed dramatically in recent years. For the preceding 50 years, sex offenders frequently were dealt with differently than other criminals under special statutes falling under such headings as sexual psychopath and mentally disordered sex offender laws. The 1960s saw the peak use of such statutes, which usually provided for specialized treatment centers for sex offenders. Enforcement of the statutes removed the offenders from the community and provided for treatment services. Indeterminate sentences were the rule, with release based on a medical finding that the offender was no longer a danger to others by virtue of cure or improvement. Weiner (1985) reported that although 16 states still had specialized sex offender laws, only 5 used them regularly (Massachusetts, Nebraska, New Jersey, Oregon, and Washington).

These specialized laws raised various legal issues. They were often challenged as being unconstitutionally vague and violating the constitutional guarantee for equal protection. Weiner (1985) noted that in order for sex offenders to be treated differently than other criminal offenders and not violate the equal protection clause, there must be a rationale for the different treatment. She reported that treatment became the rationale. Because of legal challenges such as these as well as difficulties in documenting the effectiveness of sex offender treatment, such as those reported by Furby, Weinrott and Blackshaw (1989), the use of specialized sex offender laws has declined.

In general, the present practice is that once law officers have presented their findings, a prosecutor may decide to file charges, in which case he or she would likely have considered, according to Toth and Whalen (1987): (1) the suspect's factual guilt, (2) the quality and quantity of the evidence, and (3) the likelihood of conviction. Prosecutors utilize information from law enforcement, child protective services, mental health professionals, the victim, and the victim's family to help make the decision. Decisions not to prosecute are derived in a similar manner.

The American legal system requires that the defense attorney provide his or her client with the best possible defense against the charges. Defense attorneys must act in the interest of their clients but, unfortunately, this role can be, and often is, at odds with what is best for the victim.

After a decision to prosecute has been made, a trial or a plea negotiation occurs. In a plea negotiation, the defendant pleads guilty or does not contest the charges in return for a less severe sentence than would probably occur if the defendant was found guilty in a trial. "Plea bargains," as they are often called, are arranged for a number of reasons. One reason is to avoid the lengthy delays that often occur between arrest and trials, because of crowded court dockets. Defense attorneys also may believe that the evidence against a particular client is so overwhelming that the client is likely to be found guilty at a trial. Consequently, the attorney and client may plea bargain for a less severe sentence. Another frequent reason given for the use of such negotiations is to save the victim from the trauma of trial, especially being required to confront the offender. However as Berliner and Barbieri (1984) state, based on their experience, some victims are benefited by going through the trial as it clearly assigns responsibility for the abusive behaviors to the offender. Furthermore, testifying may provide a sense of retribution and serve as a way for some victims to move on from their anger and rage to other stages of healing. A careful, individual assessment of a victim's feelings about participating in trial must be conducted by a competent, mental health professional.

Some jurisdictions (e.g., Vermont, Oregon, Washington), have diversion programs that allow certain offenders to avoid prosecution by entering specialized treatment programs or by following carefully prescribed conditions. Most programs have a mechanism to bring a case to court should an offender not participate in treatment or break other agreed-upon conditions. These programs may involve frequent monitoring of an offender by specialized probation officers. Appropriateness for a diversion program requires that information from law enforcement, child protective services, and mental health professionals who are especially trained in sex abuse issues be considered by the prosecutor. Most programs do not accept offenders with prior convictions for sexual offenses or who commit very violent crimes.

Victim witness advocates also work within the legal system. They are responsible for assisting the child victim and his or her family and help them experience the criminal justice system with the least possible trauma. This is done through: (1) establishing a supportive, trusting relationship, (2) providing information about the working of the criminal justice system, especially the court process, (3) preparing the victim and other witnesses for court, (4) preparing the victim impact statements, and (5) linking the victim and his or her family with community resources. Advocates also work for changes in the court process that recognize the unique needs of children, such as providing child-sized furniture, using videotaped testimony, and providing facilities that prevent the victim from unexpectedly confronting the offender.

Guardians *ad litem* are appointed in civil child protection proceedings to represent the best interest of the child. This objective is accomplished by the guardian by conducting an independent assessment of the child's situation and submitting a report, which includes recommendations. Court-appointed Special Advocates (CASA) are volunteer guardians *ad litem* and according to a study by the National Center on Child Abuse and Neglect, CASA programs are growing in number. Traditional guardians *ad litem* or CASAs may or may not be lawyers. The advantages of volunteer CASAs are: (1) Because they only have one or two cases, they can devote a lot of time to their task; and (2) Because of this increased time, are often able to establish a trusting relationship with a child victim. The disadvantages are: (1) Untrained CASAs can make poor recommendations to the court; (2) CASAs who are unfamiliar with legal proceedings can be intimidated by the court process and not be able to represent their child's case forcefully; and (3) Untrained and unsupervised CASAs can become emotionally involved in the family and overidentify with the parents or the child, and thereby lose their objectivity. Well-trained, supervised, and supported CASAs typically do an excellent job for children.

Both civil and criminal courts could be involved at the same time in a child sexual abuse case. The civil proceeding is designed to protect the child victim. The objective of a criminal proceeding is to determine if a crime was committed by a particular individual: the alleged offender. It is imperative that the coordination of these two processes take place to avoid conflicting or vague dispositions for the child and alleged or convicted offender.

If a case goes to criminal court, and if the accused is found guilty, it is critical for the court to have a comprehensive psychosocial evaluation. This evaluation should be conducted prior to sentencing, because sex offenders vary greatly in their ability and willingness to control their offending behavior and have different management and treatment needs. The evaluation must be completed by a mental health professional who has had specialized training in the area of sex offender evaluation and the evaluation can help the court determine the most appropriate sentence for an offender by providing information about factors that increase and decrease the risk of new offenses, describe the impact of the abuse and related events on the victim(s) and by providing information about treatment issues. Various sentencing options are available to the court. They include probation, suspended sentences, and incarceration. Criminal sentences vary from state to state. Some state statutes provide for determinate sentences (e.g., Maine). Offenders are sentenced to a specific amount of time and are released from their probation or incarceration when this time has elapsed. Other states utilize split sentencing. In these cases, part of their sentence is suspended, contingent on the offender's compliance with conditions set forth as a part of the sentence. Still other states utilize indeterminate sentences. These sentences set forth a minimum and maximum amount of time that has to be served. When offenders are incarcerated under this system, the input of the prison mental health staff often is considered by correction officials when prisoner release dates are decided. This practice may provide offenders with an incentive to participate in treatment programs. Once involved in treatment, their motivation can develop into a genuine investment in learning how not to be abusive. Unfortunately, some offenders may participate in treatment in order to obtain early release, not to learn how to control their behavior. Melton, Petrila, Poythress, and Slobogin (1987) noted that more and more states have moved away from indeterminate sentencing, in part because of the difficulties that exist when attempting to assess the appropriateness of early discharge. These difficulties often resulted in early release decisions being perceived as arbitrary.

Knopp (1984) noted that offender treatment specialists have observed that for treatment in prison to be effective, it must include a gradual community re-entry phase, followed by a significant period of community-based treatment. It is the authors' experience that some clinicians who specialize in sex offender treatment advocate for long probationary periods following prison sentences as well as in the absence of incarceration. Long probationary periods provide opportunities for supervising offenders while they reside in the community.

Until 1986, Maine had no standards for specialized sex offenders evaluations nor were evaluations requested in the majority of sex crime cases. As a result of legislation, the State of Maine established the State Forensic Service within the Department of Mental Health and Mental Retardation. In the area of abuse, the service was mandated to provide court-ordered presentence, sex offender evalutations, as well as develop a group of professionals throughout the state capable of conducting these specialized assessments. This community capability was developed through the provision of specialized training, development of a standard format for evaluations, and quality assurance mechanisms.

The establishment of this service has resulted in a dramatic increase in the number and expertise of community based evaluators of sex offenders. The recognition by the court of the service as a highly valued professional program is demonstrated by the fact that within the past year judges have been requesting that the State Forensic Service provide management and quality assurance in the evaluations of persons convicted of other than sexual crimes. The rate of referral in this category has increased substantially in recent months.

The State Forensic Service has included representatives of various state agencies and professional disciplines and provided them access to a growing forensic library. This multidisciplinary participation in training has served to impove communication and working relationships among disciplines as well as increase the knowledge of all participants.

The authors have observed disagreement among mental health professionals concerning the issue of client confidentiality. Some clinicians appear to hold the views that without client/therapist confidentiality, a therapeutic relationship will not be established. They maintain that as a consequence, the offender-client will not be free to discuss his or her deviant acts or fantasies, and consequently will not be able to gain control over such impulses through therapy. However, many clinicians who work with sex offenders argue that without the ability to communicate with the criminal justice and child protective services systems, as well as the victim's therapist and the offender's family, they are forced to rely on the offender's self-report, which as Mayer (1988) observed, is often unreliable. In some jurisdictions, judges order offenders to participate in treatment. Although some clinicians believe therapy cannot be effective if it is mandated and not voluntary, in the authors' experience, many reported sex offenders drop out of treatment unless legally required to participate. Mandated treatment, however, can pose a number of problems: (1) Some mandated offenders are not appropriate for any treatment; (2) Some offenders are not appropriate for the available services; and (3) While people can be ordered to attend treatment, they cannot be made to engage in it.

Such inappropriate or unmotivated clients can impact negatively on the therapeutic progress of other offenders who are more sincere in their motivation to make positive changes through therapy. Thus, the issues concerning mandatated treatment are complex and there is disagreement about its usefulness.

As can be seen from the preceding discussion, a state's correctional system is an integral part of a comprehensive, multidisciplinary response to child sexual abuse. At the court's request, probation officers prepare presentence reports that are reviewed by judges in order to aid their decisions concerning sentencing. These reports provide a legal and social history of the offender and require information from a variety of community and state agencies. The sentencing recommendations included in the report should reflect the availability of resources that the offender requires. If needed resources do not exist, dispositional alternatives are obviously narrowed.

When an offender is on probation, probation officers are required to supervise, monitor, and provide surveillance of the offender. If the offender is incarcerated, the probation officer has the added responsibility of coordinating release plans. It is especially important for correctional personnel to inform child protective services of release plans so that victim protection can be assured. Some specialized treatment programs for sex offenders work very closely with probation officers as they attempt to help offenders manage their abusive impulses and behaviors. Some states (e.g., Vermont, Washington, Oregon, California, and Iowa) view the failure to attend, actively participate, and make progress in court-ordered treatment reasons to pursue violation of probation proceedings vigorously or motions to modify probation, which sometimes results in incarceration or a longer period of probation.

Correctional institutions play an important part in protecting child victims of sexual abuse and prevent future victimizations by incarcerating convicted offenders, at least for the duration of the incarceration. There is no consensus in the correctional field that rehabilitation is appropriate or possible in correctional institutions. However, without prison-based treatment, offenders will not have the opportunity to develop skills that can help him or her control future abusive thoughts, impulses, or behaviors. In some states, such as Massachusetts, selected persons who commit sex offenses are treated as an inpatient in facilities run by the State Department of Mental Health. The Massachusetts Treatment Center for Sexually Dangerous Persons in Bridgewater is such an institution. This facility may be somewhat unique in that treatment is provided through the Department of Mental Health while security is the responsibility of the state Department of Corrections.

As Levy and Sheldon (1986) note, the medical community has struggled to find a role for itself in the management of child sexual abuse. The American Academy of Pediatrics did not form a standing committee on child abuse until 1988. For a number of years, numerous model programs of intervention and child abuse and neglect cases have operated, including hospital-based, multidisciplinary child sexual abuse programs. Such programs include those at the San Diego Medical Center, Children's Hospital in Philadelphia, and the Medical Center in Denver, to mention just a few. (For more information, contact Dr. Richard Krugman at the Kempe Center, Denver.) According to Levy and

Sheldon (1986), these and other similar programs delineate the following roles for physicians: (1) identification of the victim, (2) reporting the sexual abuse to the child protective services and/or law enforcement, (3) performing comprehensive, evaluative assessments of the victimized child, incorporating knowledge of medical illness, child development and obtaining pertinent laboratory evidence, and (4) assisting in the disposition and follow-up of cases. This involvement with sex abuse cases includes the responsibility of serving as an expert witness in civil or criminal court proceedings.

In many communities, obtaining physician involvement has proven to be very difficult. Illinois and North Carolina have sought a statewide solution to the problem by encouraging private physicians to gain expertise in the diagnosis and management of child abuse cases and to serve as consultants to child protective services agencies. Levy and Sheldon (1986) report that the Illinois Department of Children and Family Services established the Liaison Division of Medical Education and Consultation in cooperation with a group of physicians to establish and fund regional medical consultants. North Carolina funded two very committed physicians to travel throughout the state to provide specialized training to physicians and enlist their cooperation in assessing child victims and providing consultation to child protective services and law enforcement.

In some states (e.g., Maine, Pennsylvania, Colorado, and Massachusetts), multidisciplinary teams, known as Suspected Child Abuse and Neglect teams (SCAN), Trauma Teams, family support teams and so on, have been established. In addition to improving the hospital management of child sexual abuse cases, the teams accept referrals of possible sexual abuse from physicians who do not consider themselves skilled in this area or who simply do not want to be involved. These specialized teams often provide a place for interested physicians to gain the special knowledge and experience required to diagnose and manage child sexual abuse effectively.

In rural Maine, the medical response to child sexual abuse was dramatically improved in most communities through a commitment of a small number of physicians, hospital social workers and administrators, as well as child protective services agency staff. With a little state agency funding and the hard work and commitment of one pediatrician and one hospital administrator, a small forensic diagnostic center was established at a medical center in central Maine. This clinic not only provided expert, comprehensive examination of child victims, but it also offered a place for other physicians to obtain specialized training.

The clinic staff also facilitated the study of sexual abuse in Maine. A small amount of state funds enabled the staff to visit various communities and speak to county medical associations and other groups of interested medical professionals. A second physician soon joined this effort in the central part of the state. With the success of the clinic and its demonstrated fiscal soundness, the clinic has grown into the Diagnostic Center for Child Abuse in Maine and offers inpatient and outpatient state-of-the-art medical evaluations of victims, as well as a comprehensive, multidisciplinary evaluation of the victim and his or her family. Shortly after the clinic began, there was a successful statewide effort to establish SCAN teams in at least 5 major medical centers in Maine. The number of teams grew to 11 by 1988. These teams were overseen by a statewide, multidisciplinary committee, which undertook the additional task of developing a comprehensive protocol for the management of sexual abuse cases in hospitals and clinics. The advent of the clinic and these teams has: (1) improved the identification and medical management of child abuse cases in Maine; (2) increased reporting by physicians (especially in areas where teams exist; and (3) through the outreach educational activities by the staff of the forensic clinic, and the other team physicians, the number of Maine physicians with specialized knowledge of child sexual abuse increased, as did physician involvement with other community professionals who work with child sexual abuse.

The role of the mental health provider and the effective management of child sexual abuse is multifaceted and requires some departures from traditional methods of intervention and treatment. Mental health professionals debate among themselves the issue of becoming agents of social control in child sexual abuse cases (e.g., by reporting suspected cases of abuse).

Clinicians who work with sex offenders are familiar with their tendencies to deny, minimize, and distort their abusive behaviors. The propensity of these clients to avoid responsibility for their offenses and the fact that they are criminal offenders who victimized vulnerable, powerless children makes them nontraditional clients. Thus, many clinicians who work with them cite the importance of utilizing nontraditional methods, such as working with probation officers, protective services, caseworkers, and the courts.

As Mayer (1988) notes, in the presence of often disarming, repentant offenders who profess to be motivated to receive treatment, therapists may forget that their client population is largely diagnosed as character-disordered, and is highly manipulative and often untrustworthy. This characteristic of some offenders and the role that secrecy, coercion, and denial play in sexual abuse have led some experienced mental health providers to conclude that maintaining confidentiality regarding offender treatment represents a block to effective treatment and information must be shared with authorities that have the ability and responsibility to protect child victims. As experience with treatment of sexual offenders has increased, treatment providers have more frequently used the terms management and control to describe their goals in changing the behaviors of offenders. Some therapists, such as Carnes (1983), have drawn parallels between substance abuse and child sexual abuse as compulsive addictions.

Because of the special issues sexual offenders present, only clinicians who have specialized knowledge and experience should be involved in sex abuse cases. This requirement is true, whether the clinician works with the victim, the victim's family, or the offender. Furthermore, clinicians who work in this field must keep current with the evolving literature and knowledge base. Attending a few conferences does not make someone a specialist in this field. Ongoing training opportunities, case consultation, and peer review are also essential.

Mental health professionals are needed to provide assessment and treatment services to victims, their families, and offenders. They also are needed as evaluators and consultants for the courts, child protective services, correctional departments, as well as to provide information about identifying and intervening in child sexual abuse cases to the community. Crisis intervention services to victims and their families are critical at the time of disclosure, to support the child and his or her family. Mental health providers can expand their treatment skills by using the knowledge of adult survivors. In fact, adult survivors can provide valuable information for assessing and treating the offender and nonoffending partner.

Evaluation of the nonoffending parent by qualified mental health professionals is needed to assist in providing protection to the child victim. Assessing where the nonoffending parent places responsibility for the sexual abuse (on the offender or on the victim), his or her ability to protect the child victim from further abuse, as well as providing the nonabusing spouse with the assistance and support of dealing with the shock of disclosure, are all areas requiring mental health services.

As noted previously, specialized evaluations of offenders are critical for judicial dispositioning decisions, and are important for civil proceedings and treatment as well. They are necessary for the protection of the child victim, reducing the likelihood of further victimizations, and developing the most effective treatment and management plan for the offender. Offense-specific assessments and recommendations are necessary to provide clarity and possible direction for the treatment provider, court, probation officers, child protective services, and offender.

In addition to performing evaluations of offenders, mental health professionals also provide assessments of children, nonoffending parents as well as treatment services to victims, nonoffending parents, offenders, child victims of out-of-home abuse, and whole families. Only clinicians with extensive training in sex abuse cases should engage in this type of treatment.

As Larson and Maddock (1986) observed, while it has been fairly clearly demonstrated that traditional therapeutic interventions are not effective in child sexual abuse situations, there has been no long-term evaluation of the effectiveness of the new approaches used by the programs that have been developed. Many of these programs appear to have promise, but currently they give providers only tentative direction.

As with other specialists in the field of child sexual abuse, qualified mental health professionals are needed to provide expert testimony in civil and criminal court proceedings. Mental health providers may be asked to speak to a child's competency and to testify to the harm that a child might suffer from testifying. In some states (e.g., Alaska, Florida, Oklahoma), alternative methods of getting a child's testimony such as use of videotaped interviews and the use of a screen to block the child's view of the offender, have been developed to make giving testimony easier for a child. As Bulkley (1988) noted, a mental health provider testifying as an expert witness may not give an opinion as to the guilt or innocence, or credibility of a witness, as this invades the province of the judge and jury.

In this chapter, the roles and responsibilities for professionals involved in child sexual abuse have been described. The need for interagency cooperation and coordination is clear. Each community will have unique characteristics, resources, and limitations so that any attempt to develop a cooperative approach will need to be tailored to that community. A cooperative approach does not require that all individuals and agencies involved must be in total agreement about methods and philosophies, only that they operate in an atmosphere that encourages, as Barrett, Sykes, and Byrnes (1986) pointed out, communication, conflict resolution, and the exploration of alternative ideas. The ultimate goal of the agencies and professionals who work with these difficult cases is to prevent further abuse. We need to work together to accomplish this end.

REFERENCES

Abel, G. G., Becker, J. V., Mittelman, M., Cunningham–Rathner, J., Rouleau, J. C., & Murphy, W. D. (1987). Self-reported sex crimes of nonincarcerated paraphiliacs. *Journal of Interpersonal Violence, 2*, 3–25.

Barrett, M. J., Sykes, C., & Byrnes, W. (1986). A systemic model for the treatment of intrafamily child sexual abuse. *Journal of Psychotherapy and the Family,* 2(2), 47–63.

Berliner, L. (1987). The Child Witness: The progress and emergency limitations. *Papers from a National Policy Conference on Legal Reforms in Child Sexual Abuse Cases* (pp. 93–107). National Legal Resource Center for Child Advocacy and Protection. American Bar Association.

Berliner, L., & Barbieri, M. (1984). The testimony of the child victim of sexual assault, *Journal of Social Issues, 40,* 125–137.

Bukley, J. (1988). Legal proceedings, reforms and emerging issues in child sexual abuse cases. *Behavioral Science and the Law, 6*(2), 153–180.

Carnes, P. J. (1983). *Out of the shadows: Understanding sexual addiction.* Minnesota: Compcare Publications.

Canfield, B., & Horowitz, B. (1987). *Child abuse and the law: A legal primer for social workers.* pp. 17–24.

Child Abuse and Neglect Prevention and Treatment Act. (1974) as amended. 42 U.S.C. 5101 et seq.

Child Welfare League of America. (in press). *Standards for services to abused and neglected children and their families.*

Commonwealth of Pennsylvania, Department of Public Welfare, Office of Children, Youth, and Families. (1987). *Child Abuse Report, 2.*

Commonwealth of Virginia, Department of Social Services, Bureau of Child Welfare. (1987). *Statistical Report of Virginia's Child Welfare Program: Together for Chidren, 12.*

Cramer, R. I. (1987). *The district attorney as a mobilizer in a community approach to child sexual abuse.* Unpublished manuscript.

Furby, L., Weinrott, M. R., & Blackshaw, L. (1989). Sex offender recidivism: A review. *Psychological Bulletin, 105*(1), 3–30.

Herman, J., & Hirschman, L. (1977). Father daughter incest. *Journal of Women in Culture and Society,* 23–25.

Hindman, J. (1987). *Step by step: Sixteen steps toward legally sound sexual abuse investigations.* Ontario, OR: Alexandria Associates.

Jones, D. (1987). Reliable and ficticious accounts of sexual abuse in children. *Journal of Interpersonal Violence, 9.*

Knopp, F. M. (1984). *Retraining adult sex offenders: Methods and models.* Syracuse: Safer Society Press.

Larson, N., & Maddock, J. (1986). Structural and functional varietables in incest family services: Implications for assessment and treatment. *Journal of Psychotherapy and the Family, 2*(2), 27–42.

Laszlo, A., & Romano, L. (1988). *Investigation of out-of-home child sexual assault cases.* Alexandria, VA: National Sheriff's Association.

Levy, H., & Sheldon, S. (1986). The contribution and integration of medicine in the assessment and treatment of incest victims. Treating incest: A multiple systems perspective. *Journal of Psychotherapy and the Family, 2*(2), 45–52.

Maine Professional Statewide Child Abuse Committee. (1988). *Suspected child abuse and neglect: The role of Maine hospitals and clinics in identification and management.* Augusta, ME: Author.

Mayer, A. (1988). *Sex offenders: Approaches to understanding and management.* Holmes Beach, FL: Learning Publications.

Melton, G. B., Petrila, J., Poythress, N. G., & Slobogin, C. (1987). *Psychological evaluations for the courts: A handbook for mental health professionals and lawyers.* New York: Guilford Press.

National Association of Public Child Welfare Administrators, American Public Welfare Association. (1988). *Guidelines for a model system of protective services for abused and neglected children and their families.* Washington, DC: Author.

New Jersey Department of Human Services, Division of Youth and Family Services. (1987). *Child Abuse and Neglect Annual Report,* Trenton, (p. 16).

Spaulding, W. (1987). *Interviewing child victims of sexual exploitation.* Washington, DC: National Center for Missing and Exploited Children.

Suski, L. B. (1987). Child Sexual Abuse: An Increasingly Important Part of Child Protective Services. American Association for Protecting Children, Division of American Humane. Denver: *Protecting Children* (pp. 3–7).

Toth, P., & Whalen, M. (Eds.). (1987). *Investigation and prosecution of child abuse.* Alexandria, VA: American Prosecutors Research Institute National Center for the Prosecution of Child Abuse.

U.S. Department of Health and Human Services, Office of Human Development Services, Administration for Children, Youth, and Families, Children's Bureau, National Center on Child Abuse and Neglect. (1988). *National Study of the Incidence and Severity of Child Abuse and Neglect,* 127. Washington, DC.

Weiner, B. (1985). Legal issues in treating sex offenders. *Behavioral Science and the Law, 3*(4), 325–340.

The Generation and Corroboration of a Taxonomic Model for Child Molesters

Raymond A. Knight
Brandeis University

Whether a clinical or legal decision assigns an offender to a specific treatment modality or determines his or her release conditions, it inevitably involves the interpretation of a particular case as a member of a larger, more general group. Thus, classification, which is widely recognized as a vital precursor and sustainer of all scientific inquiry (Ghiselin, 1981; Hempel, 1965), plays a particularly important role in the study of criminal behavior, where dispositional decisions abound. If a population of offenders is heterogeneous, specific treatments may be differentially effective for subgroups in that population, particular subgroups may vary in their outcomes, and the predictive power of variables may fluctuate from group to group.

The marked heterogeneity among child molesters has frequently been acknowledged (for reviews, see Knight, Rosenberg, & Schneider, 1985; Quinsey, 1986). Clinical investigators, who have worked with these offenders and have been required to make decisions about their treatment, management, and disposition, have responded to this apparent diversity by proposing typological systems intended both to increase group homogeneity and to inform clinical judgments (e.g., Cohen, Seghorn, & Calmas, 1969; Fitch, 1962; Gebhard, Gagnon, Pomeroy, & Christenson, 1965; McCaghy, 1967). The prominent place that speculation about typological differentiation has occupied in the clinical literature (Conte, 1985; Knight et al., 1985) has not, however, been translated into concerted efforts to operationalize, apply, and test putative taxonomic models. Indeed, empirical studies of classification systems have been disproportionately underrepresented in the research on child molesters.

Consequently, when deciding what treatments are most appropriate for which offenders and when making critical decisions about which offenders should be released and which detained, clinicians and criminal justice officials have been forced to rely either on global studies of undifferentiated child molesters or, more commonly, on their personal experience with a variety of offenders. Such clinical experiences are typically unsystematic and lack the external validation that empirical research can provide. Numerous difficulties isolating the critical components of important constructs and predicting behavioral outcomes have been identified when clinical intuitions provide the only basis for judgments (e.g., Knight & Roff, 1985; Meehl, 1957, 1959; Monahan, 1981). Although in making dispositional decisions we must rely on clinical experience when more reliable and valid data are not available, it is imperative that we collect more systematic data, test the validity of our intuitions about specific groups, and identify the most appropriate groups for guiding our decisions. An empirically based classification system can provide a firm basis for enhancing the efficacy of our dispositional decisions.

Treatment and legal disposition are not the only reasons for searching for the optimal differentiators among child molesters. Understanding the taxonomic structure of such a deviant population also provides a pivotal underpinning for all other research on this population. Every study of these offenders, from simple attempts to isolate their identifying characteristics to complex investigations of the developmental antecedents of their sexually abusive behavior toward children, depends on an understanding of the taxonomic structure of the population. Failure to take subtype differences into account can lead to serious practical, methodological, and theoretical errors.

The apparently simple task of identifying distinguishing characteristics of child molesters can be confounded if typological distinctions are ignored. If one neglects the substantial heterogeneity of child molesters and employs a "known group research strategy," in which undifferentiated groups of child molesters are compared with matched, nonsexual offenders (see Earls & Quinsey, 1985), important differences between various subtypes of child molesters and other populations will inevitably be masked. Indeed, the typology we have devised indicates that particular types of molesters differ from nonsexual offenders on specific variables. Because not all subtypes differ from controls on the same variables, and indeed some subtypes differ from controls in opposite directions on some dimensions, categorizing all child molesters in a single group will conceal discriminating characteristics. Thus, this

typology provides an explanation for the unsuccessful attempts to identify distinguishing characteristics of "generic" child molesters.

The adequate classification of child molesters is also essential for
studying the etiology and life course of sexually abusive behavior toward
children. Whether one is tracking the developmental roots of a deviant
behavioral pattern or following the life course of this pattern, the failure
to distinguish among types whose abusive behavior emerges from different diatheses or formative experiences will foil attempts to unravel the
complex causal network of the determinants of sexual abuse.

Thus, both the practical exigencies of decision making and the requirements of sound methodology demand the investigation of the
taxonomic structure of child molesters. The absence of clearly operationalized, reliable typologies has forced clinicians and criminal justice officials to rely on nonoptimal decision strategies and has limited
options available to researchers studying these offenders. Despite the
evidence demonstrating the diversity of men who sexually abuse children, no agreement has emerged about what group differentiations are
most promising or even about the level at which subdivision should be
attempted. For instance, although multiple subtypes have been suggested in the clinical literature, the *Diagnostic and Statistical Manual of
Mental Disorders* (*DSM–III–R;* American Psychiatric Association, 1987)
contains only the global category of pedophilia for child molesters.
DSM–III–R does provide a mechanism for specifying the victim's gender, the exclusivity of the offender's sexual behavior with children, and
the offender's relationship with his victim (incest versus nonincest). It
also allows pedophilia to be crossed with other paraphilias, such as
sadism, thereby yielding another potential for designating subtypes of
child molesters (e.g., sadistic and nonsadistic). It does not, however,
overtly endorse these distinctions as identifying clearly defined types of
pedophiles. Consequently, clinicians are not encouraged to think of the
groups that might result from either the application of these specifica-
tions or the cross-classification with other paraphilias as distinct subtypes
of child molesters. Clearly, the critical issue of whether there are useful
subtypes of child molesters is an empirical question. One can rely neither
on the clinical intuitions that have inspired the proposed typologies nor
unsubstantiated conjectures that reject such systems.

Fortunately, a methodology for resolving this conflict has been developed. Powerful techniques for generating and testing typological
schemes of psychopathological populations have been delineated (Blashfield, 1980; Meehl, 1979; Skinner, 1981, 1986), and a detailed description of how these techniques can be applied to the study of sexual
offenders has been provided (Knight & Prentky, 1990; Knight et al.,

1985). One of the major goals of the research program at the Massachusetts Treatment Center during the last decade has been the systematic application of this approach to the study of sexual offenders. The intent of this chapter is to provide an overview of the fruits of our taxonomic investigations of child molesters. Toward that end, I briefly describe our research strategies, present the major components of the most recent version of our child molester typology (MTC:CM3), evaluate the reliability and validity data thus far generated concerning this system, discuss some of the limitations of the system, and summarize future plans for improving its criteria and structure.

CLASSIFICATION RESEARCH PROGRAM

Figure 2.1 depicts a flow chart of the plan of our research program. A detailed description of how this program was implemented has been presented elsewhere (Knight, 1988; Knight & Prentky, 1990; Knight et al., 1985). I simply outline the basic elements of the methodology here.

As shown in the diagram, we simultaneously applied two basic strategies in our taxonomic program: the deductive/rational and the inductive/empirical. Although these two strategies differ in their points of departure, their goals are the same, and ultimately they should coalesce on similar typological structures. The simultaneous application of both of these strategies to the same samples also offers distinct methodological advantages that will be amply illustrated in our program. When using the deductive approach we posit a typological system, operationalize its criteria so that classification is reliable, categorize individuals according to these criteria, and place the system at severe risk for disconfirmation by vigorously testing the validity of the types we have devised. In contrast, the inductive approach initially focuses more on the acquisition of reliable, unbiased data. Because the very determination of what data to gather requires preliminary theoretical notions, the inductive/empirical approach must be guided by some initial theory (Popper, 1972). The difference is that this initial theory can be less structured than in the deductive approach. When applying the inductive strategy, one hopes that by analyzing the critical variables with methods that are reasonable and consistent, the organizing structures sought will emerge. As indicated in the chart, the two strategies are not completely independent. They interface at several junctures, which are designated by oval shapes. Rectangular shapes indicate those operations that occur only within each strategy.

CLASSIFICATION
RESEARCH PROGRAM

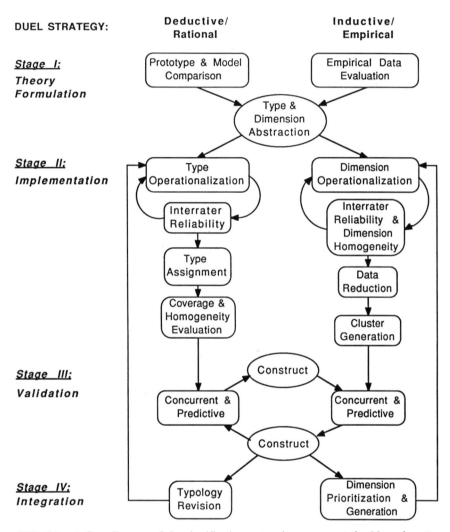

FIG. 2.1. A flow diagram of the classification research program at the Massachusetts Treatment Center.

Stage I

The first stage in applying both approaches involved the assessment of the current status of theory and research in the area and the specification of the domains that would be the focus of our investigation. After a careful consideration of the various typologies that had been proposed for child molesters, we settled on the types described by Cohen and his colleagues (Cohen, Boucher, Seghorn, & Mehegan, 1979; Cohen et al., 1969; Seghorn, 1970) as the point of departure for our deductive strategy. This system (Massachusetts Treatment Center: Child Molester Typology, Version I [MTC:CM1]) included the four types that were most frequently described in the clinical literature (see Knight, 1988; Knight et al., 1985)—the Fixated–passive type, the Regressed type, the Exploitative type, and the Aggressive or Sadistic type. Thus, these types represented the best hypotheses that clinicians had generated about what typological structures might be important in differentiating subtypes of child molesters. In the first stage of the inductive approach, we focused both on the empirical studies of child molesters and on the dimensions and the structuring of dimensions that clinicians had hypothesized to be critical to typology construction (see Knight, 1988; Knight et al., 1985). The intent of these assessments was to abstract from both the clinical and experimental literatures the most promising dimensions and taxonomic organizational principles for cluster analysis.

Stage II

With initial types and critical dimensions in hand, we moved to the second stage in Fig. 2.1, Implementation. The types and dimensions had to be operationalized so that they could be reliably assessed. The curved, reverse arrows in each strategy between reliability and operationalization indicate the cycling between revising and testing of type and dimension-defining criteria that were necessary until adequate reliability was attained.

In our attempt to operationalize the four types of our initial typology, we discovered that we could not reliably classify offenders into these types without restructuring the system. In this first revision (see Knight, 1988; Knight et al., 1985) we created a hierarchical model that employed the nature of aggression (instrumental or expressive) as a first-order, preemptory discriminator. Whereas instrumentally aggressive offenders were those who used only the amount of aggression necessary to attain the child's compliance, expressively aggressive molesters used more force than was necessary to gain compliance (see Seghorn, 1970). Instrumentally aggressive offenders were then divided into Object-related and Exploitative types on the basis of the nature of their relationship with the victim, the nature of their sexual behavior in the offense (nonorgasmic versus orgasmic), and the circumstances and style of their offense(s) (planned, seductive versus impulsive, deceptive). The expressive molesters were subdivided into sadistic and nonsadistic types on the basis of the presence or absence of eroticized aggression. All four types resulting from these secondarily applied distinctions were then subdivided into Regressed and Fixated types by the level of social competence they had attained and the degree to which children were an exclusive focus of their attention and fantasies. This first attempt to improve the reliability, homogeneity, and coverage of child molesters types (MTC:CM2) was applied to all resident child molesters at MTC.

While we were classifying offenders into MTC:CM2 subtypes, we implemented in parallel our inductive strategy. After we had established the reliability of our dimensions, the important process of data reduction ensued. Reducing the large number of variables we had measured into a smaller number of homogeneous scales was essential for ensuring that only the most reliable and relevant variables were used in our cluster analyses (Meehl, 1979; Skinner, 1981) and for facilitating the interpretation of the clusters that were generated. The resultant summary dimensions were subjected to cluster analyses, a set of statistical procedures for sorting individuals into groups (see Rosenberg & Knight, 1988).

Unfortunately, the first revision of our deductive typology, MTC:CM2, proved inadequate. Analyses of its reliability, homogeneity, and coverage indicated that our restructuring of MTC:CM1 had not resolved the difficulties we had attempted to address. Indeed, interrater reliability was not sufficient to warrant undertaking validation analyses. We had to overhaul the system again.

We now had a sufficiently large sample of child molesters assigned to MTC:CM2 types that we could introduce a more sophisticated approach to typology revision—statistical discrepancy analyses. We sorted the cases on which raters disagreed into discrepancy groups on the basis of the two judges' independently assigned types. For instance, if one judge assigned an offender to an Object-related type and the other classified him as an Exploitative type, the offender was placed in the Object-related/Exploitative discrepancy group. For our cluster analyses we had already calculated for each offender composite scores that summarized the dimensions that we had judged critical for typology generation. On these composite scores we compared the discrepancy groups with groups of agreed cases in each of the types to which the disagreeing raters had assigned the discrepant case (see Knight, 1988). For example, we compared the Object-related/Exploitative discrepancy group with both the Object-related and Exploitative agreement groups. These analyses both highlighted the problematic dimensions for discriminating among types and provided an assessment of whether new hypothetical types were required to bridge gaps between existing types.

In addition, our restructuring process was guided and informed by the cluster analyses we had done as part of our inductive strategy (see Knight, 1988; Rosenberg & Knight, 1988). The clusters that had been generated empirically provided important anchors for our revision of MTC:CM2 (see Knight, 1988). We generated our most recent typology (MTC:CM3), which is the focus of this chapter, by resolving interrater discrepancies and by integrating the results of these analyses with those of our cluster-analytical studies (Rosenberg & Knight, 1988).

Stage III

No matter how elegantly structured, intuitively sensible, and reliable a deductively and/or inductively generated typology is, it is essential that it also be valid. It must be able to advance our knowledge about etiology, provide a basis for more diversified and effective therapeutic interventions, or improve our dispositional decisions by enhancing predictive validity. If it lacked such external validity, its value would be limited to reducing the viable taxonomic options and to providing a structural foil for creating a new scheme. It is easier to build from some existing structure, no matter how inadequate, than to begin in a vacuum. Thus, Stage III in our program (see Fig. 2.1) has been focusing on the external validation of MTC:CM3. After describing the major components of this classification system, I will summarize the validity analyses we have completed on this system to date.

Stage IV

Because no typology is perfect, and because there is a good probability that different typologies will be necessary for different types of validity, the analyses of Stage III frequently induce the typology revision and the dimension prioritization and generation of Stage IV, which in turn lead to a renewal of the implementation process. After describing the limitations of MTC:CM3, I suggest the avenues of improvement that we pursue.

MTC:CM3: STRUCTURE AND MAJOR COMPONENTS

To facilitate an understanding of the discussions of MTC:CM3's reliability, validity, relation to previously proposed systems, and its limitations, I will first summarize the major components of the typology. If the reader wishes a more detailed description of MTC:CM3's classification criteria or wants to employ the system to classify offenders, he or she should refer to the full exposition of these criteria, which have been delineated elsewhere (Knight, Carter, & Prentky, 1989).

Fig. 2.2 presents a flow chart that graphically depicts the sequence of decisions that yield classifications on each of the two separate axes in MTC:CM3. The two-axis configuration of the system was designed to provide a structure within which we could both test several specific hypotheses about how the major components of the system were related and also explore as yet undetermined relations among components. For instance, previous data had suggested that social competence was orthogonal to both fixation and contact with children, but the latter two

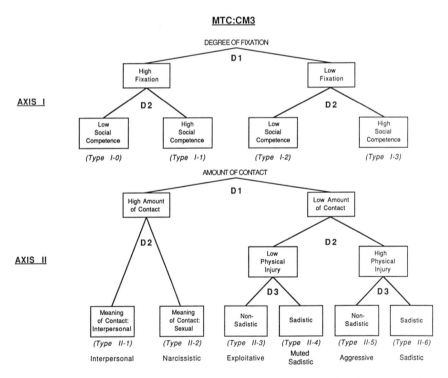

FIG. 2.2.   A flow diagram of the decision process for classifying child molesters on Axis I and Axis II of MTC:CM3. D1 = Decision 1; D2 = Decision 2; and D3 = Decision 3.

components were related. Whereas offenders with low fixation typically had little contact with children, highly fixated offenders could apparently have little or extensive contact with children. Putting fixation and contact on separate axes allowed us to test the hypotheses about how these three components were related and also to explore the relations of injury and sadism to both fixation and social competence, which were less established in previous studies.

As can be seen in this chart, Axis I requires two dichotomous decisions—the degree of fixation on children (i.e., the intensity of pedophilic interest) and the achieved level of social competence. The crossing of these two decisions yields the four Axis I types shown on the chart. The fixation distinction (see Decision 1 on Axis I) is coded as "high" if unequivocal, direct evidence indicates that children have been a central focus of the offender's sexual and interpersonal thoughts and fantasies for a protracted period (at least 6 months). In the absence of such direct evidence, the offender is considered "high" in fixation if he has demonstrated any of the following: (a) three or more sexual contacts with children in a period greater than 6 months, (b) the establishment of enduring relationships with children, and (c) the initiation of contact with children in numerous situations over his lifetime. The social competence distinction (see Decision 2 on Axis I) is coded as "high" if the offender has achieved two or more of the following: (a) a single job lasting 3 years or longer, (b) marriage or cohabitation with an adult (over 16) for 1 year or longer, (c) raising a child for 1 year or longer, (d) active membership in an organization for 1 year or longer, (e) a friendship with a peer lasting 1 year or longer.

Axis II consists of a hierarchically structured sequence of decisions. A preliminary, preemptory dichotomization (see Decision I on Axis II) is made on the basis of the amount of contact an offender has with children in both sexual and nonsexual contexts. An offender is coded as "high" in contact, if there is clear evidence that he spends time with children in multiple contexts, both sexual and nonsexual. Such contexts may be job-related (e.g., schoolteacher or day-care supervisor) or avocational (e.g., Cub or Boy Scout leader or Little League coach). It is important to distinguish this discrimination from the fixation decision made on Axis I. In the amount of contact decision, one is judging the amount of time an offender spends in close proximity to children (e.g., as a camp counselor, school bus driver, carnival worker, etc.). In contrast, the fixation discrimination attempts to assess the strength of an offender's pedophilic interest, that is, the extent to which children are a major focus of his cognitions and fantasies.

For high-contact offenders a subsequent distinction (Decision 2 for high-contact offenders) is made between those molesters who have sought to establish interpersonal relationships with children (Type II–1, Interpersonal) and those whose high contact has been exclusively sexually motivated (Type II–2, Narcissistic). If there is evidence that the offender attempted to form an interpersonal relationship with a child that was not exclusively sexual and it is determined that his offenses were predominantly nongenital with a nonorgasmic aim, he is considered an Interpersonal type (Type II–1). If there is an apparent absence of such relationships or his offenses were predominantly phallic with an orgasmic aim, he is classified Narcissistic (Type II–2).

For low-contact offenders, subsequent dichotomous discriminations are made on the degree of physical injury inflicted on the child (Decision 2 among low-contact offenders) and on the absence or presence of sadism (Decision 3 among low-contact offenders). These two decisions yield the four low-contact groups (Types II–3 to II–6 depicted at the bottom of Fig. 2.2). Decision 2 focuses specifically on the amount of physical injury inflicted on the child. Whereas the low physical injury types (Types II–3 and II–4) have limited the aggression in their sexual offense(s) to such acts as pushing, slapping, holding, and threatening the child, high physical injury types (Types II–5 and II–6) have injured the child. Decision 3 differentiates offenders according to the presence (Types II–4 and II–6) and absence (Types II–3 and II–5) of eroticized aggression (i.e., the preoccupation with and/or acting out of sadistic sexual fantasies, which include such acts as bondage, spanking, sodomy, the insertion of foreign objects, or bizarre ritualistic behavior).

EVALUATING MTC:CM3: RELIABILITY AND VALIDITY

I will use two different organizational schemes to present evaluative data about MTC:CM3. The first, which is more theoretical and construct-oriented, will focus on the three structural changes, described subsequently, that distinguish MTC:CM3 both from earlier versions of the system and from other extant typologies. The implementation of these modifications, which represent hypotheses about how the components of the system interrelate, produced the basic infrastructure of MTC:CM3. Thus, an examination of their validity affords a test of the structural aspects of the typology and provides a framework for comparing and contrasting MTC:CM3 with other proposed typologies. The second organizational scheme for evaluating MTC:CM3 will concentrate on the four Axis I and six Axis II types, providing empirically validated descriptions of the major distinguishing characteristics of each type on each axis.

Assessing the Basic Structural Components of MTC:CM3

The three major changes that provided the basic infrastructure of MTC:CM3 were:

1. The fixated–regressed distinction of MTC:CM2 was partitioned into two separate, independent factors—the degree of fixation on children (i.e., the intensity of pedophilic interest) and the level of social competence. These two judgments were placed together on a separate axis.
2. A new type, the Narcissistic, was incorporated into the system to resolve the problems we encountered in trying to differentiate between the Object-related and Exploitative types of MTC:CM2 and to represent a type that emerged in our cluster analyses. Offenders in this new type shared with the Object-related type the characteristic of seeking a high amount of contact with children. Because this high amount of contact differentiated the Narcissistic type and the Object-related type (which was now renamed the Interpersonal type) from both the Exploitative and the more aggressive types, the child-contact judgment was introduced as a major discriminator. Because the amount of time that offenders spent in contact with children was hypothesized to be independent of their social competence, but complexly related to the level of their fixation (Knight, 1989), the contact judgment was transferred to a separate axis to allow subsequent validity analyses to sort out its typological relation with fixation.
3. The violence in the sexual offense was differentiated into independent judgments of physical injury and sadism and these two violence distinctions were nested within offenders who had low contact with children.

As can be seen in Fig. 2.2, the integration and application of these three changes yielded the two axial, hierarchical structure of MTC:CM3. The unconfounding of two hypothetically independent constructs, fixation and social competence, the introduction of the child-contact judgment and its assignment to a separate axis as a first-order discrimination, and the differentiation of physical injury and sadism and their nesting within low-contact offenders on Axis II constrained the structure of MTC:CM3 to its current form.

Since the creation of this typology, approximately 280 child molesters have been assigned to its types. In a series of studies using various subsamples of these offenders we have examined the reliability and the validity of MTC:CM3. These studies, whose results will be the focus of the subsequent evaluative sections, provide a rigorous assessment of the typology and of the three relational hypotheses that determine its present structure. Reliabilities were measured by chance corrected kappa coefficients calculated on the dual, independent classifications of 177 child molesters to the MTC:CM3 types (Knight et al., 1989). Because each of the hypotheses about how the major components of MTC:CM3 relate to each other proposes a specific pattern of how offenders should be sorted into the various types in the system, we also examined in a second study (Knight, 1989) the distribution of assignments of offenders to the system. Table 2.1 presents the frequency and percentage of case assignments to each cell of the Axis I by Axis II cross-tabulation matrix from this study. It will be helpful to refer to this table during the ensuing discussions of assignment distribution.

We have also completed three validity studies, examining the developmental antecedents, the concurrent correlates, and the predictive utility of MTC:CM3. The first was a postdictive, path-analytical study of all child molesters committed to the Massachusetts Treatment Center (MTC) between 1959 and 1981 (Prentky, Knight, Rosenberg, & Lee, 1989). We assessed the family characteristics, and the child/juvenile and adult behavioral constellations that might either antecede or covary with the major components of MTC:CM3, thereby testing whether the Axis I and Axis II components of MTC:CM3 were related to different life experiences and adaptations.

In a second study (Knight & Straus, 1991) we evaluated the concurrent validity of the system. A 95-item symptom checklist that measured the presence and severity of individual symptoms over the lifespan was correlated with the major typological discriminators. A principal components analysis of the checklist items with rotation to varimax criteria yielded six theoretically meaningful, internally consistent factors. These were: (a) Impulsivity (e.g., delinquency, antisocial behavior, truancy, temper tantrums, etc.); (b) Psychosis (e.g., confusion, poor reality testing, delusions, hallucinations, etc.); (c) Anxiety/Depression (e.g., anxiety, depression, loneliness, shyness, etc.); (d) Neurocognitive Deficits (e.g., attention problems, learning problems, speech problems, mental retardation, etc.); (e) Psychosomatic Symptoms (tics, constipation, dermatitis, etc.); and (f) Paraphilias (e.g., exhibitionism, fetishism, promiscuity, voyeurism, etc.). For each factor, Likert scales were constructed, and the scales were related to the major components of the typology, using simultaneous multiple regressions.

Finally, we are now analyzing the data from a follow-up of both all offenders committed and released from MTC between 1959 and 1984 and a matched sample of those referred to MTC for evaluation, but not

TABLE 2.1
Cross-tabulation of Axis I Types with Axis II Types: Cell Frequencies and Percents

AXIS I TYPES		AXIS II TYPES					
		Interpersonal	Narcissistic	Exploitative	Muted sadistic	Aggressive	Sadistic
High fixation	Low competence	11[a] 6.2%[b]	37% 20.9%	27 15.3%	15 8.5%	14 7.9%	8 4.5%
	High competence	8 4.5%	15 8.5%	11 6.2%		2 1.1%	
Low fixation	Low competence		3 1.7%	3 1.7%	1 .6%	10 5.6%	5 2.8%
	High competence		1 .6%	5 2.8%		1 .6%	

[a]Cell frequency.
[b]Cell percent.

committed. We have been following them through multiple record sources, including FBI files, the Massachusetts Board of Probation records, the Massachusetts Parole Board Records, MTC gradual release program files, MTC clinical files, and court records whenever they were available within the other sources. We have just begun to analyze the data for the committed child molester sample. I will only discuss the recidivism rates at the end of the 10th year after release from MTC or from prison, whichever was later. This time span provides a fairly inclusive assessment of recidivism with an acceptable loss of statistical power due to the smaller *N*s that result from the exclusion of offenders who did not have the opportunity to be on the streets for 10 years. For the purpose of this chapter, I will focus primarily on the results of analyses of whether after release offenders had been charged with or convicted of a serious sexual crime or a victim-involved nonsexual crime.

In discussing the results of these studies I will indicate when the results corroborated or disconfirmed our a priori hypotheses. Because of the dearth of empirical research on child molester typologies, our hypotheses were often generated either from the speculations of clinicians working with molesters, from generic studies of these offenders (see Knight et al., 1985), or from the relations among variables found in related populations (e.g., criminal populations). Because the aim of these sections is to give an overview, I will not attempt to justify these hypotheses. The reader is referred to the studies cited for this material.

The Unconfounding of Fixation and Social Competence.   One of the most common typological discriminations proposed in the clinical literature has been the division of child molesters into types variously characterized as fixated or preferential, and regressed or situational (e.g., Cohen et al., 1979; Fitch, 1962; Groth, Hobson, & Gary, 1982; Howells, 1981; Kopp, 1962; Lanning, 1986; Swanson, 1971). The primary aim of this dichotomization has been to differentiate child molesters with a primary, long-standing orientation toward children from offenders whose involvement with children constitutes a departure under stress from a more age-appropriate sexual orientation. Implicit, or explicit, in the various fixation–regression distinctions is a judgment of the achieved level of social competence. Such an assessment can be based on behavioral data that are easily operationalized and are commonly gathered during clinical evaluations. Most typological systems have assumed that these primary orientation and social competence indicators are part of a cluster of subtype-discriminating measures that include age and sex of preferred sexual partners, age of onset and intensity of pedophilic interests, the level of planning in offenses, etc. (e.g., Groth et al., 1982).

As indicated in my summary of research strategies, our attempts to apply the fixation–regression distinction revealed its multidimensionality, and led us to redefine and restructure these constructs. The system that served as our point of departure, MTC:CM1, like many of the typologies that preceded it, employed the constructs of fixation and regression to define two separate types. When we applied this system, it became apparent that a number of distinct dimensions were confounded in this differentiation, including the molester's style of offending, his interpersonal relationships with children, the intensity of the offender's pedophilic interest, and the level of social competence he had achieved prior to his sexual assaults. On the basis of a case-by-case analysis of the discrepancies found in classifying offenders into MTC:CM1 types, we decided to separate the offender's style and relationship with children from both the intensity of his pedophilic interest and his achieved social competence. The style and relationship constructs were joined with additional characteristics that differentiated Object-related from Exploitative offense styles. Intensity of pedophilic interest and social competence were combined into a separate construct that was dichotomized to yield high-intensity, low-social-competence (fixated) and low-intensity, high-social-competence (regressed) types. From our analyses of the MTC:CM1 classifications it had appeared that this fixation–regression distinction constituted a pervasive typological discriminator, important for all child molester offense styles (see Knight, 1988; Knight et al., 1985).

As pointed out earlier, this restructuring proved insufficient. When we implemented the revised typology (MTC:CM2), we continued to encounter significant reliability problems in assigning offenders exclusively to these more precisely defined fixated or regressed groups (see Knight, 1988). Both our analyses of discrepant cases and the difficulties we experienced in reaching consensus on these decisions indicated that the strength of pedophilic interest (or "fixation" on children as sexual objects) and social competence had to be considered separately. Thus, our analyses were consistent with Finkelhor and Araji's (1983) conclusion that the fixation–regression dichotomization was inadequate and confounded two independent dimensions. We also agreed with Finkelhor and Araji about the nature of the first dimension. Our fixation distinction is now very similar to their strength of pedophilic interest. It has been purged of any implied relation to the notion of regression in psychodynamic theory and has been operationalized as the intensity of the offender's pedophilic interest in or fixation on (in the more general sense of focus of attention on) children. We disagreed with Finkelhor and Araji (1983) only on the specification of the second dimension. Instead of defining this dimension as the exclusivity of pedophilic interest, we preferred, in accord with the results of our discrepancy analyses, to concentrate on social competence as the core of the second dimension.

Our studies analyzing the reliability and the distribution of classification of offenders to Axis I types (Knight, 1989; Knight et al., 1989) strongly supported our decision to consider fixation and social competence as independent constructs. First, the unconfounding of these distinctions solved the interrater reliability problems that we had encountered in our attempts to apply the fixation–regression dichotomization in the earlier versions of the typology. In contrast to the poor reliabilities previously obtained, the fixation judgment had "good" interrater reliability (κ = .67), and the social competence decision had "excellent" reliability (κ = .84), according to Cicchetti and Sparrow's (1981) interpretive guidelines for kappa coefficients (see Knight et al., 1989). Second, in an analysis of the distribution of offenders to Axis I types (see Table 2.1) the fixation and social competence distinctions were found to be statistically independent, corroborating our hypothesis about the relation of these constructs and confirming their orthogonal configuration on Axis I (Knight, 1989).

The postdictive, path-analytical study examining the developmental antecedents and adult adaptations related to the fixation and social competence dichotomizations (Prentky et al., 1989) also provided ample support for the separate assessment of these two components. There was substantial agreement between the predicted and obtained results for these distinctions, despite one notable disconfirmation. On the basis of clinical speculations (Cohen et al., 1969; Groth et al., 1982) it was hypothesized that highly fixated offenders would show early emotional and behavior difficulties reflecting a troubled childhood and possibly involving early sexual abuse. It was predicted further on the basis of data on delinquents (Hathaway & Monachesi, 1953, 1954) that their childhood/juvenile adaptation would be characterized more by passivity and withdrawal than by impulsive acting out. Consistent with these hypotheses, fixated child molesters were rated significantly higher than less fixated offenders on the childhood and adolescence Emotional and Behavioral Instability component, but they were significantly *less* likely to manifest the aggressive and impulsive behavior measured by the School-related Acting-out component. Whereas the Emotional and Behavioral Instability factor comprised assessments of outpatient psychiatric contact, having been sexually abused, running away, arson, and problems with alcohol, the Acting-out factor measured behaviors such as assaulting peers and teachers, truancy, and vandalism. An examination of the mean levels of each of the four Axis I groups on the Emotional and Behavioral Instability component revealed that high scores on this component were most characteristic of the highly fixated, low-social-competence group, whose mean score was higher than any of the other three groups.

Contrary to expectations generated from developmental research on other deviant groups (e.g., Knight & Roff, 1983, 1985) high scores on a factor measuring early Academic and Interpersonal problems did not predict adult social competence, but rather differentiated high- from low-fixated offenders. Instead of presaging a subsequent history of inadequate interpersonal relationships and poor employment stability, this component, which comprised learning disabilities, repeating grades, and social withdrawal, apparently characterized the early adaptation of some highly fixated types, who in adulthood manifested greater psychosexual immaturity and withdrawal. A comparison of the mean Axis I group scores indicated that it was the highly fixated, low-social-competence type that was higher than the other three types on this component.

In this sample, an impulsive and aggressive childhood, rather than poor academic performance and social isolation, was associated with subsequent low social competence. Although this relation was not predicted a priori, it is not surprising that someone who was impulsive and aggressive as a child would have difficulty as an adult forming and maintaining lasting interpersonal relationships and establishing a stable work history.

Not surprisingly, because they assessed overlapping behavioral domains, high scores on Interpersonal Competence in adulthood were highly related to having been classified as high rather than low in social competence. Although the Academic and Vocational competence component did not predict social competence as we had expected, it did interact with fixation and social competence. Among the highly fixated offenders, high-social-competence molesters were significantly higher on Academic and Vocational competence than their low-social-competence counterparts. There were no differences between the high- and low-social-competence, low-fixated types on this component.

Consistent with our speculation that alcohol abuse should be more frequently found among offenders with low fixation on children, where the disinhibitory effects of alcohol or drugs should play a greater role in facilitating sexual assaults (Finkelhor & Araji, 1983), the adult Alcohol Abuse component was significantly related to lower fixation. It was not, however, related to the level of social competence. Indeed, if the fixation and social competence dimensions had remained confounded, as they are in other typologies, the confirmation of the relation of alcoholism to low fixation and the limitation of this covariation specifically to fixation rather than to social competence would have been masked. When we divided offenders into only two groups—a high-fixation, low-social-competence subgroup and a low-fixation, high-social competence sub-group—only the adult Interpersonal Competence factor was related to this simple dichotomization.

Thus, the results of this postdictive study support the separate con-sideration and crossing of fixation and social competence. First, if the two dimensions had been remained confounded the distinct de-velopmental antecedents of high fixation—high emotional and be-havioral problems, early academic and interpersonal problems, and low acting out in childhood and adolescence—would not have been detected. Thus, the unconfounding of these two constructs has not only solved the reliability problems that we had encountered, it has also provided an outcome structure whose separate types appear to have distinguishable developmental roots and by implication trait-like temporal stability. Second, both the confirmation of the hypothesis that alcoholism is re-lated to low fixation and the specification of this covariation to fixation rather than to social competence would have been masked, if the two dimensions had remained entwined.

The symptom-checklist validity study (Knight & Straus, 1991) yielded additional evidence supporting the separation of fixation and social competence, showing that each was related to different symptom com-plexes. The results of the simultaneous multiple regressions relating the checklist factor scales to Axis I fixation and social competence are de-picted in Fig. 2.3. As shown in this figure, whereas high social com-petence was related to low Impulsivity and few Neurocognitive deficits, high fixation was related to a higher prevalence and severity of Paraphi-lias and greater Anxiety/Depression. The impulsivity–social competence and the fixation–anxiety/depression (including loneliness, shyness, etc.) connections are consistent with the results of the path-analytical study, and the relation of sexual fixation to the presence and severity of paraphilias coincides with our theoretical understanding of these two manifestations of sexual preoccupation.

Finally, our 10-year follow-up study of child molesters suggests that fixation and social competence may be related to different kinds of subsequent criminal activity. The analyses comparing high- with low-fixation offenders and high- with low-social-competence offenders showed that whereas a high level of fixation predicted charges and convictions to serious sexual crimes, social competence did not predict any measure of serious sexual crimes. In contrast, lower social com-petence predicted a higher incidence of victim-involved, nonsexual charges, but fixation did not. These data support the separation of these components, because each presaged recidivism associated with a differ-ent kind of crime, and confounding these components would have obscured predictive power.

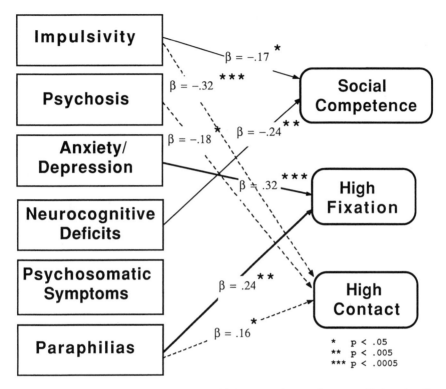

FIG. 2.3. Depiction of simultaneous multiple regression analyses, predicting the dichotomous classificatory decisions of Axis I fixation and social competence, and Axis II amount of contact with children from the six checklist symptom factor scales.

In sum, not only do the reliability and distribution analyses support the differentiation of fixation and social competence, the validity analyses exploring their developmental antecedents, their relations to concurrent adaptations, and their prognostic utility have also revealed that each is preceded by unique life experiences, correlated with specific adaptations, and predictive of different criminal outcomes. These data corroborate the hypothesis that they are separate components and suggest that each has trait-like temporal stability that is related to distinguishable life courses.

The Amount of Contact with Children and the Introduction of the Narcissistic Type. Both in MTC:CM1, the typology that served as our point of departure (Cohen et al., 1969; Seghorn, 1970), and in other classification systems (e.g., Fitch, 1962; Groth, 1978; Kopp, 1962; Swanson, 1971) a Fixated type or its equivalent was hypothesized to include passive, withdrawn men who sought children as sexual partners, and whose interpersonal attachments to children seemed to hold the same meaning for them that age-appropriate relationships held for others. In contrast, the Exploitative type or its equivalent in these typologies (e.g., Cohen et al., 1979; Fitch, 1962; Groth, 1978; Swanson, 1971) was described as someone who simply exploited the weakness of children to gratify his sexual needs. The prototypical Exploitative type purportedly attempted genital sexual acts and only used aggression to assure compliance. His victims were supposedly unknown to him, and he frequently showed many features of the antisocial personality disorder. Thus, in most of the prior systems there was a theoretical equivalency made between offenders hypothesized to be fixated on children as sexual and interpersonal objects and those who showed an immature, passive life-style (Fitch, 1962; Kopp, 1962), who were sociosexually underdeveloped (Gebhard et al., 1965), or who had a high amount of interaction with children (McCaghy, 1967). This type was contrasted to a type who was more active and antisocial, less fixated on children, and less likely to interact with children.

In our attempt to apply the original MTC:CM1 typology, we experienced significant difficulty in reliably differentiating Fixated from Exploitative types. Part of the problem was due to the presence in our sample of offenders who had an Exploitative style of offending, but still evidenced a strong fixation on children as sexual objects. As indicated in the last section, in our first revision of the typology (MTC:CM2) we distinguished offense style and the offender's relationship with children from the fixation–regression discrimination. The independent assessment of these style and fixation–regression discriminations was intended in part to address the problem of differentiating Fixated types (renamed Object-Related types in MTC:CM2) from Exploitative types (see Knight, 1988).

Classification of a sample of child molesters using MTC:CM2, which incorporated these style and fixation–regression changes, indicated that the separation of these components did not adequately resolve the problems between the Object–related and Exploitative types. Interrater discrepancy analyses of MTC:CM2 (see Knight, 1988) indicated that simply separating the intensity of pedophilic interest and level of social competence from offense style and the nature of the relationship with children was not sufficient. A more careful differentiation of the nature of the relationship between offenders and children and a better discrimination of specific aspects of offense style was required. These analyses showed that the propensity to seek contact with children had to be distinguished from the motivation for such contact and the nature of the relationships that were established.

From these analyses it was evident that there were two kinds of offenders who sought more extensive involvement with children outside the context of their offenses. The first type, which was named the Interpersonal type, conformed with the prototypical pattern of the Object-related offender. The second, which we have named the Narcissistic type, sought extensive contact with children, but for these offenders the motivation for contact appeared exclusively sexual. In contrast to the Interpersonal type, they did not seek personal relationships with children, but rather only sought the company of children to increase their opportunities for sexual experiences. They had extensive contact with children, like the prototypical Object-related type, but they also molested children whom they did not know and their sexual acts with children were typically genitally oriented, like the Exploitative offender. The importance of this new type was supported by the fact that it and an Object-related, Fixated, Interpersonal cluster had emerged as separate child molester clusters in independent analyses of these offenders (Knight, 1988; Rosenberg & Knight, 1988).

The incorporation of this Narcissistic type precipitated a restructuring of the basic structure of MTC:CM2. The fixation and social competence distinctions were separated from all other typological components by assigning them to an independent axis (Axis I). We made the amount of contact with children a first-order, preemptory discriminator in the Axis II hierarchy. This distinction was made a primary discriminator for three reasons: (a) because the new Narcissistic type and the Interpersonal type shared the characteristic of placing themselves in situations where they would have contact with children; (b) because this propensity for high-contact with children differentiated these two types from both the Exploitative and the more aggressive types; and (c) because such contact could be easily operationalized. As indicated earlier, the subsequently applied decision to discriminate the Interpersonal from the Narcissistic type was nested within the high-contact branch of Axis II. Within the low-contact branch the subsequently applied physical injury and sadism decisions were nested, to allow differentiation among the Exploitative and more aggressive types (see Fig. 2.2).

The introduction of the amount of contact with children as a major type-defining component on Axis II has been supported both by the enhanced reliability of type assignment that has resulted and by the corroboration of our a priori hypotheses about how this component related to other components of the typology. The decision to make this contact decision a preemptive discriminator on Axis II was supported by the reasonably high reliability of this judgment ($\kappa = .70$, see Knight et al., 1989). The reliability of the second-order discrimination between the Interpersonal and Narcissistic types, although not as high ($\kappa = .51$; see

Knight et al., 1989), was still "fair," and certainly acceptable by Cicchetti and Sparrow's (1981) guidelines. As might be expected from the fact that the original Fixated type anchors the high ends of both the fixation (Axis I) and the amount of contact (Axis II) distinctions, the two constructs were found to be related empirically as well as theoretically (Knight, 1989). The analyses of the distribution of type assignments (see Table 2.1) clearly illustrated the nature of this relation. Consistent with our understanding of low fixation, very few low-fixation offenders had high contact with children. In contrast, offenders rated high in fixation fell almost equally into low- and high-contact groups. Thus, the major divergence between the fixation and the amount of contact constructs centers on the existence of a substantial group of molesters who had high pedophilic interest, but who also had little contact with children outside of offense contexts. Because the majority of the child molesters in our sample were highly fixated (84%), the potential importance of dividing these highly fixated offenders into high- and low-contact subgroups is evident.

Our path-analytical validity study (see Prentky et al., 1989) provided further support for the inclusion of both fixation and child-contact distinctions. Whereas both high-fixation and high-contact shared the developmental antecedents of relatively lower School-related Acting out and more Academic and Interpersonal Problems in childhood and adolescence, only high fixation was predicted by higher Emotional and Behavioral Instability in childhood and adolescence. Moreover, consistent with McCaghy's (1967) data, a low amount of contact was related to higher adult Aggression and Impulsivity. Fixation had no such relation with this component. Thus, although the two constructs share some similarities in their developmental antecedents, they also show dissimilarities in these early experiences and they covary with somewhat different adult adaptations.

There were no differences, however, on the components measured in the path-analytical study between the two Axis II high-contact types (the Interpersonal [Type II–1] and the Narcissistic [Type II–2]). Rather, the results suggested that the offenders classified as Narcissistic were more like the Interpersonal type than they were like the Exploitative type (Type II–3). No components in the regression analyses significantly differentiated the Interpersonal type from the Narcissistic type. In contrast, the Narcissistic type manifested significantly more childhood and juvenile Emotional and Behavioral Instability and significantly less adult Aggression and Impulsivity than the Exploitative type (see Prentky et al., 1989). Analyses of other data in our data base, however, have revealed differences between the Interpersonal and Narcissistic types in other domains. Interpersonal types appear more detached and asocial in their interpersonal styles, have had a history of a higher frequency of sexual offenses, are significantly more likely to return to the Treatment Center because of parole violations or conviction of a sexual offense after release, and have greater sexual deviancy in their families of origin.

The symptom checklist study (Knight & Straus, 1991), consistent with the path-analytical study, found results that reinforce retaining both the contact and fixation distinctions. As can be seen in Fig. 2.3, this study found that child-contact, fixation, and social competence all had a different patterns of interrelations with the six symptom complexes. Contact was the only construct related to the Psychosis scale. The high-contact offenders had fewer psychotic symptoms than the low-contact offenders. Like fixation, contact with children covaried with the Paraphilia scale, and like social competence it was correlated with Impulsivity. It was not, however, related to the Anxiety/Depression scale as was fixation, and it was not, as was social competence, related to the Neurocognitive Deficits scale. Low-contact offenders showed significantly more Impulsivity than high-contact offenders, but low- and high-fixation groups did not differ on the Impulsivity scale. High-contact offenders evidenced more paraphilias than low-contact offenders, but social competence groups did not differ in the presence of paraphilias (see Fig. 2.3).

Our preliminary recidivism analyses also provide encouraging data for maintaining child contact as a typological discriminator and for retaining the Interpersonal–Narcissistic distinction within high-contact offenders. They indicate that although the amount of contact with children was not related to the incidence of subsequent charges or convictions of sexual assaults, it did predict the incidence of both charges and convictions of victim-involved nonsexual assaults. During the 10-year follow-up period, proportionately more low-contact offenders were charged with and convicted of nonsexual assaults than were high-contact offenders. Within the high-contact branch of Axis II proportionately more Interpersonal types were returned to the Treatment Center because of parole violations or new convictions for sexual offenses than were Narcissistic types during the 10-year follow-up period. Indeed, a greater proportion of Interpersonal types (78%) returned to the Treatment Center during this period because of sexual crimes or parole violations than any other Axis II type, but not all comparisons were significant because of the small ns in particular analyses.

In sum, the reliability, distribution, and validity analyses support the inclusion of the Narcissistic type and the introduction of contact with children as a preemptive discriminator on Axis II. The inclusion of the Narcissistic type resolved the reliability problems that had plagued our attempts to discriminate between the Object-related and Exploitative types in MTC:CM2. The validity analyses suggest that although the Narcissistic types share substantial similarities with the Interpersonal types, they are also sufficiently different on critical variables such as sexual deviance in their family of origin and recidivism to warrant their separate consideration. Our analyses of interrater agreement indicated that contact with children can be assessed reliably. As predicted, it was not correlated with social competence, but overlapped with fixation in complex ways. The differences in the pattern of correlations that contact and fixation had with developmental antecedents, concurrent adaptations, and recidivism support the retention of both constructs in the typology.

Separation of Sexual Sadism and the Amount of Physical Injury. The third structural change introduced into MTC:CM3 centered on the low-contact branch of Axis II, and involved a disentangling of the nature of the aggressive motivation in the offense from the amount of physical injury inflicted. A profile analysis of MTC:CM2 classifications, comparing discrepant cases (those that were judged Exploitative by one rater, but Sadistic by another) with nondiscrepant cases (those independently assigned by both raters to the Exploitative type or to the Sadistic type), and an analysis of the difficulties we encountered in reaching consensus on discrepant cases (see Knight, 1988) revealed that symbolic or "muted" sadism could occur in the absence of physical injury to the child, and high physical injury could occur for nonsadistic reasons. The need to have both of these types represented in the typology was met by crossing high and low physical injury with high and low sadism within the low-contact branch.

Interrater reliability results (Knight et al., 1989) indicated that the difficulty we encountered in assigning these hybrid cases to MTC:CM2 types has been reduced by requiring separate assessments of the amount of physical injury done to the child and the amount of sexual sadism present. The reliability of the physical injury distinction in MTC:CM3 was "excellent" ($\kappa = .76$), and the overall reliability of sadism was "good" ($\kappa = .60$). The reliability, however, of the presence of sadism for high-injury cases ($\kappa = .41$), although statistically significant, barely attained Cicchetti and Sparrow's (1981) lowest level of acceptability. Better behavioral anchors for this distinction are clearly necessary. The relative difficulty of distinguishing sadistic from nonsadistic motivation when high physical injury is present, is consistent with the problems that other investigators have experienced in rating sadism (e.g., Quinsey, Chaplin, & Varney, 1981).

The analyses of the distribution of offenders into MTC:CM3 types (Knight, 1989) corroborated our hypothesis that sadism and physical injury were distinct constructs that require separate assessment. Consistent with our a priori hypothesis, these two components of violence were found to be statistically independent. These distribution analyses also clarified the relations of each of these two constructs to other relevant constructs in the system. Injury and sadism had complex and differentiated relations with fixation and social competence (see Table 2.1). Among the low-fixated offenders there was a disproportionally high representation of high-physical-injury types, but a low representation of sadistic types. In contrast, no offenders rated high in social competence were assigned to either of the sadistic types, and an extremely low number of nonsadistic, high-injury offenders were rated as high in social competence.

The results of our path-analytical study (Prentky et al., 1989) also supported our separation of these two constructs of violence. A high degree of School-related Acting out in childhood increased the probability that an offender would be classified as sadistic, either muted or overt. In contrast, high Emotional and Behavioral Instability in childhood and high Alcohol Abuse in adulthood both increased the probability that an offender would be assigned to a high-injury type. Among the low-contact types, the Overt Sadistic types had the greatest amount of sexual deviance in their family of origin. Thus, the two components related to different developmental antecedents and adult adaptations.

As can be seen in Fig. 2.4, injury and sadism were not as clearly differentiated in the symptom checklist study (Knight & Straus, 1991) as they were in the path study. The Overt and Muted Sadistic types had the highest Impulsivity scores, but the Aggressive type was not far below them. Thus, Impulsivity in Fig. 2.4 was most strongly related to sadism (Types II–4 and II–6), but also predicted high injury (Types II–5 and II–6). Although the Overt Sadism types had the highest Psychotic symptom scores, they were followed closely by the Aggressive types, and the Muted Sadist types did not differ from the other groups. Consequently, the Psychotic scale in Fig. 2.4 predicted high injury, but not sadism.

In our follow-up study of criminal outcome, high physical injury to a victim increased the probability that an offender would be charged with and convicted of a nonsexual, victim-involved assault during the 10-year, follow-up period. In contrast, injury was unrelated to subsequent sexual assaults. Contrary to our a priori hypothesis, sadism was not related to subsequent serious sexual crimes. It also failed to predict nonsexual, victim-involved offending. The number of Overt Sadists (Type II–6) released ($n = 4$) was, however, too small to draw any firm conclusions about their recidivism. One of these four was convicted of a serious sexual offense during the 10-year follow-up period, and a second was returned because of an unspecified parole violation. Of the

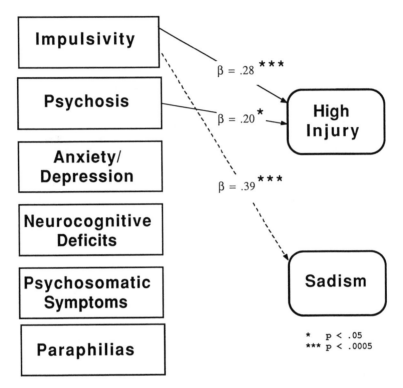

FIG. 2.4. Depiction of simultaneous multiple regression analyses, predicting the dichotomous classificatory decisions of Axis II amount of physical injury and absence or presence of sadism from the six checklist symptom factor scales.

11 released Muted Sadists (Type II–4) none was convicted of a subsequent sexual crime. Four Muted Sadists, however, were returned to prison during this period, three of these because of parole violations (one of which involved a sexual assault charge) and a fourth because of a nonsexual, victim-involved conviction.

Thus, our proposal to consider both sadism and the amount of injury as separate components has been supported by four findings: (a) the improved reliability attained by unconfounding these components, (b) the evidence in the distribution analyses that these components were independent, at least for our sample, (c) the clear demonstration in our distribution analyses that each component interacted differently with fixation and social competence, and (d) the indication of somewhat distinguishable developmental roots for these components in our path-analytical study. The recidivism data also indicate that physical injury, but not sadism, was related to subsequent nonsexual violence. Although it is not clear whether Overt Sadism is related to subsequent sexual offending, there was little evidence in our study that the Muted Sadists were at a relatively high risk for committing a subsequent serious sexual crime.

The failure to consider both the injury and sadism components might be one of the factors (along with sample differences and variations in the duration and the amount of graphic detail in stimuli across studies) contributing to discrepancies found among studies that have attempted to relate the amount of violence in the crimes of sexual offenders to differential plethysmographic responsiveness (e.g., Abel, Becker, Blanchard, & Djenderedjian, 1978; Avery-Clark & Laws, 1984; Quinsey & Chaplin, 1982; Quinsey et al., 1981). It is possible, for example, that only the sadistic component of violence correlates with sexual arousal to aggressive stimuli, and that the physical injury inflicted on the victim is not related to such arousal. Clearly, the data we have reported support the differentiation of these two components of sexual violence and suggest that efforts to improve the reliability of the assessment of sadism may be richly rewarded with an increased understanding of sexual violence.

Assessing the Major Discriminating Characteristics of MTC:CM3 Types

In contrast with the examination of the validity of the major structural components of MTC:CM3, which was the focus of the last section, in this section I will concentrate on comparisons among the various Axis I and Axis II types on selected variables that were not used to define the types. My aim here is to identify the discriminating characteristics of each type. The structural analyses have provided a convenient base, both for comparing MTC:CM3 to other systems and for assessing the infrastructure of the typology. The focus on the discriminating, descriptive characteristics of each particular Axis I and Axis II type emphasizes clinical relevance in the sense that it attempts to provide an empirically validated, prototypical picture of how each type would appear to the clinician. The descriptions of the Axis I and Axis II types that follow have been compiled by identifying the critical variables on which either Axis I or Axis II types differ significantly among themselves. To make them more readable, I have omitted the individual ANOVA or Chi-square comparisons, and have concentrated on summarizing the major differences. The specific statistical analyses are available upon request, and will be reported in future papers on the typology.

Axis I. The high-fixation, low-social-competence type (Type I–0), which includes more offenders than any other Axis I type, can be characterized as high, relative to the other Axis I types, on psychiatric symptoms, especially thought disorder and the symptoms of anxiety and depression. They also had more contact with the psychiatric establishment in childhood than other Axis I types. They were distinguished by the number and variety of neurocognitive deficits they manifested during their lifetime, by evidence of learning disabilities in childhood, and by the number of paraphilias noted in their clinical records. They were the least able of the Axis I types to maintain themselves independently and they had attained the lowest employment skill level. In the 10-year follow-up they had the greatest percent of offenders to be charged with (32.8%) or convicted of (24.1%) a subsequent serious sexual assault.

Offenders in the high-fixation, high-social-competence group (Type I–1), like offenders in the other high social competence Axis I group (Type I–3), demonstrated an ability to maintain themselves independently. They achieved the highest employment skill level of the Axis I types. Unlike their low social competence, high-fixation cogroup (Type I–0), they showed, however, few developmental problems. They had the fewest number of school-related acting-out problems, and were least likely to have had significant contacts with psychiatric establishments when they were children. Moreover, they showed little evidence of learning disabilities as children. As adults they continue to show few problems with impulse control, and manifest little evidence of severe psychiatric impairment.

The low-fixation, low-social-competence types (Type I–2) had more difficulty than other Axis I groups with impulsivity as adolescents and adults. None of the offenders in this group was even charged with a serious sexual offense during the 10-year follow-up period, but 16.7% were convicted of victim-involved nonsexual assaults during this period. Otherwise, they are relatively undistinguished.

The low-fixation, high-social-competence type (Type I–3) showed significantly fewer symptoms of anxiety and depression than all other groups. This type had the lowest amount of impulsivity, the fewest number of psychiatric and neurocognitive symptoms, and the lowest frequency of paraphilias. None of the seven offenders in this group was convicted of a serious sexual or victim-involved nonsexual offense during the 10-year follow-up, and five (71.4%) of this group were classified Exploitative type on Axis II.

Axis II. The Interpersonal type (Type II–1) was exclusively highly fixated and was split somewhat evenly into low (58%) and high (42%) social competence groups (see Table 2.1). As a group these individuals could be characterized as detached and asocial in their interpersonal style. In addition to being the lowest of the Axis II groups in sexual aggression (which is to some degree definitional), they were also the lowest group in school-related acting out, the type with the least delinquency and adult antisocial behavior, and the lowest in their adult nonsexual aggression. Although they were highly fixated, they were low on thought disorder symptoms and on the psychosis symptom factor, and relatively low on anxiety and mood symptoms. Interestingly, they were the highest group on sexual deviation in the home during their childhood. Other distinguishing characteristics included: a low number of juvenile offenses, a late onset age of drinking alcohol (18.3 years), a low frequency of drinking, the lowest coincidence of acting out and drinking alcohol, high offense planning, and the highest ability of Axis II types to maintain an independent, self-supporting life-style. Although not significantly different from all other Axis II types, they did have the distinction during the 10-year follow-up period of having a greater proportion of offenders in this group having convictions for sexual assaults (33.3%) than the remaining subtypes, and they had the greatest percent of returns to the Treatment Center (77.8%). In contrast, they had no victim-involved nonsexual convictions or charges during that same period.

The Narcissistic types (Type II–2) were almost all (93%) highly fixated, with the majority (71%) being low in social competence (see Table 2.1). Like its high-contact companion group, the Interpersonal type, these offenders were low in school-related acting out and juvenile criminal offending, low in the delinquency/adult antisocial factor, and low in unsocialized (nonsexual) aggression. They were relatively low in contact with psychiatric institutions as children, and low in alcohol abuse and psychotic and affective symptoms as adults. Their offenses were relatively unimpulsive and their sexual aggression was almost as low as that of the Interpersonal type.

Although the majority of the offenders in the Exploitative type (Type II–3) were high in fixation (82.6%), this type also included a larger number of high-social-competence, low-fixation offenders than any other Axis II type, having 71.4% of all such offenders in the entire sample (see Table 2.1). Thus, it may be considered one of the most diverse of the types. Indeed, it occupies a middle ground on most variables between the high-contact offenders and the more aggressive high-injury and high-sadism types. It shared with the Interpersonal type the distinction of having more of its members establish an independent, self-sufficient life-style than the other four Axis II types. Moreover, the offenders in this type achieved the highest level of heterosexual pair bonding of the Axis II types.

A large proportion (93.8%) of the Muted Sadistic types (Type II–4) were high-fixation, low-social-competence, Axis I types (see Table 2.1).

As might be expected from their exclusively low social competence status on Axis I, they evidenced a low level of general interpersonal competence and had the lowest level of all Axis II types of heterosexual pair bonding. Moreover, they, like the Overt Sadistic types, were poor at maintaining a stable, independent, residence outside of institutions. Although a number of distinctive characteristics suggested that this type constituted a discriminable group of child molesters, several unexpected results were not consistent with our a priori notions about the core features of this type. For instance, contrary to hypothesis, their families of origin were not high in sexual deviation, their crimes appeared to be more highly impulsive and less planned than would be expected for fantasy-driven assaults, and they had the lowest rate of recidivism for serious sexual crimes (no convictions and only 1 [9.1%] charge) during the 10-year follow-up. In contrast, like the Overt Sadists, they showed a lifelong pattern of aggressive, impulsive acting out, starting with aggressive, school-related acting out and continuing into adulthood. Like the high-injury types (Types II–5 and II–6), they were high in nonsexual aggression, and they shared with the Exploitative and Overt Sadistic types a high number of adult criminal convictions. Consistent with their defining criteria, they, like the Exploitative types, manifested significantly greater sexual aggression than the high-contact types (Types II–1 and II–2), but significantly less sexual aggressiveness than the high-injury types (Types II–5 and II–6). Although the onset of their use of alcohol was quite young (11 years old), they, like the high-contact offenders (Types II–1 and II–2), had a low incidence of alcohol abuse as adults and showed a low coincidence of drinking and acting out.

The majority (88.9%) of the Aggressive types (Type II–5) were judged to be low in social competence on Axis I, and they split relatively evenly between Axis I high- (59.3%) and low- (40.7%) fixation types (see Table 2.1). Consistent with their defining characteristics, they had the highest level of offense impulsivity (i.e., the lowest level of offense planning), and during the 10-year follow-up period they had the highest incidence of victim-involved nonsexual charges (44.4%) and convictions (33.3%), combined with one of the lower rates of convictions for serious sexual assaults (11.1%) of the Axis II groups. Like the Overt Sadists, they engaged in frequent drinking and manifested a high level of alcohol abuse. Moreover, they also showed the highest incidence of acting out while drinking alcohol of all the Axis II types. Like the sadistic types (Types II–4 and II–6), their aggression in nonsexual contexts was high, and they had evidenced high emotional and behavioral instability in childhood. Unlike these sadistic groups and unlike the high-contact types (Types II–1 and II–2), they had a low incidence of paraphilias reported in their clinical files.

All of the offenders in the Overt Sadistic group (Type II–6) were judged to be low in social competence on Axis I (see Table 2.1), and like the Muted Sadists, they had more difficulty than the other types maintaining independent living arrangements. Like the Muted Sadistic and Aggressive types, they were high in their nonsexual aggression and impulsivity, and like the Muted Sadistic types, this aggression and impulsivity began early and was clearly manifested in their school behaviors. Consistent with the finding among a mixed group of sexual offenders (Prentky et al., 1989) that the amount of injury inflicted on the victim during a sexual assault was related to the inconstancy of caregivers during childhood and adolescence, the Overt Sadists had five times more foster placements than the next closest Axis II type. Also consistent with the findings of this study, the Overt Sadists were greater than all other Axis II types except the Interpersonal types in the amount of sexual deviance in their families of origin. Finally, the Overt Sadists were distinguished by their relatively higher level of general psychopathology. They were rated highest of the Axis II groups in adult thought disorder and mood disorder symptoms. In addition, they started drinking at an early age, and like the Aggressive types, they drank frequently as adults and abused alcohol. It is difficult to make any firm conclusions about the recidivism of Overt Sadists because of the low number released from MTC. Only one (25%) committed a serious sexual offense during the 10-year follow-up, but none of the offenders from this group was charged with or convicted of a nonsexual, victim-involved offense during this period.

LIMITATIONS OF MTC:CM3

In our attempt to uncover taxonomic structures for child molesters we have followed a strategy that is now common in taxonomic research on criminals (see Brennan, 1987), that of creating a particularized system within a relatively circumscribed behavioral domain on a narrowly defined sample. Because of the greater precision and homogeneity that can be achieved within narrower populations, the potential for success is increased. We developed and validated our system on a sample of child molesters who had been judged sexually dangerous and committed for an indeterminate sentence. Although the selectivity of this sample and the extensiveness of their evaluation had distinct advantages, it also has its limitations. First, because the system was fashioned on a committed sample, generalization to broader samples of noncommitted child abusers must be empirically validated. Second, the use of the system for child abuser samples that were not included in our sample (e.g., exclusively incestuous fathers) is questionable, and might require some modifications of the system as well the empirical investigation of MTC:CM3's appropriateness for such offenders. Third, several variables, which have been hypothesized to be important in distinguishing child abusers were omitted from the MTC:CM3, because of the added complexity they introduced. Their relation to the system and possible contribution to further differentiation among types must be examined.

Generalization to Broader Nonincestuous Child Molester Samples

To resolve the first limitation problem, it must be determined empirically whether nonincestuous child molesters who have *not* been judged to be sexually dangerous or molesters who have *not* been incarcerated can be reliably classified into the MTC:CM3 types, and whether these types share the same distinguishing characteristics that have discriminated among the MTC:CM3 types thus far studied. We are currently evaluating these generalization questions by applying MTC:CM3 to three new samples. We are studying a sample of child molesters referred to MTC, but not committed, a sample of child molesters serving sentences in a general, maximum security prison, and a sample of nonincestuous child molesters who are outpatients. Preliminary results suggest that these new samples can be classified by MTC:CM3, but certain types appear less frequently in the noncommitted MTC and the outpatient samples (e.g., fewer high injury types). We have not yet begun validation analyses of these samples.

Appropriateness of MTC:CM3 for Incestuous Fathers

Men who sexually abuse children can be distinguished along a continuum assessing their social and biological relationship to their victims, from complete stranger, to casual acquintance, to close "friend," to relative, to stepfather, to biological father. Because we have been studying an incarcerated, committed sample in which incest cases have been infrequent, we have focused only on offenders who have molested children who were not their biological children or stepchildren, or who have only started sexually abusing their own children after they had molested other children. Thus, offenders who exclusively molested their biological children or stepchildren were not included in our sample. The ostensibly more circumscribed nature of the offenses of incestuous fathers or stepfathers, the fact that all of them are by definition married (or at least in a lasting relationship, if their children were born out of wedlock), and the complicating role of family dynamics (Brooks, 1982) suggest that the usefulness of MTC:CM3 for differentiating among them may prove problematic, and some of MTC:CM3's criteria may have to be amended. Some data (Erickson, Luxenberg, Walbek, & Seely, 1987; Scott & Stone, 1986) suggest further that among incestuous offenders there may be differences between biological fathers and stepfathers, with the former being less like nonincestuous offenders than the latter. Thus, the generalization of MTC:CM3 to exclusively incestuous fathers, especially natural, biological fathers, may pose more difficulties than the generalization to nonincestuous child molesters who were not determined to be sexually dangerous or who were not incarcerated for their offenses.

Recent research sheds some light on this generalization problem. A number of studies have revealed that incestuous abusers are markedly heterogeneous on a number of variables that are considered relevant to their abusive behavior (Williams & Finkelhor, 1990). Moreover, this research has identified a number of areas in which incestuous fathers as a group bear a closer resemblance to nonincestuous offenders than to controls. The substantial heterogeneity of incestuous offenders on critical variables and their similarities to nonincestuous offenders provide some empirical support for the possibility that some of the taxonomic structures that have successfully discriminated among nonincestuous offenders may, with appropriate modification, be relevant for discriminating among incest cases. A cursory identification of selected areas of heterogeneity and possible similarity illustrates this point.

An important caveat must, however, precede our consideration of these studies. The distinction between intrafamilial and extrafamilial offenders is often blurred by incomplete offense reporting and the failure to examine the differences between biological and surrogate fathers. In a confidential interview, in which offenders were provided substantial assurance that the information they disclosed would not be used against them, a significant proportion of incestuous fathers (approximately 44%) admitted that they had also molested children outside of their families (Abel, Mittleman, Becker, Cunningham-Rathner, & Lucas, 1983). This suggests the possibility that a sizable proportion of fathers reported to be exclusively incestuous in the studies reviewed herein may also have molested children outside of their immediate family, but failed to reveal this to the investigators. Also, many studies have not distinguished between biological and surrogate fathers. In our sample we found several instances of child molesters who got married simply to gain access to their wife's children by a previous marriage. This suggests the possibility that stepfathers may not constitute a pure sample of incestuous offenders and should be examined separately. Thus, because of these two sample selection and defining problems in the studies reviewed, conclusions about the similarities of intrafamilial and extrafamilial molesters must be made with caution.

The fixation discrimination of Axis I in MTC:CM3 dichotomizes child molesters into those with an enduring focus on children as sexual objects and those without such an enduring pedophilic interest. Several studies suggest that a similar discrimination may be possible among incest offenders. A subset of incestuous offenders have been found to manifest deviant patterns of sexual arousal to children and adult females (Abel, Becker, Murphy, & Flanagan, 1981; Marshall, Barbaree, & Christophe, 1986). Although this subgroup does not constitute a majority of incestuous offenders and a larger subset of nonincestuous molesters show these patterns, these data are still consistent with the hypothesis that sexual fixation on children might meaningfully discriminate among incestuous cases. Indeed, it has also been estimated that between a quarter and a third of incestuous offenders have pedophilic erotic preferences (Langevin, Handy, Day, & Russon, 1985). Although the data from all these studies indicate that the proportion of fixated offenders is likely to be smaller among incestuous than among nonincestuous offenders, the distinction might carry the same taxonomic significance in both samples. Of course, the covariation between these deviant arousal patterns and both the propensity for incestuous fathers to molest extrafamilially and the natural–surrogate father distinction needs to be examined. It may be that fixation is infrequent among exclusively incestuous natural fathers.

Nonincestuous child molesters have consistently been found deficient as a group in their social skills and competencies (Marshall & Christie, 1981; Overholser & Beck, 1986; Quinsey, 1977; Segal & Marshall, 1985), and the evidence I have presented indicates that the Axis I social competence dichotomization is a valid taxonomic discriminator for these offenders. From the fact that incestuous offenders were typically married at the time of their offenses, one might infer that they are likely to be more homogeneous than and superior to nonincestuous offenders in their social skills and competencies. Indeed, because of their marital status and possibly, but not necessarily, their involvement in parenting, incestuous fathers would have a strong propensity to be rated as high in social competence on MTC:CM3. It would be incorrect, however, to consider them to be a highly socially skilled group. Incestuous fathers have been found to have poor interpersonal relationships (Strand, 1987) and to report low levels of group involvement (Quinn, 1984; Strand, 1987). Moreover, a significant proportion (31%) of incestuous offenders report that they have almost no friends (Parker, 1984) and incestuous fathers report higher levels of introversion than controls on psychological tests (Kirkland & Bauer, 1982; Langevin et al., 1985; Scott & Stone, 1986). These data suggest that even though a larger proportion of incest than nonincest offenders might be rated as high in social competence on Axis I of MTC:CM3, incestuous offenders might not be as different from nonincestuous offenders as originally thought, and social competence may still serve as an important discriminator among incestuous offenders.

In the validity and descriptive analyses presented earlier it was evident that Axis II of MTC:CM3 included some types that were more passive and dependent in their personality, that is, the high contact types (Types II–1 and II–2), and others that exhibited more aggressive, impulsive personality traits and behaviors (e.g., Types II–4, II–5, and II–6). Several studies suggest that a similar distinction may be found among incest offenders. For instance, several investigators have found that incestuous offenders were more passive, anxious, or reserved than controls (e.g., Langevin, Paitich, Freeman, Mann, & Handy, 1978; Kirkland & Bauer, 1982; Quinn, 1984; Scott & Stone, 1986). In contrast, other research has described incestuous fathers as dominant and tyrannical. Incestuous fathers have been reported to dominate their families with the use of force (Herman, 1981). They frequently abuse their wives (Paveza, 1987; Truesdall, McNeil, & Deschner, 1986), and they are as likely (19%) to have beaten up their daughters, or to have threatened or abused them with a weapon as are the fathers of daughters referred to a juvenile court (Feltman, 1985). Such abusive, aggressive behavior is consistent with the elevation on the MMPI Psychopathy scale often found among samples of incestuous fathers (e.g., Hall, Maiuro, Vitaliano, & Proctor, 1986; Kirkland & Bauer, 1982; Scott & Stone, 1986). It is possible to resolve these discrepant descriptions of incestuous fathers as either passive and dependent or aggressive and domineering by postulating that two separate types of offenders exist among incestuous abusers that parallel the types that have emerged in nonincestuous samples.

Other similarities have been found between incestuous and nonincestuous offenders that suggest some comparability between these groups. In self-report assessments of psychopathology, subgroups of each have evidenced abnormalities, and in several investigations no substantial differences between incestuous and nonincestuous offenders have emerged (Hall et al., 1986; Kirkland & Bauer, 1982; Langevin et al., 1985). In studies that have divided incestuous offenders into biological and surrogate father subgroups (e.g., Scott & Stone, 1986), there is some evidence, however, of MMPI profile differences between these two subgroups, with the stepfathers looking somewhat more like extrafamilial offenders than biological incestuous fathers (Erickson et al.,

1987). In studies assessing intelligence, although incestuous offenders have not been found to differ from controls in average IQ (Cavallin, 1966; Lee, 1982; Maisch, 1972; Meiselman, 1978), their IQs, like those of nonincestuous child molesters (Bard et al., 1987), have been found to have a different distribution than controls' IQs, with greater proportion of cases in the sample being at the lower end of the distribution (Lee, 1982).

The early histories of both incestuous and nonincestuous offenders also have sufficient similarities to suggest that the sexually abusive behavior of subgroups of each might share specific developmental antecedents. Sizable subgroups of both incest offenders (Baker, 1985) and nonincest offenders (Bard et al., 1987; Seghorn, Prentky, & Boucher, 1987) have reported histories of sexual abuse in their own childhood. Comparably high proportions of each group have also reported that they had experienced a significant amount of physical abuse in their families of origin (Bard et al., 1987; Brandon, 1985; Parker & Parker, 1986). Indeed, for both groups there is evidence of disruptive, unstable, and rejecting relationships with parents (Baker, 1985; Bard et al., 1987; Parker & Parker, 1986; Prentky et al., 1989). It is especially interesting that paternal attitudes and behaviors have been identified as particularly problematic for both groups (Baker, 1985; Parker & Parker, 1986; Prentky et al., 1989).

Given all these similarities, it is not surprising that clinicians, speculating on the taxomony of incestuous fathers, have postulated types that are similar to some of those proposed for nonincestuous offenders. For instance, Summit and Kryso (1978) have described a variety of types of incest cases they have encountered in their clinical experience. Included in these are: "Pedophilic" types who are erotically fascinated with children and who typically limit their sexual activity with their children to body contact, fondling, and oral contacts; "Child Rape" types, who are impulsive, potentially violent men, who typically overpower their victims and are more likely to engage in intercourse; "Mysogynous" types, who are hyperaggressive, coercive males, whose anger is directed specifically at women, and who often physically as well as sexually abuse their daughters; and "Perverse" types, who involve their children in kinky, ritualized, sadistic sexual behavior. The parallels of these types to the Interpersonal, Exploitative, Aggressive, and Sadistic types in Axis II of MTC:CM3 are obvious, and suggest the possibility that MTC:CM3 might successfully capture a significant proportion of the taxonomic invariance in incest cases.

In attempting to apply MTC:CM3 to incest cases the Axis I criteria for fixation and social competence will certainly require modification. For instance, the use of the criterion of three or more sexual contacts with children over a time span exceeding 6 months to infer high fixation on children may not discriminate high- from low-fixated incestuous fathers. A longer time frame might be necessary, or this criterion might have to be replaced by a more appropriate discriminator for incest cases. Because all incestuous fathers are married, or at least in a lasting relationship, if their children were born out of wedlock, the social competence criterion of marriage or cohabitation for at least 1 year is not likely to discriminate among these offenders and the parenting criterion will certainly require greater specification.

Omitted and "Disinhibitory" Criteria

A number of the dimensions that have been excluded from the basic structure of MTC:CM3 require comment. These can be divided into two basic categories: the sex of the victim(s), which has been employed as a type defining variable by other investigators, and several dimensions that have been labeled as disinhibitors (Finkelhor & Araji, 1983), because they hypothetically weaken or evade ordinary controls and thereby increase the probability of a variety of sexual aberrations, including child molestation. Among these disinhibitors are alcoholism or other substance abuse, psychosis, organicity/senility, and mental retardation.

We did not include the sex of the child as a taxonomic characteristic even though it appears to have some discriminatory power among child molesters (Fitch, 1962; Gebhard et al., 1965; Mohr, Turner, & Jerry, 1964). There is evidence for both its concurrent (Freund, 1965, 1967a; 1967b; Laws & Osborn, 1983) and predictive validity (Fitch, 1962; Frisbie, 1969; Frisbie & Dondis, 1965). Quinsey (1986; Earls & Quinsey, 1985) has argued that a trichotomization of child molesters based on the victim's sex (homosexual, bisexual, and heterosexual) coupled with a dichotomization, based on victim relatedness (incest offenders vs. pedophiles), should serve as a "null hypothesis" comparison against which the incremental validity of any new scheme is evaluated. Because the introduction of a victim-sex trichotomization would have greatly proliferated the number of types in our system, we decided to refine the present system before examining the victim-sex distributions within these types. We have begun to analyze both the validity of this victim-sex trichotomization within our sample and the relation of such preferences to the MTC:CM3 types. We will report the results of these analyses in future papers.

Each of the disinhibitory factors cited has been found present in a notable minority of child molesters (see Bard et al., 1987; Knight et al., 1985). We were not able to specify a priori what role each of these factors would play in child abuse. Indeed, it was not clear whether they were sufficiently powerful causal factors to warrant their own types, as some have suggested (e.g., Fitch, 1962; Gebhard et al., 1965; Swanson, 1971), or whether they confound behavioral patterns to such a degree that their presence should have been considered sufficient to exclude an offender from classification in the typology. We decided to examine the relation of these factors to our typology empirically. Thus, we included these factors as "keyed" items, which were noted when classifying offenders, but were not considered in assigning offenders to particular types. The validity studies presented earlier in this chapter included analyses of the relation of measures of several of these variables to typological assignment (e.g., substance abuse, psychosis, and neuro-cognitive deficits). The pattern of these results indicate that these dis-inhibitors covary with the typological assignments in specifiable ways and suggest that these factors should not constitute criteria for exclud-ing offenders from classification. Rather, they contribute to our un-derstanding of the behavior of particular types of child molesters.

FUTURE DIRECTIONS

In addition to the generalization studies described in the last section, and the examination of the potential integration of victim sex as an addition-al typological discriminator, it is clear that we must, where possible, integrate the two axes of MTC:CM3. Currently, each offender is assigned a separate Axis I and Axis II type. Crossing the four types of Axis I with the six types of Axis II yields 24 possible two-axis com-binations presented in Table 2.1. This seems to be an unwieldy number of types. The complex interactions among Axis I and Axis II com-ponents that were described earlier indicate that our decision to set them up as separate axes was judicious. The only viable alternative, a complex nesting of some factors within others, would have required a certainty about the interrelations among Axis I and Axis II variables that we had not attained at the time MTC:CM3 was developed. The precise form of the possible interrelations was either only hypothetical (e.g., the pro-posed independence of fixation and social competence and the interac-tion of fixation with the amount of contact with children) or not known (e.g., the interaction of the Axis I variables with the sadistic and injury distinctions). Thus, the only safe initial stance was to create separate axes, to assign offenders independently to each, and to let our empirical studies provide feedback about which of the Axis I/Axis II combinations were viable.

Table 2.1 presents the frequency and percentage of case assignments to each cell of the Axis I by Axis II cross-tabulation matrix. As can be seen in this table, 11 of the 24 possible cells were either empty or so low in frequency that for practical purposes they should be considered empty. These empty or low-frequency cells, if they remain empty in our generalization studies, provide a simple, empirically based criterion for streamlining the system and integrating the two axes. As can be seen in the table, we could simply drop consideration of fixation from Types II–1 and II–2, because the overwhelming majority of these types were highly fixated, and we could drop the social competence discrimination from Types II–4, II–5, and II–6, because virtually all these offenders were low in social competence. In addition to enhancing diagnostic efficiency, the dropping of the fixation distinction for the high-contact offenders would also eliminate the current definitional overlap between these two constructs, which is definitely a taxonomic inelegance in MTC:CM3. Determination of the importance of each Axis I distinction for Type II–3 (Exploitatives) offenders will be examined empirically. Although we did not predict a priori that the Exploitative type would have the greatest diversity of Axis I types, this heterogeneity is not surprising. In essence this group of molesters occupies a middle ground between the highly fixated, high-contact groups and the more aggressive and impulsive low-social-competence, low-contact molesters.

Finally, the reliability and validity analyses indicate that some additional fine-tuning of the Axis II low-contact offenders is required. The criteria for both Muted and Overt Sadistic types need better operational anchors. The Muted Sadistic criteria, although they are identifying offenders who differ from both the Exploitative and Aggressive types, are not capturing the prototype that they were intended to identify. They are isolating a group of offenders who are generally aggressive and impulsive, but who do not appear to behave as though they are motivated by sexual fantasies. The criteria for overt sadism are not sufficiently reliable. Moreover, several offenders who were classified as Overt Sadists were also judged to be low in fixation. That is, their sexual offenses were purportedly driven by sadistic sexual fantasies about children, but children were not judged to be a primary focus of their fantasies and cognitions. This apparent inconsistency must be resolved.

CONCLUSIONS

Importance of the Taxonomic Analysis of Child Molesters

Our application of a programmatic approach to typology construction and validation has produced a taxonomic system for child molesters that has already demonstrated reasonable reliability and consistent ties to distinctive developmental antecedents and specific, theoretically coherent adult behavioral patterns. In addition, preliminary results of a 10-year follow-up criminal recidivism study of child molesters indicate that aspects of the model have important prognostic implications. The data presented on the child molester typology strongly support the subdivision of these offenders and indicate that considerable explanatory and predictive power may be gained through taxonomic differentiation. Although we have not resolved the issue of number of types that will ultimately be necessary and sufficient for uncovering the etiology of sexual abuse and for specifying the treatment and disposition of child molesters, we have nonetheless provided a partial answer to the query posed earlier in this chapter about the level of taxonomic abstraction that is appropriate for child molesters.

Viability of the Method

The data that we have presented also confirm the viability of the methodology we have been applying and illustrate the importance of implementing both deductive and inductive strategies simultaneously. Each approach has its inherent strengths and weaknesses (Brennan, 1987; Meehl, 1979; Skinner & Blashfield, 1982). When applied concurrently, the two approaches provide complementary methods with reciprocal benefits. The results of each can enrich the interpretation of the other and generate new research questions. Differences in structures, when they arise, can often lead to important advances in understanding, and convergences across methods help to highlight prepotent structures. Indeed, the comparison of multiple solutions generated from different sources enhances falsifiability. The failure of a particular model to work in an area where another is successful makes us more likely to discard the unsuccessful model. If we know only that one model has not worked, we are likely to attribute its poor showing to auxiliary theory problems or experimental particulars, especially if our theoretical biases have been disconfirmed (Meehl, 1978). Because competing systems often share auxiliary theories, when a particular system explains or predicts the behaviors in a specific domain, it is not likely that an alternative system's failure to account for these same behaviors is due to deficiencies in the shared auxiliary theories. Thus, the presence of a successful model counters the explanations that save the alternative model by attributing its failure to weak or ineffective auxiliary theories or experimental particulars. Consequently, the presence of a valid model increases falsifiability, which is, of course, the lifeblood of science (Popper, 1972).

ACKNOWLEDGMENT

The research described in this chapter was conducted at the Massachusetts Treatment Center and has been supported by grants from the National Institute of Mental Health (MH 32309) and the National Institute of Justice (82–IJ–CX–0058). Collaborators in this research program have included Leonard Bard, Richard Boucher, Daniel Carter, David Cerce, Murray Cohen, Alison Martino, Denise Marvinney, Robert Prentky, Beth Schneider, Harry Straus, Theoharis Seghorn, and Ruth Rosenberg. I thank Judith Sims-Knight and Robert Prentky for their helpful comments on a preliminary draft.

REFERENCES

Abel, G. G., Becker, J. V., Blanchard, E. B., & Djenderedjian, A. (1978). Differentiating sexual aggressives with penile measures. *Criminal Justice and Behavior, 5*, 315–332.

Abel, G. G., Becker, J. V., Murphy, W. D., & Flanagan, B. (1981). Identifying dangerous child molesters. In R. B. Stewart (Ed.), *Violent behavior: Social learning approaches to prediction management and treatment* (pp. 116–137). New York: Brunner–Mazel.

Abel, G. G., Mittleman, M. S., Becker, J. V., Cunningham-Rathner, J., & Lucas, L. (1983, December). *The characteristics of men who molest young children*. Paper presented at the World Congress of Behavior Therapy, Washington, DC.

American Psychiatric Association. (1987). *Diagnostic and Statistical Manual of Mental Disorders, DSM–III–R* (4th ed.), Washington, DC: Author.

Avery-Clark, C. A., & Laws, D. R. (1984). Differential erection response patterns of sexual child abusers to stimuli describing activities with children. *Behavior Therapy, 15*, 71–83.

Baker, D. A. (1985). Father–daughter incest: A study of the father. *Dissertation Abstracts International, 46*, 951B. (University Microfilms No. 85–10,932)

Bard, L. A., Carter, D. L., Cerce, D. D., Knight, R. A., Rosenberg, R., & Schneider, B. (1987). A descriptive study of rapists and child molesters: Developmental, clinical and criminal characteristics. *Behavioral Sciences and the Law, 5*, 203–220.

Blashfield, R. K. (1980). Propositions regarding the use of cluster analysis in clinical research. *Journal of Consulting and Clinical Psychology, 48*, 456–459.

Brandon, C. S. (1985). Sex role identification in incest: An empirical analysis of the feminist theories. *Dissertation Abstracts International, 47*, 3099B. (University Microfilms No. 86-22,829)

Brennan, T. (1987). Classification: An overview of selected methodological issues. In D. M. Gottfredson & M. Tonry (Eds.), *Prediction and classification: Criminal justice decision making* (pp. 201–248). Chicago: University of Chicago Press.

Brooks, B. (1982). Familial influences in father–daughter incest. *Journal of Psychiatric Treatment and Evaluation, 4,* 117–124.

Cavallin, H. (1966). Incestuous fathers: A clinical report. *American Journal of Psychiatry, 122,* 1132–1138.

Cicchetti, D. V., & Sparrow, S. S. (1981). Developing criteria for establishing interrater reliability of specific items: Applications of assessment of adaptive behavior. *American Journal of Mental Deficiency, 86,* 127–137.

Cohen, M. L., Boucher, R. J., Seghorn, T. K., & Mehegan, J. (1979, March). *The sexual offender against children.* Paper presented at a meeting of the Association for Professional Treatment of Offenders, Boston.

Cohen, M. L., Seghorn, T., & Calmas, W. (1969). Sociometric study of sex offenders. *Journal of Abnormal Psychology, 74,* 249–255.

Conte, J. R. (1985). Clinical dimensions of adult sexual abuse of children. *Behavioral Sciences and the Law, 3,* 341–354.

Earls, C. M., & Quinsey, V. L. (1985). What is to be done? Future research on the assessment and behavioral treatment of sex offenders. *Behavioral Sciences and the Law, 3,* 377–390.

Erickson, W. D., Luxenberg, M. G., Walbek, N. H., & Seely, R. K. (1987). Frequency of MMPI two-point code types among sex offenders. *Journal of Consulting and Clinical Psychology, 55,* 566–570.

Feltman, R. I. (1985). A controlled, correlational study of the psychological functioning of paternal incest victims. *Dissertation Abstracts International, 46,* 3592B. (University Microfilms No. 85–26,512)

Finkelhor, D., & Araji, S. (1983, July). *Explanations of pedophilia: A four factor model.* Paper presented at the American Academy of Psychiatry and Law, Portland, OR.

Fitch, J. H. (1962). Men convicted of sexual offenses against children: A descriptive follow-up study. *British Journal of Criminology, 3*(1), 18–37.

Freund, K. (1965). Diagnosing heterosexual pedophilia by means of a test for sexual interest. *Behavior Research and Therapy, 3,* 229–234.

Freund, K. (1967a). Diagnosing homo- and heterosexuality and erotic age preference by means of a psychophysiological test. *Behaviour Research and Therapy, 5,* 209–228.

Freund, K. (1967b). Erotic preference in pedophilia. *Behavior Research and Therapy, 5,* 339–348.

Frisbie, L. V. (1969). Another look at sex offenders in California. *California Mental Health Research Monograph,* No. 12. State of California Department of Mental Hygiene.

Frisbie, L. V., & Dondis, E. H. (1965). Recidivism among treated sex offenders. *California Mental Health Research Monograph,* No. 5. State of California Department of Mental Hygiene.

Gebhard, P. H., Gagnon, J. H., Pomeroy, W. B., & Christenson, C. V. (1965). *Sex offenders: An analysis of types.* New York: Harper & Row.

Ghiselin, M. T. (1981). Categories, life, and thinking. *Behavioral and Brain Sciences, 4,* 269–313.

Groth, A. N. (1978). Patterns of sexual assault against children and adolescents. In A. W. Burgess, A. N. Groth, L. L. Holmstrom, & S. M. Sgroi (Eds.), *Sexual assault of children and adolescents.* Boston: D.C. Heath.

Groth, A. N., Hobson, W. F., & Gary, T. S. (1982). The child molester: Clinical observations. *Social Work and Human Sexuality, 1,* 129–144.

Hall, G. C. N., Maiuro, R. D., Vitaliano, P. P., & Proctor, W. C. (1986). The utility of the MMPI with men who have sexually assaulted children. *Journal of Consulting and Clinical Psychology, 54,* 493–496.

Hathaway, S. R., & Monachesi, E. D. (Eds.). (1953). *Analyzing and predicting juvenile delinquency with the MMPI.* Minneapolis: University of Minnesota Press.

Hathaway, S. R., & Monachesi, E. D. (Eds.). (1954). A new approach to identifying and helping delinquent children. *Minnesota Trends, 1,* 71–79.

Hempel, C. G. (1965). *Aspects of scientific explanation.* New York: Free Press.

Herman, J. (1981). *Father–daughter incest.* Cambridge, MA: Harvard University Press.

Howells, K. (1981). Adult sexual interest in children: Considerations relevant to theories of aetiology. In M. Cook & K. Howells (Eds.), *Adult sexual interest in children.* New York: Academic Press.

Kirkland, K. D., & Bauer, C. A. (1982). MMPI traits of incestuous fathers. *Journal of Clinical Psychology, 38,* 645–649.

Knight, R. A. (1988). A taxonomic analysis of child molesters. In R. A. Prentky & V. L. Quinsey (Eds.), *Human sexual aggression: Current perspectives* (Vol. 528, pp. 2–20). New York: The New York Academy of Sciences.

Knight, R. A. (1989). An assessment of the concurrent validity of a child molester typology. *Journal of Interpersonal Violence, 4,* 131–150.

Knight, R. A., Carter, D. L., & Prentky, R. A. (1989). A system for the classification of child molesters: Reliability and application. *Journal of Interpersonal Violence, 4,* 3–23.

Knight, R. A., & Prentky, R. A. (1990). Classifying sexual offenders: The development and corroboration of taxonomic models. In W. L. Marshall, D. R. Laws, & H. E. Barbaree (Eds.), *The handbook of sexual assault: Issues, theories, and treatment of the offender* (pp. 23–52). New York: Plenum Press.

Knight, R. A., & Roff, J. D. (1983). Childhood and young adult predictors of schizophrenic outcome. In D. Ricks & B. Dowhrenwend (Eds.), *Origins of psychopathology: Research and public policy* (pp. 129–153). London & New York: Cambridge University Press.

Knight, R. A., & Roff, J. D. (1985). Affectivity in schizophrenia. In M. Alpert (Ed.), *Controversies in schizophrenia* (pp. 280–316). New York: Guilford Press.

Knight, R. A., Rosenberg, R., & Schneider, B. (1985). Classification of sexual offenders: Perspectives, methods, and validation. In A. Burgess (Ed.), *Rape and sexual assault: A research handbook* (pp. 222–293). New York: Garland.

Knight, R. A., & Straus, H. (1991). *Validating a typology for child molesters: Its relation to symptom factors.* Manuscript in preparation.

Kopp, S. B. (1962). The character structure of sex offenders. *American Journal of Psychotherapy, 16,* 64–70.

Langevin, R., Handy, L., Day, D., & Russon, A. (1985). Are incestuous fathers pedophilic, aggressive, and alcoholic? In R. Langevin (Ed.), *Erotic preference, gender identity, and aggression* (pp. 161–179). Hillsdale, NJ: Lawrence Erlbaum Associates.

Langevin, R., Paitich, D., Freeman, R., Mann, K., & Handy, L. (1978). Personality characteristics and sexual anomalies in males. *Canadian Journal of Behavioral Sciences, 10,* 222–238.

Lanning, K. V. (1986). *Child molesters: A behavioral analysis for law-enforcement officers investigating cases of child exploitation.* Washington, DC: National Center for Missing and Exploited Children.

Laws, D. R., & Osborn, C. A. (1983). How to build and operate a behavioral laboratory to evaluate and treat sexual deviance. In J. G. Greer & I. R. Stuart (Eds.), *The sexual aggressor.* New York: Van Nostrand Reinhold.

Lee, R. N. (1982). Analysis of the characteristics of incestuous fathers. *Dissertation Abstracts International, 43,* 2343B. (University Microfilms No. 82–27,677)

Maisch, H. (1972). *Incest.* New York: Stein & Day.

Marshall, W. L., Barbaree, H. E., & Christophe, D. (1986). Sexual offenders against female children: Sexual preferences for age of victims and type of behaviour. *Canadian Journal of Behavioural Sciences, 18,* 424–439.

Marshall, W. L., & Christie, M. M. (1981). Pedophilia and aggression. *Criminal Justice and Behavior, 8,* 145–158.

McCaghy, C. H. (1967). *Child molesters: A study of their careers as deviants.* New York: Holt, Rinehart & Winston.

Meehl, P. E. (1957). When shall we use our heads instead of the formula? *Journal of Counseling Psychology, 4,* 268–273.

Meehl, P. E. (1959). Some ruminations on the validation of clinical procedures. *Canadian Journal of Psychology, 13,* 102–128.

Meehl, P. E. (1978). Theoretical risks and tabular asterisks: Sir Karl, Sir Ronald, and the slow progress of soft psychology. *Journal of Consulting and Clinical Psychology, 46,* 806–834.

Meehl, P. E. (1979). A funny thing happened on the way to the latent entities. *Journal of Personality Assessment, 43,* 564–581.

Meiselman, K. C. (1978). *Incest: A psychological study of causes and effects with treatment recommendations.* San Francisco: Jossey-Bass.

Mohr, J. W., Turner, R. E., & Jerry, M. B. (1964). *Pedophilia and exhibitionism.* Toronto: University of Toronto Press.

Monahan, J. (1981). *The clinical prediction of violent behavior.* (Crime and Delinquency Issues Monograph. U.S. Government of Health and Human Services Publication No. ADM 81–921). Washington, DC: U. S. Government Printing Office.

Overholser, J. C., & Beck, S. (1986). Multimethod assessment of rapists, child molesters, and three control groups on behavioral and psychological measures. *Journal of Consulting and Clinical Psychology, 54,* 682–687.

Parker, H. (1984). Intrafamilial sexual child abuse: A study of the abusive father. *Dissertation Abstracts International, 45,* 3757A. (University Microfilms No. 85–03,876)

Parker, H., & Parker, S. (1986). Father–daughter sexual abuse: An emerging perspective. *American Journal of Orthopsychiatry, 56,* 531–549.

Paveza, G. (1987, July). *Risk factors in father–daughter child sexual abuse: Findings from a case-control study.* Paper presented at the third National Family Violence Research Conference, Family Research Laboratory, Durham, NH.

Popper, K. R. (1972). *The logic of scientific discovery*. London: Hutchinson.

Prentky, R. A., Knight, R. A., Rosenberg, R., & Lee, A. (1989). A path analytic approach to the validation of a taxonomic system for classifying child molesters. *Journal of Quantitative Criminology, 5*, 231–257.

Prentky, R. A., Knight, R. A., Sims-Knight, J. E., Straus, H., Rokous, F., & Cerce, D. (1989). Developmental roots of sexual dangerousness. *Development and Psychopathology, 1*, 153–169.

Quinn, T. M. (1984). Father–daughter incest: An ecological model. *Dissertation Abstracts International, 45*, 3957B. (University Microfilms No. 84–29,752)

Quinsey, V. (1977). The assessment and treatment of child molesters: A review. *Canadian Psychological Review, 18*, 204–220.

Quinsey, V. L. (1986). Men who have sex with children. In D. Weisstub (Ed.). *Law and mental health: International perspectives* (Vol. 2, pp. 140–172). New York: Pergamon.

Quinsey, V. L., & Chaplin, T. C. (1982). Penile responses to nonsexual violence among rapists. *Criminal Justice and Behavior, 9*, 372–381.

Quinsey, V. L., Chaplin, T. C., & Varney, G. (1981). A comparison of rapists' and non-sex offenders' sexual preferences for mutually consenting sex, rape, and physical abuse of women. *Behavioral Assessment, 3*, 127–135.

Rosenberg, R., & Knight, R. A. (1988). Determining male sexual offender subtypes using cluster analysis. *Journal of Quantitative Criminology, 4*, 383–410.

Scott, R. L., & Stone, D. A. (1986). MMPI profile constellations in incest families. *Journal of Consulting and Clinical Psychology, 54*, 364–368.

Segal, Z. V., & Marshall, W. L. (1985). Heterosexual social skills in a population of rapists and child molesters. *Journal of Consulting and Clinical Psychology, 53*, 55–63.

Seghorn, T. K. (1970). Adequacy of ego functioning in rapists and pedophiles. *Dissertation Abstracts International, 31*, 7613A–7614A. (University Microfilms No. 70–22,413)

Seghorn, T. K., Prentky, R. A., & Boucher, R. J. (1987). Childhood sexual abuse in the lives of sexually aggressive offenders. *Journal of the American Academy of Child and Adolescent Psychiatry, 26*, 262–267.

Skinner, H. A. (1981). Toward the integration of classification theory and methods. *Journal of Abnormal Psychology, 90*, 68–87.

Skinner, H. A. (1986). Construct validation approach to psychiatric classification. In T. Millon & G. L. Klerman (Eds.), *Contemporary directions in psychopathology: Toward the DSM–IV* (pp. 307–330). New York: Guilford Press.

Skinner, H. A., & Blashfield, R. K. (1982). Increasing the impact of cluster analysis research: The case of psychiatric classification. *Journal of Consulting and Clinical Psychology, 50*, 727–735.

Strand, V. (1987). Parents in incest families: A study in differences. *Dissertation Abstracts International, 47*, 3191A. (University Microfilms No. 86–23,618)

Summit, R., & Kryso, J. (1978). Sexual abuse of children: A clinical spectrum. *American Journal of Orthopsychiatry, 48*, 237–251.

Swanson, D. W. (1971). Who violates children sexually? *Medical Aspects of Human Sexuality, 5*, 184–197.

Truesdell, D. L., McNeil, J. S., & Deschner, J. (1986, March–April). The incidence of wife abuse in incestuous families. *Social Work*, 138–140.

Williams, L. M., & Finkelhor, D. (1990). The characteristics of incestuous fathers: A review of recent studies. In W. L. Marshall, D. R. Laws, & H. E. Barbaree (Eds.), *The handbook of sexual assault: Issues, theories, and treatment of the offender* (pp. 231–255). New York: Plenum Press.

Medical Detection and Effects of the Sexual Abuse of Children

Allan R. De Jong
Director, Pediatric Sexual Abuse Program, Jefferson Medical College, PA

The medical evaluation of the sexually abused child should be viewed from the perspective that it is an essential yet relatively minor part of the overall management of sexual abuse. All children being evaluated for suspected sexual abuse should have a medical examination, although most examinations will not detect abnormal physical findings or provide positive forensic medical evidence that sexual contact has occurred. The medical evaluation should be a routine part of the overall evaluation for several reasons. First, an appropriate history and physical examination can serve as documentation and validation of the child's complaint of abuse. Depending on the history, both normal and abnormal physical findings, infections, or injuries can be used to support the child's allegations of abuse. Secondly, the examination should help guide medical therapy when injuries or infections are present. Finally, and perhaps most importantly, the child may be reassured following most examinations of physical normality. We should not underestimate the therapeutic value of telling children they are not diseased, damaged, or physically different from other children.

Who should do the physical examination of the sexually abused child? The physician should be someone who understands the medical, social, and legal issues involved, who knows what information is to be collected, and who has skills in working with children. A protocol or routine examination procedure should be used, although the physician's approach should be flexible to minimize the stress and maximize the benefits of the examination. A child abuse specialist need not perform all evaluations; however, not all physicians have the training, interest, or skills to perform an appropriate interview and examination.

When is a medical evaluation indicated? Clearly a thorough evaluation is needed whenever a child states directly that sexual abuse has occurred or whenever suspicious genital or anal injury is found. A child or young adolescent who is pregnant or has a sexually transmitted disease should also initiate an evaluation as to how the child developed these "conditions." Masked presentations of abuse are common (Hunter, Kilstrom, & Loda, 1985; Krugman, 1986; Teixeira, 1981). In such cases, the child offers the history of abuse in the course of evaluation of a physical complaint or abnormal behavior, or a behavior change. Therefore, a medical evaluation is indicated in any case in which the child offers a history of abuse or if physical conditions suggest the probability of sexual contact even in the absence of a verbal complaint by the child (Seidel, Elvik, Berkowitz, & Day, 1986).

How soon should the examination be done following disclosure of abuse? The disclosure is a psychosocial emergency, but relatively few cases are medical emergencies. Immediate examination is indicated if the last episode of abuse occurred in the last 72 hours, if there is a history of acute genital or anal bleeding or injury, if there is significant risk of a sexually transmitted disease, or if there is a significant risk of pregnancy. If the criteria for immediate examination are not met, then an evaluation can be done either at that time or scheduled within the next few days (Enos, Conrath, & Beyer, 1986).

What constitutes an appropriate medical evaluation? The medical–legal or forensic evidence collected during the medical examination has four major components: (1) the history of the sexual abuse, (2) the documentation of the use of force, (3) the documentation of sexual contact, and (4) specimens to aid in proving the identity of the offender or perpetrator. The most important component is the medical interview to collect verbal information about the abuse. The results of the interview determine what additional information to collect and how this can be interpreted. The medical evaluation protocol should include methods to collect and document evidence of the use of force (physical injury) and evidence of sexual contact, (sexually transmitted diseases, sperm or seminal fluid), and evidence regarding the identity of the offender. Provisions should be made for initial medical therapy, notification of appropriate agencies, and providing options for counseling and medical follow-up (Sproles, 1985).

This chapter will discuss general information about the medical evaluation of the sexually abused child. Topics covered will include the types of medical–legal or forensic evidence in sexual abuse cases, steps in collection of this evidence and the laboratory analysis of this evidence. The information should be helpful for interpreting the presence or absence of physical injuries, sexually transmitted diseases, and forensic laboratory data in cases of suspected sexual abuse.

THE MEDICAL INTERVIEW

The ideal sexual abuse assessment interview is done by an individual who is skilled at doing a forensic interview, and who is able to cover all the questions required by the physician, social services, and the police. A single, well-executed interview, which can be videotaped and/or viewed by the others through a one-way mirror would obtain the information required by all interested parties while avoiding the stress of repeated interview for the child. Unfortunately, the medical interview is typically done separately from interviews by child protective services and law enforcement personnel (Krugman, 1986).

The medical interview is the process by which the history of the abuse is obtained. The medical interview serves many purposes when it is done appropriately. The initial purpose of the interview is to introduce the child to the supportive adults and the physical environment in which the physical examination will be done. The primary goal of the interview is to obtain a detailed history of the abuse. The history of abuse may be the only evidence in the case, since physical evidence or eyewitness accounts may not be present. A detailed history helps direct physical evidence collection and may aid in the interpretation of the results of the evidence collection. This is particularly true if a delay has occurred between the time of the last assault and the disclosure. The documented history becomes most important in cases in which the history is placed in evidence to support the child's testimony in court. Statements made by child to an adult may be admissible in court under exceptions to the hearsay rule (depending on state law), and the physician is often able to provide a more detailed and objective recollection than family members (Meyers, 1986).

The general approach to the interview will in many cases determine whether a good history of the events will be obtained. The medical interview is often conducted in the time of crisis, precipitated by disclosure or discovery of the abuse and efforts should be made to foster a sensitive, supportive, nonthreatening, unhurried approach. The interviewer should attempt to establish an empathic, trusting relationship in a private setting. Particular sensitivity is required since many children will emotionally relive the abuse as they talk about it. The interviewer should explain who he or she is and why you are interested in talking with the child today. The language used should be appropriate for the child's developmental level and initial steps should be taken to develop a common language with the child by learning what they call different body parts (Berkowitz, 1987).

A medical interview can be conducted successfully using a number of different techniques (MacFarlane & Krebs, 1987). Each technique has its advantages and disadvantages. Most of the techniques require specific training and practice, and most physicians will be experienced in the direct interview technique only. Therefore, the physician may need to refer the child for further interviews by a child psychologist, child psychiatrist, social worker, or other specialist for a more complete evaluation. The direct interview may be the most appropriate approach for the older child or the adolescent. The questions should progress from more general to more specific, with care to avoid leading questions. This direct interview technique is not as effective in younger children where interviewing the child while engaging in physical activity or play is preferred. Preprinted or spontaneously created drawings, which the child can color, label, or add cartoon-like captions to represent dialogue or to express feelings, can facilitate interviews in young children. A dollhouse can be used effectively in some children and has the advantage of allowing the child to act out scenes and relationships in different rooms of the house using the doll figures. However, some boys will refuse to "play with dolls," so puppets or stuffed animals may be useful. The dolls, puppets, or stuffed animals may be able to talk about feelings and events that the children find difficult to talk about themselves. Sexually anatomically correct (SAC) dolls are a popular interviewing device because the anatomical detail allows for a more graphic demonstration of the actual abuse. Although some recent controlled studies have begun to validate the use of these dolls, a standardized approach is required to avoid social and legal concerns about over interpretation of the child's responses (White, Strom, Santilli, & Halpin, 1986).

Regardless of the technique used, there are nine key aspects of the history that determine whether evidence is collected or found, and what immediate assessments, treatments, or referrals are required. First, who is the perpetrator? Is the perpetrator known to child or a stranger: a family member or nonfamily contact? The issue of safety needs to be addressed in cases of intrafamilial abuse for both the victim and the other children in the family. A decision needs to be made about whether the victim and other children will be safe at home while the investigation of the abuse is ongoing. Second, was force or any other form of coercion used? This is of particular importance when the victim and the assailant are of similar age, in order to determine whether the sexual contact was abusive or consensual. Also, the degree and type of force used may determine the degree of physical injuries present. Third, was this a single episode or recurrent abuse? The abuse is often recurrent and a progression of increasing intimacy of contact is common. Gentle, non-coital stretching and the use of lubricants in recurrent, progressive abuse may decrease the risk of acute physical injury. However, chronic abuse may increase the chance of finding healing scars. Fourth, when was the last abuse? Collection of evidence is time-dependent; the longer the interval from the last abuse the less likely that any physical evidence will be detected. Fifth, what has happened since that episode? Bathing, drinking, toileting, wiping may remove or destroy evidence. Sixth, is there a history that suggests current or prior injury? A present or past history of vaginal bleeding, discharges, infections, or genital or anal pain or discomfort should be documented. Current genital, urinary, or anal complaints including changes in bladder control (enuresis) or bowel control (encopresis), may have either physical or psychosomatic origins. Seventh, what type of sexual contact was attempted? The type of contact, sites of contact, whether there was pain or bleeding may help determine the location and likelihood of physical findings. Eighth, are there behavior changes or somatic complaints? Although signs of stress may be nonspecific and nondiagnostic, extreme signs of stress may direct the examiner to refer the child for emergency counseling. Ninth, what is the relative risk for pregnancy or sexually transmitted diseases? A menstrual history, use of birth control, or symptoms suggestive of infections are important. Depending on the circumstances, the physician will need to consider the use of prophylactic therapy for pregnancy and sexually transmitted diseases (Berkowitz, 1987; Enos et al., 1986; Koop, 1988; Krugman, 1986; Sproles, 1985; De Jong & Finkel, 1990).

THE PHYSICAL EXAMINATION TO DOCUMENT USE OF FORCE OR INJURY

The physical examination, like the interview, should be done in as supportive, nonthreatening, and unhurried manner as possible. Initially the examiner should explain to the child the purpose and the general components of the examination. A general physical examination should be done first with progression from least threatening and intrusive parts of the exam to the most sensitive part involving the genital areas. The child should be encouraged to assist with the exam and encouraged to ask questions. A support person should be present for the child. This individual could be either a parent or a nurse. The examination should be done as soon as possible if the last episode of abuse occurred within the last 72 hours, or if there are symptoms of vaginal discharge, vaginal bleeding, or anal bleeding. If these symptoms are absent or if more than 72 hours have elapsed, then the need for an *immediate* exam is lessened. Recent abuse victims are more likely to have positive physical evidence and symptomatic children should have their problems assessed and treated as soon as possible. However, all children should have an examination at some point, since some children with delayed reporting will have abnormal findings and those without physical evidence need to be reassured that they are not "damaged goods" and are physically normal (Berkowitz, 1987; De Jong & Rose, 1989; Enos et al., 1986; Koop, 1988).

The general physical examination serves two main purposes. First of all it helps focus the evaluation on the whole child and not just on the genital and anal areas. Secondly, physical evidence may be detected outside of the genital and anal areas. The general health, emotional state, and the nutritional and developmental status of the child should be included as part of the examination. Specific documentation of findings that suggest force or restraint may aid in corroborating child's description of events in abuse. These findings including scratches, bruises, lacerations, ligature marks, bite marks, and subconjunctival hemorrhages (often associated with choking) should be photographed or recorded on a detailed body map drawing (Enos et al., 1986; Ricci, 1988; Sproles, 1985; De Jong & Finkel, 1990).

The primary focus of the examination of the sexually abused child is the genital and anal areas. The examination may be accomplished with the child in either the knee chest position or in a modified lithotomy position (Emans & Goldstein, 1980). A brief review of the normal anogenital anatomy is appropriate here to introduce the terminology used to describe both the normal state and the abnormal findings (see Fig. 3.1). The child's own history should be recorded, using his or her own terms to identify body parts. However, the physical examination should be recorded in proper medical terminology. The *vulva* is the body area that contains the structures that are commonly called the external genitals or the external genitalia of the female. This region is external to the vagina and includes the labia majora (larger, outer lips) and labia minora (smaller, inner lips), mons pubis (the rounded prominence overlying the pubic bone), the clitoris, the urethral opening, and vaginal vestibule. The term *perineum* is often used to describe both the external genitalia or vulva as well as the area surrounding the anal opening, including the skin surfaces between the vulva and the perianal area. The *vaginal vestibule* or *fossa navicularis* is the space external to the hymen bounded on either side by the labia minora. It is important to note here that in many states, penetration into the vaginal vestibule with or without penetration through the hymen constitutes rape. Recessed within the vaginal vestibule itself is the hymen and the hymenal orifice or the vaginal ostium, the opening to the vagina through the hymen itself. The remaining vulvar structure of importance is the *posterior fourchette*, the posterior midline junction of the labia majora and labia minora. This structure forms the back or posterior wall of the vaginal vestibule.

The *hymen* is a crescent-shaped or ring-like membrane that partly covers the vaginal opening and is located at the deepest point of the vaginal vestibule. This structure is extremely variable in appearance;

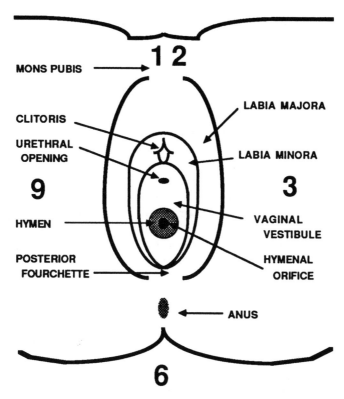

FIG. 3.1. Schematic representation of the perineum of a prepubertal girl with the child lying on her back, with legs spread and labia majora retracted laterally. The numbers (3,6,9,12) have been superimposed to show the orientation of the perineal structures with the face of a clock.

however, the normal opening through the hymen is small in most prepubertal girls. Variations include annular (ring-like with a central opening), crescentic (crescent-shaped membrane with opening at the top), fimbriated (having multiple overlapping flaps), cribriform (containing multiple holes), septate (containing two openings with a central divider), and rarely imperforate (having no opening). Recent studies have shown that the hymen is universally present in girls at birth and in nonabused prepubertal girls; there is no good documentation for the claim that the hymen can be congenitally absent (Jenny, Kuhns, & Arakawa, 1987; Pokorny, 1987). Measured transversely with the labia pulled laterally with gentle pressure to view the fossa navicularis and the hymen, the hymenal opening should probably be less than 6 or 7 mm in diameter (average = 3–4 mm; range 0–8 mm) in girls up to 8 years of age and up to 11 mm in girls older than 8. The diameter of the hymenal opening may vary with the position of the child and the degree of relaxation, and injury may result in either an enlargement or constriction of the opening, depending on scarring. The size of the opening should be documented, but should not be used as the sole criterion to establish that sexual abuse did or did not occur. Hymenal bumps and clefts are common irregularities of the hymen seen in both abused and nonabused girls (approximate frequency in both: one-fourth have bumps, one-fifth have clefts). These numerous variations in hymens make assessment of what is "normal" difficult at times (Cantwell, 1981; Emans, Woods, Flagg, & Freeman, 1987; McCann, Voris, Simon, & Wells, 1990; McCann, Wells, Simon, & Voris, 1990).

Usually the physician will describe the physiological maturation of the child as prepubertal, pubertal, or postpubertal. Often the degree of maturation is described as Tanner Stage, using the Tanner Classification System. This system defines a series of five steps or stages before and during puberty using specific physical characteristics of the genital area, breasts, and body hair, which allows for more direct comparison than the words prepubertal, pubertal, and postpubertal (Berkowitz, 1987).

The normal anal appearance depends on the integrity of the skin surrounding the opening, the pair of circular muscular sphincters that regulate opening and closing, and the fat layer lying underneath the skin. A regular pattern of folds or rugae of the skin radiating out from the anal opening give the normal "puckered" appearance to the anal opening. The sphincter muscle holds the opening in a closed position and produces an "anal wink" or a normal reflex sphincter contraction to stimulation of the surrounding skin (Berkowitz, 1987; Enos et al., 1986).

Anogenital injuries are often absent in sexually abused children. In most studies of either child or adult sexual assault victims, gross injury is reported in only approximately 25%–40% of those victims, examined following the assault. Normal examinations have been reported in from 85% to only 15% of child victims depending on the study cited (De Jong, Emmett, & Hervada, 1982; Emans et al., 1987; Enos et al., 1986; McCauley, Gorman, & Guzinski, 1986; Rimsza & Niggeman, 1982; Spencer & Dunklee, 1986; Teixeira, 1981; White, Loda, Ingram, & Pearson, 1983; Woodling & Kossoris, 1981; Muram, 1989). There are several explanations of why injury is so infrequently detected. The hymen and vulvar tissues, as well as the perianal tissues, may be damaged either acutely or permanently, or may be simply stretched during penetration. When penetration ceases, the openings may be returned to normal appearance due to the elastic properties of these tissues, much in the same way that a rubber band will return to its normal shape after being stretched. The longer the interval between the assault and examination, the less likely that acute injury will be found. The skills and experience of the physician performing the examination are also important to consider. The more experienced physician who has performed many sexual assault evaluations is more likely to detect some of the more subtle injuries than a physician who rarely does this type of examination. The pain and swelling initially may produce a falsely "normal" exam in some cases. Bruises may take 24 hours to become apparent and swelling, spasm, and patient resistance may limit a thorough exam. Since the perpetrator is often a relative or someone else known to the child, the intent of the abuse was not to hurt the child. Therefore the use of lubricants, which would help decrease friction and resultant injury, or performing only superficial penetration, and stopping when the child cries out in pain may limit injuries. The final factor that limits trauma is that vaginal or anal penetration may not have occurred, even superficially. The penis, finger, or object may be rubbed between the child's legs and over the vulva or between the buttocks without penetration (intercrural or "dry" intercourse), decreasing the risk of injury. Very young children in particular may have difficulty determining whether the penis, finger, or object was placed on them or in them.

Injury has rarely been found among victims of orogenital contact. Oral penetration in children forced to perform fellatio, may result in petechiae or fine bruises of the palate or tears in the labial frenulum. Boys who are subjected to fellatio and girls subjected to cunnilingus may show similar acute signs of injury on their external genitalia. These signs include petechiae, abrasions, swelling, or bite marks. Such injuries would be expected to resolve quickly and no chronic evidence of injury would be expected (Paul, 1977).

The most common vulvovaginal injuries include bruises, abrasions, and superficial lacerations. Similar types of injury may be produced by forceful genital fondling with or without digital penetration or penetration by a foreign body. The use of a colposcope, ophthalmoscope, otoscope, or a hand-held magnifying glass to provide magnification or the use of staining techniques may increase the detection of minor injuries. A camera attached to the colposcope gives this technique the additional feature of providing a photographic record of the findings. However, some minor injuries or irritations detected, using these enhancement techniques may be seen in nonabused children as well (Chadwick et al., 1989). Even using colposcopy, which provides magnification of up to 16 times normal size, combined with the use of vital stains such as toluidine blue to enhance very minor superficial injury, injury detection rate only increases to 40%–60% in adults. Using a similar staining technique combined with colposcopy, one published study increased the yield of positive examinations in a group of sexually abused girls from 10% without colposcopy to 30% with this technique

(McCauley et al., 1986). Other data suggest that colposcopy increases the yield of positive findings by documenting injury in 5%–10% of abuse victims who had normal examinations when viewed without magnification. Care must be taken to prevent overinterpretation of colposcopic findings that may be due to factors other than sexual abuse (Chadwick et al., 1989). Macroscopic or easily visualized findings should also not be overinterpreted. Erythema or redness of the vulvar or perianal tissues is often taken as a sign of trauma. Perineal erythema is a nonspecific finding, since it is commonly seen among both abused and nonabused children. Labial agglutination, or partial fusion of the labia minora occurs when abraided or irritated labia heal together. This may be due to sexual abuse in some cases, but nonsexual causes of irritation may produce the same end result. Erythema or labial agglutination noted on examination should be documented, but interpretations should include that they may or may not be secondary to sexual abuse (Chadwick et al., 1989; Emans et al., 1987; McCann, Wells, Simon, & Voris, 1990).

Most injuries found in girls are external injuries involving the labia minora, posterior fourchette, and hymen (Enos et al., 1986; Herman-Giddens & Frothingham, 1987). External or superficial injuries may predominate since the penetration may often be superficial, through the labia or into the vaginal vestibule, and not through the hymenal ring and more deeply into the vagina. Injuries to the hymen itself may result in scarring, which makes it look grossly intact with a normal to small orifice. Hymenal scarring may also produce asymmetry, loss of the fine elastic appearance or a thickened, scalloped appearance (caruncula hymenales) of the edges of the hymen. The scarred remnants of the hymen may be attached to the wall of the vagina by thin adhesions called synechiae. Injuries are often described by superimposing the face of a clock over the vulva or the perianal areas. Injuries located between the 3 and 9 o'clock positions clockwise on the vulva, especially between 5 and 7 o'clock (in the region of the posterior fourchette) are felt to be indicative of trauma resulting from penile penetration (Woodling & Kossoris, 1981). Injuries between 9 and 3 o'clock proceeding clockwise indicate noncoital trauma, such as digital manipulation, instrumentation, or accidental straddle injury. The pattern of accidental straddle injury usually involves bruising of mons pubis and labia majora but does not include injury to the posterior fourchette or hymen. Self-stimulation or tampon insertion *very rarely* causes trauma (Berkowitz, 1987; Enos et al., 1986; Paul, 1977).

The most common anal injuries include swelling or bruising of the anal verge or perianal tissues, initial laxity of the sphincter muscle followed by spasm within 2–4 hours, and fissures or superficial lacerations of the anal mucosa. Penetration with fingers or a foreign body may also result in similar findings. Repetitive anal penetration may be associated with unusual laxity of the rectal sphincter, perianal scarring, loss of perianal fat, or vascular or pigmentation changes. The resulting appearance is an anal opening that has lost its normal rugal pattern and "anal wink" reflex, which tends to gape open when lateral pressure is placed on the buttocks. Some dilatation of the anal opening may be seen in nonabused children; however the amount of dilatation rarely exceeds 20 mm in nonabused children (McCann, Voris, Simon, & Wells, 1989). The normal finely folded pattern of the rugae surrounding the anal opening is altered both by enlargement or hypertrophy of the individual rugae, and cupping or coving of the "valleys" between the rugae, due to loss of subcutaneous fat. An abnormal rugal pattern may also result from the flattening of some rugae, and enlargement of others. The loss of perianal subcutaneous fat may also allow for the underlying veins to become visible through the skin. This finding is sometimes called venous lakes or venous pools. Increased pigmentation of the perianal skin may also be found, but hyperpigmentation and venous pooling may not be unique to sexual abuse. These perianal findings have been reported in one-third to one-half of nonabused children (McCann et al., 1989). Unusual elasticity or laxity of the anal sphincter after repeated penetration may be demonstrated by the ability to introduce three or more fingers through the anal opening and noting the reduced strength of the sphincter muscle. The classical laceration and resulting scar due to penetration is wedge-shaped, with the apex of the wedge pointing toward the center of the opening (Berkowitz, 1987; Paul, 1977). Like vulvar injuries, anal injuries are not commonly reported among sexually abused children. The same limiting factors apply for perianal injuries as for vulvovaginal injuries. The very distensible nature of the anus and rectum limits the injury risk, even with deeper penetration.

Recurrent abuse may result in scarring, which may be detected even years after the abuse occurred. However, the severity of the acute injury and the resulting scarring may be reduced by use of gradual progression of sexual activity with gradual dilatation of orifices over time, use of lubricants, and gentle, superficial, rather than deep penetration. Scars may result from either recurrent or single episode of abuse. Scar tissue may grossly distort or subtly change the normal appearance, and in some cases may be only represented by an alteration of the vascularity of the injured area. The vascular changes in injured areas may be noted within weeks of acute injury. Increased vascularity, sometimes called neovascularity can persist for variable periods, from weeks to years. Decreased vascularity in some scars may be a permanent change. Subtle changes in vascularity or blood vessel pattern are enhanced by using a green filter and magnification with a colposcope or an ophthalmoscope

(Berkowitz, 1987; Woodling & Heger, 1986). Minor injury usually heals without scarring, and even gross injuries detectable without magnification may heal within 1 to 2 weeks by regeneration of the surface without significant scarring (Chadwick et al., 1989; Finkel, 1989; Teixeira, 1981).

A recent study in which magnification was used to detect injury not only supports the concept that physical evidence is usually missing in sexual abuse cases, but that some findings that might be determined to be injuries are nonspecific. Although genital findings distinguished some sexually abused girls from asymptomatic nonabused girls or girls with other genital complaints but not abuse histories, many findings overlap in all three groups. Findings that were unique to the sexually abused group were posterior hymenal tears (5 to 7 o'clock position), genital abrasions, and genital warts. Similar frequencies of other genital findings (erythema or redness, vaginal discharge, labial adhesions, hymenal irregularities, irritated posterior fourchette area) were noted in all three groups. Only 37% of the prepubertal sexual abuse victims in this study had any genital findings, with only 8% having the "unique injuries" that were found only in the group with a history of sexual abuse (Emans et al., 1987).

In summary, the physical examination of the sexually abused child has certain benefits and limitations. The presence of general injury or anogenital injury can be used to support the child's history of abuse. However, a normal physical examination is commonly found and is also consistent with a history of prior sexual abuse. While certain findings may only result from sexual abuse, some physical abnormalities are consistent with abuse or with other nonabusive problems. Finally, the assurance of a normal physical examination may be considered a therapeutic step in resolving the "damaged goods" syndrome experienced by the victims.

DOCUMENTATION OF SEXUAL CONTACT

The physical evaluation of the sexually abused child is not only for the purpose of documenting physical injuries. Collection of specimens for documentation of sexual contact is usually done at the same time as the physical examination. The types of evidence sought include the presence of sperm and the seminal fluid products in which the sperm is suspended, the presence of sexually transmitted diseases or pregnancy, and the detection of foreign materials found on the victim's body surface or clothing. Although such evidence is usually not found in child sexual abuse cases, a routine approach will provide documentation of sexual contact in a significant number of cases, while detecting conditions or diseases that require medical intervention.

Several general guidelines about evidence need to be addressed before outlining a more specific approach to specimen collection. First, proper consent should be obtained both from the victim and the child's parents or guardian when appropriate before performing the examination and evidence collection. Second, the number of personnel involved in handling specimens should be limited, and the handling of specimens should be documented to maintain a "chain of evidence." This includes clearly documenting names and locations of handlers of the specimens from the time of collection through the processing of the specimens in the laboratory. Third, collection kits should be standardized, whether they are one of the commercially available "rape kits" or one assembled on site. Finally, a specimen collection protocol and/or checklist should be used to ensure that all appropriate specimens will be collected. This protocol should include provisions for both the routine situation as well as circumstances for altering routine collection (Enos et al., 1986; Sproles, 1985).

Specific details of collection, labeling, and packaging of specimens should be worked out with the laboratory processing the specimens. However, the following is a brief outline of the specimen collection process (Enos et al., 1986; Sproles, 1985; De Jong & Finkel, 1990).

1. Obtain 2 or 3 swabbed specimens from each area of body assaulted (for sperm: acid phosphatase, P 30, MHS-5 antigen, blood group antigen determinations) The number of swabs required will depend on the local lab. Most laboratories require air dried specimens which require drying for 60 minutes before they can be packaged.
2. Mouth: Swab under tongue, and buccal pouch next to upper and lower molars. These areas are locations where seminal fluid is most likely to be persistent.
3. Vagina: Use dry or moistened swab, or 2 cc saline wash. These secretions may also be collected with a pipette or eyedropper.
4. Rectum: Insert swab at least one-half to 1 inch beyond anus.
5. Specimens should be taken from any other suspicious site on body or clothing. Saline moistened swabs may be used to lift any shiny stains that may be dried seminal fluid. An alternate method would be to scrape off the dried stains with the back of a scalpel blade into a clean envelope or tube.
6. Make saline wet mount of specimens from all assaulted orifices and examine immediately for presence of sperm and whether it is motile or not.

7. Some crime labs request that a dry smear be made of each secretion sample, using clean glass microscope slides, others prepare their own slides from swab specimens.

8. Collect saliva specimen to determine the victim's antigen secretion status. Saliva may be collected using 3–4 sterile swabs or a 2 × 2 gauze pad, which the victim has placed in the mouth. The value of this sample and of a blood sample from the victim will be discussed later in relation to analysis of the identity of the perpetrator.

9. Save torn or bloody clothes or any clothing when semen staining is suspected using Woods lamp. Semen may fluoresce with a blue or green color under the untraviolet light of the Woods lamp. Fluorescence under ultraviolet light is nonspecific. Various skin infections, congenital or acquired skin pigmentary changes, and chemicals including systemic and topical medications, cosmetics, soaps and industrial chemicals may fluoresce under ultraviolet light.

10. If victim was wearing a tampon, pad, or diaper during the assault, or if a fresh tampon, pad, or diaper was used following the abuse, save this for analysis. Seminal fluid products may be found on these items. These items should not be packaged in plastic bags. Sealed plastic will promote the growth of Candida and other organisms which might destroy some of the evidence.

11. Save any foreign material found upon removal of clothing.

12. Combed pubic hair or scalp hair; fingernail scrapings. These procedures are often considered optional. Although they are not really proof of sexual contact per se, pubic hair, scalp hair, or skin fragments from scratching may be used to help identify the perpetrator.

13. Swabs should also be taken for screening for sexually transmitted diseases.

The recommended procedures are detailed later in the chapter. These swabs should *not* be air dried, since air drying will kill the organisms and cause the cultures for these diseases to be falsely negative.

The interpretation of the laboratory analysis of the forensic specimens requires an understanding of the effect of delay in obtaining specimens as well as other factors that would increase or decrease the chances of documenting sexual contact. Sperm can be detected in specimens in two different forms: live, motile sperm, and dead, nonmotile sperm. Detected using a saline wet mount of a freshly collected specimen, the presence of motile sperm is the most tangible proof of recent ejaculation into the orifice. Live, motile sperm may be present for only a half-hour and are rarely seen after 6–8 hours. Therefore, detection of motile sperm requires immediate analysis of the specimen. The survival time of motile sperm is variable, depending on the body orifice. Survival time for sperm in the mouth is rarely more than a few hours, due to the cleansing and digestive action of saliva, while motile sperm may be present up to 5 days in the cervix. Nonmotile, or dead sperm usually are detectable for a longer period of time than live sperm. Nonmotile sperm may be processed by a pap smear technique or saline mount specimen. Several studies suggest that sperm may be present for up to 12–20 hours and rarely up to 48–72 hours in the vagina. Sperm are rarely present more than 24 hours in rectal specimens. Dry specimens on the other hand are stable, and sperm may be detected in stains on clothing for up to 12 months. Both motile and nonmotile sperm appear to persist for very short time in the mouth. Although no accurate figures are available for duration of persistence of this evidence, it is estimated that sperm in the mouth becomes undetectable within 6 hours (Rapps, 1980; Ricci & Hoffman, 1982; Silverman & Silverman, 1978; Sproles, 1985).

Acid phosphatase is an enzyme found in the seminal plasma or the liquid part of the semen. Acid phosphatase is important as an indicator of sexual contact because it is found in high concentration in semen, 130–1800 IU/L, but is found in only very low levels of less than 50 IU/L in vaginal secretions. Studies vary as to the amount of acid phosphatase naturally found in vaginal secretions and the length of time that elevated levels persist in the vagina following intercourse. Acid phosphatase is a more sensitive indicator of recent intercourse than sperm, because sperm are more rapidly broken down than the acid phosphatase within the body orifices. Therefore, acid phosphatase may be detected for somewhat longer periods following sexual contact. A marked elevation of the enzyme in vaginal secretions correlates with intercourse within the last 24–48 hours, and the level usually returns to normal in 72 hours. However, acid phosphatase levels may return to normal within 3 hours, so that a negative test can also be consistent with a recent sexual contact with ejaculation. Acid phosphatase is typically elevated for a much shorter duration in the mouth (perhaps only 6 hours) and in the rectum (less than 24 hours) but only estimates of the duration are available. Dried seminal fluid stains on clothing may contain acid phosphatase, which is detectable for months or even years after the deposition of the semen (Paul, 1977; Rapps, 1980; Ricci & Hoffman, 1982; Silverman & Silverman, 1978).

In recent years other tests have been developed to detect the presence of seminal fluid. Semen glycoprotein of prostatic origins, or P 30, is one substance identified by a newer test. Semen glycoprotein is a protein manufactured in the prostate gland, which is secreted into the seminal fluid. P 30 can be detected using a standardized laboratory technique involving an enzyme-linked immunosorbent assay (ELISA) after collection of fluid on dry swabs. High levels of P 30 are found in semen, ranging from 0.62 to 5.25 mg with a mean of 1.55 mg/ml of seminal plasma. Only low levels are found in the urine of males, 0.00026 mg, and it is not normally present in the vaginal fluid, urine, or saliva of females. Males who have had a vasectomy will not have detectable sperm in their semen; however, levels of P 30 in seminal fluid in normal and vasectomized males are not different. A positive P 30 test means sexual contact occurred within 48 hours, since the amount of P 30 present declines to undetectable levels within 48 hours of ejaculation into the vagina. In dried state, as in seminal stains on clothing, P 30 may be detectable for up to 12 years because the protein is extremely stable when dried. In one study, 7 of 27 rape victims with negative acid phosphatase tests had positive P 30 tests. Therefore, P 30 appears to be a more sensitive test for the presence of seminal fluid than acid phosphatase, although some studies suggest that acid phosphatase may be detectable for a day or more longer within the vagina (Graves, Sensabaugh, & Blake, 1985).

The newest test available for detection of seminal fluid is the MHS–5 antigen detection test. MHS–5 is a protein produced only in the seminal vesicles of the male. Like P 30 and acid phosphatase, MHS–5 is a component of the liquid part of the semen. The test for this protein involves a monoclonal antibody technique, and standardized laboratory kits are available for this test. This test has not come into general use at this time and there is some uncertainty of the duration of detectability of MHS–5 following sexual contact.

Laboratory tests for sexual contact have certain limitations. These tests for the presence of seminal fluid can only be interpreted properly if the limitations are kept in mind. First, if ejaculation has not occurred or if a condom is used to prevent the semen from being deposited, the tests for sperm, acid phosphatase, P 30 and MHS–5 will be negative. Second, if perpetrator has aspermia (the congenital or acquired inability to produce sperm) or has had a vasectomy, tests for sperm will be negative but acid phosphatase, P 30 and MHS–5 are positive. This occurs because the liquid part of the seminal fluid is still produced and released under these conditions. Third, if tests are obtained greater than 48 to 72 hours after intercourse, all tests are likely to be negative since sperm, acid phosphatase, P 30, and MHS–5 are rarely detectable for more than 48 to 72 hours from body surfaces. Therefore, attempts to recover seminal fluid from the body of the abuse victim are rarely made more than 72 hours after the last sexual contact. However, clothing worn during or shortly after the abuse may be inspected more than 72 hours later, since the detection of seminal fluid products in dried stains can persist for a much longer time.

The preceding information is based on both theoretical and experimental data. But what is the actual experience with detecting evidence of sexual contact. In two studies where women were examined within 24 hours following voluntary vaginal coitus, only 50%–60% had sperm and 40%–84% had acid phosphatase detected. In one study including both boys and girls who were victims of sexual abuse, 30% of a selected group had positive tests for sperm or semen (Rimsza et al., 1982). However only 16% of all the victims had samples taken. Although the criteria for testing were not specified, probably these were children who had a history of recent abuse. In a study of sexually abused boys, 5% of all victims had positive tests, and 27% examined less than 72 hours after assault had positive tests (Spencer et al., 1986). In another study of abused boys and girls, 18% had positive tests for sperm and/or acid phosphatase. The sample of abused children in this study is unusual because of an extremely low frequency of incest victims represented. Only 16% of the children studied were incest victims and therefore this was an atypical group of child victims who were subjected to abuse by strangers, where less delayed reporting might be expected (Enos et al., 1986). The conclusion that should be drawn is that sperm and acid phosphatase is usually not detected in child sexual abuse victims, and frequency of detection is likely to be even lower in unselected samples where specimen collection is done more than 72 hours following sexual contact. Data on the use of testing for P 30 or MHS–5 in child sexual abuse victims are not available. Most other studies suggest that only 2% to 5% of all sexually abused children evaluated will have positive tests for sperm or acid phosphatase (De Jong et al., 1982; De Jong & Rose, 1989; Tilleli, Turek, & Jaffee, 1980).

Table 3.1 summarizes data from a number of studies about the survival time of evidence of sperm and seminal fluid products following ejaculation. Although evidence is occasionally detected at intervals longer than the survival times listed in the chart, the times given are the

TABLE 3.1
Survival Time of Evidence

Site	Motile sperm	Nonmotile sperm	Acid phosphatase	P 30
Pharynx	½–6 hr	6 hr (?)	6 hr (?)	(?)
Rectum	½–8 hr	24 hr	24 hr (?)	(?)
Vagina	½–8 hr	7–48 hr	12–48 hr	12–48 hr
Clothing	< ½ hr	up to 12 mo.	up to 3 yr.	up to 12 yr.

intervals during which there exists a significant chance of detecting the evidence, and after which detection would be unusual.

Sexually transmitted diseases (STDs) are both a common type of physical evidence and a common stimulus to initiate an evaluation for child sexual abuse (De Jong, 1986; Centers for Disease Control, 1985; Neinstein, Goldenring, & Carpenter, 1984; White et al., 1983). The presence of an STD in a child may be the only physical evidence of sexual abuse in some cases and the infection or colonization may be associated with or without symptoms. Sexually transmitted diseases may be detected in from 2% to 20% of children examined for sexual abuse, and the variation in frequency of STDs in the children studied may be dependent on whether the study includes a large number of children referred due to their symptoms of STDs. "The diagnosis of any STD in a child who is prepubertal but not neonatal raises the strong suspicion of sexual abuse until proven otherwise" (Centers for Disease Control, 1985). Although this statement should be heeded, the amount of "proof" needed to overrule the suspicion of abuse varies from disease to disease. The following paragraphs will describe sexually transmitted diseases found among sexually abused children, and discuss the strength of their association with sexual abuse.

Gonorrhea or more appropriately gonococcal infections are caused by a small gram negative diplococcal bacteria named *Neisseria gonorrhoeae*. Infections may be present with or without symptoms, and infections of the throat (pharangitis) and of the rectum (proctitis) are typically asymptomatic. Genital infections are commonly associated with a purulent penile or vaginal discharge but infections at these sites can also be asymptomatic. Accurate diagnosis can only be made using selective culture techniques, which are readily available. The laboratory must perform appropriate confirmatory tests since similar bacteria, including *Branhamella catarrhalis, Kingella dentrificans, Neiserria meningitidis, N. lactamica, and N. cinerea,* can be misidentified as *N. gonorrhoeae.* One study reported that 14 of 40 isolates for *N. gonorrhoeae* were shown to be falsely identified because confirmatory tests were not performed appropriately to exclude other bacteria (Alexander, 1988; Whittington, Rice, Biddle, & Knapp, 1988). Reported rates of gonococcal infection range from 2.3% to 11.2% among sexually abused children (Neinstein et al., 1984). Pharyngeal infections in particular may persist despite appropriate treatment. Therefore, repeatedly positive cultures do not necessarily mean repeated exposure and repeated abuse. On the other hand, perpetrators who have taken commonly prescribed antibiotics for some other infection may eradicate the gonococci and have negative cultures when they are subsequently screened as possible sources of the child's infection. Spontaneous resolution of the infections without any antibiotic therapy can occur within weeks to months of onset, which also results in negative cultures (Alexander, Griffith, Housch, & Holmes, 1984; Folland, Burke, Hinman, & Schaffner, 1977).

Clinically unsuspected infections can be detected through routine cultures of all children regardless of the symptoms or history. In one study, 4.7% of 532 sexually abused children under 14 had routine cultures taken from all three body sites (De Jong, 1986). Eleven of the 25 cases of gonorrhea detected were in children who had no symptoms of infection, and eight infections were discovered at sites that had not been involved in the sexual contact, according to the child's initial history. Routine cultures of the throat, rectum, and genital areas are indicated in all sexually abused children (Centers for Disease Control, 1985; De Jong, 1986).

The gonococci have been shown to survive for up to 24 hours on fomites (toilet seats, towels) if the secretions containing the bacteria are not allowed to dry. This raises the possibility of nonsexual transmission in some cases, although nonsexual transmission has not been clearly documented (Neinstein et al., 1984). The physician should assume that prepubertal children with gonorrhea have acquired it by sexual contact and that most of these contacts were abusive (Alexander et al., 1984; American Academy of Pediatrics, 1983; Folland et al., 1977).

Chlamydia trachomatis, or "chlamydial" infections, are the most frequently recognized sexually transmitted disease in adolescents and adults. Therefore, infection rates of 4% to 8% among sexually abused children should not be surprising (Hammerschlag et al., 1984; Ingram, White, Occhiuti, & Lyna, 1986; Rettig & Nelson, 1981). Some infected girls will have a vaginal discharge; however, most chlamydial infections do not produce symptoms. Routine screening of sexually abused children is required to detect asymptomatic cases. Diagnosis must be made using a culture technique employing McCoy cells, rather than more commonly available rapid detection methods. Enzyme immunoassay (i.e., Chlamydiazyme®) and direct fluorescent antibody (i.e., MicroTrak®) tests are extremely unreliable for vaginal or rectal specimens in children, since falsely positive results are common using these rapid detection methods (Hammerschlag, Rettig, & Schields, 1988).

Perinatal infections are common, and positive cultures have been shown to persist for at least 3 years following exposure to *Chlamydia trachomatis* during birth process. Chlamydial infections may indicate of sexual abuse in children and adolescents; however, some infections in preschool children may represent persistence of perinatal infection, and many infections detected in adolescents may actually be the result of previous consensual sexual activity (Bump, 1985; Hammerschlag, Rettig, & Shields, 1988).

Condyloma acuminata or "venereal warts" is a common sexually transmitted disease in adults but an uncommon infection in children. This human papilloma virus (HPV) infection is characterized by soft, irregular, wart-like growths. Although most commonly seen in the perineal area, they can affect any moist skin areas or mucous membranes. Some lesions may be entirely internal, located inside the mouth, vagina, or rectum (American Academy of Dermatology, 1984; De Jong, Weiss, & Brent, 1982). Diagnosis is usually made on the typical clinical wart-like appearance of lesions and biopsy specimens, although more precise viral typing techniques are being used increasingly (Rock et al., 1986).

Nonsexual transmission of common warts (usually HPV type 2) appears to be associated with some of the typical perineal lesions in young children. However, common wart virus also could be spread from the infected hands of an individual through inappropriate genital fondling. Therefore, it cannot be assumed that all perineal lesions caused by HPV type 2 are acquired by nonabusive contact. Nonsexual transmission of the virus from infected mothers during the birth process is well documented, and the resulting lesions may take 9 or more months to develop in the infant. The interval from exposure to development of the lesions is extremely variable with the average incubation period 2–3 months in both nonsexually or sexually acquired infections. The virus can remain latent in normal appearing areas next to the skin lesions. New lesions may appear weeks to months after the old lesions are treated since the treatment is concentrated on the affected skin. Therefore, the appearance of new lesions up to several months after treatment may or may not be due to re-exposure through continuing sexual contact. The long and variable incubation period of the human papilloma virus makes it difficult to identify the child's contact, but except for those condyloma acuminata appearing during infancy, a high suspicion of sexual abuse is indicated. Lesions appearing around the anal, urethral, vaginal openings should be particularly suspect (American Academy of Dermatology, 1984; De Jong, Weiss, & Brent, 1982).

Syphilis is an uncommon sexually transmitted disease in sexually abused children, found in only 0.2% to 1.5% of reported victims (De Jong, 1986; Neinstein et al., 1984; White et al., 1983). Although infections occurring in infancy may have resulted from prenatal exposure, prepubertal children with primary or secondary stages of syphilis ocurring beyond early infancy should be presumed to be victims of sexual abuse. Accurate diagnosis can only be established using blood testing. Nontreponemal reagin tests such as the VDRL and the RPR are commonly used for screening victims, but specific antibody tests for the organism, *Treponema pallidum*, such as the FTA–ABS or the MHA–TP, must be done to confirm the screening test (Ginsberg, 1983).

"Herpes," or herpes simplex virus (HSV) infection, is characterized by painful vesicular or ulcerated lesions often accompanied by fever, which occurs 2–20 days following exposure. Primary herpes genital infection is most frequently seen among sexually active adolescents and young adults. HSV type 1 infections usually occur in the mouth, while most HSV type 2 infections occur in the genital area. Nonsexual transmission is not well studied, but HSV type 1 infections are not an uncommon childhood infection, usually involving only the mouth but occasionally the mouth and genital area simultaneously (Gardner & Jones, 1984; Kaplan, Fleisher, Paradise, & Friedman, 1984).

Routine HSV cultures from asymptomatic children have little value. Suspicious lesions (vesicles or ulcerations) must be cultured and subtyped to distinguish type 1 from type 2 infections. Nonsexual transmission of genital herpes is most reasonable in cases when a child has simultaneous oral and genital infection or when an infant or toddler has a caretaker with oral lesions. The evidence suggests that except for transmission at birth, most HSV type 2 genital infections are sexually transmitted (Gardner & Jones, 1984; Kaplan et al., 1984).

Trichomonas vaginalis infections are characterized by a purulent vaginal discharge. Infected mothers may transmit the infection to their infants during birth, but trichomonas infections are rare after infancy except in postpubertal sexually active children and adults. Nonsexual transmission has never been proven but is theoretically possible since the organism can survive up to several hours on objects (Neinstein et al., 1984). The diagnosis is usually made by examining the vaginal discharge under a microscope and observing the causative protozoan in motion. Cases of trichomonas infections in prepubertal children beyond the first months of life have high probability of having resulted from sexual abuse (Jones, Yamauchi, & Lambert, 1985; White et al., 1983).

Bacterial vaginosis or nonspecific vaginitis is characterized by a simultaneous infection with multiple anerobic organisms. Although *Gardnerella vaginalis* is one of the bacteria that may be involved in this infection, the presence or absence of this organism in a vaginal culture does not prove or disprove the diagnosis. Diagnosis cannot be made using cultures or any single test. Typical characteristics of the thin vaginal discharge are easily found using microscopic examination (the presence of "clue cells," which are epithelial cells with clusters of bacteria adhering to the surface) and simple chemical tests (the addition of 10% KOH to the discharge produces a fishy or amine aroma; Hammerschlag, Cummings, Doraiswamy, Cox, & McCormack, 1985). The infection rate is increased following sexual contact, but this entity is probably a common cause of nonsexually transmitted vaginitis in children and adolescents (Bump &

Buesching, 1988). The development of a new vaginal discharge follow-ing sexual abuse has been associated with bacterial vaginosis in several studies, but the presence of this infection in a child may be due to either sexual or nonsexual transmission (Bump & Buesching, 1988; Hammers-chlag et al., 1985).

The genital mycoplasmas, *Mycoplasma hominis and Ureaplasma urealyti-cum*, appear to be possible markers for sexual activity in adults, produc-ing colonization or asymptomatic infections following sexual contact. Symptomatic infections do not appear to be common. Colonization has been demonstrated among sexually abused children for both *Mycoplasma hominis* and *Ureaplasma urealyticum*. However, asymptomatic colonization is also common among nonabused children, and these organisms should not be considered significant markers for sexual abuse (Hammerschlag, Doraiswamy, Cox, Cummings, & McCormack, 1987).

There is limited information on other sexually transmitted diseases and their association with sexual abuse of children. At least one case of AIDS (human immunodeficiency virus; HIV) infection has been closely associated with sexual abuse, and sexual abuse has been implicated in several other cases. The potential long-term risk of AIDS among child sexual abuse victims is unknown. Some experts recommend that all sexually abused children be screened for HIV (Koop, 1988); however, others focus on the screening of the perpetrator first, and then screen-ing only a child whose perpetrator was either positive for HIV or was known to be at high risk for HIV (Berkowitz, 1987).

The U.S. Public Health Services Centers for Disease Control (CDC) recommends the following tests for STDs should be performed on all child sexual abuse victims (Centers for Disease Control, 1985):

1. Gonococcal (gonorrhea) cultures–Pharyngeal, anal, and ure-thral or vaginal sites.
2. Chlamydial cultures–Pharyngeal, anal, and urethral or vaginal sites. Cultures should be obtained from all sites for gonococcal and chlamydial infections since symptoms may not always be present, and the infections are often found in body areas not described as contact areas during the abuse.
3. RPR or VDRL blood tests for diagnosis of syphilis.
4. Examination for condyloma acuminata or venereal warts.
5. Herpes simplex virus cultures of any inflamed areas seen on physical examination.
6. In addition for females, wet mount of urine and vaginal secre-tions for microscopic examination for trichomonas, and tests for bacterial vaginosis.

SPECIMENS TO AID IN PROVING THE IDENTITY OF OFFENDER OR PERPETRATOR

Collection and analysis of saliva, semen, blood, body hair, bite marks and other materials occasionally found on the body of the victim may help to identify the offender. The collection procedures for some of this potential evidence is described earlier, and is done as part of the routine evaluation. The analysis of these tests require the expertise of a forensic pathologist or a specialized crime laboratory. If the perpetrator's saliva, seminal fluid, blood, body hair, or bite impressions are not present at the time of the examination, these tests can not be done. The fact that physical evidence is lacking in most of child sexual abuse evaluations limits the utilization of these tests in the majority of child sexual abuse cases.

Genetic markers are substances that can be used to identify the likely origin of body fluids. The basis of identification using genetic markers is the following: the majority of people are "secretors" and the pattern of secreted antigens has a variable distribution in the general population. Approximately 80% of the general population are "secretors," and all body fluids of the secretors including blood, semen, and saliva will contain blood group antigens ABO, RhD, MN, P, Lewis, and other factors, such as phosphoglucomutase (PGM) and peptidase A (pep A). At least 16 genetic markers have been identified in semen, although forensic laboratories may not test for all of them. Some of the factors and antigens representing genetic markers are common, while others are rarely seen in the general population. A pattern of genetic markers can be established for secretors and the frequency in the general population of that particular pattern of markers can be estimated. Thus, the chances of the body fluid being from the perpetrator or another individual can be estimated. This process is not as exact as fingerprinting in identifying individuals, but it can be precise enough to provide strong evidence of identity. Approximately 20% of the population are "nonsecretors"; their fluids are identified by presence of Lewis (LE) substance, but other markers are absent. Other than identifying the individual as a nonsecretor, genetic marker analysis provides little help in further characterizing the nonsecretor. Control samples of saliva and blood from the victim need to be taken to identify secretor status and genetic markers of victim accurately, so that this can be compared with the secretions of the offender. Otherwise, it may be hard to determine which genetic markers were from the victim and which were from the perpetrator. Blood found on clothing or on the body of the victim may represent blood from victim or assailant, particularly if the victim had scratched or bitten the assailant and caused bleeding. Blood samples may be analyzed, using the same procedures as other body fluids for genetic markers. Once again, these results can only be interpreted when compared with samples from the victim (Berkowitz, 1987; Rapps, 1980; Roe, 1985; Sproles, 1985).

A perpetrator's body or scalp hair occasionally may be found on the body of the victim. Hair analysis requires hair from the victim as a control, the collection of hair from the body of the victim, which is suspected to be from the perpetrator, and hairs collected from the perpetrator directly. Hair analysis typically uses direct microscopic comparison of hairs, which is much less specific than fluid analysis using genetic markers. Direct microscopic analysis is limited in specificity because of the variability of hair types from different sites in one individual. The laboratory can only conclude in the majority of cases that the sample is consistent with, inconsistent with, or inconclusive, when compared with perpetrator's hair. A second type of hair analysis technique can provide more specific identification of the source of the hair. Neutron activation analysis is an expensive but precise technique; it can identify 18 variable components common to human hair. The identification process is not as precise as fingerprinting, but is almost as reliable. Unfortunately, the cost of the instrument to perform this analysis limits the general availability of this type of test (Sproles, 1985).

Fingerprint detection is not often used in sexual abuse cases because fingerprints are difficult to obtain from the body surface. However, laser light examination of the skin may show sites of fingerprints on skin. Bite mark identification techniques can be used to identify the source of bite marks on the victim's body. Bite marks are rarely present and accurate sampling and analysis is difficult even when present. However, when good quality pictures can be obtained of the bite marks, they may be specific as fingerprints in identifying the perpetrator (Sproles, 1985).

The most recent development in the identification of the perpetrator of sexual abuse is the use of a process called DNA fingerprinting (Gill, Jeffreys, & Werrett, 1985). The DNA fingerprinting technique requires that sperm, blood, hair root (not just the shaft of the hair) or other tissue from perpetrator be found on the victim. This process uses a "gene probe" laboratory technique, which identifies the specific sequence of the DNA in the tissue (i.e., sperm) collected from the victim's body, and compares this sequence with the DNA in tissue taken from the alleged perpetrator. The results are very specific in their ability to identify the perpetrator. "Gene probe" techniques are becoming more available for a number of medical uses but are still not widely available for use in the analysis of evidence of sexual abuse.

MEDICAL LEGAL EVIDENCE SUMMARY

All children being evaluated for suspected sexual abuse should have a medical examination, although most examinations will not detect abnormal physical findings or provide positive forensic medical evidence that sexual contact has occurred. A verbal report of a history of abuse is often the only evidence present in childhood sexual assault cases; however, a physical examination should be done in all cases. Depending on the history, both normal and abnormal physical findings, infections, or injuries can be used to support the child's complaints of abuse. The examination helps to guide medical therapy when injuries or infections are present, and to reassure the child of physical normality when they are not present.

The evidence is only as good as the collection process allows it to be. Using an appropriate protocol and documentation of proper handling of all evidence is essential. The ability to document use of force and sexual contact are limited by many factors. The delay in disclosure and the type of abuse are two of the more critical factors. The identity of the offender can be suggested by forensic analysis of body fluid residues and other evidence, but body fluid residues or physical evidence must be present, and the expertise available to perform these tests. Most cases will not involve such information and analysis.

Documentation of force (injury) and documentation of sexual contact are helpful, but not necessary for conviction of the perpetrator of sexual abuse. Lack of physical evidence likewise does not assure acquittal. On the other hand, the presence of physical evidence does not assure conviction. A lack of history of abuse is the most difficult evidence to overcome in matters of child dependency and criminal proceedings. Physical injury or sexually transmitted infection may strongly indicate that abuse occurred, but without a history there is no identifiable offender or perpetrator. Appropriate child protective decisions and legal actions are dependent on the identity of the perpetrator. In many cases, physical injury or infection will raise the question of sexual abuse and a history or disclosure of the abuse will not be available. In such cases, it may be necessary to initiate the investigation of the basis of the physical evidence, and hope that the history of the abuse will be obtained in the process of the further social service and legal investigation.

REFERENCES

Alexander, E. R. (1988). Misidentification of sexually transmitted organisms in children: Medicolegal implications. *Pediatric Infectious Diseases, 7,* 1–2.

Alexander, W. J., Griffith, H., Housch, J. G., & Holmes, J. R. (1984). Infections in sexual contacts and associates of children with gonorrhea. *Sexually Transmitted Diseases, 11,* 156–158.

American Academy of Dermatology Task Force on Pediatric Dermatology. (1984). Genital warts and sexual abuse in children. *Journal of the American Academy of Dermatology, 11,* 529–530.

American Academy Of Pediatrics Committee on Early Childhood, Adoption, and Dependent Care. (1983). Gonorrhea in prepubertal children. *Pediatrics, 71,* 553.

Berkowitz, C. D. (1987). Sexual abuse of children and adolescents. *Advances in Pediatrics, 34,* 275–312.

Bump, R. C. (1985). *Chlamydia trachomatis* as a cause of prepubertal vaginitis. *Obstetrics and Gynecology, 65,* 384–388.

Bump, R. C., & Buesching, W. J. (1988). Bacterial vaginosis in virginal and sexually active adolescent females: Evidence against exclusive sexual transmission. *American Journal of Obstetrics and Gynecology, 158,* 935–939.

Cantwell, H. (1981). Vaginal inspection as it relates to child sexual abuse in girls under thirteen. *Child Abuse and Neglect, 7,* 171–176.

Centers for Disease Control. (1985). *Morbidity and Mortality Weekly Report.* Sexually Transmitted Diseases Treatment Guidelines–1985. *34* (suppl.).

Chadwick, D. L., Berkowitz, C. D., Kerns, D., McCann, J., Reinhart, M., & Strickland, S. (Eds.). (1989). *Color atlas of child sexual abuse.* Chicago: Year Book Medical Publishers.

De Jong, A. R. (1986). Sexually transmitted diseases in sexually abused children. *Sexually Transmitted Diseases, 13,* 123–126.

De Jong, A. R., & Finkel, M. A. (1990). Sexual abuse of children. *Current Problems in Pediatrics, 10,* 491–567.

De Jong, A. R., Emmett, G. A., & Hervada, A. R. (1982). Sexual abuse of children. Sex, race, and age dependent variations. *American Journal of Diseases of Children, 136,* 129–134.

De Jong, A. R., & Rose, M. (1989). The frequency and significance of physical evidence in legally proven cases of child sexual abuse. *Pediatrics, 84,* 1022–1026.

De Jong, A. R., Weiss, J. W. & Brent, R. L. (1982). Condyloma acuminata in children. *American Journal of Diseases in Children, 136,* 704–706.

Emans, S. J., & Goldstein, D. P. (1980). The gynecologic examination of the prepubertal child with vulvovaginitis; use of the knee-chest position. *Pediatrics, 65,* 758–760.

Emans, S. J., Woods, E., Flagg, N., & Freeman, A. (1987). Genital findings in sexually abused, symptomatic, and asymptomatic girls. *Pediatrics, 79,* 778–785.

Enos, W. F., Conrath, T. B., & Beyer, J. C. (1986). Forensic evaluation of the sexually abused child. *Pediatrics, 78,* 385–398.

Finkel, M. A. (1989). Anogenital trauma in sexually abused children. *Pediatrics, 84,* 317–322.

Folland, D. S., Burke, R. E., Hinman, A. R., & Schaffner, W. (1977). Gonorrhea in preadolescent children: An inquiry into the source of infection and mode of transmission. *Pediatrics, 60,* 153–156.

Gardner, M., & Jones, J. G. (1984). Genital herpes acquired by sexual abuse of children. *Journal of Pediatrics, 104,* 243–244.

Gill, P., Jeffreys, A. J., & Werrett, D. J. (1985). Forensic application of DNA "fingerprints." *Nature, 318,* 577–579.

Ginsberg, C. M. (1983). Acquired syphilis in prepubertal children. *Pediatric Infectious Diseases, 2,* 232–234.

Graves, H. C. B., Sensabaugh, G. F., & Blake, E. T. (1985). Postcoital detection of a male specific semen protein. Application to investigation of rape. *New England Journal of Medicine, 312,* 338–343.

Hammerschlag, M. R., Cummings, M., Doraiswamy, B., Cox, P., & McCormack, W. (1985). Nonspecific vaginitis following sexual abuse in children. *Pediatrics, 75,* 1028–1031.

Hammerschlag, M. R., Doraiswamy, B., Alexander, E. R., Cox, P., Price, W., & Gleyzer, A. (1984). Are rectovaginal chlamydial infections a marker of sexual abuse in children? *Pediatric Infectious Diseases, 3,* 100–104.

Hammerschlag, M. R., Doriaswamy, B., Cox, P., Cummings, M., & McCormack, W. (1987). Colonization of sexually abused children with genital mycoplasmas. *Sexually Transmitted Diseases, 14,* 23–25.

Hammerschlag, M. R., Rettig, P. J., & Shields, M. E. (1988). False positive results with the use of chlamydial antigen detection tests in the evaluation of suspected sexual abuse in children. *Pediatric Infectious Diseases, 7,* 11–14.

Herman-Giddens, M. E., & Frothingham, T. E. (1987). Prepubertal female genitalia: examination for evidence of sexual abuse. *Pediatrics, 80,* 203–208.

Hunter, R. S., Kilstrom, N., & Loda, F. (1985). Sexually abused children: Identifying masked presentations in a medical setting. *Child Abuse and Neglect, 9,* 17–26.

Ingram, D. L., White, S. T., Occhiuti, A. R., & Lyna, P. R. (1986). Childhood vaginal infections: Association of *Chlamydia trachomatis* with sexual contact. *Pediatric Infectious Diseases, 5,* 226–229.

Jenny, C., Kuhns, M. L. D., & Arakawa, F. (1987). Hymens in newborn female children. *Pediatrics, 80,* 399–400.

Jones, J. G., Yamauchi, T., & Lambert, B. (1985). *Trichomonas vaginalis* infestation in sexually abused girls. *American Journal of Diseases of Children, 139,* 846–847.

Kaplan, K. M., Fleisher, G. M., Paradise, J. E., & Friedman, H. N. (1984). Social relevance of genital herpes simplex in children. *American Journal of Diseases of Children, 138,* 872–874.

Koop, C. E. (1988). *The Surgeon General's Letter on Child Sexual Abuse.* U. S. Department of Health and Human Services, Public Health Services, Office of Maternal and Child Health, Rockville, MD., pp. 1–16.

Krugman, R. (1986). Recognition of sexual abuse in children. *Pediatrics in Review, 8,* 25–30.

MacFarlane, K., & Krebs, S. (1987). Techniques for interviewing and evidence gathering in sexual abuse of young children. In K. MacFarlane (Ed.), *Sexual abuse of young children*. New York: Guilford Press.

McCann, J., Voris, J., Simon, M., & Wells, R. (1989). Perianal findings in prepubertal children selected for nonabuse: A descriptive study. *Child Abuse and Neglect, 13*, 179–193.

McCann, J., Voris, J., Simon, M., & Wells, R. (1990). Comparison of genital examination techniques in prepubertal females. *Pediatrics, 85*, 182–187.

McCann, J., Wells, R., Simon, M., & Voris, J. (1990). Genital findings in prepubertal girls selected for non abuse: a descriptive study. *Pediatrics, 86*, 428–439.

McCauley, J., Gorman, R. L., & Guzinski, G. (1986). Toluidine blue in the detection of perineal lacerations in pediatric and adolescent sexual abuse victims. *Pediatrics, 78*, 1039–1043.

Meyers, J. E. B. (1986). Role of physician in preserving verbal evidence of child abuse. *Journal of Pediatrics, 109*, 409–411.

Muram, D. (1989). Child sexual abuse: relationship between sexual acts and genital findings. *Child Abuse and Neglect, 13*, 211–216.

Neinstein, L. S., Goldenring, J., & Carpenter, S. (1984). Nonsexual transmission of sexually transmitted diseases: An infrequent occurrence. *Pediatrics, 74*, 67–76.

Paul, D. M. (1977). The medical examination in sexual offenses against children. *Medical Science and the Law, 17*, 251–258.

Pokorny, S. F. (1987). Configurations of the prepubertal hymen. *American Journal of Obstetrics and Gynecology, 157*, 950–956.

Rapps, W. R. (1980). Scientific evidence in rape prosecution. *University of Missouri at Kansas City Law Review, 48*, 216–236.

Rettig, P. J., & Nelson, J. D. (1981). Genital tract infection with *Chlamydia trachomatis* in prepubertal children. *Journal of Pediatrics, 99*, 206–210.

Ricci, L. R. (1988). Medical forensic photography of the sexually abused child. *Child Abuse and Neglect, 12*, 305–310.

Ricci, L. R., & Hoffman, S. A. (1982). Prostatic acid phosphatase and sperm in the postcoital vagina. *Annals of Emergency Medicine, 11*, 530–534.

Rimsza, M. E., & Niggeman, M. S. (1982). Medical evaluation of sexually abused children: A review of 311 cases. *Pediatrics, 69*, 8–14.

Rock, B., Naghashfar, Z., Barnett, N., Buscema, J., Woodruff, D., & Shah, K. (1986). Genital tract papillomavirus infection in children. *Archives of Dermatology, 122*, 1129–1132.

Roe, R. J. (1985). Expert testimony in child sexual abuse cases. *University of Miami Law Review, 40*, 97–113.

Seidel, J. S., Elvik, S. L., Berkowitz, C. D., & Day, C. (1986). Presentation and evaluation of sexual misuse in the emergency department. *Pediatric Emergency Care, 2*, 157–164.

Silverman, E. M., & Silverman, A. G. (1978). Persistence of spermatozoa in the lower genital tracts of women. *Journal of the American Medical Association, 240*, 1875–1877.

Spencer, M. J., & Dunklee, P. (1986). Sexual abuse of boys. *Pediatrics, 78*, 133–138.

Sproles, E. T. (1985). National Center for Prevention and Control of Rape. *The evaluation and management of rape and sexual abuse: A physician's guide.* U. S. Department of Health and Human Services, Public Health Services, Rockville, MD, pp. 1–70.

Teixeira, W. R. (1981). Hymenal colposcopic examination in sexual offenses. *American Journal of Forensic Medicine, 2,* 209–214.

Tilleli, J. A., Turek, D., & Jaffee, A. C. (1980). Sexual abuse in children. *New England Journal of Medicine, 302,* 319–323.

White, S. T., Loda, F. A., Ingram, D. L., & Pearson, A. (1983). Sexually transmitted diseases in sexually abused children. *Pediatrics, 72,* 16–20.

White, S., Strom, G. A., Santilli, G., & Halpin, B. (1986). Interviewing young sexual abuse victims with anatomically correct dolls. *Child Abuse and Neglect, 10,* 519–529.

Wittington, W. L., Rice, R. J., Biddle, J. W., & Knapp, J. S. (1988). Incorrect identification of *Neisseria gonorrhoeae* from infants and children. *Pediatric Infectious Diseases, 7,* 3–10.

Woodling, B. A., & Heger, A. (1986). The use of the colposcope in the diagnosis of sexual abuse in the pediatric age group. *Child Abuse and Neglect, 10,* 111–114.

Woodling, B. A., & Kossoris, P. D. (1981). Sexual misuse: Rape, molestation, and incest. *Pediatric Clinics of North America, 28,* 481–499.

4

The Impact of Sexual Abuse:
A Cognitive–Behavioral Model

Tamara S. Hoier, Carita R. Shawchuck, Gina M. Pallotta, Tim Freeman, Heidi Inderbitzen-Pisaruk, Virginia M. MacMillan, Robin Malinosky-Rummell, A. L. Greene
West Virginia University

The literature on the impact of sexual abuse has highlighted a very broad range of responses observed in victims (see, e.g., Adams-Tucker, 1982; Browne & Finkelhor, 1986; Gomes-Schwartz, Horowitz, & Sauzier, 1985: Mrazek & Mrazek, 1981). Immediate outcomes for victims include responses such as depression, anxiety, fearfulness, sleep and eating disturbances, and cognitions such as self-blame and feeling damaged (Alter-Reid, Gibbs, Lachenmeyer, Sigal, & Massoth, 1986; Browne & Finkelhor, 1986; Porter, Blick, & Sgroi, 1982), as well as acting-out behaviors such as physical aggression, sexual aggression, substance abuse, and suicidal behavior (Browne & Finkelhor, 1986; Friedrich, Urquiza, & Beilke, 1986). Diverse behavior and affective disorders also are reported as long-term correlates of sexual abuse (Browne & Finkelhor, 1986; Burnam et al., 1988; Finkelhor, 1990; Gold, 1986).

Clinical reports and empirical studies of other victimized populations indicate that similar responses are observed. Self-blame, helplessness, and depression, as well as acting out and aggression seem to be common correlates of physical abuse and neglect (cf. Barahal, Waterman, & Martin, 1981; Briere & Runtz, 1988a; Kazdin, Moser, Colbus, & Bell, 1985; Wolfe & Moske, 1983). Some authors have suggested that these responses may result from a breakdown in general caretaking of children (Azar, Barnes, & Twentyman, 1988) and/or are correlates of family isolation and disruption (Harter, Alexander, & Neimeyer, 1988). Yet, many of the same responses have also been reported as correlates of stress and trauma unrelated to family dynamics (cf. Keane, Zimering, & Caddell, 1985; Lyons & Keane, 1989; Pynoos & Eth, 1984; Saigh, 1986; Terr, 1981b). Thus, as Janoff-Bulman and Frieze (1983) suggest, common responses to victimization can be identified across populations.

With such a broad range of similar responses reported across abused and traumatized populations, questions about the unique impact of sexual abuse arise. A few controlled studies have begun to differentiate the impact of sexual abuse from the impact of other stressful and traumatic events (e.g., Deblinger, McLeer, Atkins, Ralphe, & Foa, 1987; Friedrich, Beilke, & Urquiza, 1988b; Inderbitzen-Pisaruk, Shawchuck, & Hoier, in press; White, Halpin, Strom, & Santilli, 1988). Some clear differences between populations have begun to emerge. Variability of responses without populations, including sexual abuse victims, have also been reported (Friedrich & Reams, 1987; Friedrich et al., 1986; Tsai, Feldman-Summers, & Edgar, 1979; White et al., 1988). Relationships between characteristics of abuse and responses in victims are now the focus of a second wave of research into outcomes of sexual abuse (Briere, 1988).

A systematic framework is needed to explain commonalities and differences among victimized populations and to explain mechanisms by which victimization, including sexual abuse, initiates and maintains patterns of responses. To date, several authors have described processes or factors that are thought to account for responses common to trauma and victimization (Foa, Steketee, & Rothbaum, 1989; Peterson & Seligman, 1983). Among factors and processes proposed for sexual abuse are the Sexual Abuse Accommodation Syndrome (Summit, 1983); Traumagenic Factors (Briere, 1988; Finkelhor & Browne, 1986); a recent posttraumatic stress formulation (Deblinger et al., 1987; McLeer, Deblinger, Atkins, Foa, & Ralphe, 1988; Wolfe, 1990; Wolfe, Gentile, & Wolfe, 1989); and a social learning model described by Wolfe and Wolfe (1988). These conceptualizations either focus on clusters of responses that form syndromes (e.g., hyperarousal, avoidance, and re-experiencing phenomena in posttraumatic stress disorders, depression), or describe factors that are associated with different outcomes for victims (e.g., betrayal, traumatic sexualization, availability of support within the family or community). None of these formulations allows a fine-grained analysis of the mechanisms that tie specific characteristics of abuse episodes to specific responses in victims.

A cognitive–behavioral formulation will be proposed here as a way to understand antecedent–response–consequence relations that may initiate and maintain responses observed in victims. It will also be helpful in understanding commonalities across victimized populations and differences of responses among individual sexual abuse victims (McLeer et al., 1988; Sedney & Brooks, 1984; Tsai et al., 1979). The formulation discussed here takes into account cognitive mediation processes related to outcomes of stress and trauma for victims, a theoretical position that is not typical of a radical behavioristic perspective.

Many approaches to cognitive mediation of experience are possible, including information processing; attribution, expectancy, and appraisal processes; and emotional processing (cf. Foa et al., 1989; Greenberg & Safran, 1989; Holmes & St. Lawrence, 1983; Mahoney, 1974). From our perspective, cognitive mediation takes the form of covert structures referred to as rules or, more specifically, as contingency specifying stimuli (CSS; Blakely & Schlinger, 1987).[1] Therefore, this model is but one of several cognitive–behavioral conceptualizations possible.

A cognitive–behavioral formulation offers several advantages over other conceptualizations that focus on factors correlated with responses and clusters of behavior (Hoier, 1987). First, such a formulation specifies the nature of stimulus events that initiate responses in predictable ways. Second, in a cognitive–behavioral formulation, features of classical conditioning, antecedent–response–consequence contingencies, and components of CSSs can be described operationally. Thus they can be helpful in predicting and altering the responses in victims. Third, such an approach suggests that very different types of responses observed across individuals may be controlled by the same characteristics of stimuli (e.g., degree of aversiveness, degree of threat to survival, uncontrollability) or may be functionally similar (i.e., different types of behaviors, affect, and cognitive responses serve similar functions for different individuals). Fourth, a cognitive–behavioral perspective takes into consideration mechanisms such as generalization and mediation via cognitive rules (CSSs) that maintain responses over time, even after the abuse has stopped and environmental contingencies have changed. Maintenance mechanisms would be helpful in explaining the long-term problems of adult survivors now well documented in the literature. Finally, the cognitive–behavioral model to be discussed here is compatible with a whole body of research in the area of stress and coping responses in childhood and adolescence (cf. Compas, 1987a, 1987b). It is from the stress and coping perspective that this discussion will begin

SEXUAL ABUSE AS STRESS AND TRAUMA:
THE CHALLENGE–TRAUMA CONTINUUM

Aversive events in general and sexually abusive experiences in particular can be located along a continuum of severity. We propose that intensity, repetitiveness (frequency and duration), and uncontrollability of events combine to determine level of severity. Foa et al. (1989) have discussed similar dimensions in their recent discussion of posttraumatic stress and

---

[1]We will be using the terms "rules" and "contingency specifying stimuli" (CSS) interchangeably throughout the chapter.

anxiety disorders. Terr (1989) and Wolfe (1990) have also alluded to a continuum of severity in their formulations of types of trauma. In our view, exposure of a child or adolescent to developmentally in-appropriate of unwanted sexual behavior can be thought of as a signifi-cant antecedent event that challenges victims to respond with whatever adaptive responses are available. The event can be categorized as a challenge in that the event triggers responses that actually do not tax the victim. In this case, victims can make effortful and effective responses to control or terminate aversive events. Alternatively, episodes may be categorized as stressful events that involve an interaction between a person and the environment that is perceived by the victim as taxing and/or exceeding his or her adaptive resources (Compas, 1987b). Final-ly, an episode or history of repeated sexual abuse may actually be traumatic. Such an event would involve pain, threat to survival, loss of control, and/or bizarre behavior that falls outside the normal range of experience and completely exceeds the ability of the victim to employ effortful responses effectively (Briere, 1988). In a traumatic situation, automatic fight/flight and other conditioned responses are elicited. In addition, a victim can neither act successfully to alter or terminate the aversive event nor avoid punishment for effortful coping responses.

Fig. 4.1 presents the Challenge–Stress–Trauma continuum that we have suggested. Aversive events in general, and sexually abusive events in particular, can be placed along the continuum on the basis of severity. Based on a model of antecedents for anxiety proposed by Gray (1988), the particular location of an aversive/abusive event is determined by a number of victim-related factors including: (1) the degree of novelty/ bizarreness of the stimuli/event for the victim; (2) the presence of cues that signal responses will not be rewarded by positive outcomes (i.e., the victim is helpless to alter or escape the event and arousal triggered by the event); (3) the presence of cues that punishment (pain, threats to sur-vival) will be forthcoming; and (4) the actual occurrence of pain or life-threatening events.

Both contact and noncontact sexual abuse can be located along the Challenge–Stress–Trauma continuum (see Fig. 4.1). At the challenge end of the continuum are events that involve novel sexual events that are not physically intrusive and do not provide cues of nonreward or punishment to the victim. In addition, sexual events that are challenging involve situations in which the victim can carry out effortful responses. These result in some control over outcomes for the victim. Exhibition-ism, exposure to pornography, and accidental observation of sexual behavior between consenting partners might be located at this point on the continuum.

Borrowing from Russell (1983) and others (Briere, 1988; Friedrich et

Challenge	Stress	Severe stress	Trauma	Severe trauma	Bizarre trauma
exposure to pornography	photographed	simulated intercourse	vaginal intercourse	oral sex	bondage
observing sex	observing rape	genital fondling	multiple perpetrators	anal sex	bestiality
inappropriate kissing	nongenital fondling	mutual masturbation		anilingus	ritual/cult sex
exhibitionism		digital penetration of anus/vagina		rape	penetration with sharp objects.

FIG. 4.1. The Challenge-Stress-Trauma Continuum of sexual abuse.

al., 1986; Juell, 1983; McLeer et al., 1988), abuse involving contact can be located farther along the continuum. Stressful abuse would involve contact abuse that varies in degree of novelty/bizarreness, decreased control for the victim, and threat to the victim (i.e., cues of nonreward or punishment). These characteristics elicit unconditioned arousal and escape/avoidance responses in the victim. Genital and nongenital fondling of clothed and unclothed victims, mutual masturbation, digital penetration (without pain) of the vagina and anus, simulated intercourse, and observing sexual assault of another would be located in the "Stressful Abuse" range.

Severe/traumatic abuse may involve intercourse, rape, anilingus, cunnilingus, and oral/anal penile penetration (Juell, 1983), as well as more bizarre behavior, such as bondage, painful insertion of objects, presence of multiple perpetrators, ritualistic or cult-related sex, and bestiality (Briere, 1988). At this point, the sexual behavior involved may be extremely bizarre and life threatening from the perspective of the victim, pain may be involved, and autonomic arousal associated with fear is predominant. Overt escape and avoidance behaviors are not rewarded; that is, the victim is helpless to terminate or alter events.

In addition to the type of contact, the temporal characteristics of the abuse are important. Compas (1987b) has suggested that stress may be acute or chronic. From a cognitive–learning perspective, chronic abuse would represent repeated learning trials for the victim and would interact with the severity of the stress/trauma to strengthen some responses (e.g., conditioned emotional responses such as fearful arousal, reexperiencing phenomena) and to decrease other responses (e.g., overt attempts to fight or escape). Repeated learning trials involving stressful or traumatic events can also strengthen responses to the point they become automatic, that is, responses are rapidly and strongly evoked and may be relatively resistant to change (Compas, 1987a).

The notion that the intensity, uncontrollability, and recurrent qualities of the abuse are associated with greater negative impact on victims is supported by several empirical studies. Conte and Schuerman (1987), Wolfe et al. (1989), and Friedrich et al. (1986), among others, have reported that more intrusive contact (i.e., severity of contact as defined by the challenge-trauma continuum) is associated with more emotional symptoms (e.g., anxiety) and behavioral problems. Similar conclusions have been drawn in other research involving populations of adults abused as children (Briere, 1988; Herman & Hirschman, 1981; Herman, Russell, & Trocki, 1986; Juell, 1983).

Repetitious abuse has been shown in a number of studies to have a greater impact on victims than a single incident. For example, Friedrich et al. (1986) reported that frequency of abuse was one of the predictors of internalizing and sexual problems in their pediatric population. Externalizing problems (e.g., acting out, aggression, destructive acts) also were positively correlated with frequency of abuse. Juell (1983), using a multivariate analysis, found that duration and frequency predicted more relationship, emotional, and sex problems in her adult survivors. Briere (1988) reported that extended abuse, in combination with characteristics of intensity (bizarreness of abuse and concurrent physical abuse) was related to a variety of psychological problems. Herman and colleagues (1986) reported that duration of childhood sexual abuse was greater on the average for female survivors seeking treatment than for survivors not in therapy. Finally, abuse by multiple perpetrators over time has been linked to greater emotional and adjustment problems in victims (cf. Briere, 1988; Browne & Finkelhor, 1986; Friedrich et al., 1986; Seidner, Calhoun, & Kilpatrick, 1985).

Uncontrollability may be related to the use of force, of age of onset, and identity of the perpetrator. Results of a path analysis reported by Juell (1983) suggested that victims abused as young children by someone who had easy access to them (i.e., a family member) tended to be abused longer and more severely over time. Thus, the identity of the perpetrator may be important because that individual may have greater opportunity to abuse more intensely and extensively. A perpetrator within the family also may control reinforcement and punishment contingencies that can be used to gain compliance from the victim. Similarly, the age of onset may be related to compliance with authority and may be a predictor of intensity and duration of abuse, which in turn predicts impact on victims. Further, coercion and force have been associated with more severe outcomes for victims in a number of studies (Briere & Runtz, 1988b; Finkelhor, 1979; Herman et al., 1986; Seidner et al., 1985).

Taken together, a number of studies support the traumatic learning model. The younger the victim, the use of force and coercion, and the involvement of a perpetrator who controls access to food, shelter, and other family members appear to be factors that combine to increase the uncontrollability of abusive events for victims. Force, coercion, penetration, and bizarreness of abusive contact combine as aspects of intensity that appear to increase impact as predicted by the model. Finally, recurrence of the abuse (frequency/duration) and involvement of multiple perpetrators represent repeated learning trials that seem to strengthen and generalize the impact of traumatic learning. The mechanisms that tie specific responses to characteristics of abuse histories and a discussion of responses associated with abuse will be described in the following sections.

LEARNING MECHANISMS: THE LINK BETWEEN ABUSE AND RESPONSES IN VICTIMS

In this section we will propose a model that includes both learning and cognitive mediation processes (see Fig. 4.2). In conditioning processes stimuli may evoke responses or operate as consequences that change the probability a response will reoccur. Several responses may occur simultaneously. They may be overt (e.g., motor and verbal responses) or covert (images, self-statements); and they can function as stimuli for other responses. The two basic learning processes that evoke responses are classical conditioning (respondent learning) and contingencies of reinforcement and punishment (instrumental learning). Behavioral accounts of victimization and posttraumatic stress disorders in adult populations typically include both learning processes (Holmes & St. Lawrence, 1983; Keane et al., 1985; Kilpatrick, Resick, & Veronen, 1981; Kilpatrick, Veronen, & Resick, 1982; Mowrer, 1947, 1960; Wirtz & Harrell, 1987). In addition, processes that maintain responses over time, such as generalization, complexity of conditioned stimuli, and higher-order learning, are hypothesized to be important factors for the maintenance of traumatic and stress-generated responses over time.

Mediational processes also operate to regulate responses to environmental stimuli. As antecedent–response–consequence sequences are established, cognitive rules (CSSs) are established that describe those sequences. These rules mediate responses in several ways. First they act as stimuli that compete with environmental contingencies for control of behavior. Second, CSSs act as complex behavioral programs that describe how the world operates. Third, they include descriptions of probabilities and valence of outcomes for individuals. We see the operation of CCCs as similar to relational, attributional, expectancy, and appraisal processes, and fear structures or cognitive maps described by other authors (cf. Finkelhor, 1990; Foa et al., 1989; Holmes & St. Lawrence,

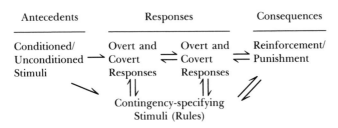

FIG. 4.2. Conditioning processes and response clusters with mediation by contingency specifying stimuli.

1983; Mahoney, 1974). Contingency specifying stimuli are more specific, however, as they involve information about antecedent–response–consequence relations and probabilities. These cognitive rules also operate to increase generalization and maintenance of a variety of responses. Conditioning and cognitive mediation processes are described in greater detail in the following sections.

Classical Conditioning

Behavioral accounts of responses in sexual assault and war-related traumata suggest classical conditioning as one of two learning factors operating in traumatic experiences (Holmes & St. Lawrence, 1983; Keane et al., 1985; Lyons & Keane, 1989). Classical conditioning occurs when an unconditioned stimulus (US) that involves pain, injury, and/or overwhelming and uncontrollable threats to survival or physical integrity elicits autonomic arousal. Unconditioned emotional responses (UCRs) include increased heartrate and other autonomic changes. Cognitive changes, such as time distortion, sharpening of perception, and greater attention to the environment, also may occur as well as cessation of behavior that was ongoing prior to the onset of the US (Gray, 1988; Pynoos & Eth, 1984; Terr, 1981b). Neutral stimuli associated with the unconditioned stimulus (e.g., thoughts, images, environmental cues) come to elicit similar arousal in the victim, operating as conditioned stimuli (CS). Based on reports by clients in treatment with the first author, both internal events (self-statements, images, and arousal/affect) and external cues (e.g., time of year, time since last sexual episode, smells, rooms in a house, running water, contact with perpetrator during supervised visitation) can come to operate as conditioned stimuli that elicit arousal, re-experiencing phenomena, and other classically conditioned responses. These observations are supported by research in the area of state-dependent learning (Bower, 1981) and clinical interventions for posttraumatic stress (cf. Blanchard & Abel, 1976; Fairbank & Keane, 1982; Hoier, in press; Hoier & Shawchuck, 1987; Keane & Kaloupek, 1982).

Even after the unconditioned (aversive) stimulus is removed, conditioned stimuli can elicit conditioned responses reliably, particularly if the US and CS have been repeatedly paired in multiple stressful or traumatic episodes. Thus, for a sexual abuse victim, cognitions, imagery, affect, types of touching, facial expressions, times of the day, and so on, can trigger automatic responses associated with aversive events. Autonomic arousal and other conditioned responses may be similar across victims of trauma (Janoff-Bulman & Frieze, 1983). However, conditioned cues that trigger conditioned responses are unique for individuals as a function of their individual learning histories.

While classical conditioning accounts for some immediate physiological, motor, and cognitive responses, this mechanism does not account for either the variety of effortful responses observed in victims of stress and trauma (e.g., escape, avoidance responses, sexual acting out, social withdrawal), or for the persistence of responses in victimized populations long after the stress/trauma has stopped.

Contingencies of Reinforcement and Punishment

To account for the breadth of responses that are associated with aversive conditioning histories, behavioral accounts of aversive conditioning include a second process. This process, instrumental learning, occurs when behavior is controlled by consequences. For example, individuals respond so as to avoid or reduce arousal and/or to terminate aversive external events (Hoier, in press; Holmes & St. Lawrence, 1983; Keane et al., 1985; Lyons & Keane, 1989).

Successful avoidance of, escape from, or reduction of distressing events (negatively) reinforces these responses in victims. That is, a victim would tend to respond in the same way in the future to cope with cues and affect/arousal previously associated with stressful/traumatic events. Cognitive responses, such as dissociation and suicidal ideation, substance abuse, somatic numbing, phobic avoidance of social situations, running away, and aggression, are all potential responses that may alter, avoid, or terminate distressing events. Similarly, some individuals may comply with or initiate sexual activity to "get it over with," a strategy observed by the first author in her own clients. All of these escape/avoidance responses may be controlled by negative reinforcement.

Positive reinforcement may operate concurrently with negative reinforcement schedules to shape responses in victims. In this case, behavior that is followed by consequences that are valued or sought by the victim would tend to increase. For example, compliance with abusive contacts may be expected to increase when they are associated with physical pleasure, material rewards, attention from significant others, and privileges not available to siblings.

The effects of punishment and noncontingent aversive events on instrumental responses must also be considered. Behavior that is followed by an aversive consequence (punishment) tends to be suppressed or decreased. Thus, for some victims, attempts to resist or escape may be decelerated over episodes of repeated abuse if those behaviors are punished either by force or threats of other aversive consequences for the victim (e.g., withdrawal of love and nurturance). Generally, the more severe and consistent the punishment for the victim, the greater the behavioral suppression of instrumental behavior (Walters & Grusec, 1977). In addition, suppression may occur if aversive events are delivered independently of responses. In this case, there is no relationship between the specific behavior of the victim and the onset of an aversive event. This type of learning mechanism underlies the cluster of behavioral deficits and cognitive rules associated with learned helplessness (Peterson & Seligman, 1983).

Extinction refers to a process in which effortful responses are not followed by reinforcement or other consequences. As a result of absence of consequences, responses are extinguished. For example, protests from a victim that do not result in change in the perpetrator's behavior would be expected to decrease over time. Similarly, when reporting abuse produces no response in caregivers, reports by victims would be expected to decrease.

For each victim, the relationship between antecedents, responses, and consequences, the type of antecedents and consequences, and the response capabilities of the victim are unique. Ratios of reinforcement and/or punishment to responses may vary as a function of schedules of these contingencies (i.e., the regularity with which responses are elicited, reinforced, and/or punished). In addition, the temporal characteristics of uncontrollable traumatic events (e.g., the frequency, average time between episodes, seasonal variation of episodes) may be operating concurrently to control response clusters in victims. The particular characteristics of the classical conditioning, reinforcement, and response capabilities of the individual victims would create a unique clinical picture for each case. Victims of stress and trauma may be most similar in respect to classically conditioned arousal, anxiety, and fear. Victims within and across different victimization experiences may be less similar in terms of cognitive responses (e.g., specific memories, themes in images, self-statements about self and the meaning of victimization) and behavior that has been reinforced, punished or extinguished.

Maintenance of Responses: Long-term Impact

Several authors have documented the "core of distress" that may continue for many months or years after a traumatic experience (Kilpatrick et al., 1981; Sales, Baum, & Shore, 1984; Wirtz & Harrell, 1987) and after sexual abuse has stopped (Briere, 1988; Formuth, 1986; Juell, 1983). Several mechanisms may account for the resistance to extinction of fear/arousal, escape/avoidance, and other responses after sexual abuse has ceased. As has been described, repeated abuse may strengthen responses in victims. In addition, the involvement of multiple perpetrators may facilitate generalization of responses across persons, time, and settings and may contribute to longer-term and more severe distress in victims.

Generalization occurs when neutral stimuli that share common characteristics with the original conditioned stimuli also evoke trauma-related responses. In addition, contingency specifying stimuli (discussed later) may facilitate generalization. Thus, a victim of sexual abuse who has been abused by a grandfather may come to fear older men or all men as a result of the abuse. Higher-order learning is a related mechanism in which neutral stimuli are paired with conditioned stimuli at a point in time after the original conditioning events. Therefore, a victim may begin to fear coming to a survivors' group or to individual therapy as a result of discussing events associated with fear and trauma in the past.

The nature of the conditioned stimuli associated with trauma can contribute to maintenance of conditioned responses long after the original trauma occurred. Two important stimulus features, the sequence of stimuli and the complexity of stimuli associated with the abuse, contribute to maintenance of traumatic responses by impeding normal desensitization and extinction processes (Levis & Hare, 1977; Stampfl & Levis, 1967). If a sequence of events comes to signal a traumatic or abusive episode, any one of these events may later evoke arousal or avoidance/escape and other coping behaviors. For example, a sexual abuse victim may learn that at a particular time of day, several times a month the perpetrator will run the bathwater, remain in the bathroom, stare at the victim as he or she undresses, and then begin to fondle or penetrate the child. At another point in time, any or all of these stimulus events may elicit abuse-related responses in the victim. For the power of these cues as controlling variables to decrease (extinguish), the victim would have to be exposed to the same or a similar sequence that evokes conditioned responses without molestation occurring. The degree to which the victim will avoid the first stimulus in the sequence will reduce the likelihood that habituation to that stimulus and later stimuli in the sequence will occur. Further, pairing of previously "normalized" cues with cues that still prompt arousal, and so on, can reinstate the control of the normalized cues as conditioned stimuli. Thus, to reduce arousal and other abuse-related responses permanently, the abuse victim must be exposed to the entire sequence of events associated with the trauma and escape/avoidance prevented before the sequence is complete (as in clinically directed abreaction or flooding experiences). Research exploring the avoidance of attack-similar stimuli in rape victims supports the hypothesis that postassault exposure to traumatically conditioned stimuli facilitates recovery (Wirtz & Harrell, 1987).

Exposure to all the components of a stimulus complex (e.g., a complete and elaborated memory or analog of the trauma) must also occur to reduce the persistence of conditioned responses and other coping behaviors that follow these responses. Components of a traumatic stimulus complex involve not only external stimuli associated with the person(s) and setting of the trauma or abuse, but also internal stimuli such as the level of affect, rules, visual, olfactory, kinesthetic, and auditory perceptions. Some of these may be associated with developmentally specific internal cognitions such as "feeling 4 years old." State-dependent learning may have occurred such that the stimulus complex is only elicited if the victim is returned to the state in which events occurred (Bower, 1981; Greenberg & Safran, 1989; Keane et al., 1985). Thus, if stimuli are conditioned in a heightened state of arousal, if conditioning occurs at a specific developmental level, or if events become paired with particular physical and affective states such as inebriation, illness, and dissociative states, subsequent exposure to and reduction of responses may only occur if these conditions are reinstated (e.g., via flooding, hypnotherapy, or perhaps via traumatic play and reenactment).

A final mechanism that may control and maintain trauma-related responses is the acquisition and operation of contingency specifying stimuli. According to Blakely and Schlinger (1987), CSSs are similar to but operate differently from discriminative stimuli. First, discriminative stimuli (SDs) evoke behavior immediately. In contrast, CSSs can evoke behavior after long delays. Second, SDs only evoke behavior. Once CSSs are established, they can alter the functional relationships among the stimuli and responses they describe and can therefore change or distort the manner in which external stimuli evoke behavior. For example, a socially active child may acquire a rule such as "I am dirty. Others will see this and hate me" as a result of sexual abuse. Subsequently, the child will withdraw from once welcome social overtures and praise by others. Finally, unlike SDs, CSSs alter the function of stimuli that evoke behavior. We propose this occurs because CSSs contain information about the probabilities of occurrence and aversiveness of environmental events, for example, contact with once trusted nonabusing adults may become aversive for a child who has developed a rule "all adults probably hurt (exploit) children."

As outlined, contingency specifying stimuli are cognitions constructed by individuals to describe relations between antecedents, responses, and consequences. Therefore, CSSs function to provide meaning and predictability to events and the world.[2] We propose that they are analogous to the "fear structures" described by Foa et al. (1989) and others. Because CSSs control behavior differently than environmental antecedents and consequences, they can operate to make behavior of individuals insensitive to changes in environmental conditions (Baron & Galizio, 1983; Zettle & Hayes, 1985). For example, the victim of abuse may continue to use escape strategies in the presence of genuinely safe stimulus conditions long after the abuse has stopped. Similarly, the victim may develop a rule that identifies himself or herself as the cause for the abuse. Subsequently, the victim irrationally may blame oneself for bad events unrelated to the abuse.

These special regulating cognitions also may heighten the control of external antecedents and consequences by making the connection between events and behavior more explicit for the victim. For example, if the victim is told that he or she will be injured or restrained if he or she does not cooperate during molestation, that warning may become internalized as a CSS or rule. Subsequent behavior may become rule governed during that episode and across many other episodes. The important feature of cognitive rules is their ability to regulate responses of individuals independently of environmental events. Thus, cognitive rules may be among the most important responses to victimization and may be fundamental to the long-term response patterns in victims.

RESPONSES TO VICTIMIZATION: SEXUAL ABUSE AND OTHER TRAUMA

Past reviews of the literature concerning the short- and long-term impact of sexual abuse typically have discussed categories of responses and symptoms, basing these categories on topographic similarity (cf. Alter-Reid et al., 1986; Browne & Finkelhor, 1986; Finkelhor, 1990). Alternatively, lists of adjustment problems or disorders have been reported (cf. Adams-Tucker, 1984; Mrazek & Mrazek, 1981). The following review is

---

[2]Several authors have discussed the "meaning" of traumatic events at length. Janoff-Bulman and Frieze (1983), for example, suggested that victimization shatters beliefs about self and the world. According to their conceptualization of responses to victimization, cognitive coping processes following victimization involve the establishment of an "assumptive world" that can include the victimization experience. That is, victims must generate a new set of beliefs about how the world operates and about self that incorporate what they learned during traumatic events. This description is quite compatible with the less cognitive, more behavioral view of the development of rules and rule-governed behavior (CSS-controlled behavior) discussed by radical behaviorists.

organized around mechanisms that may contribute to the development of specific responses. That is, responses that may be functionally similar are discussed together as are responses that may be controlled by the same conditioned stimuli. Studies that report responses in victims of trauma in general are also discussed in an effort to highlight common outcomes of stress/trauma and to identify possible differences between sexual abuse victims and other populations.

Very few studies have linked severity of abuse as defined by the Challenge–Stress–Trauma continuum to levels of response in victims. Rather, most studies reviewed here have assessed the impact of the presence or absence of a history of sexual abuse rather than looking at correlates of severity (but see, e.g., Briere, 1988; Wolfe et al., 1989). Therefore, based on the available data, few conclusions can be drawn concerning impact as a function of severity of victimization. The notion that characteristics of abusive antecedents are critical determinants of responses in victims' conclusions are suggested by the model but must await further research for validation.

Previous reviews of the literature have included data from uncontrolled clinical studies as well as results from the first few controlled studies that began to appear a decade ago. Virtually every review has listed the many methodological problems with the outcome research in the area of sexual abuse (e.g., Finkelhor, 1986; Lamphear, 1986; Mrazek & Mrazek, 1981). In the past 3 to 5 years, however, better-designed studies that have included comparison groups and psychometrically sound measures have begun to appear in the literature. Further, in addition to studies that describe differences in symptomatology between sexual abuse victims and comparison groups, research that examines the relationship between characteristics of abuse and different outcomes for victims has begun to appear (Briere, 1988). Therefore, it is now possible to begin to identify general responses to trauma and victimization. It is also now possible to draw some preliminary conclusions about specific sequelae of sexual abuse and to speculate about cause-and-effect relationships between sexual abuse and the adjustment of victims.

Classically Conditioned Responses

One of the most frequently reported responses to trauma of any kind is increased arousal and short-term disruption of appetitive and other physiological functions. These responses are described as components of fear or anxiety and are assumed to be initiated by unconditioned stimuli and, eventually, by conditioned stimuli. Posttraumatic hyperarousal has been most carefully described in single-case studies involving physiological assessment of adult survivors of incest, rape, and war (cf. Becker, Skinner, & Abel, 1982; Blanchard & Abel, 1976; Fairbank & Keane, 1982; Keane & Kaloupek, 1982). In these studies, a causal relationship between exposure to trauma-related stimuli and conditioned physiological responses has been demonstrated in multiple baseline single-subject research. Interview-based reports of similar autonomic arousal in child witnesses to violence and in victims of sexual abuse have also been reported (cf. Deblinger et al., 1987; Einbender & Friedrich, 1989; Pynoos & Eth, 1984; Rosenberg, 1987).

Deblinger and her associates (1987) found that the clinical records of sexually abused pediatric inpatients contained significantly more indexes of autonomic arousal (e.g., sleep disturbance, distractibility, hyperalertness, startle responses, physiological changes) than did the records of matched samples of physically abused and nonabused inpatients in the same facility. Similarly, in an uncontrolled study, Wolfe et al. (1989) reported higher-item scores for symptoms of posttraumatic stress (e.g., difficulty sleeping, concentration problems, somatic complaints) in their sample of sexually abused children, compared with a normative sample. Einbender and Friedrich (1989) reported higher scores on a measure of hyperactivity in sexually abused girls ages 6 to 14 than in a comparison sample of nonabused, nonreferred girls matched on the basis of age, race, family income, and family disruption (single versus two-parent homes). As an index of autonomic arousal, hyperactivity does not appear to be specific or sensitive to differences between history of trauma and other types of stress. For example, if sexually abused children are compared to conduct-disordered or other clinic-referred children, it appears sexually abused children are as hyperactive or less so than the comparison samples (Friedrich et al., 1988a, 1988b; Gomes-Schwartz et al., 1985).

Other nonspecific indicators of hyperarousal such as sleeplessness and concentration problems have been reported as specific short- and long-term sequelae of sexual abuse. Sleeplessness has been reported as more prevalent in sexually abused children and adolescents compared with nonabused control groups (cf. Conte, 1988; Edwall, Hoffmann, & Harrison, 1989). Hoier and Shawchuck, (1987) documented the onset of sleep disturbance and night wandering immediately following visitation with the perpetrators in a 6-year old sexual abuse victim. Sleep disturbance has also been reported to be more prevalent in adult survivors of sexual abuse than in nonabused adult comparison groups (Briere, 1988; Briere, Evans, Runtz, & Wall, 1988; Sedney & Brooks, 1984). Conte (1988) reported concentration problems were more prevalent in sexually abused children than in a nonabused comparison group. Murphy, Saunders, and McClure (1986) reported that self-reported concentration problems were also more prevalent in sexually abused children than in their nonabused siblings. Studies that report specific symptoms in other populations suggest that sleep disturbance and concentration problems are common outcomes of stress and victimization (e.g., Kolko, Moser, & Weldy, 1988).

Increases in somatic complaints that may indicate physiological disturbance and hyperarousal have often been reported as sequelae of sexual abuse (cf. Brown & Finkelhor, 1986). Some studies suggest somatic complaints and somatization are more prevalent in sexual abuse victims than in nonabused community comparison samples (Briere & Runtz, 1988b; Conte, 1988). However, other studies comparing sexual abuse victims with clinical populations and nonabused community samples have found that somatic complaints are either less frequent in cases of sexual abuse or are comparable with complaints in clinical comparison groups (Friedrich et al., 1988b; Gomes-Schwartz et al., 1985). Studies of other maltreated adults and children also have reported somatic complaints be common in these populations (Briere & Runtz, 1988a; Wirtz & Harrell, 1987; Wolfe & Moske, 1983). It appears that somatic phenomena may be general indicators of stress and are not specific to either sexual abuse or physical trauma.

Based on the preliminary evidence, general heightened activity (e.g., hyperactivity) and specific arousal problems such as sleep disturbance, concentration problems, and somatic phenomena appear to be common short-term outcomes of severe distress and trauma of any kind. Few studies attempt to identify specific stimuli that may increase arousal over baseline levels (but see Hoier, in press; Hoier & Shawchuck, 1987; Keane & Kaloupek, 1982). Stressed and traumatized populations may not differ in terms of general arousal levels. They may differ, however, in terms of the specific stimuli that evoke arousal, sleeplessness, and so on. A fine-grained functional analysis of the antecedents for arousal in specific cases would be helpful to identify differences between sexual abuse victims and other populations.

Eating disturbances in victims of trauma have not been widely reported since changes in appetitive behaviors tend to be grouped together with indicators of depression, a frequently reported outcome of victimization. However, Edwall et al. (1989) reported differences in eating patterns between sexually abused and nonabused chemically dependent adolescents. Further, Becker et al. (1982) and Hoier and Shawchuck (1987) have observed significant increases in eating behavior in children following sexual abuse and/or exposure to abuse-similar stimuli. Again, these single-case studies suggest that abuse-related stimuli triggered the onset of appetitive changes in the children studied. Further longitudinal and single-subject replication research must be completed, however, to support the notion that eating behavior changes are outcomes of traumatic classical conditioning processes.

Enuresis has been reported in both sexually abused children and a matched sample of neglected children (White et al., 1988), suggesting multiple controlling variables may be operating in respect to elimination problems in children. However, *changes* in bladder control in children following sexual abuse have been reported for some child and adolescent victims (cf. Blanchard & Abel, 1976; Friedrich & Reams, 1987). Like studies of changes in eating behavior, the temporal relationship between abuse and onset of these problems suggests a cause-and-effect relationship. Further controlled research and longitudinal studies are needed to support this hypothesized causal relationship.

Re-experiencing phenomena have been described in victims of trauma (Keane et al., 1985; Lyons & Keane, 1989; Pynoos & Eth, 1984; Saigh, 1986; Terr, 1981a, 1981b). These phenomena appear to be common to all victimized populations and are apparently controlled by internal and external trauma-related conditioned stimuli and rules (cf. Bower, 1981; Foa et al., 1989; Keane et al., 1985). Re-experiencing phenomena appear to be classically conditioned responses rather than functional behaviors that are controlled by their consequences. In traumatized adults, nightmares involving themes related to the trauma or actual images of the trauma have been reported (Fairbank & Keane, 1982; Keane et al., 1985; Wirtz & Harrell, 1987). Flashbacks, defined as detailed memories that are triggered by conditioned stimuli during nonsleep periods, also have been reported in traumatized populations (Becker, Skinner, Abel, & Cichon, 1986; Keane et al., 1985). Waking and sleep-related replays of stressful/traumatic episodes seem to be common in child, adolescent and adult survivors of childhood sexual abuse as well. Further, they have been observed to occur more frequently in these victims, compared with other nonabused populations (Becker et al., 1986; Sedney & Brooks, 1984, Wolfe et al., 1989).

In contrast to adults and adolescents, reexperiencing phenomena have a greater variety of modes of expression in children (Pynoos & Eth, 1984). For example, traumatic themes and details of traumatic events have been reported in the play of child victims of kidnap and other trauma (Terr, 1981a, 1981b, 1983) and in structured and unstructured doll and toy play of sexually abused young children (White et al., 1988; White, Strom, Santilli, & Halpin, 1986). Traumatic themes in play vary from child to child in terms of the elements included. In one of the first controlled studies involving sexually abused children, White and colleagues (1986) compared use of anatomically correct dolls during structured interviews in sexually abused and nonreferred children. They found that sexual material appeared to be specific to the play of sexual abuse victims. In two other studies, use of dolls to demonstrate sexual acts was observed in a significantly greater number of sexually abused young boys and girls than in comparison groups of neglected and nonreferred young children and relatively rarely in nonabused children (Sivan, Schor, Koeppl, & Nobel, 1988; White et al., 1988).

A related reexperiencing phenomenon, reenactment, also has been observed in traumatized pediatric populations. In this type of behavior, the victim actually role plays or motorically re-creates the traumatic episodes. In uncontrolled studies of kidnapped children and child witnesses to homicide, Terr (1981b) and Pynoos and Eth (1984) have observed many types of event-specific reenactment of traumatic events. Deblinger and colleagues (Deblinger et al., 1987; McLeer et al., 1988) have defined some types of sexual acting out and repetitive talking about the abuse as reexperiencing/reenactment phenomena. Deblinger et al. (1987) compared the clinical records of sexually abused inpatients, ages 3 to 13, with the clinical records of physically abused and nonabused inpatients. Using a 17–item symptom checklist drawn from the DSM-III-R criteria for posttraumatic stress disorder, the authors found that significantly more sexually abused children engaged in sexual aggression toward others, compared with physically abused and nonabused populations. In addition, significantly more sexually abused children engaged in sexually inappropriate behavior such as excessive masturbation, compared with physically abused and nonabused inpatients.

The finding that sexual aggression and some sexualized behaviors are rare (Friedrich, Grambsch, Broughton, & Kuiper, in press) and much more frequent in sexually abused children, compared with physically abused, neglected, conduct-disordered, other clinical and nonreferred populations frequently has been reported (Friedrich et al., 1986, 1988a, 1988b; Inderbitzen-Pisaruk et al., in press; White et al., 1988). In addition, single-case studies in which a preabuse baseline for sexual behavior could be established suggest that sexual abuse and exposure to abuse-related stimuli, such as supervised visitation with the perpetrator, evoke masturbation and sexual aggression in these cases (Becker et al., 1982; Hoier & Shawchuck, 1987). Overall, sexualized behavior in play and reenactment of sexual abuse appear to be among symptoms that clearly distinguish sexually abused children and adolescents from other stressed and traumatized populations.

Other types of behaviors also may present as reenactment phenomena such as self-injurious and dangerous behavior reported in uncontrolled studies of witnesses to homicide (Pynoos & Eth, 1984) and in sexually abused children. In their single-case study, Becker et al. (1982) reported that self-injurious behavior began after the onset of sexual abuse in their 4-year-old subject. White et al. (1988) found that sexually abused young boys were significantly more accident-prone and more likely to put themselves in dangerous situations than were groups of neglected and nonreferred boys of the same age. This finding did not hold, however, for girls in their study.

Two other studies have explored the differences in incidence of self-injury between sexually abused children receiving inpatient treatment and other pediatric and adolescent psychiatric inpatients. Kolko et al. (1988) reported that sexually abused child psychiatry inpatients took unnecessary risks and hurt themselves more often than nonabused children on the same inpatient unit. Lesaca and Fuller (1989) presented clinical data that suggest self-injury (particularly hand injury) was much more frequent in sexually and physically abused inpatient adolescents than in nonabused adolescents hospitalized on the same unit. In addition, they reported that sexually abused girls in particular were significantly more likely to injure themselves during hospitalization than physically abused and nonabused girls. Finally, the abused male group was more than three times more likely to self-injure than nonabused inpatient males. This difference was not statistically significant, however, due to the small sample size. The sample of males was also too small to look at differences between the incidence of self-injury in physically and sexually abused boys.

Reports of self-injurious and mutilating behavior have just begun to appear in the literature on adult survivors of sexual abuse (Briere, 1988; Gil, 1988). Based on the few studies available, however, it appears that sexually abused children and adolescents and perhaps adults may self-injure more frequently than nonabused comparison groups. Other controlled studies of self-injurious behavior need to be completed to support the notion that these behaviors may be conditioned re-enactment/ reexperiencing responses and are functionally different from self-injurious behavior reported in nontraumatized populations, such as among individuals with developmental disabilities. Further, studies that compare the incidence of self-injurious behavior in male and female children exposed to different intensities of violence and abuse would be helpful understanding the controlling variables of self-injury and mutilation across various traumatized and sexually abused populations.

Generalized fear and anxiety are commonly reported outcomes of sexual abuse (Brown & Finkelhor, 1986). The results of studies on fearfulness in sexually abused children and other populations can only be understood in the context of the measures used in these studies. Fearfulness and anxiety are often measured by self-reports on psychometrically sound fear and anxiety questionnaires. These questionnaires combine many items involving a variety of motor, physiological, and cognitive responses into a fear or anxiety score. Therefore, they do not measure responses to specific traumatic stimuli nor do they measure individual-specific patterns of responses (but see Wolfe et al., 1989, for a measure of sex-related fears). In contrast, some studies of fearfulness have employed a more individualized measure, self-reported subjective units of distress (SUDS), in response to the presence or absence of a trauma specific stimuli. The SUDS measures may be more sensitive to individual conditioned distress.

Generalized fear and fear of victimization appear to be problems common to stressed and traumatized children and adolescents. For example, Friedrich and colleagues (1988b) used the parent-report Anxiety/Obsessiveness subscale of the Child Behavior Checklist (CBCL; Achenbach & Edelbrock, 1983) to compare groups of sexually abused boys and girls (ages 3–12) with samples of nonabused, referred and nonabused, nonreferred children. They found that sexually abused boys and girls did not differ significantly from other referred children on this measure. Both treatment groups were significantly more anxious/fearful than the community sample, however. In another study, Friedrich et al. (1988a) compared sexually abused boys with boys diagnosed as conduct-disordered, using the CBCL Anxiety measure. Again they found that the abused and clinic groups did not differ in terms of anxiety. Gomes-Schwartz et al. (1985), using another standardized questionnaire, found that sexually abused children from 4 to 13 were more fearful, compared with norms for community populations, but were less fearful compared with norms for clinic populations. Finally, Wolfe et al. (1989) reported that interpersonal discomfort scores on their Sexual Abuse Fear Scale (SAFE) for a sample of sexually abused children did not differ from scores for a nonreferred school sample. However, the abused sample did report more sex-related fears and rated themselves as more anxious than nonclinical normative samples.

The possibility that generalized fear and anxiety in children may be outcomes of family and environmental variables other than specific trauma and stress episodes is suggested by most of these data. Two recent studies have attempted to control for family disruption and other variables in an attempt to look at this issue. Murphy et al. (1986) studied similarities and differences between sexually abused children and their nonabused siblings ages 6–17. The two groups shared the same environment. However, the groups differed in terms of their mean ages and sex ratio (the sexually abused group was somewhat older and contained significantly more females). Both groups completed two psychometrically sound measures of fear and anxiety. The authors found that the two groups did not differ on these measures. A recent study completed by Inderbitzen-Pisaruk et al. (in press) involved nonsibling samples of children. Sexually abused children were matched with a community sample of nonabused peers on the basis of age, sex, and family disruption (single-parent versus two-parent homes). Both groups completed a measure of general fear and a new measure developed to tap sex abuse-related fears (Wolfe & Wolfe, 1988). There were no significant differences between groups on these measures, suggesting that global measures of fearfulness do not differentiate sexually abused populations from other stressed populations of children, even when measures of fear victimization are used. Together, these findings suggest that factors (e.g., family variables) other than characteristics of specific abuse episodes may contribute to generalized, nonspecific fear and anxiety in children. Individual- and event-specific responses might be found, however, if individualized measures such as galvanic skin responses and Subjective Units of Distress (SUDS) were used in future research designed to observe responses in the presence or absence of abuse and trauma-specific stimuli (cf. Rychtarik, Silverman, Landingham, & Prue, 1984; Saigh, 1986). Traumatized groups also may be found to differ if the specific content of fearful cognitions are assessed (cf. Hoier, in press; Terr, 1983; Wolfe et al., 1989).

Some studies suggests that a history of sexual abuse contributes to generalized anxiety in adulthood. For example, Burnam et al. (1988) reported results from an epidemiological study in which they analyzed the predisposing factors for a variety of mental disorders, including anxiety disorders (phobia, panic, and obsessive–compulsive disorders), schizophrenia, manic episodes, and substance abuse. They found that sexual assault, particularly assault in childhood, predisposed victims to later anxiety disorders, but not to disorders associated with genetic transmission (mania, schizophrenia) or to antisocial activity. In another study, Tsai et al. (1979) compared MMPI profiles of three groups: adult survivors of sexual abuse who sought treatment, adult survivors who were not in treatment, and a nonsexually abused community sample. The authors reported that, compared with the other two groups, adult survivors of sexual abuse who sought treatment scored significantly higher on the Pa scale (paranoia scale) of the MMPI. The mean scores for all groups were not clinically significant, however. Neither of these studies controlled for family or community variables; therefore, the contribution of these variables to the development of fear and anxiety cannot be considered.

Few if any studies attempted to analyze fear functionally in adult populations. Most studies of adult survivors of sexual abuse have not used narrow-band measures to assess fear, anxiety, or specific phobic symptoms in abused, stressed, and nonabused populations. Rather, studies of adult survivors have tended to use more general indexes of psychological functioning (cf. Gold, 1986; Harter et al., 1988; Juell,

1983; Seidner et al., 1985). Though items concerning fear, anxiety, or other specific symptoms may have been embedded in these measures, the level and pattern of specific responses present in these populations is not possible to identify. Thus, both the child and adult literature offer little help in identifying the unique contributions of trauma, sexual abuse, family, and other variables to the development of fearfulness and anxiety.

While aggression has been described as one of the automatic responses to aversive stimuli by a number of authors (e.g., Walters & Grusec, 1977), aggression does not appear to be specific to trauma or traumatic abuse. For example, Friedrich et al. (1988a, 1988b) reported higher levels of aggression in conduct-disordered boys than in either sexually abused or community populations. Similarly Gomes-Schwartz et al. (1985) reported that sexually abused children were more aggressive than community norms but were less aggressive, compared with clinical norms. In their study of adults, Burnam et al. (1988) reported antisocial personality was not related to a history of sexual assault in childhood for either men or women. As Wolfe and Wolfe (1988) suggested, aggression may be controlled by consequences and may develop independently of sexual abuse episodes. These processes will be discussed later.

Negative Reinforcement

Escape and avoidance have been described as primary responses to overwhelming stress and trauma. These responses develop and are maintained because they are effective in removing the victim from the stressful/traumatic stimuli. A variety of escape and avoidance behaviors have been reported in both trauma and sexual abuse victims. The most obvious are the phobias and avoidance of trauma-specific stimuli observed in children and adults (cf. Becker et al., 1986; Saigh, 1986; Wirtz & Harrell, 1987). For example, sexual dysfunction has been found to be more prevalent in adults with a history of sexual abuse than in nonabused comparison samples (Becker et al., 1986; Gold, 1986; Tsai et al., 1979). Becker and colleagues (1986) found that victims of sexual assault and incest victims had more problems with sexual dysfunctions involving avoidance of sexual contact than nonabused clients with sexual dysfunction. The groups also differed in terms of types of other sexual problems experienced. The predominant other problems in victims of abuse and assault included onset of flashbacks and pain during intercourse. In contrast, other problems for nonassaulted clients generally involved boredom with sex. The groups were comparable in terms of incidence of orgasmic dysfunction, however. The Becker et al. study did not report differences between sexually abused clients and those assaulted as adults. However, their work suggests that sexual dysfunctions reported in survivors of sexual abuse are of a type that would inhibit or interfere with sexual activity.

Some studies have found social withdrawal to be more frequent in victims of sexual abuse, compared with other populations (Conte, 1988; Einbender & Friedrich, 1989; Kolko et al., 1988; White et al., 1988). For example, among children ages 2–6, White et al. (1988) found that significantly more male and female sexual abuse victims withdrew socially than either neglected or nonreferred children of the same age. In addition, they found that significantly more abused girls preferred to play alone, compared with neglected and nonreferred females. In contrast, some studies suggest that child and adolescent victims may be no more withdrawn than other distressed populations. For example, Friedrich et al. (1988a, 1988b) found that sexually abused children were as socially withdrawn as other clinical groups. However, all clinical groups, including sexually abused children, were more depressed/withdrawn on the CBCL than nonreferred community samples.

Wolfe et al. (1989) reported their sexually abused sample was rated as less socially competent on the CBCL, compared with the normative population described by Achenbach and Edelbrock (1983). In the Friedrich studies described earlier, sexually abused children were rated as more socially competent than were clinical comparison groups. Together, these data suggest that variables related to social withdrawal/ participation measures for comparison groups and sexually abused children may be very different. On the one hand, conduct-disordered children may be less socially competent, more aggressive, and, therefore, more rejected than sexually abused and other peers. On the other hand, sexually abused peers may have adequate social skills but may choose to avoid social participation more than nonabused, normal peers. Some support for this hypothesis comes from the adult literature. For example Wirtz and Harrell (1987) have reported avoidance of attack-similar stimuli in adult rape victims, including reduction of social contacts following assaults. To identify the controlling variables for social withdrawal and social competence in different populations, social participation/withdrawal, social anxiety, and social skill levels of sexually abused children and adults should be assessed and compared with participation and skill in other populations.

Some studies of sexual abuse victims have suggested that survivors tend to have earlier peer sex, more casual sex, and/or more partners than other populations (cf. Becker et al., 1986; Wyatt, 1988). While increased sexual acting out may involve reexperiencing phenomena for some victims, or may reflect inappropriate rules about the meaning and function of sexual intimacy (more later), sexual acting out may also be negatively reinforced. For example, the first author has observed that a number of adolescent and adult clients in her clinical practice have initiated unsatisfying sexual contacts. They have reported that they initiated these contacts because they predicted that sex was inevitable and they wanted to "get it over with," thereby removing anxiety. This function of sexual acting out is based on clinical reports and on the cognitive–behavioral model. Empirical data are lacking to date. To account for the different functions and controlling variables of sexual behavior in survivors of sexual abuse and other populations, assessment of the immediate antecedents of behavior, the function of sexual behavior, and rules about sexual contact in different populations is needed.

Other escape/avoidance responses possible in victims of trauma and stress include running away, drug and alcohol use, suicide, and dissociative processes. In a comparison study of 40 adult survivors of sexual abuse and 20 nonsexually abused women who had "seductive" fathers, Herman and Hirshman (1981) reported a significantly greater number of sexually abused women had run away, compared with nonabused women. A similar difference between groups was reported by Meiselman (1978). She found that 50% of the adult victims of incest left home before age 18, compared with 20% of the nonabused comparison group. In a study of residents of a shelter for runaways, McCormack, Janus, and Burgess (1986) reported the incidence of male and female victims of sexual abuse was much higher than incidence reported in the literature. Cavaiola and Schiff (1988) reported that a higher percentage of chemically dependent abused adolescents had run away, compared with nonabused, chemically dependent and nonchemically dependent groups. Finally, Conte (1988) reported that a higher percentage of sexually abused children had run away, compared with their nonabused comparison sample. Most of these studies reported differences in incidence of running away without reference to whether these differences were statistically significant. Replication of these findings, using comparison groups such as physically abused and neglected children, would help identify whether sexually abused children are more likely to run than other children in dysfunctional families. Further, reports of statistical differences between comparison groups would strengthen the findings of between-group differences.

Some recent research has suggested that sexual abuse is associated with specific patterns of drug and alcohol abuse. For example, Herman and Hirschman (1981) reported a higher percentage of abused women in their sample abused drugs and alcohol, compared with nonabused women. This difference was not statistically significant, however. Using a much larger sample of randomly selected community members, Burnam et al. (1988) found that a history of sexual assault in childhood increased the probability of subsequent alcohol and drug dependence, particularly in males. In another study of 444 adolescent girls admitted to chemical dependency programs, Harrison, Hoffmann, and Edwall (1989) found that sexual abuse victims were significantly more likely to use stimulants, sedatives, tranquilizers and hallucinogens, compared with nonabused chemically dependent girls. Further, sexually abused girls began to use drugs at a much earlier age than nonabused residents (see also Cavaiola & Schiff, 1988). Finally, inspection of their data reveals that incest and incest plus extrafamilial sexual abuse histories were associated with wider use of drugs, compared with nonabuse and extrafamilial-abuse-only histories. The authors asked residents to identify the reasons why they used substances. Many more of the victims of incest and victims of incest plus extrafamilial sex abuse reported use to reduce tension, to get away from problems, and to reduce physical pain or discomfort, compared with nonabused and extrafamilial abuse victims. The authors propose incest victims and victims of multiple perpetrators used substances to "self-medicate," that is, to cope with aversive internal or external events.

Suicidal ideation and behavior and dissociative disorders have been reported in victims of sexual abuse. These responses appear to be closely associated with a history of sexual abuse and with the severity of sexual trauma. Several authors have reported a higher rate of suicidal ideation and attempts in sexual abuse victims, compared with other nonabused populations (Briere, 1988; Briere & Runtz, 1986, 1988b; Conte, 1988; Edwall et al., 1989; Herman & Hirschman, 1981; McCormack et al., 1986; Sedney & Brooks, 1984). For example, in the McCormack et al. (1986) study of runaways, there was a trend toward greater suicidality among sexually abused runaways than among nonabused runaways. Edwall et al. (1989) identified four groups of chemically dependent adolescents (nonabused, extrafamilial abuse alone, incest victims, and incest plus extrafamilial abuse). Based on multivariate research (e.g., Briere, 1988; Juell, 1983), the latter two groups could be assumed to have experienced more extensive and intensive abuse than the other two groups. Results reported by Edwall et al. suggest a relationship between the type of sexual abuse, defined by group membership, and suicidality. Suicide attempts occurred in a higher percentage of sex abuse cases involving incest or incest plus abuse by others than in cases of extrafamilial abuse or cases with no sexual abuse history. The greatest percentage of suicide attempts was reported by victims of incest only. Briere (1988) studied relationships among abuse variables and measures of symptomatology in an adult population. Results of his multivariate analysis suggested a strong relationship between the occurrence of intercourse in an abuse history and subsequent suicidality. Based on these preliminary data, traumatic sexual abuse, (i.e., repeated and highly intrusive sexual contact, particularly within the family) appears to increase substantially the probability of escape through suicidal ideation and behavior.

Cognitive processes of dissociation have also been reported as a means to escape from trauma, severe abuse, and intense noncontingent punishment (Briere, 1988; Kluft, 1985; Malinosky-Rummell & Hoier, 1990, in press; Spiegel, 1984). Putnam (1985) described dissociation as a complex process that changes consciousness so that feelings and experiences are not integrated into memory in a normal way. He suggested that dissociation is one coping response when overwhelming assault occurs and if fight/flight is prevented. Malinosky-Rummel and Hoier (1990, in press) do not emphasize changes in "unity of consciousness" as the critical process in dissociation. Rather, using a behavioral framework, they defined dissociation as an escape response to trauma-related stimuli involving a breakdown in the normal correspondence between and/or within three response modes (i.e., cognitive, physiological, and motor). The behavioral definition offers the advantage of operationally defining dissociation and important antecedents.

Several authors have suggested that dissociative processes are maintained by negative reinforcement and that unpredictable physical and sexual assault can result in episodic dissociation or in persistent compartmentalization of arousal, cognitions, and motor behavior as is seen in multiple personality disorder (Braun & Sachs, 1985; Briere, 1988; Frischolz, 1985; Malinosky-Rummell & Hoier, 1990). The frequency of the trauma and repeated use of dissociation to reduce the experience of trauma is assumed to contribute to the severity of the dissociative disorder that results (Braun & Sachs, 1985). Mention of dissociative phenomena has just begun to appear in the sexual abuse literature (Briere, 1988; Briere & Runtz, 1988b; Gil, 1988). Historically the study of dissociative phenomena, particularly those associated with the development of multiple personality disorders (MPD), has been restricted to the psychiatric literature. Descriptive studies appearing in that body of research have linked trauma, especially sexual abuse, to dissociation and MPD (cf. Bowman, Blix, & Coons, 1985; Braun & Sachs, 1985; Kluft, 1985). Assessment of dissociative phenomena in sexually abused and other distressed children and adults, using psychometrically sound instruments (cf. Branscomb & Fagan, 1988; Carlson & Putnam, 1988), would be useful direction for future research. Such a study has been reported by Malinosky-Rummell and Hoier (in press). In addition to exploring the psychometric properties of two measures of dissociative experiences in children, the authors assessed differences in parent and self-reported dissociation in females ages 7 to 12. Scores from 10 sexually abused girls were compared to those obtained from 50 nonabused girls in a community sample. The authors found that the sexually abused females scored significantly higher on measures of dissociation than did the nonabused community females. Further, in a regression analysis, the estimated number of abusive incidents experienced by the abused girls predicted higher dissociation scores.

The Malinosky-Rummel and Hoier study involved a small number of fairly severely abused girls. Further studies, perhaps using the same or comparable parent and self-report measures, would be important to support these initial findings. Also, based on the clinical experience of the first author with dissociative sexually abused clients, a functional analysis of dissociation is possible and could be explored via behavioral single-case studies in the future (cf. Hoier, in press).

Aggression and related externalizing behaviors (e.g., hostility, tantrums, anger, delinquency) have been suggested as outcomes of sexual abuse (see Browne & Finkelhor, 1986; Conte, 1988). In fact, empirical studies suggest that levels of aggression and antisocial activity are no greater for sexually abused individuals than for other distressed populations (Burnam et al., 1988; Friedrich et al., 1986, 1988a, 1988b; Gomes-Schwartz et al., 1985; Kolko et al., 1988). It is more likely that aggression and acting out are developed and maintained by coercive processes operating in the family system in nonabuse situations rather than by processes specific to sexual abuse episodes (Patterson, 1976; Wolfe & Wolfe, 1988). In a coercive family system, aggression is negatively reinforced across a wide range of interactions among siblings and between children and parents. Greater aggression results in termination of conflict as the less aggressive party gives in. For some victimized individuals, however, aggression may be a strategy to avoid future victimization. In our own work, several sexual abuse victims have reported that they take a "best defense is a good offense" approach when moving into new or threatening social situations. These, of course, are anecdotal data. However, future research might study the antecedents of aggression (rather than the level of aggression and acting out) to help identify differences in function and situational expression of aggression between sexually abused and other populations.

Positive Reinforcement

Many adaptive as well as maladaptive responses are developed and maintained by contingencies of reinforcement. Responses that are positively reinforced may include reporting the abuse to responsive others, and seeking social support to ventilate feelings and experiences resulting from trauma (Keane et al., 1985). Research suggests that victims who receive support (e.g., have more friends, receive positive consequences for disclosure, protection) seem to do better than those who had no support or received punishment from parents for disclosure (Browne & Finkelhor, 1986; Conte & Schuerman, 1987). These conclusions are drawn from a small number of studies and, therefore, are tentative. Support and other positive consequences that elicit adaptive responses (e.g., problem solving, networking for support and protection) may compete with negative consequences that elicit avoidant and destructive responses. Research is needed on different reinforcement contingencies as they affect behavior and adjustment.

Two processes have been described as supporting sexualized behavior in sexually abused children and adolescents: classical conditioning of reexperiencing phenomena and negative reinforcement. Positive reinforcement may also account for some types of sexualized behavior. Masturbation may be reenactment. However, it also may be maintained by the physical pleasure the child or adolescent experiences when masturbating. Sexual behavior and compliance with sexual requests may also increase because they have been reinforced by attention, special favors, or material rewards offered by the perpetrator (cf. Herman & Hirschman, 1981; Tharinger, 1990). Thus, sexual behavior may be elicited and maintained by a variety of contingencies. Those operating to control sexual behavior in individual victims must be carefully assessed for each individual case (cf. Hoier & Shawchuck, 1987).

Punishment and Extinction

Aversive consequences of coping responses in victims may decrease the likelihood that victims will respond with that particular coping strategy in the future. For example, the ability to defend oneself against sexual advances and sexual assault may be punished or extinguished during abuse episodes. Therefore, self-defensive behaviors and active avoidance of "risky" situations may disappear from the repertoires of some victims. One indicator that self-defensive behavior has decreased is the incidence of revictimization. Several authors have reported that victimization and sexual assault occurring in adulthood is more frequent in victims of childhood sexual abuse than in other populations (Briere, 1988; Burnam et al., 1988). While self-defensive behavior in adulthood may be maintained by contingency specifying internal stimuli and other cognitions described later, the original punishment or extinction of self-defensive behavior during sexual abuse episodes could have given rise to the initial cessation of active self-defense.

Noncontingent punishment and low rates of reinforcement of active responses have been linked to depressive behaviors, such as low activity, withdrawal, decreased interest in previously valued activities, and cognitions of reduced control over a threatening environment. These processes are described in behavioral conceptualizations of depression in victimized populations (cf. Kilpatrick et al., 1982; Peterson & Seligman, 1983). Some authors have reported that sexual abuse in childhood predicts major depression in adults (Burnam et al., 1988). Further, sexually abused children and adolescents have been reported to score higher on measures of depressive cognitions than sibling and community populations (Murphy et al., 1986; Inderbitzen-Pisaruk et al., in press). However, other authors have found that self-reported depressive cognitions are no more common in children and adolescents who have been sexually abused than in other clinical populations (Edwall et al., 1989; Einbender & Friedrich, 1989). Studies that have assessed depressive behaviors have found no differences between sexually abused children and adolescents and other stressed and abused populations (Einbender & Friedrich, 1989; Friedrich et al., 1986, 1988a, 1988b). Further, depressive behaviors and cognitions appear to be common among physically abused children (Allen & Tarnowski, 1989; Kazdin et al., 1985) and among survivors of sexual assault in adulthood (Burnam et al., 1988; Kilpatrick et al., 1981). Thus, depression, a term that refers to specific overt behavior patterns and to cognitions, may not be specific to sexual abuse, but rather is an outcome of trauma and/or other stressful conditions. Future research might assess cognitions and contingencies operating for depressed abuse victims and compare them with victims who do not develop depression. It is possible that the severity of the trauma, combined with the relative absence of reinforcing contingencies, contribute to the development of depressive responses in some sexual abuse victims.

CSS and Other Cognitive Processes

As described in an earlier section, rules (CSSs) can be acquired via learning mechanisms and, once established, they can mediate the impact of other environmental conditions on behavior. We have also suggested that once established, CSSs can establish control over responses rendering these responses relatively insensitive to environmental stimuli. A number of authors have reported specific cognitions observed in victims of trauma. For example, Terr (1981b) and Pynoos and Eth (1984) have reported that child victims of trauma will retrospectively identify omens or specific antecedents of traumatic events. The designation of some antecedent to trauma by victims also has been described by authors who have studied the "search for meaning" following victimization (cf. Silver,

Boon & Stones, 1983). For the children of the Chowchilla kidnapping, many omens or rules/attributions of cause involved identification of their own behaviors or traits as cause for the kidnapping (Terr, 1981b, 1983). Such cognitive (mis)representations of antecedent–response–consequence relations may underlie the guilt, self-blame, and low evaluation of self (self-esteem) reported in both adult and child sexual abuse victims.

For example, Gold (1986) reported that, compared with a sample of nonabused women, survivors of sexual abuse made more internal attributions of cause for bad events. In addition, she found that attributions or rules about the self as cause, in conjunction with the view that bad events were highly probable and danger was omnipresent (referred to as internal–stable–global attributions), predicted the level of distress and low self-esteem in these women. Similar results were reported by McGarry (1988), who compared attributions of sexually abused and nonabused adolescent inpatients of a psychiatric unit. He found that sexually abused inpatients made more internal–stable–global attributions (i.e., the clients felt at cause for highly probable bad events occurring across settings) than did comparison groups. Finally, Wolfe et al. (1989) reported that sexually abused children tended to hold rules that sexual abuse is probable across settings and that adults exploit children. They also found that an attributional style (set of rules) that one is personally predisposed to recurrent bad events (e.g., "bad things happen to me, I cause bad things to happen") predicted decreased social competence, greater depression, and self-rated anxiety in their sexually abused sample.

The rule or expectation that danger is omnipresent was observed by Terr in the Chowchilla children (1981b). The view that danger is unavoidable may have implications for the long-term adjustment problems and "core of distress" reported in some victim populations (cf. Sales et al., 1984). For example, Seidner et al. (1985) reported that adult survivors of sexual abuse who made stable attributions for the cause of the abuse (i.e., danger was assumed to be omnipresent) had lower levels of adjustment than those survivors who defined threat as specific to time and place. Few other studies have attempted to assess systematically types of cognitions about how the world operates in victims of trauma and sexual abuse. Based on the model of learned helplessness proposed by Peterson and Seligman (1983), specific classes of cognitions should commonly appear across victimized populations as a function of traumagenic processes. Therefore, some rules (CSSs) may be general outcomes of trauma rather than specific to sexual abuse.

In addition to internal–stable–global rules/attributions, sexual abuse victims may develop other specific dysfunctional rules about antecedents, behavior, and consequences. For example, sexual assault and compliance may be labeled as inevitable and the only coping option, respectively. Alternatively, sexual behavior may be misidentified as the means to obtain much-needed attention and nurturance. Sex also may be identified as a consequence or behavioral expression of anger. Therefore, victims may inappropriately expect sexual initiations to follow anger in self or others. (Also see Finkelhor, 1990; and Tharinger, 1990, for discussions of cognitive aspects of traumatic sexualization). The development of rules that predict the behavior of others (e.g., identification of behaviors that signal consistent responses in others, the basis of "trust") may be impaired by trauma or abuse, particularly if victimization was unpredictable and not contingent on the behavior of the victim. Finally, rules about the behavior of others may develop during abuse. These rules about the attributes of perpetrators may eventually make the victim insensitive to appropriate behavior in nonabusing others.

Many different antecedent–response–consequence rules and rules that classify the world may be acquired. Previous little research has been conducted to go beyond depressive cognitions and those associated with the learned helplessness paradigm (Peterson & Seligman, 1983). A few rules we have observed in our work with clients and those referred to as "issues" by other clinicians have been offered here (cf. Porter et al., 1982). Research into cognitions might develop a taxonomy of rules and attributions that develop in victims in general and in sexual abuse in particular.

Maintenance Variables

The contribution of cognitions to the long-term maintenance of other responses in survivors of trauma has been mentioned. Other processes, such as generalization and higher-order learning, have been fairly neglected in the research on outcomes of sexual abuse. Generally research studies do not ask questions about the immediate conditioned antecedents of responses. However, behaviorally oriented treatment studies of various posttraumatic problems do offer support for the notion that complex and multicomponent stimuli come to control responses in victims over time (cf. Becker et al., 1982; Rychtarik et al., 1984; Blanchard & Abel, 1976). Further, studies such as that completed by Wirtz and Harrell (1987) support the hypothesis that avoidance of trauma-related stimuli maintains avoidance and conditioned responses over time. Conversely, exposure to traumatic stimuli appears to reduce both classically conditioned and negatively reinforced behaviors (cf. Blanchard & Abel, 1976; Fairbank & Keane, 1982; Saigh, 1986). These maintenance mechanisms are probably operating in all survivors of trauma. Individuals may differ in their willingness to contact trauma-related stimuli and in terms of specific clusters of rules they generate postvictimization. These differences may then contribute to variability of long-term outcomes within populations.

Clinical Disorders: Multiple Response Clusters

Syndromes such as multiple personality disorder, dissociative disorders, and posttraumatic stress disorder (with subcategories: reexperiencing, hyperarousal, and avoidant behavior) have been associated with a history of sexual abuse in the psychiatric literature (cf. Braun & Sachs, 1985; Frischolz, 1985). These disorders identify stress as the antecedent to responses and they imply cause-and-effect relationships between trauma and responses in victims. The problem with research exploring the incidence and severity of syndromes or disorders associated with sexual abuse lies in the breadth of responses associated with diagnostic categories. As Conte (1988) points out, discussing the impact of sexual abuse in terms of broad diagnostic categories loses the detail and in-dividual-specific organization of cognitive, motor, and physiological responses possible in victims. An approach that associates diagnostic categories with sexual abuse also may distort the relationship between specific characteristics of abuse and specific responses in victims. Multi-variate studies involving specific responses, such as that recently reported by Briere (1988), would serve to elaborate relationships between trauma and responses in general and between characteristics of sexual abuse and responses in victims in particular.

SUMMARY AND CONCLUSIONS

All victimized populations seem to experience classically conditioned increases in arousal, sleep disturbance, and changes in some biological functions, such as appetite and elimination. Based on the model described here, the severity of these disruptions is hypothesized to be a direct function of the severity of the trauma as defined by the Challenge–Stress–Trauma continuum. Reexperiencing phenomena also appear to be common across traumatized populations. However, the content and topography of nightmares, flashbacks, and reenactments appear to be specific to the type of trauma and, to a lesser extent, the age of the victim.

Sexualized behavior appears to be much more disturbed and prevalent in sexually abused children and adolescents, compared with other distressed populations. As has been noted earlier, sexual behavior may be categorized as reexperiencing phenomena. It also may be under the control of several other variables, such as cognitions about the use of sex and reinforcement contingencies. The hypothesis that sexualized behavior is under the control of several learning processes may account for the diversity of sexual behavior reported in sexually abused children and adolescents. While less well documented, specific and possibly unique forms of sexual dysfunction appear in adult sexual abuse victims. This area may need more attention in the future.

Escape and avoidance behaviors such as social withdrawal, phobic responses to trauma-specific stimuli, substance abuse, running away, increased suicidality, and dissociation have all been reported as sequelae of stress/trauma. The specific conditioned stimuli that later come to control avoidance and escape may be individual-specific. That is, individual victims of trauma may differ more in terms of the specific *complex* and *sequence of cues* that elicit avoidance and escape responses than in terms of level or incidence of these responses. Further, some escape/avoidance behaviors may appear to be topographically similar and common across populations. However, they may be *functionally* different for individuals. For example, low social participation (a measure of social withdrawal) may be the outcome of social anxiety in competent children (as has been suggested is the case for some sexually abused children) or it may be the result of rejection by peers of a socially incompetent and aggressive child. Similarly, running away might serve to terminate abuse, or may allow escape from a repressive and dysfunctional family system. Finally, the *pattern* rather than incidence of some of these responses (e.g., substance abuse, suicidality, dissociation) may be unique for sexually abused individuals.

While substance abuse appears to be a correlate of sexual abuse as well as many other variables, the pattern of chemical use appears to vary as a function of abuse history. Preliminary data suggest that sexually abused adolescents use earlier and are more likely to become involved in polysubstance abuse than nonabused adolescents. Further, abuse of chemicals may vary directly with level of sexual trauma. Similarly, other self-damaging behaviors, such as suicide and self-injury, may be elicited by more severe abuse and the sexual nature of trauma in sexual abuse. For example, some data suggest traumatic sexual abuse, as indicated by intercourse and inescapability, may increase the probability of final escape attempts through suicide and dissociation. Clearly research is needed to clarify the patterns of specific symptoms and their controlling variables in victimized populations and in sexually abused individuals.

Other responses in victimized populations that seem to be common include depression, aggression, and specific rules about antecedent–response–consequence relations. Again, attention to the function of aggression across various populations would be helpful in identifying any unique contribution of sexual abuse to interpersonal violence. Depressive responses are common but not unique outcomes of sexual abuse. Research into depression in sexual abuse victims might begin to explore the specific cognitions these individuals report and compare them with depressive cognitions in other populations. Assessment of differences in cognitive rules between sexual abuse and other victims is in its infancy. So far, cognitions concerning internal–stable–global attributions associated with the learned helplessness conceptualization have received the most attention. Other cognitions/rules assumed to be specific outcomes of sexual abuse have been described in clinical reports. We propose that the operation of cognitive rules is a very powerful process that mediates responses and adjustment in the short and long term. Therefore, empirical studies of cognitive rules and their contribution to short- and long-term responses to sexual abuse and other types of victimization need to be completed.

Finally, the cognitive–behavioral model assumes that most learning processes will operate independently of the gender of the victim. The one exception may be cognitive responses to abuse associated with sexual identity and expression of sexuality. Most of the research reviewed here did not address the question of differences in impact of sexual abuse on male versus female victims. A few studies have begun to appear that explore responses in boys and men abused as children (e.g., Briere et al., 1988; Finkelhor, 1990; Friedrich et al., 1988a). Fewer investigations have compared responses in males and females (but see Briere et al., 1988; Burnam et al., 1988; Finkelhor, 1990; White et al., 1988). We have found only one study that has systematically assessed and reported significant *differences* between male and female children (White et al., 1988) and that was described as an initial investigation that needed replication. Clearly, further research is needed to highlight gender-linked responses and to explore abuse in males versus females.

DIRECTIONS FOR FUTURE RESEARCH

Several of the conclusions drawn in the previous section are based on preliminary data originating in the "first wave" of research into the impact of sexual abuse (Briere, 1988). Based on that research, it appears that sexual abuse victims as a group present with a variety of short- and long-term symptoms and disorders, some of which may be specific sequelae of the severity sexual nature of the trauma suffered. Among the most important questions for continuing research is the issue of similarities and differences across traumatized populations. To this end, investigators should continue to compare the effects of sexual abuse with effects of other types of victimization within the family as well as to extrafamilial victimization that occurs independently of family dynamics. Better assessment of the pattern of responses in individuals, assumed by this model to be, in part, a result of specific traumatic learning histories, should be undertaken. Assessment of the link between severity of trauma, as defined by the Challenge–Stress–Trauma continuum proposed here, and classes of responses (unconditioned, conditioned, and consequence-controlled responses) also is now a reasonable direction for the "second wave" of research (Briere, 1988). Finally, we have suggested the powerful influence of CSSs on victim responses. As the model in Fig. 4.2 implies, rules impact responses and their contingencies on many different levels and serve to filter or distort environmental contingencies. Some research into the types of CSSs that develop in the course of victimization and their impact has begun. Perhaps this represents a "third wave" of research in the area of sexual victimization.

While a number of methodological problems with research in the area of sexual abuse have been detailed by several authors (e.g., Finkelhor, 1986; Mrazek & Mrazek, 1981), some of these problems might be solved if the goals of future investigations were directed toward answering some of the questions posed here. For example, samples might be selected on the basis of levels of severity of abuse and/or victimization as defined by the Challenge–Stress–Trauma continuum. This might allow better control over the contribution of type of history than selecting on the basis of the presence or absence of a sexual abuse history. Further, selection of dependent measures that are sensitive to different patterns of specific symptoms rather than level or occurrence/nonoccurrence of symptoms is recommended to provide a finer-grained analysis of outcomes. Dependent measures that assess more globally defined problems (e.g., depression, hyperactivity, aggression, sex problems) might be replaced by measures of more narrowly defined symptoms (e.g., suicide attempts, suicidal ideation with or without a plan, dissociation with or without amnesia, initiates aggression, uses aggression in self-defense, sexual touching of others, sexual themes in play, avoidance of touching, excessive masturbation, social withdrawal versus social rejection, etc.). Finally, multivariate, longitudinal, and single-subject methodologies might be considered as the tools of choice for future research efforts. The first two methodologies would allow us to answer questions concerning the contribution of characteristics of specific histories and other variables to variability of response patterns in subjects. Single-subject methods would allow conclusions to be drawn about specific responses and the antecedents and consequences that control them. Finally, single-subject treatment research designed to alter relations between responses, controlling environmental contingencies, and cognitive rules may also highlight variables that control responses in sexual abuse victims.

REFERENCES

Achenbach, T., & Edelbrock, C. R. (1983). *Manual for the Child Behavior Checklist and Revised Child Behavior Profile.* Burlington, VT: University of Vermont, Department of Psychiatry.

Adams-Tucker, C. (1982). Proximate effects of sexual abuse in children. A report on 28 children. *American Journal of Psychiatry, 139,* 1252–1256.

Adams-Tucker, C. (1984). The unmet psychiatric needs of sexually abused youths. Referrals from a child protection agency and clinical evaluations. *Journal of the American Academy of Child Psychiatry, 23,* 659–667.

Allen, D. M., & Tarnowski, K. J. (1989). Depressive characteristics of physically abused children. *Journal of Abnormal Child Psychology, 17,* 1–11.

Alter-Reid, K., Gibbs, M. S., Lachenmeyer, J. R., Sigal, J., & Massoth, N. A. (1986). Sexual abuse of children: A review of the empirical findings. *Clinical Psychology Review, 6,* 249–266.

Azar, S. T., Barnes, K. T., & Twentyman, C. T. (1988). Developmental outcomes in physically abused children: Consequences of parental abuse or the effects of a more general breakdown in caregiving behaviors? *Behavior Therapist, 11,* 27–32.

Barahal, R. M., Waterman, J., & Martin, H. P. (1981). Social cognitive development of abused children. *Journal of Consulting and Clinical Psychology, 49,* 508–516.

Baron, A., & Galizio, M. (1983). Instructional control of human operant behavior. *Psychological Record, 33,* 495–520.

Becker, J. V., Skinner, L. J., & Abel, G. G. (1982). Treatment of a four-year-old victim of incest. *American Journal of Family Therapy, 10,* 41–46.

Becker, J. V., Skinner, L. J., Abel, G. G., & Cichon, J. (1986). Level of postassault sexual functioning in rape and incest victims. *Archives of Sexual Behaviors, 15,* 37–49.

Blakely, E., & Schlinger, H. (1987). Rules: Function-altering contingency-specifying stimuli. *Behavior Analyst, 10,* 183–187.

Blanchard, E. E., & Abel, G. G. (1976). An experimental case study of the biofeedback treatment of rape-induced psychophysiological cardiovascular disorder. *Behavior Therapy, 1,* 113–119.

Bower, G. H. (1981). Mood and memory. *American Psychologist, 36,* 129–148.

Bowman, E. S., Blix, S., & Coons, P. M. (1985). Multiple personality in adolescence: Relationship to incestuous experiences. *Journal of the American Academy of Child Psychiatry, 24,* 109–114.

Branscomb, L., & Fagan, J. (1988, August). *Development and validation of a childhood dissociative predictor scale*. Paper presented at the annual meeting of the American Psychological Association, Atlanta, GA.

Braun, B. G., & Sachs, R. G. (1985). The development of Multiple Personality Disorder: Predisposing, precipitating, and perpetuating factors. In R. Kluft (Ed.), *Childhood antecedents of multiple personality* (pp. 37–64). Washington, DC: American Psychiatric Press.

Briere, J. (1988). The long-term clinical correlates of childhood sexual victimization. *Annals of the New York Academy of Sciences, 328,* 327–334.

Briere, J., Evans, D., Runtz, M., & Wall, T. (1988). Symptomatology in men who were molested as children: A comparison study. *American Journal of Orthopsychiatry, 58,* 457–461.

Briere, J., & Runtz, M. (1986). Suicidal thoughts and behaviours in former sexual abuse victims. *Canadian Journal of Behavioural Science, 18,* 413–423.

Briere, J., & Runtz, M. (1988a). Multivariate correlates of childhood psychological and physical maltreatment among university women. *Child Abuse and Neglect, 12,* 331–341.

Briere, J., & Runtz, M. (1988b). Symptomatology associated with childhood sexual victimization in a nonclinical adult sample. *Child Abuse and Neglect, 12,* 51–59.

Browne, A., & Finkelhor, D. (1986). Impact of child sexual abuse: A review of the literature. *Psychological Bulletin, 99,* 66–77.

Burnam, M., Stein, J., Golding, J., Siegel, J., Sorenson, S., Forsythe, A., & Telles, C. (1988). Sexual assault and mental disorders in a community population. *Journal of Consulting and Clinical Psychology, 56,* 843–850.

Carlson, E., & Putnam, F. W. (1988, August). *Further validation of the Dissociative Experiences Scale.* Paper presented at the meeting of the American Psychological Association, Atlanta.

Cavaiola, A. A., & Schiff, M. (1988). Behavioral sequelae of physical and/or sexual abuse in adolescents. *Child Abuse and Neglect, 12,* 181–188.

Compas, B. E. (1987a). Coping with stress during childhood and adolescence. *Psychological Bulletin, 101,* 393–403.

Compas, B. E. (1987b). Stress and life events during childhood and adolescence. *Clinical Psychology Review, 7,* 275–302.

Conte, J. R. (1988). The effects of sexual abuse on children. Results of a research project. *Annals of the New York Academy of Sciences, 528,* 310–326.

Conte, J. R., & Schuerman, J. R. (1987). Factors associated with an increased impact of child sexual abuse. *Child Abuse and Neglect, 11,* 201–211.

Deblinger, E., McLeer, S. V., Atkins, M. S., Ralphe, D., & Foa, E. B. (1987, November). *Posttraumatic stress in sexually abused, physically abused, and nonabused children.* Paper presented at the annual meeting of the Association for Advancement of Behavior Therapy, Boston.

Edwall, G. E., Hoffmann, N. G., & Harrison, P. A. (1989). Psychological correlates of sexual abuse in adolescent girls in chemical dependency treatment. *Adolescence, 24,* 279–288.

Einbender, A. J., & Friedrich, W. A. (1989). Psychological functioning and behavior of sexually abused girls. *Journal of Consulting and Clinical Psychology, 57,* 155–157.

Fairbank, J. A., & Keane, T. M. (1982). Flooding for combat-related stress disorders: Assessment of anxiety reduction across traumatic memories. *Behavior Therapy, 13*, 499–510.

Finkelhor, D. (1979). *Sexually victimized children.* New York: Free Press.

Finkelhor, D. (1986). Designing new studies. In D. Finkelhor (Ed.), *A sourcebook on child sexual abuse* (pp. 199–223). Beverly Hills, CA: Sage.

Finkelhor, D. (1990). Early and long term effects of sexual abuse: An update. *Professional Psychology: Research and Practice, 5*, 325–330.

Finkelhor, D., & Browne, A. (1986). Initial and long-term effects: A conceptual framework. In D. Finkelhor (Ed.), *A sourcebook on child sexual abuse* (pp. 180–198). Beverly Hills, CA: Sage.

Foa, E. B., Steketee, G., & Rothbaum, B. O. (1989). Behavioral/cognitive conceptualizations of post-traumatic stress disorder. *Behavior Therapy, 20*, 155–176.

Formuth, M. E. (1986). The relationship of childhood sexual abuse with later psychological and sexual adjustment in a sample of college women. *Child Abuse and Neglect, 10*, 5–15.

Friedrich, W. N., Beilke, R., & Urquiza, A. J. (1988a). Behavior problems in young sexually abused boys: A comparison study. *Journal of Interpersonal Violence, 3*, 21–28.

Friedrich, W. N., Beilke, R., & Urquiza, A. J. (1988b). Children from sexually abusive and distressed families: A behavioral comparison. *Journal of Interpersonal Violence, 2*, 391–402.

Friedrich, W. N., Grambsch, P., Broughton, D., & Kuiper, J. (in press). Normal sexual behavior in children. *Pediatrics.*

Friedrich, W. N., & Reams, R. (1987). Course of psychological symptoms in sexually abused young children. *Psychotherapy, 24*, 160–170.

Friedrich, W. N., Urquiza, A. J., & Beilke, R. (1986). Behavior problems in sexually abused children. *Journal of Pediatric Psychology, 11*, 47–57.

Frischolz, E. J. (1985). The relationship among dissociation, hypnosis, and child abuse in the development of Multiple Personality Disorder. In R. Kluft (Ed.), *Childhood antecedents of Multiple Personality* (pp. 99–126). Washington, DC: American Psychiatric Press.

Gil, E. (1988). *Treatment of adult survivors of childhood sexual abuse.* Walnut Creek, CA: Launch Press.

Gold, E. R. (1986). Long term effects of sexual victimization in childhood: An attributional approach. *Journal of Consulting and Clinical Psychology, 54*, 471–475.

Gomes-Schwartz, B., Horowitz, J. M., & Sauzier, M. (1985). Severity of emotional distress among sexually abused preschool, school-age, and adolescent children. *Hospital and Community Psychiatry, 36*, 503–508.

Gray, J. A. (1988). The neuropsychological basis of anxiety. In C. Last & M. Hersen (Eds.), *Handbook of anxiety disorders* (pp. 10–37). New York: Pergamon Press.

Greenberg, L. S., & Safran, J. D. (1989). Emotion in psychotherapy. *American Psychologist, 44*, 19–29.

Harrison, P. A., Hoffmann, N. G., & Edwall, G. E. (1989). Differential drug use patterns among sexually adolescent girls in treatment for chemical dependency. *International Journal of the Addictions, 24,* 499–514.

Harter, S., Alexander, P. C., & Neimeyer, R. A. (1988). Long-term effects of incestuous child abuse in college women: Social adjustment, social cognition, and family characteristics. *Journal of Consulting and Clinical Psychology, 56,* 5–8.

Herman, J., & Hirschman, L. (1981). Families at risk for father–daughter incest. *American Journal of Psychiatry, 138,* 967–970.

Herman, J., Russell, D., & Trocki, K. (1986). Long-term effects of incestuous abuse in childhood. *American Journal of Psychiatry, 143,* 1293–1296.

Hoier, T. S. (1987). Child sexual abuse: Clinical interventions and new directions. *Journal of Child and Adolescent Psychotherapy, 4,* 179–185.

Hoier, T. S. (in press). The course of treatment of a sexually abused child: A single case study. *Behavioral Assessment.*

Hoier, T. S., & Shawchuck, C. R. (1987, December). *The natural history and treatment of behavioral problems in sexually abused children: A case study.* Paper presented at the Rivendell Conference, Memphis.

Holmes, M. R., & St. Lawrence, J. S. (1983). Treatment of rape-induced trauma: Proposed behavioral conceptualization and review of the literature. *Clinical Psychology Review, 3,* 417–433.

Inderbitzen-Pisaruk, H., Shawchuck, C. R., & Hoier, T. S. (in press). Behavioral characteristics of child victims of sexual abuse: A comparison study. *Journal of Clinical Child Psychology.*

Janoff-Bulman, R., & Frieze, I. H. (1983). A theoretical perspective for understanding reactions to victimization. *Journal of Social Issues, 39,* 1–17.

Juell, H. M. (1983). A descriptive model of the emotional, sexual, physical, and relational effects of childhood sexual molestation on adult females. *Dissertation Abstracts International, 44,* 3936B. (University Microfilm No. 84–04–365)

Kazdin, A. E., Moser, J., Colbus, D., & Bell, R. (1985). Depressive symptoms among physically abused and psychiatrically disturbed children. *Journal of Consulting and Clinical Psychology, 94,* 298–307.

Keane, T. M., & Kaloupek, D. G. (1982). Imaginal flooding in the treatment of a Posttraumatic Stress Disorder. *Journal of Consulting and Clinical Psychology, 50,* 138–140.

Keane, T. M., Zimering, R. T., & Caddell, J. M. (1985). A behavioral formulation of posttraumatic stress disorder in Vietnam veterans. *Behavior Therapist, 8,* 9–12.

Kilpatrick, D. G., Resick, P. A., & Veronen, L. J. (1981). Effects of a rape experience: A longitudinal study. *Journal of Social Issues, 4,* 105–122.

Kilpatrick, D. G., Veronen, L. J., Resick, P. A. (1982). Psychological sequelae to rape: Assessment and treatment strategies. In D. M. Doleys, R. L. Meredith, & A. R. Ciminero (Eds.), *Behavioral medicine: Assessment and treatment strategies* (pp. 475–497). New York: Plenum Press.

Kluft, R. P. (1985). Childhood Multiple Personality Disorder: Predictors, clinical findings, and treatment results. In R. Kluft (Ed.), *Childhood antecedents of Multiple Personality* (pp. 167–198). Washington DC: American Psychiatric Press.

Kolko, D. J., Moser, J. T., Weldy, S. R. (1988). Behavioral/emotional indicators of sexual abuse in child psychiatric inpatients: A controlled comparison with physical abuse. *Child Abuse and Neglect, 12,* 529–541.

Lamphear, V. S. (1986). The psychosocial adjustment of maltreated children: Methodological limitations and guidelines for research. *Child Abuse and Neglect, 10,* 63–69.

Lesaca, T., & Fuller, M. (1989). *The relationship of phsyical and sexual abuse to self-injury in adolescent inpatients.* Manuscript submitted for publication.

Levis, D. J., & Hare, N. (1977). A review of the theoretical rationale and empirical support for the extinction approach of implosive (flooding) therapy. In M. Hersen, R. Eisler, & P. Miller (Eds.), *Progress in behavior modification* (Vol. 4, pp. 299–376). New York: Academic Press.

Lyons, J. A., & Keane, T. M. (1989). Implosive therapy for the treatment of combat-related PTSD. *Journal of Traumatic Stress, 2,* 137–152.

Mahoney, M. J. (1974). *Cognition and behavior modification.* Cambridge, MA: Ballinger.

McCormack, A., Janus, M. D., & Burgess, A. W. (1986). Runaway youths and sexual victimization: Gender difference in an adolescent runaway population. *Child Abuse and Neglect, 10,* 387–395.

McGarry, M. S. (1988, August). *Sexual abuse and power dynamics: Learned helplessness in adolescent populations.* Paper presented at the annual meeting of the American Psychological Association, Atlanta.

McLeer, S. V., Deblinger, E., Atkins, M. S., Foa, E. B., & Ralphe, D. L. (1988). Post-traumatic Stress Disorder in sexually abused children. *Journal of the American Academy of Child and Adolescent Psychiatry, 27,* 650–654.

Malinosky-Rummell, R. R., & Hoier, T. S. (1990). *Dissociation in sexual abuse victims: Current conceptualizations, assessment, and research.* Manuscript submitted for publication.

Malinosky-Rummell, R. R., & Hoier, T. S. (in press). Dissociation in children: A validation study of measures of dissociation in community and sexually abused children. *Behavioral Assessment.*

Meiselman, K. C. (1978). *Incest: A psychological study of causes and effects with treatment recommendations.* San Francisco: Jossey-Bass.

Mowrer, O. H. (1947). On the dual nature of learning: A reinterpretation of "conditioning" and "problem-solving." *Harvard Educational Review, 17,* 102–148.

Mowrer, O. H. (1960). *Learning theory and behavior.* New York: Wiley.

Mrazek, P. B., & Mrazek, D. A. (1981). The effects of child sexual abuse: Methodological considerations. In P. Mrazek & C. H. Kempe (Eds.), *Sexually abused children and their families* (pp. 235–245). New York: Pergamon Press.

Murphy, S. M., Saunders, B. E., & McClure, S. (1986, August). *Victims of incest: An individual and family profile.* Paper presented at the annual meeting of the American Psychological Association, Washington, DC.

Patterson, G. R. (1976). The aggressive child: Victim and architect of a coercive system. In E. Mash, L. A. Hamerlynck, & L. C. Handy (Eds.), *Behavior modification and families: Theory and research* (pp. 267–316). New York: Brunner Mazel.

Peterson, C., & Seligman, M. E. P. (1983). Learned helplessness and victimization. *Journal of Social Issues, 39,* 103–116.

Porter, F., Blick, L., & Sgroi, S. (1982). Treatment of the sexually abused child. In S. Sgroi (Ed.), *Handbook of clinical intervention in child sexual abuse* (pp. 109–146). Lexington, MA: Lexington Books.

Putnam, F. W. (1985). Dissociation as a response to extreme trauma. In R. Kluft (Ed.), *Childhood antecedents of multiple personality* (pp. 65–98). Washington, DC: American Psychiatric Press.

Pynoos, R. S., & Eth, S. (1984). The child as witness to homicide. *Journal of Social Issues, 40,* 87–108.

Rosenberg, M. S. (1987). Children of battered women: The effects of witnessing violence on their social problem-solving abilities. *Behavior Therapist, 10,* 85–89.

Russell, D. E. H. (1983). The incidence and prevalence of intrafamilial and extrafamilial sexual abuse in female children. *Child Abuse and Neglect, 7,* 133–146.

Rychtarik, R. G., Silverman, W. K., Landingham, W. P., & Prue, D. M. (1984). Treatment of an incest victim with implosive therapy: A case study. *Behavior Therapy, 15,* 410–420.

Saigh, P. A. (1986). In vivo flooding in the treatment of a 6-year old boy's post-traumatic stress disorder. *Behaviour Research and Therapy, 24,* 685–688.

Sales, E., Baum, M., & Shore, B. (1984). Victim readjustment following assault. *Journal of Social Issues, 40,* 117–136.

Sedney, M. A., & Brooks, B. (1984). Factors associated with a history of childhood sexual experience in a nonclinical female population. *Journal of the Academy of Child Psychiatry, 23,* 215–218.

Seidner, A. L., Calhoun, K. S., & Kilpatrick, D. G. (1985, August). *Childhood and/or adolescent sexual experiences: Predicting variability in subsequent adjustment.* Paper presented at the meeting of the American Psychological Association, Toronto.

Silver, R. L., Boon, C., & Stones, M. H. (1983). Searching for meaning in misfortune: making sense of incest. *Journal of Social Issues, 39,* 81–102.

Sivan, A. B., Schor, D. P., Koeppl, G. K., & Nobel, L. D. (1988). Interaction of normal children with anatomical dolls. *Child Abuse and Neglect, 12,* 292–309.

Spiegel, D. (1984). Multiple personality as a Posttraumatic Stress Disorder. *Psychiatric Clinics of North America, 7,* 101–110.

Stampfl, T. G., & Levis, D. J. (1967). Essentials of Implosive Therapy: A learning-theory-based psychodynamic behavioral therapy. *Journal of Abnormal Psychology, 72,* 496–503.

Summit, R. C. (1983). The Child Sexual Abuse Accommodation Syndrome. *Child Abuse and Neglect, 7,* 177–193.

Terr, L. C. (1981a). Forbidden games: Post-traumatic child's play. *Journal of the American Academy of Child Psychiatry, 20,* 741–760.

Terr, L. C. (1981b). Psychic trauma in children. *American Journal of Psychiatry, 138,* 14–19.

Terr, L. C. (1983). Chowchilla revisited: The effects of psychic trauma in a group of "normal" children. *Journal of the American Academy of Child Psychiatry, 22,* 221–230.

Terr, L C. (1989). Treating psychic trauma in children: A preliminary discussion. *Journal of Traumatic Stress, 2,* 3–20.

Tharinger, D. (1990). Impact of child sexual abuse on developing sexuality. *Professional Psychology: Research and Practice, 21,* 331–337.

Tsai, M., Feldman-Summers, S., & Edgar, M. (1979). Childhood molestation: Variables relating to differential impacts on psychosocial functioning in adult women. *Journal of Abnormal Psychology, 88,* 407–123.

Walters, G. C., & Grusec, J. E. (1977). *Punishment.* San Francisco: W. H. Freeman.

White, S., Halpin, B. M., Strom, G. A., & Santilli, G. (1988). Behavioral comparisons of young sexually abused, neglected, and nonreferred children. *Journal of Clinical Child Psychology, 17,* 53–61.

White, S., Strom, G. A., Santilli, G., & Halpin, B. M. (1986). Interviewing young sexual abuse victims with anatomically correct dolls. *Child Abuse and Neglect, 10,* 519–529.

Wirtz, P. W., & Harrell, A. V. (1987). Effects of postassault exposure to attack-similar stimuli on long-term recovery of victims. *Journal of Consulting and Clinical Psychology, 55,* 10–16.

Wolfe, D. A., & Moske, M. D. (1983). Behavioral comparisons of children from abusive and neglectful families. *Journal of Consulting and Clinical Psychology, 51,* 702–708.

Wolfe, V. V. (1990, November). *Type I and Type II PTSD: A conceptual framework for sexual abuse sequelae.* Paper presented at the meeting of the Association for the Advancement of Behavior Therapy, San Francisco.

Wolfe, V. V., Gentile, C., & Wolfe, D. A. (1989). The impact of sexual abuse: A PTSD formulation. *Behavior Therapy, 20,* 215–228.

Wolfe, V. V., & Wolfe, D. A. (1988). The sexually abused child. In E. J. Mash & L. B. Terdal (Eds.), *Behavioral assessment of childhood disorders* (2nd ed., pp. 670–714). New York: Guilford Press.

Wyatt, G. (1988). The relationship between child sexual abuse and adolescent sexual functioning in Afro-American and White American women. *Annals of the New York Academy of Sciences, 528,* 111–122.

Zettle, R. D., & Hayes, S. C. (1985). Rule-governed behavior: A potential theoretical framework for cognitive behavioral therapy. In P. C. Kendall (Ed.), *Advances in cognitive–behavioral research and therapy* (Vol. 1, pp. 73–118). New York: Academic Press.

5

Psychological Assessment of Sexually Abused Children

Vicky Veitch Wolfe
Children's Hospital of Western Ontario
Carole Gentile
University of Ottawa

As a society, we have awakened to the reality that childhood sexual abuse is a major social problem, and that policies must be established to assure protection of our children. Growing public awareness has resulted in an amazing increase in reported cases of sexual abuse (Cantwell, 1981; National Center on Child Abuse and Neglect, 1981). Unfortunately, as mental health professionals are keenly aware, we are sorely underequipped to cope with the demands for services brought forth by these disclosures. Not only are agencies understaffed for managing sexual abuse cases, the technology for assessment and intervention is grossly underdeveloped. A pivotal cornerstone to the development of adequate social and therapeutic interventions is a development of adequate assessment technology. The purpose of this chapter is to provide a conceptual framework for assessing the sexually abused child, with a particular emphasis on understanding the interplay of contextual factors as they relate to sexual abuse sequelae. Assessment methodology will be reviewed regarding the context of the abuse, veracity of allegations, impact of sexual abuse, and factors mediating the impact of sexual abuse.

Assessing sexually abused children can be conceptualized as a threepart, building block process. The first task is to define the context for the assessment. The second is assessing the child's current psychological adjustment. The third task is assessing those factors that may mediate the impact of sexual abuse for a particular individual. Each of these aspects of assessment will be described in detail in the following sections.

Many of the assessment procedures described in this chapter were developed as a part of a line of research designed to assess the impact of

sexual abuse on children. This project, conducted in collaboration with
D. A. Wolfe, involves the assessment of all cases of sexual abuse investigated by a team of social workers in a lower-income section of
London, Ontario. Currently 100 cases have been followed from the time
of disclosure, and at 3-month and 9-month follow-up periods. Assessments include a series of questionnaires and structured interviews for
both the child and the nonoffending parent.

CONTEXT

What are the goals for assessment and who will use the results and for
what purpose? At what point in time is a child being assessed, as related
to the abuse, disclosure, court, and treatment? What were the circumstances surrounding the sexual abuse, and what happened sexually?
What other stressors are occurring that might affect psychological
adjustment? What other forms of maltreatment or trauma have affected
the child? Inherent in conducting an assessment of contextual variables
is obtaining accurate historical information from knowledgeable in-
formants, interviewing the child about the details of the abuse, assessing
the veracity of the child's allegations, and ascertaining the demands that
will be placed upon the child from the society, including courtroom
testimony. Each of these issues will be addressed in the following sections.

Wolfe and Wolfe (1988) developed a conceptual model for sexual
abuse trauma and recovery, in which various factors affecting adjustment are considered along a time continuum from sexual victimization
and predisclosure to a crisis phase at disclosure, followed by a recovery
and adjustment period. From this model it is proposed that the child's
development of either adaptive or maladaptive behavior patterns reflects the interplay of past and current stress and support factors. These
stress and support factors fall into four categories: aspects of the sexual
abuse, characteristics of the child, familial characteristics, and community stressors and resources. For example, during the abuse period and
prior to disclosure, the nature of the abuse, child and family circumstances, and community attitudes and resources interplay to determine
whether and when a child reports the abuse and how the child will be
affected psychologically and emotionally. At the time of disclosure,
stress and support factors include the circumstances leading to the
disclosure, familial reactions to the disclosure (e.g., belief vs. disbelief),
community demands (e.g., multiple interviews, courtroom testimony),
and community resources (e.g., trained investigators, stress management programs, group therapy). Long-term adjustment may relate to

the child's ability to overcome associated posttraumatic stress symptoms through a supportive family environment, appropriate treatment regimens, and the attainment of a stable, less stressful life-style. Resolution of abuse-related symptoms may be hindered by long, protracted court-related regimens, family upheaval, and continued contact with a perpetrator who has not acknowledged the abuse or its consequences.

"Context" refers to more than the circumstances surrounding the abuse. Familial and community environments prior to the abuse may have contributed to the child's risk for abuse, or may be directly responsible for the problems, aside from the abuse. Some maladaptive behavior observed among sexually abused children may relate more to environmental and familial conditions that precipitated, and perhaps facilitated, the abuse. For example, children from disorganized families may be more prone to delinquent behavior, and may be less protected against sexually opportunistic individuals (Gruber & Jones, 1981). Children who do not have a close, accepting relationship with at least one parental figure may be more susceptible to the attentions of abusive individuals, and may fear punishment or disbelief if they disclose their abuse. Children without strong, supportive primary relationships may be prone to depression, poor self-esteem, and helplessness (Kazlow & Racusin, 1990).

Depending on the circumstances, much of the contextual information may be available from other professionals, such as police or social workers who have already investigated the case. Otherwise, the information maybe obtained from interviews with the nonoffending parent or the child. As part of the study mentioned earlier, two assessment instruments have been developed to gather some of this contextual information, one for social workers and the other for nonoffending mothers: The *History of Victimization Form* (Wolfe, Gentile, & Bourdeau, 1987) and the *Parent Impact Questionnaire* (V. V. Wolfe, 1985). Each of these will be discussed, followed by a discussion about interviewing the child about his or her sexual abuse.

History of Victimization Form

In lieu of interviewing the child directly about the details of the abuse, the examiner may request such information from other professionals involved with the child (e.g., police, social workers). The *History of Victimization Form* was developed to obtain detailed information from social workers regarding the child's maltreatment, and allow for objective assessment of the severity of various forms of child maltreatment. The form has five scales: sexual abuse, physical abuse, neglect, exposure to family violence, and psychological abuse. In addition to providing objective data about the events associated with each form of maltreatment, the social workers are also asked to rate the severity of the abuse from 1 to 5, using their own experiences with similar cases as the standard of comparison.

Each scale contains a Gutman-like checklist of several abusive behaviors, listed in an escalating order of severity. Along with each checklist are several questions designed to tap factors related to the severity of maltreatment: physical sequelae to the abuse, the relationship of the child to the perpetrator, the emotional "closeness" of the perpetrator to the child, and the time frame, duration, and frequency of the abuse. For the Sexual Abuse scale, the type and extent of force or coercion used to gain compliance is also assessed. Also, the informant is asked whether he or she believes the sexual involvement eventually elicited the child's sexual response resulting in eroticism.

A factor analysis of the *History of Victimization Form* Sexual Abuse scale, based upon 48 subjects (Gentile, 1988), revealed two orthogonal factors. The first labeled "course of abuse" included duration, frequency, and relationship between child and perpetrator. The duration and frequency variables appear to relate to the relationship to perpetrator variable because those perpetrators who were closer to the child tended to live within the same home as the child and therefore had more unsupervised access to the child. The second factor, "seriousness of abuse," included type of sexual acts, force or coercion, and number of perpetrators. The course of abuse factor accounted for 31% of the total variance, and the seriousness of abuse factor accounted for 34% of the variance, altogether accounting for 65% of the total variance.

Parent Impact Questionnaire. This form was designed to provide an objective format for gathering contextual information from mothers during the assessment of their child's sexual abuse sequelae. Maternal reactions to the abuse disclosure may relate strongly to the child's ability to recover from the sexual abuse. Therefore, it is important to assess the mother's response to the trauma, her belief of the child's story, and her experiences since the time of disclosure. For those mothers who had experienced either sexual abuse or other forms of maltreatment as a child, their own child's abuse may elicit unresolved issues. These conflicts may hinder a mother's ability to act as an ally and protector after disclosure.

The *Parent Impact Questionnaire* is completed in interview with the mother, and like the *History of Victimization Form,* all response options are objectified either through checklists or Likert-like ratings. The *Parent Impact Questionnaire* has four sections: a brief account of the family-related problems that the mother experienced during childhood and as an adult, the mother's history of sexual abuse as a child, the impact of the disclosure for the mother and the family, and the mother's perception of events regarding the sexual abuse. For the first section, two sets of questions are asked: "As a child, did you experience any of the following family-related problems?" Response options include parental separations or divorce, excessive parental arguing, physical fighting between parents, inadequate housing, parental alcohol or drug abuse, parental mental health problems, inadequate attention to physical needs (e.g., poor nutrition), and excessive physical punishment. If the parent responds affirmatively to any items, further questioning can be pursued, including information about what happened and when, their age at the time of the abuse, and how the experience affected them. The next question is "As an adult, have you experienced any of the following?" Response options include: marital separations or divorce, physical violence from your partner or boyfriend, drug or alcohol dependence, and mental health problems or sufficient magnitude to see a mental health professional.

The second section regards the mother's history of sexual abuse or assault. Adapted from the interview format developed by Finkelhor and his colleagues (Finkelhor, 1979) for assessing the epidemiology of childhood sexual abuse experiences by interviewing adults, the following questions are asked: "Do you recall any sexual experience or set of experiences that occurred before the age of 16, which you did not consent to? That is, a sexual experience which was forced on you, done against your will, or which you did not want to happen?" If the respondent indicates "yes," then she is asked "How many sets of experiences?" A follow-up question is asked: "Do you recall any sexual experience or set of experiences before the age of 16 that involved someone at least 5 years older than you and was/were *not* imposed on you against your will?" If the mother responds "yes" to either question, the following information is obtained: age of respondent at the time of the abuse, age and sex of perpetrator, relationship to the perpetrator, time span over which the abuse occurred, whether the mother disclosed the abuse to anyone or to an official agency, and whether charges were filed and the result of those charges.

The third section regards the impact of the sexual abuse and disclosure on the family and the mother. The first part of the section asks "As a result of what happened to your child, how have things changed for your family?" Thirty-one situations are listed, categorized as family constituency, family relationships, involvement with social agencies, legal proceedings, therapeutic interventions, and social relations. The second part of this section is the *Impact of Event Scale* (Horowitz, Wilner, & Alvarez, 1979). This scale contains 15 items that relate to intrusive thoughts and avoidance regarding a traumatic event, in this case the child's sexual abuse, disclosure, and resulting sequelae. Respondents rate the frequency of symptoms on a 4-point scale from not at all, to rarely, sometimes, and often.

The fourth section contains five main questions designed to assess the mother's perception of events about the sexual abuse, personal responsibility and guilt, treatment by investigative and legal agencies, and type of interventions the parent would like to see available to her child and family. With the exception of the last question, all questions require rated responses, which are provided along an anchored 5-point continuum.

Investigative Interviewing

Often, one of the primary reasons for the referral is to establish the details of a child's story about the sexual abuse. This is generally referred to as an investigative interview. Investigative interviews should be conducted with two primary goals in mind. First, a detailed account of the sexual abuse experience should be obtained, taking care not to influence the child's story by differential reactions to various aspects of the story, or by using leading questions unneccessarily. Second, an investigative interview serves as a child's introduction to the "helping" community and should be conducted in a therapeutic atmosphere that would facilitate further involvement with helping professionals. Despite the legalistic aspect of the interview, the key to a successful interview is to obtain the information in a therapeutic manner.

Investigative interviews are often conducted by a number of professionals, including police, social workers, and psychologists. Investigative interviewing should be considered a specialized skill that is reserved for those specifically trained in child sexual abuse, child development, cognitive processes, and therapeutic interviewing of children.

Gilgun (1984) suggests that investigative interviews be conducted over several sessions, progressing at a rate comfortable to the child. The first session should focus on building rapport, general development, and adjustment to school, peers, and family. A general principle for facilitating rapport is to assess a child as a "whole person" and avoid connotations that the only important aspect to the child is that he or she was sexually abused. Achenbach and McConaughy (1985) developed a semi-structured interview format that is recommended for children ages 6 to 10. For that interview, children are first asked to talk about their favorite activities, sports, hobbies, television programs, and musicians. From there the child is asked about school, peers, and family; then presented with assessment tools such as the Kinetic Family Drawing; asked to make three wishes; asked what he or she would like to be when grown up; and given a self-perception series of questions in which he or she is asked to describe what makes him or her happy, sad, mad, and scared.

When interviewing the child about the sexual abuse details, important information includes the name of the perpetrator, the child's relationship to the perpetrator, duration and frequency of the abuse, details of the sexual behavior including places and circumstances surrounding the abuse, date and time of the last occurrence (to assess feasibility of obtaining specimens), whether anyone else was involved or observed the abuse, whom did the child tell about the abuse, and the sequence of disclosure, who knows about the abuse, methods used to gain the child's compliance, reasons for disclosure, and the child's understanding of the current situation and upcoming events (Wells, 1984).

Considering the investigative interview as the initial step in therapy, children can also be asked about what they felt before, during, and after the abuse and perceptions of their role in the abuse. The child's understanding of the perpetrator's deviance, as well as the child's understanding of human sexual interaction can also be explored (Gilgun, 1984). Gilgun suggests that a child's right to self-determination in the interview be placed at par with the goal to obtain complete and accurate information. Interviews should not last too long; Gilgun suggests that children be reminded frequently that they can terminate the interview or change topics whenever they feel uncomfortable. Paradoxically, she found children were actually more likely to provide information when she provided many opportunities for them to avoid the topics.

To maximize accuracy of the information, the interviewer should take steps to ensure that he or she does not influence the child's story (Underwager, Wakefield, Legrand, Bartz, & Erickson, 1986). White (1986) recommends that the interviewer should remain relatively uninformed about the case until after the interview with the child. Underwager et al. (1986) suggest videotaping the interview not only to avoid multiple interviews by other professionals, but also to be used as a reliability check when reviewing the interview. Open-ended questions help avoid leading the child's response, and tend to produce the most accurate, although incomplete, accounts of events (Dent & Stephenson, 1979). Asking the child to recall the event soon after it occurred can have the advantage of facilitating recall several months later. Nevertheless, even when questioned after several months for the first time, children's recall for important and salient events is usually accurate, although less complete. As the presence of a parent might influence a child's story, interviews should be conducted without their presence. Once the investigative interview is complete, however, some professionals suggest interviewing the child in the presence of both parents, particularly when there is a custody and access dispute (Green, 1986). However, interviewing the child in the presence of the accused perpetrator magnifies the potential for retraction of the story or alteration of the story such that the accused parent is no longer implicated (Wolfe, 1990).

Because children may have difficulty verbally describing the abuse, such tools as drawings, pictures, and anatomically correct dolls can be used to facilitate communication. Anatomically correct dolls can be particularly helpful as interview aids, as they are a nonthreatening medium that facilitates descriptions of body parts and sexual acts. Generally, at least four dolls are involved in the interview: a male and a female adult and a male and female child. As part of the investigative interview, the child is encouraged to play with the dolls, and then undress them. White, Strom, Santilli, and Halpin (1986) used a five-part standard protocol for interviewing children with the anatomically correct dolls: (1) naming the doll and labeling it male or female; (2) naming body parts and function; (3) knowledge of private parts; (4) abuse evaluation, including questioning the child if she or he has ever been touched or hurt in the private areas or threatened to keep a secret; and (5) abuse elaboration. White et al. (1986) evaluated the validity of the doll interview process, by asking the interviewers to complete an anchored rating scale of suspicion of sexual abuse following the interview. Confirmed cases of sexual abuse received significantly higher ratings than those resulting from interviews of children not suspected of having been sexually abused. Older sexually abused children were more likely to report abuse that was consistent with other sources of information.

Use of anatomically correct dolls in a projective fashion as part of an investigative interview is contraindicated. Jampole and Weber (1987) compared sexually abused children ages 3 to 8 with nonsexually abused children in solitary free play with anatomically correct dolls. Although 90% of the sexually abused children demonstrated sexual behavior with the dolls, 20% of the nonabused group also demonstrated sexual behavior. Some of the nonabused children even acted out vaginal and oral intercourse. Therefore, sexual play with anatomically correct dolls should not by itself, be used as evidence of sexual abuse.

Assessing the Veracity of a Child's Allegations

There is a strong consensus in the sexual abuse literature (derived from clinical case studies and arguments based on norms of sexual development) that children almost never make up stories about being sexually abused (Faller, 1984; Kerns, 1981; Melton, 1985; D. A. Mrazek, 1981; Sgroi, 1982), and that sexual allegations of preadolescent children, in particular, should be taken at face value (Kempe & Kempe, 1984). Although it is often assumed that children never lie about sexual abuse, children's testimony in court is often suspect and children are generally thought to make poor witnesses. Thus, although most people assume that children do not lie about the abuse, prosecution of offenders is often not pursued unless corroborating evidence is available. Recent statistics provide a clearer picture about the potential for children to accuse someone falsely of sexual abuse. Jones and McGraw (1987) found that only 8% of sexual abuse allegations could truly be considered fictitious, and three-fourths of those reports were generated by adults, often in custody disputes. Nevertheless, 47% of reported cases of sexual abuse went unfounded; that is, reports to protection agencies did not yield enough information to confirm or disconfirm abuse. Of unfounded abuse cases, 24% of the cases did not produce enough information to determine that abuse had occurred, and 17% of the cases followed a legitimate suspicion that was not substantiated during the investigation.

When considering the credibility of a child's report, several issues can be examined (see also DeYoung, this volume). Faller (1984; 1988) suggests that a child's credibility is enhanced if he or she can provide details about the abuse and if the emotional responses are consistent with the topics discussed. Sgroi (1982) suggested that credibility is enhanced when the child's story corresponds to what is generally known about the process of sexual abuse (i.e., multiple incidents over time, progression in the severity of sexual activities, secrecy, pressure and coercion, and the ability to provide specific information about the sexual behaviors that occurred). Other sources of evidence that may corroborate a child's story (Faller, 1984) include the child's report to other significant adults, sexualized doll play or drawings, age-inappropriate knowledge of sexual behaviors, stress or trauma-related symptoms, such as wetting the bed, fearing darkness, refusing to be left alone, nightmares, increased dependency, and uncomfortableness with men and boys. Sometimes physical evidence obtained through medical examination can be helpful in corroborating a child's allegation. However, fewer than one-third of sexually abused girls and one-half of sexually abused boys show positive evidence of physical trauma related to the abuse (DeJong, this volume; Kerns, 1981; Sgroi, 1982).

Although fictitious reports of sexual abuse are often related to custody and access disputes, careful evaluation in such cases is necessary because sexual abuse of young children occurs more frequently in the context of marital dissolution, with fathers the primary perpetrators

(Mian, Wehrspann, Klajner-Diamond, LeBaron, & Winder, 1986). Therefore, no allegation of sexual abuse in a custody and access dispute can be disregarded, and assessments should be expanded beyond the abuse allegation to ensure that marital conflict is not exacerbating the child's trauma. Complications arise in the investigation of sexual abuse with noncustodial fathers because access must be denied long enough to allow for a proper investigation. Care must be taken to balance the accused parents' right to visit the child with the need to formulate a clear impression about the abuse. If visitations are restored prematurely, and the child's story subsequently changes, it is unclear whether the child has been pressured to recant or whether the original story was a fabrication.

Bresee, Stearns, Bess, and Packer (1986) suggest two interviewers become involved in cases of sexual abuse in which custody and access issues are involved. Interviewers of accused fathers can look for personality characteristics consistent with that of sexual offenders: poor impulse control, self-centeredness, strong dependency needs, poor judgment, and difficulty monitoring and directing emotions. They suggested that vindictive mothers may display several characteristics that might suggest the child had been coached. The mother may not be able to describe what made her suspicious of the sexual abuse, may resist allowing the child to be interviewed alone, resist alternate explanations for the abuse, seem overly eager to have the child testify in court, and pursue the matter, despite the potential for a negative impact on the child. In contrast, mothers who have not coached their child were described as tending to express remorse at not protecting the child, expressing concern about the impact of courtroom testimony on the child, allowing the child to be interviewed alone, and were willing to consider alternate explanations.

ASSESSING THE IMPACT ON THE CHILD

When assessing the impact of sexual abuse on children, a two-pronged approach is recommended, both for developing an assessment protocol and for interpreting information. These two facets include assessing global adjustment and assessing adjustment specific to the sexual abuse. This allows for assessing general adjustment that may relate to ongoing problems of the child, as well as symptoms that can more clearly be related to the sexual abuse. An assessment strategy for each will be outlined.

ASSESSING GLOBAL ADJUSTMENT

Parent and Teacher Report

One of the easiest methods to assess global adjustment is to ask the child's parent or guardian to complete a checklist of behavior problems. The most commonly used measure with sexually abused children is the *Child Behavior Checklist* (CBCL; Achenbach & Edelbrock, 1983), although research studies have also used the Louisville Child Behavior Checklist (Miller, 1977) and the Revised Behavior Problem Checklist (Quay, 1983). The CBCL consists of 118 items reflecting a variety of child behavior problems. Each item has three response options: *not true, somewhat true,* and *very true.* The checklist yields a Social Competence profile and a Behavior Problem profile. The Social Competence profile provides scales on socialization, organized activities and interests, and academics. The Behavior Problem profile is divided into Internalizing and Externalizing Scales. Each scale is subdivided into a number of subscales that vary in content, depending on the child's age and sex. As a result, the CBCL yields T scores for each of the scales, which reflect norms for six groups: male and female for each of three age levels—4–5, 6–11, and 12–16. Computer scoring programs are available. There are two versions of the CBCL: the *Parent Report Form* and the *Teacher Report Form.* Some evidence suggests that when parents are distressed or depressed themselves, they tend to overreport child behavior problems (Griest, Forehand, Wells, & McMahon, 1980; Griest, Wells, & Forehand, 1979). Therefore, since many parents are usually extremely distressed following the disclosure of child sexual abuse, caution should be used in interpreting the CBCL–PRF. The *Teacher Report Form* may provide an alternative picture of the child. Nevertheless, discrepancies between teacher and parent report should not automatically be interpreted as exaggeration on the part of the parent. Situational factors at home or school may serve to exacerbate or attenuate problems, and children may indeed behave or express emotion differently in the two situations.

Empirical Findings with Sexually Abused Children. Several studies investigating the impact of sexual abuse on children have used parent-completed behavior problem checklists. These studies yield several tentative conclusions, which call for more careful examination through longitudinal and comparative research designs. One of the major outcomes of these studies is the large percentage of sexually abused children who have problems of clinical significance. It appears that a quarter to a third of sexually abused children experience clinically significant levels of behavioral and emotional problems or significant deficits in areas of social competence. These problems are evident relatively soon after the abuse disclosure (Wolfe, Gentile, & Wolfe, 1989), and tend to persist over time and may actually increase if the child does not receive treatment (Friedrich & Reams, 1986; Tong, Oates, & McDowell, 1987). Not surprisingly, the subset of sexually abused children who are referred to mental health facilities tends to score higher on parent-report behavior problem checklists than the population of sexually abused children as a whole (Friedrich, Urquiza, & Beilke, 1986; Hart, Mader, Griffith, & de Mendonca, 1989).

These results presage a surge of mental health referrals seeking help for sexually abused children. Considering the incidence of childhood sexual abuse, and the percentage of those children who have significant psychological sequelae, major alterations to the delivery of mental health services for child victims seem necessary.

Self-report Questionnaires

Self-report measures can be used to assess a number of constructs related to global adjustment. The *Youth Self Report* (YSR; Achenbach & Edelbrock, 1981) provides a global assessment that can easily be compared with the CBCL–PRF and the CBCL–TRF. Like the other forms, the YSR yields Social Competence and Behavior Problem profiles. The Behavior Problem profile of the YSR yields Internalizing and Externalizing scale scores, with subscales roughly corresponding to those of the CBCL–PRF and CBCL–TRF.

Other child report measures are designed to assess one specific aspect of adjustment. Several scales assess negative affect, such as depression and anxiety. Commonly used instruments include the *Children's Depression Inventory* (CDI; Kovacs, 1983), the *Revised Children's Manifest Anxiety Scale* (*RCMAS;* Reynolds & Paget, 1981), and the *State–Trait Anxiety Inventory for Children* (STAIC; Spielberger, 1973). A recent psychometric analysis of these scales suggests that all three scales assess a similar construct, *negative affectivity*, which relates to the Internalizing scale of the *CBCL–TRF* (Wolfe et al., 1987). Therefore, caution should be made in interpreting any one of the instruments as indicative of depression of anxiety, per se.

Other important constructs for assessment include the child's sense of self-esteem and competence. Two commonly used instruments for these purposes are the *Piers-Harris Self-concept Scale* (Piers-Harris; Piers, 1984) and a series of perceived competence measures developed by Harter (1985). Each of the child self-report measures are described here.

Children's Depression Inventory (CDI). The CDI consists of 27 items designed to assess components of depression, including sleep disturbance, appetite loss, and dysphoria. Each item includes three sentences describing normal affect, moderate symptoms, and severe, clinically significant symptoms. The child chooses the sentence that best describes him or her over the past 2 weeks.

Revised Children's Manifest Anxiety Scale (RCMAS). The RCMAS includes 37 statements written in first-person form; 27 depict anxiety symptoms (e.g. "I have trouble making up my mind") and 10 assess social desirability (e.g., "I never get angry). Response options are "yes" and "no." With the exception of the social desirability items, all "yes" responses are scored in the anxiety direction. The five subscales are labeled physiological anxiety, worry and oversensitivity, concentration, total anxiety, and lie. Norms are available for males and females, Blacks and whites, age 6 to 16.

State–trait Anxiety Inventory for Children (STAIC). The STAIC includes two scales: The State Anxiety Scale and the Trait Anxiety scale. The State Anxiety Scale instructs the respondent to consider his or her feelings at that moment, while the Trait Anxiety Scale asks the child to consider how he or she usually feels. For the State Anxiety Scale, half of the items reflect nonanxiety states (e.g. calm) and half reflect anxiety states (e.g., upset). Each item begins with the words "I feel" and is followed by response options along a 3-point continuum from "very" to "not" with the same descriptor. For example, item *1* reads "*I feel very calm, calm, not calm.*" The Trait Anxiety Scale items are all posed in the first person ("I am shy") with response options *hardly ever, sometimes, often.*

Piers-Harris Self-concept Scale. Subtitled "The Way I feel about Myself," the *Piers-Harris* is an 80-item, self-report questionnaire designed to assess how children and adolescents feel about themselves. Children respond to statements about feelings with "yes" or "no" as true or not true of themselves. Six cluster scales are scored: behavior, intellectual and school status, physical appearance and attributes, anxiety, popularity, and happiness and satisfaction. Higher scores reflect more positive self-esteem. Reliability analyses with the Piers-Harris indicate adequate temporal stability and internal consistency. Validity investigations of the Piers-Harris have supported the scale in terms of content validity, concurrent validity, convergent and discriminant validity, and construct validity. Factor analyses have upheld the cluster scores and have demonstrated greater within-scale correlations than across scales, although all scales tend to correlate moderately.

Harter Scales. The Harter Scales include several versions of a scale originally developed to assess perceived social competence during childhood. The most widely researched and used version is the *Self-perception Profile for Children* (SPPC; Harter, 1985), originally named the *Perceived Social Competence Scale for Children* (Harter, 1982), which is appropriate for grade 3 to grade 8. This version includes six subscales: scholastic competence, social acceptance, athletic competence, physical appearance, behavioral conduct, and global self-worth. Global self-worth is independent of the other subscales and does not represent a summation of the other scales. Rather, it is intended to measure a "gestalt-like" evaluation about the self.

Two other versions of the scale are available, as well as a teacher rating scale. The teen-ager version, the *Self-perception Profile for Adolescents* (Harter, 1986), includes three additional domains: Romantic appeal, close friendships, and job competence. The *Pictorial Scale of Perceived Competence and Social Acceptance for Young Children* (Harter & Pike, 1984) has two versions, one for preschoolers and kindergartners, and one for grades 1 and 2. Subscales include social competence, physical competence, peer acceptance, and maternal acceptance. Harter (1985) indicates that a revision will add Father Acceptance and Behavioral Conduct. The teacher-rating version (*Teacher's Rating Scale of Child's Actual Behavior,* 1985) was designed to assess actual behavior displayed in the classroom, and reflects the same domains as the self-report counterparts, without the global self-worth rating.

The *Self-perception Profile* questions are presented with two alternative descriptors, from which the child is asked to select the one most like him or her. Then, the child indicates if that descriptor is *Really True* or *Sort of True* of him or her. The question format is designed to reduce the tendency to respond in a socially desirable manner by legitimizing either choice (Harter, 1985). As an example, one item reads "Some kids often forget what they learn—but—other kids can remember things easily."

Psychometric analyses of the *SPPC* reveal adequate internal consistency for all six subscales. Factor-analytical studies support all domains, as well as the independent self-worth scale. Various intercorrelations among the scales appear to relate to differing interests and activities of different age groups.

Empirical Findings with Sexually Abused Children. Recent evidence suggests that children are not likely to report elevated levels of global symptoms such as anxiety, depression, or poor self-concept immediately following disclosure of sexual abuse. Both Cohen and Mannarino (1988) and V. Wolfe et al. (1989) reported using the CDI and the STAIC. Cohen and Mannarino (1988) also administered the Piers-Harris, and

Wolfe et al. (1989) used the RCMAS. Compared with the respective normative samples of each measure, no measure showed consistent elevations for sexually abused children. Interestingly, Tong et al. (1987), who administered the Piers-Harris an average of 2.6 years after the abuse, did find significant elevations for the sexually abused girls, compared with a control group on overall scores, as well as all cluster scores. However, they did not find differences between the groups on the Youth Self Report questionnaire. Although these data are not conclusive, perhaps global adjustment problems develop over time following the abuse and abuse disclosure, and are not recognized or felt by children during the initial stages following disclosure.

Professional Evaluation

Given that parent report and child report may vary, it is often necessary to utilize professional expertise in evaluating the child in order to obtain a clear conceptualization of the child's range of problems. To objectify the diagnostic interview, several structured interview formats have been developed with accompanying interviewer completed rating scales. One example is the *Diagnostic Interview Schedule for Children* (DISC). The DISC is a structured interview with response options coded as 0–1–2 corresponding to "no," "sometimes," and "yes." The items correspond to the DSM–III diagnostic constructs. Sansonnet-Hayden, Haley, Marriage, and Fine (1987) conducted DISC assessment with 17 adolescent sexually abused psychiatric inpatients, and 37 nonabused inpatients. The sexually abused inpatients showed evidence of several significant differences from the rest of inpatient population: more conduct problems, more hallucinations, more suicide attempts, and more likely to be recommended for long-term treatment. Other diagnostic interview schedules include the *Children's Affective Rating Scale* (McKnew, Cytryn, Efron, Gershon, & Bunney, 1979) and the *Diagnostic Interview for Children and Adolescents* (Herjanic, Herjanic, Brown, & Wheatt, 1975).

ABUSE-RELATED SYMPTOMS

Measures of global adjustment with sexually abused children allow for documentation of the magnitude of the problems experienced by these children, compared with nonabused children and other clinic populations. Unfortunately, these measures have not been able to define a pattern of symptoms unique to sexually abused children, and therefore fail to provide a framework for conceptualizing the sequelae to child-hood sexual abuse. As an alternative, several assessment strategies have been developed that specifically address the problem of sexual abuse. These instruments correspond to one or more of three conceptual models useful in understanding sexual abuse sequelae: Post-traumatic Stress Disorder (Wolfe et al., 1989), traumagenic factors (Finkelhor & Browne, 1985), and eroticization (Yates, 1982). Each of these models will be discussed, followed by sections describing corresponding assessment strategies.

Conceptual Framework—PTSD:

Wolfe et al. (1989) supported the PTSD formulation of the impact of sexual abuse based upon three premises. First, childhood sexual abuse meets the criteria for "trauma" as defined by the Diagnostic and Statistical Manual–III–Revised (DSM–III–R, American Psychiatric Association, 1987). That definition of trauma is "an event that is outside the range of usual human experience and that would be markedly distressing to almost anyone" (p. 230). Second, clinical descriptions of sexually abused children indicate that a substantial number of victims show at least some PTSD symptoms, if not clear symptoms in all domains defined by the DSM–III–R for PTSD. These diagnostic characteristics include intrusive thoughts, avoidance of trauma-related stimuli and numbing of responsivity, and hyperarousal as shown by sleep disturbance, irritability, and concentration difficulties. Associated features include fears, anxiety, depression, and guilt. Third, current literature from studies of adults who were sexually abused as children (Gold, 1986; Seidner & Calhoun, 1984, July; Silver, Boon, & Stones, 1983) suggests that individual differences in response to childhood sexual abuse relate to three mediating variables: severity of the abuse, availability of social support, and attributional styles regarding the cause of negative life events. These three sets of variables have also been shown to mediate the impact of other stressful life events, such as rape (Baker & Peterson, 1977; Steketee & Foa, 1987) and combat (Cluss, Boughton, Frank, Stewart, & West, 1983; Foy, Sipprelle, Rueger, & Carroll, 1984).

PTSD has been studied most extensively with adults, but the DSM–III–R acknowledges that children are not immune to the disorder. However, children may display parallel yet different symptoms and behaviors (American Psychiatric Association, 1987). Although psychogenic amnesia and numbing are common PTSD symptoms with adults, such symptoms are difficult to assess with children who may recall the events but refuse to talk about what happened. Children generally do not have flashbacks in the forms that adults report. However, children tend to relive the events through play, dreams, and intrusive recall. Dreams about the trauma may change overtime from trauma themes to more generalized fears and monsters. Children may display their guilt by believing that they did not heed imagined omens of the upcoming trauma. Some children develop an overwhelming sense of vulnerability and are unable to view themselves in the future or make future plans (Terr, 1981, 1983a, 1983b, 1985a, 1985b). Like adults who experience deteriorations in job performance, children's school performance may deteriorate, especially for those of lower premorbid intellectual functioning (Garmezy, Masten, & Tellegen, 1984).

The DSM–III–R (American Psychiatric Association, 1987) cautions that children tend to underestimate such symptoms as somatic complaints, diminished interest in significant activities, and constriction of affect, although these symptoms may be noted by parents or guardians. This is consistent with the findings of recent assessment studies using both parent-report and child-report measures. As noted earlier, these studies generally find significant elevations on parent-report measures, yet child-report measures are within the average range (Cohen & Mannarino, 1988; Friedrich et al., 1986; Tong et al., 1987; Wolfe et al., 1989).

One of the major criticisms of the PTSD model is that sexual abuse does not truly count as trauma. Although sexual abuse fits the DSM–III–R definition of trauma, others have defined trauma as a "sudden, discrete, overwhelming event" (Kiser et al., 1988; Terr, 1985a). Pynoos and Eth (1985) described PTSD as resulting from "an overwhelming event resulting in helplessness in the face of intolerable danger, anxiety, and instinctual arousal" (p. 38).

Finkelhor (1986) contrasted such a view of trauma to what he perceived children experience in sexual abuse. He posited that much sexual abuse does not generally occur under conditions of danger, threat, or violence. Instead, many children respond with trust to a perpetrator's misuse of authority or manipulation of moral standards. He suggests that the trauma is significantly different from trauma usually associated with PTSD in that sexual abuse trauma is more related to the social meaning of the act or the abnormal relationship surrounding the abuse, compared with danger per se.

Terr (1987), in response to this discrepancy in the concept of trauma, suggested a dual classification for patients suffering from trauma-related disorders. Type I disorders follow from exposure to a single traumatic event, while Type II disorders result from multiple or long-standing experiences with extreme stress such as sexual abuse. While both Type I and Type II PTSD patients experience similar symptoms,

Type II patients were thought to develop abnormal coping strategies for dealing with the ongoing stressors, such as denial or psychogenic numbing, rage, and unremitting sadness.

Conceptual Framework: Traumagenic Factors

In addition to criticizing the PTSD formulation on the ground that sexual abuse represents a different form of trauma, Finkelhor (1986) criticized the model for failing to account for all symptoms associated with PTSD and as not applying to all victims. As an alternative he presented the Four Traumagenic Dynamics Model. The model posits that four dynamics—traumatic sexualization, betrayal, stigmatization, and powerlessness—cause trauma by distorting a child's self-concept, world-view, and affective capacities. These traumagenic factors relate to the child's development of abnormal coping styles and behavioral difficulties.

According to Finkelhor (1986), traumatic sexualization may result in sexual preoccupation, sex play, excessive masturbation, and exploitation of peers or younger children. Betrayal may come from many sources—the offender, those who do not believe the child's story, those who did not act to protect the child, and those whose actions on behalf of the child were viewed as intrusive and disruptive. Disenchantment, disillusionment, and loss of a trusted figure may relate to feelings of depression and vulnerability to subsequent victimization. Also, betrayal may lead to hostility and anger and distrust of men.

Stigmatization may relate to negative messages communicated to the child about himself or herself—evilness, worthlessness, shamefulness, or guilt. Abusers may blame or denigrate the victim by saying such things as the child seduced him or her. Such labels as "spoiled goods" or "queer" may be associated with the abuse and contribute to the child's feelings of self-blame. Stigmatization may result in lowered self-esteem and identification with other stigmatized levels of society, such as drug abusers or prostitutes. Stigmatization may also relate to self-destructive behavior and suicide attempts.

Finkelhor (1986) notes that sexually abused children experience powerlessness in that the child's will, wishes, and sense of efficacy were repeatedly overruled and frustrated during the abuse. As part of the abuse, the child may have been threatened with injury or death. Powerlessness was proposed to relate to three effects: fear and anxiety, impairment of coping skills resulting in decreased social and academic effectiveness, and compensatory reactions stemming from extreme needs to control or dominate. This compensatory reaction may relate to male victims' propensity toward becoming sexual perpetrators themselves.

Conceptual Framework: Eroticism

A third area where child sexual abuse appears to have an impact is the child's sexual adjustment. Heightened sexual activity, such as compulsive masturbation, precocious sexual play, knowledge of sexual matters inappropriate to age and developmental level, and overt sexual acting out toward adults, has been associated with sexual abuse and may be detected even in very young children (Adams-Tucker, 1982; James & Nasjleti, 1983; Justice & Justice, 1979; Meiselman, 1978, Mrazek & Mrazek, 1981). James and Nasjleti (1983) found that sexually abused children not only expressed more overt sexuality, but also tended to express coexisting themes of sexuality and violence in their artwork, written schoolwork, language, and play. Yates (1982) suggests that sexually abused children become atypically eroticized as a result of their sexual victimization, and that most of these children cannot distinguish erotic from nonerotic relationships. Ordinary activities such as climbing on playground equipment and sitting on an adult's lap may be sexually arousing to a sexually abused child.

Assessment of Abuse-related Symptoms

Like global adjustment, abuse-related symptoms can be assessed by parent-report, child-report, and professional evaluation. Like global adjustment, multimethod, multitrait, multi-informant assessment is essential in order to have a clear sense of trauma-related adjustment.

CBCL PTSD Subscale. At this point, there is no established method of assessing abuse-related symptoms via parent-report. However, by examining items from the CBCL-PRF, a number of abuse-related symptoms may be revealed. In fact, the CBCL usually reveals elevations across the board for the CBCL scales, yet no clear pattern emerges in terms of specific subscale elevations. It serves to reason that CBCL scales, as they currently exist, do not conceptually relate to the sequelae of sexual abuse nor were they developed with that intent or purpose. However, a cluster of items spread across different scales may relate more meaningfully to the abuse sequelae, and therefore yield a posttraumatic stress disorder subscale.

In an attempt to examine parent-reported PTSD symptoms, Wolfe et al. (1989) developed such a scale from the CBCL-PRF items. Using the

DSM–III–R as a guide, the following 20 CBCL items were selected to comprise a PTSD scale: difficulty concentrating; obsessive thoughts; feels too guilty; moody; difficulty sleeping; nightmares; irrational fears; clinging to adults; nervous; anxious; sad or depressed; withdrawn; secretive; feels persecuted; irritable; argues a lot; and somatic complaints, including headaches, nausea, stomachaches, and vomiting. Based upon a sample of 68 sexually abused children, the PTSD scale had an alpha value of .89.

With a sample of 63 sexually abused girls, composite scores of the CBCL PTSD scale were calculated by averaging responses across the 20 items. As a comparison sample, item means from the CBCL normative sample (N = 2500) were obtained for girls ages 8 to 11 and 12 to 16. Composite means and the standard deviations from the sexually abused sample reflected substantial elevations, compared with the CBCL normative sample. For young girls, 8 to 11, the average item score for the PTSD scale was .734 (s.d. = .468) for the sexually abused children and .156 for the normative sample. For older girls, the average item score for the sexually abused children was .765 (s.d. = .320) and .157 for the normative sample. At this point, further psychometric evaluations for the PTSD scale are being conducted, with CBCLs from several sites across Canada and the United States.

PTSD: Child Report

Sexual Abuse Fear Evaluation Subscale (SAFE). In order to assess fears and phobias associated with the sexual abuse, Wolfe and Wolfe (1986) developed the *SAFE*, which is a 27-item scale embedded into the 80-item *Fear Survey Schedule for Children-Revised* (Ollendick, 1983). Items were originally developed to assess three types of abuse-related fears: sexual fears, fears related to the disclosure and investigation, and fears of revictimization. Like the FSSC-R, children respond to each fear with a 3-point rating of "none," "some," or "a lot." A recent psychometric evaluation of the SAFE (Wolfe, Gentile, & Klink, 1988), with a sample of 171 schoolchildren and 62 sexually abused children, revealed two orthogonal factors that were subsequently labeled Sex-associated Fears (11 items) and Interpersonal Discomfort (13 items). Alpha values for the two scales were .80 and .81, respectively. The Sex-associated Fear Scale included: being alone on a playground, watching people kiss on TV, talking or thinking about sex, someone kissing or hugging me, naked people, taking my clothes off, being tickled, having older boys or men look after me alone, taking a bath, sleeping alone, and mom not at home. The Interpersonal Discomfort scale included: mean looking people, doing something nasty, people not believing me, telling on someone for bothering me, saying "no" to an adult, mom finding out about something I did, someone in my family getting into bad trouble, being lied to by someone I trust, being told to do something I shouldn't do, going to court to talk to a judge, being blamed unfairly, being taken away from my parents, and someone getting drunk.

For the SAFE, composite scores from the Sex-associated Fear scale and the Interpersonal Discomfort scale were compared with the scores from the normative sample. Comparisons were limited to girls since the number of boys in the sexually abused sample was relatively small. Out of 13 items of the Interpersonal Discomfort scale, the mean composite score for both groups was 27 (school sample s.d. = 6; sexual abuse sample s.d. = 4.5), indicating that most children have at least "some" fear of each of those items. Out of 11 items on the Sex-related Fears Scale, the mean composite score for the normative sample was 16 (s.d. = 3.9) and for the sexually abused children 18 (s.d. = 4.3). T-tests comparing the two subscales for the school sample and the sexually abused sample revealed a significant group difference for the Sex-associated Fear scale ($p < .041$) but not for the Interpersonal Discomfort scale. These findings suggest that most children experience substantial discomfort with those aspects of abuse that related to the interpersonal facets of abuse (i.e., being lied to by someone trusted, saying "no" to an adult). Even though sexually abused children reported significantly more sex-related fears than the normative group, the difference between the means of the two groups was not substantial. The extent to which nonabused children endorsed SAFE items underscores the degree of discomfort children expect to experience during and after the sexual experiences. Given that most children would find many of the SAFE items distressing, the fact that the sexually abused children experienced those events accentuates the importance of assessing these items, as they may be quite relevant to treatment.

Children's Impact of Traumatic Events Scale-Revised (CITES-R). (Wolfe & Gentile, 1991). The CITES-R provides a structured format for interviewing children about their perceptions and attributions concerning their sexual abuse. The original instrument included 54 statements such as "I try not to think about what happened" to which the child can respond "very true," "somewhat true," and "not true." The CITES was originally designed to yield nine subscales, six related to impact (betrayal, guilt, helplessness, intrusive thoughts, sexualization, and stigmatization) and three related to attributions about the abuse (internal–external, global–specific, and stable–unstable). Development of the CITES was based on the three models previously described: the

Finkelhor and Browne (1985) model in which the impact of sexual abuse is thought to relate to four traumagenic factors (betrayal, guilt, sexualization, and stigmatization), the PTSD model (intrusive thoughts and numbing of responses), and the Eroticization model. The Intrusive Thoughts scale was based on the *Impact of Events Scale* developed by Horowitz et al. (1979) to assess intrusive thoughts with adults. Attributional scales were based on the Abramson, Seligman, and Teasdale (1981) model.

A recent factor analysis of the CITES with 144 children (Wolfe, Gentile, Sas, Michienzi, & Wolfe, in press), revealed a factor structure similar to that of the original scales. Based upon that factor analysis, the scale items and names were altered to: Intrusive Thoughts, Avoidance, Negative Reactions by Others, Social Support, Self Blame and Guilt, Dangerous World, Empowerment, Personal Vulnerability, Sexual Anxiety, and Eroticism.

Three of the scales of CITES appear to be particularly strong: Intrusive thoughts, Negative Reactions by Others, and Self Blame and Guilt. All have relatively high alpha values and include between 6 and 13 items. The remaining scales have between 2 and 6 items and alpha values range from .57 to .84. Based upon these analyses, several new items have been added to the CITES in order to improve the psychometric properties of those scales. As well, an additional scale was added; Hyperarousal, in order to reflect the DSM-III-R criteria for PTSD symptoms. Table 5.1 lists the original items, the new items, and the current alpha values for each scale. Table 5.2 provides the CITES scale means and standard deviations.

The means and standard deviations from the CITES scale scores reflect the diversity of symptoms sexually abused children reported following the disclosure of their abuse. With a possible range of 1 (not true) to 3 (very true), the mean endorsement of items per scale ranged from 1.37 (eroticism) to 2.49 (Dangerous World). On the average, the sexually abused children reported some symptoms per scale, but only some of them reported the majority of items as "somewhat true" or "very true." Two exceptions were the Dangerous World and the Intrusive Thoughts scales. As reflected by a mean of 2.49 (s.d. = .83) on the Dangerous World scale, the sexually abused children tended to report a belief that sexual abuse is pervasive and that adults tend to exploit children. As reflected by a mean of 1.94 (s.d. = .67) on the Intrusive Thoughts scale, the majority of the sexually abused children reported intrusive, ruminative thoughts about the abuse, triggered by frequent reminders of what happened to them. These intrusive thoughts included involuntary thoughts about what happened, pictures of what

TABLE 5.1
Children's Impact of Traumatic Events Scale (CITES): Scale Items and Alpha Values

I. *Intrusive thoughts* (Alpha = .91)
- Pictures of what happened often pop into my head.
- I have trouble falling asleep because pictures or thoughts of what happened keep popping into my head.
- I think about what happened to me even when I don't want to.
- I have dreams or nightmares about what happened.
- Many things remind me of what happened.
- I sometimes want to cry when I think of what happened.

II. *Avoidance* (Alpha = .72)[b]
- I try to stay away from reminders of what happened.
- I try not to think about what happened.
- [a] When I'm reminded of what happened, I try to think of something else.
- [a] I have tried to forget about what happened.
- [a] I sometimes pretend this never happened or that it was a dream.
- [a] I sometimes have trouble remembering what happened during the sexual abuse.
- [a] I am not as interested in some things I used to like before the sexual abuse happened.
- [a] It is more difficult for me to love people than it was before the sexual abuse.

III. *Negative reactions by others* (Alpha = .94)
- As a result of what happened, people who use to care about me no longer do.
- Some people think I was to blame for what happened.
- Some people blame me for what happened.
- People who I trusted let me down.
- People who know what happened think bad thoughts about me.
- After people learned about what happened, they no longer wanted to spend time with me.
- Some people think I am lying about what happened.
- Some kids at school make fun of me because of what happened.
- Some people believed I did a very bad thing.

IV. *Self-blame and guilt* (Alpha = .83)
- I was to blame for what happened.
- This happened to me because I acted in a way that caused it to happen.
- I feel I should be punished for what I did.
- This happened to me because I was not smart enough to stop it from happening.
- I was not to blame for what happened (reverse order scored).
- *(Perpetrator)* was to blame for what happened (reverse order scored).
- I feel guilty about what happened.
- This happened to me because I was too young to do anything about it.
- I feel I have caused trouble to my family.
- This happened to me because I was bad and needed to be punished.
- I am embarrassed when I see people who know what happened.
- I feel I have caused problems for many people.
- This happened to me because I always have bad luck.

V. *Dangerous World* (Alpha = .67)
- People often take advantage of children.
- These kinds of things happen to a lot of children.
- There are many people do bad things to children.
- [a] I worry that other children will also be sexually abused.
- [a] Children should not trust adults because they might sexually abuse them.

TABLE 5.1
(Continued)

VI. *Empowerment* (Alpha = .68)
- If something like this happens again, I CAN stop it.
- Things like this WILL NOT happen again.
- Things in my life will get better.
- If adults bother me, I can stop them.
- If something like this happens again, I think I KNOW what to do to stop it.
[a] I know enough about sexual abuse now that I can protect myself in the future.
[a] My family will protect me from being sexually abused again.

VII. *Personal Vulnerability* (Alpha = .64)
- I dislike or feel uncomfortable spending time alone with older boys or men.
- Something like this might happen to me again.
- Things in my life will get better (reverse order scored).
- These kinds of things happen often.
- No matter what I do, I can't stop such things from happening.
- I don't trust people the way I used to.
[a] I often worry that I will be sexually abused again.
[a] I feel I have to know people for a long time before I can trust them.

VIII. *Social Support* (Alpha = .57)
- Most people who know about what happened are nice and understanding.
- Most people believe me when I talk about what happened.
[a] I have someone with whom I feel comfortable talking about the sexual abuse.
[a] I feel good about how my family treated me after I told about the sexual abuse.
[a] Since people found out about the sexual abuse, they have tried to protect me from it happening again.
[a] Social workers, police, and/or doctors have helped me since I told about the sexual abuse. (If child only had contact with one or two of above, limit question to whomever child has had contact).

IX. *Sexual Anxiety* (Alpha = .84)
- Thinking about sex upsets me.
- I get frightened when I think about sex.
[a] Sex is dirty
[a] I hope I never have to think about sex again.
[a] I wish there was no such thing as sex.

X. *Eroticism* (Alpha = .57)[c]
- I have more sexual feeling than my friends.
- I think about sex even when I don't want to.
[a] I have sexual feelings when I see people kiss on TV.
[a] I like to look at naked people in books or in movies.

XI. *Hyperarousal*[d]
[a] I often feel irritable for no reason at all.
[a] I have difficulty concentrating because I often think about what happened.
[a] I am easily startled or surprised.
[a] I often feel restless or jumpy.
[a] I am easily annoyed by others.
[a] When I am reminded of what happened, I sometimes feel very scared.

[a]New items not included in psychometric analyses presented in this chapter.
[b]Alpha conducted for 9-month folow-up; children rarely endorsed items prior to that time.
[c]Administer these items after ascertaining if child knows meaning of sexual feelings or sex.
[d]New scale added after factor analysis; no alpha value available.

TABLE 5.2
Means and Standard Deviations for CITES Scales

Scales	Number of items in scale	Scale mean	Standard deviation	Average item mean
1. Intrusive thoughts	6	11.62	4.06	1.94 (.67)
2. Avoidance[a]	2	4.87	1.32	2.43 (.66)
3. Negative reactions	9	12.89	4.41	1.43 (.49)
4. Self-blame/guilt	13	18.20	4.55	1.40 (.35)
5. Dangerous world	3	7.47	1.42	2.49 (.47)
6. Empowerment	4	6.20	2.08	1.55 (.52)
7. Personal vulnerability	5	8.70	2.20	2.09 (.44)
8. Social support	2	2.66	1.27	1.33 (.63)
9. Sexual anxiety	2	3.50	1.55	1.75 (.78)
10. Eroticism	2	2.70	1.08	1.37 (.54)

[a]Conducted at the 9-month, follow-up assessment, rather than earlier after disclosure.

happened popping into their heads, difficulty falling asleep or staying asleep because of abuse-related thoughts, and dreams and nightmares during which the abuse was relived. Interestingly, the Avoidance Scale showed poor reliability at the first and second assessment periods (1 and 3 months), but good reliability at 9 months (alpha = .74). Theoretically, the pattern makes sense, in that children generally develop strategies to inhibit the intrusive thoughts over time, and avoidance of abuse-related issues may be a commonly employed strategy. Therefore, this scale may only be appropriate for children who were abused at least 9 months prior to the assessment, and may reflect an adaptive, rather than pathological response.

PTSD Professional Evaluation

McLeer et al. (1988) developed a method for diagnosing sexually abused patients as having PTSD. Following structured interviews, a PTSD symptom checklist was completed. Items fell into one of three subcategories of symptoms: (1) *re-experiencing behaviors*, including repetitive conversations about the abuse, repetitive play, flashbacks, nightmares, inappropriate sexual behavior or talk, and fears of places, people, or things symbolic of the abuse; (2) *avoidant behavior*, including avoidance of people, places, and things associated with the abuse, unwillingness to discuss the abuse, limited memory of the abuse, concentration difficulties, and diminished interest in activities; and (3) *autonomic hyperarousal*, including difficulty falling asleep or staying asleep, irritability, anger, aggression, distractibility, hyperalertness, anxiety or startle responses, and physiological symptoms. Scoring was dichotomous, and judged as the symptom being present or absent. To meet criteria for PTSD, the child had to demonstrate at least one symptom of re-experiencing behavior, three or more symptoms of avoidant behavior, and two or more symptoms of autonomic hyperarousal. Of the 31 clinic-referred sexually abused children interviewed, 48.4% met criteria for PTSD. In a separate analysis of 87 inpatient psychiatric patients, sexually abused patients were compared with physically abused and nonabused patients using the PTSD diagnostic method. In that study, 20% of the sexually abused children met PTSD criteria, whereas 7% of the physically abused met the criteria, and 10% of the nonabused.

Conte and Schuerman (1987) also developed a checklist of symptoms for social workers to complete after concluding the intake/assessment process after disclosure. Less theoretically driven than the McLeer et al. (1988) checklist, Conte and Schuerman selected 38 symptoms from those most frequently reported in the literature. From asessments of 369 sexually abused children, Conte and Schuerman found the average number of symptoms per child to be 3.5. The most commonly reported symptoms were low self-esteem (33%), fearfulness of abuse stimuli (31%), emotional upset (23%), nightmares and sleep disorders (20%), repressed anger/hostility (19%), depression (19%), withdrawal from activities (15%), academic problems (15%), daydreaming, loss of memory, inability to concentrate (14%), overly compliant, anxious to please (14%), behavior regression (14%), aggressive behavior (14%), generalized fear (12%) and psychosomatic complaints (10%).

Assessing Sexuality

Assessment of sexual behavior is very difficult for two primary reasons: (1) sexual behavior is generally private behavior that is not readily reported by children; and (2) norms of sexual behavior among various age groups are not available. Nevertheless, there is substantial evidence that sexually abused children exhibit higher rates of inappropriate sexual behavior, compared with their peers (Friedrich et al., 1986; Tufts, New England Medical Center, 1984). However, until recently the rating scales available lacked breadth and detail.

Purcell, Beilke, and Friedrich (1986) addressed this concern by developing the *Child Sexual Behaviour Inventory* (CSBI). The CSBI has two parts. Part I asks about various sources of sexual information available to the child. It includes questions about the availability of sexually explicit movies or television shows, opportunities to view naked people in books or in the home, and whether the child has ever viewed sexual intercourse in real life or on television. Part II consists of 42 items that tap the type and frequency of sexualized behaviors exhibited by children. Each item is rated as occurring "never," "less than once a month," "1–3 times a month," and "at least once a week." The CSBI yields five factors: Boundary permeability, sexual aggression, self-stimulation, sexual inhibition, and sex-role confusion. Of the 42 items, 26 differed significantly from a control group of nonabused children.

At this point, there is no well-established method of assessing sexual knowledge or sexuality directly with children. Less directly, two teams of investigators have examined children's drawings for indicators of abnormal sexuality. Both Sidun and Rosenthal (1987) and Yates, Beutler, and Crago (1985) compared Draw-a-Person tests of sexually abused children to those nonabused children. Yates et al. (1985) found that sexually abused children tended to either overemphasize or minimize sexual features in their drawings. Although Sidun and Rosenthal (1987) did not find a difference between groups regarding oversexualization, they did find a greater number of enclosed circles among the drawings of sexually abused children. Abbenante (1983) also noted a preponderance of enclosed circles among rape victims. Other differences between the groups included a greater tendency for sexually abused children to omit hands or fingers and to exert excessive pencil pressure (Sidun & Rosenthal, 1987). Omission of hands and fingers was thought to relate to feelings of guilt and helplessness, whereas excessive pencil pressure was related to tension and anxiety. Although provocative, the findings should be interpreted cautiously because of the small numbers of subjects and the lack of psychometric rigor applied to these forms of assessments.

SEXUAL ABUSE SEQUELAE

As noted earlier, four types of factors have the power to influence the sequelae of child sexual abuse: abuse-related factors, child factors, family variables, and community-related stressors and supports (Wolfe & Wolfe, 1988). In the following sections, assessment strategies for mediating variables are reviewed along with the studies that have empirically investigated the relationship of these factors to sexual abuse sequelae.

Abuse-related Factors

As described earlier, several factors appear to be very important when assessing the sexual abuse: seriousness, frequency, duration, number of perpetrators, emotional closeness to perpetrator, and level of coercion or force used to ensure compliance. Two studies have investigated these factors as they relate to sexual abuse sequelae, with fairly discrepant results. Friedrich et al. (1986) conducted a series of multiple regression analyses to determine abuse variables that predicted CBCL–PRF Internalizing, Externalizing, and Sexual Problem scores. Higher Internalizing scores were associated with more serious forms of abuse, more frequent abuse, emotional closeness to the perpetrator, and girls, compared with boys. Higher Externalizing scores were related to longer duration of abuse, emotional closeness to the perpetrator, less time since the abuse occurred, and boys, compared with girls. Sexual problems were predicted by the frequency of the abuse and the number of perpetrators.

Wolfe et al. (1989) also conducted a series of multiple regression analyses designed to assess the extent to which abuse factors, as well as several other sets of variables, related to several measures of global adjustment and abuse-specific symptoms. Included among the dependent variables were the CBCL–PRF Internalizing, Externalizing, Social Competence scales, and PTSD items, as well as the following child-report measures: CDI, RCMAS, STAIC–S, STAIC–T, SAFE Sex-related Discomfort and Interpersonal Discomfort scales, and the original scales of the CITES: Guilt, Stigmatization, Betrayal, Intrusive Thoughts, and Negative Sexualization. The first step of the multiple regression was the abuse composite variables "Course of Abuse" and "Seriousness of Abuse." "Course of Abuse" included duration, frequency, and relationship between child and perpetrator, and "Seriousness of Abuse" included type of sexual abuse, use of force or coercion, and number of perpetrators. Three other steps were entered subsequent to abuse-related factors: Attributional style, attributions specific to the abuse, and age of the child. Interestingly, two other abuse-related factors did not correlate with any sequelae measure and therefore were not entered into the analyses: time since abuse and time since disclosure.

Unlike the results from the Friedrich et al. (1986) study, Wolfe et al. (1989) did not find that CBCL scores were significantly related to either abuse factor. However, the STAIC–T was predicted significantly by entry of the two severity of abuse factors, with an R of .54. Partial correlations of Course of Abuse and Seriousness of Abuse variables were .26 and .75, respectively, suggesting that postabuse anxiety may relate primarily to such abuse factors as the seriousness of the abuse, the extent of coercion or force used during the abuse, and the number of perpetrators. The CITES Negative Sexualization was also predicted by abuse factors, with an R of .54, with partial correlations for Course of Abuse and Seriousness of Abuse of .27 and .51, respectively. Like anxiety, discomfort with sex appears to be related most strongly to the seriousness of the abuse.

It is possible that the two abuse-related variables have different effects at different points in time. Seriousness of abuse may relate more to the immediate and enduring posttraumatic stress disorder symptoms such as abuse-related fears and anxieties, whereas Course of Abuse may relate more to long-term, global adjustment problems, such as depression, global anxiety, and chronic behavior problems. This may account for the fact that the variables of relationship to perpetrator, and frequency and duration of abuse that predicted the CBCL scores in the Friedrich study, did not predict adjustment in the Wolfe study. Friedrich's sample was comprised of clinic-referred children who had reported their abuse during the past 2 years, whereas the Wolfe et al. (1989) sample included a more comprehensive sample of children who had reported their abuse at a mode of 2 months earlier. It is possible that more global adjustment problems related to sexual abuse take time to develop subsequent to disclosure, and therefore abuse-related factors would not predict such scores until a substantial time had elapsed from the time of abuse or abuse disclosure to the time of assessment.

Child-related Factors; Developmental Issues

Age and cognitive maturity are important variables in understanding three domains of sexual abuse: (1) the child's ability to recall and express the abusive events; (2) the child's understanding of the abuse and the abusive relationship; and (3) the impact of the abuse on personality, and social and sexual development. Each of these issues is discussed in detail in the following sections with regard to predominant developmental theory and supporting research.

Recall of Traumatic Events. Understanding a child's ability to recall events has importance in two ways. Obviously, the child's ability to provide testimony is at stake if the veracity of their statements is questionable. Secondly, the child's ability to recall events will affect the process of therapy. If the child cannot or will not describe what happened, then discussions about the abuse are restricted. A balance must be taken between assisting the child with his or her recall of events, and suggesting to the child aspects of abuse that may not have occurred.

Two primary issues arise when considering developmental changes that may affect a child's recall of a traumatic event: (1) How much detail can the child recall; and (2) How susceptible is a child's recall of events to distortion? Regarding the former question, much of the research sug-gets that adults are more efficient at remembering than children (John-son & Foley, 1984; Loftus & Davis, 1984). Adult superiority appears to relate to two main factors: (1) more sophisticated use of encoding and retrieval memory strategies, and (2) enriched knowledge structures that facilitate use of memory strategies. However, simple information about events of which the child is knowledgeable may be remembered equally well by children as adults. Familiarity may be one of the key determi-nants of adult–child differences in memory. Children's recall of events for which they are familiar (e.g., a child's game) is usually greater than an adult's recall of the same events, if the adult was not familiar with the situation (Loftus & Davies, 1984).

The second question relates to the child's distortion of information. Distortion appears to occur with both adults and children, but perhaps under different circumstances. Children may have difficulty distinguish-ing between what actually happened and what they thought. However, compared with adults who use previous knowledge to facilitate storage and recall, children are less susceptible to distortions of recall based upon previously held precepts or prejudices (Johnson & Foley, 1984). Both adults and children appear to be susceptible to distortions in their memories when provided contrary information after the fact. Loftus and Davies (1984) suggest that children, like adults, are more susceptible to memory distortions when the original event was not encoded well to begin with, or if delays occur between the event and attempts to recall. In such cases, spotty recall of the event may give way to suggestion in recalling other details.

The Child's Understanding of the Abuse and Disclosure Sequelae.   One of the keys to overcoming trauma-related symptoms may well be the ability to gain a conceptual framework for what happened, and place various aspects of the abuse and abusive relationship into perspective (Silver et al., 1983). This concept is similar to the Freudian notion that symptoms relate to underlying conflicts, and that as long as the conflicts remain unresolved the symptoms will persist. Given the complexity of human social and sexual relationships, particularly those associated with sexual abuse, children may have extreme difficulty coming to terms with sexual abuse. Children's logic, social cognitions, and concepts of morality vary with age. In order to expand on those concepts, three leading de-velopmental theories will be briefly reviewed with regard to children's developmental stages and their perspectives on sexual abuse.

Cognitive Development.   Piagetian theory (Piaget, 1954) describes how logical thought changes over the course of childhood, with four major stages: preconceptual, intuitive, concrete-operational, and formal operational. The preconceptual child, from age 2 to 4, is characterized by transductive thinking and egocentricism. Transductive thinking refers to the tendency to assume a causal relationship between two events that occur together. Egocentrism refers to a tendency to view the world from one's own perspective and to have difficulty recognizing another's point of view. Therefore with young children, their causal attributions about the abuse may be tied to events coincidental to the abuse, such as playing tickling or wrestling games or their mother going out to play bingo and leaving them with a babysitter or stepfather.

From ages 4 to 7, the intuitive child's thinking is characterized by centration, or a tendency to focus on a single aspect of a problem while ignoring other information that would help to answer a multifaceted question. Centration is responsible for a child's difficulty with conservation problems, in which children are asked about differences in size, volume, or mass based upon changes in form, such as from tall and thin to short and wide. Not until a child develops a cognitive operation called compensation is he or she capable of focusing on several aspects of a problem simultaneously. Because sexual abuse involves very complex processes, a preschooler's ability to entertain simultaneously two or more aspects of the situation is seriously compromised.

Between the ages of 7 and 11, the concrete-operational stage, children gain many logical "operations" that are tied to "concrete" objects, situations, and events. During this period, children are more capable of understanding relationships among objects and events, but may continue to have difficulty understanding relationships between abstract principles and concepts. For example, the child may be able to understand the relationship between a series of events associated with the abuse (e.g., a series of events beginning with the perpetrator coming to babysit, putting other children to bed, sexual abuse, followed by threats not to tell), but have difficulty understanding such abstract principles as the necessity of "consent" in sexual relationships.

It may not be until children reach adolescence that they are able to understand the abstract principles behind the taboos against sexual abuse, or understand the principles governing the legal and social system responses. During the formal operations stage, adolescents acquire the ability to perform operations with abstract concepts. As well, adolescents gain the ability to use scientific reasoning of hypothetical-deductive reasoning. It is at this point, that children who were abused at a younger age, may experience a resurgence of abuse-related symptoms, as the adolescent attempts to resolve the more abstract aspects of their abuse experience.

Social Cognition.   Sexually abused children may experience particular difficulty understanding the abuser's actions, as well as the reactions of others once the abuse is discovered. Selman (1980) developed a paradigm for understanding a child's development of social role taking and understanding of other's perspectives. According to Selman, until age 6, children do not have the ability to recognize that others have a different perspective from theirs. From 6 to 8, children may attribute differences in perspectives simply to differences in information. For the abused child faced with an abuser who denies the abuse, the child may feel that the abuser needs to be reminded of "the facts" and then the accused will naturally share their concept of events. From 8 to 10, children can recognize that others may hold different opinions even given the same information. They are usually able to "step into someone else's shoes," but still have difficulty simultaneously entertaining both their own and someone else's perspective. Therefore, a sexually abused child may have a sense for why a perpetrator denies the abuse, but cannot integrate the perpetrator's perspective with one's own. Around age 10, children learn to view and compare simultaneously two different perspectives, as well as that of a neutral party. At around age 12, children gain an appreciation of what the perspective would be of most people given a certain situation, and can compare their own and others' views of a situation with the view that most people would take. At this point, adolescents may be quite concerned that others share their perspective on the abuse, and be quite motivated to prove this through public policy and courtroom resolution.

Morality.   Sexual abuse is fraught with moral dilemmas for the child. While the abuse is occurring and prior to disclosure, moral conflicts may relate to the contrast between two sets of actions that can have both positive and negative consequences. The child may view acquiesing to sexual abuse demands as a way to obtain attention, rewards, or privileges, avoid criticism and physical abuse, and abide by the authority of a parental figure. On the other hand children may sense that sex is "naughty," "dirty," or "sinful," and that they should not keep secrets from their mothers. Still, they may fear the repercussions of telling. They may have been threatened personally, or may have been told others would be hurt if they told. Depending on the child's level of reasoning about moral issues, a child's personal conflicts may differ greatly.

Kohlberg's (1981) theory provides a conceptual framework from which to view how children view sexual abuse. Kohlberg's theory sets out three levels of moral thinking, each with two stages. At the preconventional morality stage, the child views morality based upon the consequences of the act. Any behavior that is punished is "bad," and the stronger the punishment, the worse the act (stage 1). Behaviors that result in rewards or positive consequences are viewed as "good" (stage 2).

During level 2, conventional morality, is judged according to the social consequences of the act. Moral behavior is that which is intended to please or help others or that which receives approval from others (stage 3). Moral behavior is also viewed as complying with rules in order to maintain order and abide by social custom (stage 4). During level 3, or postconventional morality, moral behavior is that which maximizes social welfare or complies with the wishes of the majority (stage 5). At the highest stage of moral development, morality is defined according to internal moral principles of universal justice (stage 6).

Although assessment of various aspects of developmental stages is beyond the scope of this chapter, the interested reader is referred to the following materials for comprehensive reviews of assessment of sociomoral development: Colby and Kohlberg (1987), Gibbs and Widaman (1982), and Gibbs, Widaman, and Colby (1982).

Although research studies have not examined developmental constructs per se in investigating the impact of sexual abuse, age has been investigated with some discrepant results. Wolfe et al. (1989) found that when age entered into prediction equations, it was the younger children who showed the greater symptomology. Younger children were more distressed by sex-related situations, with higher numbers of endorsements on the SAFE Sex-associated Fear scale and the CITES Negative Sexualization scale. Younger children were also more likely to report feelings of stigmatization on the CITES, and more anxiety on the CMAS–R. Wolfe et al. (1989) queried whether younger children have greater difficulty understanding sexual behavior and thus are more bothered and anxious as a result of such events.

Nevertheless, the foregoing study contrasts to the findings of Friedrich et al. (1986), who found that age was not significantly correlated with sexual problems. To complicate matters further, Sirles, Smith, and Kusama (1989) found that among outpatient psychiatry patients, older children who had been sexually abused, compared with younger sexually abused children, were more likely to display symptoms of sufficient magnitude to be diagnosed with a DSM–III axis I clinical disorder.

Attributional Style

The development of depressive symptomology and negative self-concept among victims of child sexual abuse can be conceptualized along the lines of the reformulated learned helplessness model (Gold, 1986;

Seidner & Calhoun, 1984). The reformulated learned helplessness model attempts to account for individual differences in responses to uncontrolled events. It also addresses the loss of self-esteem that frequently accompanies helplessness and negative affect. Individual differences in response to traumatic events are related to three dimensions of causal attributions about uncontrolled events (Peterson & Seligman, 1983): internal–external, stable–unstable, and global–specific. Loss of self-esteem is related to tendencies to attribute a helpless situation to something about oneself (i.e., internal), as opposed to something else (i.e., external). Chronic feelings of helplessness are related to the attribution that the causes of a helpless situation are persistent across time (i.e., stable), as opposed to transient (i.e., unstable). Pervasive deficits in functioning are related to the attribution that the cause of the helpless situation is such that other areas of life will also be affected. For a more thorough discussion of this model as it relates to child sexual abuse, see Wolfe and Wolfe (1988).

Attributions are determined by situational factors, such as the nature of the victimization, as well as dispositional factors, such as a previous tendency to attribute negative events to personal characteristics (Peterson & Seligman, 1983). Therefore, when assessing attributions as a mediator of sexual abuse sequelae, both levels of attributions should be assessed.

The most widely researched attributional measure for children is the *Attributional Style Questionnaire for Children,* also known as the KASTAN (Kaslow, Tannenbaum, & Seligman, 1978). The KASTAN is a 48-item questionnaire that assesses the child's tendency to attribute positive events to internal, global, and stable factors and negative events to external, specific, and unstable factors. Each item depicts either a fortunate or unfortunate event for which the child selects one or two possible causes. A self-enhancing attributional style is reflected by the difference between the number of internal, stable, and global attributions given for fortunate events minus the number of internal, stable, and global attributions given for unfortunate events.

In accordance with the revised learned helplessness theory, the CITES has three scales developed to assess abuse-related attributions. The original CITES scales were labeled Internal Negative, Stable Negative, and Global Negative. The revised scales are labeled Guilt and Self-blame, Dangerous World, and Personal Vulnerability and Empowerment, respectively. The Guilt and Self-blame scale assesses the child's tendency to view something about himself or herself as responsible for the abuse. The Dangerous World scale assess the child's tendency to view the world as dangerous for children and believe that many adults take advantage of children. The Personal Vulnerability scale assesses the child's view that he or she is particularly prone to negative life events and victimization, whereas the empowerment scale assessed the child's belief that he or she can prevent or stop their own re-victimization.

As noted previously, V. Wolfe et al. (1989) investigated the extent to which attributional variables predicted a number of measures of child adjustment. The KASTAN predicted several scores: CBCL Social Competence Scale, CDI, STAIC–S, STAIC–T, and the CITES Betrayal and Guilt Scales. Not surprisingly, the CITES Internal Negative scale predicted the CITES Guilt Scale, as well as the Negative Sexualization scale from the CITES. Stable Negative scores predicted the CBCL Social Competence Scale scores, and the CITES Intrusive thoughts, Stigmatization, and Betrayal scales. The CITES Global Negative scale predicted the STAIC–T and the CITES Intrusive thoughts, Stigmatization, and Betrayal scales. Interestingly, the direction of the correlations between the CITES Global Negative scale and the impact variables was opposite to that predicted. It had been predicted that believing the world to be dangerous and believing that many people exploit children would relate to negative affect. Results suggested that such beliefs may have a comforting effect for the sexually abused child. That is, feeling that similar things happen to other children and one is not alone in one's experience may buffer against negative affective symptoms.

Family Relationships

Probably the most fundamental variables affecting the sequelae of sexual abuse is the emotional support that the child receives from family and friends. Having a positive relationship with one or both parental figures can help a child feel safe enough to disclose their abuse early in the process. Believing the child's story and acting to protect the child can be fundamental to the child's sense of security and safety. As the child shows more and more trauma-related symptoms, sympathetic parents who respond sensitively and constructively can help the child overcome the trauma of sexual abuse.

On the other side, however, are cases of incestuous abuse in which children may fear disclosure, both in terms of the father's reaction, but also that of the mother. Children may fear their mother will not believe them, or will punish them for doing "nasty" things. In some cases, mothers indeed do not believe their child's story or fail to act to protect their child from further abuse. Even when the abuser is removed from the home, the child and the nonoffending parent are faced with many stressful situations. The mother's ability to cope with extreme stress, while remaining supportive of her child, can play a key role in aiding the child's recovery.

In many ways, the key to recovery from intrafamilial sexual abuse lies within the relationship between the child and the mother. The mother must act as protector for her child, yet must be sensitive and allow for open communication about relationships and sex. This is a very tall order for anyone, especially a mother whose world has recently collapsed.

Several assessment instruments can be used to assess the quality of parent–child relationships. Assessment requires input from both the parent and the child, preferably along the dimensions of parent and child attitudes toward each other and parent and child interactions and exchanges of positives and negatives. Furthermore, assessment of family dimensions such as adaptability and cohesion can aid in predicting how well the family will cope with the demands placed upon them by the disclosure and by decisions to prosecute the offender.

A set of three questionnaires are available to assess family attitudes toward one another: *Child's Attitude Toward Mother (CAM)*, *Child's Attitude Toward Father (CAF)*, and the *Index of Parental Attitudes* (IPA; Giuli & Hudson, 1977; Hudson, 1982). Each scale consists of 25 brief statements about family attitudes, such "My mother gets on my nerves," "I like being with my father," or "My child interferes with my activities." Two-thirds of the items reflect positive characteristics, and one-third reflect negative characteristics. Respondents rate the extent to which each statement is true for themselves from 1 ("rarely" or "none of the time") to 5 ("most or all of the time"). Norms are available for both males and females from 11 to 19 years of age. Internal consistency for the scales range from .94 to .95. Psychometric evaluations provide evidence of both discriminant and construct validity (Giuli & Hudson, 1977; Saunders & Schuchts, 1987).

For children younger than 11, an alternative method of assessing parent–child relationships is the *Family Relationships Test* (FRT; Bene & Anthony, 1957). Two child-report versions are available. The version for older children assesses two levels of positive contact—moderate friendly approval and "sexualized or sensualized feeling associated with close physical contact and manipulation" (p. 4), and two levels of negative contact—moderate disapproval, and hate and hostility. Attitudes of overindulgence and overprotection are also assessed. For younger children, the FRT assesses positive and negative feelings both experienced by the child and coming from the child, as well as feelings of dependency. According to the authors, the test material was designed to give a concrete representation of the child's family. The test includes 20 figures representing people of various ages, shapes and sizes, designed to represent members of the child's family. The characters range from grandparents to babies, and one character is labeled "Mr. Nobody." The child labels the characters according to his or her views of family members. Each character is attached to a box with a slit in the top. Items are printed on small individual cards. The child's job is to put each "message" into the "person" whom the message best fits.

Although the test has extensive information about interpretation from a theoretical perspective, validation efforts have been meager. The authors suggest that interpretation of the FRT involves considerations of the psychological importance of family members as related to the number of messages to that figure, egocentrism by number of messages sent to oneself, and ambivalence as related to conflicting outgoing feeling.

While the CAM, CAF, and IPA, in addition to the FRT, assess attitudes, the *Parent Perception Inventory* (PPI; Hazzard, Christensen, & Margolin, 1983) assesses the child's perception of the frequency of specific types of parenting behaviors. The PPI consists of 18 items depicting nine positive parenting behaviors, such as praise, time together, and affection, and nine negative parenting behaviors, such as criticism, ignoring, and physical punishment. The PPI is administered in interview format by asking how frequently each set of behaviors occurs. Response options range along a 4-point scale from "never" to "a lot." The PPI is completed separately for mothers and fathers. Scores include Mother Positive, Mother Negative, Father Positive, and Father Negative. Alpha values for the scales range from .78 to .88. Discriminant validity has been demonstrated by comparisons of distressed and nondistressed families, and convergent validity with measures of self-concept and externalizing behavior problems. Norms are available for children ages 5 to 13.

Several questionnaires are available to assess dimensions of family interactions. The three most commonly used are the *Family Environment Scale* (FES; Moos & Moos, 1976, 1983), the *Family Adaptability and Cohesion Scale–III* (FACES–III; Olson et al., 1985), and the *McMaster Family Assessment Device* (FAD; Epstein, Baldwin, & Bishop, 1983; Miller, Epstein, Bishop, & Keitner, 1984). The FES has 90 true–false items, and yields 10 scales: cohesion, expressiveness, conflict, independence, organization, control, achievement orientation, intellectual-cultural orientation, moral-religious emphasis, and active-recreational orientation. Psychometric analyses provide evidence of discriminant validity for the cohesion, independence, expressiveness, conflict, and control subscales. The scales have been shown to be sensitive to family changes resulting from counseling. Furthermore, the conflict scale has demonstrated concurrent validity with frequency counts of family conflict (Foster & Robin, 1988).

The FACES–III has 20 items and yields two scales: adaptability and cohension. The FACES–III is the result of substantial factor-analytical studies and was derived from the Family System Circumplex Model of dysfunctional family processes. Olson et al. (1985) reported evidence that the two scales are indeed orthogonal, and that both scales distinguish dysfunctional families from nonproblem families.

The FAD is a 53-item, self-report scale designed to assess seven dimensions of family functioning: Problem solving, communication, roles, affective responsiveness, affective involvement, behavior control, and general functioning. Alpha values of the subscales range from .72 to .92, with test–retest at 1-week intervals of .66 to .76. It correlates moderately with the predecessor of the FACES–III, the FACES II. Discriminant validity was demonstrated with significant differences on the majority of FAD scales, comparing psychiatric and nonpsychiatric families (Miller et al., 1984).

Unfortunately, data reflecting the use of these measures are not available at this point. Our own project has included the CAM, CAF, IPA, and PPI, as well as a direct observation measure of mother–daughter relationships. However, those findings are not ready for reporting. Nevertheless, clinically, the measures have been very useful, particularly for detecting mother–daughter relationship disturbances. These measures have been essential for organizing the therapeutic process, with regard to decisions about group, individual, and/or family modes of treatment.

CONCLUSIONS

From this chapter it is clear that assessment of childhood sexual abuse is a complex problem that involves expertise in a number of areas: child development, cognitive development, child and adult responses to stress and trauma, child psychopathology, and knowledge of sexual abuse and other forms of maltreatment. Expertise in interviewing children and parents is also essential.

Although the chapter has focused on "what to assess," interpretation of the results requires the ability to examine many sources of information, some potentially contradictory, the ability to create and test hypotheses, and the ability to draw proper conclusions. The examiner must come to the assessment armed with a conceptual framework that provides structure and organization to the tasks. This chapter has attempted to provide such a framework. However, the data available to draw conclusions are sparse and inconsistent. As our assessment technology improves, our ability to test this conceptual model, and alter it, will further our ability to understand the sexually abused child.

ACKNOWLEDGMENT

The authors would like to express their appreciation to Teresa Michienzi for her assistance with the literature search and data analyses. Requests for reprints should be directed to Vicky Veitch Wolfe, Department of Psychology, Children's Hospital of Western Ontario, 800 Commissioners Rd. E., London, Ontario N6A 4G5.

REFERENCES

Abramson, L. Y., Seligman, M. E. P., & Teasdale, J. D. (1978). Learned helplessness in humans: Critique and reformulation. *Journal of Abnormal Psychology, 87*, 49–74.

Abbenante, J. (1983). Art therapy with victims of rape (summary). *Art therapy: Still growing.* Proceedings of the 13th annual conference of the American Art Therapy Association, p. 34.

Achenbach, T. M., & Edelbrock, C. (1981). *Youth self-report for ages 11–18.* University of Vermont, Burlington, VT.

Achenbach, T. M., & Edelbrock, C. (1983). *Manual for the Child Behavior Checklist and Child Behavior Profile.* Burlington: University of Vermont, Department of Psychiatry.

Achenbach, T. M., & McConaughy, S. H. (1985, March). *Semistructured clinical interview for children aged 6–11, Protocol Form.* Dept. of Psychiatry, University of Vermont, Burlington, VT.

Adams-Tucker, C. (1981). The socioclinical overview of 28 sex-abused children. *Child Abuse and Neglect, 5*, 361–367.

Adams-Tucker, C. (1982). Proximate effects of sexual abuse in childhood: A report on 28 children. *American Journal of Psychiatry, 139*, 1252–1256.

American Psychiatric Association. (1987). *Diagnostic and Statistical Manual for Mental Disorders* (3rd Ed., Rev.). Washington, DC: Author.

Baker, A. L., & Peterson, C. (1977). Self-blame by rape victims as a function of the rape's consequences: An attributional analysis. *Crisis Intervention, 8*, 92–104.

Bene, E., & Anthony, E. J. (1957). Manual for the *Family Relations Test.* National Foundation for Educational Research in England and Wales, Slough.

Bresee, P., Stearns, G. B., Bess, B. H., & Packer, L. S. (1986). Allegations of child sexual abuse in child custody disputes: A therapeutic assessment model. *American Journal of Orthopsychiatry, 56*, 560–569.

Cantwell, H. B. (1981). Sexual abuse of children in Denver, 1979. *Child Abuse and Neglect, 5*, 75–85.

Cluss, P. A., Boughton, J., Frank, L. E., Stewart, B. D., & West, D. (1983). The rape victim: Psychological correlates for participation in the legal process. *Criminal Justice and Behaviour, 10*, 342–357.

Cohen, J. A., & Mannarino, A. P. (1988). Psychological symptoms in sexually abused girls. *Child Abuse and Neglect, 12*, 571–577.

Colby, A., & Kohlberg, L. (1987). *The measurement of moral judgement. Vol. 2: Standard Issue Scoring Manual,* Cambridge, England: Cambridge University Press.

Conte, J., & Schuerman, J. R. (1987). The effects of sexual abuse on children: A multidimensional view. *Journal of Interpersonal Violence, 2,* 380–390.

Dent, H. R., & Stephenson, G. M. (1979). An experimental study of the effectiveness of different techniques of questioning child witnesses. *British Journal of Social and Clinical Psychology, 18,* 41–51.

Epstein, N. B., Baldwin, L. M., & Bishop, D. S. (1983). The McMaster Family Assessment Device. *Journal of Marriage and the Family, 9,* 171–180.

Faller, K. C. (1984). Is the child victim of sexual abuse telling the truth? *Child Abuse and Neglect, 8,* 473–481.

Faller, K. C. (1988). Criteria for judging the credibility of children's statements about their sexual abuse. *Child Welfare, 67,* 389, 401.

Finkelhor, D. (1979). *Sexually victimized children.* New York: Free Press.

Finkelhor, D. (1986). The trauma of child sexual abuse: Two models. In G. Wyatt & G. J. Powell (Eds.). *The lasting effects of child sexual abuse.* Sage: Newbury Park.

Finkelhor, D., & Browne, A., (1985). The traumatic impact of child sexual abuse: A conceptualization. *American Journal of Orthopsychiatry, 55,* 530–541.

Foster, S. L., & Robin, A. L. (1988). Family conflict and communication in adolescence. (pp. 717–775). In E. J. Mash & L. G. Terdal (Eds.), *Behavioural assessment of childhood disorders:* (2d Ed.). New York: Guilford Press.

Foy, D. W., Sipprelle, R. C., Rueger, D. G., & Caroll, E. M. (1984). Etiology of postraumatic stress disorder in Vietnam veterans: Analysis of premilitary, military, and combat exposure influences. *Journal of Consulting and Clinical Psychology, 52,* 79–87.

Friedrich, W. N., & Reams, R. A. (1987). The course of psychological symptoms in sexually abused young children. *Psychotherapy: Theory, Research, and Practice, 24,* 160–170.

Friedrich, W. N., Urquiza, A. J., & Beilke, R. L. (1986). Behaviour problems in sexually abused children. *Journal of Pediatric Psychology, 11,* 47–59.

Garmezy, N., Masten, A. S., & Tellegen, A. (1984). The study of stress and competence in children: A building block for developmental psychopathology. *Child Development, 55,* 97–111.

Gentile, C. (1988). *Factors mediating the impact of child sexual abuse: Learned helplessness and severity of abuse.* Unpublished master's thesis. University of Western Ontario, London, Ontario

Gibbs, J. C., & Widaman, K. S. (1982). *Social intelligence: Measuring the development of sociomoral development.* New Jersey: Prentice-Hall.

Gibbs, J. C., Widaman, K. S., & Colby, A. (1982). Construction and validation of a simplified group-administratable equivalent to the Moral Judgement Interview. *Child Development, 53,* 875–910.

Gilgin, J. F. (1984). *A non-coercive method of helping children discuss their own sexual abuse. Pt. 2: An example of intervention by multiple qualitative case studies.* Unpublished manuscript. School of Social Work, University of Minnesota, Minneapolis.

Giuli, C. A., & Hudson, W. W. (1977). Assessing parent–child relationship disorders in clinical practice: The child's point of view. *Journal of Social Service Research, 1,* 77–92.

Gold, E. R. (1986). Long-term effects of sexual victimization in childhood: An attributional approach. *Journal of Consulting and Clinical Psychology, 54,* 471–475.

Green, A. H. (1986). True and false allegations of sexual abuse in child custody disputes. *Journal of the American Academy of Child Psychiatry, 25,* 449–456.

Griest, D. L., Forehand, R., Wells, K. C., & McMahon, R. J. (1980). An examination of differences between nonclinic and behavior problem clinic-referred children and their mothers. *Journal of Abnormal Psychology, 89,* 497–500.

Griest, D. L., Wells, K. C., & Forehand, R. (1979). An examination of predictors of maternal perceptions of maltreatment in clinic-referred children. *Journal of Abnormal Psychology, 88,* 277–281.

Gruber, K. J.; & Jones, R. J. (1981). Does sexual abuse lead to delinquent behavior: A critical look at the evidence. *Victimology: An International Journal, 6,* 85–91.

Hart, L. E., Mader, L., Griffith, K., & de Mendonca, M. (1989). Effects of sexual and physical abuse: A comparison of adolescent inpatients. *Child Psychiatry and Human Development, 20,* 49–57.

Harter, S. (1982). The Perceived Competence Scale for Children. *Child Development, 53,* 87–97.

Harter, S. (1985). *Manual for the Self-Perception Profile for Children:* University of Denver.

Harter, S. (1986a). *Self-perception Profile for Adolescents.* University of Denver.

Harter, S. (1986b). *Teacher's Rating Scale of Child's Actual Behavior.* University of Denver.

Harter, S., & Pike, R. (1984). The pictorial scale of perceived competence and social acceptance for young children: *Child Development, 55,* 1962–1982.

Hazzard, A., Christensen, A., & Margolin, J. G. (1983). Children's perceptions of parental behaviours. *Journal of Abnormal Child Psychology, 11,* 49–60.

Herjanic, F., Herjanic, M., Brown, F., & Wheatt, T. (1975). Are children reliable reporters? *Journal of Abnormal Child Psychology, 3,* 41–48.

Horowitz, M. J., Wilner, N., & Alvarez, W. (1979). Impact of event scale: A measure of psychosomatic stress. *Archives of General Psychiatry, 32,* 85–92.

Hudson, W. W. (1982). *One clinical measurement package: A field manual.* Homewood, IL: Dorsey Press.

James, B., & Nasjleti, M. (1983). *Treating sexually abused children and their families.* Palo Alto, CA: Consulting Psychologists Press.

Jampole, L., & Weber, M. K. (1987). An assessment of the behavior of sexually abused and nonabused children with anatomically correct dolls. *Child Abuse and Neglect, 11*, 187–192.

Johnson, M. K., & Foley, M. A. (1984). Differentiating fact from fantasy: The reliability of children's memory. *Journal of Social Issues, 40*, 33–50.

Jones, D. P. H., & McGraw, J. M. (1987). Reliable and fictitious accounts of sexual abuse of children. *Journal of Interpersonal Violence, 2*, 27–45.

Justice, B., & Justice, R. (1979). *The broken taboo.* New York: Human Sciences Press.

Kaslow, N. J., Tannenbaum, R. L., & Seligman, M. E. P. (1978). *The KASTAN–R: A Children's Attributional Style Questionnaire (KASTAN–R CASQ).* Unpublished manuscript. University of Pennsylvania.

Kazlow, N. J., & Racusin, G. R. (1990). Childhood depression: Current status and future directions. In A. E. Kazain, A. S. Bellack, & M. Hersen (Eds). *Interpersonal handbook of behavior modification and therapy* (pp. 649–668). New York: Plenum Press.

Kempe, R. S., & Kempe, C. H. (1984). *The common secret: Sexual abuse of children and adolescents.* San Francisco: Freeman.

Kerns, D. L. (1981). Medical assessment in child sexual abuse. In P. B. Mrazek & C. H. Kempe (Eds.), *Sexually abused children and their families* (pp. 126–141) Oxford, England: Pergamon.

Kiser, L. J., Ackerman, B. J., Brown, E., Edwards, N. B., McColgan, E., Pugh, R., & Pruitt, D. B. (1988). Post-traumatic stress disorder in young children: A reaction to purported sexual abuse: *Journal of the American Academy of Child and Adolescent Psychiatry, 27*, 645–649.

Kohlberg, L. (1981). *Essays on moral development* (Vol. 1). New York: Harper & Row.

Kovacs, M. (1983). *The Children's Depression Inventory: A self-rated depression scale for school-age youngsters.* Unpublished manuscript.

Kovacs, M. (1986). A developmental perspective on methods and measures in the assessment of depressive disorders: The clinical interview. In Rutter, M., Izard, C. E., & Read, P. B. (Eds.), *Depression in young people: Developmental and clinical perspectives* (pp. 435–469). New York: Guilford Press.

Loftus, E. F., & Davies, G. M. (1984). Distortions in the memory of children. *Journal of Social Issues, 40*, 51–68.

Lyons, J. A. (1987). Post-traumatic stress disorder in children and adolescents: A review of the literature. *Developmental and Behavioural Pediatrics, 8*, 349–357.

Meiselman, K. C. (1978). *Incest: A psychological study of causes and effects with treatment recommendations.* San Francisco: Jossey-Bass.

Melton, G. B. (1985). Sexually abused children and the legal system: Some policy recommendations. *American Journal of Family Therapy, 13*, 61–67.

McKnew, D. H., Cytryn, L., Efron, A. M., Gershon, E. S., & Bunney, W. E. (1979). Offspring of patients with affective disorders. *British Journal of Psychiatry, 134*, 148–152.

McLeer, S. V., Deblinger, E., Alkins, M. S., Foa, E. B., & Ralphe, D. L. (1988). Post-traumatic stress disorder in sexually abused children. *Journal of the American Academy of Children and Adolescent Psychiatry, 27*, 650–654.

Mian, M., Wehrspann, W., Klajner-Diamond, H., LeBaron, D., & Winder, C. (1986). Review of 125 children 6 years of age and under who were sexually abused. *Child Abuse & Neglect, 10,* 223–229.

Miller, I. W., Epstein, N. B., Bishop, D. S., & Keitner, G. I. (1984, November). *The Family Assessment Device: Reliability and Validity.* Paper presented at the Association for the Advancement of Behaviour Therapy convention, Philadelphia.

Miller, L. C. (1977). *Louisville Behavior Checklist.* Los Angeles: Western Psychological Services.

Moos, R. H., & Moos, B. S. (1976). A typology of family social environments. *Family Process, 15,* 357–371.

Moos, R. H., & Moos, B. S. (1983). Clinical applications of the *Family Environment Scale.* In E. E. Filsinger (Ed.) *Marriage and family assessment: A source book for family therapy* (pp. 253–273). Beverly Hills, CA: Sage.

Mrazek, D. A. (1981). The child psychiatric examination of the sexually abused child. In P. B. Mrazek & C. H. Kempe (Eds.), *Sexually abused children and their families* (pp. 143–154). New York: Pergamon Press.

Mrazek, P. B., & Mrazek, D. A. (1981). The effects of child sexual abuse: Methodological considerations. In P. B. Mrazek & C. H. Kempe (Eds.), *Sexually abused children and their families* (pp. 235–245). New York: Pergamon Press

National Center on Child Abuse and Neglect. (1981). *Study findings: National study of the incidence and severity of child abuse and neglect* (DHHS Publication No. OHDS 81–30325). Washington, DC: U.S. Government Printing Office.

Ollendick, T. H. (1983). Reliability and validity of the revised fear survey schedule for children (FSSC-R). *Behavior Research and Therapy, 21,* 65–692.

Olsen, D. H., McCubbin, H. I., Barnes, H., Larsen, A., Muxen, M. & Wilson, M. (1985). *Family inventories,* St. Paul, MN: University of Minnesota, Department of Family Social Science.

Peterson, C., & Seligman, M. E. P. (1983). Learned helplessness and victimization. *Journal of Social Issues, 39,* 103–116.

Piaget, J. (1954). *The construction of reality in the child.* New York: Basic Books.

Piers, E. V. (1984). *Piers-Harris Children's Self Concept Scale. Revised Manual.* Los Angeles: Western Psychological Services.

Purcell, J., Beilke, R. L., & Friedrich, W. N. (1986, August). *Sexualized behaviour in sexually abused and non-sexually abused children.* Poster presented at the American Psychological Association conference, Washington, DC.

Pynoos, R. S., & Eth, S. (1985). Children traumatized by witnessing acts of personal violence: Homocide, rape, or suicidal behaviour. In S. Eth & R. S. Pynoos (Eds.). *Post-traumatic stress disorder in children* (pp. 19–43). Los Angeles: American Psychiatric Association.

Quay, H. E. (1983). A dimensional approach to behavior disorder: The Revised Behavior Problem Checklist. *School Psychology Review, 12,* 244–249.

Reynolds, C. R., & Paget, K. D. (1981). Factor analysis of the *Revised Children's Manifest Anxiety Scale* for blacks, whites, males, and females with a national normative sample. *Journal of Consulting and Clinical Psychology, 49,* 352–359.

Sansonnet-Hayden, H., Haley, G., Marriage, L., & Fine, S. (1987). Sexual abuse and psychopathology in hospitalized adolescents. *Journal of the American Academy of Child and Adolescent Psychiatry, 26,* 753–757.

Saunders, B. E., & Schuchts, R. A. (1987). Assessing parent–child relationships: A report of normative scores and revalidation of psychometric properties of two clinical scales. *Family Process, 26,* 373–381.

Seidner, A. L., & Calhoun, K. S. (1984, July). *Childhood sexual abuse: Factors related to differential adult adjustment.* Paper presented at the second annual National Family Violence Research Conference, Durham, NH.

Selman, R. L. (1980). *The growth of interpersonal understanding.* New York: Academic Press.

Sgroi, S. M. (1982). *Handbook of clinical intervention in child sexual abuse.* Lexington, MA: D. C. Heath.

Sidun, N. M., & Rosenthal, R. H. (1987). Graphic indicators of sexual abuse in *Draw-a-Person* tests of psychiatrically hospitalized adolescents. *Arts in Psychotherapy, 14,* 25–33.

Silver, R. L., Boon, C., & Stones, M. H. (1983). Searching for meaning in misfortune: Making sense of incest. *Journal of Social Issues, 39,* 81–102.

Sirles, E. A., Smith, J. A., & Kusama, H. (1989). Psychiatric status of intrafamilial child sexual abuse victims. *Journal of the American Academy of Child and Adolescent Psychiatry, 28,* 225–229.

Spielberger, C. D. (1973). Preliminary manual for the *State–Trait Anxiety Inventory for Children* ("How I Feel Questionnaire"). Palo Alto, CA: Consulting Psychologists Press.

Steketee, G., & Foa, E. B. (1987). Rape victims: PTSD responses and their treatment: A review of the literature. *Journal of Anxiety Disorders, 1,* 69–86.

Terr, L. C. (1981). Psychic trauma in children: Observations following the Chowchilla school-bus kidnapping. *American Journal of Psychiatry, 138,* 14–19.

Terr, L. C. (1983a). Chowchilla revisited. The effects of psychic trauma four years after a school-bus kidnapping. *American Journal of Psychiatry, 140,* 1543–1550.

Terr, L. C. (1983b). Child snatching: A new epidemic of an ancient malady. *Journal of Pediatrics, 103,* 151–156.

Terr, L. C. (1985a). Children traumatized in small groups. (pp. 45–70). In S. Eth & R. S. Pynoos (Eds.), *Post-traumatic stress Disorder in children* (pp. 45–70). Washington, DC: American Psychiatric Press.

Terr, L. C. (1985b). Psychic trauma in children and adolescents. *Psychiatric Clinics of North America, 8,* 815–835.

Terr, L. C. (1987). *Severe stress and sudden shock—the connection.* Sam Hibbs Award Lecture, American Psychiatric Association Convention, Chicago.

Tong, L., Oates, K., & McDowell, M. (1987). Personality development following sexual abuse. *Child Abuse and Neglect, 11,* 371–383.

Tufts New England Medical Center, Division of Child Psychiatry. (1984). *Sexually exploited children: Service and research project.* Final report for the Office of Juvenile Justice and Delinquency Prevention. Washington, DC: U. S. Department of Justice.

Underwager, R., Wakefield, H., Legrand, R., Bartz, C. S., & Erickson, J. (1986, August). *The role of the psychologist in the assessment of cases of alleged sexual abuse of children.* Presented at the American Psychological Association convention, Washington, DC.

Wells, M. (1984). *Guidelines for investigative interviewing of child victims of sexual abuse.* The metropolitan chairman's special committee on child abuse, Toronto.

White, S. (1986). Uses and abuses of the sexually anatomically correct dolls. *Division of the Child, Youth, and Family Services Newsletter, American Psychological Association, 9,* 3–6.

White, S., Strom, G. A., Santilli, G., & Halpin, B. M. (1986). Interviewing young sexual abuse victims with anatomically correct dolls. *Child Abuse and Neglect, 10,* 519–529.

Wolfe, V. V. (1985). *Parent Impact Questionnaire.* Unpublished assessment instrument. Children's Hospital of Western Ontario, London, Ontario.

Wolfe, V. V. (1990). Sexual abuse of children. In A. E. Kazdin, A. S. Bellack, & M. Hersen (Eds.), *International handbook of behaviour modification and therapy* (pp. 707–730). New York: Plenum Press.

Wolfe, V. V., & Gentile, C. (1991) *The Children's Impact of Traumatic Events Scale-Revised.* Unpublished assessment instrument. Children's Hospital of Western Ontario, London, Ontario.

Wolfe, V. V., Gentile, C., & Klink, A. (1988). *Psychometric properties of the Sexual Abuse Fear Evaluation.* Unpublished manuscript. Children's Hospital of Western Ontario, London, Ontario

Wolfe, V. V., Gentile, C., Sas, L., Michienzi, T., & Wolfe, D. A. (in press). The Children's Impact of Traumatic Events Scale: A measure of post-sexual abuse PTSD symptoms. *Behavioral Assessment.*

Wolfe, V. V., Gentile, C., & Wolfe, D. A. (1989). The impact of sexual abuse on children: A PTSD formulation. *Behavior Therapy, 20,* 215–228.

Wolfe, V. V., & Wolfe, D. A. (1986). *The Sexual Abuse Fear Evaluation.* Unpublished assessment instrument. Children's Hospital of Western Ontario, London, Ontario.

Wolfe, V. V., & Wolfe, D. A. (1988). The sexually abused child. In E. J. Mash & L. G. Terdal (Eds.), *Behavioral assessment of childhood disorders* (2nd ed., pp. 670–714). New York: Guilford Press.

Wolfe, V. V., Gentile, C., & Bourdeau, P. (1987). *History of Victimization Form.* Unpublished assessment instrument. Children's Hospital of Western Ontario, London, Ontario.

Yates, A. (1982). Children eroticized by incest. *American Journal of Psychiatry, 139,* 482–485.

Yates, A., Beutler, L. E., & Crago, M. (1985). Drawings by child victims of incest. *Child Abuse and Neglect, 9,* 183–189.

6

Instrumentation and Methodological Issues in the Assessment of Sexual Arousal

William R. Farrall
Farrall Instruments, Inc., Grand Island, NE

The penile plethysmograph is not a sexual lie detector. Used properly, the penile plethysmograph can provide an accurate determination of the sexual interest and arousal patterns of offenders and nonoffenders. This valuable information greatly enhances the fair disposition and the effective treatment of offenders. In some cases, plethysmograph data provide the only accurate method of insight to the offender's disorder.

Considerable literature has been published that demonstrates the effectiveness of the penile plethysmograph in detecting sexual arousal. The practical application of this information in assessing and treating clients with paraphilias and illegal sexual activity is shown in many publications including: Blanchard et al. (1986), fetishes; Fedora (1986), exhibitionists; Fedora et al. (1987), sexual sadists; Sakheim (1985), gender preference; Abel et al. (1984), pedophilia; and Farrall and Card (1988), sex offenders.

As Earls and Marshall (1983) have stated:

> To treat a sexual offender, one must understand the process through which he arrived at the level of sexual arousal that motivated the act. This includes not only varieties of stimuli but levels of responding penile tumescence as well. There is a growing body of experimental literature revolving around measuring the sexual components of erectile responses to arousal. Such measurement techniques not only have been found to be reliable indices of early stages of such sexual arousal, important in considering treatment approaches, but also permit differentiation between appropriate and deviant arousal. (p. 336)

Pithers and Laws (1989) specify the various uses of the penile plethysmograph as (1) identification of individuals who manifest excessive arousal in response to stimuli depicting sexual abuse, (2) discernment of lack of arousal to stimuli of consenting sex, (3) determination of offenders whose arousal disorder necessitates specialized behavioral therapies, (4) minimization of distortions evident in self-reported levels of arousal, (5) evaluation of therapeutic efficiency, and (6) use in certain forms of behavior therapy.

Perhaps the most important contribution the penile plethysmograph can make to therapy is providing information concerning the relative strength of arousal to all of the possible categories of sexual stimulation. This can be particularly important in an evaluation of therapeutic progress. As stated by Murphy and Barbaree (1987):

> When a man engages in sexually deviant behavior, he may or may not be expressing a preference for deviant sexual activity, because in his natural environment there may not have been an alternative choice available. Or, a man might prefer deviant sexual behavior in another context, but engage in normative sexual behavior because of strong social sanctions against deviant behavior. (p. 14)

Stated another way, often an offense is situational simply because of the lack of availability of more desirable and socially sanctioned partners. If treatment is based solely on arrest records or confession, then it may be misdirected because it is based on apparent preference for the wrong age or gender.

As Murphy and Barbaree (1987), stated:

> The concept of stimulus control of sexual arousal is central to the clinical assessment of sexual deviants. The DSM–III declares that the paraphilias are characterized by sexual arousal in response to sexual objects or behaviors which are not part of normative arousal-activity patterns. For example, a paraphiliac rapist is classified as such because he is sexually aroused by non-consent and violence rather than normal sexual cues. The laboratory assessment attempts to provide information about men which will assist the clinician in diagnosis; if a catalogue of stimulus control of arousal could be constructed for a man, a DSM–III diagnosis could be made with more confidence. (p. 14)

The penile plethysmograph can be of great assistance in demonstrating improvements in arousal control and partner preference by making periodic assessments during the therapy process. Monthly assessments are recommended. Changes in arousal during treatment may indicate that the client has returned to his deviant activity either in fantasy or real life, or that counterconditioning therapy is proceeding as expected. Most relapse prevention programs use the penile plethysmograph to monitor progress and to determine if the client is returning to deviant fantasies. Three important relapse prevention programs are described by Pithers (1988, 1989), Laws (1985), and Marques et al. (1989).

A paper presented at the Association for the Behavioral Treatment of Sexual Abusers in Newport, Oregon, May 3–6, 1987, by the Sexual Abuse Clinic of Portland, Oregon, provides treatment outcome data on 3,000 male sex offenders that had gone through this treatment program since 1978. Treatment successes were defined as individuals who had met all of the following criteria:

> Completed all treatment sessions; demonstrated no sexual arousal (under 20 percent of full tumescence) to three test stimuli; demonstrated no deviant sexual arousal on plethysmograph testing at any annual follow-up testing session; reported no deviant covert or overt sexual behavior at any time since treatment ended; and had no legal record of any charges of, or arrests or convictions for, deviant sexual activity, even if unsubstantiated. (Sexual Abuse Clinic, p. 29)

Abel et al. (1984) showed a success rate of 79.2% for child molesters 6 to 12 months following treatment. These programs involve very comprehensive behaviorally oriented treatments; all of them use the penile plethysmograph for the original assessment and to monitor therapy.

It should be noted that client admittance to these programs is usually

TABLE 6.1

Percentage of Offenders Satisfying Criteria for Successful Treatment Outcome
($N = 3,000$)

Diagnostic category	Percent successful at time of last follow-up
Heterosexual pedophilia ($n = 1,719$)	94.7%
Homosexual pedophilia ($n = 513$)	86.4%
Heterosexual and homosexual pedophilia combined ($n = 112$)	75.7%
Exhibitionism ($n = 462$)	93.1%
Rape ($n = 87$)	73.5%
Public masturbation ($n = 45$)	91.1%
Voyeurism ($n = 42$)	88.1%
Frotteurism ($n = 36$)	80.6%
Transvestism ($n = 36$)	91.7%
Fetishism ($n = 18$)	88.8%
Obscene telephone callers ($n = 15$)	100%
Sadomasochism ($n = 15$)	80.0%
Zoophilia ($n = 12$)	100%

Source: Sexual Abuse Clinic of Portland, OR (1987).

very selective. Clients who participated in very aggressive or violent activities are usually excluded. Thus the success figures are not representative of the general population of sex offenders.

A national survey by Knopp and Stevenson (1990) of sex offender treatment programs reported that penile plethysmography was used by 21% of all juvenile treatment providers and 32% of the adult providers. In the case of the use with juveniles this was an increase of 7%, and for adults 6%, over the 1988 survey.

BRIEF DESCRIPTION OF PLETHYSMOGRAPHIC ASSESSMENT

The client sits in a comfortable chair in a small room and is presented with audio or visual stimuli, or both. A strain gauge on his penis measures his erection with such high sensitivity that the recording can show arousal even before the client can sense it. This sensitivity allows the therapist to determine both the subconscious and conscious arousal patterns. Because of the novelty, many people who are assessed have some response to the first slide, even though there is little interest in that particular model. Another problem with obtaining accurate data from a single visual image occurs when clients have an extreme preference or dislike to a particular body characteristic, such as color of hair or weight. These factors can be controlled by using several stimulus slides in the same age category and by using a combination of both audio and visual stimuli. Diagnosis is made by comparing responses of the client to various classes of stimuli. Thus, high arousal to a child's picture with low arousal to the picture of an adult is taken to be indicative of a preference to the child as a sex partner.

Conventional and Fast Run Assessments

The past 20 years shows that there are almost as many ways of doing an assessment as there are people who write papers about the penile plethysmograph. These variations can be broken down into two distinctive methods that are based on different points of view. For the purpose of this discussion, we will assume that visual stimuli are being used. The two methods will be called Conventional, because it is the most widely used technique, and Fast Run.

The major differences in these types of assessments are the amount of time the client is allowed to view the stimulus material and the way the information is interpreted. In the Conventional penile plethysmographic assessment, the time each slide is presented may range from 30 to 120 seconds, the most common being 120 seconds. In Fast Run, the stimulus times are generally 30 seconds or less. When Gene Abel (personal communication, 1988) is doing his Fast Run he presents the stimulus for only 7 seconds.

It should be noted that all the information that can be collected in the Fast Run is also collected in the Conventional Assessment. However, significant details are usually ignored in evaluating the Conventional Assessment, when the diagnostic factor is usually the highest arousal level obtained. On the Fast Run Assessment, the data are derived from both the maximum arousal in the first 7 seconds of stimulus presentation and the maximal arousal in the 14 seconds following the stimulus period. This is called poststimulus time and should not be confused with detumescence time. Perhaps the most significant aspect of the Fast Run diagnostic technique is the theory that small, but significant, arousal levels can be detected in the first 7 seconds, and that these erection levels correspond to the nonvoluntary arousal or subconscious levels of arousal. The author is convinced, through experiments with normals and offenders, that a person cannot selectively suppress an erection until tumescence reaches approximately 10% of his maximum erection. This is because the 10% level must be reached before the individual is consciously aware that he is becoming erect. Until he has this feedback, he cannot exercise control. Further, a person who is trying to produce an erection through fantasy, or to reduce the erection through some process of thought stopping, will be unable to produce or reduce an erection for approximately 15 seconds after a stimulus presentation. The therapist who understands these factors is not likely to be fooled by clients who attempt to manipulate the data.

One of the advantages of the Fast Run is that it takes less time to do an assessment. This is extremely important, especially with juveniles, who the author has found often require long detumescence periods. Usually the erection levels found in the Fast Run are smaller than those encountered in the Conventional Assessment. This does give the advantage of a shorter detumescence time after a stimulus that produces significant arousal.

A controversial issue in the field is the matter of setting the equipment for maximum arousal. Many therapists require the client to observe very exciting pornographic movies or to masturbate to obtain what is theoretically called the 100% arousal. The author sees significant problems with this procedure and furthermore, in some cases, it may be counterproductive. Some clients object to masturbation and refuse to be assessed on the ground that masturbation is against their religion. This is a very big problem with parents of teen-agers who are going to be assessed. Avoiding asking clients to masturbate will eliminate a major objection to the assessment.

INTERPRETATION OF DATA

The most commonly used indicator of sexual preference derived from the penile plethysmograph is the maximum tumescence. This measure has certain problems associated with it. For example, for some clients the arousal peak may be quite similar in several or all stimulus categories. When this happens, alternative scoring procedures that extract more information from the erection data may prove useful. These include average erection, area under the curve, detumescence time, and the rate of rise of the erection. In an experiment, Earls, Quinsey, and Castonguay (1987), compared three methods of scoring penile circumference changes. The highest proportion of variance, 52.7%, was found using z scores. When using percentage scores, the same data yielded 32.5%, while the raw scores produced 30.1%. As they stated:

> The choice among scoring methods depends on the specific objectives of the researcher/clinician. If, for example, we wish to know whether a particular subgroup of sexual offenders (rapists, pedophiles, etc.) can be distinguished from non-sex offenders, based on their patterns of penile response, a z-score transformation seems to be the logical choice, i.e., this method of data scoring is more sensitive to differences between stimulus categories thus reducing the probability of Type II errors. Furthermore, this type of research question does not require a consideration of the absolute magnitude of response. Rather, it is the relative levels of responses among stimulus categories that is of interest.
>
> Nevertheless, absolute levels of responding should not be entirely disregarded. For example, the magnitude of responses can be useful when interpreting possible ceiling effects. Absolute levels of responding are also necessary when making decisions regarding either the need for treatment or when evaluating the success of treatment. Although as yet not empirically justified, high levels of deviant sexual arousal are generally interpreted as indicating increased risk for recidivism and therefore a need for treatment; conversely, low levels of deviant arousal are rarely targeted in treatment since it is difficult to evaluate treatment success (due to floor effects). As mentioned earlier, z-scores do not provide this type of information. (p. 499)

Barbaree (Murphy & Barbaree, 1987), on the other hand, argued that z scores are not an appropriate way to present data from studies of sexual arousal because,

They distort the basic data in the raw scores and add to the "error" variance. The problem is that subjects who show very small variance due to stimulus presentations (little difference in responding to different stimuli; or "weak" stimulus control) are made to have a between stimulus variance equal to subjects who show large differences in strength of responding to different stimuli ("strong" stimulus control). This has the effect of magnifying error variance. Subjects who show minimal, or random fluctuating responding to the various stimulus presentations, have their between stimulus variance increased to match that of subjects who show strong stimulus control. In the end, subjects who respond randomly contribute as much to the group data as do subjects who respond strongly to only one class of stimuli. (p. 25)

The information derived from an accurate penile plethysmographic assessment only shows the genital arousal patterns or sexual preference of the person tested. This information cannot be used to confirm the occurrence of a past act or to predict future behavior absolutely. However, it can, in most cases, show if the individual has deviant thought patterns or fantasies. In most cases, the arrest records and the responses to the deviant behavior that precipitated the arrest agree. However, in

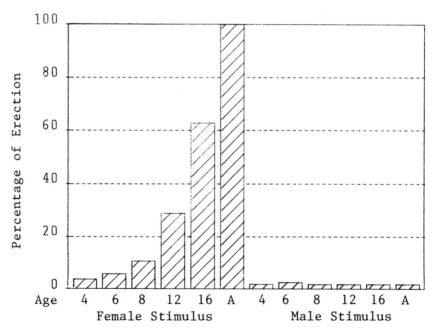

FIG. 6.1.   The sexual arousal profile for a typical, 30-year-old male nonoffender.

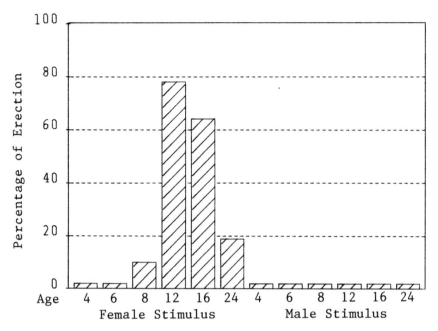

FIG. 6.2.   The sexual preference profile of a 28-year-old pedophile rapist whose victims were 12–16-year-old females.

the case of a situational victim, the plethysmographic data will most likely not agree with the arrest record or confession.

No large studies appear in the literature that compare arousal patterns of deviants and nondeviants. Richard Laws is nearing the end of a 5-year study of a large number of offenders in a treatment program. It is likely that that work will provide significant answers to many questions (Laws, 1985). Lacking this comparative information across subject populations, another approach is used in which the individual is used as his own control. To illustrate, nondeviant males usually have some degree of erection to pictures of nude females of all ages. Figure 6.1 shows the typical arousal response of an adult male nonoffender to an age range of male and female nude photographs. As the age of the model in the picture increases, the arousal increases.

Sex offenders often have very low arousal to adults and teens, but high arousal to the age group of their victims. For diagnostic purposes it is suggested that one look at the ratio of the erection of acceptable to nonacceptable victims or the ratio of nondeviant to deviant behavior. (Figs. 6.2, 6.3, and 6.4 illustrate the use of penile responses to assess sexual interests.)

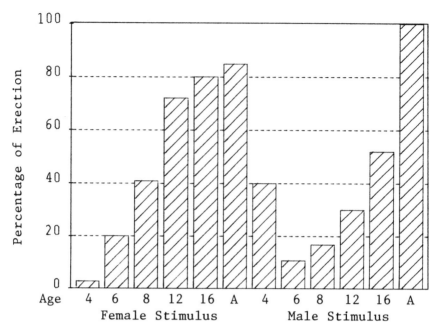

FIG. 6.3.   The sexual preference profile of a 58-year-old man denying an arrest report of fondling a 4-year-old boy. He claimed to be heterosexual and was married, but had not had sex with his wife since a heart attack 10 years previous. When confronted with the assessment data, he admitted to an incident with a 6-year-old neighbor boy, to masturbating with adult homosexual material, and claimed to have been "experimenting" with the boy to determine if he was a homosexual himself.

STIMULUS CHARACTERISTICS AND SELECTION

Julien and Over (1988) studied the effects of penile circumference change from five different modes, film, slides, spoken text, written text, and fantasy. The study reports, "The differences between modes related primarily to level of response. The highest level of physiological and subjective arousal was generated by film, while fantasy produced the lowest level of arousal. Slides, spoken-text, and written-text were equally potent, and these three modes had intermediate influence on arousal. That all modes can elicit measurable arousal in the laboratory, and at different levels, has important implications clinically and for research. Selection of the mode of stimulus presentation must depend on the aim of therapist or experimenter."

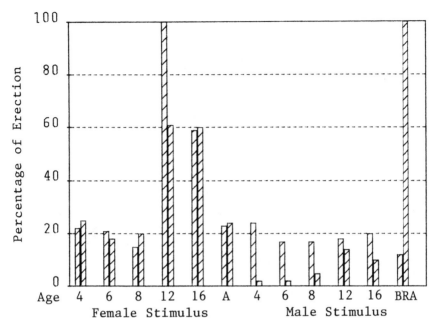

FIG. 6.4.   The sexual preference profile of two teen-age fraternal twin males. The bars on the left are the erection scores of the nondeviant twin who dates, is a good student, and is very well liked. The scores on the right are for the twin who was arrested, and admits stealing girls' underclothes for masturbation. This twin does not date, is a poor student, is not well liked, and is considered weird by his peers. The last stimulus response plotted on the extreme right is a picture of a young man wearing women's panties and holding a bra. The score to the left of it is a picture of a pair of women's panties.

Visual Still Pictures

It is generally believed that still photographs are the most useful form of stimulus presentation. Because they are so easy to control, 35-mm slides are usually chosen. The major advantage of still photographs over audio or video presentations is the ability to time the onset and duration of the stimulus. Thus, there is no possible ambiguity over the moment of presentation of the stimulus. Another advantage to using still photographs is the purity of their stimulus value. In any continuously changing stimulus, such as audio or video, it is not exactly clear to which component of the stimulus complex the client is responding. Another important characteristic of the still visual stimulus, as opposed to audio scripts, is that it more clearly defines the age, size, and appearance of the person in the stimulus for the client, not leaving this to his imagination.

In order to conduct accurate assessments, the selection of visual photographs is extremely critical. Each photograph in a given stimulus battery should have the same erotic level. The best way to do this is to have control over variables such as degree of nudity, pose, and setting. Extraneous cues must not be present. It should be obvious that results will be unreliable if a child is shown open-legged with open vagina and an adult is shown sitting nude, cross-legged in a chair. Equally unreliable would be showing an adult with an erection if this is then compared with a stimulus of a 10-year-old boy without an erection.

A set of 44 slides chosen especially for assessments has been prepared for a multisite study group and is available from Farrall Instruments. The study is under the direction of Gene Abel and Vernon Quinsey (personal communication, 1988). The study is described as follows:

> Aim: Various treatment centers for paraphiliacs have traditionally used their own, idiosyncratic sexual stimuli when evaluating the age and gender preferences of clients. This lack of standard stimuli makes it difficult to compare assessment results from different centers and may account for some of the variants in assessment outcome studies. The aim of this study was to develop a set of standard stimuli that could be used in assessing the age and gender preferences of paraphiliacs.
>
> Methods: Nine treatment centers agreed by consensus that the stimuli should be colored slides, each depicting a nude, single person of caucasian race, easily identifiable as male or female, each facing the camera and not in a sexually provocative pose. All persons depicted would have completed photographic releases. The slide images would occupy proportionally the same percentage of the slide and all stimuli other than the human image would be replaced by a dull, grey background. In addition, stimuli depicting neutral landscapes would be developed. For each gender, there were four slides per age category of 4, 8, 12, 16, and 24 years of age plus the neutral landscapes, for a total of 44 slides. From a pool of 80 slides, 102 individuals rated slides according to their age and attractiveness, deficit categories were replaced and the final 44 slides were rated according to the Tanner sexual maturity scale. The final set was then randomized into two independently randomized sets.

The Tanner Scale (1962) is an index of human developmental growth which includes physical changes from birth to maturity. It is used by pediatricians to describe physical developmental stages. At a National Institute of Mental Health meeting in Tampa, the author proposed using the Tanner Scale as a supplemental description for visual stimulus materials (Farrall, 1986). The use of the Tanner Scale has also been suggested by Fuller et al. (1988).

Pornography Laws Affect Therapists

There is one caution regarding the possession and use of photographs of nude children. The Child Protection Act of 1984 makes sale, possession, and use of photographs of nude children illegal. There are no exclusions for therapeutic use of these materials. Most states have also enacted similar legislation. However, laws in Colorado and Illinois do have exclusions for therapists. Therapists should work with local authorities to protect themselves from prosecution.

The Society for the Scientific Study of Sex has published a statement regarding the use of pornographic materials for research and therapy (1987). Reimer (1984) of the Congressional Research Service can provide an "Issue Brief on Child Pornography." A privately published paper, "Dealing with Pornography Laws" is available from Farrall (1985). This paper presents a plan of advising law enforcement officials in the therapist's area that materials that are considered illegal pornographic materials are being used in the treatment of sex deviants. When law enforcement agents understand the usefulness of the materials in controlled therapeutic situations, there is a good possibility that the pornography laws will be selectively enforced. A bulletin of the National District Attorneys Association (NDAA, 1990) discusses this issue in light of the Supreme Court's decision in the Ohio v. Osborne case. The case does not directly deal with the use of child pornography for scientific purposes but may signal that truly legitimate scientific or educational uses of otherwise prohibited material does not violate the law.

Audiotapes

Audio is the second most common stimulus modality presently used. It often supplements assessment data gained using visual stimuli. Many sexual and aggressive acts are not easily photographed and thus are not available in photographic form. It is difficult to convey aggressive acts in a still photograph, especially in ethically proper ways. Even a vast collection of visual stimuli would never cover the full range from normal to bizarre activities in which deviates can participate. Audio stimuli can, in most cases, solve these problems. Audiotapes are available for the usual sexual and aggressive types of behavior (Abel, 1989; Jensen, 1989), and it is relatively easy for the therapist to customize a tape for an individual client with an unusual paraphilia or behavior. At present, there are no legal restrictions to this type of recording when used in a therapeutic or assessment setting. The preparation of audiotapes usually starts with the client being asked to narrate his fantasy or to describe an acknowledged deviant act. In the case of a client in denial, police records of the crime or the victim's statements can be used to develop a scenario. The narration is then edited by the therapist to remove extraneous material and to condense it. The final narration is then recorded by the client, therapist, or an actor. Most scripts are around 3 minutes in length. Some clients will not become aroused in less than 2 minutes and arousal does not usually increase after 3 minutes.

Videotapes

Videotapes or motion pictures are seldom used as stimulus material in the plethysmographic assessment. Using moving pictures makes it difficult to determine exactly when the onset of stimulus occurred. The major reason that motion pictures are not used is because they produce so much arousal that the ability to discriminate responses is very poor. Stated another way, both normal and offenders tend to "turn on" with high arousal to both normal and deviant stimuli. Some therapists use video presentations to determine the client's maximum arousal to calibrate the equipment and to select the proper size of strain gauge.

Video Stills

Videotapes with still pictures and an audioscript are a new type of stimulus presently being used in assessment centers. One available type is known as the Card-Farrall Stimulus Tape (version IV, 1989). In this method a matrix of 19 segments each provide 85 seconds of audio followed by four still pictures showing four different individuals designed to elicit a heightened response to the audio material. The stimulus matrix includes males and females, with ages ranging from infant, preschool, grammar school, adolescents, and adults. In all but the infant segments, persuasive and coercive segments are counterbalanced. The 19th segment depicts pure violence. One study using these stimuli discriminated perfectly between experimental normals and deviants, but failed to discriminate across other dimensions, possibly due to the very small size of the experimental population. A new study with a larger N and more refined stimuli is under way.

EQUIPMENT

Early plethysmograph apparatus were assembled by researchers using general purpose physiological recorders of the type commonly used in medical schools. Some of this type of equipment is still being used by

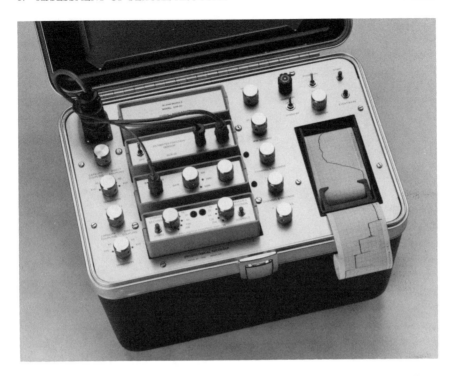

PHOTOGRAPH 6.1. A strip chart recorder, the SP-300, manufactured by Farrall Instruments, Inc.

those interested in basic assessment research. Today, two classes of assessment apparatus are in common use. They can be characterized as the strip chart recorder and the computer-aided recorder. The most common type is illustrated in Photograph 6.1. The recording is made on a 50-mm width of heat-sensitive paper.

The erection-sensing gauges all require a Wheatstone bridge circuit in the input amplifier so the resistance of the gauge in the flaccid condition can be matched to produce a reading of zero on the recorder. The strip chart recorder is a self-contained apparatus with the bridge circuit, gauge, amplifier, and recorder.

The computer-aided recorder is shown in Photograph 6.2. The computer receives the physiological data from a special converter, which has the same type of input section as the strip chart recorder. An analog to digital converter feeds the computer via RS 232 serial port with an optical isolator for safety. Personal computers were not designed or manufactured with isolation circuits that would enable them to have input circuits safely connected to humans. Leakage currents that may

PHOTOGRAPH 6.2.   Computer-type assessment apparatus being used.

present a risk of heart failure to patients are present in apparatus that is operated from the powerline.

Safety standards for the plethysmograph apparatus are established by three groups; FDA (1976, 1990), The Association for the Advancement of Medical Instrumentation (1985), and Underwriters' Laboratories (1985). The standards are basically the same. Because the plethysmograph connects to the human body and it is used to diagnose people for treatment, the manufacture and distribution of the equipment is regulated by FDA. The Association for the Advancement of Medical Instrumentation is a non-profit organization composed of doctors, engineers and manufacturers that set standards of performance and safety for medical devices. Its standards are generally accepted by FDA and UL. Underwriters' Laboratories is a non-profit testing laboratory that assists in establishing standards for electronic medical devices, electrical components, and materials associated with fire or fire fighting. Electronic apparatus used in accredited hospitals and in several major cities must pass UL specification and be "listed."

In order to assure client safety, some method of circuit isolation is necessary between the computer and any metal parts that are in contact with the client, that is, electrodes or gauges. Most medical devices use a device called an optical isolator. The optical isolator is a component in which the signal to be transmitted illuminates a light-emitting diode and is received by a photo diode. There is a transparent high-voltage insulator between the two diodes. Light is the "contact" between the input and output of the optical isolator. No electrical connection is present between the input and output.

Even if a computer has a UL listing, it probably is not safe for connection to humans. Computers are usually listed by UL under a business machine category that does not require the high standard of a medical device.

The computer also acts as a stimulus timer to control either a slide projector, tape player or videocassette recorder. The erection plot is shown on a cathode ray tube screen, stored on floppy disks and printed out on a printer. At the end of the session, a printout provides linearized data for each stimulus presentation. The data include minimum, maximum, area under the curve, standard deviation and detumescence time.

ERECTION SENSING

As a man becomes sexually aroused, several physiological parameters change. Zuckerman (1971) demonstrated that the best indicator of male arousal is penile tumescence. Two general types of transducers have been used to measure erectile response: volumetric and circumferential. The most accurate measure is the phallometric, or volumetric, device. This consists of a glass cylinder into which the penis is inserted. Erection forces air out of the closed cylinder and is detected by a sensitive pressure transducer. This device was invented by Freund and described by Freund, Sedlack, and Knob (1965). It is used at the Clark Institute of Psychiatry in Canada and at Prince of Wales Hospital, Randwick, Australia. Due to the cumbersome aspect of the glass tube and the fact that it may inhibit the erectile response, this sensor is not widely used.

Circumferential erection sensors are widely used because they are easy to use and to calibrate. Their major advantage is that they do not restrict the vertical movement of the penis. Barlow, Becker, Leitenberg, and Agras (1970) invented the metal clip gauge, which uses two strain elements cemented to a metal clip. These elements are used by engineers to test strain on mechanical elements such as airplane wings and bridges. As an erection occurs, the semicircular sections on the clip, which are in contact with the penis, transmit a bending movement to the saddle part of the gauge where the strain elements are located. One of the elements is in stress and the resistance increases while the other element is in compression and the resistance decreases. The gauge resistance is around 120 ohms. The Barlow gauge is very stable and easy to calibrate.

Fisher, Gross, and Zuch (1965) developed the mercury-in-rubber strain gauge. A sylastic rubber tube with electrodes at each end is filled with mercury. As an erection occurs, the tube stretches, causing the electric current flowing through the mercury to drop due to a smaller cross-section and a longer length of the conductor. The resistance of the mercury-in-rubber gauge is around 0.3 ohms.

A recent modification in the mercury-in-rubber gauge substitutes an indium/gallium alloy in place of the mercury. Mercury gauges are not very stable and have a limited shelf life, due to the chemical interaction between the mercury and the electrodes. The indium/gallium-in-rubber gauge does not have this problem. The indium/gallium gauge has a resistance of 0.6 ohms. Both types of rubber gauges are difficult to calibrate but are widely used. Because their cost is about one-fifth that of the Barlow gauge, they are used when it is desirable to assign a gauge to one client for his exclusive use.

When used with the appropriate circuitry, all three types of gauges have the same sensitivity. They are shown in Photograph 6.3. The aluminum step cylinder in this photograph is called a "cone." It is used as a physical standard for calibration of the gauges.

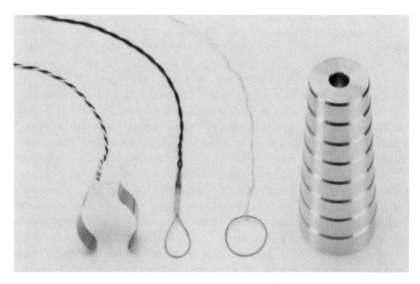

PHOTOGRAPH 6.3. Erection sensing sensors and calibration cone. Sensors left to right; Barlow, Indium-Gallium and Mercury gauges.

LABORATORY

Room Variations

Great variations are possible in the design of assessment rooms. Fig. 6.5 shows an ideal room. Rooms have been made in closets, corners of rooms, and free-standing cubicles. One therapist has four small client rooms adjoining a master control room, where one technician can test four clients at the same time. Laws and Osborne (1983) has published a comprehensive paper on setting up an assessment laboratory. A description of Laws's latest assessment laboratory is described in "Relapse Prevention with Sex Offenders" (Laws, 1989, pp. 272–273). The major consideration in the design of a room is to provide a client with space that will reduce the anxiety and trauma of the assessment. The client is well aware of the serious consequences of "failing" the test. It can be a very frightening experience. This anxiety is probably one of the reasons why approximately 20% of those assessed fail to develop penile response to erotic stimuli. Even though careful psychological preparation of the client by the personnel doing the assessment is the most important factor in reducing the fear, room design can be a big factor. The following considerations should be given to construction of an assessment room.

Size

The room should be at least 4 × 6 feet; a better size is 5 × 7 feet. This size seems big enough to prevent claustrophobic feelings, and yet is small enough to make the client feel intimate with the projection screen or television.

Sound Reduction

It is very important to reduce or eliminate extraneous sounds. If a new room is to be constructed, it is suggested that it have a wood, 2-×-4 stud wall with ⅝-inch dry wall on both sides. The studs should be on 12-inch or 16-inch centers and the space filled with fiberglass insulation. If noxious odor conditioning is not anticipated to be used in the room, an excellent sound-reducing wall and ceiling covering is carpet. Any cracks in the wall, such as holes through which to project slides, or clearance under the door will defeat the best sound reduction measures. A small glass window can be used for the projector port. Some noise reduction is possible by having the client wear a good-quality headphone. In some

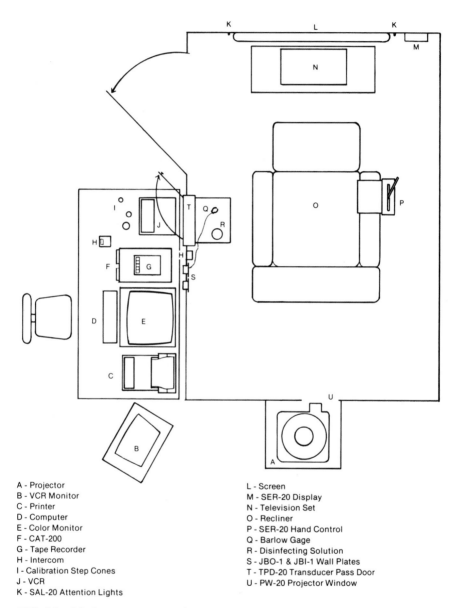

A - Projector
B - VCR Monitor
C - Printer
D - Computer
E - Color Monitor
F - CAT-200
G - Tape Recorder
H - Intercom
I - Calibration Step Cones
J - VCR
K - SAL-20 Attention Lights

L - Screen
M - SER-20 Display
N - Television Set
O - Recliner
P - SER-20 Hand Control
Q - Barlow Gage
R - Disinfecting Solution
S - JBO-1 & JBI-1 Wall Plates
T - TPD-20 Transducer Pass Door
U - PW-20 Projector Window

FIG. 6.5.   Ideal assessment room layout.

situations, it may be necessary to mask extraneous sounds. This can be done through the use of a small, white noise generator.

Ventilation

If the room is not served by both a forced air inlet and outlet, a small blower should be placed in the wall. This blower should run during the assessment and will provide an extra advantage of providing a small masking noise.

Projector Location

The projector can be located in the client's room but the preferred location is outside the client's room, either by projecting through a small glass window or projecting on a back projection screen. The main advantage of placing the projector on the outside is that stimulus slides can be changed without entering the client's area. When projecting through a window, as shown on the room drawing, the window should be wide enough to allow one to sight along the projector for focusing. A 100- to 150-mm zoom lens is very convenient for adjusting the projector to the exact screen size.

Screen

A high-quality screen should be used to make the stimulus slides appear as life-like as possible. The screen should be large enough to fill the horizontal width of the wall. If a television is to be used, it should also be as large as reasonable. Generally a video monitor will produce a better quality picture than a standard television. Most videotape recorders have the capability of directly driving a monitor and eliminate a great deal of interference and noise that occur when using the VHF output to the television set.

Room Locks/Security

While the client may feel better if the door is provided with a lock, it is not advisable. If the client becomes violent or suicidal, it will be necessary to enter the room without delay.

Observation Window

There is considerable controversy about using a one-way vision window
in the side of the assessment room. Rooms usually do not have windows
because it is an invasion of client privacy. There is no question that a
window will add to the anxiety of the client. Although a window is very
useful as a safety measure and is helpful in seeing if the client is
attending to the screen, it necessitates that the technician operate in
semidarkness.

Transducer Pass Door

An 8-inch × 10-inch pass door should be installed in the side of the wall
of the client's room. The transducer can be calibrated on the equipment
desk outside of the client's room and passed through the door to the
client. After the session, the client can drop the transducer into a con-
tainer of disinfectant, which is placed on the ledge extending from the
door. This is a great convenience to the technician.

DISINFECTION OF THE STRAIN GAUGES
AND VAGINAL SENSORS USED IN MEASURING
SEXUAL AROUSAL

According to the United States Disease Control Center in Atlanta (personal communication, June 3, 1985) all sexually transmitted diseases that
might contaminate either penile or vaginal sensors can be destroyed by a
10-minute disinfection with a dialdehyde solution. For additional information on disinfection techniques see "Chemical Disinfection," by
Favero (1983).

There are many disinfecting materials that are available, but many of
them will damage the delicate strain gauges and vaginal sensors. Extensive trials have been conducted using Cidex 7, manufactured by Surgikos (1984), and the author recommends it as both meeting the manufacturer's criteria for not damaging the electronic sensors, and also
meeting the disease center's requirements. Overnight immersion of sensors in Cidex 7 will damage the sensors. The best disinfecting technique
is to place a small plastic cup of Cidex in the assessment chamber. When
the assessment is finished the client is told to remove the sensor and
place it in the cup of Cidex. The technician, using rubber gloves, takes
the sensor to a sink and washes it with tap water to make certain that, if

there is any contamination on the gauge or on its cable, it is washed away. After this rinse, the sensor should again be placed in the Cidex solution and left for 10 minutes. It is then removed, rinsed again with tap water and allowed to dry.

Some of the anxiety caused by the assessment can be traced to the client's fear that he or she may pick up a STD (sexually transmitted disease) by using a reusable sensor. Usually a frank, knowledgeable discussion regarding the precautions that are being taken to prevent this will be sufficient. In some cases, especially in prisons, a different approach is used. In this case, the clients purchase their own gauge, which is used only on them. One caution: This procedure does not protect the therapist from coming in contact with a contaminated gauge; therefore the disinfection procedures should still be used.

STEP-BY-STEP DESCRIPTION OF A TYPICAL ASSESSMENT PROCEDURE

This section describes the plethysmographic assessment step by step. Detailed explanation of each step is given in specific sections to follow.

1. The client is brought into the room and told to make himself comfortable in the reclining chair.

2. The client is given a brief explanation of the room, the equipment visable in the room and the procedure to be used.

3. The client is then asked to sign the informed consent agreement.

4. He is told that the therapist will leave the room and is given instructions to remove his pants and underwear. He is instructed how to obtain an accurate measure of his flaccid penis. One procedure for measuring the flaccid penis is to use a small scotch tape dispenser and a pen that will mark the tape. Place a pen mark across the tape about half an inch from the end of the tape. The client is instructed to pull off a length of tape and wrap it around his penis. Then he is to mark a line across the tape exactly over the first line. He then removes the tape and places it on a strip of paper. Using a metric ruler, the therapist measures between the lines. This distance is considered the flaccid circumference.

5. After this measurement is obtained the client is instructed to sit down and to relax.

6. The correct gauge is selected, based on the size of the client's penis and connected to the recording equipment.

7. The recording equipment is turned on and allowed to warm up for 2 minutes before calibration. Preliminary equipment adjustments can be made at this time and the gauge should be placed on the calibra-

tion cone on the step that is 5-mm smaller than the measured flaccid penis size.

8. The gauge is calibrated using the procedure in the section on Calibration.

9. The gauge is removed from the calibration cone set and given to the client with instructions regarding placement. A board is placed between the arms of the chair, giving the client someplace to place his hands and help prevent efforts to fake responses.

10. The client is told to relax as much as possible but to remain alert and not to go to sleep. He should try not to move. There will be a 5-minute relaxation period to obtain a baseline and to help calm the client.

11. During the relaxation the therapist should make certain the recording is not below the zero or baseline of the recording instrument. If the measured flaccid value is incorrect, the calibration will have to be redone. The therapist should also make certain there is some fluxion, or small movement, of the plethysmographic trace. Lack of some small variation may signal that the client has not placed the gauge on his penis. If there is a small regular oscillation of the trace it may be due to the gauge being on a small artery. When this is the case, the client should be asked to move the gauge a short distance. Usually this will correct the problem. If not, the assessment can still be effectively done with this artifact being only a small annoyance.

12. When the 5 minutes are up the final instructions should be read or presented by tape recording to the client. The instructions provided by the Multi-site Study Group (Abel, 1987) are a good example:

"I am going to show you a series of slides that includes males and females of various ages. You will see each slide for 30 seconds. During each slide presentation I want you to imagine yourself sexually involved with the person shown in the slide. That is, I want you to visualize as clearly as possible that you are having a sexual interaction with the person in the picture. If you find yourself becoming sexually aroused, just let it happen. After each slide I will ask you to do two things. First, I want you to tell me how mentally aroused you became by estimating a percentage between zero and 100%. Second, I want you to estimate to the nearest 5% how much penile erection you produced. Do this also on a scale between zero and 100%. Remember, if you become upset or uncomfortable during the session, just let me know and we will stop. Do you have any questions?"

13. The assessment is started by showing the first slide. When using noncomputerized equipment it will be necessary for the therapist to time the stimulus and detumescence periods accurately. An instant reset stopwatch is essential for this timing.

14. If an erection does not diminish to meet the detumescence criterion, (near baseline) by 30 seconds following termination of the slide presentation, the client should be encouraged to use mental arithmetic such as counting down from 1,000 or talking about a nonsexual subject. If the criterion is not reached after 3 minutes, proceed, scoring the next erection based on the lowest recorded point during the new presentation.

15. At the conclusion of the last detumescence period in the set of slides the client should be told to carefully remove the gauge and place it in the cup of disinfecting solution.

16. The client should be given any debriefing he may need.

CALIBRATION

None of the gauges presently available for sensing male arousal is linear. This means that an erection reading of 20 may not be twice as physically large as a reading of 10. Figure 6.6 shows typical error readings in the three types of gauges. It is not uncommon to find errors of 15% of full scale.

If nonlinearized data are used in diagnosis of the differential responses to deviant and nondeviant behavior, an incorrect diagnosis may

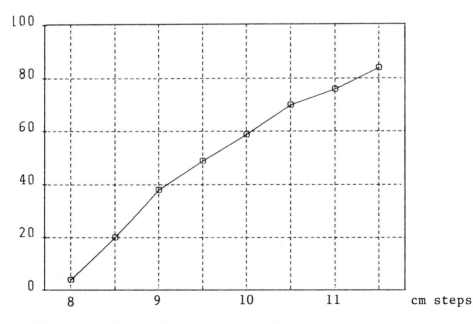

FIG. 6.6.   Linearity error of a typical strain gauge for sensing erection. Note the bow in the mid range. Each point on the X axis is an equal change in circumference. A perfectly linear gauge would have a straight line. Correct techniques eliminate this error.

result. Often the significant arousal values between deviant and nondeviant stimuli are rather close. This is especially true in the case of age-related stimuli, for example, teen-agers and adults of the same sex. An accurate assessment may be impossible if the effect of the nonlinearity is not considered.

A mathematical adjustment of the data to compensate for this error is called linearization. The first step in linearization requires calibration of the gauge to a physical standard. Briefly, the calibration procedure is as follows:

1. The client is instructed to measure the circumference of his penis. The gauge size is chosen to be 5-mm smaller than the measured size.

2. The gauge is placed on the cone circumference, which is 5-mm smaller than the flaccid penis as measured in Step 1. The smaller size is chosen because the client often produces a small penile change during the measuring process and the gauge must have some deflection so it doesn't become loose.

3. The baseline of the recording equipment is adjusted to zero using the bridge balance control.

4. The gauge is moved to the cone step which is estimated to be the maximum erection. Most clients will have a maximum erection change of within 30-mm of the flaccid state. Run a short strip of the recording paper.

5. The recording indicator will deflect and the sensitivity control should be adjusted so the indicator is at the predicted full-scale maximum erection point on the recording system. A short strip of recording paper should be run.

6. The gauge is moved to the next 5-mm smaller circumference on the cone. At this point, and from now on during the calibration and assessment, NO control settings should be changed. Run a short strip of paper.

7. The same procedure should be followed on each of the smaller steps running a short strip of paper on each step and marking the circumference size near the corresponding line on each step.

8. When the gauge has been moved back to the cone size which was chosen to represent the baseline, or unaroused state, the trace should come back within 2% of baseline. At this point, run another short strip of paper to indicate the final baseline. Assume the full scale or left side of the recording paper to be 100%. If the apparatus is properly calibrated and the error data determined in the calibration are used to compensate for the nonlinearity, the data will have no more than 3% error. In other words, when the calibration and linearization procedure is followed the system has an accuracy of 3% of the maximum anticipated erection (full scale or lefthand side of the chart).

Linearization of Data

As stated, because neither the rubber tube type of gauges or Barlow gauges gives equal electrical change for equal changes of circumference, it is necessary to calibrate the gauge to the chart paper. It is then possible to develop a ruler that can be used to measure an individual's recording at any point and accurately compare it from test to test and with other clients. In order to interpolate between calibration steps and to make it more convenient to read the printout, an individual "calibration ruler" must be constructed. This ruler can then be placed at any place on the printout and allow easy determination of the value. The Farrall CAT system performs the data correction steps automatically. Linearization of the data in noncomputer systems is as follows.

Take a 1-inch strip of chart paper and position it at the start of the calibration overlapping the righthand and lefthand grid marks. Using a pen, mark the 1-inch "ruler strip" to correspond with the mark the pen drew when the gauge was on zero, then mark each calibration step. Label each mark with the actual size of the circumference at each step.

This ruler can now be used to measure the pen trace made during the collection of patient data. Interpolation will be necessary between steps. Using this procedure will give accurate measures of arousal from time to time and from client to client. The arousal is thought of in terms of millimeters of change.

When a chart is to be "read," the calibration ruler is laid on the chart with the baseline mark of the calibration ruler lined up with the baseline on the chart. See where the erection trace intersects the edge of the calibration ruler. Read the value from the calibration ruler. Interpolate if necessary. This value is the erection value corrected for the nonlinearity of the gauge.

COMBATING FAKING

There is a great deal of concern over the possibility that clients can control the outcome of the plethysmographic assessment. This concern is well founded. However, experienced penile plethysmograph operators and readers can, in most cases, determine if the client is attempting to influence the data to his advantage. Even successful attempts to fake the data will be seen by the experienced person and often the real data can be discerned. In some cases, the operator can change the instructions or stimulus materials during the assessment in order to obtain accurate response information. In the worst case, the attempt to control will result in an invalid assessment but the operator will know that it is invalid. The following describes some of the strategies or maneuvers that people use in an attempt to fake or obscure their data.

COGNITIVE IMAGERY

In cognitive imagery, the client attempts to suppress his true arousal to deviant stimuli and, occasionally, to enhance the erection to nondeviant stimuli. It seems easier to suppress arousal than to enhance arousal. When a deviant stimulus is presented, the client concentrates on a disagreeable thought such as having his teeth drilled, being punished, vomiting, or other unenjoyable experiences. If the client tries to enhance responses to a stimulus depicting an adult who is not of interest to him, he may visualize the woman as a child, concentrating on the face and ignoring signs of adult development.

Selective suppression of arousal to deviant stimuli is usually easy to spot. It shows up on the chart in two ways; usually both clues are present but either can be alone. First, arousal is shown by the characteristic increase in erection followed by a decrease. In selective suppression, a maximum penile excursion occurs in the range of 10% to 20% of full scale. After 5 to 10 seconds of suppression, arousal goes back up. It is believed that the following takes place: The client sees the stimuli and determines to suppress arousal. The process of imagining the noxious counterimage and concentrating on it until becoming detumescent usually requires 10 to 15 seconds.

When the erection drops below approximately 10%, the client cannot control his erection because he loses the feedback necessary for control. Often the erection goes up; the client senses this, and starts suppression again. It is not unusual to see four to six of these sequences of tumescence–detumescence in a 2-minute erotic stimulation period. Earls and Marshall (1983) studied low-level arousal and suggested that males can detect circumferential tumescence below 10%, but are unable to control its occurrence.

A second suggestion of selective suppression in this situation is seen by examining the detumescence period. The stimulus period may show little or no arousal. During the detumescence period, the erection goes up, usually in the first few seconds. It appears that in this case, the client has been able to suppress during the stimulus but relaxes when the stimulus goes away, allowing himself to respond to a pleasurable after-image. This effect also may be caused by his relaxation in the absence of the stimulus. He feels he does not have to fight his interest any longer.

Apparently some offenders are unable to suppress selectively, but can suppress all stimulus segments by using such cognitive methods. This is

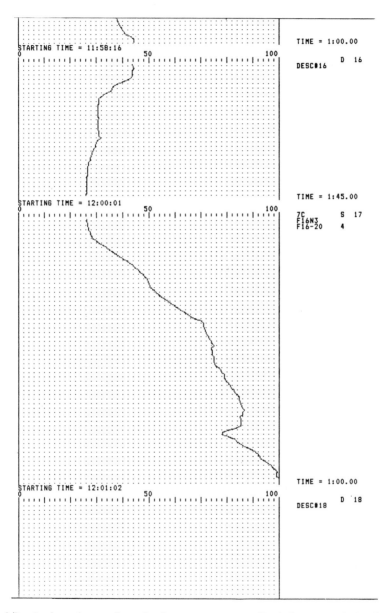

FIG. 6.7.   Analog printout of erection from a computer penile plethysmograph showing a natural response to a visual stimulus.

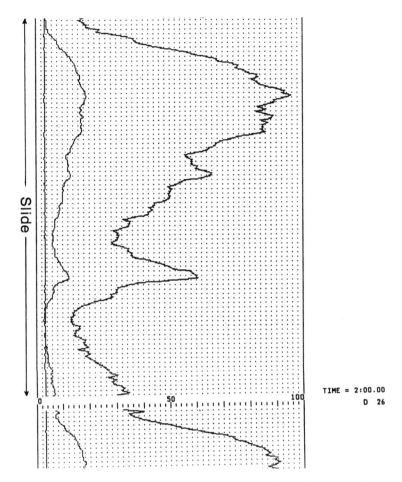

Slide

TIME = 2:00.00

D 26

FIG. 6.8.   Analog printout of erection from a computer penile plethysmograph system.
The client is suppressing as evidenced by the increase and decrease in penile circumference and the upward swing when the stimulus is removed. The lower trace is the calibrated
circumference change on the base of 30-mm change as an anticipated maximum. The
upper trace is the value of the lower trace multiplied by 5.

the most difficult type of faking to detect. Using a high sensitivity
sometimes helps with these individuals. Since there is almost always
some arousal, setting the instrument's sensitivity at a level that requires
more than 30-mm change from baseline to full scale will dull the sensitivity to the point that small arousal changes will not be seen. It is difficult
for clients to maintain this "blanket" suppression over a long session.
Therefore, continue the session to the end even when it looks as if there
is no arousal.

Physical Manipulation

In one case, the client placed the gauge on a short length of pipe obtained from the prison shop, which he carried into the room in his pocket. This was very easy to detect since the penile plethysmograph trace was an absolutely straight line.

Clients sometimes try to tug on the strain gauge wire to show an increase in erection during the "nondeviant" stimulus. This does not work at all with the Barlow gauge but is somewhat effective with the indium/gallium or mercury gauges. This is easy to detect because the trace changes abruptly. An easy counter to this type of faking is to use a board between the arms of the chair. This gives the client a place to rest his arms and keeps his hands aways from the gauge.

Closing Eyes

During visual stimulus presentations, clients often close their eyes or look away from the screen to avoid responding to visual stimuli. A good strategy to obviate this type of cheating is to ask the client to describe the stimulus he is viewing. Often all that is necessary is to ask a simple question, such as "What color of hair does the girl have?". While not necessary, some laboratories use a television monitor to observe the eyes or have the room arranged to allow visual observation.

Holding Breath

Some clients try holding their breath with the idea it will affect erection. It will not. It is a good indication, however, that the client is trying to influence the recording. This behavior can be detected by either a numotach or monitoring galvanic skin resistance. This is not a common problem and actually has little, if any, effect on outcome.

Muscle Constriction

Clients often constrict their rectal sphincter by manipulation of the pubococcygeus muscle. This introduces artifact but does not control erection. It usually shows up on a galvanic skin response channel.

Drug Usage

Some clients use various prescription or nonprescription drugs in an attempt to reduce overall arousal. Others masturbate as much as possible before the assessment. In institutions, these factors can be reduced by not making an assessment appointment in advance.

Clients with diabetes have lower arousals, but the differential between deviant and nondeviant stimuli are still usually significant diagnostically. Deperovora and other hormone-type drugs also affect arousal. It has not been demonstrated whether this is selective or general. If a client is on medication it is important to determine how the drug may affect arousal.

SPECIAL PROBLEMS IN ASSESSING ADOLESCENT CLIENTS

Adolescents have arousal patterns similar to adults, except that they are more easily aroused and their detumescence time is considerably longer than adults. It is thus necessary to use "talk down" procedures after arousal in order to shorten the detumescence time. It has been the author's experience that it is not uncommon for some adolescents without this sort of assistance to require more than 10 minutes to detumesce. Another consideration with adolescents is that some critics argue adolescents shouldn't be subjected to the sadomasochistic stimulus materials that are used in an adult assessment. If the adolescents were not involved in the adult-type crimes or behavior, the chances are they would not be in a situation of having to go through an assessment (also, see the remarks concerning masturbation under "Conventional and Fast Run Assessments" in this chapter).

CHALLENGES AND DEFENSE OF THE USE OF THE PENILE PLETHYSMOGRAPH IN ASSESSING OFFENDERS

Hall (1988) questioned the validity of the plethysmograph basically on the grounds that some subjects can alter their arousal response at will. In spite of an overwhelming body of literature proving the validity and usefulness of plethysmography in treatment and assessment of sex offenders, Simon and Schouten (1991) stated:

> The validity and clinical utility of plethysmography in the assessment and treatment of sexual deviance remain to be established. At the same time, basic questions relating to the significance of physiological aspects of the human sexual response must be addressed. Future work in this area should focus not only on the appropriateness of plethysmography in

typical clinical and research applications with forensic populations but also should respond to the need for empirical and theoretical knowledge about human sexuality in general.

McConaghy (1989) provided a critical review of the validity and ethics of penile circumference measurement and sexual arousal.

On the positive side of using the penile plethysmograph, a monograph by Murphy and Barbaree (1987) concluded, "Studies which compare the erectile responses of rapists, child molesters, and incest offenders with nonoffenders are reviewed as are studies which relate erectile responses of offenders to their offense history, and to recidivism. These studies speak to the criterion validity of these measures."

Annon (1988) in discussing the reliability and validity of penile plethysmography in rape and child molestation cases states, "It is the author's opinion that the methods and procedures involved in psychophysiological measurement of genital blood flow (plethysmography) in males and females in general, and in sex offenders in particular, have been sufficiently established so as to have gained general acceptance in the fields of psychology and psychiatry and in the area of assessment and treatment of sexual offenders, in particular, thus meeting the Frye standards (1923). The author has performed such assessments at the request of prosecuting and defense attorneys, parole boards, and circuit and family court judges. He has testified at length on these procedures and their results in the federal, circuit, district, and family courts of Hawaii."

Laws and Osborne (1983) summarize the possibility of over-interpretation of the data and thus drawing unwarranted conclusions.

Does the presence of high levels of arousal to rape, pedophilic, or other deviant stimuli in a laboratory mean that surely the person will rape, molest children, or otherwise disport himself in a deviant fashion? Of course, it does not. Undeniably, sexual arousal is considerably more than just penile erection. The erection response is not even present during the commission of some deviant sexual acts and, when present, the offender may or may not use his genitals in the act itself. Nonetheless, if in an assessment . . . a males shows a very large erection response to a deviant sexual stimulus, and very little or no response to a nondeviant stimulus, this is more than presumptive evidence that he is more sexually attracted to the former than the latter. This would be a particularly reasonable conclusion if the man had a known history of sexual deviance. Such data, however, do not mean that he will necessarily act upon his arousal; they do mean that he may be at risk to do so, and in the case of a known sex offender, that is reason enough to justify therapeutic intervention. . . . Deviant sexual arousal is deviant sexual behavior. That is what the data show.

USE OF THE PENILE PLETHYSMOGRAPH IN THE CRIMINAL JUSTICE SYSTEM

It is the author's opinion, which is shared by many but not all of those doing assessments, that penile plethysmograph data should be used in court only after the client is found guilty. The data obtained cannot prove innocence or guilt. It does show deviant interest patterns, which could indicate that the client may act on the deviant thoughts. It is important to know that some offenders do not show arousal to deviant stimuli when tested with a penile plethysmograph and some nonoffenders who show arousal to deviant stimuli during this test do not offend. Clearly, lack of arousal does not prove lack of interest or innocence. On the other hand a response to deviant stimuli does at least demonstrate inappropriate arousal, which in itself is clinically important.

The deviant arousal profile of an offender obtained from a penile plethysmograph can provide extremely useful information to the criminal justice system, but should be limited to recommendations or disposition of the convicted offender. The problem for attorneys and plethysmographic assessors is to see that the information is used in a manner that will enhance justice.

In some cases the assessor can resolve ethical issues by becoming a friend of the court. Assessment results are provided to the plaintiff's and the defendant's counsel and to the judge. The assessor should enter into this type of agreement with the court before the assessment is conducted.

Use of the Expert Witness

The U. S. court system is an adversarial system. It was designed to pit one side against the other as a sort of check and balance. This is usually played to the extreme. The attitude of the attorneys is to seek justice by, on one side, trying to prove guilt and, on the other side, to ensure that guilt has been proven. Procedural and technical matters can sometimes overshadow the facts. In court the penile plethysmograph data are presented by the expert witness. The witness could be called by either the plaintiff's attorney or the defense attorney. An outstanding paper by Jensen and Jewell (1988) illuminates the role and responsibility of the sex offender expert.

Travin, Cullen, and Melella (1988) discussed the admissibility of expert testimony and problems of the ethical use of the penile plethysmograph in the legal context in their paper, "The Use and Abuse of Erection Measurements: A Forensic Perspective."

An attorney will use an expert witness for several reasons: (1) when the burden of proof is too complex for the average person, (2) to smuggle in hearsay or otherwise inadmissible "evidence", (3) when evidence is more believable from an expert and (4) when proof needs an impressive, professional touch (Hillsman, 1988).

The opposing attorney's job is to discredit the expert witness by (1) challenging his or her credentials, (2) discrediting the state of scientific knowledge by arguing that a reasonable opinion cannot be asserted, even by an expert witness, and (3) eliminating hypothetical questioning (Goodier, 1988).

Undermining credibility may be based on licensing, the expert's educational level, specialized education, publications, continuing education and by any kind of questionable ethical behavior by the expert. Licensing is an important aspect to the credibility of the witness. Every state requires the M.D. (psychiatrist) to be licensed. Most states have licensing requirements for psychologists. Because of the mystique regarding physicians, psychiatrists usually have the least amount of worry concerning objections to their credibility or education. Clinical psychologists will generally be recognized without too much difficulty; but experts whose backgrounds are in social work or who have master's degrees could face considerable difficulty, especially if the opposition has an expert witness with more education. Unfortunately, the people who win in court are often those who have the best experts or those who are successful in achieving rapport with the jury and/or the judge.

To survive as an expert witness, one should carefully lay a foundation for credibility long before the court date. The expert should attend national and regional meetings in the field and obtain continuing education certificates, read the current literature, and maintain records so that specific answers can be given to questions regarding credentials.

The field of assessing offenders using plethysmograph techniques dates back at least 20 years. Formal training programs are not offered at any universities since only a small number of people are interested in learning the field. Many people doing assessments have been trained as apprentices in the laboratories of one of the pioneers in the field: Freund, Abel, Barlow, Laws, and others. Comprehensive short courses lasting 2 to 3 days have been taught by Steve Jensen of the Center for Behavioral Intervention in Beaverton, Oregon; William Farrall at Farrall Instruments in Grand Island, Nebraska, or by Farrall at the Institute for the Advanced Study of Human Sexuality in San Francisco. These courses are nonaccredited. More than 300 people have been trained in these courses. Both the Farrall and Jensen courses teach equipment operation, assessment techniques, and interpretation of the data. However, it is possible to become knowledgeable in assessment techniques without going through a course. Many people have purchased the equipment and learned how to use it from the manufacturer's instruction manuals, workshops, and the extensive literature in the field.

Credibility is also enhanced by membership in national professional organizations, such as the American Psychiatric Association, American Psychological Association, Association for the Treatment of Sexual Abusers, Network of Kempe National Center for Prevention and Treatment of Child Abuse and Neglect, Society for the Scientific Study of Sex, American Association of Sex Educators Counselors and Therapists (AASECT), and the Association for Advancement of Behavior Therapy (AABT). Another measure of credibility is provided by the expert's publications and lectures in the field.

Penile Plethysmograph Introduced as Evidence

As of July 1, 1989, a search of Westlaw (™), a national legal data base, reveals only two reported cases in which results of a penile plethysmograph were offered to prove innocence, and in both cases the court correctly rejected the offer. No cases are in the record where the penile plethysmograph was used to prove guilt. Anecdotally, the author has heard that trial courts (whose rulings are generally not reported) have admitted penile plethysmograph evidence. However, for reasons discussed previously, this should not be allowed.

The following is a summary of the two reported cases where an attempt to introduce penile plethysmograph evidence to prove innocence. In a California case, *People v. John W.* (1986), the Superior Court of Napa County ruled to exclude penile plethysmograph evidence. The Court of Appeals affirmed with the following explanation:

> In a prosecution for committing a lewd and lascivious act upon a child and a related sexual offense, the trial court did not err in excluding the expert opinion testimony of a defense psychologist that defendant was not a sexual deviant, and that the alleged crimes therefore did not occur, where the psychologist's opinion was primarily based on an electronic physiological test that measured whether defendant responded to deviant stimuli, and the reliability of the test had not been established. The psychologist was the only witness who testified to the general acceptance of the test in the scientific community; he, as a proponent of the new test, was therefore likely to be biased, and his testimony established that one-fifth of subjects given the test had no response to either deviant or nondeviant sexual stimuli.

> The admissibility in a criminal action of expert testimony based upon the application of a new scientific technique traditionally involves a two-step

process: the reliability of the method must be established, usually by expert testimony, and the witness furnishing such testimony must be properly qualified as an expert to give an opinion on the subject. Moreover, the proponent of the testimony has the burden of demonstrating the reliability of the new technique.

Although statements made as the result of an unreliable scientific technique may be used to establish a basis for expert opinion, those statements are not admissible to prove the truth of the matter asserted. (p. 185)

In a family court case in Dutchess County, New York, *T. G. Petitioner v. Mr. G. and Mrs. G.* (1988), a clinical psychologist testified he had examined Mr. G. with a penile plethysmograph and concluded that since Mr. G. did not become sexually aroused by either male or female chidren, the child in question would not be at risk living with him. An opposing expert testified, "that the penile plethysmograph has not gained acceptance by the scientific community as a reliable predictor of future behavior, and that recent studies have borne out that lack of confidence" (p. 69).

The family court judge ruled,

Results of penile plethysmograph could not be considered as predictor of father's behavior toward children and could not be considered to detemine whether to terminate his parental rights for sexually abusing a child; plethysmograph received questionable professional recognition and had margin of error that was too great to forecast the child's safety. (p. 64)

Examples of Possible Questions

This section includes typical questions a knowledgeable attorney might ask the opposition's expert witness. For the correct answer, see the appropriate sections of the text listed as a reference following the question.

Question 1. Does the instrument have adjustments that, if set incorrectly, could cause an incorrect reading or diagnosis? Reference: "Calibration." Additional comment: This instrument has a zero or baseline adjustment and a full scale or sensitivity adjustment. The zero should be set so the recorded trace is on one side of the chart paper and the full scale on the other. If the sensitivity is not set high enough, an erection may not be detected. There are various ways of setting the sensitivity but usually 30-mm of erection reaches the full scale side of the chart.

Question 2. How were the data compensated for the nonlinearity of the gauge? Reference: "Calibration." Additional comment: New transducers can have errors of as much as 15%. While some manufacturers claim to produce linear mercury-in-rubber gauges, the author has found this not to be true. The use and abuse of the gauge can cause very large errors. Data that have not been corrected for those errors can be very misleading and will sometimes result in an incorrect indication of arousal patterns.

Question 3. What type of stimulus was used in the assessment? Reference: "Stimulus Selection and Characteristics." Additional Comment: Usually slides are used to determine partner age and gender preference and audio is used to determine preference for an activity. The correct answer depends on the person being tested.

Question 4. Is the penile plethysmograph a sexual lie detector, which will prove if a person has or has not committed a crime or done a specific sexual act? Reference: The answer is NO and it is so important to stress this that it is the first sentence in this chapter. Additional Comment: The information derived from an accurate penile plethysmograph assessment only shows the arousal patterns or sexual preference of the person tested. This cannot be used to confirm an act or to predict future behavior absolutely. In most cases it can show if the individual has deviant arousal patterns. Frequently arrest records agree with the results of the testing. There is also a high correlation between the penile plethysmographic data and the deviant's admitted deviant behavior. There are times when the victim is "situational." There was simply someone available who was not the offender's ideal choice. In this case, the arousal pattern may not agree with the arrest records.

Question 5. Were standardized stimulus materials used? Reference: "Stimulus Selection and Characteristics." Additional Comment: At present there are few standardized stimulus materials available. However, therapists who are experienced in the field of treatment of sex offenders should have data indicating what normal arousal patterns would look like when using their own stimulus materials. This data on normal arousal patterns can then be used for comparison with someone whose arousal patterns are deviant.

Question 6. Did the stimulus set that was used in the assessment have equal explicitness across age and gender? Reference: "Stimulus Selection and Characteristics." Additional Comment: Only one variable should change in a given test. Every visual image should have the same degree of nudity and the same general pose. Example: Results will be skewed if one age group shows a crotch or open vagina while others show a standing nude or clothed person. Standardized stimulus sets are available which have similar poses across age and gender.

ASSESSMENT OF FEMALES

There is a photoplethysmograph for measuring arousal patterns in females. It has been around almost as long as the male measuring devices. It was developed by Geer, Morokoff, and Greenwood (1974) in the United States and a somewhat similar version was developed about the same time in the Netherlands by van Dam, Honnebier, and van Zalinge (1971). A number of other investigators through the years have developed somewhat similar devices. They all function basically the same way. A light source is used to illuminate the vaginal wall. The light reflected back from the wall undergoes a color change caused by an increase in the supply of the oxygenated blood in the tiny veins in the wall of the vagina. This reflected light is detected by a light-sensitive resistor or photodiode.

Unlike the simple physical change that occurs in the male, female arousal is tracked by changes in the amplitude of the pulse height of the signal picked up by the photoplethysmograph. This signal closely follows the blood pressure pulse wave form. The raw output from the photoplethysmograph thus is a complex signal, which is affected by respiration, movement, and the blood pressure pulse. The detection of arousal is based on measuring the point from the most negative side of the blood pressure pulse to the positive peak. Ordinarily this is done by taking three consecutive measurements and averaging them. Thus, the complexity of the signal and the fact that computation must be made on each pulse provides a bigger challenge to the interpretation of data. Of course, with computer programs this determination is quite easy.

At the present time there are very few therapists working with female sex offenders. Most of them do not use the photoplethysmograph. Interest is growing as more and more female deviants are being discovered. A recent study by Annon and Brinton (1989) compared sexual arousal of 34 women, some of whom were involved in incest with nondeviant women. They reported:

> Responses of an alleged female incest offender were compared to the mean responses of similar age nonoffender females and were found to be significantly different. These findings suggest that is possible to assess female sexual deviance patterns using procedures analogous to those currently used to assess male sexual deviance.

CONCLUSION

Techniques for measuring both male and female sexual response to erotic and semierotic stimuli has advanced to a degree that makes it a

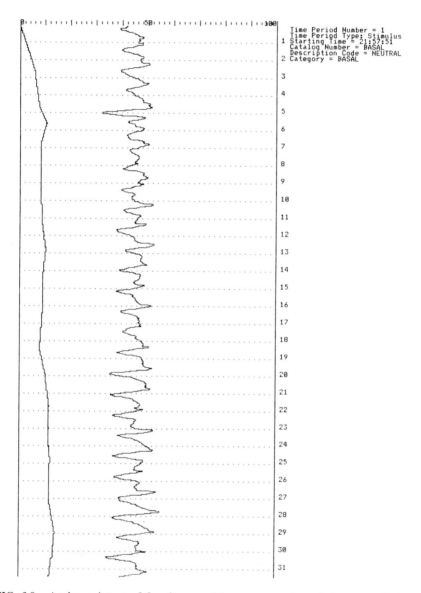

FIG. 6.9. Analog printout of female arousal by computer photoplethysmograph. No arousal condition.

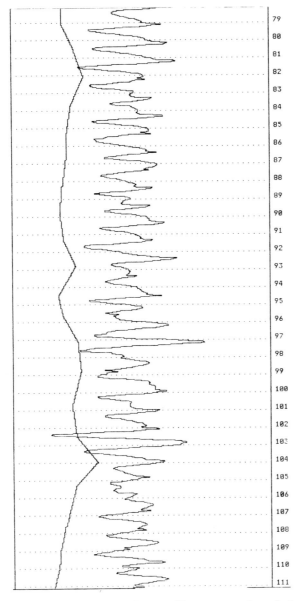

FIG. 6.10.   Analog printout of female arousal by computer photoplethysmograph. Showing arousal to a fantasy.

227

necessary part of any program attempting to treat sex offenders. While sexual arousal information will never be able to provide an accurate answer to the question of innocence or guilt, for most clients, it offers the following information that is not obtained by any other methods:

1. It can indicate the most likely type of victim or preferred sex partner.
2. It can provide some information on the possible degree of violence or coercion the offender might use.
3. It can often reduce the denial period.
4. It can give insight to the progress or lack of progress in the treatment process.

REFERENCES

Abel, G. (1989). Paces Pavilion, Suite #202, 3193 Howell Mill Road, N.W., Atlanta, GA 30321–4101.

Abel, G. (1987). *Multi-site study group.* Behavior Medicine Institute, Atlanta.

Abel, G. G., Becker, J. V., Cunningham-Rathner, J., Rouleau, J. L., Kaplan, M., & Reich, J. (1984). *The treatment of child molesters.* Unpublished manuscript.

Annon, J. S. (1988). Reliability and validity of penile plethysmography in rape and child molestation cases. *American Journal of Forensic Psychology, 6*(2), 11–25.

Annon, J. S., & Brinton, C. (1989, May). *Physiological assessment of female sexual arousal using male sex offender and gender identity cues.* Paper presented at the First International Conference on the Treatment of Sex Offenders, Minneapolis, MN.

Association for the Advancement of Medical Instrumentation. (1985). *AAMI standards and recommended practices.* Arlington, VA: Association for the Advancement of Medical Instrumentation.

Barlow, D. H., Becker, R., Leitenberg, H., & Agras, W. S. (1970). A mechanical strain gauge for recording penile circumference change. *Journal of Applied Behavior Analysis, 3*, 73–76.

Blanchard, R., Racansky, I. G., & Steiner, B. W. (1986). Phallometric detection of fetishistic arousal in heterosexual male cross-dressers. *Journal of Sex Research, 22*, 452–462.

Card-Farrall (1989). *Stimulus tapes.* Farrall Instruments, Inc., P.O. Box 1037, Grand Island, Nebraska 68803.

Earls, C. M., & Marshall, W. L. (1983). The current state of technology in the laboratory assessment of sexual arousal patterns. In J. G. Greer & I. R. Stuart (Eds.), *The sexual aggressor: Current perspectives on treatment* (pp. 336–362). New York: Van Nostrand Reinhold.

Earls, C. M., Quinsey, V. L., & Castonguay, L. G. (1987). A comparison of three methods of scoring penile circumference changes. *Archives of Sexual Behavior, 16*, 493–500.

Farrall, W. R. (1985). *Dealing with new pornography laws, a therapist's problem* (Available from Farrall Instruments, Inc., Grand Island, NE). Grand Island, NE.

Farrall, W. R., & Card, R. D. (1988). Advancements in physiological evaluation of assessment and treatment of the sexual aggressor. In R. A. Prentky & V. L. Quinsey (Eds.), *Human sexual aggression: Current perspectives* (Vol. 528, pp. 261–273). New York: New York Academy of Science.

Favero, M. S. (1983). Chemical disinfection of medical and surgical materials. In S. S. Block (Ed.), *Disinfection, sterilization and preservation* (3rd ed., pp. 469–491). Philadelphia: Lea & Fabiger.

Federal Food, Drug, and Cosmetic Act. (1976). 21, U.S.C. §513 (1976).

Fedora, O., Reddon, J. R., Morrison, J. W., Fedora, S. K., Pascoe, H., & Yeudall, L. T. (1987). *Penile tumescence to themes of domination, denigration, and infliction of pain: Relationship to sexual sadism.* Research Bulletin #137, Department of Neuropsychology & Research Alberta Hospital, Edmonton, Canada.

Fedora, O., Reddon, J. R., & Yeudall, L. T. (1986). Stimuli eliciting sexual arousal in genital exhibitionists: A possible clinical application. *Archives of Sexual Behavior, 15*, 417–427.

Fisher, C., Gross, J., & Zuch, J. (1965). Cycle of penile erection synchronous with dreaming (REM) sleep. *Archives of General Psychiatry, 12*, 29–45.

Food and Drug Administration. (1990). *Safe Medical Devices Act of 1990* (Public Law 101–629). 101st Congress, Washington, DC.

Frye V. United States, 293F.1013 (D.C. Cir. 1923).

Freund, K., Sedlack, F., & Knob, D. (1965). A simple transducer for mechanical plethysmography of the male genital. *Journal of Experimental Analysis of Behavior, 8*, 169–170.

Fuller, A. K., Barnard, G., Robbins, L., & Spears, H. (1988). Sexual maturity as a criterion for classification of phallometric stimulus slides. *Archives of Sexual Behavior, 17*, 271–276.

Geer, J. H., Morokoff, P., & Greenwood, P. (1974). Sexual arousal in women: The development of a measurement device for vaginal blood volume. *Archives of Sexual Behavior, 3*, 559–564.

Goodier, G. G. (1988). The defense perspective on expert witnesses. *The Brief*, pp. 45–50.

Hall, G. C. N., Proctor, W. C., & Nelson, G. M. (1988). The validity physiological measures of pedophilic sexual arousal in a sexual offender population. *Journal of Consulting and Clinical Psychology, 56*, 118–122.

Hillsman, J. R. (1988). The plaintiff's perspective on expert witnesses. *The Brief*, pp. 51–56.

Jensen, S. H. (1989). 4560 SW 110th, #200, Beaverton, OR 97005.

Jensen, S. H., & Jewell, C. A. (1988). The sex offender experts. *The Prosecutor,* pp. 13–20.

Julien, E., & Over, R. (1988). Male sexual arousal across five modes of erotic stimulation. *Archives of Sexual Behavior, 17,* 131–143.

Knopp, F. H. & Stevenson, W. F. (1990). *Nationwide survey of juvenile & adult sex-offender treatment programs.* The Safer Society Program.

NDAA. (1990). Will strong child porn ruling hurt some professionals? *National District Attorneys Association Bulletin, 9*(2).

Laws, D. R. (1985). *Prevention of relapse in sex offenders.* (Project No. 1 RO1 MH42035), National Institute of Mental Health.

Laws, D. R., & Osborne, C. A. (1983). How to build and operate a behavioral laboratory to evaluate and treat sexual deviance. In J. G. Greer & I. R. Stuart (Eds.), *The sexual aggressor: Current perspectives on treatment* (pp. 293–335). New York: Van Nostrand Reinhold.

Marques, J. D., Day, D. M., Nelson, C., & Miner, M. H. (1989). The sex offender treatment and evaluation project: Calfornia's relapse prevention program. In D. R. Laws (Ed.), *Relapse prevention with sex offenders* (pp. 247–267). New York: Guilford.

McConaghy, N. (1989). Validity and ethics of penile circumference measures of sexual arousal: A critical review. *Archives of Sexual Behavior, 18,* 357–369.

Murphy, W. D., & Barbaree, H. E. (1987). *Assessments of sexual offenders by measures of erectile response: Psychometric properties and decision making* (Order No. 86M0506500501D). Rockville, MD: National Institute of Mental Health.

People v. John W., 229 Cal. Rptr. 783 (Cal. App. 1 Dist. 1986).

Pithers, W. D., & Cumming, G. F. (1989). Can relapses be prevented? Initial outcome data from the vermont treatment program for sexual aggressors. In D. R. Laws (Ed.), *Relapse prevention with sex offenders* (pp. 313–326). New York: Guilford.

Pithers, W. D., Kashima, K. M., Cumming, G. F., Beal, L. S., & Buell, M. M. (1988). Relapse prevention of sexual aggression. In R. A. Prentky & V. L. Quinsey (Eds.), *Human sexual aggression: Current perspectives* (Vol. 528, pp. 244–260). New York Academy of Sciences.

Pithers, W. D., & Laws, D. R. (1989). The penile plethysmograph: Uses and abuses in assessment and treatment of sexual aggressors. In B. Schwartz (Ed.), *A practioner's guide to the treatment of the incarcerated male sex offender* (pp. 83–91). Washington, DC: National Institute of Corrections.

Reimer, R. A. (1984). *Child pornography: Legal considerations* (Order code: IB83148). Washington, DC: Congressional Research Service.

Sakheim, D. K., Barlow, D. H., Beck, J. G., & Abrahamson, D. J. (1985). A comparison of male heterosexual and male homosexual patterns of sexual arousal. *Journal of Sex Research, 21,* 183–198.

Sexual Abuse Clinic of Portland, Ore. (1987, May). *Data generated by an outpatient sexual abuse clinic.* In proceedings of Association for the Behavioral Treatment of Sexual Abusers first annual conference, Newport, Oregon.

Simon, W. T., & Schouten, G. W. (1991). Plethysmography in the assessment and treatment of sexual deviance: An overview. *Archives of Sexual Behavior, 20(1),* pp. 75–91.

Society for the Scientific Study of Sex. (1988). Policy statement regarding legal restrictions on the use of sexually explicit materials in criminal assessment and therapy, scientific investigation, and professional education. *Siecus Report, 16*(3), 17.

Surgikos. (1984). *How to use Cidex 7.* Arlington, TX: Author.

T. G. Petitioner v. Mr. G. and Mrs. G., 534 N. Y. Supp. 64 (1988).

Tanner, J. M. (1962). *Growth at adolescence* (2nd ed.). Oxford, England: Blackwell Scientific Publications.

Travin, S., Cullen, K., & Melella, J. T. (1988). The use and abuse of erection measurements: A forensic perspective. *Bulletin of the American Academy of Psychiatry Law, 16,* 235–250.

UL 544 (July 25, 1972). *Standard for safety, medical and dental equipment.* Underwriters' Laboratories, Inc.

van Dam, F., Honnebier, W., & van Zalinge, E. (1971). *An investigation comparing the effect of sexual stimulation on a group of patients suffering from amenorrhea grade I and a group of normal menstruating women.* (translated from Dutch). Personal Communication.

Zuckerman, M. (1971). Physiological measures of sexual arousal in the human. *Psychological Bulletin, 75,* 297–329.

7

Clinical Issues in the Psychological Assessment of Child Molesters

Christopher M. Earls
University of Montreal, Québec

INTRODUCTION

One of the major preconditions for solving any problem is its precise definition. For example, it is rare that an auto mechanic, when faced with a car that will not start, will begin by replacing the engine. Rather, a diagnosis would begin by an assessment of the various components known to be related to the starting behavior of cars (the presence or absence of gasoline, the presence or absence of electrical power, etc.). The logic used by mechanics generally consists of a combination of inductive and deductive reasoning that leads to specific guesses, or hypotheses, concerning the origin of the problem. Each of these hypotheses is, in turn, tested (using the appropriate tools and measurement devices) until the problem has been isolated. Once the nature of the problem is identified, there is a specific set of decision rules and procedures that can be used to rectify the malfunction.

In principle, a psychological evaluation proceeds in much the same manner. The health professional begins an assessment by examining the component behaviors that are thought to be necessary for the well-being of the individual. As with the car, a combination of inductive and deductive logic is used to generate various testable hypotheses. Each of these hypotheses is tested until the problem is identified. Once identified, there is a specific set of procedures (treatment) that can be used to bring about changes in behavior.

Unfortunately, although the automobile analogy serves well in explaining the procedures and logic of general problem solving, a psychological evaluation is, in practice, much more complicated than diagnosing a mechanical malfunction. This complication arises from two factors: (1) Our knowledge of human behavior is considerably less complete than our knowledge of cars; and, (2) Our diagnostic tools are subject to more error than are those of the mechanic. The purpose of this chapter is to examine both the knowledge base and the diagnostic tools that are currently available for the assessment of men who have had, or who are alleged to have had, sexual interactions with children. In the following sections, some of the major diagnostic techniques are reviewed: The first two sections outline the use of self-report (i.e., the clinical interview, psychological tests); the last two describe some of the work that has been done with physiological measures (lie detection and phallometric measurement).

However, it should be noted at the outset that although there are some offenders who seek professional help for problems related to inappropriate sexual behavior, the vast majority have been referred by the legal system; that is, they may not necessarily be cooperative or active participants in the evaluation process. This reticence on the part of the offender is different from most clinical situations, in which it is the client who enters assessment and treatment in an effort to reduce or eliminate distress; it also poses difficulties when attempting to determine the nature and magnitude of the problem. In other words, our diagnostic tools must not only be considered from the perspective of their ability to identify problem areas in the behavior of sexual offenders, but also to be accurate in assuming only minimal cooperation on the part of the offender.

A further complication arises from the fact that there is a variety of different reasons for assessing sexual offenders, for example:

1. To assist the court in a determination of guilt or innocence;
2. To provide additional information in custody disputes;
3. To determine whether there is a need for treatment;
4. To identify those areas of behavior that could be targeted in treatment;
5. To estimate the potential danger the individual poses to the community.

Each of these possible mandates implies that some decision will be made concerning the disposition of the offender and that the assessment will reduce the uncertainty of each kind of decision.

THE INTERVIEW

Although there is considerable overlap in interviews concerned with assessment and those conducted in treatment, the main objective of the *initial assessment* interview is to gather information relevant to the problem at hand (Sundberg, 1977). This information should include a description of the individual's background (e.g., family, criminal, psychiatric, and health history), mental status, and basic demographic information, such as age, marital status, and so on. In addition, questioning should focus on the reasons why the client has been referred and by whom. In the case of sexual offenders against children, information is required concerning sexual history, details of the sexual aggression, modus operandi, number of previous victims, a description of the sexual behaviors with the victim, and a complete description of the victim(s).

Despite its almost universal use as an initial assessment tool, there is surprisingly little empirical research concerning the reliability and validity of the information obtained in a clinical interview. Turning first to the issue of reliability, Hay, Hay, Angle, and Nelson (1979) had four highly trained advanced graduate students interview four clients. The design was completely counterbalanced with respect to the order of the interviews by each interviewer. All interviews were audiotaped and each interviewer was asked to give a general summary at the end of the session. The data were rated by two independent judges with respect to the clients' history and life problem areas. The results indicated that there were no significant difference between interviewers in terms of the number of problems identified; however, the mean interrater agreement scores for the identification of type of problem was .55 (range .25 to .76). In other words, everyone agreed that there were problems but there was little agreement as to their nature.

There are no studies bearing directly on the reliability of sex offenders' self-reports in the interview (for an interesting case study account, see Marshall & Christie, 1981). However, there is indirect evidence to suggest that the information obtained within a forensic setting is not interpreted by interviewers in the same manner. To give just one example, Quinsey and Ambtman (1979) attempted to determine the extent to which experts agreed among themselves when making predictions concerning the likelihood that a forensic psychiatric patient, if released, would commit either a property offense or assault against another person. A total of 30 patient files (including 9 child molesters) were studied by a group of four experienced forensic psychiatrists and nine secondary schoolteachers. For each patient, the amount of available information (e.g., the patients' histories, test results, general demeanor in the interview, and progress notes concerning general functioning within the hospital) was systematically varied. There were two findings of interest: First, correlations between averages of the two occupational groups' ratings were high, indicating that psychiatrists and teachers made essentially the same judgments; and second, although agreement among the members of the two groups was highest when a maximum amount of information was available, overall agreement between individuals, regardless of their occupational group, was very low. These findings are particularly discouraging because, when evaluating the complete file data, raters had access to considerably more information than would normally be obtained in a typical intake interview (see also Goldberg, 1968; Golden, 1964; Faust, 1984, 1985; Oskamp, 1965; Sines, 1959).

With respect to the validity of the clinical interview, there are some general concerns that would lead us to expect unwanted error due to both interviewer and client characteristics. For example, the data obtained are subject to errors that can be either intentional or unintentional. Examples of unintentional error would include problems of recall that could result in either a lack of information or a distortion of the information, responses to leading questions, and the failure to focus questioning on pertinent areas of functioning.

In addition, although it is often implicitly assumed that the interviewer is an unbiased measurement agent, a large body of evidence suggests that the conclusions of interviewers tend to be affected by a number of interpersonal factors totally unrelated to what is said by the client, for example, sex, race, socioeconomic status, client attractiveness, and the general theoretical orientation of the interviewer (for reviews of research pertaining to the influence of these factors see Arvey & Campion, 1982; Ziskin, 1981).

Perhaps the most serious threat to the validity of the information obtained in a clinical interview would be the unwillingness of the client to disclose embarrassing or socially undesirable behavior. Obviously, the amount of dissembling is likely to vary as a function of both the particular client, the reason for referral and the presenting problem. However, given the very real threat of legal consequences to a sexual offender if he admits to the offense for which he has been charged, or additional sexual offenses against children, we can expect that the validity of data obtained in the initial interview is fairly low.

Research concerning the validity of sexual offenders' self-reports is sparse. One of the major problems in verifying self-reports is an absence of "ground truth," that is, some objective criterion by which we could compare the self-report of the offender. Nevertheless, there is evidence to suggest that under some circumstances we may approach a semblance of ground truth in interviews with sexual offenders. For example, studies that have attempted to describe the demographic characteristics of incarcerated sexual offenders often include data pertaining to previous arrests or convictions for a sexual offense. To simplify, these studies generally report that about 50% of the sample is made up of first-time offenders with the remainder having a history of between one and three previous arrests (Christie, Marshall, & Lanthier, 1977; Earls et al., (1989); Wormith, 1983). These studies provide data concerning what is already known about large groups of sexual offenders. In an effort to obtain detailed information concerning was not yet known, Abel et al. (1987) used an elaborate procedure, not only to ensure the confidentiality of information disclosed in the interview, but also to convince the offender that the data would not be divulged to the criminal justice system. Subjects were 561 nonincarcerated men, referred to the authors for evaluation and treatment; of these, 377 were extrafamilial child molesters. The 244 men who had molested female children reported an average of 19.2 victims (median = 1.3); men who had molested male children averaged 150.2 victims (median = 4.4). In another published report using the same sample, Abel, Becker, Cunningham-Rathner, Mittelman, and Rouleau (1988) showed that a self-report of only one sexual deviation was relatively rare for child molesters. Rather, it appeared that these men, at some point in their lives, had engaged in a variety of illegal sexual acts.

Although the sample studied by Abel and his colleagues may not be representative of the population of sexual offenders, these data have important implications for the assessment of men who have sex with children. Specifically, they suggest that we would be less likely to obtain information from the offender (other than that which is already known) if the interview was being conducted within a forensic context; any honesty on his part could be almost immediately punished with additional charges. Even if the offender was self-referred, we would not be assured of an accurate self-report unless there was an explicit understanding as to what the therapist would do with information that had not, as yet, come to the attention of the legal authorities.

Taken together, the available data concerning the validity of sexual offenders' self-reports suggest that if the subsequent assessment procedures are based on what the offender chooses to disclose, the end result may underestimate the frequency and seriousness of the client's previous sexual offences. Of course, information supplied by the offender can (and should) be verified by using police reports, victim reports, interviews with significant others, and so on; however, this additional data may only confirm what is already known, that is, the crimes for which he has been arrested and/or convicted. In the case in which the offender denies any and all sexual involvement with children, and there is no additional proof that can be brought to bear on the question, a clinical interview will be of little or no use, irrespective of the assessment mandate.

PSYCHOLOGICAL TESTS

With the exception of the clinical interview, psychological tests are probably the most often used assessment technique in the clinic. Although there appears to be considerable variability of the types of tests used to assess child molesters, reports in the literature can be divided into two main categories: "objective" paper-and-pencil personality tests and projective tests.

Personality tests are essentially a self-administered interview in which the client is asked to describe himself (by endorsing a fixed number of self-descriptors or other statements); the characteristics measured are traits that are common to all people in varying degrees. There are a number of different personality tests currently available; however, the Minnesota Multiphasic Personality Inventory (MMPI) is, without a doubt, the most common paper-and-pencil test used with clinical populations. In 1976, Anastasi estimated that there were more than 3,500 published reports concerning the MMPI; and, in 1986, Quinsey predicted that by the year 2000 every man, woman and child on earth would have published an MMPI study. This popularity stems from the fact that the MMPI was developed specifically to measure various personality characteristics associated with psychopathology.

The research pertaining to the use of psychological tests with child molesters has been extensively reviewed by Langevin (1983), Levin and Stava (1987), Lester (1975) and Quinsey (1977, 1986). Therefore, we will only briefly outline some of the major findings; in addition, we will describe one test that has been marketed since the publication of these reviews.

With respect to studies using personality tests other than the MMPI, Levin and Stava (1987) have succinctly summarized the findings as follows:

> There is some evidence that pedophiles tested in the community are more introverted than normal males. Rapists and pedophiles, regardless of the sex of the victim, tend to score higher on the EPPS [Edwards Personal Preference Schedule] scale of abasement than nonsex offenders. Further, rapists and heterosexual pedophiles obtain low scores on aggression. It also appears that heterosexual pedophiles score high on deference and low on heterosexuality, whereas homosexual pedophiles tend to be high on both succorance and nurturance. (p. 74–75)

However, as noted by Levin and Stava, these general findings may be more related to the subjects' current situation (e.g., under evaluation or on the bottom rung of the prison hierarchy) and a desire to appear contrite and reformed (for a similar argument, see Quinsey, 1986).

Studies using the MMPI that have attempted to differentiate between child molesters and nonoffenders have yielded mixed results. For example, a number of authors have reported successful discrimination using an MMPI profile consisting of an elevated scale 4 (psychopathic deviate), scale 8 (schizophrenia; Armentrout & Hauer, 1978; Erickson, Luxenberg, Walbek, & Seely, 1987; McCreary, 1975; Kirkland & Bauer, 1982; Panton, 1978). However, in a specific search for the predominance of elevated two-point profile among child molesters, Hall, Maiuro, Vitaliano, and Proctor (1986) examined the profiles from 406 men incarcerated for sexual offenses against children. The results indicated statistical differences related to both the sex and age of the victim but no predominant two-point MMPI code was found. Similarly, Quinsey, Arnold, and Pruesse (1980) compared the MMPI profiles of four groups of offenders: two groups of murderers (intrafamilial and extrafamilial), extrafamilial child molesters, and men convicted of property offenses. The result indicated no significant differences between groups.

Because the MMPI was not designed to be used with sexual offenders, it may be unreasonable to expect large and significant differences when attempting to identify individuals who have committed a specific type of offense. In an effort to develop a self-report instrument that would provide information particular to sexual offenders, Nichols and Molinder (1984) constructed a 300-item test known as the Multiphasic Sex Inventory (MSI). This test is similar in presentation to the MMPI and includes three sexual deviance scales (child molestation, rape, and exhibitionism, as well as subscales to measure sexual interest in a variety of paraphilias (fetishism, voyeurism, sadomasochism, bondage, and obscene phone calls). In addition, there is a scale designed to detect sexual dysfunction as well as six validity scales. The authors report that the reliability (test–retest) coefficients of the various scales range from .58 to .91; and, to date, they have conducted a number of validity studies comparing large groups of different subgroups of sex offenders and nonoffenders (see MSI manual). The results indicate that the MSI can successfully differentiate among rapists, child molesters, exhibitionists and college students (see also, Kalischman, Szymanowski, McKee, Taylor, & Craig, 1989). However, one disturbing aspect of the MSI is that there are large and statistically significant effects due to treatment. Specifically, the more an offender progresses in treatment, the more he scores deviant on the various scales. These findings suggest that the results obtained using the MSI may be heavily influenced by the "openness" of the client to admit that he is responsible for his behavior.

Partly because of the transparency of many paper-and-pencil tests, some authors have employed projective tests in the assessment of child molesters. Projective tests involve the presentation of ambiguous stimuli that are designed to elicit a wide variety of responses from the client. It is believed that these responses will contain elements of conscious and unconscious thoughts and fantasies that, when interpreted by a trained clinician, will provide indexes as to the psychological functioning of the client. Examples of projective tests include the Rorschach Inkblot Test, the Thematic Apperception Test (TAT) and the Draw-a-Person Test.

There have been few published reports of the responses of sexual offenders to projective tests. Wysocki and Wysocki (1977) administered the Draw-a-Person test to a group of rapists, pedophiles, and incest offenders; Hammer (1954) obtained drawings for a similar test (the House-Tree-Person) from pedophiles and rapists. However, both studies were so hopelessly impoverished in terms of experimental control (e.g., lack of comparison groups, no specification as to scoring method, and failure to have drawings evaluated by blind raters) that no meaningful conclusions are possible.

Using the Rorschach, Stricker (1964) reported that the responses of incarcerated child molesters were guarded but not substantially different from other groups that he had previously tested (outside of the experimental context presented in his article). Prandoni, Jensen, Matranga, and Smith-Waison (1973) compared 58 sexual offenders with 58 incarcerated nonoffenders and found that the only differences between groups were in terms of the number of rejections (refusal to respond) and reaction time to various cards.

However, these results should not be considered surprising, given that projective tests were not designed or meant to be used as a method for discriminating among various subgroups of clinical patients. Rather, their main function in the assessment process is intended to help the clinician to obtain a more descriptive clinical portrait of the client. As Exner (1974), one of the leading authorities on the Rorschach, has noted:

> It would seem that, too frequently, clinicians have been enticed, by the intrigue of questions . . . into issuing verdicts about people and their behaviors which have little relevance to data found in most Rorschach records. Descriptions of religious preference, hobbies, class standing, grade point average, supervisor ratings, job satisfaction, or frequency of intercourse are not items to which even the most experienced Rorschacher will address himself. These may all be intriguing questions, but most Rorschach data would be only very indirectly related to them. (p. 20)

To summarize, psychological tests have not been shown to be very useful when attempting to identify either sexual offenders or characteristics that are specific to the offender. Although the MMPI has some clinical utility in terms of diagnosis within the major categories of psychosis versus neurosis as well as providing general indexes of psychopathology, there is little indication that it provides data that would be of use either in identifying a child molester or in the prediction of future sexual behavior.

"LIE DETECTION"

The validity of polygraphy, or "lie detection," has been the subject of long debate within the scientific community (Lykken, 1979; Podlesny & Raskin, 1977; Raskin & Podlesny, 1979). Major reviews of this literature are available by Saxe, Dougherty, and Cross (1985) and Furedy and Heslegrave (1988). In their review, Saxe et al. identified approximately 250 published references concerning the validity of polygraph testing; of these, they note that only 10 field studies met the criteria for the U.S. Office of Technology Assessment. These reports, as well as an additional 12 analog studies, were critically evaluated. After an exhaustive review, the authors concluded that,

> [U]nder certain conditions [Control Question Tests] can detect deception at rates significantly better than chance, although the data also suggest that substantial rates of false positives, false negatives, and inconclusives are possible. What appears to be very important are the conditions of the test. These probably include, at a minimum, a narrowly focused question, an experienced examiner/investigator, and a subject who believes in the efficacy of the test.[1] (p. 363)

Similarly, Furedy and Heslegrave note that, "as a *scientific tool*, [Control Question Technique] polygraphy is of questionable validity, although it is probably a better-than-chance detector of guilt" (p. 219). It seems that although there are a number of legal, moral, and scientific

---

[1]The Control Question Technique refers to a procedure in which the subject's physiological responses to three types of questions are compared: Irrelevant questions, e.g., "Were you born on June 25th, 1950?"; relevant questions, e.g., "Have you ever inserted your finger into *child's name* vacina?"; and, control questions, e.g., "Before the age of 18, did you ever lie to avoid being in trouble?". Because control questions are specifically chosen to be emotionally charged, innocent subjects are expected to respond equally to the relevant and control questions. When responses to relevant questions exceed those elicited by control questions, lying or guilt is inferred (for a detailed discussion of the assumptions underlying the Control Question Technique, see Lykken, 1981).

arguments with respect to the use of polygraphy, one of the major concerns is an unsettling number of false positives, that is, truthful subjects who are mistakenly identified to be lying (Horvath, 1977; Kleinmuntz & Szucko, 1982; Lykken, 1981; Saxe et al., 1985).

No empirical studies exist concerning the ability of "lie detection" techniques to discriminate between child molester and nonoffenders. There have been, however, suggestions that lie detection methods should be used when assessing sexual offenders (Jensen & Jewell, 1988) or that offenders be periodically monitored with polygraphy while on probation (Abrams, 1989; Knowlton, 1972).

There is only one study that has addressed the issue of the effectiveness of polygraphic surveillance of sex offenders. Abrams and Ogard (1986) studied a group of 14 men convicted of sexual offenses and placed on a 2-year probation. The subjects were divided into two groups: an experimental group that was evaluated at 90-day intervals and a control group that followed normal probationary procedure. The results indicated that two of the seven experimental subjects recidivated during the 2-year period, as opposed to four of the seven control subjects. Although the groups were too small to permit statistical analyses, the authors noted that "the probation officer was particularly impressed" (p. 181).

The greatest danger of any technology is, of course, abuse. In a particularly brutal account of his courtroom practices, Judge Clarence E. Partee describes how he adopted the procedure of asking defendants petitioning the court for probation whether or not they had ever committed other crimes for which they had not been apprehended:

In about fifty cases in which this proceeding [sic] has been used, all but two or three have answered the question. In those cases where the answer is refused, probation is immediately denied. In those cases where answers are received, the answer is "No" . . . each who answers the question lies. However, after each answers the question, I state that it is necessary for me to be satisfied whether their answer is true or false, and that I can see no reason why I should accept their answer as true, and that if they still wish that I consider their application for probation, that I will require that they submit themselves to a polygraph examination. . . . All but two have taken the polygraph. Those who refused were denied probabion and sentenced.

After getting the report from the polygraph examiner . . . I resume the proceedings and ask the applicant for probation to state his offenses one by one. His pride at being able to outsmart the law is now deflated completely. His cloak of secrecy has been stripped away, and his past, and his true self exposed so that the judge, his friends, relatives, the officers, and he also can see him as he really is -. . . a liar before the court.

Whenever the examiner tells me of tough nuts that are now whipped pups, that bawl and cry like a baby in their admissions to him, I think we are dealing with people who can be rehabilitated, whose conscience, though calloused, can be regenerated. (Partee, 1975, pp. 34–35)

For the moment, polygraphy should not be considered any more than an experimental assessment procedure. The fact that there exists no empirical demonstration that sexual offenders can be distinguished from nonoffenders, combined with the potential for a high rate of false positives suggests that lie detection methods would lead to a considerable amount of error.

PHALLOMETRIC TESTS OF SEXUAL PREFERENCE

Research concerning the sexual preferences of child molesters has been extensively reviewed elsewhere (Earls, 1988; Quinsey, 1986). It will be reviewed here partly because a number of studies have been published since these reviews and because the methodology, as used in empirical studies, is sometimes not well understood when applied in the clinic.

Description of the instrumentation used to measure sexual arousal in males can be found in Earls and Marshall (1983), Rosen and Keefe (1978) and Farrall (Chapter 6, this volume). To summarize briefly, there are essentially two methods used to evaluate penile responses: (a) true plethysmography (also referred to as the volumetric method), in which the entire volume change in the penis is measured during erection (Freund, Sedlacek, & Knob, 1965); and (2) an approximation of plethysmography, using devices that measure penile circumference changes only (Bancroft, Jones, & Pullen, 1966; Barlow, Becker, Leitenburg, & Agras, 1970). Most investigators and clinicians have chosen to employ the circumferential devices and there is evidence to indicate that both work equally well (Wheeler & Rubin, 1987).

Validity

Freund (1961, 1963) was the first to use penile tumescence as a measure of sexual preference. His initial work consisted of the presentation of photographic slides depicting nude adults of both sexes while measuring changes in penile volume. Soon after, this procedure was extended to include stimuli in which both sex and age were systematically varied. The results of these experiments have consistently shown that it is possible not only to differentiate among men having homosexual *versus* heterosexual preferences but also to identify inappropriate sexual age preferences among extrafamilial child molesters (Freund, 1967a, 1967b). These findings have since been replicated in other laboratories using penile circumferential measures (Marshall, Barbaree, & Christophe, 1986; Quinsey, Steinman, Bergersen, & Holmes, 1975).

During the later part of 1970s, investigators from a variety of fields began to reconsider previous conceptions of child molesters as relatively nonagresssive and nonviolent individuals. Evidence from a number of demographic studies (De Francis, 1969) clinical studies (Marshall & Christie, 1981) and historical accounts (Quinsey, 1986) suggest that, for some men, sexual interest in children can be aggressive and violent. In an effort to explore these observations experimentally, Abel, Becker, Murphy, and Flanagan (1981) developed a series of six audiotaped stimuli describing interactions between an adult male and a female child in which the level of force required to obtain victim compliance was systematically varied. Using penile tumescence as the dependent variable, these investigators identified (among a group of heterogeneous sexual offenders) a percentage of child molesters who were more sexually excited by descriptions of sexual violence against children than by "mutually consenting" sex with a child. While no between group statistical analyses were provided, indexes of aggression were calculated (penile responses to descriptions of aggressive sexual interaction with children divided by responses to descriptions of nonaggressive sex) that appeared to be related to sexual offense history.

In a subsequent experiment, Avery-Clark and Laws (1984) also developed a series of five audiotaped stimuli describing various nonviolent and violent interactions between an adult male and a child. Two sets of audiotapes were constructed: one for homosexual child molesters and a second for heterosexual child molesters. Stimuli were presented to two groups of extrafamilial child molesters previously classified on the basis of offense history as being either "more dangerous" or "less dangerous." In this experiment, the focus of the data analysis was on aggression indexes. The data showed that child molesters classified as more dangerous responded at significantly higher levels to the aggressive cues than the child molesters classified as less dangerous. Unfortunately, the investigators did not include a nonoffender comparison (the importance of using a normal comparison group will be discussed in more detail).

Using similar audiotaped descriptions, Marshall et al. (1986) included a control group of nonsex offenders and compared their penile responses with a group of heterosexual child molesters and a group of incest offenders. Although heterosexual child molesters evidenced less arousal to descriptions of nonsexual violence than to episodes describing sexual interactions with children, they responded at higher levels over all stimulus categories than the nonsexual offender group (there were no significant differences between the nonsex offenders and the incest offenders). Also reported was a significant correlation ($r = .40$) between degree of force used by these men in previous sexual encounters with children and the ratio of responses to forced sex to "consenting" sex with children (pedophile aggression index). Similar results have been reported for heterosexual child molesters by Quinsey and Chaplin (1988a) and for homosexual child molesters by Marshall, Barbaree, and Butt (1988). Of particular importance, both Marshall et al. (1986) and Quinsey and Chaplin (1988a) report significant correlations between arousal to sexually violent stimulus episodes and previous victim injury.

The research pertaining to the differentiation of intrafamilial (incest) offenders is less clear. There are two studies (Marshall et al., 1986; Quinsey, Chaplin, & Carrigan, 1979) that have compared normals with both extra- and intrafamilial offenders. As mentioned earlier, the results of these experiments showed significant differences between extrafamilial child molesters and normals; however, neither study found differences between the incest offenders and the normals. In two other studies (Abel, Becker, Murphy, & Flanagan, 1981; Murphy, Haynes, Stalgaitis, & Flanagan, 1986), comparisons between extra- and intrafamilial offenders revealed that both groups responded equally to descriptions of sexual activity with children. It is noteworthy that the two studies reporting no differences between extra- and intrafamilial offenders both used the same stimulus set (i.e., Abel et al., 1981) and neither employed a normal comparison group.

To date, there has been only one study that has failed to show that extrafamilial child molesters can be differentiated from normals using erectile measures. Hall, Proctor, and Nelson (1988) compared 25 incarcerated rapists and 97 child molesters, using audiotapes "similar to those used by Avery-Clark and Laws." The results indicated no differences between these two groups and the authors concluded that, "the ability of physiological measures [penile tumescence] to discriminate between sexual offenders and normal subjects . . . remains to be investigated" (p. 122).

This study provides an example of some of the ways in which methodological errors can lead to confusion in the literature. There are two major problems with the experiment report by Hall et al. First, the authors failed to include an appropriate control group. As mentioned, the audiotapes were similar to those used by Avery-Clark and Laws. But because Avery-Clark and Laws also did not test their stimuli on a nonoffender comparison group, it is difficult to determine the significance of a sexual response to these stimuli. Second, Hall et al. introduced a fatal confound into their experimental design: All audiotaped descriptions of sexual interactions with children were 2 minutes in duration; stimulus episodes describing mutually consenting sex with a female adult were 4 minutes long. Given the substantial difference in stimulus duration, it is not terribly surprising that the results showed no statistical differences between penile responding to female adults and children (for a more detailed critique of Hall et al.'s study, see Quinsey & Laws, 1989).

An example from our laboratory will be useful to illustrate more fully the problems inherent in the foregoing study. In 1983, we began testing clients in Quebec. The population of this Canadian province is primarily French speaking; therefore, our first task was to construct audiotaped stimulus material in French. At that time, the most complete stimulus set available was that of Avery-Clark and Laws. We hired a professional to translate the transcripts, and began testing incarcerated child molesters. After the 15th assessment, we felt that we had a potentially useful stimulus set: All offenders tested showed high levels of arousal to almost all episodes describing sexual interactions with children and no arousal to sexually neutral stimuli. We then began testing nonoffender community volunteers. We tested 20 normals; and, to our chagrin, the results indicated that these subjects were *more* aroused to the child categories (but not significantly so) than the child molesters.

The results of our experiment generated three hypotheses: (1) There is no difference between child molesters and normals in terms of the sexual arousal to audiotapes describing a sexual interaction between a child and an adult (Hall et al.'s conclusion); (2) French-speaking men are deviant; or (3) There was something wrong with our stimulus material.

Unlike Hall et al., we concluded that the first hypothesis seemed unlikely because at about this time many of the aforementioned studies (Marshall et al., 1986, 1988; Quinsey & Chaplin, 1988a) that had successfully discriminated child molesters from normals were being submitted for publication. The second hypothesis was also troublesome not only because of its "culturalist" connotation but also because we had previously shown that francophone rapists and nonrapists could be differentiated (Earls & Proulx, 1986). Therefore, we concentrated on the third hypothesis. We put the Avery-Clark stimuli on the shelf and translated the stimuli used by Quinsey and Chaplin (1988a). The experiment was repeated (Degagné & Earls, 1989), using 28 homosexual child molesters and 21 homosexual nonoffenders. The results were identical in almost every respect to those reported by Marshall et al. (1988) who also studied homosexual child molesters. This episode shows the importance of using normal control groups to establish the validity of a particular stimulus set before using that set to assess sexual offenders.

Reliability

To date, there are few studies concerning the reliability of penile assessment techniques with child molesters alone. Wormith (1986) assessed 12
pedophiles, 12 rapists, and 12 nonsexual offenders, using two sets of
slides. The sets included two slides in each of the following categories;
male child, male adult, female child, female adult, couples, and neutral.
Testing was conducted on two occasions, separated by a 1-week interval.
Results, in terms of internal consistency (correlations between slides in
the same category), varied between .53 and .92; test–retest correlations
(i.e., among slide sets) ranged from .59 to .83. There are also data
concerning the reliability of phallometric measures with rapists. For
example, Quinsey and Chaplin (1984) alpha coefficients (a measure of
internal consistency) ranging from .50 to .89 (mean, .75) for audiotapes
describing both consenting and nonconsenting sex with a female adult
(for a more complete review of the reliability of phallometric measures
with rapists, see Murphy & Barbaree, 1988). Although more data are
required concerning the reliability of phallometric assessment techniques, the results to date suggest a reasonable degree of consistency
both within and between sessions.

Response Control

There is at least one major threat to the validity of measures of sexual
arousal, that is, some men can quite successfully exert voluntary control
over their erectile response (Abel, Blanchard, & Barlow, 1981; Abel,
Barlow, Blanchard, & Mavissakalian, 1975; Freund, Chan, & Coulthard,
1979; Henson & Rubin, 1971; Laws & Holman, 1978; Laws & Rubin,
1969; Quinsey & Bergersen, 1976; Quinsey & Carrigan, 1978; see also
Geer & Fuhr, 1976). Of course, we need hardly call into question the
validity of assessment results if the individual is known to have engaged
in sexual behavior with children and he shows high levels of sexual
arousal to inappropriate sexual stimuli involving children (it is improb-
able that anyone is going to attempt to fake a response profile in the
direction of deviance). However, in a case where the results of the
assessment indicate a normal profile for a known sexual offender there
are three possible interpretations of the data: (1) The individual is
genuinely not sexually aroused by children; (2) We were not astute
enough to present him with stimuli depicting children in the right sexual
context (e.g., the case where only slides are presented and the individual
is mainly aroused to descriptions of sexual violence); or (3) the client
successfully controlled any signs of deviant sexual arousal. Although

there are some interesting techniques available for the detection of faked profiles (Freund, Watson, & Renizo, 1988) and for the prevention of faking (Quinsey & Chaplin, 1988b), the assessment of sexual arousal can be influenced by voluntary control.

The difficulties of voluntary control can also be exacerbated by varying instructions to clients. Specifically, there are some laboratories that attempt to obtain an estimate of the extent to which the client is able to control his arousal voluntarily. This estimate is obtained by presenting a one set of stimuli (most often audiotapes) while instructing the client to "relax, and let himself become aroused" and a parallel set of stimuli with the instructions to "control his arousal." It is thought that by comparing the result obtained under relax instructions with those observed under the control condition that the investigator will obtain an index of the individual's capacity to influence the results voluntarily (see, for example, Wormith, Bradford, Pawlak, Borzecki, & Zohar, 1988). Some researchers will also ask their clients to engage in a cognitive task such as "counting backward by threes" if the interstimulus interval is protracted due to residual arousal to a previous stimulus. As we (Earls & Proulx, 1986) have pointed out, such procedures not only alert the client to the possibility of voluntary control but also give him the opportunity to practice such control. If an index of voluntary control is required for the assessment session *and* the clinician does not anticipate having to reassess or treat the client, then it may be more worthwhile to follow the example of Hall et al. (1988). At the end of their assessment sessions, these investigators presented the stimulus that elicited highest arousal during the evaluation and asked subjects to control their arousal.

Individual vs. Group Data

To this point, the discussion has focused on data concerning the identification of child molesters and nonoffenders in terms of group data. However, what is of primary interest to the clinician is the ability of phallometric measures to identify problem areas in the individual — especially those individuals who deny any sexual interest in children.

Freund and Blanchard (1989) have conducted one of the only experiments to examine the relationship between measures of penile tumescence and the degree to which an individual admits to having committed a sexual crime (see also, Freund et al., 1979); because of its importance, this study will be presented in detail. The investigators tested 210 men who had been *accused* of either sexual offenses against children ($n = 154$) or against women ($n = 56$; the authors referred to this group as the control subjects). The experiment was divided into two parts: In the first phase, 47 child molesters and 26 control subjects were used to develop diagnostic criteria; in the second phase 107 child molesters and 30 controls were used to cross-validate these criteria. Only the results of the cross-validation will be reported here.

Each subject was administered a questionnaire that contained two items pertaining to sexual fantasies involving both children and adults. On the basis of their responses to these questions, subjects were classified as full admitters (the endorsement of both questions), partial admitter (the endorsement of only one question), and nonadmitters (the rejection of both questions). Following this, sexual arousal to films, slides, and audiotapes was measured over two sessions and the data were analyzed in terms of ratio scores (a "sex-preference" ratio, i.e., males relative to females; and, a "age-preference" ratio, i.e., adults relative to children). The result indicated that admitters were more likely to show sexual interests in children than the nonadmitters and offenders against male children were more likely to manifest deviant sexual arousal than offenders against female children. Of the 40 nonadmitter subjects, 55% were diagnosed as either pedophilic (preference for prepubescent children) or hebephilic (preference for pubescent children); only 1 of the "control" subjects was misclassified. Thus unlike the results obtained using "lie detection" methods, there appears to be only a small number of false positives. Combining the data presented by the authors in Table 1 (p. 102) and Table 2 (p. 103), it can be seen that of the total sample, 114 subjects (83.2%) produced interpretable data; of the 92 child molesters for whom data was obtained 66 (71.7%) were identified as having deviant sexual arousal (these calculations included admitters, partial admitters, nonadmitters).

However, it is important to note that in Freund and Blanchard's study, there was no ground truth: Their subjects had simply been accused of a sexual crime and no further proof as to the veracity of the accusation was considered by the authors. Therefore, it is difficult to determine the significance of deviant arousal in the 55% of nonadmitters. It would indeed be a hapless individual who was unjustly accused of child molestation and evidenced deviant sexual arousal in the laboratory. In addition, as pointed out by the authors, the remaining 45% may be made up of: (1) Men who may have had a sexual interaction with a child as a "surrogate" (i.e., those men who do not have a genuine sexual interest in children but who approached a child as a substitute for an adult partner); (2) Subjects who were able to falsify the results; and, (3) Those individuals who had been falsely accused.

In any case, Freund and Blanchard conclude that "a phallometric diagnosis of pedophilia or hebephilia should not be interpreted as evidence that a man has committed the specific offense (or offenses) for which he has been charged" (p. 104).

To summarize, studies that have directly measured the sexual arousal patterns of child molesters indicate that there are reliable and significant differences between extrafamilial child molesters and nonoffenders. These studies have also shown that there is a significant relationship between the sex and age of the victim and responses to deviant sexual stimuli; and, that there is a correlation between victim damage scores and arousal to descriptions of coercive sex with children. The data concerning deviant patterns of sexual arousal among intrafamilial child molesters are less conclusive. However, men who molest children do not *necessarily* manifest deviant sexual arousal in the laboratory (either because they are genuinely not aroused by children or because they can successfully control such arousal). Finally, although they appear very few in number, there are men who may evidence such arousal but never act on it. Therefore, the presence or absence of such arousal cannot be considered as unequivocal proof of behavior outside of the testing situation.

CONCLUSION

Of the currently available techniques, phallometric measurement appears to be the most specific in terms of identifying sexual offenders. However, if an individual is accused of a sexual crime and denies any wrongdoing, a psychological evaluation will be of little use in a determination of guilt or innocence. None of the existing techniques is sufficiently refined to make such a determination with an acceptable degree of error.

If, on the other hand, an accusation or conviction of a sexual crime is accompanied by an admission of guilt, a psychological assessment may be extremely useful in designing treatment strategies that may reduce the risk of continued sexually inappropriate behavior (for descriptions of current treatment approaches, see Abel et al., 1984; Marshall, Earls, Segal, & Darke, 1983; Quinsey, Chaplin, Maguire, & Upfold, 1987).

An assessment of sexual preferences may also be useful in both custody disputes and in the determination of dangerousness. For example, in decisions concerning which parent should be legally responsible for children, the presence of deviant sexual arousal in the father would not be an encouraging sign. Similarly, men who already found guilty of sexually violent behavior, a profile of high arousal to nonconsenting sex with either a child or an adult can serve as a predictor of future sexual behavior (Rice, Quinsey, & Harris, 1989). Nevertheless, in all of these cases the direction of the results is important: Because there are sexual offenders who may not evidence deviant sexual arousal in the laboratory, a "normal" profile provides no additional information in the assessment.

ACKNOWLEDGMENT

I would like to thank Martin Lalumière for his technical assistance in conducting the literature review and V. L. Quinsey for his comments on an earlier version of this manuscript.

REFERENCES

Abel, G. G., Barlow, D. H., Blanchard, E. B., & Mavissakalian, M. (1975). Measurement of sexual arousal in male homosexuals: The effects of instructions and stimulus modality. *Archives of Sexual Behavior, 4*, 623–629.

Abel, G. G., Becker, J. V., Cunningham-Rathner, J., Mittelman, M., & Rouleau, J. L. (1988). Multiple paraphilic diagnoses among sex offenders. *Bulletin of the American Academy of Psychiatry and the Law, 16*, 153–168.

Abel, G. G., Becker, J. V., Cunningham-Rathner, J., Rouleau, J. L., Kaplen, M., & Reich, J. (1984). *The treatment of child molesters.* Department of Psychiatry. Emory University, School of Medicine, Atlanta.

Abel, G. G., Becker, J. V., Mittelman, M., Cunningham-Rathner, J., Rouleau, J. L., & Murphy, W. D. (1987). Self-reported sex crimes of nonincarcerated paraphiliacs. *Journal of Interpersonal Violence, 2*, 3–25.

Abel, G. G., Becker, J. V., Murphy, W. D., & Flanagan, B. (1981). Identifying dangerous child molesters. In R. B. Stuart (Ed.), Violent behavior: Social learning approaches to prediction, management, and treatment. (pp. 116–137). New York: Brunner/Mazel.

Abel, G. G., Blanchard, E. B., & Barlow, D. H. (1981). Measurement of sexual arousal in several paraphilias: The effects of stimulus modality, instructional set and stimulus content on the objective. *Behavior Research and Therapy, 19*, 25–33.

Abrams, S. (1989). Probation polygraph surveillance of child abusers. *The Prosecutor, 22*, 29.

Abrams, S., & Ogard, A. (1986). Polygraph surveillance of probationers. *Polygraph, 15*, 174–182.

Anastasi, A. (1976). *Psychological testing* (4th ed.). New York: Macmillan.

Armentrout, J. A., & Hauer, A. L. (1978). MMPIs of rapists of adults, rapists of children, and non-rapists sex offenders. *Journal of Clinical Psychology, 34*, 330–332.

Arvey, R. D., & Campion, J. E. (1982). The employment interview: A summary and review of recent research. *Personnel Psychology, 35,* 281–322.

Avery-Clark, C. A., & Laws, D. R. (1984). Differential erection response patterns of sexual child abusers to stimuli describing activities with children. *Behavior Therapy, 15,* 71–83.

Bancroft, J. H. J., Jones, H. G., & Pullen, B. R. (1966). A simple transducer for measuring penile erection with comments on its use in the treatment of sexual disorder. *Behavior Research and Therapy, 4,* 239–241.

Barlow, D. H., Becker, R., Leitenberg, H., & Agras, W. S. (1970). A mechanical strain gauge for recording penile circumference change. *Journal of Applied Behavior Analysis, 3,* 73–76.

Christie, M. M., Marshall, W. L., & Lanthier, R. D. (1977). *A descriptive study of incarcerated rapists and pedophiles.* Report to the solicitor general of Canada.

De Francis, V. (1969). *Protecting the child victim of sex crimes committed by adults.* Denver: American Humane Association, Children's Division.

Degagné, R., & Earls, C. M. (1989). *The differentiation of homosexual child molesters and normals.* Unpublished manuscript, University of Montreal.

Earls, C. M. (1988). Aberrant sexual arousal in sexual offenders. *Annals of the New York Academy of Sciences, 528,* 41–48.

Earls, C. M., Aubut, J., Laberge, J., Bouchard, L., Castonguay, L. G., & McKibben, A. (1989). Etude déscriptive des delinquants sexuels [A descriptive study of sexual offenders]. *Revue québécoise de psychologie, 10,* 30–40.

Earls, C. M., & Marshall, W. L. (1983). The current state of technology in the laboratory assessment of sexual arousal patterns. In J. G. Greer & J. R. Stuart (Eds.), *The sexual aggressor: Current perspectives on treatment* (pp. 336–362). New York: Van Nostrand Reinhold.

Earls, C. M., & Proulx, J. (1986). The differentiation of francophone rapists and nonrapists using penile circumferential measures. *Criminal Justice and Behavior, 13,* 419–429.

Erickson, W. D., Luxenberg, M. G., Walbek, N. H., & Seely, R. K. (1987). Frequency of MMPI two-point code types among sex offenders. *Journal of Consulting and Clinical Psychology, 55,* 566–570.

Exner, J. E. (1974). *The Rorschach: A comprehensive system.* New York: Wiley.

Faust, D. (1984). *The limits of scientific reasoning.* Minneapolis: University of Minnesota Press.

Faust, D. (1985). Declarations versus investigations: The case for the special reasoning abilities and capacities of the expert witness in psychology/psychiatry. *The Journal of Psychiatry & Law, 13,* 33–59.

Freund, K. (1961). Laboratory differential diagnosis of homo- and heterosexuality — An experiment with faking. *Review of Czechoslovak Medicine, 7,* 20–31.

Freund, K. (1963). A laboratory method for diagnosing predominance of homo- or hetero-erotic interest in the male. *Behaviour Research and Therapy, 8,* 85–93.

Freund, K. (1967a). Diagnosing homo or heterosexuality and erotic age-preference by means of a psycho-physiological test. *Behaviour Research and Therapy, 5,* 209–228.

Freund, K. (1967b). Erotic preference in pedophilia. *Behaviour Research and Therapy, 5,* 339–348.

Freund, K., & Blanchard, R. (1989). Phallometric diagnosis of pedophilia. *Journal of Consulting and Clinical Psychology, 57,* 100–105.

Freund, K., Chan, S., & Coulthard, R. (1979). Phallometric diagnosis with "nonadmitters." *Behaviour Research and Therapy, 17,* 451–457.

Freund, K., Sedlacek, F., & Knob, K. (1965). A simple transducer for mechanical plethysmography of the male genital. *Journal of Experimental Analysis of Behavior, 8,* 169–170.

Freund, K., Watson, R., & Rienzo, D. (1988). Signs of feigning in the phallometric test. *Behaviour Research and Therapy, 26,* 105–112.

Furedy, J. J., & Heslegrave, R. J. (1988). Validity of the lie detector: A psychophysiological perspective. *Criminal Justice and Behavior, 15,* 219–246.

Geer, J. H., & Fuhr, R. (1976). Cognitive factors in sexual arousal: The role of distraction. *Journal of Consulting and Clinical Psychology, 44,* 238–243.

Goldberg, L. R. (1968). Simple models or simple processes? Some research on clinical judgements. *American Psychologist, 13,* 483–496.

Golden, M. (1964). Some effects of combining psychological tests on clinical inferences. *Journal of Consulting Psychology, 28,* 440–446.

Hall, G. C., Maiuro, R. D., Vitaliano, P. P., & Proctor, W. C. (1986). The utility of the MMPI with men who have sexually assaulted children. *Journal of Consulting and Clinical Psychology, 54,* 493–496.

Hall, G. G., Proctor, W. C., & Nelson, G. M. (1988). Validity of physiological measures of pedophilic sexual arousal in a sexual offender population. *Journal of Consulting and Clinical Psychology, 56,* 118–122.

Hammer, E. F. (1954). A comparison of H-T-P's of rapists and pedophiles. *Journal of Projective Techniques, 18,* 346–354.

Hay, W. M., Hay, L., Angle, H. V., & Nelson, R. O. (1979). The reliability of problem identification in the behavioral interview. *Behavioral Assessment, 1,* 107–118.

Henson, D. E., & Rubin, H. B. (1971). Voluntary control of eroticism. *Journal of Applied Behavioral Analysis, 4,* 37–44.

Horvath, F. (1977). The effect of selected variables on interpretation of polygraph records. *Journal of Applied Psychology, 62,* 127–136.

Jensen, S. H., & Jewell, C. A. (1988). The sex offender experts. *The prosecutor, 21,* 13–20.

Kalichman, S. C., Szymanowski, D., McKee, G., Taylor, J., & Craig, M. E. (1989). Cluster analytically derived MMPI profile subgroups of incarcerated adult rapists. *Journal of Clinical Psychology, 45,* 149–155.

Kirkland, K. D., & Bauer, C. A. (1982). MMPI traits of incestuous fathers. *Journal of Clinical Psychology, 38,* 645–649.

Kleinmuntz, B., & Szucko, J. J. (1982). On the fallibility of lie detection. *Law & Society Review, 17,* 85–104.

Knowlton, J. O. (1972). The polygraph and probation. *Idaho Law Review, 9,* 74–84.

Laws, D. R., & Holman, M. L. (1978). Sexual response faking by pedophiles. *Criminal Justice of Behavior, 5,* 343–356.

Laws, D. R., & Rubin, H. B. (1969). Instructional control of an autonomic sexual response. *Journal of Applied Behavioral Analysis, 2,* 93–99.

Langevin, R. (1983). *Sexual strands: Understanding and treating sexual anomalies in men.* London: Lawrence Erlbaum Associates.

Lester, D. (1975). *Unusual sexual behavior: The standard deviations.* Springfield, IL: Thomas.

Levin, S. M., & Stava, L. (1987). Personality characteristics of sex offenders: A review. *Archives of Sexual Behavior, 16,* 57–79.

Lykken, D. T. (1979). The detection of deception. *Psychological Bulletin, 86,* 47–53.

Lykken, D. T. (1981). *A tremor in the blood.* New York: McGraw–Hill.

Marshall, W. L., Barbaree, H. E., & Butt, J. (1988). Sexual offenders against male children: Sexual preferences. *Behaviour Research and Therapy, 26,* 383–391.

Marshall, W. L., Barbaree, H. E., & Christophe, D. (1986). Sexual offenders against female children: Sexual preferences for age of victims and type of behavior. *Canadian Journal of Behavioural Science, 18,* 424–439.

Marshall, W. L., Christie, M. M. (1981). Pedophilia and aggression. *Criminal Justice and Behavior, 8,* 145–158.

Marshall, W. L., Earls, C. M., Segal, Z., & Darke, J. L. (1983). A behavioral program for the assessment and treatment of sexual aggressors. In K. Craig & R. McMahon (Eds.), *Advances in clinical behavior therapy* (pp. 148–174). New York: Brunner/Mazel.

McCreary, C. P. (1975). Personality differences among child molesters. *Journal of Personality Assessment, 39,* 591–593.

Murphy, W. D., & Barbaree, H. E. (1988). *Assessments of sexual offenders by measures of erectile responses: Psychometric properties and decision making.* Washington, DC: National Institute of Mental Health.

Murphy, W. D., Haynes, M. R., Stalgaitis, S. J., & Flanagan, B. (1986). Differential sexual responding among four groups of sexual offenders against children. *Journal of Psychopathology and Behavioral Assessment, 8,* 339–353.

Nichols, H. R., & Molinder, I. (1984). *Multiphasic sex inventory manual.* Tacoma, WA, 437 Bowes Drive.

Oskamp, S. (1965). Overconfidence in case-study judgements. *Journal of Consulting and Clinical Psychology, 29,* 261–265.

Panton, J. H. (1978). Personality differences appearing between rapists of adults, rapists of children and non-violent sexual molesters of female children. *Research Communications in Psychology, Psychiatry and Behavior, 3,* 385–393.

Partee, C. E. (1975). Probation and the polygraph. In N. Ansley (Ed.), *Legal Admissibility of the polygraph* (pp. 31–39). Springfield, IL: Charles C. Thomas.

Podlesny, J. A., & Raskin, D. C. (1977). Physiological measures and the detection of deception. *Psychological Bulletin, 84,* 782–799.

Prandoni, J. R., Jensen, D. E., Matranga, J. T., & Smith-Waison, M. O. (1973). Selected Rorschach response characteristics of sex offenders. *Journal of Personality Assessment, 37,* 334–336.

Quinsey, V. L. (1977). The assessment and treatment of child molesters: A review. *Canadian Psychological Review, 18,* 204–220.

Quinsey, V. L. (1986). Men who have sex with children. In D. N. Weisstub (Ed.), *Law and Mental Health: International Perspectives* (Vol. 2, pp. 140–172). New York: Pergamon Press.

Quinsey, V. L., & Ambtman, R. (1979). Variables affecting psychiatrists' and teachers' assessments of the dangerousness of mentally ill offenders. *Journal of Consulting and Clinical Psychology, 47,* 353–362.

Quinsey, V. L., Arnold, L. S., & Pruesse, M. G. (1980). MMPI profiles of men referred for pre-trial psychiatric assessment as a function of offense type. *Journal of Clinical Psychology, 36,* 410–417.

Quinsey, V. L., & Bergersen, S. G. (1976). Instructional control of penile circumference in assessments of sexual preference. *Behavior Therapy, 7,* 489–493.

Quinsey, V. L., & Carrigan, W. F. (1978). Penile responses to visual stimuli: Instructional control with and without auditory sexual fantasy correlates. *Criminal Justice and Behavior, 5,* 333–341.

Quinsey, V. L., & Chaplin, T. C. (1984). Stimulus control of rapists' and non-sex offenders' sexual arousal. *Behavioral Assessment, 6,* 169–176.

Quinsey, V. L., & Chaplin, T. C. (1988a). Penile responses of child molesters and normals to descriptions of encounters with children involving sex and violence. *Journal of Interpersonal Violence, 3,* 259–274.

Quinsey, V. L., & Chaplin, T. C. (1988b). Preventing faking in phallometric assessments of sexual preference. *Annals of the New York Academy of Sciences, 528,* 49–58.

Quinsey, V. L., Chaplin, T. C., & Carrigan, W. F. (1979). Sexual preferences among incestuous and nonincestuous child molesters. *Behavior Therapy, 10,* 562–565.

Quinsey, V. L., Chaplin, T. C., Maguire, A., & Upfold, D. (1987). The behavioral treatment of rapists and child molesters. In E. K. Morris & C. J. Braukmann (Eds.). *Behavioral approaches to crime and delinquency* (pp. 363–382). New York: Plenum Press.

Quinsey, V. L., & Laws, R. D. (1989). *The validity of phallometric measures: A response to Hall, Proctor, and Nelson.* Manuscript submitted for publication.

Quinsey, V. L., Steinman, C. M., Bergersen, S. G., & Holmes, T. F. (1975) Penile circumference, skin conductance, and ranking responses of child molesters and "normals" to sexual and nonsexual visual stimuli. *Behavior Therapy, 6,* 213–219.

Raskin, D. C., & Podlesny, J. A. (1979). Truth and deception: A reply to Lykken. *Psychological Bulletin, 86,* 54–59.

Rice, M., Quinsey, V. L., & Harris, G. (1989). *Predicting sexual recidivism among treated and untreated extra-familial child molesters admitted to a maximum security psychiatric facility.* Penatang Mental Health Centre Research Reports, 6(3).

Rosen, R. C., & Keefe, F. J. (1978). The measurement of human penile tumescence. *Psychophysiology, 15,* 366–376.

Saxe, L., Dougherty, D., & Cross, T. (1985). The validity of polygraph testing. *American Psychologist, 40,* 355–366.

Sines, L. K. (1959). The relative contribution of four kinds of data to accuracy in personality assessment. *Journal of Consulting Psychology, 6,* 483–492.

Stricker, G. (1964). Stimulus properties of the Rorschach to a sample of pedophiles. *Journal of Projective Techniques and Personality Assessment, 28,* 241–244.

Sundberg, N. D. (1977). *Assessment of persons.* Englewood Cliffs: Prentice-Hall.

Wheeler, D., & Rubin, H. B. (1987). A comparison of volumetric and circumferential measure of penile erection. *Archives of Sexual Behavior, 16,* 289–299.

Wormith, J. S. (1983). A survey of incarcerated sexual offenders. *Canadian Journal of Criminology, 25,* 379–390.

Wormith, J. S. (1986). Assessing deviant sexual arousal: Psychological and cognitive aspects. *Advances in Behaviour Research and Therapy, 8,* 101–137.

Wormith, J. S., Bradford, J. M. W., Pawlak, A., Borzecki, M., & Zohar, A. (1988). The assessment of deviant sexual arousal as a function of intelligence, instructional set and alcohol ingestion. *Canadian Journal of Psychiatry, 33,* 800–808.

Wysocki, A. C., & Wysocki, B. A. (1977). Human figure drawings of sex offenders. *Journal of Clinical Psychology, 33,* 278–284.

Ziskin, J. (1981). *Coping with psychiatric and psychological testimony.* Venice, CA: Law and Psychology Press.

8

Credibility Assessment During the Sexual Abuse Evaluation

Mary deYoung

Associate Professor, Sociology, Grand Valley State University, Allendale, MI

There is a paradoxical character to an allegation of child sexual abuse: The substantiation of its truth in any one case only engenders doubt that truth will be found in any other. Certainty and skepticism are juxtaposed. This paradox is neither an invention of the current time nor an artifact of the moment; it is, instead, a contradiction that has persisted unresolved for the century that child sexual abuse has been defined as a social problem.

This paradox arose in the middle of the 19th century. It had been customary for medical and legal authorities, in particular, routinely to assume a child's allegation of sexual abuse was false, especially if it were made against a parent. Even medical evidence that would seem to indicate the child indeed had been sexually abused, including such clinically remarkable evidence as vaginal or rectal trauma, often was presumed to be the result of a self-injury that was motivated by a coldly calculated desire to extort money or some other material advantage from the accused (Masson, 1985).

That conventional wisdom was challenged in the 1860s by Ambroise August Tardieu, professor and dean of legal medicine at the University of Paris. His court-ordered medical examinations and autopsies of children revealed anatomical sequelae of sexual abuse that, in his opinion, could not have been simulated or contrived; the psychic trauma of the children he interviewed showed emotional pain unmitigated by even the prospect of material advantage. His conclusion was as unshakable as it was startling: The majority of the allegations of sexual abuse made by children, even very young children, could be corroborated and substantiated by medical evidence.

The paradox was made more bold in the 1880s by Alexandre Lacassagne, chair of legal medicine at the University of Lyons, who with his students investigated hundreds of cases of sexual abuse. His careful medical examinations led him to the conclusion that a child actually could be sexually abused frequently and over a rather considerable period of time *without* demonstrating any physical evidence or symptoms of that abuse. A lack of medical evidence, he hypothesized, should not in every case be used as a reason to impugn the credibility of the child's allegation. In his words, "The experiences we have undergone confirm this manner of seeing things and prove the truth of the assertions of the child" (cited in Masson, 1985, p. 26).

Doubts arose almost immediately. While medical and legal experts could only debate the diagnostic value of the physical sequelae of sexual abuse, many of them remained adamant that an allegation made in the absence of these physical symptoms was still suspect. Most outspoken of those skeptics was Alfred Fournier, who in an 1880 address to the Academy of Medicine urged fellow physicians to regard an uncorroborated accusation as a symptom of *Pseudologia phantastica,* that is, a fiction or a fantasy that was, by definition, both pathological and untrue.

His colleague, Claude Etienne Bourdin, agreed. He zealously urged physicians and educators to join together to destroy the myth of the infallible veracity of the child by recognizing an allegation of sexual abuse for what it most likely was—a lie originating in the evil instinct and passion of a jealous and hateful child. One colleague to join him in that mission was physician Paul Brouardel, who in 1883, delivered a sustained and oft-cited polemic against the credibility of a child's allegation of sexual abuse:

> One often speaks of the candor of children. Nothing is more false. Their imagination likes to invent stories in which they are the hero. The child comforts herself by telling herself fantasies which she knows are false on every point. . . . This child, to whom one ordinarily paid only the most minor attention, finds an audience that is willing to listen to her with a certain solemnity and to take cognizance of the creations of her imagination. She grows in her own self esteem, she herself becomes a personage, and nothing will get her to admit that she deceived her family and the first people who questioned her. Her lie will be all the more difficult to unmask since the child lies without troubling herself over the improbabilities which one finds in her account. (cited in Masson, 1985, pp. 44–45)

These pathological lies thus were offered as explanations for what Fournier and Brouardel, among many others, believed were the large number of false allegations of sexual abuse made by children. And in so offering them, they subtly enhanced the image of the falsely accusing child; perceived not only as capable of engaging in a cold, rational calculus in order to maximize rewards, the accusing child now also was envisioned as suffering from disturbance, confusion, even pathology. And the developing lexicon of psychiatry and psychoanalysis reinforced that image with words such as pathological lying, *pseudologia phantastica*, hysteria, *mythomanie* and genital hallucinations, all of which located the origin of an allegation of sexual abuse in the dark pathology of childhood and, in so doing, painted it once again with suspicion.

These diagnoses were offered by the most eminent psychiatrists of the early 20th century, most notably, by Sigmund Freud. His own discomfort with his patients' painful disclosures of childhood sexual abuse, and his fear of collegial rejection of his theory that it was that very abuse that was the root of his patients' psychopathology, caused him to abandon his seduction theory and relegate those allegations of sexual abuse to the richly sexualized fantasies of children (Herman, 1981; Masson, 1985; Rush, 1980). Less a theory than a strategy, it nonetheless darkened the paradox with lines drawn so boldly and enduringly that nearly a century would pass before an allegation of sexual abuse made by a child was viewed with a less jaundiced eye.

The alliance between psychiatry and the law in alleged cases of sexual abuse was forged in heavy chains; the language of one became the language of the other, the image of the child in one was reflected in the image of the child in the other. Concepts such as pathological lying, hysteria, and genital hallucinations found their way into courts of law and were used by psychiatric experts to impugn the credibility of a child's testimony. The image of the child as "the most dangerous of all witnesses" (Whipple, 1911, p. 305) mirrored the psychiatric image of the child as cunning, vengeful, and disturbed. And this oft-quoted plea that has echoed through courtrooms for decades, "When are we going to give up, in all civilized nations, listening to children in courts of law?" was voiced by neither lawyer or judge, but by a psychiatrist (Varendonck, 1911, p. 133).

Shading this bold stroke of skepticism in the credibility of a sexual abuse allegation made by a child was another, more subtle line that was captured in the words of Fournier. The men accused of sexual abuse by children, he wrote, were "all too often excellent and perfectly honorable . . . absolutely incapable of ignominious action" (cited in Masson, 1985, p. 43). That opinion resonated very well with the patriarchy of the times and was shared by many of Fournier's colleagues in medicine and in law. Patriarchy, in fact, was a kind of ideational envelope that held skepticism and doubt in children's veracity and in men's culpability. This was an envelope that had to be ripped open by a new generation of social scientists and once its contents were spilled and examined, the paradoxical character of an allegation of sexual abuse was evident again.

This historical legacy of skepticism was confronted in the most organized fashion in recent years. Armed with surveys and questionnaires that were expedient and relatively nonintrusive methods of obtaining sensitive personal information about childhood sexual experiences from large samples of people, social scientists began documenting the prevalence of this type of victimization (Peters, Wyatt, & Finkelhor, 1986). Their data, although far from consistent due to the methodological variations in their research, nonetheless were as startling in their impact as were those first few cases described by Tardieu a century before.

And they were now much more difficult to dismiss. Unencumbered by psychoanalysis and psychiatry's historical mantle of skepticism and doubt, social scientists were more inclined to believe that their data reflected actual experiences rather than childhood fantasies or self-serving distortions of memory. The recent ebb and flow of social change also had created a historical moment conducive to the questioning of tradition, ideology, and custom; a historical moment open to advocacy, challenge, and justice. Children, so long overlooked by society, disbelieved by psychiatry and ignored by the law, became a *cause célèbre* and allegations of sexual abuse made by them often were believed without question and pursued with passion. The failure to do either of those, as a matter of fact, often was viewed as tantamount to having bought into that century-old agenda rooted in doubt and patriarchal ideology (Brownmiller, 1975; Rush, 1980).

It may require the buffer of years to evaluate the consequences of this recent and dramatic change in attitude and practice. It already has been predicted that the unquestioning belief in any child's allegation and the active pursuit of justice in courts of law will be favorably compared with the Salem witchcraft trials of the 17th century (Underwager & Wakefield, 1985). It has been anticipated by some that certain professions that have close and sustained personal contact with children will be increasingly vulnerable to suspicion, rumor and even legal harassment (Sale, 1984). And others still forecast that what now appears to be an epidemic of child sexual abuse will be analyzed in the future as nothing more than an artifact of the frenetic activities of misguided professionals who fancy themselves experts in the field (Hechler, 1988).

Quite aside from future judgments, the present poses its own problems. This is an era where many marriages fail and child custody and visitation issues are determined daily in courts of law; where the sexually scintillating images from television and films can be found in virtually every home; where many children spend most of their day in the custodial care of nonfamilial people; where professionals are mandated by law to report suspected cases of sexual abuse and risk malpractice suits if they fail to do so. This is an era of motivations for false allegations by both adults and children; an era of programs and laws for responding to them. This is an era where the substantiation of truth in any one case of child sexual abuse only engenders doubt that truth will be found in any other. The century-old paradox persists.

IN THE MIDDLE OF THE PARADOX

Some contemporary professionals would characterize the dilemma discussed in this admittedly thumbnail sketch of historical reactions to children's allegations of sexual abuse as a battle between disbelievers and believers (Hechler, 1988; Herman, 1981; Summit, 1988). They would argue that there always have been those who disbelieve the estimated prevalence of child sexual abuse, and those who believe it. The disbelievers, their argument continues, can only maintain that position by denying the veracity of children's allegations of sexual abuse, thus refuting the official statistics; the believers, on the other hand, can only concede the official statistics by believing the allegations made by children.

The dichotomy suggested by this argument, however, is painted with too wide a brush. A Century ago Fournier determined that the *majority* of the allegations made by children could be dismissed as the products of fantasy; and even Brouardel conceded that *some* of the allegations corroborated by medical evidence would have to be accepted as true. Even those contemporary professionals who would most ardently characterize themselves as believers conclude that *most* children do not lie, but grant that *some* children can be coerced or inveigled by adults into making false allegations of sexual abuse (Corwin, Berliner, Goodman, & Goodwin, 1987; Faller, 1984).

Those qualifying words are important. They indicate that even along the outer facet of this paradox no absolute statements have been made that can be used conveniently to dichotomize professionals into believers and disbelievers. The issue at hand is not whether all allegations are true or false, but *which* ones are. It is that persistent issue that draws attention to the middle of the paradox and to a shared concern: How can the credibility of a child's allegation of sexual abuse be assessed?

And this is a major concern. Peters (1976) determined that 6% of the 64 children evaluated in a hospital emergency room had falsely alleged they had been sexually abused. That same percentage of false allegations was reported by Goodwin, Sahd, and Rada (1978) in their analysis of 46 cases of children referred to a sexual abuse treatment center. In a review of 576 reports of child abuse made to a metropolitan department of social services, Jones and McGraw (1987) calculated that 8% were false. These estimated rates of false allegations increase significantly in child custody and visitation cases, when acrimonious feelings between estranged or divorcing parents are aired in the adversarial setting of a courtroom (Awad, 1987; Dwyer, 1985; Guyer & Ash, 1986; Kaplan & Kaplan, 1981), and where motivations for making false allegations are apparent. Current data suggest that up to 10% of all of these types of cases involve an accusation and often a counteraccusation of sexual abuse (Thoennes & Pearson, 1988). Yet many of these accusations are determined to be false. Benedek and Schetky (1985), for example, were unable to substantiate the sexual abuse allegations in 55% of the 18 visitation and custody cases they examined; Green (1986) failed to do so in 36% of the 11 cases he reviewed. An even alarmingly higher rate was calculated by Yates and Musty (1987). In their study of child custody cases in which sexual abuse was alleged, they were unable to verify the allegations made in 79% of the 19 cases they analyzed.

Other cases that involve the alleged sexual abuse of what are often large numbers of children within a single setting, such as a preschool or day-care center, also raise concerns about false allegations. Many of these types of cases have come to public view under the unrelenting glare of national and international media coverage, yet few of them have remained in that light unchanged. Rather, time sees the adding and dropping of criminal charges, the making and retracting of accusations, and the waxing and waning of suspicions and rumors, and the only thing that persists unchanged over the months and even years of public attention is the paradoxical character of these sexual abuse allegation:

> One of the reasons sexual abuse in day care inspires so much controversy is that allegations are often difficult to substantiate. In virtually every case, there are both people convinced that abuse occurred and people (if only allies of the accused) who remain doubtful. Even dealing with the issue in the abstract, there are those professionals who believe that almost any allegation of abuse coming from a child so young must have some truth, and there are others who believe that many day-care workers are being unfairly "tarred and feathered" today by mistaken allegations. (Finkelhor, Williams, & Burns, 1988, p. 13)

No single discipline owns child sexual abuse as a matter of concern, therefore more than one discipline may be called upon to make an assessment of a single case of alleged child sexual abuse, a process that only adds to what is already a significant degree of confusion. Thus, professionals from a variety of different fields, with varying levels of skill, are each making judgments as to the credibility and veracity of a child's disclosures of sexual abuse (Herbert, 1987; Renshaw, 1987; Stone, Tyler, & Mead, 1984). These assessments are necessary, of course, for the creation of a phenomenological understanding of the experiences of a sexually abused child so that effective intervention and treatment strategies can be implemented. A problem arises, however, with the fact that these professionals approach the assessment process from perspectives as diverse as the disciplines they represent, and often come to conclusions that are odds with those reached by others.

Even that is not the end to the problem. An alliance once again is being forged between these various professionals and the legal system so that information gleaned during the assessment process is used by the legal system to determine what, if any, criminal charges will be placed against the alleged perpetrator, and whether the child will make a credible witness in a court of law. That these various professionals too often are untrained in evidentiary rules, that they infrequently have all of the necessary information and facts they need to come to a certain conclusion regarding the truthfulness of an allegation, and that they use a variety of different models in arriving at a judgment (Mantell, 1988; Wehrspann, Steinhauer, & Klajner-Diamond, 1987) only makes what the poet Milton described as "confusion worse confounded."

That latter point regarding the variety of models that can be used to assess the credibility of an allegation deserves closer attention. In recent years, and in keeping with the paradoxical character of an allegation of child sexual abuse, a number of models have been developed to guide professionals through the morass of difficulties inherent in an assessment process. To date, none of these models is quantitative in nature, that is, none is capable of generating a statistical prediction. Instead, each is a conceptual model that creates qualitative categories. The final judgment at which the professional will arrive, then, will be stated on a conjectural continuum between "the allegation is definitely false" on one end, and "the allegation is definitely true" on the other (Bresee, Sterns, Bess, & Packer, 1986; deYoung, 1986, 1988; Klajner-Diamond, Wehrspann, & Steinhauer, 1987).

And that final judgment may be suspect. Because there is no standard model or scheme for evaluation purposes, professionals are inclined to develop their own; each researcher and practitioner, therefore, arrives at a judgment from a different path. Yates and Musty (1987), for example, used the following checklist for determining false accusations: the presence of a persuasive caretaker who has something to gain from the child's allegation of sexual abuse; the presence of sexualized perceptions originating in the oedipal conflict of the child; the appearance of primary process material in the language, thoughts, and ideas of the child; and the involvement of the child in the projective identification of a dominant caretaker. Researchers with a less psychoanalytic bent would find this checklist arguable, at best; practitioners would find it unworkable, and both would be inclined to question the conclusion that 79% of the sexual abuse allegations studied were false.

Even less ideologically influenced models should raise serious questions as to their viability because most consist only of checklists of some kind, against which the researcher or evaluator can compare both the putative facts of the case and the child's allegation. Jones and McGraw (1987), for example, conclude that false allegations of sexual abuse are characterized by the absence of detail; also emotion, and description of threats, and by the presence of a hysterical or paranoid mother. Green and Schetky (1988) add to that list the lack of symptoms of sexual abuse in the child, a discrepancy between the child's angry accusation and his or her apparent comfort in the father's presence, and the unwillingness of the child to discuss the alleged sexual abuse unless so prompted by the mother. Child protective service workers tend to work from a different checklist. Everson and Boat (1989) find that more than half of the workers they surveyed used retraction of the allegation as the primary, if not sole reason for determining that the original allegation was false, even while they acknowledged that a child can be pressured by skeptical professionals and unsupportive adults to withdraw the allegation. The researchers, disturbed by these findings, conclude that an examination of the criteria used in assessing the validity of the child's allegation "raises serious questions in several cases about the adequacy of the evaluation and the accuracy of the ultimate determination" (p. 16).

As is typical in other types of approaches to determining the truthfulness of an allegation, none of those guidelines provides direction for *how* information is to be gathered, let alone assessed. And, except for rather broad caveats "to be aware of the impact of the child's cognitive limitations on his (or her) perception and recall of the events of the molestation," (Green & Schetky, 1988, p. 107), the influences of the developmentally based skills of the complaining child rarely are taken into consideration. Different models indeed may lead to different conclusions. Thus neither a retracted nor an unsubstantiated allegation of sexual abuse should be summarily evaluated as false.

There is considerable consensus among the various professionals who are being called upon to do this assessment task that the development of a systematic guideline for gleaning information that can be used to assess the credibility of a sexual abuse allegation is necessary. Such a model would guide their understanding of the nature and effects of sexual abuse, help them through the labyrinths of conflicting ideologies, liberate them from the dead facts and worn-out myths that have plagued this concern for more than a century and, most importantly, allow them to come to a judgment about the credibility of an allegation that is based on something more rigorous than a checklist and more reliable than mere hunch.

A CONCEPTUAL MODEL

The proposed conceptual model for assessing the credibility of a child's allegation of sexual abuse is a logical, systematic template that directs the professional, regardless of discipline, to the relevant features of the experience of sexual abuse, to the interactions between them, and to the child's developmental and life-course issues that may impact on these features. This guide outlines a series of investigative steps and assesses the type and quality of information that is needed at each step before a final judgment as to the credibility of the allegation can be made.

Allegation of Sexual Abuse

This model begins with the allegation of sexual abuse. It assumes that it may originate with the child or with another person, most likely a parent or some other trusted adult. While the source of the allegation is impor-tant to this model, it nonetheless directs the professional to begin with the child's version of the abuse, and to be guided by the helpful organiz-ing schemes provided in the child development literature that may affect the unfolding of this account (deYoung, 1987; Summit, 1983).

Clarity. The clarity of an allegation of sexual abuse may be precluded by the cognitive style of a young child who is between the ages of 2 and 5. In this preoperational stage of development, a child tends to engage in such distinctive thought processes as egocentrism, concreteness, trans-ductive reasoning, centering and lack of conservation (Phillips, 1981; Singer & Reveson, 1978), any one of which is likely to render the allegation unclear.

That allegation, in fact, may become lost in a stream of consciousness style of communication in which words and ideas have idiosyncratic referents and illogical associations. As the young child reasons from one particular idea to another with no discernible connection between them, the professional may lose the thread of the allegation that winds often too vaguely through what may sound like a free-associative mode of communication. This cognitive and communicative style, of course, is developmentally based and reflects the young child's tendency toward egocentrism, concreteness, and transductive reasoning.

Even if the allegation is clear, other features of the young child's cognitive style may cast doubts on his or her credibility. Centering, for example, refers to the tendency to perceive and define an object only in relation to its particular function. In alleging sexual abuse, then, the young child may refer to ejaculation as urination because that is the perceived function of the penis. There is also a lack of conservation in this preoperational cognitive style. Unable to understand that objects remain the same despite changes in physical appearance, the young child may believe that an erect penis is no longer a penis because of its change in shape and in size.

These developmental factors, then, diminish the likelihood that an allegation of sexual abuse will be so clear that it could stand alone as a measure of truth. But what about the clarity of an allegation made by an older child? A vague, obfuscated accusation should be carefully examined and questioned by the professional conducting the evaluation because there are no compelling developmental reasons why an older child's allegation would lack clarity. There may be other reasons why it does, however. An older child who has been pressured to secrecy by the perpetrator of the abuse, or who has been coerced or manipulated by another person to lie, may make vague and confusing statements. The reason why the allegation lacks clarity, however, cannot be determined until further investigative steps have been taken.

Despite recent concerns that a sexually frank family environment and/or the exposure to sexually explicit media may provide a child of any age with sexual knowledge that is incommensurate with his or her developmental level (Green, 1986), the child's demonstration of age-inappropriate sexual knowledge generally is considered to be an indicator that the allegation is credible (Corwin, 1989). And there is preliminary empirical verification for this assumption. In her examination of 103 cases of child sexual abuse, Faller (1988) determined that a child's ability to describe the sexual behavior in a manner that is explicit, that demonstrates advanced sexual knowledge, and that is in the child's own language is highly correlated with an allegation whose truth is substantiated by the perpetrator's confession.

Celerity. The literature demonstrates that a child of any age may not make an accusation until days, months or, in some cases, even years after the alleged event (Conte & Berliner, 1981; deYoung, 1981; Hunter, Kilstrom, & Loda, 1985). Delays in allegations largely are attributed to the pressures for secrecy placed on the child by the perpetrator, and the child's fear of not being believed or of being blamed. More the rule than the exception, a lack of celerity should not be used to dismiss summarily an allegation as false.

Suspicions typically are raised when an older child or an adolescent delays making an accusation. What Bourdin a century ago described as the child's susceptibility "to cupidity, to hatred, to vengance, to enmity, to jealousy" (cited in Masson, 1985, p. 48) underlies the concern that the timing of an allegation may be deliberately and propitiously calibrated to other life events. And, in fact, that must be considered a possibility. An older child or adolescent can make a false allegation out of spite or anger, or can be pressured into doing that by someone else who will gain from it, and that indeed may affect the timing of the accusation. The professional, however, is encouraged to suspend any judgment regarding the credibility of the allegation until such other factors as the motive or pressure to lie have been carefully examined and considered.

Certainty. Perhaps there is no other feature that more illustrates the parodoxical character of an allegation of child sexual abuse than its certainty. Historically, a young child's reticence and timidity in making an allegation was reason alone to dismiss it summarily as false. Bourdin's classic case of the mute child, published over a century ago, is a sterling example of this facet of the paradox. He described a boy, 6 or 7 years old, who upon admission to a hospital was able to understand and obey the medical personnel but was unable to communicate with them verbally. He remained mute for a year. One day, however, he uttered a word in the presence of a nurse who painstakingly worked with him until he was again able to talk and when he could, he hesitantly and reluctantly alleged that he had been sexually abused by his father who had purchased his year of silence with threats to his life. Once that allegation finally was voiced, however, the child refused to elaborate upon it or to give his father's name or his family's address and Bourdin, noting his uncertainty and diffidence, dismissed the allegation as false (Bourdin, 1880).

What Bourdin did not understand a century ago is that the same cognitive style that clouds the clarity of a young child's allegation also will obscure its certainty. What he did not appreciate is that some of the attendant features of the sexual abuse experience — the pressure for secrecy, the attribution of blame, the reinterpretation of morality (deYoung, 1981, 1982; Lister, 1982; Summit, 1983) — may leave a child, particularly a young child, confused both as to the nature of the abuse and its consequences.

Professionals today seem to be guided less by the judgments of Bourdin than the words of the poet Yeats: "The best lack all conviction, while the worst are full of passionate intensity." A hesitant, uncertain allegation now is considered more the rule than the exception and often is taken as prima facie evidence of credibility; a bold, passionate allegation, on the other hand, often is perceived as an overcompensatory attempt to disguise Machiavellian machinations and coldly calculated lies.

It is to the middle of the paradox that attention must be focused. The certainty with which an allegation is offered varies from one child to another and is dependent on factors that the professional always must keep in mind. These include, but are not limited to, the nature of the alleged sexual abuse, the pressure for secrecy, the motivation for lying, and the cognitive style and language skills of the child. There is no evidence that in and of itself, certainty or lack of same is a sufficient criterion for a judgment as to the credibility of an allegation.

Consistency. A recent survey of 212 child protection workers, mental health therapists, and legal professionals indicates that 96% agree that the consistency of a child's allegation of sexual abuse over time is a valuable criterion for assessing its credibility (Corwin, 1989). They reason that an allegation that persists without embellishment or abridgment in the face of repeated questioning by what very well may be a number of skeptical professionals, must bear the weight of truth.

Yet a caveat must be offered. Despite the wisdom of these professionals, a wisdom that is derived from training and experience, there is case study and empirical evidence in the literature that a child may be inclined to amend or even retract an allegation in response to the reactions of others, or to the fears of the consequences of disclosure (Conte & Berliner, 1981; DeJong, 1985; Hunter et al., 1985). In the light of that evidence, therefore, neither consistency nor inconsistency can be considered a sufficient criterion for judging the credibility of an allegation.

The evaluation of the allegation is simply the first of a number of investigative steps that must be taken. The professional is advised to take to heart the wisdom offered by the playwright Fry: "Critical judgment is so exquisite it leaves us nothing to admire except opinion." After all, there is no compelling evidence that an allegation alone, whether given by a young or an older child, will provide enough information for the purpose of evaluating its credibility. There is only compelling evidence that a judgment made on an allegation alone is just the stuff of opinion, susceptible to bias and error.

Elaboration of Details

The second series of investigative steps in this conceptual model involves the elicitation from the child of elaborated details about the alleged sexual abuse. These details should be systematically and rigorously explored because they provide the opportunity for the professional to check and cross-check information in such a way as to enhance the certainty of judgment.

Specific Details. Inquiries should be made of the child as to the nature of the abuse that he or she allegedly experienced. With a young child this process can be greatly facilitated with the use of props that will help to distinguish a sexually abused child from a nonabused child. Anatomically correct dolls are particularly useful. Research consistently has shown that a sexually abused child is more likely to focus on the genitals of the dolls, to simulate sexual behavior with the doll or between dolls, to make sexual references in language while playing with the dolls, and to disclose personal incidents of sexual abuse than is a nonabused child (Sivan, Schor, Koeppl, & Noble, 1988; White, Strom, Santilli, & Halpin, 1986). Professionals who want to use the dolls for assessment purposes are well advised to seek training in doing so, since there is evidence that the accuracy of professional judgment is highly related to the skill of use and the sophistication of interpretation (Boat & Everson, 1988). Other assessment tools, such as drawings, are shown to be helpful in distinguishing a sexually abused child from a nonabused child (Kelley, 1985; Yates, Beutler, & Cargo, 1985), and require an advanced skill for interpretation.

Perhaps the most useful advice to give a professional regarding the use of these props is that they will not serve as assessment tools unless the professional is trained to use them as such. Without that training, they should be used cautiously, if at all, and whatever interpretation the professional is tempted to come to by virtue of their use should be considered speculative and tentative, and should not bear the total weight of the final assessment.

A description by a child of any age of a progression of sexual acts over time is noteworthy. A child who is lying or is being manipulated or coerced by an adult into making a false allegation is certainly not likely to know that the literature demonstrates that multiple acts over a period of time often advance along a continuum that begins with fondling and/or masturbation, proceeds to oral contact, penetration with objects or fingers, and then possibly to vaginal and/or rectal intercourse (DeJong, 1985; Faller, 1984). Also, any single act or series of acts described by the child in language that exhibits age-inappropriate knowledge about sexual behavior is especially noteworthy and should be carefully explored.

The older the child, however, the more likely that sexual information has become part of his or her general knowledge and, particularly in the case of an adolescent, sexual activity may have become a part of personal experience. In either case, the child may be able to give a believable description of sexual abuse without having experienced it. The additional investigative steps of this model will provide a check and balance against a concocted allegation that is made at this level of inquiry.

Contextual Details. Information about who is alleged to have perpetrated the sexual abuse, where it occurred, and when are the contextual details that next should be pursued with the child. Recent studies have reinforced the wisdom of professionals that the absence of details or the presence of greatly conflicting details are correlated with false allegations (Bresee et al., 1986; Faller, 1984, 1988; Jones & McGraw, 1987).

For any child, but most especially for a young child, these details are best elicited through short, direct questions, which have been shown to stimulate memory retrieval cues (Kabasigawa, 1974; Marin, Holmes, Guth, & Kovac, 1979). While the susceptibility of any child to interviewer suggestion probably has been greatly overestimated (Cohen & Harnick, 1980), leading questions nonetheless should be strenuously avoided.

The child should be asked to describe the place in which the alleged act of sexual abuse occurred. Details such as the location, the color of the room, the arrangement of the furniture, as examples, enhance the credibility of the allegation and can be used as a check on the identification of the alleged perpetrator. For a young child, in particular, significant confusion is likely to arise if there were allegedly mutliple acts in different locations over a period of time.

Time is a difficult concept for a young child to master. At the preoperational stage of development, time is often confused with distance or length; it is often thought of as a place, such as suppertime in the kitchen or bedtime in the bedroom; and the past is simply perceived as the time before and has no sequential order. For older children, however, time concepts in general will be less of a problem.

However, for a child of any age, time concepts again become problematical if the child indeed has been traumatized, in the clinical sense of that term, by sexual abuse, or by some other traumatic event. Recent research shows that psychic trauma can significantly impair a child's perception of the duration and sequence of time (Terr, 1981, 1983), so a professional who encounters this problem during an assessment of a child is advised to make careful inquiries as to the nature and seriousness of the alleged abuse and as to a recent history of any other psychically disorganizing or overwhelming event in the life of the child.

Time-honored concerns regarding what this model refers to as contextual details must be addressed at this point. A hundred years has not mitigated the worry that a child of any age may render details that are the product of imagination and fantasy rather than of reality. Brouardel gave voice to that concern in 1883: "Their imagination likes to invent stories in which they are the hero. The child comforts herself by telling herself fantasies which she knows are false on every point" (cited in Masson, 1985, p. 44), and it was echoed by Green in 1986: "The child creates an aura of secrecy and excitement, often accompanied by a plethora of sexualized fantasies" (Green, 1988, pp. 116–117).

This issue of fantasy is only raised in this model, and unfortunately not resolved. The persistence of the belief that a child fantasizes about sexual behavior and may relate that fantasy as fact is well documented in the literature (Freud, 1965; Masson, 1985; Rosenfeld, Nadelson, & Krieger, 1977, 1979). What is considerably less clear, however, is whether a child fantasizes about sexual *abuse* and, just as importantly, whether that fantasy is then likely to be related as fact especially in the face of what often is adult skepticism and the concerted interventions of professionals who are strangers to the child.

The evidence would seem to weigh against that latter possibility. Child development research shows that a child of any age is highly dependent on actual experiences for the images of fantasies. It also demonstrates that fantasies are closely tied to the pleasure principle and therefore tend to have a hedonistic tone; that they tend to have themes of mastery, competence, and victory; and that they are easily distinguishable from reality by the child (Arieti, 1976; Freud, 1965; Jersild, 1968; Singer & Reveson, 1978).

A century also has not diminished the concern that a child could displace the responsibility for an actual act of sexual abuse on an innocent person. Since the recent construction of posttraumatic stress disorder as a clinical diagnostic category (Figley, 1985), new concerns have been raised that a child who was traumatized by a prior act of sexual abuse could attach his or her vivid memories of traumatization to a different, and innocent, person (Jones & McGraw, 1987) and then could relate specific details in making this new allegation. This is an intriguing and disturbing hypothesis that must be carefully researched, but at this point is considered too tentative to be included as an investigative step in this conceptual model.

Secrecy Details. In any case of child sexual abuse, a conspiracy of silence develops by a cabal of participants: The adult, eager to avoid public discovery and censure, pressures the child into silence; the child, eager to avoid the threatened consequences of disclosure, keeps their secret; and society, eager to sustain the bliss of ignorance, all too often looks the other way. That bond of secrecy that holds all together must be carefully and skillfully unraveled by the professional.

Only if a child feels protected from the negative consequences of disclosure will he or she talk freely about the secrecy surrounding the sexual abuse. More often, the child will be reticent, even vague, and will only unravel the account when that bond of secrecy loosens over time (deYoung, 1981; Lister, 1982). Professionals should inquire about a range of secrecy pressure techniques that may include threats of death or bodily harm; second-party threats against the child's family or friends; warnings about abandonment or withdrawal of love; bribes that may include toys, clothing, money, or special favors; the reinterpretation of reality that defines the sexual abuse as normal, healthy, or desirable; and the attribution of blame that holds the child responsible for the act and its consequences.

Secrecy pressure techniques that are calibrated to the developmental level and intelligence of the child are especially effective in gaining the child's silence. A young child, for example, may be intimidated by the tone of voice or the facial expression of a sexually abusive adult who threatens death if the secret is disclosed, but because a young child typically does not have an abiding and enduring concept of death the threat may be idle, if only because it is unmatched to the developmental level of the child. An older child or adolescent, as another example, may be effortlessly pressured to keep the secret by an offending adult who blames the child for the sexual abuse. In this case, the older child's moral development and attribution skills would not only predict the acceptance of responsibility for the abuse, but also the motivation to keep the secret. Secrets that are gauged to the developmental level and intelligence of the child, then, are particularly noteworthy for assessment purposes.

Affective Details. Feelings are critically distinguishing factors in this conceptual model. A child who has been sexually abused not only will experience many emotions in general as a result of the victimization, but particular emotions in regards to the different relevant features of that experience. A child who is making a false allegation or who is being pressured or coerced by an adult into doing so, is unlikely to know or to reveal convincingly the subtleties and nuances of these affective details.

The professional carefully should inquire as to the child's feelings about the sexually abusive act(s) per se. Experience shows that these acts can be placed along a continuum from nonintrusive abuse, such as fondling and masturbation, to intrusive abuse, such as vaginal and/or rectal intercourse. All things held constant, the more intrusive the abuse the more likely the child will report negative feelings, such as anger or fear; the less intrusive the abuse, the less negative the reported feelings are likely to be. The trick, of course, is in the holding of all things constant. Any child can be greatly influenced by the way that significant others interpret the abuse and may take their definition of it as his or her own. Professionals should remember that if warm, supportive, and trustworthy, they quickly can become significant others to a sexually abused child, therefore it is very important that they not provide significant emotional cues that the child will respond to or imitate.

Affective responses to the context of the alleged act(s) and to the pressure for secrecy also should be elicited. As a rule of thumb, the more commensurate the described feelings are with the details of these features of the abuse experience, the more credible the allegation. Yet even rules of thumb have exceptions. Feelings about the alleged perpetrator of the abuse often are not commensurate with descriptions of the abuse experience. A child of any age, in fact, often endures a great deal of ambivalence about the perpetrator. If that person is a parent, for example, strong affectionate bonds may be present even long after the sexual abuse has been disclosed; if that person is otherwise a trusted adult whose relationship with the child has proved to be occasionally rewarding, positive feelings may linger for a considerable time.

What only complicates this further is that a young child is not generally able to predict or judge the character of another person because that ability is based upon attribution skills that are not yet part of that child's developmentally based repertoire of talents. Unable to use stable, dispositional constructs in the description of another person, the young child tends to judge others by possessions or appearance rather than by behavior or character (Peevers & Secord, 1973; Rholes & Ruble, 1984), and therefore may be inclined to describe positive feelings about the alleged perpetrator despite the victimizing nature of the sexual abuse.

All of these affective details are held in a bundle of contradictions. A child who reports feeling frightened and hurt by an act of sexual penetration, also may report feeling happy about the toy he or she received for keeping the secret. A child who relates feelings of physical pleasure from an act of gentle, that is, nonintrusive molestation and a fondness for the perpetrator, also may relate feelings of fear because of the threats to keep the sexual abuse secret. This model hypothesizes that a child who is lying or who is being pressured into lying will not know the nuances of these affective details and may be more inclined to report consistent and unwavering negative emotions about each relevant feature of the abuse experience.

Supporting Details. Any evidence of details that support the allegation made by the child should be noted by the professional and aggressively pursued. The child should be asked if anyone, child or adult, witnessed the abusive act, and if he or she knows of other children who also were sexually abused by the alleged perpetrator. If similar accusations are being made by other children to other people, or if the alleged perpetrator has a criminal history of sexual offenses against children, the child's allegation is supported and its credibility is enhanced.

Indicators of Sexual Abuse

In a recent and frantic rush to address the problem of child sexual abuse, researchers have focused on the behavioral, emotional, and physical symptoms that it may engender and then have encouraged the use of these symptoms as indicators that the abuse indeed did take place. The vast majority of these earlier studies on symptoms were not empirical in nature but were, instead, clinical assessments of samples of sexually abused children; retrospective reviews of hospital, mental health, or court records; theoretical approaches to the nature of sexual abuse symptomatology; and case studies of small samples of sexually abused children with similar symptomatology (Adams-Tucker, 1982; Conte & Berliner, 1981; deYoung, 1984).

And this "catalog phase" of research, as Finkelhor (1988) refers to it, produced a long inventory of the indicia of sexual abuse that recalls the lament of the essayist Pope: "Here am I, dying of a hundred good symptoms." Some of these symptoms found in the literature are reported with some degree of consistency from one study to another, others are not, and still others are unique and abstruse at best. This veritable grab bag of indicators of sexual abuse has lent itself to misapplication and most certainly to false positive predictions. In the more recent "documentation phase" of this research, statistical measurements of the impact of sexual abuse are being compared with recognized indexes of psychopathology (Browne & Finkelhor, 1986) and those symptoms that cannot be empirically verified as sequelae of sexual abuse are being emptied out of the grab bag.

While much more documentation type of research yet needs to be done, some researchers already are moving into a "modeling phase" in which lines of influence between the phenomenology of the sexual abuse experience and the attitudes, feelings, and behaviors of the child are being sketched into general theoretical models of the process of traumatization. It is this approach that promises to create a deeper and richer understanding of the effects of child sexual abuse, and although still tentative, it organizes clinical observations and empirical research in such a way that reduces the chance that a professional will blindly reach into that grab bag of so-called indicators and pull out one or two that may not be indicators at all.

One of the most useful models for distinguishing the symptoms of sexual abuse is that of Finkelhor and Browne (1985) who posit four traumagenic features of the experience of sexual abuse that will alter a child's cognitive and emotional orientation and create trauma by distorting the child's self-esteem, world-view, and emotional capacities. A child's attempt to cope with the world through these distortions will result in symptoms that can be assessed as indicators of sexual abuse and that, if present or reported, will add to the credibility of a child's allegation.

One of those traumagenic features is traumatic sexualization. Characteristic of the abuse experience, it occurs when the child is rewarded by the perpetrator for sexual behavior and when parts of the child's anatomy are fetishized. As a result, the child's sexual feelings and attitudes are shaped in developmentally and interpersonally inappropriate ways, creating symptoms that may include sexual aggression, compulsive masturbation, or repetitious play with sexual themes. The second traumagenic feature is betrayal. The child's trust and dependency are betrayed by the offending adult as a result of the sexual abuse and the child may react with symptoms of grief, depression, dependency, or regressive behaviors.

Disempowerment is the third traumagenic factor of sexual abuse. Arising from the fact that in a sexually abusive relationship the child's needs, desires, and will are contravened by the offending adult, it tends to produce symptoms of anxiety, fear, phobias, nightmares, and hypervigilance. The final traumagenic factor of sexual abuse is stigmatization. Messages that have to do with culpability, blame, and fault often are communicated to the child by the offending adult. Resultant symptoms, then, may include guilt and shame, low self-esteem, suicidal ideation, and self-injuring behavior.

Using a scheme such as this really empties out the grab-bag of indicators and helps the professional to distinguish symptoms related to the sexual abuse experience from those that are not. But knowing what the symptoms are is only part of the task; the other is having some kind of objective measure of them. Relying on the report of the child or of the parents may not give the most accurate information. A child or a parent who is lying, or a child who is being pressured to lie may exaggerate and even concoct symptoms; parents who anxiously consider the possibility that their child may have been sexually abused may retrospectively interpret the child's behavior so it appears to be more symptomatic than it is. Thus more objective measures are needed in this critical area of assessment.

A variety of tests can be used which measure the child's self-concept, behavioral problems, relationship to parents, and body image, any one or more of which could be significantly altered by the traumagenic features of the sexual abuse experience (Adams-Tucker, 1982; Bressee et al., 1986; Friedrich, 1989). A child between the age of 3 and 5 can be given the Child Sexual Behavior Inventory, the Draw-a-Person or Draw-a-Family Test, the Conger Children's Completion Test, the Children's Apperception Test, or the Louisville Behavior Checklist. A child between the ages of 6 and 12 can take that same battery of tests as well as the Children's Manifest Anxiety Scale, the Piers-Harris-Children's Self-concept Test, or the Robert's Apperception Test. While no test, in and of itself, is able to differentiate a sexually abused child from a nonabused child, measures more objective than description are needed to assist the professional in determining the credibility of an allegation.

Vulnerability of the Child. The fact that one child is sexually abused and another is not may be more than just a matter of circumstances or fate. There is evidence in the literature that certain types of children indeed are more at risk for sexual abuse, so the vulnerability of the child should be the next assessment made by the professional.

It is axiomatic that any child can be sexually abused. Even if an adult lacks persuasive skills, his or her superior strength and power can bring about the victimization of the child. But research and other evidence demonstrate that the use of brute force and violence is *not* typical in cases of child sexual abuse; rather, a child is more likely to be cajoled, manipulated, lured, or enticed by an adult into a sexually abusive act. Therefore, assessing the vulnerability of a child to these techniques is a critical step in this conceptual model.

Research shows that a child with little accurate sexual knowledge (Gilgun & Gordon, 1985), few self-protective coping skills (deYoung, 1982), a history of prior sexual victimization (Miller et al., 1978) and a weak, conflictual bond with the parents (Paveza, 1988) are psychologically vulnerable to sexual buse. And there is also a kind of familial vulnerability that has been shown in the literature. A child who has a stepfather (Finkelhor, 1980; Gruber & Jones, 1983), who has a parent who is absent from the home or unavailable for a length of time (Finkelhor, 1984), or whose family is socially or geographically isolated (Finkelhor, 1984) appears to be at more risk for sexual victimization both inside and outside of the family than are other children.

If none of these factors exists, it will be necessary to re-examine carefully details regarding the context of the alleged abuse and the pressure for secrecy. A child who would not generally be thought of as at risk for sexual abuse, very well could have had his or her repertoire of coping skills overwhelmed by the offending adult. If these and other elaborated details do not bolster this hypothesis, however, then the last step in this conceptual model may be the litmus test for assessing the credibility of a child's allegation of sexual abuse.

Motivation for Lying. This is an era where the substantiation of truth in any one case of child sexual abuse only engenders doubt that truth will be found in any other. The century-old paradoxical character of an allegation of sexual abuse persists. But once again it is to the middle of the paradox that attention must be drawn: Not every child who alleges sexual abuse is lying, neither is every child telling the truth. Therefore, inquiries into the motivation to lie must be examined in this conceptual model.

The weight of evidence would argue against a child spontaneously concocting a lie about having been sexually abused, as well as against a child innocently reporting a fantasy as if it were the truth. Since these are still debatable, and therefore researchable assertions, they should be treated as such. For the purposes of this conceptual model, however, it is more important and more instructive to look again at the middle of the paradox and into that gray area where pressures to lie abound.

The power of an adult to inveigle or coerce a child into making a false allegation is indisputable. In the vast majority of research that has been done on false allegations, the person making the original complaint is the adult, not the child. The task of the professional, then, is to determine if such a pressure to lie exists and with whom it originates. A sexual abuse allegation made in the context of a divorce or custody battle is particularly suspect, as has been previously explained in this model; however there are other reasons why an adult may manipulate or force a child to make a false allegation. Any list of these reasons would be as incomplete as it would be spurious, so the professional is advised to examine carefully the family and relationship networks of the child with an eye to uncovering any of these motivations.

The personality of the players in this allegation also is a factor to be taken into consideration. If it is an adult who makes, sustains, and embellishes the allegation, leaving the child to do nothing more than simply confirm it, a suspicion should be entertained by the professional that the allegation is false. If it is the adult who clearly gains by the consequences of the allegation being accepted as true, the possibility that it is really false must be carefully considered. Finally, if it is the adult who is suffering from the lingering trauma of childhood sexual victimization or from a psychiatric disorder, the likelihood that the child's allegation is false increases. These assertions should be treated as probabilities rather than as axioms; as such, they should be considered only *after* the other investigative steps in this model have been taken, and should always be weighed against the other details that have been elicited.

A child who is being forced or manipulated into lying will experience that pressure as stress (Dwyer, 1985; Kaplan & Kaplan, 1981). Because a child tends to become behaviorally disorganized under stress, he or she is likely to exhibit symptoms of that disorganization; symptoms that will be different, in fact, from those that arise from the traumagenic features of the sexual abuse experience. Here lies another reason why the emptying of that grab bag of indicators of sexual abuse is so important to the prevention of false positive predictions.

If a reason to pressure the child into making a false allegation can be determined, then the focus needs to be placed on the person who is applying that pressure. The professional must consider whether that person should be clinically evaluated and what kinds of therapeutic strategies must be designed to intervene in what surely must be an emotionally abusive experience for the child. In this final step in the conceptual model, as in every other, the welfare of the child is the preeminent concern.

The guide that has been developed in this chapter is not a conceptual lie detector. It is, instead, a logical systematic template that outlines a sequence of investigative steps that should be taken by a professional who has been given the unenviable task of assessing the credibility of a child's allegation of sexual abuse. Once taken, these steps will lead the professional to make with some confidence a qualitative judgment as to credibility of the child's allegation.

FUTURE RESEARCH PROSPECTS

The final judgment at which the professional will arrive using any model will be stated on a conjectural continuum between "the allegation is definitely false" on one end, and "the allegation is definitely true" on the other. What is needed to increase the validity of that conclusion are judgment categories that are clinically and/or empirically based. Conte (1989) is moving in that direction with a national survey of validation practices that is being disseminated to investigators and mental health practitioners throughout the country. The cumulative wisdom gleaned from that survey, coupled with a careful examination of the literature, should assist in the development of a model that eventually can be subjected to empirical verification.

CONCLUSION

The poet Meredith once lamented: "Ah, what a dusty answer gets the soul when hot for certainties in this our life!" In these chaotic times when child sexual abuse appears to be of an epidemic proportion and where motivations to accuse innocent people abound, we are hot for certainties in this our professional life.

The conceptual model developed in this chapter will not relieve that heat because it is only an answer, and an admittedly dusty one at that. Yet it is an answer that arises from the middle of the paradox, away from its outer facets that have been drawn during the last century in bold, ideological strokes. For it is in the middle of this paradox that questions are being raised, challenges to dead facts and worn-out myths are being thrown down, and intellectual excitement is being stirred. It is in this dusty and uncertain middle where the future of the discipline lies.

REFERENCES

Adams-Tucker, C. (1982). Proximate effects of sexual abuse in childhood: A report on 28 children. *American Journal of Psychiatry, 139,* 1252–1256.

Arieti, S. (1976). *Creativity: The magic synthesis.* New York: Basic Books.

Awad, G. (1987). The assessment of custody and access dispute in cases of sexual abuse allegations. *Canadian Journal of Psychiatry, 32,* 539–544.

Benedek, E., & Schetky, D. (1985). Allegations of sexual abuse in child custody and visitation disputes. In D. Schetky & E. Benedek (Eds.), *Emerging issues in child psychiatry and the law* (pp. 145–146). New York: Brunner/Mazel.

Boat, B. W., & Everson, M. D. (1988). Use of anatomical dolls among professionals in sexual abuse evaluations. *Child Abuse and Neglect: The International Journal, 12,* 295–304.

Bourdin, C. E. (1880). Les enfants menteurs (Children who lie). *Annales Medico-psycholiques, 6,* 53–67, 374–386.

Bresee, P., Sterns, G. B., Bess, B., & Packer, L. (1986). Allegations of child sexual abuse in custody disputes: A therapeutic assessment model. *American Journal of Orthopsychiatry, 56,* 560–569.

Browne, A., & Finkelhor, D. (1986). Impact of child sexual abuse: A review of the research. *Psychological Bulletin, 99,* 66–77.

Brownmiller, S. (1975). *Against our will.* New York: Simon & Schuster.

Cohen, R. L., & Harnick, M. A. (1980). The susceptibility of child witnesses to suggestion. *Law and Human Behavior, 4,* 201–210.

Conte, J. R., & Berliner, L. (1981). Sexual abuse of children. Implications for practice. *Social Casework, 62,* 601–607.

Corwin, D. L. (1989). New research: Survey explores consensus among experts evaluating suspected cases of child sexual abuse. *Advisor, 2*(1), 8–9.

Corwin, D. L., Berliner, L., Goodman, G., & Goodwin, J. (1987). Child sexual abuse and custody disputes: No easy answer. *Journal of Interpersonal Violence, 2,* 95–105.

DeJong, A. R. (1985). The medical evaluation of sexual abuse of children. *Hospital and Community Psychiatry, 36,* 509–512.

deYoung, M. (1981). Promises, threats and lies: Keeping incest secret. *Journal of Humanics, 9,* 61–71.

deYoung, M. (1982). Innocent seducer or innocently seduced? The role of the child incest victim. *Journal of Clinical Child Psychology, 11,* 56–60.

deYoung, M. (1984). Counterphobic behavior in multiply molested children. *Child Welfare, 63,* 333–339.

deYoung, M. (1986). A conceptual model for judging the truthfulness of a child's allegation of sexual abuse. *American Journal of Orthopsychiatry, 56,* 550–559.

deYoung, M. (1987). Disclosing sexual abuse: The impact of developmental variables. *Child Welfare, 66,* 217–223.

deYoung, M. (1988). Issues in determining the veracity of sexual abuse allegations. *Children's Health Care, 17,* 50–57.

Dwyer, M. (1985). New custody gambit: Mother alleges sexual abuse by father. *Sexuality Today, 8,* 1–2.

Everson, M. D., & Boat, B. W. (1989). False allegations of sexual abuse. *Advisor of the American Professional Society on the Abuse of Children, 2,* 15–16.

Faller, K. C. (1984). Is the child victim of sexual abuse telling the truth? *Child Abuse and Neglect: The International Journal, 8,* 473–481.

Faller, K. C. (1988). Criteria for judging the credibility of children's statements about their sexual abuse. *Child Welfare, 67,* 389–401.

Figley, C. R. (Ed.). (1985). *Trauma and its wake: The study and treatment of post-traumatic stress disorder.* New York: Brunner/Mazel.

Finkelhor, D. (1980). Risk factors in the sexual victimization of children. *Child Abuse and Neglect: The International Journal, 4,* 265–273.

Finkelhor, D. (1984). *Child sexual abuse: New theory and research.* New York: Free Press.

Finkelhor, D. (1988). The trauma of child sexual abuse: Two models. In G. E. Wyatt & G. J. Powell (Eds.), *Lasting effects of child sexual abuse* (pp. 61–82). Beverly Hills, CA: Sage.

Finkelhor, D., & Browne, A. (1985). The traumatic impact of child sexual abuse: A conceptualization. *American Journal of Orthopsychiatry, 55,* 530–541.

Finkelhor, D., Williams, L. M., & Burns, N. (1988). *Nursery crimes: Sexual abuse in day care.* Beverly Hills, CA: Sage.

Freud, A. (1965). *Normality and pathology in childhood.* New York: International Universities Press.

Friedrich, W. N. (1989). The child sexual behavior inventory: Preliminary normative data. *Advisor, 2,* 9, 11.

Gilgun, J. F., & Gordon, S. (1985). Sex education and the prevention of child sexual abuse. *Journal of Sex Education and Therapy, 11,* 46–52.

Goodwin, J., Sahd, D., & Rada, R. (1978). Incest hoax: False accusations, false denials. *Bulletin of the American Academy of Psychiatry and Law, 25,* 449–456.

Green, A. H. (1986). True and false allegations and sexual abuse in child custody disputes. *Journal of the American Academy of Child Psychiatry, 25*, 449–456.

Green, A. H., & Schetky, D. H. (1988). True and false allegations of sexual abuse. In D. H. Schetky & A. H. Green (Eds.), *Child sexual abuse: A handbook for health care and legal professionals* (pp. 104–124). New York: Brunner/Mazel.

Gruber, K., & Jones, R. (1983). Identifying determinants of risk of sexual victimization of youth. *Child Abuse and Neglect: The International Journal, 7*, 17–24.

Guyer, M., & Ash, P. (1986). *Child abuse allegations in the context of adversarial divorce.* Paper presented at the annual meeting of the American Academy of Psychiatry and the Law, Los Angeles.

Hechler, D. (1988). *The battle and the backlash: The child sexual abuse war.* Lexington, MA: Lexington Books.

Herbert, C. P. (1987). Expert medical assessment in determining probability of alleged child sexual abuse. *Child Abuse and Neglect: The International Journal, 11*, 213–221.

Herman, J. L. (1981). *Father-daughter incest.* Cambridge, MA: Harvard University Press.

Hunter, R. S., Kilstrom, N., & Loda, F. (1985). Sexually abused children: Identifying masked presentations in a medical setting. *Child Abuse and Neglect: The International Journal, 9*, 17–25.

Jersild, A. T. (1968). *Child psychology.* Englewood Cliffs, NJ: Prentice-Hall.

Jones, D. P., & McGraw, J. M. (1987). Reliable and fictitious accounts of sexual abuse to children. *Journal of Interpersonal Violence, 2*, 27–45.

Kabasigawa, A. (1974). The utilization of retrieval cues by children in recall. *Child Development, 45*, 127–134.

Kaplan, S. L., & Kaplan, S. J. (1981). The child's accusation of sexual abuse during a divorce and custody struggle. *Hillside Journal of Clinical Psychiatry, 3*, 81–95.

Kelley, S. J. (1985). Drawing: Critical communication for sexually abused children. *Pediatric Nursing, 11*, 421–426.

Klajner-Diamond, H., Wehrspann, W. H., & Steinhauer, P. D. (1987). Assessing the credibility of young children's allegations of sexual abuse: Clinical issues. *Canadian Journal of Psychiatry, 32*, 610–614.

Lister, E. D. (1982). Forced silence: A neglected dimension of trauma. *American Journal of Psychiatry, 139*, 872–876.

Mantell, D. P. (1988) Clarifying erroneous child sexual abuse allegations. *American Journal of Orthopsychiatry, 58*, 618–621.

Marin, B. V., Holmes, D. L., Guth, M., & Kovac, P. (1979). The potential of children as eyewitnesses: A comparison of children and adults in eyewitness tasks. *Law and Human Behavior, 3*, 295–306.

Masson, J. M. (1985). *The assault on truth: Freud's suppression of the seduction theory.* New York: Penguin Books.

Miller, J., Moeller, D., Kaufman, A., DiVasto, P., Pathak, D., & Christy, J. (1978). Recidivism among sex assault victims. *American Journal of Psychiatry, 135*, 1103–1104.

Paveza, G. J. (1988). Risk factors in father–daughter sexual abuse. *Journal of Interpersonal Violence, 3,* 290–306.

Peevers, B. H., & Secord, P. F. (1973). Developmental changes in attribution of descriptive concepts to persons. *Journal of Personality and Social Psychology, 27,* 120–128.

Peters, J. J. (1976). Children who are victims of sexual assault and the psychology of the offender. *American Journal of Psychotherapy, 30,* 398–421.

Peters, S. D., Wyatt, G. E., & Finkelhor, D. (1986). Prevalence. In D. Finkelhor et al. (Eds.), *A sourcebook on child sexual abuse* (pp. 15–59). Beverly Hills, CA: Sage.

Phillips. J. L. (1981). *Piaget's theory: A primer.* San Francisco: Freeman.

Renshaw, D. C. (1987). Evaluating suspected cases of child sexual abuse. *Psychiatric Annals, 17,* 262–270.

Rholes, W. S., & Ruble, D. N. (1984). Children's understanding of dispositional characteristics of others. *Child Development, 55,* 550–560.

Rosenfeld, A. A., Nadelson, C. C., & Krieger, M. (1977). Incest and sexual abuse of children. *Journal of the American Academy of Child Psychiatry, 16,* 327–339.

Rosenfeld, A. A., Nadelson, C. C., & Krieger, M. (1979). Fantasy and reality in patient reports of incest. *Journal of Clinical Psychiatry, 40,* 159–164.

Rush, F. (1980). *The best kept secret: Sexual abuse of children.* Englewood Cliffs, NJ: Prentice-Hall.

Sale, J. (1984). *Child care and child abuse: What is the connection?* Testimony presented to the U. S. House of Representatives Select Committee on Children, Youth, and Families.

Singer, D., & Reveson, T. (1978). *How a child thinks.* New York: New American Library.

Sivan, A. B., Schor, D. P., Koeppl, G. K., & Noble, L. D. (1988). Interaction of normal children with anatomical dolls. *Child Abuse and Neglect: The International Journal, 12,* 71–179.

Stone, L. E., Tyler, R. P., & Mead, J. J. (1984). Law enforcement officers as investigators and therapists in child sexual abuse: A training model. *Child Abuse and Neglect: The International Journal, 8,* 75–82.

Summit, R. C. (1983). The child sexual abuse accommodation syndrome. *Child Abuse and Neglect: The International Journal, 7,* 177–193.

Summit, R. C. (1988). Hidden victims, hidden pain: Societal avoidance of child sexual abuse. In G. E. Wyatt & G. J. Powell (Eds.), *Lasting effects of child sexual abuse* (pp. 39–60). Beverly Hills, CA: Sage.

Terr, L. C. (1981). Psychic trauma in children: Observations following the Chowchilla bus kidnapping. *American Journal of Psychiatry, 138,* 14–19.

Terr, L. C. (1983). Time sense following psychic trauma. *American Journal of Psychiatry, 53,* 244–261.

Thoennes, N., & Pearson, J. (1988). Sexual abuse allegations in domestic relations cases: The research perspective. *Children's Legal Rights Journal, 9,* 16–26.

Underwager, R., & Wakefield, H. (1985, June). Sexual Abuse. *Playboy,* p. 59.

Varendonck, J. (1911). The testimony of children in a famous trial. *Archives de Psychologie, 11,* 129–171.

Wehrspann, W. H., Steinhauer, P. D., & Klajner-Diamond, H. (1987). Criteria and methodology for assessing credibility of sexual abuse allegations. *Canadian Journal of Psychiatry, 32,* 615–623.

Whipple, G. M. (1911). The psychology of testimony. *Psychological Bulletin, 8,* 307–309.

White, S., Strom, G. A., Santilli, G., & Halpin, B. M. (1986). Interviewing young sexual abuse victims with anatomically correct dolls. *Child Abuse and Neglect: The International Journal, 10,* 519–529.

Yates, A., Beutler, L. E., & Cargo, M. (1985). Drawings by child victims of incest. *Child Abuse and Neglect: The International Journal, 9,* 183–189.

Yates, A., & Musty, T. (1987). *Young children's false allegations of molestation.* Paper presented at the 140th annual meeting of the American Psychiatric Association, Chicago.

II

TREATMENT

9

Applications of Psychoanalytic Theory in the Treatment of the Victim and the Family

Arthur H. Green
Family Center and Therapeutic Nursery, Presbyterian Hospital, New York City

INTRODUCTION

Child Sexual Abuse as a Traumatic Event

Freud's early psychoanalytic theories were based on his observations that the hysterical symptoms of his adult female patients could be traced to childhood experiences of seduction at the hands of nurses, maids, adult strangers, siblings, and adult family members. In "The Etiology of Hysteria" (1896, 1952, p. 203). Freud stated, "I put foreward the thesis that at the bottom of every case of hysteria there are one or more occurrences of premature sexual experiences, belonging to the earliest years of childhood, which can be reproduced through the work of psychoanalysis in spite of the intervening decades." Freud's psychoanalytic treatment of these patients consisted of establishing a linkage between the hysterical symptoms and the childhood sexual experiences through the uncovering of repressed memories. Therefore, psychoanalysis was originally a "trauma" theory.

Freud (1905/1952) subsequently de-emphasized the importance of childhood sexual seduction in producing neuroses after he discovered that many of the symptoms of his hysterical patients had their origins in fantasy rather than in actual sexual experiences. However, he never discarded the traumatic potential of actual external events. He refined his concept of psychological trauma in "Beyond the Pleasure Principle" (1920/1955) and in "Inhibitions, Symptoms, and Anxiety," (1926/1959). He regarded the infant's high threshold for the perception of stimuli as a protective shield, or stimulus barrier, and described as traumatic any excitation powerful enough to break through the protective shield. The traumatic situation was defined as the experience of helplessness on the part of the ego in the face of accumulation of excitation, whether of external or internal origin. The pleasure principle is put out of action, and a regression ensues in which primitive modes of functioning are utilized in order to master and bind the traumatic stimuli. The repetition compulsion, or need to repeat painful traumatic events, was ultimately regarded as a manifestation of the death instinct, or primary masochism. In "Moses and Monotheism" (1939/1964), Freud noted the importance of the interaction between constitutional factors and experiences, and contrasted the positive and negative effects of traumata. Positive effects are described as attempts to repeat the painful trauma, while negative effects are defensive reactions designed to avoid the traumatic experience. Freud postulated that both the positive and negative reactions represent fixations to the trauma.

More recent psychoanalytic observations of children have broadened the concept of trauma to include chronic adverse conditions that do not involve a breakthrough of the stimulus barrier and an ensuing state of helplessness. Kris (1956) described the term "strain trauma" to demonstrate the effect of long-lasting situations that cause traumatic effects by the accumulation of frustrating tensions. Khan (1963) stressed the mother's role as a protective shield and auxiliary ego for the vulnerable infant. The mother's chronic failure to carry out this protective role may lead to subtle deficits in the child's ego functioning on the basis of "cumulative trauma." There is often a time lag between the maternal deficiencies and the onset of symptoms. Boyer (1956) also stressed the mother's role as a supplementary stimulus barrier and cited her potential to traumatize the infant through overstimulation. Winnicott (1960) described the mother's protective role as the "good-enough" holding environment, which is necessary for the child's optimal ego development. Therefore, the failure of a mother to recognize and respond to the child's needs in a predictable manner and to safeguard the child from abnormal levels of stimulation constitutes a deficiency in the protective role and a potential for long-term trauma.

Traumatic Elements in Child Sexual Abuse

Intrafamilial child sexual abuse appears to contain both the acute and long-term traumatic components previously described. The acute sexual assault can result in a shock-like overwhelming of the ego, producing fearfulness, and anxiety-related symptoms, such as nightmares, sleep disorders, hypervigilance, psychosomatic symptoms, and in some cases posttraumatic stress disorder. The sexual assault is superimposed upon a chronic background of pathological family interaction, including stigmatization and betrayal, which can give rise to guilt, shame, and low self-esteem, and a paranoid, mistrustful quality to subsequent object relationships. The tendency to re-enact the sexual encounter actively or passively might be derived from acute posttraumatic stress disorder and long-term (identification with the aggressor) traumatic elements. The premature sexual arousal inherent in both the acute molestation and the chronic sexual overstimulation may result in inappropriate hypersexual behavior. The interaction between these acute and long-term variables is likely to potentiate their pathological impact.

This psychoanalytically derived hypothesis regarding the traumatic nature of sexual abuse is not dissimilar to the model proposed by Finkelhor and Browne (1986), based on learning theory. These investigators identified four "traumagenic" factors operating in child sexual abuse: (1) Traumatic sexualization, occurring through the sexual stimulation and reinforcement of the child's sexual response so that the child learns to use sexual behavior to gratify a variety of nonsexual needs. This leads to inappropriate and premature sexual activity and deviant patterns of sexual arousal. (2) Powerlessness, due to the child's helplessness during the sexual assault, and his or her inability to stop it, leading to fear and anxiety. (3) Stigmatization, describing the victim's sense of being "damaged" and blamed for the molestation, leading to shame, guilt, and low self-esteem. (4) Betrayal, occurring when the victim experiences cruelty and disregard at the hands of a trusted caretaker from whom love and protection are expected. Betrayal may lead to distrust of others, hostility and anger. Finkelhor and Browne's conceptualization lacks a temporal perspective, that is, there is no differentiation between immediate and long-term responses to trauma.

Severity of both acute and long-term symptoms of child sexual abuse might vary as a function of the age and developmental level of the child, the onset, duration, and frequency of the abuse, the degree of coercion and physical trauma, the child's pre-existing personality, and the relationship between the child and the perpetrator, the familial and institutional responses to the disclosure, and the impact of the therapeutic intervention.

Psychoanalytically oriented treatment is designed to deal with both the immediate and long-term sequelae of child sexual abuse. The therapist helps the child link current anxiety-related symptoms back to the original traumatic experiences, and facilitates the uncovering and remembering of the victimization. The child is encouraged to verbalize and "work through" memories and painful affects associated with the sexual abuse as an alternative to their compulsive re-enactment. In-

terpretation of the child's play, dreams, fantasies, and artistic pro-
ductions may be used as an effective therapeutic agent. A psychoanalytic
understanding of these phenomena may also provide a means of assessing the traumatic impact of the sexual abuse. The pathological impact of
longstanding deviant family interactions on the child's object relationships, identifications, personality development, and defensive operations can be modified through the interpretation of transference
distortions and the child's participation in a "corrective emotional
relationship" with the therapist. The greater part of this chapter will be
devoted to a discussion of the most salient treatment issues encountered
by psychoanalytically oriented psychotherapists working with sexually
abused children.

MAJOR TREATMENT ISSUES

Acute Traumatization

If the child is being seen soon after the disclosure of the sexual abuse,
the child's vulnerability to further victimization must be carefully assessed. The abusive environment must be modified so that the child is no
longer at risk of molestation, that is, the perpetrator should no longer
have access to the child. Furthermore, active steps should be taken to
reduce the impact of the postdisclosure phase. The disclosure of incest
usually results in a series of traumatic events that may equal or surpass
those resulting from the molestation itself. For example, if the perpetrator is the father, he is forced to leave the house, or face incarceration. The breakup of the marriage often leaves the mother feeling
angry, depressed, and betrayed, and in some cases she might blame the
child for the dissolution of the family unit. If the mother, on the other
hand, colludes with the perpetrator and fails to protect the child, foster
placement of the victim might be required. The child is usually in-
terrogated by child protective case workers, sexual abuse "validators,"
and pediatricians, as well as the police or district attorneys. The child is
often compelled to testify in court. If the child is genitally damaged, or
sustains a sexually transmitted disease as a result of the molestation, he
or she might face hospitalization and medical procedures reminiscent of
the original traumata. Therapeutic efforts with the child can only be
effective when he or she is safe from further molestation and the
postdisclosure crises are recognized and dealt with.

The beginning phase of therapy is designed to establish a supportive
trustful relationships with the child, who may be initially fearful and
suspicious of the therapist. The child, so recently betrayed by the sexual-

ly abusive parent, might generalize his or her mistrust to all adults. This mistrust might be especially pronounced if the therapist is of the same gender as the offender. If a girl was molested by a father or stepfather and exihibited a marked aversion to adult males, it would be advantageous to provide her with a female therapist. On the other hand, some sexually abused children may benefit from a corrective emotional experience with a therapist of the same sex as the offender, as this might help them overcome their negative generalization. The therapeutic setting should be unpressured, and the child should be able to talk about the molestation at his or her own pace. The child will frequently be unable to or unwilling to remember anything about the victimization and present the therapist with a wall of denial, while simultaneously re-enacting and repeating traumatic elements of the sexual abuse in spontaneous play activities. The original sexual experiences may be expressed in doll or puppet play, drawings, or clay modeling. They may also occur in dreams and fantasies. According to Terr (1981), this type of re-enactment of a trauma in play, or "posttraumatic play" often fails to relieve the anxiety it was designed to control. In fact, this type of play may increase the child's agitation. These empirical observations have not yet been tested by controlled studies. The ultimate therapeutic goal is to identify and interpret the unconscious link between the compulsive, repetitive play activity and the original traumatic experiences. Once the child is able to make this connection, he or she will be in a position to verbalize the traumatic memories and express the painful effect in words rather than in actions.

Case Illustration

Betty, a seductive and rather hyperactive 6-year-old girl lived with her father after the marital separation because her mother became involved with drugs. However, he reverted to a homosexual life-style and forced this child to participate in frequent orgies, where she was sexually used by gays and lesbians. At first she was unable to talk about these events, but her play consisted of scribbling heavy lines in a driven, intense manner. Betty called these drawings "squiggly lines." which had no apparent meaning. After some time, she added heads and bodies to the scribbles, and it was apparent that the "squiggly lines," connected the genital areas of the two figures. This represented the genital contact and fondling that she experienced with the adults of both sexes during the orgies. After the therapist made this connection, Betty was able to verbalize some of the feelings that she experienced during these perverse activities, such as fear, shock, disgust, and sexual excitement.

These re-enactments are not limited to play and drawings or other symbolic expressions, but may be manifested in actual sexual acting out with others. The sexually traumatized child may actively engage other children and adults in sex play, and this seductive behavior is usually directed to the therapist as well. In this active repetition of the passively endured trauma, the child attempts to achieve some mastery and control of these frightening experiences, using the defense mechanism of "identification with the aggressor." The sexualized behavior may serve other purposes for the child such as an attention-getting device, or as a means of expressing affection, due to the sexually abused child's inability to differentiate sexual from nonsexual affectionate feelings. The child may exhibit seductive behavior in the therapeutic setting as a means of testing the therapist. The child tries to ascertain if the male therapist would respond in a sexual manner, or if the female therapist would act protectively. The therapist must set limits on the sexualized behaviors, and establish their linkage to the sexual molestation. When this is accomplished, the therapist can interpret how the child uses "identification with the aggressor" as a major defense mechanism. Such comments as "when you act like daddy you don't have to be so afraid," or "when you try to touch me that way you want me to know how badly you felt when daddy did this to you" focus on the child's feelings of helplessness and vulnerability that mobilize the sexually aggressive defenses. The sexual acting out occurs more frequently with a male therapist, whose presence readily elicits the powerful incestuous transference as well as phase-specific oedipal fantasies. The major transference themes occurring with a female therapist deal with a lack of protectiveness, and with guilt, and abandonment.

Some sexually abused children will react to their traumatic experiences with a contrasting coping style dominated by phobic and avoidant defenses. Instead of repeating and re-enacting their molestation, they tend to avoid and withdraw from persons or situations associated with sexuality, such as heterosexual social activities, for example, dancing, dating, and undressing in front of others. Some sexually abused girls will avoid contact with males, others will refuse to wear dresses or skirts, which would label them as "sexual," and therefore vulnerable. These children might also exhibit generalized anxiety, nightmares, sleep disturbances, and psychosomatic complaints. Some of the phobic anxiety will gradually subside, providing that the child is safe from further molestation. However, the sexual inhibition and avoidance may persist and ultimately interfere with the establishment of intimacy and future sexual relationships. The therapist might explain to the child that the phobic, avoidant, hypervigilant coping style which was adaptive in the incestuous environment is burdensome and unnecessary in normal settings. The child should be taught to differentiate benign individuals from sexual predators. The development of a trusting, empathic relationship with the therapist (especially if the therapist is male) and the interpretation of transference distortions can help the child to gradually modify these avoidant patterns.

The use of primitive defense mechanisms such as denial, projection, splitting, and dissociation is common among sexually abused children. These defenses are necessary to protect the child from the awareness that the parent upon whom he is entirely dependent is essentially malevolent. The pervasive use of denial, projection, and splitting enables the child to maintain the fantasy of having a "good parent" while the badness is projected onto some other person or attributed to himself or herself. The predominance of these defenses impairs the child's ability to integrate the positive and negative characteristics of his parents and others, leading to an overcategorization of objects into "good" and "bad." In extreme cases, the child may resort to depersonalization or the creation of alternate personalities to deal with the trauma, resulting in multiple personality disorder. The child's need for these primitive defense mechanisms diminishes when he becomes less fearful of victimization. As the child develops affectionate ties to the therapist and begins to regard him as an ally, he comes to represent a benign "good" parental figure and an object for identification. Gradual internalization of the therapist's attitudes and values leads to the emergence of more effective defenses such as repression, sublimation, and reaction formation. As the child becomes less vulnerable, he is able to appraise the behavior of the abusing parent and others more realistically. Therapeutic interventions must consistently identify and reverse the distortions of reality caused by the primitive defenses.

Stigmatization.   The stigmatization of the child during the incestuous relationship results in shame, guilt, and low self-esteem, and depression. Self-destructive behavior in the form of suicide attempts and suicidal gestures, can be observed in older children and adolescents. These feelings of shame and guilt are intensified if the child is blamed by the mother or other family members for participating in the sexual activity, or if the child experiences some sexual pleasure. Boys who are victimized by their fathers or other males might experience more guilt and feel more stigmatized because of the homosexual nature of the molestation. The therapist must challenge the victim's perception that he or she is responsible for the sexual acts. It should be emphasized that the child who is coerced and pressured into sexual activity by a parent or other adult cannot be regarded as culpable in any way. The child must be told that the offender's behavior is "sick" and inappropriate. If possible, it is helpful to the child if the offender acknowledges his culpability and apologizes to him or her.

The depression and stigmatization are often associated with feelings of bodily damage, especially when the child sustains genital trauma or a sexually transmitted disease during molestation. This "damaged goods syndrome" was described by Sgroi (1982). These children fear that they have been permanently damaged by the sexual activity. They often believe that they will never to able to have normal sexual relations or get married when they become adults. Some of these children fear that they will never get pregnant, or bear normal babies. The therapist must address these concerns, and the children require reassurance that they are not permanently impaired.

Suicidal behavior must be taken seriously, and at times antidepressant medication or even hospitalization may be required. Runaway behavior, heavy risk taking, and substance abuse may be regarded as additional forms of self-destructive behavior. Depression and self-hatred are often a result of internalized anger, which can be externalized in the therapeutic setting. The child should be encouraged to ventilate his or her anger toward the perpetrator and the nonabusing parent for failing to protect the victim. Often the child will cling to self-blame in order to deny the culpability of the parent. This form of denial also gives the child a sense of illusory control. She might say, "if I wasn't so sexy, my father wouldn't have slept with me." The therapist may acknowledge the child's wish to protect the parent, but the burden of guilt does not belong with the victim.

Betrayal. The experience of exploitation and sexual coercion by a parent from whom tenderness and nurturance is expected generates a feeling of betrayal in the victim. The child feels equally betrayed by the mother for failing to protect him or her from the molestation. This sense of betrayal is especially pronounced if the mother denies the incident or blames the child. Feelings of betrayal are easily generalized and displaced onto other parental and authority figures, which leads to an inability to trust others. In adolescence and adulthood, potential love objects and spouses might be considered untrustworthy and unpredictable. The theme of betrayal or mistrust is inevitably encountered in the therapeutic relationship. The child is often afraid of being exploited or seduced by a male therapist, and is concerned about the ability of the female therapist to act in a protective manner. The child might act in a seductive manner with the male therapist to see if he becomes sexually aroused. Sexual acting out by the child in the presence of a female therapist might be an attempt to gauge her protectiveness. The therapist can eventually interpret these transferences reactions, that is, by tracing them back to their original feelings of betrayal and disillusionment with their parents. After a long period of testing behavior, the child can then usually begin gradually to relax his vigilance and learn that the therapist is reliable, predictable, and trustworthy. This newly acquired sense of trust may then be applied to extratherapeutic relationships. Positive changes in the behavior of the parents will also help the child overcome his or her sense of betrayal.

Role Confusion. The child's experiences in an incestuous family easily leads to role confusion. When a young girl is treated like a spouse or confidante by her father and her mother becomes psychologically or physically unavailable, the normal processes of attachments and identifications are altered significantly. The child is made to feel responsible for her father's happiness while simultaneously assuming some of the household and caretaking responsibilities of her mother. In addition to the premature burden of assuming parental roles, the child is often given the responsibility of keeping the family intact. Needless to say, these role reversals are in direct conflict with the child's needs for protection, nurturance, and dependency gratification. In a sense, the child is thrust into adulthood before completing the tasks of childhood and adolescence, that is, the achievement of a stable gender identity, and a healthy self-concept as a reflection of receiving nurturance from predictable, loving parents, and the attainment of separation and individuation, with the relinquishing of infantile ties to the parents. The child victim of incest maintains the infantile attachment to the father in spite of the "pseudoadult" facade and is prevented from establishing normal peer relationships, which are prerequisites for independent functioning.

In the treatment setting, the child will usually act in a very solicitous manner toward the therapist. The child's need to please and ingratiate the therapist occurs at the expense of his or her own needs. This transference reaction may be interpreted to the child and linked to the child's previous need to please and "perform" for the parents. The therapist should provide the child with the opportunity to engage in age-appropriate childhood activities and to foster positive peer relationships. These goals can only be achieved with the cooperation of the mother, who must resume her role as caretaker and protector of the child.

Premature Sexualization. Sexually abused children frequently exhibit hypersexual, highly eroticized behavior, which includes compulsive masturbation (MacVicar, 1979), and promiscuity (Browning & Boatman, 1977), which may lead to prostitution in adolescence and adulthood (James & Meyerding, 1977). Yates (1982) described the eroticization of preschool children by incest, in which the degree of eroticization was proportional to the duration and intensity of the incestuous relationship. These preschoolers were orgastic and maintained a high level of sexual arousal. They often failed to distinguish affectionate relationships from sexual ones and became sexually aroused by routine physical or psychological closeness. This sexually "acting-out" behavior may be explained in various ways. First of all, the intense premature sexual overstimulation inherent in the incestuous relationship might be difficult to control by the child's ego defenses, that is, repression, sublimation, and intellectualization, and so on. In these children, the drive to repeat the sexual behaviors clearly overrides their ability to control them. The traumatic impact of the incest contributes to the need to repeat, that is, the repetition compulsion. The child also makes use of the defense mechanism of "identification with the aggressor," which appears to be embedded in the compulsion to repeat the traumatic sexual themes. The tendency of the sexually abused child to re-enact his or her victimization with others seems to represent an active attempt to master a passively endured trauma. From a social learning point of view, the child learns that sexualized behavior is an important way of obtaining attention and control, and this is selectively reinforced by the perpetrator and the family.

At the other end of the spectrum are studies citing phobic reactions and sexual inhibition as major sequelae to incest (Herman, 1981; Tsai, Feldman-Summers, & Edgar, 1979). Such children avoid experiences and stimuli reminding them of their sexual victimization. For example, female incest victims might avoid social contact with boys or men. Boy and girl victims may exhibit anxiety in situations in which they are given routine physical affection, for example, kissing, hugging, hand holding. Some of these children will refuse to get undressed or change clothing in front of others, or wear a bathing suit. Clearly, these children seek mastery by avoiding any stimuli evoking memories of the incest experience. Long-term patterns of avoidance are associated with sexual inhibition and sexual dysfunction, which may undermine sexual and marital relationships. In essence, the experience of premature sexual stimulation, elicits two contrasting styles of adaptation in child incest victims, one seeking mastery through active repetition of the trauma and the other by avoiding sexual stimuli. Alternating phases of repetition and avoidance may be encountered in the same child. Each of these contrasting styles, however, is based on the same mechanism: a weakening of normal repression, which results in the acting out or complete avoidance of traumatic memories. The aim of psychotherapy is to curtail the acting-out and avoidant patterns while encouraging the use of higher-level defenses, such as repression, sublimation, and intellectualization.

This may be carried out by a variety of therapeutic maneuvers, such as limit setting, educational techniques, interpretation, and desensitization. The key to successful intervention is to make the child gradually aware of frightening and conflictual memories of the incest experience along with the associated painful affect. The child is then encouraged to verbalize the memories and feelings instead of acting them out or avoiding them completely. The therapist must set limits on the hypersexual, seductive behavior of the child when it inevitably appears during therapy sessions. The child is gradually able to internalize these prohibitions while strengthening superego functioning. The child's tendency to identify with the "aggressor" during this seductive behavior may be interpreted. The child is also taught to differentiate routine physically affectionate behavior from behavior with a sexual intent, and is encouraged to respect his or her own bodily privacy and the privacy of others. Younger children need to be informed about "good" and "bad" touching of the body, as a means of preventing future victimization.

Case Illustration

Sharon, a 6-year-old girl, had been sexually molested by her father. Sharon's precocious sexual behavior at school was alarming to the staff, and her classmates, whom she seduced by taking them into the bathroom and fondling their genitals. The seductive school behavior launched the investigation that uncovered the incest. During the second month of play therapy, Sharon became increasingly preoccupied with polishing her nails and applying her mother's lipstick and makeup. The therapist questioned the appropriateness of this activity for a 6-year-old and prohibited it. However, the child began to improvise her makeup by using crayons and magic markers. She made herself a cardboard crown and called herself "the queen of Europe." She made a crown for her male therapist, invited him to be the "king" and tried to color his nails with the markers. Finally, she tried to sit on the therapist's lap, and had to be gently restrained. Careful questioning and exploration by the therapist revealed that Sharon's father used to dress her up in women's clothing and helped her apply lipstick and makeup as a prelude to their sexual activity. The therapist commented that Sharon was repeating with the therapist the same "makeup" game that her father played with her, and perhaps she wondered if he was going to give her "bad touches" as her father had. Sharon responded "that's what people do when they like each other, Daddy told me that, and I wanted you to like me." The therapist was then able to discuss more appropriate, nonsexual ways of showing affection.

Avoidant children have frequently been traumatized by threats of violence, or dire consequences should they disclose the molestation. They often require reassurance that they will be safe from punishment or retaliation if they talk about their victimization.

Countertransference Problems

Working with sexually abused children may elicit the therapist's own incestuous feelings either as a child or an adult. The therapist must be aware of his or her own feelings about child sexual abuse and sexuality. If the therapist is uncomfortable about sexual matters, this might be communicated to the child, who would then be reluctant to disclose his or her own molestation. Such a therapist might also ascribe the child's description of incest to sheer fantasy. On the other hand, some therapists will overidentify with the victim and develop exaggerated rescue fantasies. This may lead to an intolerance of the child's positive feelings toward the perpetrator, or impatience with the progress of therapy. These therapists also cannot tolerate patient resistance and hostility, which threatens the rescue mission. They may also express their vindictiveness toward the perpetrator. Some male therapists might over-identify with the father and blame the victim for the incest. Female therapists may defend the mother and overlook the pathological mother–child relationship commonly encountered in incest families. Many therapists are unable to tolerate the seductiveness and precocious sexuality of sexually abused children because they fear becoming sexually aroused.

Therapists working with sexually abused children should have access to supervision or the ability to discuss their cases with peers. This will result in a greater awareness of their feelings and should reduce the likelihood of major countertransference errors.

SPECIAL ISSUES

Dealing with the Incest Family

While each individual member of the incest family exhibits prominent psychopathology, the family itself is severely dysfunctional. Therefore, treatment of the child is usually supplemented by intervention with the family members. Under certain conditions family therapy and dyadic treatment can be useful. In most cases following the disclosure of incest, the father is removed from the home. He may benefit from individual psychotherapy, or a behavioral treatment if there is a substantial pedophilic component to his incestuous behavior. The incest father should either be in treatment or have successfully completed therapy before being reintegrated into the family. It is also imperative that he acknowledges his sexual misconduct before resuming contact with the victim. Some incest fathers may benefit from a family systems approach pioneered by Giaretto (1982). Fathers are selected for family therapy on the basis of their willingness to accept responsibility for their sexual misconduct and a commitment to save the marriage. The use of psychoanalytic treatment alone has usually proved to be ineffective for the sexually abusing parent.

The mother is a key figure in the incestuous family and must be a focus for intervention. The mother is often insufficiently involved with the incest victim, due to preoccupation with work or career, depression, or discomfort with the maternal role. When the incest is disclosed, many incest mothers disbelieve the child or blame the child for "provoking" the sexual contact. These mothers are reluctant to acknowledge their spouse's culpability because of their strong dependency. Intervention with these mothers is designed to promote a more supportive and protective maternal response to the child victim. Other important therapeutic issues that must be confronted in the incest mothers are feelings of guilt or anger at the spouse, the experience of loss with the break-up of the marriage, and anger toward the child for usurping her role as the spouse's sexual partner. Dyadic treatment (with the child), marital counseling, and family therapy may supplement the individual psychotherapy of the mother.

Siblings of the incest victim may require psychiatric evaluation in order to determine if they had also been victimized by the incest offender, or if they had witnessed the molestation. Nonabused siblings may exhibit a variety of responses to the incest, such as "survivor guilt," guilt regarding their failure to protect the victim, anger toward the parents, or jealousy of the attention generated by the victim.

Preparation of the Child for Court Testimony

It is often the responsibility of the therapist to decide whether or not the child is competent to offer testimony in court, and if it is in the child's best interest to testify. Berliner and Barbieri (1984) offer guidelines from a prosecutor's standpoint stating, "The child victim should testify only when that testimony will substantially increase the chance of conviction and will not do serious harm to the child."

Common fears expressed by child witnesses, as described by Schetky

(1988) are the fear of retaliation by the defendant, particularly if he has threatened the child, the fear that the victim will not be believed, the feeling that she is on trial, which may be reinforced by aggressive cross-examination, feelings of guilt if she blames herself for the molestation, and embarassment from the nature of the questions asked and the presence of the jury. Some clinicians believe that detailed questions about the molestation may retraumatize the child. Potential advantages of a child testifying in court are: (1) it provides the child with an active role in mastering the trauma; (2) it offers her a chance to be believed and to see justice work; and (3) it may provide a constructive outlet for her anger.

The therapist can be helpful in preparing the child for court testimony by introducing her to the courtroom prior to the hearing and by rehearsing the anticipated courtroom procedures through role playing. If possible, the therapist should accompany the child to the courtroom. Some states have implemented the use of two-way, closed-circuit television in which the child and the defendant are in separate rooms but can see one another on the television monitor.

SUMMARY

The treatment of sexually abused individuals provided Freud with the theoretical framework for the establishment of psychoanalytic theory. Psychoanalysis was essentially a "trauma" theory and Freud's psychoanalytic treatment consisted of uncovering repressed memories of sexual abuse during childhood by caretakers and family members. Although Freud and his followers subsequently de-emphasized the importance of actual sexual trauma in the genesis of neurosis, the recent increase in reporting of child abuse leads one to reconsider Freud's original treatment of adult sexual abuse victim and explore its suitability in the psychoanalytic treatment of sexually abused children.

Intrafamilial child sexual abuse produces both immediate (anxiety disorders) and longterm (guilt, loss of self-esteem, and stigmatization) sequelae, ultimately resulting in abnormal sexual behavior and impaired object relationships. The major treatment issues encountered by psychoanalytically oriented therapists working with sexually abused children were outlined. These include acute traumatization, primitive defense mechanisms, stigmatization, betrayal, role confusion, premature sexualization, and mind countertransference problems. This chapter also suggested a strategy of intervention with the parents and siblings of the sexually abused child and a plan for preparing the victim for court testimony. Although psychoanalytically oriented intervention with the sexually abused child has been widely used, there have not as yet been any outcome studies regarding its efficacy.

REFERENCES

Berliner, L., & Barbieri, M. (1984). Testimony of the child victim of sexual assault. *Journal of Social Issues, 40*, 125–137.

Boyer, L. B. (1956). On maternal overstimulation and ego defects. *Psychoanal. Study Child, 11*, 236–256.

Browning, D., & Boatman, B. (1977). Incest: Children at risk. *American Journal of Psychiatry, 134*, 69–72.

Finkelhor, D., & Browne, A. (1986). Initial and long-term effects: A conceptual framework. In D. Finkelhor (Ed.), *Sourcebook on child sexual abuse*. Beverly Hills, CA: Sage Publications.

Freud, S. (1896/1952). *The etiology of hysteria*. Standard Edition, *3*, 191–221. London: Hogarth Press.

Freud, S. (1905/1952). *Three essays on the theory of sexuality*. Standard Edition 7, 125–243. London: Hogarth Press.

Freud, S. (1920/1955). *Beyond the pleasure principle*. Standard Edition, *18*, 1–64. London: Hogarth Press.

Freud, S. (1926/1959). *Inhibitions, symptoms and anxiety*. Standard Edition, *20*, 75–175. London: Hogarth Press.

Freud, S. (1939/1964). *Moses and monotheism*. Standard Edition, *23*, 3–137. London: Hogarth Press.

Giaretto, H. (1982). A comprehensive child abuse sexual treatment program. *Child Abuse and Neglect, 6*, 263–278.

Herman, J. (1981). *Father-daughter incest*. Cambridge, MA: Harvard University Press.

James, J., & Meyerding, J. (1977). Early sexual experiences as a factor in prostitution. *Amer. J. Psychiat., 134*, 1381–1385.

Khan, M. (1963). The concept of cumulative trauma. *Psychoanal. Study Child, 11*, 286–306.

Kris, E. (1956). The recovery of childhood memories in psychoanalysis. *Psychoanal. Study Child, 11*, 54–88.

MacVicar, K. (1979). Psychotherapy of sexually abused girls. *Journal Amer. Acad. Child Psychiatry, 18*, 342–353.

Schetky, D. (1988). The child as witness. In D. Schetky, & A. Green (Eds.), *Child sexual abuse: A handbook for health care and legal professionals*. New York: Brunner/Mazel.

Sgroi, S. (1982). *Handbook of clinical intervention in child sexual abuse*. Lexington, MA: Lexington Books.

Terr, L. (1981). "Forbidden games": Post-traumatic child's play. *Journal American Acadamy Child Psychiatry*. 20: 741–760.

Tsai, M., Feldman-Summers, S., & Edgar, M. (1979). Childhood molestation variables related to differential impacts on psychosexual functioning in adult women. *Journal of Abnormal Psychology, 88*, 407–417.

Winnicott, D. (1960). The theory of the parent–infant relationship. In *The Maturational Processes and the Facilitating Environment*. New York: International Universities Press, pp. 37–55.

Yates, A. (1982). Children eroticized by incest. *American Journal of Psychiatry, 139,* 482–485.

Behavioral Treatment Approaches for Offenders and Victims

Raymond C. Rosen
Kathryn S. K. Hall
Department of Psychiatry, University of Medicine and Dentistry, NJ

"Now then," said Dr. Brodsky, "how do you think this is done? Tell me, what do you think we're doing to you?"

"You're making me feel ill," I said. "I'm ill when I look at those filthy pervert films of yours. . . . If you'll stop these films I'll stop feeling ill."

"Right," said Dr. Brodsky. "It's association, the oldest educational method in the world."

Anthony Burgess: *A Clockwork Orange*
(1962, 1986, p. 114)

INTRODUCTION

The protagonist in Burgess's futuristic novel, *A Clockwork Orange*, is Alex, a 15-year-old sadistic rape-murderer who becomes the involuntary subject of a primitive psychological rehabilitation approach known as the "Ludovico technique." The goal of treatment is to create a conditioned aversion in Alex to all stimuli associated with anger and hostility, thereby suppressing his compulsive urges for sex and violence. Despite the caricature of "Dr. Brodsky," and the overly simplistic view of conditioning therapy presented, Burgess powerfully portrays the central dilemmas and controversies surrounding behavioral treatment of offenders. When and how should such therapy be administered? Who is an appropriate candidate for treatment? Under what circumstances should treatment be substituted for incarceration? What are the risks to the offender, potential victims, and society at large of such treatments? Ultimately, can psychologically based treatments be effective for criminal or sexual deviance? Curiously, *A Clockwork Orange* has been published with two alternative endings. In the original U. S. version, Alex escapes from the treatment facility to recover his passion for violence. The English edition, however, ends on a more optimistic note, as Alex finally becomes bored with his life of violence, and ends up wishing for a wife and family: "But now as I end this story, brothers, I am not young, not no longer, oh no. Alex with groweth up, oh yes" (1962/1986, p. 191).

A central theme of *A Clockwork Orange*, and a key issue for discussion in the present chapter, is the supposed relationship between habitual patterns of emotional/physiological arousal to deviant stimuli in offenders, and the commission of specific acts of physical or sexual aggression. This so-called "deviant arousal hypothesis" (Rosen & Beck, 1988) has served as the dominant theoretical framework for the bulk of behavioral theory and research in the field to date. Particularly in the treatment of child molesters with documented pedophilic arousal patterns, behavioral interventions have traditionally been aimed at *response suppression* of deviant arousal (e.g., Abel, Blanchard, & Becker, 1978; Quinsey & Marshall, 1983). A number of behavioral techniques have been developed for this purpose, the most recent of which is *masturbatory satiation* (Marshall, 1979). The rationale for this approach will be reviewed in some depth and a detailed case study is provided.

Whereas behavioral treatment approaches in the past had tended to rely on aversive conditioning procedures for reduction or elimination of deviant arousal, most authors currently recommend the concomitant use of *positive behavior change* techniques, such as social skills enhancement, stress management procedures, and assertiveness training in the treatment of selected offenders. Social–cognitive and marital therapy techniques are also employed with increasing frequency. Clearly, there is an overall trend toward more broad-spectrum and flexible approaches to the treatment of offenders (e.g., Wincze, 1989; Bancroft, 1989). Comprehensive intervention approaches have similarly been emphasized in the area of *relapse prevention training* (Pithers, Marques, Gibat, & Marlatt, 1983; Laws, 1989), which is seen increasingly as a critical component of treatment. How one selects a specific behavioral technique for use with an individual offender remains a key question, which has not been sufficiently addressed to date.

In contrast to the image portrayed in *A Clockwork Orange*, behavior therapy is no longer viewed as a passive and involuntary treatment approach, which can be effective regardless of the client's motivation for treatment. Nowadays, clinicians strongly emphasize the need for client participation in all phases of treatment planning and execution. Wincze (1989), for example, recommends that a prospective client's motivation for treatment should be carefully evaluated at the outset, and that treatment should be withheld until a satisfactory commitment to change has been obtained. This is not to deny that most offenders are reluctant to "give up" their preferred deviant behaviors, but that there needs to be a clear acknowledgment by the offender of the personal and societal reasons for change.

Perhaps the most striking development in the field in recent years is the application of behavioral concepts and interventions to the treatment of child victims. In general, the use of behavioral approaches for child victims has lagged considerably behind developments in the treatment of offenders. Although numerous authors have documented the variety of emotional sequelae associated with child sexual abuse, little attention had previously been paid to the potential use of behavioral interventions with child victims. In part, this may reflect the lack of attention until recently to conceptualizing the effects of child sexual abuse in explicitly behavioral terms. Some of the initial manifestations include heightened levels of anxiety, as shown by nightmares, phobias, somatic complaints, and fears of being harmed, as well as guilt, shame, inappropriate sexual and aggressive behavior, sleep and eating disturbances, and a variety of regressive behaviors (Browne & Finkelhor, 1986). As indicated by several recent case reports (e.g., Becker, Skinner, & Abel, 1982; McNeill & Todd, 1986; Kolko, 1986), certain sequelae of child sexual abuse appear to be amenable to behavioral treatment interventions. Unfortunately, however, there is a paucity of controlled outcome studies demonstrating the effectiveness of behavioral treatments for child victims of sexual abuse.

Overall, behavioral approaches for offenders and victims of sexual abuse share a number of important common features: (1) An emphasis on *learning theory concepts* in accounting for the etiology of problem behaviors, (2) A reliance on *behavioral assessment* techniques as the basis for planning treatment interventions and evaluating outcome; (3) A treatment focus on *specific symptoms* or behavioral manifestations, such as anxiety or interpersonal deficits, as opposed to underlying psychodynamic processes or family systems issues. Behavioral group interventions are also increasingly emphasized, as will be illustrated in the case studies offered herein. Regrettably, there is a paucity of controlled outcome research on behavioral interventions with child victims, and we conclude this chapter with recommendations for future research.

Behavioral Treatment Approaches for Offenders

The Role of Deviant Arousal

Despite the increasing emphasis on the use of broad-spectrum or flexible approaches to treatment (e.g., Wincze, 1989; Bancroft, 1989), therapists have traditionally focused on deviant arousal patterns in offenders as the key determinant of sexual aggression against both adult and child victims. Deviant arousal is generally seen as resulting from early conditioning experiences, which are typically reinforced by repetition of deviant fantasy themes during sex play and masturbation. In the first systematic exploration of this hypothesis, McGuire, Carlisle, and Young (1965) reviewed the case histories of 45 patients with mixed paraphilias. Due to the high frequency of deviant masturbatory fantasies reported in this group, it was concluded that fantasy rehearsal during masturbation had played a key role in conditioning deviant arousal in virtually every instance. The authors also noted a high incidence of early sexual victimization among the offender group, although the effects of these early molestation experiences appeared to be mediated, according to the authors, by fantasy rehearsal during masturbation. Early laboratory studies by Rachman (1966), and Rachman and Hodgson (1968) similarly demonstrated the potential role of classical conditioning factors in the development of deviant arousal. Specifically, it was shown that previously neutral stimuli, such as a pair of women's boots, can become a strong stimulus for deviant arousal after repeated pairings with slides of nude females. In the past 20 years, the deviant arousal hypothesis has played a central role in guiding behavioral theory and practice in the field.

A common clinical observation is that overt acts of sexual deviance, such as child molestation, are typically preceded by a complex *chain* of antecedent components leading up to and including physiological activation, and ultimately, overt behavior. As one offender described the process: "It really begins when I leave the house. Riding to the park, I have only one thing on my mind. I know exactly what I'm doing, but there's no way to stop it." Most behavioral treatment approaches are accordingly aimed at interrupting the chain of antecedent arousal as early as possible, substituting appropriate alternative behaviors wherever possible. Wincze (1989), for example, recommends careful assessment via behavioral recording of *all* antecedent events associated with deviant arousal, along with the development of alternative responses to high-risk situations. This approach is also emphasized as an important component of *relapse prevention training*, which we will discuss.

It should be noted that deviant arousal patterns may manifest differently in repetitive pedophiles, compared with patients with a history of incest or intrafamilial offences. Empirical support for this hypothesis comes from a study by Quinsey, Chaplin, and Carrigan (1979). These authors found that extrafamilial child molesters could be clearly distinguished from a comparable group of incestuous offenders by the greater responsivity of the former group to age-inappropriate partners (i.e., the incest offenders were *less strongly* aroused by pedophilic stimuli).

Freund and Langevin (1976) and Freund, Scher, Chan, and Ben-Aron (1982) have similarly shown that bisexual arousal patterns are far more common in pedophilic, as opposed to androphilic (preference for post-pubescent children) or hebephilic offenders (preference for pubescent children), suggesting that offenders against young children are primarily aroused by the *age* of the victim, and might be more likely to choose victims of either sex.

Markedly different findings have been reported by Abel, Becker, Murphy, and Flanagan (1981). These authors evaluated arousal patterns in 10 heterosexual pedophiles, 6 matched incest offenders, and a control group of 11 subjects with mixed sexual deviations. Arousal patterns in the nonincestuous and incestuous offenders were almost identical overall, and incest offenders showed significant levels of arousal to pedophilic stimuli. Incest offenders also showed subnormal levels of arousal to adult heterosexual stimuli. Diagnostic groups were carefully assigned on the basis of *multiple* sources of information, including self-report, psychiatric records, police records, and interviews with relatives. The authors conclude that: "incest is a special subset of pedophilia" (Abel et al., 1981, p. 126). Unfortunately, the relatively small sample sizes in the study limit the generalizability of this provocative finding.

Further contradictory evidence to the deviant arousal hypothesis comes from a recent large-scale study investigating patterns of deviant arousal in incarcerated child molesters (Hall, Proctor, & Nelson, 1988). These authors measured penile tumescence responses in 122 male offenders during presentation of laboratory erotic stimuli. All subjects in the study were receiving inpatient treatment at the time, and offenders were classified according to age and gender of their preferred victims. Two findings from this study stand out as presenting major difficulties for the deviant arousal hypothesis: First, when subjects were instructed to suppress voluntarily arousal to deviant stimuli, about 80% demonstrated substantial, if not complete suppression of arousal. Second, the arousal measures used failed to discriminate between the different offender classifications. For example, arousal patterns in offenders who characteristically used force against their victims were not significantly different from arousal patterns in those child sex offenders who rarely if ever used force. Commenting on these findings, the authors suggest that "sexual arousal among sex offenders may occur in a generalized, rather than in a stimulus-specific, manner. It may often be that exhibited deviant arousal is reflective of general arousability rather than of a history of or potential for specific types of sexually aggressive behavior" (p. 122).

It could be argued, however, that several design features of this study contributed to the negative findings. For example, while most investigators specifically exclude patients who show little or no response to baseline stimuli ("nonresponders"), these individuals were all included in the Hall et al. (1988) study. Including such patients may have obscured the differences between groups in response to specific stimuli, thus highlighting the "general arousability" factor noted by the authors. Second, the audiotaped stimuli used in the study were of relatively brief duration (2 minutes for nondeviant, 4 minutes for deviant stimuli), and this too may have tended to obscure possible arousal differences between the groups. The ability of almost all patients in the study to suppress arousal voluntarily also suggests that the stimuli used may have been lacking in erotic intensity.

Overall, the deviant arousal model has greatly influenced behavioral theory and practice in the area to date, despite the increasing concern with theoretical assumptions and empirical evidence. In particular, we have recently discussed major advantages of the model in at least two areas (Rosen & Beck, 1988). First, current laboratory methods for measuring male sexual arousal are easily adapted to assessing responses to deviant stimuli and can readily be used to compare response patterns of different groups of deviant (e.g., pedophilic) and nondeviant subjects. Second, a wide range of intervention techniques has been developed for modifying deviant arousal, and the effectiveness of these techniques can be determined by laboratory evaluations. A key assumption of the model, however, is that arousal in the laboratory will be predictive of the occurrence of sexually deviant behavior in the external environment ("the real world"). However, several authors have emphasized the dangers of assuming a one-to-one relationship between laboratory arousal and the proclivity to act inappropriately in external situations. Laboratory measures may be of value in determining sexual preferences, but not the likelihood of an individual's acting on these preferences. According to Laws (1984), deviant arousal patterns are predictive in a qualitative, rather than a quantitative manner: "The measures (of deviant arousal) will *not* reliably and validly predict the probability of future offending, although . . . they *will* rather accurately describe the quality of that offending" (p. 129).

Response Suppression Techniques

A wide variety of behavior change techniques have been recommended at one time or another for suppressing deviant arousal in pedophilic offenders, and these techniques are generally viewed as the cornerstone of effective behavioral treatment. For example, one reviewer (Kelly, 1982) observed that approximately 75% of published reports on behavioral treatment for pedophilia have included a major emphasis on aversion therapy or other response suppression techniques. In part, this emphasis on aversive conditioning originated with early attempts to modify sexual preference in homosexuals (Max, 1935), and fetishists (Raymond, 1956). These early case reports indicated the possibility of modifying sexual interest in motivated individuals through classical conditioning techniques involving systematic pairing of deviant stimuli with aversive consequences. Similar findings were reported by the Maudsley group in the late 1960s, in a series of classic case studies of transvestites, exhibitionists, and other paraphilias (Marks & Gelder, 1967; Marks, Gelder, & Bancroft, 1970). Subsequent changes in public and professional attitudes toward modification of sexual preference, however, have severely curtailed the use of aversion therapy in this context (Kelly, 1982). The necessity for adequate *treatment motivation* and commitment for change on the part of the offender has also been increasingly emphasized by various authors (e.g., Wincze, 1989; Bancroft, 1989).

The first systematic application of aversion therapy to the treatment of pedophilia was described in a single-case study by Marshall (1971). This author adapted the avoidance conditioning paradigm originally used by Feldman and MacCullough (1965) with homosexual patients, and combined it with desensitization for heterosexual anxiety and a program of positive social skills training. Approximately 30 treatment sessions were provided over an intensive 3-week period to a single male patient with a chronic history of pedophilic offenses. Successful outcome, as indicated by elimination of deviant fantasies and increasing contacts with age-appropriate females, was correlated with self-reported changes in masturbatory fantasies to adult females.

Similarly, Rosenthal (1973) reported results of a single-case study comparing two forms of electrical aversion therapy for suppression of pedophilic arousal in a 31-year-old, mildly retarded male offender. Specifically, a fixed pairing ("punishment") procedure, consisting of presentation of pedophilic slides followed by electric shock, was compared with a response contingent ("shaping") technique, in which increased latencies of deviant arousal were paired with decreasing durations of electric shock. Whereas the fixed pairing ("punishment") paradigm was found to be relatively ineffective in modifying deviant arousal, the shaping procedure was associated with relatively complete suppression of pedophilic arousal and self-report of successful outcome at 2-year posttreatment.

Over the next decade, several variations in the aversive conditioning paradigm were developed, including the use of signaled punishment (Callahan & Leitenberg, 1973; Quinsey et al., 1980), covert sensitization (Barlow, Agras, Leitenberg, Callahan, & Moore, 1972; Brownell, Hayes, & Barlow, 1977) and assisted covert sensitization (Maletzky, 1980). Various forms of biofeedback training of erections have similarly been used as a means for controlling deviant arousal in pedophilic offenders (Laws, 1980; Quinsey et al., 1980). Attempts to differentiate between specific response suppression techniques in terms of efficacy or outcome, however, have been generally inconclusive. For example, Callahan and Leitenberg (1973) compared the effects of contingent shock for erections with deviant slides with covert sensitization, an imagery-based aversive conditioning procedure. The subjects for this study included a variety of paraphilic offenders, including at least one chronic pedophile. Despite the heterogeneity of subjects studied, results indicated that both treatment conditions produced substantial levels of erectile suppression to the deviant stimuli. Similarly, Quinsey et al. (1980) compared the effects of signaled punishment of deviant arousal with biofeedback in the treatment of a more homogeneous group of child molesters. The signaled punishment procedure again proved to be moderately effective, as assessed by both erectile response and follow-up reports of clinical outcome. In this study, however, a combination of both signaled punishment and biofeedback proved to be optimally effective.

Biofeedback alone had previously been shown to be effective for training of response suppression in a laboratory analogue study with normal males (Rosen, 1973). Subsequently, Laws (1980) used visual analog feedback for training self-control of arousal in a bisexual pedophile. A multiple-baseline case study approach was used to target specific changes in tumescence to deviant stimuli during an intensive training period, lasting more than 88 days. In the course of this lengthy treatment period, the patient appeared to have improvised a form of self-administered covert sensitization, which may have been the critical therapeutic element, with the biofeedback procedure adding only confirmation of treatment effectiveness. This took the form of specific images such as the following:

> When I'd see those slides of boys I'd imagine doing my usual things and I'd start to get turned on. Then I'd imagine the kid saying I was hurting him or crying and that response pen would go right down. After a while I couldn't get an erection any more. (Laws, 1980, p. 210)

The most recent application of the response suppression paradigm is *masturbatory satiation therapy*. This innovative treatment method was first described by William Marshall (Marshall, 1979; Marshall & Barbaree, 1978), and appears to be rapidly gaining acceptance as an effective and cost-efficient approach for reducing deviant arousal in selected offenders. As described by Marshall, the technique was originally intended to associate boredom and masturbatory satiation effects with the patient's preferred deviant fantasies. The initial evaluation was conducted in a psychophysiological laboratory setting, and the patient's arousal responses were assessed prior to and following treatment. During treatment, the patient was seated in a darkened room and instructed to commence masturbating, while simultaneously verbalizing aloud all imaginable variations of the deviant fantasy script. The verbalized fantasies were monitored throughout via an intercom system to assess thematic content and to ensure compliance. Treatment sessions were continued for at least 1 hour at a time, and included continuous masturbation and verbalization: "Even if he ejaculated he was to continue, stopping only to wipe himself clean if he found this necessary" (Marshall, 1979, p. 380).

Findings from two controlled case studies of chronic pedophiles indicated that the masturbatory satiation technique is associated with rapid and complete suppression of deviant arousal, and that the suppression effects appear to be specific to the targeted fantasies. In one instance, masturbatory satiation was associated with a concomitant increase in arousal to appropriate stimuli, while in a second case it was not. In general, the author has recommended using the technique in conjunction with other interventions designed to facilitate positive behavior change, such as social skills and assertiveness training (Marshall, 1979).

We have recently begun to apply masturbatory satiation training on an outpatient basis with motivated offenders, having modified the original Marshall technique in a number of ways. Specifically, we have found that masturbation sessions can be conducted by the patient in private *at home,* provided that the therapist monitors compliance throughout by means of video or audiotapes of all treatment sessions. Patients are instructed to tape all sessions, and each tape is made available for review by the therapist on at least a weekly basis. Second, the patient's nonverbal or affective responses to the treatment process should be carefully assessed. When effective, the treatment is normally associated with high levels of subjective discomfort, which should be noticeable by the second or third week of treatment. Additionally, other sources of validation, such as partner reports of compliance and progress, should be obtained where possible.

Masturbatory satiation is generally regarded as less ethically objectionable than other forms of response suppression, such as electrical aversion. Nonetheless, it can be experienced by certain patients as extremely aversive, and therapists are cautioned about the possible occurrence of hostile or paranoid reactions. In general, offenders should be carefully screened before exposure to *any* aversive conditioning procedure. These treatment techniques are generally not recommended for patients with a history of thought disorder or other major psychopathology.

Case Example[1]

J.P. is a 36-year-old married male who initiated treatment at the request of his wife. Although he described his problem as primarily involving a lack of self-esteem and inadequate sexual relationship with his wife, Mr. P. acknowledged that he engaged in frequent acts of genital exposure to young children, and that he had recently been "caught in the act" by his wife. He had once previously been apprehended, when exposing himself in a girls' music school, and was reported by one of the girls' mothers. He was referred for psychiatric evaluation at the time, after which all legal charges had been dropped. Mr. and Mrs. P. have been married for the past 14 years, and have 3 children, aged 4 through 11.

Sexual history taking revealed that the present pattern of deviant behavior began when the patient was in his mid- to late-teens, at which time he developed a strong desire to expose himself to young girls. The victims of this exposure were usually in the 4- to 6-year-old age range, and he had occasionally masturbated to orgasm in the presence of very young children. The exposure usually took place in suburban shopping malls or amusement parks, where Mr. P. would seek out children who were playing alone or had been separated from a caretaker. He reports that his exhibitionism is not impulsive, but is "calculated," and that he carefully chooses victims who are young enough and of the "type who wouldn't tell." He also has difficulties in the control of anger, and has frequently hit and screamed at his own children in the course of sudden outbursts of anger. He acknowledges that he frequently verbally abuses his children in an effort to "wipe out of them any bad parts of myself that I see in them." Mr. P. claimed that he had never exposed himself to either of his own children. There was also no evidence that the patient had been molested or subjected to exposure as a child.

According to Mr. P., he has always been shy and awkward with women of his own age. He dated infrequently in college and was introduced to wife Jill by a friend of his mother. She is 2 years older than him, and had taken the initiative in their relationship soon after they met. Jill reports being attracted by her husband's determined personality and "quiet good looks." She was extremely distraught at the discovery of his exhibitionism, and threatened to divorce him unless he immediately entered treatment.

---

[1]Clinical management of this case was provided by Dr. Susan Shafer.

Following the initial 2-week evaluation, approximately four addition-al sessions were spent in reviewing the patient's motivation for treat-ment. A strong therapeutic stance was taken on the need for immediate control of his inappropriate sexual and child disciplinary behaviors. The patient was also strongly urged to reconsider his role in the marriage at the present time, and to undertake a future commitment to marital therapy. At the end of this postevaluation phase, and after several discussions with his wife, Mr. P. elected to receive masturbatory satiation therapy for control of exhibitionistic urges, in conjunction with ongoing individual treatment for developing greater self-control of anger and improved marital/interpersonal skills.

Satiation therapy was conducted over a 4-month treatment period. The patient was instructed to masturbate in privacy at home, for at least 30 minutes at a time, using a hierarchy of preferred deviant fantasies. During the course of each satiation session, he was instructed to ejaculate as rapidly as possible, and to continue masturbation beyond the point of ejaculation. He was further told to verbalize aloud all deviant fantasies during satiation sessions, and to tape-record these verbalizations. Treat-ment sessions were to be conducted at least four times weekly, and were interspersed with biweekly review sessions with the therapist. Treatment audiotapes were monitored at each of these sessions in order to assess compliance and possible changes in fantasy content over the course of treatment.

Like other patients who have engaged in this technique, J. P. ex-pressed surprise at the extreme aversiveness of the procedure. After 2 weeks of treatment he angrily confronted the therapist about his dislike for the procedure and questioned the need for further treatment. He attempted to rationalize his previous behavior and to question the ther-apist's motivation in administering the technique. With some encourage-ment and reassurance, however, he was able to resume therapy and remained compliant for the remainder of the treatment program.

It is important to emphasize that masturbatory satiation therapy should *always* be combined with positive behavior change techniques for improving coping skills and enhancing interpersonal relationships. In the present case, 3 months of additional therapy was provided to im-prove marital communication and assertiveness skills. Significant posi-tive reinforcement was provided in these sessions and the patient re-ported substantial improvements in self-esteem as a result. No evidence of relapse was apparent at 6-month follow-up.

Positive Behavior Change Techniques

In addition to the use of response suppression procedures, Barlow (1974, 1977) and others have emphasized the importance of heterosocial/heterosexual skills deficits and gender role deviations as key areas for intervention. It has frequently been observed, for example, that reducing deviant arousal alone will not necessarily motivate offenders to seek more appropriate forms of sexual contact. Instead, we find an increasing focus in the literature on positive behavior change techniques, as noted by Bancroft (1989):

> Whenever possible, it is desirable and more effective to take a constructive, positive approach to treatment, to help the individual build up or reinforce new and more adaptive behaviors rather than simply to eliminate old, undesirable ones. . . . The assumption is that if "normal" sexuality becomes more rewarding, there will be less need for the anti-social forms of sex. (p. 724)

Along these lines, various methods have been recommended for developing age-appropriate arousal patterns in pedophilic clients. In one of the earliest case studies of this type, Beech, Watts, and Poole (1971) employed a classical conditioning paradigm for developing sexual arousal to nondeviant stimuli in a heterosexual pedophile. Using nude pictures of adult females as the CS, and photographs of young girls as the UCS, the authors were able to demonstrate increases in erection to the adult stimulus after 3 weeks of treatment. This age-appropriate arousal pattern was found to generalize outside the laboratory, as the patient experienced heterosexual intercourse for the first time shortly after treatment. Unfortunately, subsequent attempts to replicate this procedure with larger clinical samples have been generally unsuccessful (Herman, Barlow, & Agras, 1974; Marshall, 1973). A similar technique based on operant conditioning principles, known as *stimulus fading*, has been used successfully for increasing heterosexual arousal in male homosexuals (Barlow & Agras, 1973). However, this approach has not been used to date with child molesters.

The most widely used technique at present for increasing nondeviant arousal in offenders is *masturbatory conditioning*. This technique was originally introduced by Marquis (1970), who taught his patients to shift their masturbatory fantasies from a deviant to a nondeviant theme, initially at the moment of orgasmic inevitability. Over the course of therapy the patient is instructed to introduce the nondeviant stimulus at progressively earlier intervals, until he is able to masturbate with nondeviant fantasies throughout. The first controlled study to evaluate this procedure was reported by Conrad and Wincze (1976), who evaluated masturbatory conditioning in the treatment of four male homosexuals. Despite reports of improved sexual adjustment in three cases, laboratory erection measures failed to show any significant changes. Perhaps because of its use in the context of changing sexual preference in homosexual patients, the authors concluded that the technique is relatively ineffective and of little clinical value.

More positive results have been obtained by Laws and coworkers (Laws & O'Neill, 1981; Laws, 1985), using a variation of masturbatory conditioning for the development of nondeviant arousal in pedophiles and rapists. This variation is described as "sexual fantasy alternation," and consists of controlled trials of masturbation to orgasm, in which weekly blocks of five trials with a deviant theme are alternated with blocks of trials including nondeviant fantasy themes. Psychophysiological assessments of deviant and nondeviant arousal are conducted before and after each treatment session. Laws and O'Neil (1981) have presented controlled case-study results on the use of this procedure with six hospitalized pedophiles, all of whom showed marked reductions of deviant arousal associated with increased responding to nondeviant themes. Similarly, Abel, Mittelman, and Becker (1985) have recommended this procedure as the treatment of choice for increasing nondeviant arousal in a wide range of paraphilic patients, including child molesters.

For those offenders with established relationships, a brief course of marital or sex therapy may be strongly indicated (Wincze, 1989). Common sexual difficulties, such as premature ejaculation or erectile difficulties, are often encountered among child molesters, and may benefit from a variety of short-term, sex therapy treatment approaches (e.g., Leiblum & Rosen, 1989). Similarly, marital distress may be present as either an antecedent or an effect of child molestation, and is a further important area for treatment. Bancroft (1989) has observed that pedophiles tend to marry women who are dominant in the relationship, suggesting that marital therapy should be focused on restoring a more equal power balance in the relationship. Although most authors strongly endorse the potential value of marital and sex therapy interventions for offenders, there is a surprising dearth of controlled outcome research in this area to date.

In addition to treatment approaches for suppressing deviant arousal or for increasing heterosexual responsiveness, a wide range of positive behavior change techniques have been used for improving interpersonal skills, developing assertiveness, and coping more effectively with stress (e.g., Becker, Abel, Blanchard, Murphy, & Coleman, 1978; Whitman & Quinsey, 1981). In particular, we have recommended the use of *tension reduction training* in conjunction with other modalities of treatment (Rosen & Fracher, 1983). Tension reduction is broadly defined to include a wide range of negative arousal states, ranging from anger to anxiety. These negative arousal states frequently serve as precursors to sexual aggression, and may play an important mediating role in the chain of deviant arousal that has been described. Techniques for coping with tension range from specific somatic procedures, such as EMG biofeedback or progressive muscle relaxation (PMR), or the use of cognitive–behavioral approaches for coping with interpersonal stressors. Additionally, it has frequently been noted that alcohol and drug abuse contribute significantly to child sexual abuse (e.g., Abel et al., 1985), and referral for concurrent treatment of these problems is often indicated.

Case Study

Paul G. is a 42-year-old, never-married man who currently lives with his parents and younger brother. Mr. G. was referred for inpatient therapy following discovery that he had sexually molested his two nieces, aged 4 and 6. The sexual abuse consisted of breast and genital fondling in both cases. Although he did not deny that the abuse had occurred, he claimed that he was completely unable to account for his behavior. Laboratory assessment of penile tumescence supported Mr. G.'s claim of sexual preference for adult women.

In the course of initial evaluation, severe deficits were revealed in the areas of social skills and assertiveness. Paul appeared to be extremely anxious in social situations and to harbor major misconceptions about heterosexual relationships. He had little dating experience, and had generally grown up in a very sheltered family environment. He had worked for many years in a neighborhood grocery store, but had been passed over for promotion on several recent occasions, probably due to his lack of assertiveness and social ineptitude. Based upon these findings, treatment was focused on four specific areas: (1) Challenging the client's misconceptions about adult female behavior and expectations; (2) Improving his social skills, especially with women; (3) Assertiveness training; and (4) Relapse prevention. Each of these interventions were conducted primarily in a group therapy setting over a 4-month period of treatment.

Cognitive restructuring was directed at the patient's deep-seated, irrational beliefs about adult female behavior. For example, Paul believed strongly that *all* women were opportunists at heart, who would spend time with a man *only* until someone better (i.e., wealthier or more powerful) should come along. Paul also stated that he believed any woman would readily "trade" sex for opportunities to date or marry a man with financial means. These entrenched beliefs were targeted for change, primarily because they justified the patient's avoidance of adult women. Indeed, Paul presented himself as "too moral" to be associating with women, and denied that his avoidance of dating might be related to his not owning a car, living with his parents, and working in a low-paying, low-status job. By his own definition, he was clearly unattractive to women.

Irrational beliefs about adult women were confronted in the context of a group-based, rational–emotive treatment approach. For example, specific beliefs were analyzed as follows: "All women are only interested in men for money. Since I have no money, no women will be interested in me." When presented in this manner, Paul was readily confronted with exceptions from his own experience. Additionally, he was confronted by other group members, who frequently challenged his irrational beliefs about women. Toward the end of treatment, Paul allowed that he was interested in meeting a woman and that there might be a woman who would be interested in him for himself.

A second component of treatment involved social skills and assertiveness training. The group format was used for modeling of appropriate behaviors by the more skilled and assertive members. In addition, nursing and clinical staff participated in role-playing sessions to enhance generalization of training. Initially, Paul refused to role play scenarios involving either adult men or women. At this point the staff constructed a hierarchy of anxiety-producing situations for Paul, ranging from initiating a conversation with a woman, to asking someone out on a date. Each of these situations was carefully rehearsed until he was able to attempt role playing with other members of the group.

In the area of social skills, the most difficult items consisted of meeting a woman, asking a woman out on a date, and engaging in conversation on a date. Additional assertiveness items consisted of refusing an unreasonable request from his brother-in-law, or asking for a raise at work. Least difficult items in both hierarchies involved interactions with casual male acquaintances. Paul role played various scenarios from each of these hierarchies over a period of weeks. He was also given "homework" assignments to carry out on the unit and eventually on passes with his family. For example, Paul was able to ask his roommate to stop occupying his chair; he was able to meet and play cards with new patients on the unit; and finally, on a weekend pass he refused a request from his brother-in-law to help in a construction work job.

The final component of treatment consisted of relapse prevention training, following the model described by Pithers et al. (1983). The major emphasis of this approach is to prevent a recurrence of the child molestation by intervening as early in the chain of antecedents as possible. Paul initially claimed that the previous incidents with his nieces were unpremeditated and spontaneous occurrences. In analyzing the sequence of events leading up to each of the assaults, however, this was obviously not the case. Paul had carried out elaborate maneuvers to ensure that he would be alone with the girls, and that he would have uninterrupted access to them for a period of time. Specifically, he had frequently encouraged his sister and brother-in-law to go out at night, and had eagerly volunteered to babysit at any time. The sexual abuse itself consisted of a series of graded activities, that typically began with a benign "tickle" game, and culminated in genital fondling. From this response prevention analysis, Paul began to realize that his sexual abuse had stemmed from sexual curiosity, his fear and hostility toward adult women, and the power he came to exercise over his two small nieces. He was carefully instructed in the importance of avoiding unsupervised access to children, for example, by refusing future requests to babysit. Moreover, Paul re-examined his "apparently irrelevant decision" to befriend couples who had young children.

At termination, Paul had decided to attempt independent living in a small town, in which one of his sisters lived. This particular sister was childless and the client agreed to avoid scrupulously further contact with young children. He was able to find a job without much difficulty, and had gradually begun dating. No further offenses were noted at 1-year follow-up.

It is noteworthy that treatment in this case was focused almost exclusively on the cognitive and interpersonal dimensions, and that no specific response suppression techniques were employed. The client's previous offenses were conceptualized as predominantly related to his interpersonal skills deficits, particularly in the areas of heterosocial and heterosexual functioning, and his lack of assertiveness in work and social situations. In addition, the group therapy intervention served as a powerful source of modeling and social reinforcement for treatment gains.

Behavioral Approaches to Relapse Prevention

A major advance in recent years has been the application of relapse prevention concepts and methods to the treatment of sex offenders (see Laws, 1989, for comprehensive reviews of this burgeoning area). Based on the observation that recidivism rates are unacceptably high in many treatment programs (Furby, Weinrott, & Blackshaw, 1989), several authors have recommended the use of structured relapse prevention training as an integral component of treatment (George & Marlatt, 1984; Pithers et al., 1983). Although developed originally as a maintenance program for use with alcoholism and other addictive disorders, the RP approach seems well suited for application in this area. Certainly, the potential consequences of relapse are nowhere as important as in the treatment of sex offenders. While a complete discussion of the training system is beyond the scope of the present chapter, a few key concepts are worth noting here.

To begin with, a distinction is drawn between the terms "lapse" and "relapse," with the latter concept being reserved for a full-blown return to the problem behavior. In applying this distinction to sex offenders, George and Marlatt (1989) suggest that a lapse be defined as engaging in any related antecedent activities, such as fantasizing about sex with children or seeking situations in which such activities might be possible. A continuum of behavioral lapses can be conceptualized in this way, ranging from a brief urge or fleeting thought about reoffending, to formulation of a specific plan of action prior to commission of an actual offense. Naturally, relapse prevention training is focused on intervention at the *earliest step* in the chain of antecedent lapses—typically the use of deliberate fantasy or imaginal rehearsal of the problem behavior.

A second important concept is the role of *high-risk situations* in determining the possible occurrence of both lapses and relapses. According to George and Marlatt (1989): "An HRS may be broadly defined as any situation that poses a threat to perceived control and thereby increases the probability of lapse or relapse" (p. 7). Examples of high-risk situations are situations of intense negative affect (e.g., anger, depression), interpersonal conflict, particularly with a spouse or significant other, and social pressure to engage in deviant behavior. A key assumption of the relapse prevention model is that the likelihood of relapse is inversely related to the client's ability to cope effectively with such high-risk situations. Accordingly, training incorporates a major emphasis on developing coping stategies for a wide range of situations. Steenman, Nelson, and Viesti (1989), for example, have recommended the following eight specific strategies:

1. Avoidance of drug and alcohol abuse;
2. Improving stress management through relaxation and self-monitoring techniques;
3. Enhancing social skills for developing more satisfactory adult relationships;
4. Maintaining self-esteem through positive self- statements;
5. Augmenting assertiveness skills;
6. Improving or developing anger management techniques in order to facilitate better conflict resolution;
7. Increasing victim empathy;
8. Combating distorted attributions to the victim. (Steenman et al., 1989, p. 183)

Two other concepts that have been used to explain specific instances of relapse are *apparently irrelevant decisions* and the *problem of immediate gratification*. The former refer to sequences of behavior that may increase the probability of relapse, such as deciding to take a walk through a neighborhood schoolyard, which the offender fails to link consciously with the problem behavior. Another example in the case study described earlier was the client's decision to babysit for his sister and brother-in-law. The problem of immediate gratification, as defined by Marlatt (1989), refers to the intense cravings or states of negative arousal that many offenders experience, which may be temporarily relieved through sexual or aggressive outlets. This often leads a vicious cycle:

> Once the craving has been gratified by the consummatory act, the individual is plunged into a contrasting emotional state, characterized by negative emotions. . . . Once again, the seeds of craving grow in this soil of discomfort and decreased self-efficacy, and the cycle is set to repeat itself. As in any addiction cycle, the quick fix of the [problem of immediate gratification] is followed by a downside that sets the stage for another bout of craving and indulgence. (Marlatt, 1989, pp. 61–62)

In order to deal more effectively with both the apparently irrelevant decisions and the problem of immediate gratification, the client's rationalizations and denial are vigorously challenged in treatment, and alternative (i.e., more realistic) attributions are substituted where possible. Again, techniques for stress management and enhanced self-esteem are also recommended for the control of cravings. Finally, structured *relapse rehearsal training* has been used for development and practice of alternative coping responses in offenders (Hall, 1989).

Behavioral Approaches to the Treatment of Child Victims

Learning Models of Postabuse Sequelae

An important trend in recent years has been the use of learning theory concepts, such as conditioned anxiety or two-factor theory, to account for specific behavioral sequelae of sexual abuse in child victims and adult survivors. Surprisingly, there have been scant reports in the treatment literature of clinical applications based on these important concepts. Overall, there has been a disproportionate emphasis in the field on development of behavioral treatment approaches for offenders, as opposed to victims. This may be due, in part, to the lack of awareness, until recently, of a distinct pattern of emotional and behavioral sequelae resulting from sexual abuse. An important goal of the present chapter is to highlight the need for further research on behavioral treatment of child victims.

Recently, a number of conceptual models have been proposed for understanding the emotional consequences of child sexual abuse (e.g., Conte & Schuerman, 1987; Finkelhor & Browne, 1986). Of these conceptual approaches, the learning theory paradigm is perhaps the most highly developed to date. This approach was first applied to the conceptualization of emotional sequelae of sexual assault in adult female survivors (e.g., Holmes & St. Lawrence, 1983; Kilpatrick, Veronen, & Resick, 1979), and subsequently to the interpretation of these symptoms as evidence of posttraumatic stress disorder (Foa, Steketee, & Rothbaum, 1989).

Several authors have attempted to apply Mowrer's two-factor theory (Mowrer, 1960), to the persistent symptoms of anxiety frequently observed in victims. According to Berliner and Wheeler (1987), fear and anxiety are conditioned during the sexual assault (UCS) to previously neutral stimuli (CS) that are present during the sexual abuse (e.g., a particular adult, items of clothing, a specific time of day or place, etc.). The principles of stimulus generalization and higher-order conditioning are then invoked to account for the generalization of fear and anxiety responses to other related stimuli. The conditioning of anxiety, according to this model, sets the stage for subsequent instrumental conditioning of anxiety-reducing avoidance behaviors. The symptomatic avoidance behaviors of a given victim are said to be maintained because they enable him or her to escape the classically conditioned anxiety-eliciting cues. Regressive behaviors, such as thumbsucking or bedwetting, as well as aggressive behaviors, temper tantrums, and self-mutilations may be additional ways in which child victims learn to cope with conditioned anxiety.

There are several shortcomings to this theory as a causal explanation of emotional consequences of child sexual abuse. Holmes and St. Lawrence (1983), for example, note that for adult victims of sexual assault, the symptoms of anxiety tend to be particularly resistant to extinction, despite repeated unreinforced exposure to the conditioned stimulus. The same observation appears generally true for child victims. Fear of the dark, or of adult men, may persist despite the fact that many dark nights have elapsed and numerous adult males have been present without additional assaults occurring. To account for this observation, Holmes and St. Lawrence draw upon Stampfl and Levis' (1967) "serial stimulus hypothesis" to account for the phenomenon of resistance to extinction. According to this hypothesis, the anxiety CS is never a discrete stimulus, but rather a series of internal and external cues sequentially ordered in time. Effective extinction would only occur with repeated presentations of the entire cuing series of stimuli, followed by the absence of the UCS. However, it is unlikely that the complete cuing series would ever be presented to the child solely by chance.

A more serious limitation of two-factor theory is that it focuses only on *anxiety* and anxiety-reducing behaviors as the important sequelae of child sexual abuse. This approach also assumes that there is nothing unique about the effects of sexual abuse, as opposed to other emotional traumata that a child might endure. However, as Finkelhor (1986) noted, the sequelae of child sexual abuse encompass a wide range of affective reactions other than anxiety, and include anger, rage, and depression, as well as behavioral problems such as lethargy, anhedonia, truancy, low self-esteem, and inappropriate sexual behavior.

Berliner and Wheeler (1987) have recently expanded the conditioning model to include social learning processes in accounting for sequelae of sexual abuse other than anxiety. Specifically, these authors speculate that:

> Through the offender's modeling, instruction, direct or differential reinforcement, and punishment or threat of punishment, abused children acquire a repertoire of sexual behaviors and experiences before they have the necessary emotional, cognitive, or social capabilities to regulate their own sexuality. (p. 420)

This social learning addition to the original two-factor theory implies that the unique circumstances of the abuse, beyond the fact that sexual abuse represents an emotional trauma to the child, results in the particular pattern of psychosocial sequelae. Finkelhor and Browne (1986) have similarly suggested that the circumstances of the abusive situation will determine the ultimate behavioral consequences. For example, a child may learn that sexual behaviors are used to obtain reinforcement or to avoid punishment. This "premature and distorted sexualization" (p. 421) can disinhibit the child's control and expression of sexual behaviors. This may, in turn, lead to social ostracism, stigmatization, revictimization, or abuse of other children, and potentially long-term sexual dysfunction (Berliner & Wheeler, 1987).

In terms of possible cognitive sequelae, sexual abuse frequently affects the child's self-concept, concept of others, and expectations for relationships. A sense of powerlessness and diminished self-efficacy may also be created. Peterson and Seligman (1983), for example, have applied the learned helplessness model to explain the apparent passivity of some victims. Sexual abuse is perceived by some victims as beyond their control in terms of onset, duration, and termination, as well as the specific sexual acts performed. Child victims learn that their actions have no relation to outcome and they may become hopelessly passive, even if the situation changes, and failing to develop coping strategies in new and potentially controllable situations. A "self-deprecatory" attributional style has also been described in response to sexual victimization (Wolfe, Gentile, & Wolfe, 1989).

Implications for Treatment

Each of the foregoing models can be viewed as having specific treatment implications. These include an emphasis on anxiety-reducing techniques, procedures for enhancing self-esteem and self-efficacy, and skills-training to develop or restore behavior that is developmentally appropriate for the child. Additionally, it is important to encourage behaviors that may reduce the risk of revictimization. Contingency management procedures have also been used to eliminate undesirable behaviors, and to develop appropriate alternatives.

In the first case report of this type, Becker, Skinner, and Abel (1982) described the behavioral treatment of a 4-year-old female victim of father–daughter incest. The child victim in this case showed a severe emotional reaction to the abuse, including symptoms of anxiety and depression, self-injurious behavior, sleep difficulties, and significant weight loss. Previous attempts by the mother to talk about her abuse and to reassure the child were of no avail. After consultation with a rape crisis center, mother and daughter were referred for behavioral treatment.

Treatment in this case was conducted primarily by the child's mother, with ongoing consultation from the authors. The mother was initially instructed on the importance of behavioral assessment and recording, and a number of specific behaviors were targeted for observation. An overall rating of mood ("happiness scale") was also instituted. Behavioral observations were conducted on a daily basis throughout treatment and during a 2-month follow-up period. Treatment was based on operant conditioning principles, and consisted essentially of ignoring, where possible, problem behaviors such as phobic and self-injurious responses, while reinforcing positive behaviors, such as eating at mealtime. A token reinforcement program was set up, with colored stars and pennies being provided as rewards.

Marked improvements in the child's behavior were noted during the course of the 18-week treatment program, most of which were maintained at follow-up. Positive behaviors, such as the number of meals eaten per week and rating of overall happiness, were gradually increased over treatment, while phobic and self-injurious behaviors were reduced. A temporary setback was observed at weeks 7–10, which appeared to be associated with two visits from the child's paternal grand-mother. After all visitation rights for the father were waived at week 13, no further relapses were observed. In addition to providing direct treatment for the child's posttraumatic stress disorder, the child's mother appeared to have benefited considerably through her direct involvement in the therapy process. Specifically, Becker, Skinner, and Abel (1982) note that: "The patient's mother was able to serve as data collector to document the impact of the assault and therapy, and to serve as the 'therapist', giving the mother a feeling of helping and control" (p. 46).

Similar results were obtained by McNeill and Todd (1986) in a case study of behavioral treatment for a 5-year-old female victim of extrafamilial sexual abuse. The victim in this case had been abused over a period of about a year prior to disclosure, and showed various symptoms of distress. These included excessive rumination about the molestation and extreme dependency behaviors. The child's mother was again utilized for behavioral observation and contingency management training, and treatment was focused on stimulus control techniques for dealing with the ruminative behavior, coupled with positive reinforcement for alternative activities. Using a multiple baseline assessment approach, the authors were able to demonstrate specific changes in the targeted behaviors. Treatment effects were maintained at 12-month follow-up assessment.

Social–cognitive interventions may also be of value in the treatment of child victims. Noting that sexually abused children frequently display interpersonal difficulties subsequent to the abuse, Kolko (1986) described the use of a social–cognitive skills training program with an 11-year-old male victim of sexual abuse. Treatment in this case was conducted in a psychiatric inpatient facility, due to the patient's hospitalization for molesting a neighborhood girl. The boy had a history of parental neglect and was sexually abused at age 9 by a maternal uncle, following which he had been removed from the custody of his biological mother and placed in foster care. In addition to displaying inappropriate sexual behavior, he was frequently caught fighting with other children and had become socially withdrawn and suspicious.

Using an innovative analog role-playing procedure for assessment of social skills, the author focused on several target behaviors for treatment intervention. These included voice quality, eye contact, physical gestures, and verbal content in a variety of interpersonal situations. An intensive program of social and cognitive skills training was then introduced, including didactic instruction, coaching, modeling, role playing, and feedback components. Results indicated a significant increase in social skills following treatment, which were associated with dramatically improved interpersonal adjustment and self-esteem. As noted by the authors, treatment in this case may have been effective not only in alleviating specific symptoms of sexual abuse in this child, but also in decreasing the likelihood of his becoming a future offender.

Finally, two recent reports have described *behavioral group treatment* approaches for coping with emotional sequelae of sexual abuse in child victims. Burke, Jackson, and Townsley (1988) evaluated the effectiveness of a six-session group treatment program, which included education about sexual abuse, progressive muscle relaxation, anxiety reduction training, and instructions for coping with inappropriate advances by adults. Treatment outcome was assessed in 12 girls aged 8–13, who had been sexually abused during the past 2 years. Compared with a matched waiting-list control group, the treatment group showed a significant reduction in self-reported depressive symptoms, anxiety, sexual abuse fears, and parent-ratings of negative affect. Similarly, Hoier, Inderbitzen-Pisaruk, and Shawchuck (1988) evaluated a short-term, cognitive–behavioral group intervention for male and female child victims. The children in this study ranged in age from 5 to 15, and males and females were combined in two treatment groups. Group sessions emphasized cognitive restructuring, behavior rehearsal and role playing, and modeling of appropriate interpersonal behaviors. In contrast to Burke et al. (1988), these authors observed significant improvements in depressive and fear-related symptoms, but no change in aggressive or inappropriate sexual behaviors.

Taken together, these studies suggest that behavioral interventions may be of considerable value in alleviating emotional and interpersonal sequelae of sexual abuse. Behavioral approaches for child victims are potentially more efficient and cost-effective than other forms of individual therapy, and are amenable to controlled outcome evaluation. Behavioral approaches are now widely used in the treatment of adult survivors of rape and sexual assault (e.g., Becker, 1989; Koss, 1983), and we anticipate increased application of these techniques to child victims in the future. Further research is urgently needed, however, to determine which aspects of treatment are likely to be effective for which individuals, and whether treatment results are maintained at long-term follow-up. Controlled comparisons have also not been conducted to date with more traditional forms of treatment, such as play therapy or family therapy.

Case Example

John P. is a 5-year-old boy who was referred for treatment following his disclosure that he had been sexually abused by two 10-year-old girls in his neighborhood. The abuse had taken place about a year previously and had involved repeated digital penetration of the anus. At the time of evaluation, John's mother complained that her son was extremely anxious and exhibited a number of obsessive–compulsive behaviors. He picked lint off carpeting and chairs, was frequently fearful that he would swallow dirt and become ill, and checked repeatedly whether his food was contaminated. During early treatment sessions, John presented as a shy, compliant, and generally well-behaved boy. He was contented to sit alone and draw pictures with crayons.

John was extremely reluctant, at first, to disclose the particulars of the abuse. Anatomically detailed drawings and dolls, as well as a role-playing game about sexual abuse, were utilized to assess the extent of abuse he had suffered. John's mother reported an exacerbation in his symptoms during the initial evaluation; he refused to eat without his mother's assurance that no harm would come to him, and he insisted that she check all his bowel movements and pronounce them normal before he would flush the toilet. Recognizing that these symptoms were likely related to John's anxiety and distress at recalling the sexual abuse, several behavioral interventions were introduced to deal with specific problem behaviors. A contingency management program was set up whereby John was instructed to color a circle for every meal he was able to eat without checking with his mother for germs or dirt. If all three meals received color circles, John was given an extra half-hour of play time with his parents before bedtime. John, his mother, and the therapist each signed a written contract to that effect.

At the end of the first week of this program, Mrs. P. stated that she had been unable to comply with the contract as she found it impossible to refuse her son's requests for additional playtime, even if he had not achieved the criterion behavior. Accordingly, the contingency was modified so that if John colored circles for every meal and snack time of the day, he would receive a quarter. John used his quarters for playing video games at the corner store. Within 3 weeks, he was able to complete all his charts and the problem behavior appeared to have been eliminated.

At this time Mrs. P. complained that John had escalated in his concern about his bowel movements and requested that this behavior be targeted next for intervention. It was explained to John that since he had done so well in controlling his mealtime behavior, we would now begin working on bathroom behavior as well. The new contingency was set up to include that he not ask his mother to examine his bowel movements, in addition to not checking his food. Again, he would receive a quarter for each day with all colored circles, as well as a half-hour of additional playtime at the weekly therapy session if he achieved a perfect week. The compulsive toilet behavior quickly improved, so that within 2 weeks John was no longer asking his mother to check his bowel movements. When asked about his mealtime and toilet behavior, John stated: "I don't even think about it anymore!"

Despite some concern that these behavioral interventions might inhibit further disclosure on John's part, he regularly chose to play the role-playing game about sexual abuse issues, as a reward for coloring all his circles. Furthermore, he began openly to express anxiety and doubts about sexual issues, and to display inappropriate sexual behavior at home, such as exposing his penis to his parents or grabbing at their genitals. Two additional interventions were introduced for dealing with these new problem behaviors. First, John was placed in a behavioral group therapy program for other young male victims in his age group. This group was aimed to enhance positive peer-interaction behaviors and to develop age-appropriate ways of dealing with sexual feelings.

The group functioned well, fostering positive peer interactions in John at this time. However, there appeared to be little generalization to the home environment, where he continued to act out sexually with both of his parents. Before introducing a specific behavioral intervention in this area, the parents were encouraged to request John firmly to stop each time he initiated inappropriate sexual behavior with either Mr. or Mrs. P. This appeared sufficient to bring the behavior under control.

Behavioral techniques were used in this case primarily to gain control over obsessive–compulsive symptoms (e.g., checking his food for germs and dirt), and inappropriate social and sexual behaviors. The contingency management program allowed us to deal directly with John's obsessive–compulsive behaviors. It also provided some measure of control over these behaviors for his parents, thereby encouraging their commitment to a more long-term program of therapy for John. At 6-month follow-up there appeared to be no evidence of return of his obsessive behaviors.

Conclusion

In contrast to the stereotyped image of behavior therapy presented in books and films such as A Clockwork Orange, we have attempted in this chapter to represent the breadth and diversity of treatment methods currently included in this category. Certainly, behavior therapy approaches to both offenders and victims have become more flexible and broader in spectrum in recent years. Social–cognitive interventions are being used with increasing frequency, as are behavioral group therapy approaches. In the area of offender treatment, there has been a noticeable shift away from response suppression techniques, with greater attention being paid to interpersonal deficits and inadequate coping mechanisms. Relapse prevention training has also become a major focus of treatment, as a variety of innovative procedures are being used to ensure maintenance of treatment gains.

Behavioral treatment approaches for child victims appear to be most useful in coping with emotional sequelae of sexual abuse, and in restoring the child's self-esteem and interpersonal functioning. Several case studies have included the child's mother in the treatment process and specific benefits of this approach have been noted. Two studies have made use of behavioral group treatment approaches for victims, which we have also found to be a valuable treatment modality. Unfortunately, there is a paucity of controlled outcome research in this area to date. Hopefully, future studies will be conducted to determine which components of treatment are most effective in particular patient groups. There is also a pressing need for long-term follow-up studies of behavioral treatment for child victims.

ACKNOWLEDGMENT

Support for the Family Relations Center is provided by a grant from the Robert Wood Johnson Foundation.

REFERENCES

Abel, G. G., Becker, J. V., Murphy, W. D., & Flanagan, B. (1981). Identifying dangerous child molesters. In R. Stuart (Ed.), *Violent behavior* (pp. 116–137). New York: Brunner/Mazel.

Abel, G. G., Blanchard, E. B., & Becker, J. V. (1978). An integrated treatment program for rapists. In R. Rada (Ed.), *Clinical aspects of the rapist* (pp. 161–214). New York: Grune & Stratton.

Abel, G. G., Mittelman, M. S., & Becker, J. V. (1985). Sexual offenders: Results of assessment and recommendations for treatment. In M. H. Ben-Aron, S. J. Hucker, & C. Webster (Eds.), *Clinical criminology: The assessment and treatment of criminal behavior* (pp. 191–205). Toronto: M & M Graphics.

Bancroft, J. (1989). *Human sexuality and its problems.* New York: Churchill Livingstone.

Barlow, D. H. (1974). The treatment of sexual deviation: Towards a comprehensive behavioral approach. In K. S. Calhoun, H. E. Adams, & K. M. Mitchell (Eds.), *Innovative treatment methods in psychopathology* (pp. 121–148). New York: Wiley.

Barlow, D. H. (1977). Assessment of sexual behavior. In R. A. Ciminero, K. S. Calhoun, & H. E. Adams (Eds.), *Handbook of behavioral assessment* (pp. 461–508). New York: Wiley.

Barlow, D. H. & Agras, W. S. (1973). Fading to increase heterosexual responsiveness in homosexuals. *Journal of Applied Behavior Analysis, 6,* 355–366.

Barlow, D. H., Agras, W. S., Leitenberg, H., Callahan, E. I., & Moore, R. C. (1972). The contribution of therapeutic instruction to covert sensitization. *Behavior Research and Therapy, 10,* 411–416.

Becker, J. V. (1989). Impact of sexual abuse on sexual functioning. In S. R. Leiblum & R. C. Rosen (Eds.), *Principles and practice of sex therapy: Update for the 1990's* (pp. 298–318). New York: Guilford Press.

Becker, J. V., Abel, G. G., Blanchard, E. B., Murphy, W. D., & Coleman, E. (1978). Evaluating social skills of sexual aggressives. *Criminal Justice and Behavior, 5,* 357–367.

Becker, J. V., Skinner, L. J., & Abel, G. G. (1982). Treatment of a four-year-old victim of incest. *American Journal of Family Therapy, 10,* 41–46.

Beech, H. R., Watts, F., & Poole, A. D. (1971). Classical conditioning of sexual deviation: A preliminary note. *Behavior Therapy, 2,* 400–402.

Berliner, L., & Wheeler, J. R. (1987). Treating the effects of sexual abuse on children. *Journal of Interpersonal Violence, 2,* 415–434.

Browne, A., and Finkelhor, D. (1986). Impact of child sexual abuse: A review at the research. *Psychological Bulletin, 99,* 66–77.

Brownell, K. D., Hayes, S. C., & Barlow, D. H. (1977). Pattens of appropriate and deviant sexual arousal: The behavioral treatment of multiple sexual deviations. *Journal of Consulting and Clinical Psychology, 45,* 1144–1155.

Burgess, A. (1962). *A clockwork orange.* New York: Norton.

Burke, M., Jackson, J., & Townsley, R. (1988). *Behavioral treatment for negative affect in sexually abused girls.* Paper presented at the World Congress of Behavior Therapy, Edinburgh, Scotland.

Callahan, E. J., & Leitenberg, H. (1973). Aversion therapy for sexual deviation: Contingent shock and covert sensitization. *Journal of Abnormal Psychology, 81,* 60–73.

Conrad, S. R., & Wincze, J. P. (1976). Orgasmic reconditioning: A controlled study of its effects upon sexual arousal and behavior of adult male homosexuals. *Behavior Therapy, 7,* 155–166.

Conte, J. R., & Schuerman, J. R. (1987). Factors associated with an increased impact of child sexual abuse. *Child Abuse and Neglect, 11,* 201–211.

Feldman, M. P., & MacCullough, M. J. (1965). The application of anticipatory avoidance learning to the treatment of homosexuality. *Behaviour Research and Therapy, 2,* 165–183.

Finkelhor, D. (1986). *A sourcebook on child sexual abuse.* Beverly Hills, CA: Sage.

Finkelhor, D., & Browne, A. (1986). The traumatic impact of child sexual abuse: A conceptualization. *American Journal of Orthopsychiatry, 55,* 530–541.

Foa, E. B., Steketee, G., & Rothbaum, B. O. (1989). Behavioral/cognitive conceptualizations of post-traumatic stress disorder. *Behavior Therapy, 20,* 155–176.

Freund, K., & Langevin, R. (1976). Bisexuality in homosexual pedophilia. *Archives of Sexual Behavior, 5,* 415–423.

Freund, K., Scher, H., Chan, S., & Ben-Aron, M. (1982). Experimental analysis of pedophilia. *Behaviour Research and Therapy, 20,* 105–112.

Furby, L., Weinrott, M. R., & Blackshaw, L. (1989). Sex offender recidivisim: A review. *Psychological Bulletin, 105,* 3–30.

Hall, G. C. N., Proctor, W. C., & Nelson, G. M. (1988). Validity of physiological measures of pedophilic sexual arousal in a sexual offender population. *Journal of Consulting and Clinical Psychology, 56,* 118–122.

Hall, R. L. (1989). Relapse rehearsal. In D. R. Laws (Ed.), *Relapse prevention with sex offenders* (pp. 197–206). New York: Guilford Press.

Herman, S. H., Barlow, D. H., & Agras, W. S. (1974). An experimental analysis of classical conditioning as a method of increasing heterosexual arousal in homosexuals. *Behavior Therapy, 5,* 33–47.

Hoier, T. S., Inderbitzen-Pisaruk, H., & Shawchuck, C. (1988). *Short-term cognitive–behavioral group treatment for victims of sexual abuse.* Unpublished manuscript, (W. Virginia Univ.).

Holmes, M. R., & St. Lawrence, J. S. (1983). Treatment of rape-induced trauma: Proposed behavioral conceptualization and review of the literature. *Clinical Psychology Review, 3,* 417–433.

Kelly, R. J. (1982). Behavioral reorientation of pedophiliacs: Can it be done? *Clinical Psychology Review, 2,* 387–408.

Kilpatrick, D. G., Veronen, L. J., & Resick, P. A. (1979). Assessment of the aftermath of rape: Changing patterns of fear. *Journal of Behavioral Assessment, 1,* 133–148.

Kolko, D. J. (1986). Social–cognitive skills training with a sexually abused and abusive child psychiatric inpatient: Training, generalization, and follow-up. *Journal of Family Violence, 1,* 149–165.

Koss, M. (1983). The scope of rape: Implications for the clinical treatment of victims. *Clinical Psychologist, 36,* 88–91.

Laws, D. R. (1980). Treatment of bisexual pedophilia by a biofeedback-assisted self-control procedure. *Behaviour Research and Therapy, 18,* 207–211.

Laws, D. R. (1984). The assessment of dangerous sexual behaviour in males. *Medicine and Law, 3,* 127–140.

Laws, D. R. (1985). Sexual fantasy alternation: Procedural considerations. *Journal of Behavior Therapy and Experimental Psychiatry, 16,* 39–44.

Laws, D. R. (Ed.). (1989). *Relapse prevention with sex offenders.* New York: Guilford Press.

Laws, D. R., & O'Neill, J. A. (1981). Variations in masturbatory conditioning. *Behavioural Psychotherapy, 9,* 11–136.

Leiblum, S. R., & Rosen, R. C. (Eds.) (1989). *Principles and practice of Sex Therapy.* New York: Guilford Press.

Maletzky, B. M. (1980). Self-referred versus court-referred sexually deviant patients: Success with assisted covert sensitization. *Behavior Therapy, 11,* 306–314.

Marks, I. M., & Gelder. M. G. (1967). Transvestism and fetishism: Clinical and psychological changes during faradic aversion. *British Journal of Psychiatry, 113,* 711–730.

Marks, I. M., Gelder, M. G., & Bancroft, J. H. (1970). Sexual deviants two years after electric aversion therapy. *British Journal of Psychiatry, 117,* 173–185.

Marlatt, G. A. (1989). Feeding the PIG: The problem of immediate gratification. In D. R. Laws (Ed.), *Relapse prevention with sex offenders.* New York: Guilford Press.

Marlatt, G. A., & George, W. H. (1984). Relapse prevention: Introduction and overview of the model. *British Journal of Addiction, 79,* 261–273.

Marquis, J. (1970). Orgasmic reconditioning: Changing sexual object choice through controlling masturbation fantasies. *Journal of Behavior Therapy and Experimental Psychiatry, 1,* 263–271.

Marshall, W. L. (1971). A combined treatment method for certain sexual deviations. *Behaviour Research and Therapy, 9,* 293–294.

Marshall, W. L. (1973). The modification of sexual fantasies: A combined treatment approach to the reduction of deviant sexual behavior. *Behaviour Research and Therapy, 11,* 557–564.

Marshall, W. L. (1979). Satiation therapy: A procedure for reducing deviant sexual arousal. *Journal of Applied Behavior Analysis, 12,* 377–389.

Marshall, W. L., & Barbaree, H. E. (1978). The reduction of deviant arousal. *Criminal Justice and Behavior, 5,* 294–303.

Max, L. W. (1935). Breaking up a homosexual fixation by the conditioned reaction technique. *Psychological Bulletin, 32,* 734.

McGuire, R. J., Carlisle, J. M., & Young, B. G. (1965). Sexual deviations as conditioned behaviour: An hypothesis. *Behaviour Research and Therapy, 2,* 185–190.

McNeill, J. W., & Todd, F. J. (1986). The operant treatment of excessive verbal ruminations and negative emotional arousal in a case of child molestation. *Child and Family Behavior Therapy, 8,* 61–69.

Mowrer, O. H. (1960). *Learning theory and behavior.* New York: Wiley.

Peterson, C., & Seligman, M. E. P. (1983). Learned helplessness and victimization. *Journal of Social Issues, 2,* 103–116.

Pithers, W. D., Marques, J. K., Gibat, C. C., & Marlatt, G. A. (1983). Relapse prevention with sexual aggressives. In J. G. Greer & I. R. Stuart (Eds.), *The sexual aggressor: Current perspectives on treatment* (pp. 214–239). New York: Van Nostrand.

Quinsey, V. L., Chaplin, T. C., & Carrigan, W. F. (1979). Sexual preferences among incestuous and non-incestuous child molesters. *Behavior Therapy, 10,* 562–565.

Quinsey, V. L., Chaplin, T. C., & Carrigan, W. F. (1980). Biofeedback and signaled punishment in the modification of inappropriate sexual age preferences. *Behavior Therapy, 11,* 567–576.

Quinsey, V. L., & Marshall, W. L. (1983). Procedures for reducing inappropriate sexual arousal: An evaluation review. In J. G. Greer & I. R. Stuart (Eds.), *The sexual aggressor: Current perspectives on treatment* (pp. 267–292). New York: Van Nostrand.

Rachman, S. (1966). Sexual fetishism: An experimental analogue. *Psychological Record, 16,* 293–296.

Rachman, S., & Hodgson, R. J. (1968). Experimentally-induced "sexual fetishism": Replication and development. *Psychological Record, 18,* 25–27.

Raymond, M. J. (1956). A case of fetishism treated by aversion therapy. *British Medical Journal, ii,* 854–856.

Rosen, R. C., & Beck, J. G. (1988). *Patterns of sexual arousal: Psychophysiological processes and clinical applications.* New York: Guilford Press.

Rosen, R. C., & Fracher, J. C. (1983). Tension-reduction training in the treatment of compulsive sex offenders. In J. G. Greer & I. R. Stuart (Eds.), *The sexual aggressor: Current perspectives on treatment* (pp. 144–159). New York: Van Nostrand.

Rosen, R. C. (1973). Suppression of penile tumescence by instrumental conditioning. *Psychosomatic Medicine, 35,* 509–514.

Rosenthal, T. L. (1973). Response-contingent versus fixed punishment in aversion conditioning of pedophilia: A case study. *Journal of Nervous and Mental Disease, 156,* 440–443.

Stampfl, T. G., & Levis, D. J. (1967). Essentials of implosive therapy: A learning-theory-based psychodynamic behavioral therapy. *Journal of Abnormal Psychology, 72,* 157–163.

Steenman, H., Nelson, C., & Viesti, C. (1989). Developing coping strategies for high-risk situations. In D. R. Laws (Ed.), *Relapse prevention with sex offenders* (pp. 178–187). New York: Guilford Press.

Whitman, W. P., & Quinsey, V. L. (1981). Heterosocial skills training for institutionalized rapists and child molesters. *Canadian Journal of Behavioral Science, 13,* 105–114.

Wincze, J. P. (1989). Assessment and treatment of atypical sexual behavior. In S. R. Leiblum & R. C. Rosen (Eds.), *Principles and practice of sex therapy: Update for the 1990's* (pp. 382–404). New York: Guilford Press.

Wolfe, V. V., Gentile, C., & Wolfe, D. A. (1989). The impact of sexual abuse on children: A PTSD formulation. *Behavior Therapy, 20,* 215–228.

11

Group Treatment of Child Sexual Abuse Victims: A Review

Kinly Sturkie
Clemson University, Clemson, SC

Since a recognition of the pervasiveness of child sexual abuse first captured our attention, a number of models of intervention have been used with this problem. This multiplicity of approaches reflects, in part, the ideological and conceptual diversity of the many different practitioners and social activists who first brought child sexual abuse to professional and public awareness and who helped elevate it to the status of a social problem. These persons included researchers and clinicians in the child maltreatment and family violence fields who were broadening their previous focus from physical child abuse and the battered child syndrome (De Francis, 1969; Kempe, 1977), feminists who were providing a revisionist view of rape and other forms of sexual violence against women (Brownmiller, 1975; Herman & Hirshman, 1977), persons in the family therapy field who were applying cybernetic concepts to the problem of incest (Eist & Mandel, 1968; Machotka, Pittman, & Flomenshaft, 1967), clinicians and historians who were critically re-evaluating the work of Sigmund Freud (Masson, 1984; Rosenfeld, 1977; Rush, 1980), and persons who began treating child victims and their families because of an unconventional willingness to acknowledge the existence and magnitude of this problem (Burgess, Groth, Holmstrøm, & Sgroi, 1978; Giaretto, 1976; Summit & Kryso, 1978). Importantly, during the formative years of the field, each of these groups worked in relative isolation and each approached the problem of child sexual abuse with its own unique set of conceptual and political premises and its own political agenda. Not surprisingly, the therapeutic approaches that were developed by these groups were often philosophically antagonistic and methodologically varied (Sturkie, 1986).

Despite these differences, group treatment soon emerged as one of the more widely used forms of intervention with a variety of client groups. These client groups have included preschool children (Carozza & Heirsteiner, 1982; Damon & Waterman, 1986; Mitchum, 1987; Mrazek, 1981; Nelki & Watters, 1989; Pescosolido & Petrella, 1986; Steward et al., 1986); latency-aged children (Berliner & Ernst, 1984; Boatman, Borkan, & Schetky, 1981; Delson & Clark, 1981; Mandell & Damon, 1989; Sturkie, 1983); adolescents (Berliner & MacQuivey, 1983; Blick & Porter, 1982; Boatman et al., 1981; Furniss, Bingley-Miller, & van Elburg, 1988; Gagliano, 1987; Gottleib & Dean, 1981; Hazzard, King & Webb, 1986; James, 1977; Knittle & Tuana, 1980; Verleur, Hughes, & De Rios, 1986; Wayne & Weeks, 1984); adult survivors of incest and other forms of sexual assault (Bergart, 1986; Cole, 1985; Cole & Barney, 1987; Courtouis, 1988; Deighton & McPeek, 1985; Fowler, Burns, & Roehl, 1983; Goodman & Nowak-Scibelli, 1985; Gordy, 1983; Hays, 1987; Herman & Schatzow, 1984; Tsai & Wagner, 1978); and the parents of sexually abused children (Giaretto, 1976, 1982; Haugaard & Reppucci, 1988; Herman, 1981; MacFarlane & Waterman, 1986).

The purpose of this chapter is to review critically the group treatment approaches for child victims of sexual abuse that have emerged during the last decade. The chapter begins by examining the rationale for this form of intervention and by describing the major models of group treatment currently evident in the field. The premises regarding why group treatment is curative are also presented and the limited empirical research on the utility of this form of intervention is reviewed. The focus then shifts briefly to a comparison of child and adult treatment groups, exploring how the temporal proximity of the abuse experience, the presence or absence of long-term effects, and the developmental maturity of the clients affect the conduct and outcome of treatment.

As the various treatment themes and techniques in this literature are explored, representative references for the many contributors are provided. However, no effort has been made to connect each author with each of the many recurrent ideas that are presented in this literature.

THE RATIONALE FOR GROUP TREATMENT

As children grow from toddlers through latency-age into adolescence, peer relationships become increasingly pre-eminent. Therefore, group treatment with its peer focus has long been recognized as a developmentally appropriate form of intervention for children with a variety of behavioral and emotional difficulties (Johnson, Rasbury, & Siegel, 1986). However, group treatment has a particular relevance and salience for child victims of sexual abuse. First, as Herman (1981) and Courtois (1988) have elaborated, certain elements of a traditional, individual, psychotherapeutic relationship are isomorphic to elements of an abusive relationship. Both an individual treatment relationship and an abusive relationship involve an emotionally intense dyad in which the client—in this case a child—is in a one-down position with a significant authority figure. The therapeutic relationship, like a child's relationship with a parent, is also constructed on a requirement of trust, though the child has learned through the molestation experiences that parental and adult trust can be violated. The child often harbors the fear that he or she will be hurt and exploited again, even though he or she may be not fully aware of these feelings. Additionally, if the child has experienced the initial investigation of his or her case as pressured or manipulative, he or she may be very cognizant of these feelings. The consequent fear creates a dilemma, since even the most supportive, well-intentioned behavior on the part of the therapist may be interpreted by the child as a precursor for the sexualization of the relationship or as a preface for betrayal or abandonment. Furthermore, since the therapeutic relationship is defined as "private" and "confidential," it is also shrouded in secrecy, just as the abusive relationship may have been. Though many children may have difficulty understanding confidentiality in the abstract sense, they still have to contend with the feelings that are evoked as the door to the therapy room is closed (Knittle & Tuanna, 1980). The recognition of the influence of these "abuse dynamics" on the therapy process challenges the early maxim that traumatized children need the undivided adult attention afforded them by individual treatment (Jorne, 1979; Steward, Farguhar, Dicharry, & Glick, 1986).

The use of a group format counters these potentially noxious elements of the individual treatment relationship in a number of ways: by providing a place in which dependency needs can be met without the threatening level of intimacy or intensity associated with individual treatment (Hazzard et al., 1986); by opening up the therapeutic relationship to the scrutiny of multiple persons; by emphasizing egalitarian rather than authoritarian relationships; by allowing trust to be cultivated rather than to be required or assumed; by providing a safe forum for the appropriate expression and sharing of physical affection; and by enhancing the child's own sense of efficacy by explicitly sharing the responsibility for treatment with her.

The disclosure of sexual abuse often creates social upheaval and turmoil for the child, who may be confronted with parental and sibling rejection and changes in residence, schools, and peer relationships (Lubell & Soong, 1982). During these tumultuous times, the group may be one of the more stable and supportive aspects of the child's social existence. Several writers have even suggested that the group becomes something of a surrogate family for the child with male and female cotherapists functioning as parental surrogates (Steward et al., 1986). In addressing this issue, Gottlieb and Dean (1981) have also emphasized that child victims of sexual abuse, especially incest, may have confused ideas about relationships involving adults in general and between women and men in particular. The treatment group affords the opportunity for cotherapists to work together in a way that individual therapy usually does not, with the cotherapists actively modeling mutual support, respect, and cooperation that the children's parents may not have.

In addition to the objective isolation and abandonment the child may experience through the crisis of disclosure, it is the nature of this problem that the child may experience a subjective sense of isolation and estrangement during the course of the molestation incidents (Blick & Porter, 1982). The child may feel abandoned and unprotected by significant adults and may view herself as different from and therefore estranged from peers. The group allows the child a forum for "universalizing" her experiences and establishing significant peer connections that were previously unavailable (Knittle & Tuanna, 1980; Pescosolido & Petrella, 1986).

Giaretto (1976, 1982), Sgroi (1982), and others have advocated a multimodel approach to the treatment of child sexual abuse victims and their families that includes the use of family therapy, mother–daughter dyad meetings, marital therapy, and a self-help component, in addition to individual and group treatment. However, the use of family therapy and mother–daughter dyad meetings has an unbridled potential for further victimizing the child if they are employed too early in the treatment process. For example, it might be premature to use these interventions before the offender is willing to admit responsibility for his conduct through the provision of a therapeutic apology. As will be elaborated, the group format with its emphasis on active interventions such as role playing furnishes the child with an indispensable opportunity and safe place to anticipate, prepare for, and practice her involvement in these relationally focused forms of treatment.

It has also been noted that the group format aids the therapist in relation to what are usually referred to an countertransference issues (Steward et al., 1986). As Holleman (1983, p. 159) has noted in describing therapy with the victims of child maltreatment in general, "the seriousness of the child's plight and the therapist's desire to make restitution and relive pain" inevitably lead to "rescue fantasies" or other distortions in the relationship. The structure afforded by the group process and the presence of a cofacilitator helps the therapist modulate her or his own feelings, enhancing the ability to be emotionally available to the child without being unrealistic or emotionally crowding.

Finally, the astronomical increase in the number of children referred for treatment during the last decade has far out distanced the available treatment resources in many communities. In addition to the sound, dynamic reasons for using this method of intervention, the group format also maximizes the number of children that can be provided services with a finite number of resources (Haugaard & Reppucci, 1988).

MODELS OF GROUP TREATMENT

Even the most cursory review of the group psychotherapy literature reveals tremendous variation in the ways in which treatment is conceptualized and undertaken with identical presenting problems. As might be anticipated, there are also differences in the basic organization and treatment processes of the group approaches examined here. At the same time, these approaches are far more striking in their similarities than in their differences. Virtually none contains elements that are truly unique and differences tend to be more in emphasis and sophistication than in substance.

A principal source of the continuity in these approaches relates to the fact that most appear to have been developed pragmatically with few pre-existing philosophical or theoretical allegiences. The conceptual foundations of these eclectic approaches are seemingly based in the clinical findings of the child sexual abuse field, rather than in more general theories of human behavior, such as a behaviorism, psychodynamic theory, or family systems theory. Even the philosophical antagonisms between the feminist and family approaches that dominate other areas of the sexual abuse literature are rarely evident in these group approaches.

Based on their relative emphases and the ages of the clients for which they are designed, five principal models of group treatment for children can be discerned.

Traditional Group Model

A number of authors have described their efforts to adapt traditional group approaches to work with sexually abused children (for example, Berliner & MacQuivey, 1983; Blick & Porter, 1982; Delson & Clark, 1981; Furniss et al., 1988; Gagliano, 1987; Hazzard et al., 1986; James,

1977; Knittle & Tuanna, 1980; Lubell & Soong, 1982). In these approaches, the facilitators provide a basic framework for the experience, but the participants move the group in the direction that they choose at the pace they choose. These approaches may be so nondirective, in fact, that the adult professional may serve more as a convenor than a facilitator (see e.g., James, 1977). Though special consideration is given to the virulent influences that the abuse may have had on the child's sense of self and her interactions with others in the group, these themes tend to be addressed as they emerge from the group process rather than being introduced presumptively.

Developmental-Play Group Model

This model of treatment is very similar to the traditional model, though it is used primarily with younger children. This approach emphasizes play, fantasy, and games as the principal methods of intervention with verbal exchange, explanation of abuse dynamics, and interpretations of the participant's behavior being less dominant (Mitchum, 1987; Pescosolido & Petrella, 1986; Steward et al., 1986). This model of therapy tends to be more growth than problem-oriented, with the primary goal of treatment being to return the child to his or her normal developmental course. Less explicit emphasis is placed on the issue of the molestation per se, with broader disruptions in parent–child interactions organizing assessment and intervention.

Structured Group Treatment

The structured group approaches are distinguished by their higher levels of organization and directivity relative to the more traditional approaches. This model also places more responsibility on the adults to lead rather than simply facilitate the process. Sturkie (1983), for example, has described a brief treatment model with eight sessions, each of which is organized around a predetermined treatment theme and related exercises. Berliner and Ernst (1984) present a similar approach, based on six sessions. The structured model allows a broad array of treatment themes to be pursued in a relatively short span of time. This is an important consideration in a field in which children and their families often leave treatment in advance of the time professionals might recommend. At the same time, Haugaard and Reppucci (1988) have expressed concern that the use of the structured format has the potential for suggesting to the child symptoms and feelings that he or she does not have. For example, a thematic emphasis on responsibility or anger may be very confusing to children who have not experienced these feelings. This may result in the children trusting their own perceptions even less, thereby creating a negative, iatrogenic, treatment outcome.

Group-arts Therapy

The use of the arts as a means for sorting through and expressing complex, ineffable feelings is, along with role playing, the most common set of techniques used in all of the group approaches. However, the group-arts model as described by Carozza and Heirsteiner (1982) is distinguished by its organization around forms of media rather than around thematic content (also see Mayer, 1983). These media include drawing, painting with water colors, finger-painting with flavored, edible, pudding, sculpturing with clay, and creating box collages out of magazines and wallpaper. Critical treatment issues are then identified, reflected, and interpreted, based on this graphic expression. Though the use of any particular medium requires obvious preparation, the actual use of these media is largely unrestricted. Since this model emphasizes the indirect and symbolic expression of ideas and feelings (including unconscious material and therapeutic regression), it might be regarded as one of the more psychodynamically oriented models of group treatment.

Parallel Group Treatment

This model of treatment, developed by Damon and Waterman (1986), represents a synthesis of the clinical and empirical knowledge that is embodied in the group treatment literature as a whole (also see Nelki & Watters, 1989; Mandell & Damon, 1989). The terminology "parallel" refers to the simultaneous use of children's and caretaker's groups, each of which addresses the same treatment themes through 13 highly developed, curricular modules. Though there are few elements in this model that are novel, its level of clinical sophistication, organization, and scope is noteworthy. The field's overall transition from unstructured, to structured, to structured-interlocking group approaches is also exemplified in this treatment model.

GROUP FORMATION AND RELATED LOGISTICAL CONSIDERATIONS

Despite its many putative advantages relative to other forms of intervention, group treatment is also suggested to have several disadvantages. First, as has been noted, concern has been expressed that it may influence the participants to have feelings and symptoms they have not experienced. Second, in a field dominated by multimodel approaches, there has been concern that a major emotional investment in a therapy group may result in diminished involvement in other modalities. Blick and Porter (1982), for example, found that an intense group commitment sometimes led to a division of loyalties between the group and the child's individual therapist. Such complicated cross-commitments may prove unmanageable for some children who are already experiencing competing demands for loyalty within their own families. Third, precourt group involvement has the potential for creating special problems for children waiting to participate in judicial proceedings. Young children may inadvertently incorporate some elements of other children's narratives into their own or be subject to accusations of coaching and prompting. Fourth, concern has been expressed that the differing and competing languages, rules, and emotional affiliations of the treatment group might actually confound efforts to help families reconstitute (Haugaard & Reppucci, 1988). Finally, Nelki and Watters (1989) have expressed concern that prolonged treatment in a "victims' group" may perpetuate the child's identification and role as a victim.

Another, more practical disadvantage of group treatment is that it is often more difficult to implement, manage, and purposefully complete. As a result, this literature devotes substantial attention to the issues associated with pregroup formation. The most critical issues include: (1) creating a basic group structure; (2) recruiting, screening, and admitting potential participants; (3) selecting, training, and supporting adult facilitators; and (4) involving parents in the treatment process.

Creation of a Basic Group Structure

The development of a group requires that a number of therapeutic decisions be made and related logistical tasks be accomplished. These include establishing the frequency, length, and content of the sessions, determining the number of sessions the group will continue, deciding how many children will participate, locating a suitable group meeting place with treatment materials, establishing adequate, consistent blocks of meeting time, organizing and providing transportation, and others.

As with most children's groups, meetings are usually held weekly, ranging in length from 1 to 2 hours. A review of these groups reveals that an hour is the modal meeting length for preschool-children while 90 minutes is the modal length for older participants. Group size varies considerably from as few as three to more than a dozen members. Some groups with an open admission policy report having allowed group membership to quadruple over time, a decision seemingly shaped more by need than a specific therapeutic rationale (Blick & Porter, 1982). However, the clinical consensus in this literature is that optimal group size for younger children is about six members while the optimal size for older children is about eight members.

The greatest structural variability involves the number of sessions that are regarded as constituting a full-group experience. This number ranges from 6 to 30 sessions, though there are references to groups lasting as long as 4 years (Wayne & Weeks, 1984). The most common pattern involves scheduling a group for a specified number of sessions (6 to 12), taking several weeks off, and then beginning again. Subsequent series of meetings may contain both old and new members. Several advantages for using a brief therapy model with a prespecified ending date have been cited—most notably that it provides the child with a sense of closure and completion that may not be present in other areas of her life.

Selecting and Screening Members

A central task in the development of any treatment group involves defining the criteria for membership. Few specific criteria are offered in the children's group treatment literature, presumably because of a desire to make treatment as inclusive as possible. Similarly, only Mandell and Damon (1989) discuss the use of formal pregroup interviews or other screening procedures for selecting potential group members. Since group treatment is most often used in the context of multiple forms of intervention, however, there is the implicit assumption that the child's emotional and behavioral functioning have already been scrutinized through the investigatory process or during individual treatment.

The criteria for group membership that are presented are rather straightforward and unsophisticated. First, all participants should have either experienced some form of sexual molestation or be at risk for it (Damon & Watterman, 1986). Though children who have experienced other forms of developmental trauma such as physical abuse, divorce, or parental death may manifest symptoms similar to those of child sexual abuse victims, it is not recommended that these children be placed in the same group. Though most children dealing with severe developmental disruptions experience some guilt, betrayal, and loss, these feelings are so pronounced for child sexual abuse victims that separate treatment groups are warranted. A principal exception is a group described by Wayne and Weeks (1984) that contained physically abused and neglected as well as sexually abused adolescents.

As common sense would also dictate, some severely, emotionally disturbed and behaviorally disruptive children may not be able to benefit from the group experience and may actually undermine it for others (Boatman et al., 1981; Hazzard et al., 1986). These children are not placed in a group until they have stabilized through other methods of intervention. Berliner and Ernst (1984) and Mandell and Damon (1989) also caution against groups containing both males and females. Because male victims have been underidentified historically and since the dynamics of this kind of abuse may vary from female victimization, the treatment needs of males are often very different (Vander Mey, 1988). Regrettably, with the exception of the more recent work of Mandell and Damon (1989), the principal form of group treatment for male child sexual abuse victims to date has been those developed for juvenile sexual offenders (see, for example, Smets & Cebula, 1987). As this literature develops more fully, group treatment for boys may constitute still another model of victim treatment.

Little attention has been given to the influence of class, race, and related variables on group composition, though Hazzard et al. (1986) have concluded these issues become more critical as group size decreases. They suggest any striking difference has the potential for isolating a member, a problem to which the facilitators must remain attentive.

A major area of consensus in terms of membership is that groups should contain children who are functioning at comparable emotional and intellectual levels. Age differences up to 7 years have been found to be workable if the participants are focusing on the same developmental issues and dilemmas (Blick & Porter, 1982). For example, though the issues of sexuality and sexual expression are virtually always explored in these groups, the ways in which these issues are broached with younger children, latency-aged children, and adolescents are very different. Young children should not be exposed to developmentally inappropriate, adolescent material associated with dating, for example. Too much developmental disparity may also lead older children to be overly responsible for younger participants, which may exacerbate problems the older child is already experiencing at home.

There is great variability in the forms of molestation children experience, the duration of these experiences, and the nature of the child's relationship to the offender and other significant adults (Summit & Kryso, 1978). Though some authors report problems treating in the same groups children who have experienced extrafamilial abuse and children who have experienced incestuous molestation (Blick & Porter, 1982), others have reported no adverse effects on group functioning because of this kind of heterogeneity (Pescosolida & Petrella, 1986). The differences in the experiences within groups are often profound enough to obscure differences between groups (Sturkie, 1983).

Clinical experience also suggests one should be cautious about including in the same group siblings with severely conflictual relationships. These siblings have a high potential for regularly introducing into the group idiosyncratic issues to which the other participants may have trouble relating. Children who reside together in residential facilities may also attempt to bring into the group unresolved conflicts from their living situations that subvert the group process as a whole. The group setting may provide a useful forum for addressing and dealing with some conflicts. However, if these conflicts are so chronic as to create severe rifts or factions within the group, it may be beneficial for these children to be placed in separate groups.

One should also consider the appropriateness of including in a treatment group children who are awaiting initial participation in a legal proceeding. The credibility of child victims is virtually always subject to judicial challenge. Exposure to other children and their accounts of abuse has the potential for further undermining the credibility of the individual child by increasing allegations that he or she has been coached. At the same time, the many benefits attributed to group participation for the purposes of preparing for and practicing court involvement are almost universally described in this literature.

A related membership issue involves the process by which members join and terminate from the group. Children need therapeutic support immediately following the disclosure of abuse. At the same time, the introduction "midgroup" of new members may create "backtracking" (Hazzard et al., 1986). Backtracking may provide the opportunity for a helpful reiteration of treatment themes, but it can also disrupt the normal flow and development of the group process. These tradeoffs have been handled in several ways. For example, Blick and Porter (1982) describe an open-ended format in which adolescent members were added as the disclosure of abuse made it appropriate. Gagliano (1987), in contrast, recommends the use of a closed format with members being added at the end of a fixed number of sessions. This latter approach is the most common one reported.

Selecting and Supporting Adult Facilitators

The literature gives even less attention to the issues involved in selecting potential facilitators than it does to selecting child participants. It is generally advised, however, that potential facilitators be well grounded in the basics of victim treatment *prior* to the group experience. It is also generally recommended that these groups employ at least two adult facilitators. The complexity, intensity, and occasional unpredictability of the group experience are such that the mutual support and multiple vantage points afforded by the presence of cofacilitators have been regarded as indispensable. Mayer (1983) has also suggested that the presence of two facilitators allows for team interventions in which one person may act in a more supportive role while the other may be more confrontive. However, she does not clarify the circumstances in which this form of intervention might be useful. Damon and Waterman (1986) also note that in complex role playing or vignette presentations, it may be helpful to have two facilitators available so one can set up the scenario while the other helps process it.

Having cofacilitators also makes it possible for the group to meet even if one facilitator must be absent. In ongoing or open-ended groups, the use of cofacilitators also enhances consistency if one facilitator has to be permanently replaced. This is a critical consideration with children like sexual abuse victims who have experienced extensive social upheaval and loss and for whom continuity in relationships is essential.

The major controversy in this area relates to the sex of the facilitators—more specifically, whether or not it is appropriate to use male facilitators. As was noted earlier, Gottlieb and Dean (1981), Lubell and Soong (1982), and Pescosolido and Petrella (1986), among others, have suggested that the use of a male cofacilitator can provide a corrective emotional experience for children whose experiences with males have been characterized by betrayal and whose conceptions of heterosexual relationships are skewed. In contrast, Boatman et al. (1981), Blick and Porter (1982), Mayer (1983), and Berliner and Ernst (1984), among others, have argued that the inclusion of a male facilitator, especially in the early stages of treatment, has an inhibiting effect on the group process and elicits sexually stylized and seductive behavior from the participants. Boatman et al. (1981) and Gottlieb and Dean (1981) have also noted that adolescents are often preoccupied with the nature of the relationship between the facilitators—generally, whether they are sexually involved with one another and specifically if the female facilitator is being sexually exploited by the male. Furniss et al. (1988) also noted that the participants in their groups attempted to split the adults regardless of whether they choose to align with the male or female facilitator. In general, those persons opposed to the regular use of male and female cofacilitators recommend the introduction of the male later in the treatment process and for clearly defined therapeutic reasons.

This controversy has seemingly evolved from the pragmatics of group work, but also reflects broader concerns about the rightful treatment role of males in a field created primarily by male abusiveness. Interestingly, in a study of the curative factors in group therapy for former incest victims, Bonney, Randall, and Cleveland (1986) found that having male and female facilitators was defined by group members as being helpful, even though they had not asked about this aspect of treatment. In the children's literature, this remains one of the important empirical questions for which there are not even preliminary answers as yet.

Regardless of the sex of the facilitators, when a team is used, each must be experienced and comfortable in working with the other. Facilitator disorganization or conflict may parallel the home experiences for some participants (Hazzard et al., 1986). Additionally, Steward et al. (1986) describe the importance of providing ongoing support for the facilitators through a supervisory group. The group is used for planning sessions, sharing literature, working through countertransference issues that emerge through the groups, and for training other agency staff. Wayne and Weeks (1984) have also emphasized that the group experience can create intense feelings of incompetence and frustration in the facilitators. They recommend the use of a consultant to facilitate the exploration and resolution of these feelings in a group context. Zimpfer (1987) has described a similar professional consultation-support group for persons working in the field.

Eliciting Parental Support and Involvement

As Mrazek (1981) has noted, it is difficult to help child sexual abuse victims unless their life circumstances change. Without parental involvement in and commitment to treatment, gains will be minimal.

Several authors have elaborated the reasons why some parents may not be supportive of treatment in general and of group treatment in particular. First, parents in incestuous families may fear that the group will elicit information that is incriminating to one or both of the parents (Blick & Porter, 1982; Haugaard & Reppucci, 1988). Parents may also be reluctant to have their children exposed to the stories of other children who have been molested. It is also common for children in treatment to express the wish that the issue of their abuse not be belabored. This pressure to move on may eminate from the child's own wish for things to be "normal" in her life or from parents who have not resolved their own feelings about the incidents. The latter is particularly a problem for parents with unresolved molestation experiences of their own. Some parents may also be threatened by the support implicit in the childrens' group. They may believe that it provides the child a level of attention and nurturance they can not, or for which they have longed themselves but never received.

Parents may also be threatened by the content of the groups. For example, material dealing with sexuality may be perceived as too provocative. Parents who have experienced management problems with their children may also believe that exercises intended to empower the child and to increase body integrity undermine their disciplinary perogatives. Furthermore, parents may be unsure how to deal with the strong affective responses that some of the exercises may provoke. For example, exercises intended to help the child express anger openly may appear counterproductive to some parents.

Once these potential parental concerns are recognized, a number of methods for addressing them are available. Berliner and Ernst (1984) suggest that the facilitators convene a meeting of the participants' parents in advance of the initial group meeting to anticipate and deal with these issues. Blick and Porter (1982) recommend that parents be forewarned of specific sessions that have potentially provocative content. Giaretto (1976), Mrazek (1981), Sturkie (1983), Damon and Waterman (1986), Mandell and Damon (1989), and Nelki and Watters (1989) have described the use of concurrent or parallel caretakers' groups. Hazzard et al. (1986) recommend the inclusion of the parents in some form of therapy, even if it is not group therapy. Finally, Steward et al. (1986) have advocated quarterly home visits and Pescosolido and Petrella (1986) have noted that the mothers of some very young children can actually be invited to participate in the children's treatment group.

CURATIVE ELEMENTS OF GROUP TREATMENT

It has been well documented that children who are sexually abused suffer a number of grave emotional, behavioral, and interpersonal consequences (Finkelhor & Browne, 1985; Haugaard & Reppucci, 1988; Meiselman, 1978). The molestation experience can pervade and color every aspect of the child's intrapersonal and social existence. At the same time, the particular constellation of symptoms manifested by any given child and the relative prominence of these symptoms can vary widely, depending on the nature and duration of the abuse, the child's age, sex, and premorbid history, the familial reaction to disclosure, and a number of other variables.

The group approaches examined here have a number of process and outcome goals, many of which are pursued simultaneously and subsequently in other forms of treatment. These include:

1. Clarifying and validating the ambiguous and conflicting feelings and sensations associated with the molestation experiences and the aftermath of disclosure;
2. Facilitating the verbal, physical, and graphic expression of previously ineffable thoughts and feelings;
3. Universalizing and detoxifying the experiences through appropriate sharing;
4. Offering explanations for the abuse that help the child organize his or her thoughts about the experience and which help transcend his or her own solipsistic view;
5. Teaching age-appropriate methods for eliciting, expressing, and receiving physical affection and nurturance;
6. Enhancing the child's sense of physical control, body integrity, and individual efficacy; and
7. Establishing and practicing a protection plan to minimize the potential for future molestation.

There are a variety of ways of distinguishing the treatment methods and techniques used to pursue these goals: whether they are active or reflective, whether they are facilitator-originated or group-driven, whether they involve verbal expression or another medium, whether they focus on a real-life concern or symbolic representations, and so on. For the purposes of this review, these techniques are distinguished according to the mechanisms by which they are hypothesized to work. Though this list is not exhaustive, five primary curative elements are identified according to theory of change upon which they are based. As should become clear, the pragmatic, eclectic quality evident elsewhere in this literature also dominates the technical domain. "Healing" for these children is suggested to occur in a variety of different ways and no unified theory has been developed.

Curative Elements Intrinsic in the Group Process

It is axiomatic in this literature that any meaningful involvement in group treatment has a significant potential for diminishing feelings of isolation and estrangement and for enhancing the child's sense of interpersonal competence. These benefits accrue as a function of the child's immersion into the group process, by entrance into what Bergart

(1986) has referred to as a "hall of mirrors," in which a client's seemingly idosyncratic experiences are expressed, reflected, and validated by others.

The healing process within the group begins with the development of cohesion and foundational trust through the processes of gathering and ice breaking (Carozza & Hiersteiner, 1982 Blick & Porter, 1982). Though the specific exercises may vary with the developmental levels of the participants, common ice-breaking techniques include the use of name circles, passing a "good touch" (a hug or handshake) around the circle, having the child describe or make a picture of an animal that he or she believes he or she is most like, or having the participants break into dyads, interview one another, and then report back to the group something they have learned about their partner (Gagliano, 1987; Hazzard et al., 1986; Mitchum, 1987). Though most groups establish a rule that no one must talk, share, or otherwise participate unless she wants to, these kinds of techniques create participation and encourage the members to take manageable risks.

Through the use of these exercises, the implicit rule is also established that initial sharing will occur in sheltered ways that protect against coerced participation or destructive overexposure. New members often have the expectations that they will only deal with the "grisly details" of their abuse, even when pregroup information to the contrary is provided. These gathering techniques help to emphasize early that a principal consideration is that the groups be fun. Making the groups fun increases the probability that the members will want to continue. It also enhances efforts to increase spontaniety and self-expression, thereby helping the child return to his or her normal developmental course (Pescosolido & Petrella, 1986). The sharing and validation of feelings with more provocative and threatening content necessarily come much later.

Even simplistic tasks such as doing a name circle will inevitably overwhelm some members who may respond with withdrawal, regression, or even disruptive behavior. These occasions provide the opportunity for the child to be given explicit permission to request and use the help of others. Many children in incestuous families have never cultivated this skill that is essential for the purpose of establishing a meaningful protection plan. In short, even difficulties in the ice-breaking process can offer special moments for experimential learning that are simply not available in some other forms of treatment.

Many sexually abused children have been underparented in general and the structure of the group provides an important socialization experience (Sturkie, 1983; Wayne & Weeks, 1984). The problem of sexual abuse is, in part, a failure of an adult to understand or respect appropriate limits, a problem that may be manifest in many other aspects of the adult's life (Summit & Kryso, 1978). This confusion about acceptable limits is also conveyed to the child through the abusive act, a problem the use of explicit limit-setting attempts to counter.

Because of their curative, socialization value, most treatment groups employ explicit ground rules that safeguard both the participants and the group process. The primary rule usually involves the issue of confidentiality—the explicit provision that "what is said within the groups stays within the group." This rule is essential since some children may attempt to master the anxiety of their abuse by inappropriately divulging the details. Other important issues addressed by group rules typically concern: (1) Basic conduct and personal safety (e.g., no running, yelling, or hitting other participants; no mistreatment of toys, facilities, or facilitators; Berliner & Ernst, 1984; Wayne & Weeks, 1984); group participants must wear age-appropriate, nonprovocative attire; (Mandell & Damon 1989); (2) In-group conduct (e.g., no one has to share if he or she doesn't want to; only one person may talk at a time; Sturkie, 1983); (3) Group commitment (e.g., members must agree to attend consistently; participants must be punctual and the group must end on time; Blick & Porter, 1982); and (4) Out-of-group conduct (e.g., members are not to socialize outside of the group until after the group terminates; Gagliano, 1987). Out-of-group contacts are regulated for at least two reasons: so that an adult can be present to monitor the emotional reactions to the member's early exchanges and because the development of factions, coalitions, and cliques has the potential for undermining the group process as a whole.

None of these rules would be invoked without a need, but their use creates something of a dilemma. If the group is too fluid and chaotic, this may duplicate the child's experience within his or her family and be unnecessarily anxiety provoking. At the same time, child sexual abuse victims may be overly compliant and too many rules may exacerbate this quality. For example, these children may raise their hands before contributing to a group discussion even when this has been defined as unnecessary (Sgroi, 1982). As common sense dictates, the problems associated with the development and enforcement of rules are minimized when the group members are encouraged to help create, reiterate, and safeguard their rules themselves. Participating in the rule-making process is also hypothesized to contribute to the child's sense of efficacy and control (Sturkie, 1983).

Another important dimension of the group process is the opportunity it affords for the adult facilitators to provide unconditional attention and concern. Refreshments are almost universally provided as a concrete sign of nurturance intended to address feelings of deprivation

(Pescosolido & Petrella, 1986). The sharing of refreshments by group members also teaches an important social skill (Hazzard et al., 1986) to a population of children who may manifest an impairment in empathy (Steward et al., 1986). Refreshments are also used to influence subtly the group process. When served at the beginning or end of a session, for example, they can facilitate a transition or a slowing of the group process, or mark the beginning of reflection on the days accomplishments.

Validating the Child's Reality

Children who have been sexually abused are required, ipso facto, to subjugate their needs and feelings to those of the abusive adult. Since no child can ever be prepared for the occurence of sexual abuse, he or she may also accept the adult's construction of the event, even when the subjective experience is totally different from that construction (Summit, 1983). The child may also have to deny and counterfeit one's own feelings and sensations in order to keep the molestation a secret. This pressure may emanate from fear of retribution or withdrawal of love by the offender, fear of separation from her family, or fear of stigmatization by others. A second curative element in group treatment, then, is the elicitation, clarification, and validation of critical feelings and sensations as one method of helping the child re-establish confidence in his or her own perceptions. This process includes identifying and openly expressing feelings such as anger, grief, humiliation, powerlessness, and betrayal. These feelings are also elicited and expressed indirectly through various media. For example, Carozza and Heirsteiner (1981) have used psychodrama techniques to elicit and explore these feelings. Damon and Waterman (1986) have described a similar process using written vignettes to which the group members react. Mayer (1983) has also described the use of the "unsent letter." In this technique, the child writes a letter to the person who abused him or her detailing his or her feelings. This letter is then presented to the group and then kept by the facilitator. (The letter isn't actually mailed since it is a tool for focusing feelings rather than a means of confrontation.) Feelings are also evoked through the use of films and books which describe the feelings of adult incest survivors (Berliner & Ernst, 1984; Carozza & Heirsteiner, 1982; Hazzard et al., 1986).

More indirect methods for eliciting and addressing the feelings associated with the molestation experiences are also employed. Steward et al. (1986), for example, emphasize the use of unstructured play as a means of allowing children to express whatever thoughts and feelings are preoccupying them. They found that the themes of trust, nurturance, and aggression were expressed far more often than issues relating directly to the molestation experiences themselves.

Feelings are also elicited indirectly through the use of artwork. Exercises include drawing any important feeling (Hazzard et al., 1986), drawing a self-portrait (Berliner & Ernst, 1984), drawing one's family, and drawing the abuser (Mayer, 1983). Group murals have also been used enhance group cohesion while feelings and sentiments are being expressed.

As has been noted, a number of writers have described the problems associated with presenting and emphasizing feelings that some members may not have. Haugaard and Reppucci (1988), among others, have noted that a critical aspect of the validation process is emphasizing the variability and acceptability of different responses. Though feelings of anger are very common (Lubell & Soong, 1982), for example, as Herman (1981) has emphasized, it is critical that anger not be presented as the only "innocent" response. Herman's caveat regarding anger can be extended to virtually any feeling that may surface within the group.

Providing an Alternative View of Reality

Though a central goal of treatment is to validate the child's experience and to make it as comprehensible as possible, a number of techniques are also used to expand the child's understanding of oneself and his or her situation. In many ways, these methods attempt to challenge the child's narrow view of reality, but in a nonthreatening manner. For example, Gagliano (1987), in her work with female adolescents, includes discussions of male physiology, the symbolic significance of the penis, and the typical modes of male sexual expression. Gagliano (1987) and Hazzard et al. (1986) also focus on the kinds of offender motivations that create sexualized adult–child relationships and the kinds of family dynamics that perpetuate them. These didactic approaches shift the focus away from the child victim to those elements of the problem that exist far beyond him or her.

Lamb (1986), MacFarlane and Waterman (1986), and others have discussed the problems associated with attempting to talk children out of their feelings of responsibility and guilt. Efforts to diminish feelings of responsibility may also diminish feelings of efficacy. Feelings of extreme powerlessness may have graver, long-term implications for some children than feelings of responsibility. Children who feel responsible but are told they should not may also feel unheard and further invalidated. The feelings of responsibility for some children are also exacerbated by the fact that they have victimized younger children themselves. The discussion of adult motivations and family patterns widens the child's field of understanding, thereby indirectly challenging the feelings that "I have caused this to happen to me." Of course, there is no magical expectation that a child can easily develop "a sociological imagination" and comprehend all the broad social forces (such as patriarchy, poverty, and an increasing number of blended families) that may have contributed to her victimization. These techniques begin to lay the foundation for that task, however.

Feelings of guilt and responsibility can also be exaggerated if the child experienced aspects of the abuse as physically pleasurable. Sturkie (1983) describes the use of a technique developed by Rosensweig-Smith to counter these feelings. The child is informed that sexual arousal is a physical response that one's body makes and that occurs automatically. Sexual arousal is then made analogous to tickling. If tickled, children usually laugh or twitch even if they don't wish to, a finding that can be readily demonstrated by asking the members to tickle one another. In the same way, even after one learns that the sexual touching of a child by an adult is not acceptable, the child may find the touching physically pleasureable. Since this is an automatic response from the body, it is not something to feel bad or embarrassed about.

Another approach to expanding the child's reality is to have the participants bring in pictures of themselves as babies or smaller children (Berliner & Ernst, 1984). Literally seeing oneself as smaller can be used as a means for helping the child to understand the inability to subdue an assailant physically. The child's having "allowed" the abuse to occur is often one source of feelings of responsibility and guilt. As Carozza and Heirsteiner (1982) have noted, this problem may also be worsened by the fact that children often think of themselves as having had the same developmental capabilities when they were being molested as they have in the present. Having the participants bring in photographs of themselves as babies and smaller children helps to underline their own developmental differences, why abuse may have been unavoidable in the past, but why reabuse is avoidable now.

Still another method of influencing the child's perceptions is through the use of concretized metaphors. These methods, borrowed in part from the family therapy literature, involve the presentation of the subtleties of relationships in observeable forms. For example, if a group member continuously makes it clear that he or she must protect and emotionally carry an adult in the family, he or she may be asked to pick up and physically carry an adult facilitator across the group room. The members then discuss what this means and how it relates to their families (Sturkie, 1986). The participants can also role-play family interactions expressing emotional distance physically, an inability to discuss key issues as mutism, and the inability to be heard as deafness. These scenarios lay a foundation for working through feelings, preparing for therapeutic encounters with other family members, and for establishing and practicing a workable protection plan.

Symbolic Mastery

As has been noted, the experience of being molested can result in feelings of powerlessness and lack of control that can linger for years, creating a destructive, self-fulfilling prophesy. The process of discarding one's status as a victim and becoming a survivor is closely related to the mastery of these feelings. Adults may surmount these feelings through confronting their abuser, ending emotional cutoffs from their families of origins, speaking publicly about this problem, and through helping other victims (Deighton & McPeek, 1985; Herman, 1981). For children, however, these feelings, persons, and situations are often mastered symbolically. For example, Steward et al. 1986, describe role playing role reversals, in which the group members have the facilitators take on the role of abusive or unprotective parents who are then rehabilitated, punished, or dismissed. Similarly, Mayer (1983) has noted that the offender can be fashioned out of modeling clay and then be handled as the child sees fit. Knittle and Tuanna (1980) describe re-enacting the abuse sequence but having the child stop the abuse before it occurs. Delson and Clark (1981) and others have also described yelling "no" and physically pushing away someone who has invaded the child's physical space and other methods in which the child is symbolically empowered.

Mayer (1983) has described the use of the "Worst Concept Drawing." In this technique, the group participants are asked to imagine the worst thing that has or could happen to them, or to remember their worst dream. They then draw a picture of the event, describe it in writing, and present it to the group. This procedure seems to be grounded in the same premises as flooding and implosion techniques, in which anxiety is mastered through exaggeration. Clinical experience reveals that feelings of mastery and competency can almost be contagious as the participants examine and share their strengths.

Mass Practice

It is sometimes easier to help children behave into a new way of thinking than to help them think into a new way of behaving. Patterson (1971), for example, has described extensively the importance of creating prosocial, adaptive behaviors in small children who haven't as yet developed an understanding of their importance. In the same way, programs in which children are drilled in the skills of "yelling, running, and telling" are built upon the assumption that self-protective behaviors and related skills may be learned and habituated, even before the child fully comprehends their significance. Though a wide variety of themes and techniques are presented in these groups, reiterating and reworking them is regarded as invaluable as the treatment process and the child's emotional functioning progress.

THE EFFECTIVENESS OF GROUP TREATMENT

Group treatment has regularly been touted as one of the most effective forms of intervention for child and adolescent sexual abuse victims (see, e.g., Berliner & Ernst, 1984; Steward et al., 1986; Gagliano, 1987). Despite the extensive testimonial endorsement that it has received, however, relatively little empirical evidence has been offered in support of its use. As has been noted, the majority of the treatment groups described in the literature were developed in response to the clinical needs of the children in their respective geographical areas at a time when such services were not readily available. With only a few notable exceptions (for example, James, 1977; Carozza & Heirsteiner, 1982; Verleur et al., 1986), systematic evaluation of treatment outcome was simply not regarded as a central priority when most of these groups were being organized and implemented.

One major force influencing the relatively limited amount of research into treatment outcome may be the ongoing concerns in the field over false allegations of abuse. Historically, when faced with a sexual abuse allegation, the judicial system has manifested more of a willingness to make a type I error (that is, to reject an allegation that is true) than a type II error (that is, to accept an allegation that is false). Child welfare professionals, in contrast, have been more willing to risk a type II error. Because of this basic philosophical conflict, recent research in the field has seemingly focused more on the problems involved in validating allegations than in testing treatment methodologies. For example, there have been recent empirical efforts to distinguish abuse and nonabuse victims by their drawings (see e.g., Cohen & Phelps, 1985) and by the ways in which they interact with anatomically correct dolls (see e.g., Jampole & Weber, 1987). Though of questionable scientific value, scales have even been developed to distinguish legitimate from fabricated allegations by adults (Gardner, 1987). When the problems associated with the validation of allegations are more fully resolved, treatment outcome research may become a higher priority.

Another problem involving outcome research is the astonishingly ahistorical quality of this literature. For example, neither the work of Damon and Waterman (1986) nor the work of Gagliano (1987), two of the more recent contributions to this literature, contain even a single, explicit reference to one of the dozen other group treatment articles and chapters published between 1977 and 1985. This ahistorical quality, observable throughout this literature, may have a variety of origins. First, the principal treatment needs of most sexually abused children should be rather obvious to anyone who spends as long as 3 months working in this field and who is open to understanding them. Though there are shadings and subtleties, the conspicuousness of these primary needs has made it possible for a number of practitioners working in isolation to make the same "discoveries" at about the same time. The child sexual abuse field is also multidisciplinary and a number of the articles examined here appeared in social work, psychology, education, and other kinds of journals. Many of the authors may have been unaware of the literature outside of their separate disciplines and therefore did not reference it. Third, in a field of practice crowded with "experts," concerns about the politics of ideas may also have led to a conservative approach to acknowledging previous sources. Regardless of the causes of this phenomenon, however, the later literature has done relatively little to extend the earlier literature and more resources have seemingly been expended reinventing the wheel than in systematically evaluating and improving it.

Systematic analysis of the effectiveness of group treatment is also confounded by the fact that whether it is regarded as a primary or an adjunctive form of intervention, group treatment is virtually always used in conjunction with individual therapy, family therapy, mother–daughter dyad meetings, or some other form of intervention. It is therefore difficult to discern the contributions, problems, and interactive effect of each modality on outcome (Sturkie, 1983). Several treatment paradigms for using and sequencing different modalities have been described, but these have never been tested comparatively (see, for example, Giaretto, 1982).

The limited outcome data that do exist can be placed in four categories: (1) data derived from the use of standardized instruments, (2) data drawn from systematic ratings or observations of clients by clinicians and caretakers, (3) impressionistic "data" based on unstructured observations of clients by clinicians, and (4) conclusions based on the unstructured observations and reports of the child clients and their caretakers.

Data from Standardized Instruments

Only two of the groups described in this literature used standardized instruments or clinician-developed rating scales to evaluate the usefulness of treatment and reported it. In an early study, James (1977) developed an index that measured the participants' comfort in discussing the issues and problems associated with their abuse. Her subjects, seven institutionalized females, also completed an index of self-esteem. These scores were then compared with two comparison groups comprised of institutionalized and noninstitutionalized girls who had not been sexually abused. The treatment group increased the girl's comfort in discussing the many abused-related issues, a critical finding since this occurred prior to the widespread acknowledgment of this problem. The group experience also increased the level of self-esteem for six of the seven participants. The overall level of self-esteem enhancement was higher in the treatment group than in the two comparison groups.

Verleur et al. (1986) provide the most explicit standardized measures and the rationale for their use. They measured participants' levels of self-esteem, using the Coopersmith Self-Esteem Inventory, and their knowledge of human sexuality (birth control, venereal disease, and the like) with the Anatomy/Physiology Sexual Awareness Scale. Pre- and postmeasures were taken and contrasted to the findings of a matched-comparison group of girls who had been sexually abused but did not participate in the group. However, the members of the comparison group were receiving other forms of treatment through a residential program. The authors reported a significant, posttest increase in the levels of self-esteem for both the treatment and the comparison groups. The treatment group also had a significant increase in awareness and knowledge of sexuality issues, though this change was not also observed in the comparison group.

These commendable efforts do have some limitations, however. The principal methodological issue involves group assignment and the problems associated with availability sampling. Furthermore, since the symptoms of sexual abuse are often enduring, these kinds of studies provide little information about the durability of positive results.

In addition to these two studies, several authors make reference to collecting standardized data but don't report it (see, e.g., Mrazek, 1981; Hazzard et al., 1986; Webb, 1986). Mrazek actually lists almost a dozen different instruments used to evaluate her group participants. She also offers interpretations of each child's individual functioning at an 8-month follow-up. No objective data derived from these instruments are reported. However, Mrazek seemingly believed that presenting these data might be misleading, given the many family problems these children were experiencing. To borrow from Jay Haley, to examine these girls' adjustment by using these data would be like comparing poems by counting the number of words in each.

Systematic Rating

A second category of outcome data involves the rating of variables such as reported recidivism, stated willingness to report recidivism, time in foster care, and the ability to provide necessary information during judicial proceedings (see, e.g., Blick & Porter, 1982; Sturkie, 1983). These measures are more directly related to the issue of abuse, but may not have the reliability levels of the standardized instruments reported earlier.

Carozza and Heirsteiner (1982) also used ratings of pre- and post-group drawings to measure outcome. They report a number of trends reflective of "change and growth" including: "an increase in figure size of persons; addition of a body in post-tests by girls who initially drew a floating head to represent a person . . . less emphasis on clothing to conceal the body," and others (p. 173). These findings were consonant with their clinical observations of their group participants whose day-to-day functioning was regarded as improved.

Nelki and Watters (1989) requested that the primary caregivers for their group participants rate their child using a 33-item problem list. Each behavior was designated as being absent, minor, or major and given a corresponding numerical value. Pre- and postgroup ratings were made and compared and a significant decline in problematical behaviors was observed overall. There was actually an increase in several behaviors, however, including clingingness, increased sexual play, and increased sexual references. These changes were framed positively as a manifestation of the children's increasing expressiveness during the early stages of treatment. These findings and conclusions were based on a total N of only six, however. Small sample sizes of 10 or fewer generally plague this literature.

Unstructured Observation

The most common form of outcome information reported involves impressionistic data based on the facilitator's unstructured observations of the group members' behaviors and interactions. These include increased assertiveness (Damon & Waterman, 1986; Gagliano, 1987); decreased sexualized interactions and play (Damon & Waterman, 1986; compare the results of Nelki & Watters, 1989, earlier); better frustration management (Gagliano, 1987); more openness in discussing the molestation-related issues (Pescosolido & Petrella, 1986); enhanced ability to express anger (Knittle & Tuana, 1980); more appropriate expression of needs for nurturance (Damon & Waterman, 1986); diminished pseudomature behaviors and decreased anxiety (Furness et al., 1988); and experiencing adults as caring (Steward et al., 1986). The group experience was suggested to be effective in all of these areas. However, in addition to the notorious level of unreliability of such "measures," they tend to be based on selective retrospection rather than on longitudinal observation. Their primary value, then, is in generating testable hypotheses.

Furniss et al. (1988) did initiate a follow-up study with nine girls involved in an adolescent therapy group. The study was initiated approximately 3 years after the completion of the group and was carried out by persons *not* affiliated with the group treatment team. These persons interviewed the girls' caretakers and the professionals who were still involved with them and rated eight aspects of their emotional, behavioral, and family functioning. Seven of the nine girls were found to be essentially symptom-free. They were regarded as improved, compared with their pregroup functioning. The two remaining girls manifested several problems including sexualized behavior and dependency.

Client and Parent Self-Report

The fourth category of outcome information is based on the unstructured observations of the child and adolescent clients and their caretakers. These have included a decrease in self-destructive behaviors (Knittle & Tuanna, 1980), feelings of anger and sadness that had lessened in intensity; more optimism about the future (Lubel & Soong, 1982), and a neutralization of feelings of guilt (Gagliano, 1987). Mrazek (1981) has also noted that her group participants reported more concerns (somatic complaints, excessive worrying) than their adult caretakers had observed. Among other things, this finding highlights some of the problems involved in using impressionistic evaluations of a child's functioning.

In summary, it is incumbent upon a practitioner to demonstrate that her or his treatment approach is effective. Though some group treatment models have been tested and modified based on a cumulative body of "clinical wisdom" that has grown out of thousands of hours of client contact, the systematic evaluation of these models is woefully lacking. Empirical measures of process and outcome have been used with and reported on only a minute proportion of the children who have been treated in groups. Given the total monetary resources committed to the child sexual abuse treatment industry in the past decade, the amount expended on this kind of research is startlingly insignificant.

The research to date has also been exceedingly narrow and myopic, typically emphasizing some limited aspect of children's subjective experience, their behavior, or life circumstances. An additional priority in the field is the development of multidimensional evaluative tools that tap each of these elements simultaneously.

A BRIEF COMPARISON OF ADULT AND CHILDREN'S GROUPS

Treatment groups for adult survivors of child sexual assault have proliferated in much the same way that groups for children have. Though these groups are exceedingly similar in their basic goals, structure, and methods, several important differences do emerge when adult groups are compared with children's groups.

Conceptual Allegiances are More Explicit in the Adult Group Literature

While most groups for children have been established within mainline social service agencies, many women's groups have been rooted in feminist self-help or rape crisis organizations. As a result, the ideological foundations of these groups are often more explicit which is reflected in their overall texture (see, for example, Herman, 1981). Interestingly, however, several adult groups are more explicitly grounded in the family therapy field than any of the children's groups are (see, for example, Deighton & McPeek, 1985; Goodman & Nowak-Scibelli, 1985).

Adults Often Manifest More Serious Symptomatology, Which Results in More Rigorous Pregroup Screening Procedures

The processes and criteria for screening potential members are much more extensive and exclusionary for adults. Adults seeking admission often manifest more chronic, serious psychological disturbances than children (for example, borderline personality disorder, dissociative tendencies), even though these conditions may exist in an inchoate form in some children. Patterns of self-destructive behavior including sub-stance misuse, suicidal tendencies, and others may also be much more chronic and ingrained for prospective adult members leading them to be excluded from group participation (Courtois, 1988; Herman & Schat-zow, 1984). Furthermore, while concurrent individual treatment is usually encouraged for children at particular points in the treatment sequence, concurrent individual therapy is almost universally required for adult group participants.

Increased Adult Autonomy Influences the Organization of Treatment

As might be anticipated, many of the differences that exist between these groups are simply a function of the amount of autonomy that adults typically enjoy relative to children. For example, the group screening process for children is essentially unilateral. A facilitator de-cides whether the child will participate or not. With adults, however, the decision is usually bilateral—the prospective member also has the option of joining or declining. Cole and Barney (1987) have noted a high percentage of adults opt out of treatment, a prerogative most children can not exercise. Furthermore, children are usually unsophisticated about the therapy experience and may have few positive expectations about it, though their caseworkers are sometimes viewed as un-realistically powerful (Delson & Clark, 1981). In contrast, some adults have unrealistically high expectations, which must be tempered during screening to forestall disappointment (Cole & Barney, 1987).

Courtouis (1988) has reviewed the rules employed in adult groups. By and large, these rules are synonymous with those of the children's groups. A major exception is that members may make the decision regarding whether or not out-of-group contacts are permissible. If members do choose to allow outside contact, they are prohibited from discussing group members who are not present. Herman (1981) also notes that some adult groups have explicit prohibitions against out-of-group sexual liaisons between members.

The Group Process for Adults is More Explicitly Managed

One of the principal reasons that group treatment has been advocated for children is because it relieves the intense pressure implicit in in-dividual treatment to propel the therapeutic process and to deal with the issues of dependency and disclosure. However, Cole and Barney (1987) have noted that this may actually be viewed as a liability for some adult group members who feel *more* in control in individual therapy.

Several authors have noted that adult survivors often oscillate between periods of denying their pain and being overwhelmed by it. The group process is therefore structured to manage these extremes—to diminish intensity in some areas and to increase it in others—and to promote growth during the stable period in between. These mechanisms are seemingly related to the more chronic symptomotology evident in adults noted earlier. An example of a procedure intended to limit and contain involves touching. Touching is often an integral part of group treatment with children (see, e.g., Delson & Clark, 1981). However, Cole and Barney (1987) note that touching is explicitly prohibited in their groups because the members may find it too threatening or confusing. Intensification can involve techniques that are more demanding and confrontational. For example, while some children's groups encourage a sharing of the molestation experience, most adult groups require it. Even the use of the "photograph technique" described earlier may be more confrontational. After members bring in and exchange photographs of themselves dating from the time of their abuse, they are informed, "if you can blame this child for her incest experience, you can keep blaming yourself for yours" (Woods, in Bergart, 1986).

Adult and Children's Groups Vary in the Ways the Members Deal with the Experience Beyond the Therapy Room

The experience of being in treatment with all its attendant support, validation, and direction can be very empowering. Group participants often want to move the experience beyond the therapy room. As was noted earlier, adults may wish to end family cutoffs, confront family members, or in some other way demonstrate the ongoing process of integrating and mastering their molestation experiences. This is a threatening process, but occurs at the adult's pace. The process is threatening in a different way for children who may be required by demands for family reconstitution or other external pressures to move along. The child's dependence on the adults in his or her life is literal, not symbolic, and the requirement to confront family issues must often take place before integration and mastery have occurred internally.

SUMMARY

The last decade has witnessed the emergence of a number of promising forms of treatment for victims of child sexual abuse. The foundations of these approaches have largely been borrowed from the child and family therapy and rape crisis fields, modifying the treatment process and thematic focus to address the dynamics and peculiarities of this special problem. At first glance, no method of intervention has been more promising for child victims than group treatment and the clinical experience of the dozens of practitioners who have reported their work have lent considerable credibility to this approach. At least five different models of group treatment have emerged.

Some major limitations in the current group treatment literature are also evident, however. Most groups have been developed on an ad hoc basis, failing to incorporate and build upon the insights culled by the practitioners who had previously implemented and experimented with this approach; virtually no methodologically sound outcome research has been performed on the use of group treatment, either as a primary or adjunctive approach; and few group models have taken into account the special needs of male victims. The contributions of group treatment to the child sexual abuse field are unquestionable, but the therapeutic and research priorities for the future are equally clear.

ACKNOWLEDGMENT

The author would like to express appreciation to Ann Hazzard, PhD., Carol Layman, and Brenda Vander Mey, PhD., who reviewed earlier drafts of this manuscript and made a number of helpful comments.

REFERENCES

Bergart, A. (1986). Isolation to intimacy: Incest survivors in group therapy. *Social Casework, 67*(5), 266–275.

Berliner, L., & Ernst, E. (1984). Group Work with preadolescent sexual assault victims. In I. Stuart & J. Greer (Eds.), *Victims of sexual aggression: Treatment of children, women, and men.* New York: Van Nostrand Reinhold.

Berliner, L., & MacQuivey, K. (1983). A therapy group for female adolescent victims of sexual abuse. In R. Rosenbaum (Ed.), *Varieties of short-term therapy groups* (pp. 110–116). New York: McGraw-Hill.

Blick, L., & Porter, F. (1982). Group therapy with female adolescent sexual abuse victims. In S. Sgroi (Ed.), *Handbook of clinical intervention of child sexual abuse* (pp 147–176). Lexington, MA: Lexington Books.

Boatman, B., Borkan, E., and Schetky, D. (1981). "Treatment of Child Victims of Incest." *American Journal of Family Therapy, 9*(4), 43–51.

Bonney, W., Randall, D., & Cleveland, D. (1986). An analysis of client-perceived curative factors in a therapy group of former incest victims. *Small Group Behavior, 17*(3), 303–321.

Brownmiller, S. (1975). *Against our will: Men, women, and rape.* New York: Simon & Schuster.

Burgess, A., Groth, N., Holmstrom, L., & Sgroi, S. (Eds.). (1978). *Sexual assault of children and adolescents.* Lexington, MA: Lexington Books.

Carozza, P., & Heirsteiner, C. (1982). Young female incest victims in treatment: Stages of growth seen with a group art therapy model. *Clinical Social Work Journal 10*(3), 165–175.

Cohen, F., & Phelps, R. (1985). Incest markers in children's artwork. *Arts in Psychotherapy, 12*(4), 394–402.

Cole, C. (1985). A group design for female victims of childhood incest. *Women and Therapy, 4*(3), 71–82.

Cole, C., & Barney, E. (1987). Safeguards and the therapeutic window: A group treatment strategy for adult incest survivors. *American Journal of Orthopsychiatry, 57*(4), 601–609.

Coutouis, C. (1988). *Healing the incest wound.* New York: Norton.

Damon, L., & Waterman, J. (1986). Parallel group treatment of children and their mothers. In K. McFarlane & J. Waterman, (Eds.), *Sexual abuse of young children* (pp. 244–298). New York: Guilford Press.

DeFrancis, V. (1969). *Protecting the child victims of sex crimes committed by adults.* Denver: American Humane Society.

Deighton, J., & McPeek, P. (1985). Group treat: Adult victims of childhood sexual abuse. *Social Casework, 66*(7), 403–410.

Delson, N., & Clark, M. (1981). Group therapy with sexually molested children. *Child Welfare LX*(3), 175–182.

Eist, H. I., & Mandel, A. (1968). Family treatment of ongoing incest behavior. *Family Process, 7,* 216–232.

Finkelhor, D., & Browne, A. (1985). The traumatic effect of child sexual abuse: A conceptualization. *American Journal of Orthopsychiatry, 55*(4), 530–541.

Fowler, C., Burns, S., & Roehl, J. (1983). The role of group therapy in incest counceling. *International Journal of Family Therapy, 5*(2), 127–135.

Furniss, T., Bingley-Miller, L., & van Elburg, A. (1988). Goal-oriented group treatment for sexually abused adolescent girls. *British Journal of Psychiatry, 152,* 97–106.

Gagliano, K. (1987). Group treatment for sexually abused girls. *Social Casework, 68*(2), 102–108.

Gardner, R. (1987). *The parental alienation syndrome and the differentiation between fabricated and genuine child sex abuse.* Cresskill, NJ: Creative Therapeutics.

Giarretto, H. (1976). Humanistic treatment of father–daughter incest. In R. Helfer & Henry Kempe (Eds.), *Child abuse and neglect: The family and the community* (pp. 143–158). Cambridge, MA: Ballinger.

Giaretto, H. (1982). *Integrated treatment of child sexual abuse.* Palo Alto, CA: Science & Behavior Books.

Goodman, B., & Nowak-Scibelli, D. (1985). Group treatment for women incestuously abused as children. *International Journal of Group Psychotherapy, 35*(4), 531–544.

Gordy, P. (1983). Group work that supports adult victims of childhood incest. *Social Casework, 64*(5), 300–307.

Gottlieb, B., & Dean, J. (1981). The co-therapy relationship in group treatment of sexually molested adolescent girls. In P. Mrazek & H. Kempe (Eds.), *Sexually abused children and their families* (pp. 211–217). Elmsford, NY: Permagon Press.

Haugaard, J., & Repucci, D. (1988). *The sexual abuse of children.* San Francisco: Jossey-Bass.

Hays, K. (1987). The conspiracy of silence revisited: Group therapy with adult survivors of incest. *Journal of Group Psychotherapy, Psychodrama and Sociometry, 39*(4), 143–156.

Hazzard, A., King, H., & Webb, C. (1986). Group therapy with sexually abused girls. *American Journal of Psychotherapy, 40*(2), 213–223.

Herman, J. (1981). *Father–daughter incest.* Cambridge, MA: Harvard University Press.

Herman, J., & Hirschman, L. (1977). Father-daughter incest. *Signs: An International Journal of Women in Culture and Society, 2*, 735–756.

Herman, J., & Schatzow, E. (1984). Time-limited group therapy for women with a history of incest. *International Journal of group Psychotherapy, 34*(4), 605–616.

Herman, J., & Schatzow, E. (1987). Recovery and verification of memories of childhood sexual trauma. *Psychoanalytic Psychology, 4*(1), 1–14.

Holleman, B. (1983). Treatment of the child. In N. Ebeling & D. Hill (Eds.), *Child abuse and neglect* (pp. 145–181). Boston: John Wright.

James, K. (1977). Incest: The teenager's perspective." *Psychotherapy: Theory, Research, and Practice, 14*(2), 146–155.

Jampole, L., & Weber, K. (1987). An assessment of the behavior of sexually abused and nonsexually abused children with anatomically correct dolls. *Child abuse and neglect, 11*(2), 187–192.

Johnson, J., Rasbury, W., & Siegel, L. (1986). *Approaches to child treatment.* New York: Pergamon Press.

Jorne, P. (1979). Treating sexually abused children. *Child Abuse and Neglect, 3*(3), 285–290.

Kempe, H. (1978). Sexual abuse: another hidden pediatric problem. *Pediatrics, 62*(3), 382–389.

Knittle, B., & Tuana, S. (1980). Group therapy as the primary treatment for adolescent victims of intrafamilial abuse. *Clinical Social Work Journal, 8*(4), 237–242.

Lamb, S. (1986). Treating sexually abused children: issues of blame and responsibility. *American Journal of Orthopsychiatry, 56*(2), 303–307.

Lubell, D., & Soong, W. (1982). Group psychotherapy with sexually abused adolescents. *Canadian Journal of Psychiatry, 27*(4), 311–315.

MacFarlane, K., & Waterman, J. (1986). *Sexual abuse of young children.* New York: Guilford Press.

Machotka, P., Pittman, F., & Flomenshaft, K. (1967, March). Incest as a family affair. *Family Process, 6*, 98–116.

Mandell, J., & Damon, L. (1989). *Group treatment for sexually abused children*. New York: Guilford Press.

Masson, J. (1984). *The assault on truth: Freud's suppression of the seduction theory*. New York: Farrar, Straus, & Giroux.

Mayer, A. (1983). *Incest: A treatment manual*. Holmes Beach, FL: Learning Publications.

Meiselman, K. (1978). *Incest: A psychological study of cause and effects with treatment recommendations*. San Francisco: Jossey-Bass.

Mitchum, B. (1987). Developmental play therapy: A treatment approach for child victims of sexual molestation. *Journal of Counseling and Development 65*(6), 320–321.

Mrazek, P. (1981) Group psychotherapy with sexually abused children. In P. Mrazek & H. Kempe (Eds.), *Sexually abused children and their families* (pp. 199–210). Elmsford, NY: Permagon Press.

Nelki, J., & Watters, J. (1989). A group for sexually abused young children. *Child Abuse and Neglect, 13*, 369–377.

Patterson, G. (1971). *Families: Applications of social learning to family life*. Champaign, IL: Research Press.

Patterson, G. (1971). *Families*. Champaign, IL: Research Press.

Pescosolido, F., & Petrella, D. (1986). The development, process, and evaluation of group psychotherapy with sexually abused pre-school girls. *International Journal of Group Psychotherapy, 36*(3), 447–469.

Rosenfeld, A. A. (1977). Sexual misuse and the family. *Victimology: An International Journal, 2*, 226–235.

Rush, F. (1980). *The best kept secret: Sexual abuse of children*. New York: McGraw-Hill.

Sgroi, S. (1982). *Handbook of clinical intervention in child sexual abuse*. Lexington, MA: D. C. Health.

Smets, A., & Cebula, C. (1987). A group treatment program for adolescent sexual offenders. *Child Abuse and Neglect, 11*(2), 247–254.

Steward, M., Farguhar, L., Dicharry, D., & Glick, D. (1986). Group therapy: A treatment of choice for young victims of child abuse. *International Journal of Group Psychiatry, 36*(2), 261–277.

Sturkie, K. (1983). Structured group treatment for sexually abused children. *Health and Social Work, 8*(4), 299–308.

Sturkie, K. (1986). Treating incest victims and their families. In B. Vander Mey & R. Neff (Eds.), *Incest as child abuse* (pp. 126–165). New York: Praeger.

Summit, R. (1983). The child sexual abuse accomodation syndrome." *Child Abuse and Neglect, 7*(1), 177–193.

Summit, R., & Kryso, J. (1978). Sexual abuse of children: A clinical spectrum. *American Journal of Orthopsychiatry, 48,* 237–251.

Tsai, M., Feldman-Summers, S., & Edgar, M. (1979). Childhood molestation: Variables related to differential impacts on psychosexual functioning in adult women. *Journal of Abnormal Psychology, 88,* 407–417.

Tsai, M., & Wagner, N. (1978). Therapy groups for women sexually molested as children. *Archives of Sexual Behavior, 7,* 412–427.

Vander Mey, B. (1988). The sexual victimization of male children: A review of previous research. *Child Abuse and Neglect, 12*(1), 61–72.

Verleur, D., Hughes, R., & De Rios, M. (1986). Enhancement of self-esteem among female adolescent incest victims: A controlled study. *Adolescence, 21*(84), 843–854.

Wayne, J., & Weeks, K. (1984). Groupwork with abused adolescent girls: a special challenge. *Social Work with Groups, 6*(1), 83–104.

Zimpfer, D. 1987). Group treatment for those involved with incest. *Journal for Specialists in Group Work, 12*(4), 166–177.

12

Relapse Prevention: Application and Outcome

Diane D. Hildebran and William D. Pithers
Burlington Bay Psychological Associates, Burlington, VT.
Center for Prevention and Treatment of Sexual Abuse, South Burlington, VT.

The typical sex offender comes to treatment under the shadow of a profound contradiction: He recognizes that his actions periodically move past his control, apparently leaving him subject to sexual and aggressive urges that he does not understand. At the same time, he may be convinced that the shock and shame of discovery and the possibility or reality of arrest and incarceration are so frightening that he will never again indulge those urges. However great his awareness of the contradiction, he must ultimately accept the reality: If will alone were enough to deter him, more than likely he would have already drawn on the power of that will and not engaged in sexual aggression.

Herein lies both the fundamental premise and challenge of Relapse Prevention (RP). The sexual aggressor, regardless of his intention, finds himself locked into a habitual pattern of abuse. He feels drawn to aggressive sexual acts like an alcoholic, or a compulsive overeater is to binges. He is unable to change his behavior by simply activating his intention. His "problem" has become larger than his will.

RP is a therapeutic modality developed by Marlatt and colleagues (Marlatt, 1982; Marlatt & Gordon, 1980) for treatment of clients with addictions. It has been applied in the treatment of smokers (Shiffman, Read, Maltese, Rapkin, & Jarvik, 1985), alcoholics (McCrady, Dean, Dubreuil, & Swanson, 1985) and overeaters (Sternberg, 1985), all of whom share the experience of inability to overcome the addiction through strength of will alone. A fundamental premise of RP is that the addictive process is manifested and reproduced through specific behaviors, which feed the process, subverting the intention of the individual. If these behaviors are altered, the process will be interrupted and the individual's self-control enhanced.

Sexual aggressors experience a behavioral process that is in many ways similar to the patterns of addicted individuals. Both groups engage in behaviors that are self-defeating but *apparently* beyond their control. Unlike most addicts whose behaviors are self-damaging and may indirectly cause hardship for others, the sexual aggressor's behavior is not only self-defeating but physically and emotionally damaging to others.

The RP model, as applied to the treatment of sex offenders, provides the paradigm within which the Vermont Treatment Program for Sexual Aggressors (VTPSA) was established (Pithers, Martin, & Cumming, 1989). This chapter may be seen as divided into two sections. In the first part we will present the conceptual framework for RP, as we have expanded and refined it over the past decade of clinical experience at the VTPSA. In the second part we will tie the model to data related to offender recidivisim.

RP is based on the theory that while the sexual offense, taken as a whole, may seem to the offender to be beyond his control, when it is broken into component parts, control over each of those parts becomes manageable. An offender may experience his offense as an event so complex that it has taken possession of his life. His sense of powerlessness to interrupt his destructive addictive behavior may encourage him to abdicate any degree of control. When broken into individually recognizable components, however, the pattern loses much of its compelling power. No longer experienced as an external event that happened to him, it is recognized by him as a series of smaller decisions and directed behaviors that he orchestrated.

Reducing the overall experience into manageable affective, cognitive, behavioral and situational precursors removes the power from the event and returns it to the offender. Redefining the offense in terms of its precursors creates a structure in which the offender can be held responsible for each of his separate decisions within his offense process. Far from absolving him of responsibility for the abuse, analyzing the precursors to relapse requires the offender to assume responsibility for all of the mismanaged feelings, thoughts, and actions that enabled him to enter a situation in which he could choose to abuse sexually. Conversely, therapeutic interventions focused on these offense precursors (or "risk factors") provide the client with many opportunities to recognize the earliest signs of his relapse process, and to take action to minimize the likelihood of further abuse.

THE RELAPSE PROCESS

Offense Precursors

The chain of precursors leading to sexual aggression follows a predictable pattern (Pithers, Buell, Kashima, Cumming, & Beal, 1987). Typically, the sequence begins with an alteration in affective state. For pedophiles, this change is most commonly manifested as depression or anxiety. Rapists frequently experience an exacerbation of chronic anger (Pithers, Kashima, Cumming, & Beal, 1988). Although darkening of mood is not unique to this population, many sex offenders attempt to cope with negative affect, not interpersonally, but through abusive sexual fantasies (Pithers et al., 1988). A predominance of abusive sexual fantasies is the first precursor of the relapse process that differentiates the abuser and nonabuser. Negative affect, the first actual element, does not distinguish sex offenders from nonoffenders. The relapse process (also referred to as the relapse chain) is the sequence of affective, cognitive, and behavioral developments that precede reoffense (relapse).

Abusive sexual fantasies, frequently accompanied by masturbation, may provide temporary release of negative affect (Rosenberg, 1989). Masturbation to abusive fantasies may reinforce the fantasy by creating an artificial world in which the offender has total power over others. It provides only fleeting relief from negative affect, however. Offenders may report that negative affect actually becomes stronger post-orgasm (Rosenberg, 1989). The third element of the process usually involves cognitive distortions that justify and feed the masturbatory fantasies. It is in this stage, for instance, that the offender may convince himself that the child victim in his fantasy is seductively inviting sexual advances or that violent invasiveness is necessary punishment for childish misbehavior (Pithers, Marques, Gibat, & Marlatt, 1983). These distortions feed his excitement and deflect any potential guilt, facilitating the fourth stage of the process, passive development of a plan by which to act on the fantasy. The repeating nature of the process involves the offender in a cascading progression toward relapse, the fifth stage. What may have begun as depression, spirals to become eventually what the offender perceives to be a rational and well-justified plan to find and aggress against a victim.

An offender entering treatment may have repeated his relapse process often enough that he believes it is automatic and beyond his control. Nevertheless, he is likely to be aware of some aspects of his pattern (e.g., abusive masturbatory fantasies) even though he may be reluctant to acknowledge them to others. Because he has exercised restraint in some situations but not in others, the relapse process can never be regarded as being beyond his control. Treatment within RP requires him to assume full responsibility for every aspect of his relapse process. At the same time, it works to build skills in identification of elements of his relapse process, improved problem solving, and the use of specific coping strategies in high-risk situations. Through treatment, the offender learns to gain power by developing and using personal skills rather than by exerting abusive control over others.

Over his months or years in treatment, he becomes expertly knowledgeable of his own patterns of offending. With the help of treatment staff, he learns to identify his offense precursors and to recognize them as they appear in increasingly subtle forms. He also learns to examine his decision-making processes, exploring in greater detail how some decisions lead to risky situations and others lead to finer control over his behavior.

Lapses

Though realistic self-confidence can be a desirable reflection of a positive self-image, eventually the offender's self-assurance will lead to unrealistic optimism. When his self-assurance outpaces his fear of relapse, his caution will diminish and he will permit himself to enter a high-risk situation (i.e., a situation in which his ability to self-regulate is challenged and he is at risk of reoffending). The presence of risk factors (e.g., pornography, alcohol, children) increases the likelihood that the abuser will experience a lapse (e.g., deviant fantasy, decreasing inhibition through alcohol consumption, or isolating with a potential victim; Pithers et al., 1983). These precursory components of his relapse process are referred to as lapses. Lapses are affective and cognitive responses as well as behaviors that initiate or continue the relapse process. While lapses may represent regression in treatment, they are to be expected as the offender develops new skills in recognizing and interrupting his relapse chain. Lapses can provide a rich opportunity for fine-tuning coping skills as well as a vehicle for realistic self-appraisal.

A decisive positive response to a lapse can reinforce healthy empowerment. Not only may the offender have a more realistic respect for his continuing vulnerability to relapse, he is likely to have affirmed his ability to halt his relapse process. His treatment will be reinforced if he can maintain a sense of realism about both the ongoing presence of situational risk and his continued susceptibility to it. He will discover that

his newly affirmed self-assurance must be balanced with healthy anticipation of future dangers.

Abstinence Violation Effect

The offender who is not able to activate coping skills in response to risk
may begin a downward spiral as he experiences the lapse as an entry
point into his relapse chain. Subsequent self-statements determine
whether he moves further toward relapse (Pithers et al., 1983). Lapses,
even relatively minor ones, which might generally be viewed as necessary
learning experiences, have the dangerous potential of activating what
is known as the Abstinence Violation Effect (AVE). When the AVE is
operating, the individual's experience of his inability to cope with risk is
interpreted as either personal failure or global ineffectiveness of treatment. Cognitions reinforcing his sense of defeat may devlop into a
self-fulfilling prophecy: "I knew I couldn't make it. This just proves I'm
a failure. It's only a question of time before I reoffend." Negative
self-statements, if not countered promptly, will lead to the conclusion, "I
failed this time. I'm going to keep on failing. What's the point in fighting
it?" The more he perceives that relapse is inevitable, the more likely it
becomes unless his thinking can be reversed.

GOALS OF TREATMENT

The fundamental premise of RP is that intention not to reoffend is a
necessary but insufficient factor in abstention from sexual aggression.
Though the offender feels entangled in a pattern of compulsive behaviors, as the component parts of the behaviors are defined, the process assumes manageable dimensions. In order to achieve that differentiation, RP principles are applied toward the following goals: realistic
expectations of treatment, expanded awareness, a broadened range of
choices, self-monitoring, anticipation and avoidance of high-risk situations, and development of coping skills.

Realistic Expectations of Treatment

It is imperative that the client begins treatment understanding the
enduring nature of his deviancy. Unless he gives up his belief that he will
someday be cured, he will eventually stumble over an inevitable sense of
failure when lapses occur. If his expectation is realistic (i.e., that he will

always need consciously to manage his inclination toward sexual aggression), he will be able to build cumulatively the self-esteem and coping skills necessary for avoiding relapse.

Expanded Awareness

The client who is new to treatment is likely to have a myopic perception of himself. Though he knows that he is aroused to sexual aggression, he is probably not fully aware of the entire process that leads to his acting on his arousal pattern. Once in treatment, his awareness is directed to the full range of affective, cognitive, behavioral, and situational factors in his relapse pattern.

Broadened Range of Choices

Expansion of the offender's repertoire of behavior choices provides him with reliable alternatives to previous, self-defeating behaviors. For example, an offender for whom loneliness is an affective precursor may have a history of isolating, a behavior that has been dangerous for him in the past. As he develops a variety of healthier coping responses (e.g., calling a member of his support network), he replaces the need for abusive control of others with self-control and enhances his perception that he can accomplish self-change.

Self-monitoring

Basic to maintaining aggression-free behavior is the tenet that the client must take responsibility for monitoring his own internal processes. Because early precursors are experienced as affective change (e.g., depression or anger) and in fantasies of sexual abuse, the client alone is in a position to observe and report them. It is a precarious task to find a therapeutic balance wherein the client is consistently held accountable for cognitive distortions and behavior choices that re-engage him in his relapse chain, but at the same time feels supported enough to report internal lapses. It is wise to avoid reinforcing the perception that it is the job of treatment staff to catch the client's lapses. Unless the client realizes that disclosure is his responsibility, he may sustain a continuing involvement in his risk cycle, holding fast to a fantasy life that will be hidden from the prying questions of the therapist. In addition to the risk of the fantasies themselves, secrecy will lead to a destructive sense of control over the therapeutic relationship. Paradoxically, when he accepts responsibility for reporting lapses, authentic control may be enhanced and channeled into self-motivated change.

Anticipation and Avoidance of High-Risk Situations

The potential for high-risk situations is constant. It is essential that the offender realize that his progress in treatment will not remove the risk from some situations. Rather than hoping for these situations to shrink magically in their threat to his self-maintenance, he is encouraged to acknowledge their risks and to develop strategies for avoiding them. Preparedness will foster a sense of adequacy that will serve him even in those situations that have not been anticipated. The client who must abstain from contact with young children, for instance, might take care to shop for groceries in the late evening hours when he is likely to encounter only other adults. He must nevertheless be prepared with predetermined coping strategies (e.g., removing himself from the situation), for those unanticipated circumstances when, despite his best efforts, he finds himself in the presence of children.

Development of Coping Skills

Though some high-risk situations may be avoided, others (e.g., girl scouts arriving at his front door to sell cookies) may be beyond his control to prevent. In order to develop a reliable sense of self-management, the offender must be able to draw from a number of coping skills to emerge sucessfully from such situations. On finding girl scouts on his doorstep, for example, he might repeat a preprepared, short statement that he prefers to not be approached by salespersons. Preparation for unavoidable or unexpected circumstances is likely to foster client competence in controlling his response when exposed to risk.

INTRODUCING RELAPSE PREVENTION IN TREATMENT

In the initial stages of treatment, primary attention is given to addressing issues of client trust of the treatment program and therapist control of the direction of therapy. Once these issues have been resolved and client/therapist rapport-building is under way, treatment focuses on development of offender empathy for sexual abuse victims in general and his victims in particular. We have found that victim empathy is necessary to the implementation of RP (Hildebran & Pithers, 1989). Unless the offender develops a sense of the damage done to his victims, he will limit himself to an intellectualized experience of treatment, one that will not provide the motivation required for a lifetime of self-maintenance.

Identification of the Relapse Process

Once the offender has begun to develop empathy for his victim, he begins the process of differentiation of the elements of his relapse cycle. This work can be done in individual therapy sessions or in groups focusing on the relapse process. Each client examines his offense(s) to identify the specific factors that comprised his movement toward sexual aggression, usually beginning with his progressive change in affect, sometimes commencing months or years before the actual offense. He is trained to identify those conditions and events that triggered the change and the distorted cognitions that followed it. In directing this process, the therapist draws on a variety of resources including case records, the structured interview, the penile plethysmograph, and offender self-monitoring.

Case Records

Case records may hold significant information about the offender's history, including police reports, presentence investigation information, the victim's affidavit, a computerized check of his prior criminal record, psychological evaluations, and clinical notes from prior treatment. Careful analysis of these records can reveal a composite image of the offender's relapse process as well as specific personality or behavioral characteristics that may identify inappropriateness for treatment (e.g., the development of criminal behaviors over a prolonged period).

Structured Interview

Used to screen applicants for treatment, this procedure is a valuable tool for collecting information and assessing the client's level of denial or readiness for treatment (Pithers, Beal, Armstrong, & Petty, 1989). If the evaluator has had access to case records, the structured interview can serve two functions: (1) It provides firsthand information concerning the offender's cognitive and affective states, as well as his attitudes toward his offense, his victims, and his family and social relationships.

Clinical factors such as deficient social skill, criminal thinking or suicidal tendencies may be observed and targeted for attention in treatment. (2) In addition to its value in the collection of data, the structured interview is usually the setting in which the client first interacts with treatment staff. Previously acquired case information arms the interviewer with the means by which to measure the client's account of his offense and to confront possible cognitive distortions or lies.

Penile Plethysmograph

Use of the penile plethysmograph makes possible a direct measurement of sexual arousal patterns. Such observation is crucial for accurate targeting of arousal disorders, which the offender may be motivated to conceal or minimize in the interest of early discharge from treatment. In one case, a pedophile, whose offense against a 6-year-old girl indicated no tendency toward violence, revealed strong arousal to rape scenarios during plethysmographic evaluation. Had not this information been gained, he might have spent many fruitless months in treatment for an offense pattern centered only on child victims. Instead, the treatment staff was able to encourage his disclosure of several unreported rapes, making accessible his entire sexual abuse pattern to exploration and analysis in the process of conceptualizing his relapse process.

Plethysmographic data may reveal victim gender and age preferences that the offender has attempted to conceal. Periodic monitoring of arousal patterns is also useful in tracking changes in these patterns over the course of treatment and throughout aftercare.

Self-monitoring

When used in tandem with other evaluative measures, the offender's own report of his individual risk factors is an essential ingredient in the conceptualization of his relapse chain. His participation in the initial definition of the relapse process is preparation for the self-monitoring necessary for him to take responsibility for maintaining his own self-management. Unless he recognizes himself as solely responsible for an aggression-free life-style, he may attribute to therapists, family members and friends, the responsibility for detecting and reporting lapses.

The client who conscientiously monitors his susceptibility to lapses discovers a pattern of internal and external experiences that form the subtle structure of his relapse chain. Journaling techniques, such as those developed by MacDonald and Pithers (1989), provide an effective self-monitoring procedure by which clients maintain a daily record of external events and internal and external responses to these events. The record includes body sensations, self-statements (including identified cognitive distortions), affect, sexual and aggressive fantasies, and response planning. As he learns to recognize patterns to his reactions to daily events, he begins to discern similar patterns to previous abusive behaviors.

The wide range of assessment procedures makes possible a detailed breakdown of each client's offense process. Case records, structured interviews, plethysmographic observation, and self-monitoring yield an extensive collection of data, the strength of which lies in its diversity of sources. Considering information from any one source in isolation carries the potential risk that, although the information may be technically accurate, it may also create a skewed representation of the offender or his offense.

IDENTIFYING HIGH-RISK SITUATIONS

As the client examines the relationship among affect, sexual fantasies, cognitive distortions, and sexual aggression, he develops a more inclusive perception of what constitutes a high-risk situation. For example, participation in worship services in a family oriented church is identified as inherently risky for a fixated pedophile because of the presence of children. Having recognized the risk, the client is encouraged to seek a church in which the congregation is primarily adult.

In learning how to assess high-risk situations, the offender is continuously confronted by seemingly unimportant decisions[1], decisions that appear superficially unrelated to relapse but in reality are pivotal to his putting himself at risk. An example is the pedophile who decides, apparently in a random way, to take a different route home from work. As he explores an unfamiliar neighborhood, he discovers an elementary school and stops his car to observe children leaving at the end of the school day. He may be inclined to believe that finding himself parked in front of a school is unrelated to the earlier decision to alter his route, but as he develops a finer sensitivity to the subtleties of his relapse process, he will begin to realize that decisions that seem initially irrelevant may lead either directly or indirectly to relapse. When these seemingly unimportant decisions can be recognized before they are put into action, the client is in a position to monitor and control even his earliest precursors.

---

[1]In earlier publications, these decisions were identified with the acronym AIDs (apparently irrelevant decisions). Due to the seriousness of the disease which also goes by that name, Auto-immune Deficiency Syndrome, we have chosen another name.

A necessary component of the differentiation of the relapse cycle is an exploration of the determinants of the sexual expression of the client's aggression, for it is not aggression itself that defines him as a sex offender, but his sexualization of aggression. Case records and structured interviews can provide infomation about such factors as gender-oriented hostility, sexual dysfunction, early traumatic experiences, or compulsive masturbation to deviant fantasies. These records will also be useful in assessing the client's life-style to identify contributory circumstances such as chronic substance abuse, deficient social skills, and obsessive control of family members.

ASSESSMENT OF COPING SKILLS

As the client develops proficiency in identifying precursors and assessing high-risk situations, he begins an assessment of his skills for coping with them. Development and tracking of coping skills is done with situational competency tests, self-efficacy ratings, and relapse fantasies.

Situational Competency Tests

The client is presented with descriptions of common high-risk situations and asked to design coping responses. His competency at contending with risk is determined by the degree to which he is able to articulate a response strategy that is likely to be successful. Delay in formulating a realistic response, or elaboration of the circumstances of risk, signal the need for improvement.

Self-Efficacy Ratings

Studies of substance abusers (Condiotte & Lichtenstein, 1981) confirm the assumption that if the client is motivated, he or she is best able to measure his or her susceptibility to lapses. Using a seven-point scale, the offender is asked to study a list of high-risk situations and to predict the likely ability to cope with each one without engaging in a lapse.

Relapse Fantasies

The offender is asked to articulate possible relapse scenarios, beginning with his earliest precursors. Such exercises give him the opportunity to adapt learned coping skills to a variety of hypothetical conditions. His responses are monitored to identify problematic situations.

Encouragement is useful to deflect shame and guilt, which sometimes surface as the client retells actual seemingly unimportant decisions and offense planning. When guilt and shame build, they can be distractions from the skills building process, for they draw the client's attention from preparing for future coping back to the hopelessness he associates with his offense.

Each of these measures for assessing the client's coping resources aids in developing both a healthy respect for the immediacy of potential risks and an awareness of individual vulnerability to particular risks. The ultimate goal in skills training is the teaching of strategies that enable the offender to reduce the frequency and seriousness of lapses so that he will be able to interrupt them before they lead to relapse.

TREATMENT PROCEDURES

Although the primary goal of treatment is prevention of relapse, it is important to realize that lapses ae unavoidable as the client tackles a new field of self-control. Lack of expertise in developing and applying unfamiliar skills will inevitably expose him to situations involving risk. In addition, familiar negative attitudes and cognitive and affective patterns should be expected to sidetrack him occasionally. The frequency and severity of his lapses are reliable gauges of the efficacy of self-management. An important focus of treatment is the identification and utilization of lapses as learning experiences that can instruct the motivated offender in increasingly competent self-management.

A lapse may take many forms. It may be the experience of an affective state characteristic of an individual's early stages of relapse (e.g., loneliness or anxiety). It may also present as cognitive distortions (e.g., "that child needs to learn about sex. She ought to have someone who loves her show her how good it can be."). Frequently lapses are most apparent to the treatment staff when the client intentionally places himself in a high-risk situation (e.g., a trip to a music store for an offender whose victims are children or adolescents), or when some combination of precursors is present (e.g., masturbating to fantasies of aggression while angry). Whichever form the lapse takes, it is evidence that the client has re-entered his relapse process.

INTERRUPTING THE RELAPSE PROCESS

Those measurements employed in identifying the client's offense precursors (case records, structured interviews, the penile plethysmograoh, and offender self-monitoring) are also used to assist him in discerning increasing subtleties of his relapse chain. Once identified, lapses become cautionary signals to the client that he is at risk, both in his immediate circumstances and possibly in his larger pattern of self-maintenance. His response to the lapse is key, as it may determine whether his progress in treatment will be reinforced or whether he will begin a downward spiral of self-defeating cognitions and behaviors that lead to relapse. It is essential that the client know to expect that lapses will occur and that he may not always cope with them as well as he would like. A comprehensive range of primary and fallback strategies are necessary to equip him fully to contend with both predictable and unanticipated risk and lapses. These include stimulus control, avoidance and escape strategies, programmed coping responses, interruption contracts, maintenance manuals, and responses to urges.

Stimulus Control

External stimuli that serve as catalysts of aggression (e.g., alcohol, narcotics, pornography) may interfere with conscientious self-maintenance. Realistic stimulus control includes restriction of the client's exposure to others using the stimulus.

Avoidance Strategies

The client is trained to incorporate his knowledge of his offense precursors into his strategies for avoiding those circumstances that facilitate lapses. For instance, the man for whom loneliness is a precursor learns to contact appropriately supportive friends when he feels lonely. Avoidance strategies may range from the subtle (e.g., anticipating and preparing for a shift toward negative affect in stressful situations) to larger life-style decisions (e.g., deciding not to take employment in a school).

Escape Strategies

Because even careful planning is sometimes insufficient to enable the offender to avoid all situations with risk, preplanned escape maneuvers are essential. They should be activated at the earliest recognition of risk. The offender who intentionally prolongs exposure to the risk by staying in the situation to test himself or to understand all the dynamics of the experience reveals seriously distorted thinking, which calls into question his ability to safely manage himself.

Programmed Coping Responses

As with the relapse fantasies described earlier, the client is encouraged to anticipate and walk through a comprehensive range of likely relapse scenarios. Working in a supportive and appropriately confrontive group, the offender brainstorms possible coping responses and assesses the reliability and probable consequences of each one. He travels the entire scenario, designing a matrix of alternatives that will allow him to make appropriate choices of behavior regardless of the turns the situation may take. He creates a series of fallback options for each possible development so that he is able to exercize as much self-control within the event as possible. Repeated drilling is used to instill overlearned responses that allow the client to respond appropriately to risk even when he is not in top form cognitively or affectively.

Responses to Urges

A common thinking error for sex offenders new to treatment is that the memory of recently experienced negative consequences of sexual aggression (e.g., public humiliation, costly court proceedings, and incarceration) will in the future be sufficient to dissipate his urge to reoffend. Unfortunately, the offender who relies solely on his fear of consequences is discounting his powerful compulsion to aggress sexually. When faced with the choice of immediate gratification over avoiding future negative consequences, his arousal to deviant sexual behavior is likely to obscure his fear, at least temporarily. This dynamic may have been strengthened by several years of orgasmic reinforcement, either through masturbation to fantasies of sexual abuse or through actual offenses. While in a state of high sexual arousal, his fear of negative consequences diminishes in the face of the expected sexual gratification (Pithers et al., 1983).

It is important for the client to anticipate the continuance of deviant sexual urges so that he not interpret them as signs of failure, triggering the AVE. Despite their persistence, he learns that they will not inevitably build until they overwhelm him and that there are alternatives to acting out sexually.

To diminish the impact of his arousal pattern, he is taught to recognize clearly and honestly label the urge. He is then encouraged to monitor his experience of arousal in the same way he monitors other parts of his life, using the journaling techniques mentioned earlier. Deciphering the deviant urge in his journal helps him realize that relapse is a not a consequence of the urge itself, but of the decisions he makes in response to the urge.

Behavior therapy procedures employing masturbatory satiation, orgasmic reconditioning, and olfactory aversion can be effective in altering disordered arousal patterns. Plethysmographic measurement of arousal changes is vital to the tracking of progress in treatment (Laws & Osborn, 1983; Quinsey & Marshall, 1983; Rosen & Fracher, 1983).

Interruption Contracts

Delay in acting on the impulse to re-enter his relapse process can serve to diminish the strength of the impulse to a point where he is again thinking clearly and intentionally. Delays may be created by the use of a prior contract, whereby the client agrees to take predetermined action when risk is encountered. For instance, he may agree in advance that whenever he feels compelled to purchase or read pornography, he will remove himself from the situation for at least 10 minutes. During that time, he will weigh carefully the benefits versus the risks of proceeding with the urge. Once out of the immediate situation, he is likely to think more clearly about the consequences of either choice and move safely out of the lapse. If, at the end of the 10 minutes, he decides to move into a more serious lapse by buying or using the pornography, he has clearly labeled his choice and can be confronted in treatment on consciously choosing to stay in the relapse process.

Delay may also be affected with the use of positive self-statements such as, "Lapses are bound to happen. I just need to use the tools I have to cope with this one." While in the midst of a lapse involving deviant urges, constructive self-statements are most impactful if used in conjunction with other previously rehearsed coping responses.

Maintenance Manuals

As a means of sustaining his progress following treatment, each client develops a guidebook that provides him with instant access to many of the self-maintenance tools he has developed. This resource may include a detailed description of strategies for coping with high-risk situations, statements to counteract the AVE, a list of his past seemingly unimportant decisions and offense precursors, and the names and telephone numbers of appropriate emergency support contacts. The manual is particularly useful for the offender in the community, for it provides a link with his treatment program. He should be encouraged to modify gradually and update it as he encounters new risks, and with them, new successes and failures.

ADMISSIBILITY TO TREATMENT

RP cannot be employed effectively with every sex offender. Therefore, thorough screening of applicants to treatment is vital. We recommend consideration of the following criteria: acceptance of responsibility, self-awareness, intelligence, absence of a history of criminal life-style, and extensiveness of high-risk factors.

Acceptance of Responsibility

Though it is common for offenders to enter treatment minimizing to some extent the details of their offenses and denying full responsibility for the damage they have inflicted on their victims, the man who refuses to acknowledge that he committed his offense is considered unready for treatment. He must have some sense of personal responsibility for his crime before he will be able to engage in the process of intentional self-change. It is impossible to treat someone for a problem he claims he does not have.

Self-awareness

The client must have sufficient ability to monitor his own cognitive and affective states to allow him to track modulations in his internal processes. Without such skill, he will be unable to monitor internal risk factors and his responses to external factors.

Intelligence

Though intelligence testing is an important part of the offender's profile, it should not be given disproportionate weight in considering him for treatment under the RP model. Men with limited cognitive abilities may require more time, and in some cases, more attention from staff to understand subtle dynamics of the relapse process. Once RP concepts are understood and put into practice, however, these men may be more likely to maintain lapse-free behavior than men with superior intelligence who are better able to develop elaborately distorted cognitions.

Absence of a History of Criminal Life-style

Men whose police records indicate a lifetime history of impulsive criminal activity or who display persistent criminal thinking during the assessment interview are unlikely to activate the motivation necessary to relinquish their criminal mindset during and after treatment (Pithers, 1982). They display an enduring absence of empathy, without which RP principles are hollow, intellectual exercises.

Manageable Number of High-Risk Factors

Men who have so many high-risk factors that they are rarely in risk-free situations are poor candidates for RP treatment. Whereas a limited number of individual risks may be avoided or encountered with appropriate escape strategies, the person who experiences pervasive high risk (e.g., consistent rage in situations that are, for most people, only mildly irritating) will not be able to detach himself from his risk process sufficiently to respond wisely. Likewise, the polymorphic offender may have such a diverse range of potential victims that he will have difficulty limiting his contacts to people whom he is not liable to abuse.

LIMITATIONS OF SELF-MANAGEMENT

Although an informed and highly motivated offender is in the best position to track his therapeutic progress precisely and his ability to maintain aggression-free behavior, he is not always the most reliable source of information about himself. If he believes that the treatment staff expect him to achieve perfection in his handling of risk, he may resist reporting lapses out of a sense of personal failure, fear of disappointing treatment the staff, or anxiety over punishment.

Because the integrity of the individual's treatment rests on access to reliable information about his behavior in the community, external supervision is a vital component of successful application of the principles of RP. Probation and parole officers should be trained in the RP model and should function as members of the treatment team, for they provide essential links between therapeutic services and the client's support system in the community. Drawing on contact with employers, teachers, vocational counselors, friends, and family members, these professionals are able to maintain a supervisory relationship that is solidly grounded in specific knowledge of the client's risk factors. That knowledge is shared with members of the offender's employment and social network, who are encouraged to disclose information that allows for professional monitoring of his progress in treatment. To this end, offenders are required to sign waivers of confidentiality at the beginning of treatment. As precursors reappear in the client's daily life, they are quickly identified, disclosed to other members of the treatment team and discussed with the client. It thus becomes possible to recognize and interrupt lapses as soon as they occur. Weekly meetings of the therapists, probation and parole officers, caseworkers, and other profesionals involved in treatment and supervision eliminate the offender's opportunity to manipulate individual members of the team by distributing disparate information. A more detailed description of the external supervisory component of RP is provided by Pithers et al. (1989).

RECIDIVISM OF UNTREATED SEX OFFENDERS

In order to demonstrate that RP is something more than a good idea, its use must be experimentally shown to decrease recidivism rates of sexual aggressors. In order to provide a context for this comparison, the following section of this chapter presents recidivism data for: (1) untreated sex offenders, (2) treated sex offenders, and (3) sex offenders treated under the RP model.

Recidivism of Untreated Sex Offenders

Guthman (1980) reviewed an outcome study of sex offenders (Strugeon & Taylor, 1980) that reported a 5-year follow-up of every sex offender released from a California prison or state hospital in 1973. More than half (55%) of all untreated sex offenders had been convicted of new crimes involving interpersonal assault, with 36% having been convicted of at least one more sexual offense and 19% for nonsexual assaults.

Additional information concerning recidivism of untreated offenders comes from a variety of sources. A special report entitled "Examining Recidivism" (Bureau of Justice, 1985), found that 43.6% of the rapists incarcerated for sex offenses in 1974 and 1979 had previous convictions for sexual aggression. Groth and Burgess (1977), studying the characteristics of 133 "dangerous sexual offenders," determined that 53% had at least one prior rape conviction. Abel (personal communication, February, 1986) noted that rape relapse rates, after a 5-year follow-up, range between 35% and 70%. Marshall and Barbaree (1988) reported recidivism among untreated offenders reaches nearly 40% within a 4-year follow-up. Freeman-Longo and Wall (1986), in an article concentrating upon treatment modalities employed with sex offenders, indicate that 80% of untreated sex offenders commit additional acts of sexual abuse.

Research conducted in countries with lower crime rates than the United States generally confirms a high incidence of recidivism among untreated sex offenders. In Canada, Mohr, Turner, and Jerry (1964) reported reconviction rates as high as 55% within 3 years of release. Radzinowicz (1957), performing a 4-year follow-up of 1,919 British sex offenders who went untreated, found relapse rates of 10.8% for first-time offenders, 33.3% for men who had committed solely sexual offenses, and 42.6% for individuals previously convicted of both sexual and nonsexual crimes. Evaluating 58 Danish sexual offenders who received no treatment, Sturup (1953) discovered a relapse rate of 43%. Cornu (1973), reporting on 50 Swedish sex offenders 10 years after their refusal to engage in treatment, identified a 52% relapse rate. Langeluddeke (1963), who followed the status of 685 untreated offenders for as long as 20 years, found that 39.1% of his sample offended again.

In contrast to the research reporting high relapse rates, far lower recidivism rates have been identified in some studies. Amir (1971) found that, whereas 50% of his sample of rapists had been arrested previously, only 12.5% had prior sexual abuse convictions. Reporting data from a 3.5-year follow-up study, Frisbie (1969) noted that 14.7% of the untreated sex offenders released from California prisons had been reconvicted for sex abuse. Jacks (1962), reporting on 3,423 Pennsylvanians who had been incarcerated between 1947 and 1962, suggests that only 3.7% of the sample committed subsequent sex offenses within 15 years of release; another 5.5% of the sample reportedly were convicted for nonsex crimes.

Discrepancies among these outcome studies may be attributed to several factors. Studies reporting lower recidivism rates followed only rapists. Abel et al. (1985), who obtained self-reports from abusers who had been assured that their confidentiality would be protected, found that rapists had victimized an average of 7.5 people, whereas pedophiles had abused approximately 75.8 children. Thus, the relative infrequency of rapists' acts may lead to deceptively low relapse rates in comparison with studies involving a more diverse sample of sex offenders. The fewer offenses performed, the lower the probability of apprehension.

Research suggesting low recidivism rates was conducted in the early 1970s at the latest (e.g., Amir, 1971), before the full impact of the social movement encouraging reporting of sexual victimizations, and more compassionate treatment of victims by police and advocacy groups. Therefore, early studies underestimated relapse rates because many victims chose not to report their abuse. The increased rate of reporting of sexual offenses (40% of all rapes being reported currently, Bureau of Justice, 1985; versus approximately 10% in the mid-1970s) would appear to yield more accurate information about recidivism.

Early studies reflecting high recidivism rates (e.g., Sturup, 1953) typically were conducted in Europe, where tolerance of crime is considerably less than in the United States. We propose that intolerance of crime is positively correlated with an increased likelihood of crime reporting and, therefore, higher recidivism rates.

Two conclusions may be drawn from studies examining recidivism of untreated sex offenders: (1) Many untreated sex offenders have a high likelihood of performing another assault; and (2) Compassionate and respectful intervention with victims of abuse may also produce increasingly accurate estimates of the incidence and repetition of sex offenses.

Recidivism of Treated Sex Abusers

Furby, Weinrott, and Blackshaw (1989) recently reviewed controlled outcome studies of the efficacy of early sex offender treatment models. Furby et al. properly assert that their conclusions must be regarded as tentative since every study reviewed contained significant methodological flaws. With that caveat, they conclude,

> Nevertheless, we can at least say with confidence that there is no evidence that treatment effectively reduces sex offense recidivism. Treatment models have been evolving constantly, and many of those evaluated in the studies reviewed here are now considered obsolete. Thus, there is always the hope that more current treatment programs are more effective. That remains an empirical question.

Against these studies, the impact of relapse prevention, when used as part of an integrated program of treatment and supervision, can be compared.

Recidivism of Offenders Treated
with Relapse Prevention Model

The first adaptation of RP for use with sex offenders occurred within the Vermont Treatment Program for Sexual Aggressors (VTPSA; Pithers, 1982). RP serves as the common thread uniting the 2 residential and 27 outpatient groups of the VTPSA.

Over the past 7 years, the VTPSA has provided services to 332 clients. Of these, 57 initially entered residential treatment and 275 were seen in outpatient therapy only. A total of 65 clients (28 residents and 37 outpatients) either withdrew from therapy or were terminated unfavorably for various reasons (e.g., consistently failing to show up for group, unwillingness to acknowledge harm to victim, etc.). Thus, 81% of the offenders entering treatment either continue their involvement or have favorably progressed out of formal therapy. Fifty men have progressed out of the treatment program, whereas 217 maintain some therapeutic involvement.

During this time, four abusers have been convicted of additional offenses while in treatment and three have been convicted after their favorable release; 210 clients appear to have refrained from further abuse. If recidivism is defined as a reoffense (not reconviction) occurring at any point during or after treatment, relative to the total number of offenders who either are in treatment or who have progressed favorably out of formal therapy, then the recidivism rate for offenders treated under the RP model within the VTPSA is 3% (i.e., seven relapses out of 217 clients). If recidivism is computed solely on the basis of clients who have progressed out of formal treatment, the relapse rate is 6% (i.e., three relapses out of 50 released clients).

Of the 65 men who have left treatment on an unfavorable basis, 25 remain in prison. Of the 40 men who live in the community and have had access to potential victims, 13 have reoffended within the follow-up period while 27 have refrained from further abuse. Thus, the recidivism rate for untreated sex offenders reached 48%. Effective treatment and RP appear to lead to decrease the recidivism rate of sexual offenders by a factor ranging between 8 and 16. The difference between the proportion of relapses committed by treated and untreated sex offenders is statistically significant, $\chi2$ (1, $N = 90$) = 4.40, $p < .05$. Treated sex offenders relapsed at a significantly lower proportions than untreated offenders. Relative to recidivism data for untreated offenders and offenders treated under earlier therapeutic models, RP seems to diminish reoffense rates effectively.

EFFECT OF RELAPSE PREVENTION ON RAPISTS AND PEDOPHILES

Separately examining the recidivism rates of pedophiles and rapists who have participated in the VTPSA may yield important information. That is, RP may possess differential efficacy with rapists and pedophiles. Of the 20 rapists in our follow-up sample, three (18%) performed an additional sexual assault during the 6-year follow-up period. In comparison, of the 247 pedophiles, four (2%) have reoffended.

Statistical comparison of the proportion of relapses relative to sample size of each of the two offender subtypes (i.e. pedophile and rapist), reveals a significant difference, χ^2 (1, $N = 267$) = 12.94, $p < .01$. In comparison to their overall representation within our treatment program, rapists have greater than expected frequency of relapse whereas fewer pedophiles than expected have relapsed.

THEORETICAL BASIS FOR DIFFERENTIAL EFFECT OF RELAPSE PREVENTION

Possibly, differences in the dynamics and precursors of rapists and pedophiles may explain the discrepancy in impact of relapse prevention on the two offender subtypes. The greater recidivism rate for rapists may reflect the influence of anger and power as the predominant motivations for sexual violence. Eruptions of anger and disempowerment have precipitous, explosive onsets that often represent exacerbation of chronic states. In individuals for whom these issues are problematic, loss of behavioral control can take place rapidly.

Nearly all therapeutic programs for rapists offer some variety of anger management. In such groups, strategies for dealing with anger resulting from conflictual situations typically are devised. Thus, clients learn to stand up for their own rights while respecting those of others. Unfortunately, the much more fundamental hostility of an individual who believes life has been unfair to him, victimizing him at every turn, remains untouched. If an offender's anger can be compared with fire, the situation is comparable with extinguishing all forest fires on the earth's surface, but forgetting about the eternally molten core deep within the heart of the planet.

Extending this premise to the efficacy of relapse prevention as a maintenance procedure for rapists, one can envision how the model may be challenged. Rapists may manifest few precursive risk factors prior to offending. They may move from periods of adequate self-management to relapse within a relatively short time. Few opportunities to observe signs of anger exist prior to relapse. As with our planet, the surface may be tranquil until moments before a cataclysmic volcanic eruption.

The lower recidivism rate for pedophiles may reflect their misguided efforts to obtain "intimacy" and "relationships." Many pedophiles groom victims, gaining the familiarity that enables sexual access. Development of any human relationship, even the profoundly disturbing interaction of a pedophile with a victim, takes time. The greater quantity of time consumed by the etiology of pedophilic acts may be responsible for the later period of highest risk of relapse for child molesters than rapists. Pedophiles are most likely than rapists to display precursive risk factors over a relatively lengthy time. This affords greater opportunity for identification of precursors, therapeutic intervention, and restoration of self-control.

RELAPSE PREVENTION COMPARED
WITH TRADITIONAL TREATMENT MODELS

Multiple Sources of Information Versus Reliance on Self-report

Exclusive reliance on a sex offender's self-report to assess extent of behavioral change, and maintenance of change, is a flawed concept. Sex offenders have numerous incentives to misrepresent their progress in treatment. To the extent that the client likes, and wishes to please his therapist, an offender may be tempted to propose that he has made great progress when he has not. An individual paying for outpatient treatment may need to justify (or attempt to end) the expense by fictitiously claiming attitudinal and behavioral change.

Traditional treatment relies almost exclusively on client's self-reports and therapist's intuitions to evaluate improvement. Because sex offenders have a strong incentive to misrepresent their gains, and therapists' intuitions have never been empirically validated, professionals working with sex offenders must access additional sources of information. RP formalizes mechanisms for acquiring information from others who frequently observe the offender's behaviors. In this fashion, the offender's behavioral maintenance and therapeutic compliance may be examined more thoroughly. The therapist will be less likely to make important decisions about the offender on the basis of misinformation.

Relapse Prevention Versus other Addictions Models

Although one might assume sex offender treatment models based on therapeutic approaches to addictive behaviors would be similar, comparison of RP and "Twelve Steps" programs (Carnes, 1983) reveals major differences in orientation and implication.

Carnes provides superb insight into the phenomenology of sexual "addicts." He proposes that sexual addicts may be treated through adaptation of the Alcoholics Anonymous' Twelve Steps. Under Carnes' treatment model, participants attend self-help groups, with ancillary therapy for "coaddicts" (i.e., spouses). Following the Twelve Steps model, sex offenders are encouraged to subscribe to tenets advocating total abstinence from all behaviors remotely related to sexual victimization.

The model advocates that troubled individuals must be in total control of their problematical behavior at all times. The alcoholic is considered either in absolute control, or absolutely out of control. No intermediate stages exist. As long as an alcoholic maintains perfect behavioral control, the tenets of Alcoholics Anonymous represent useful concepts. However, anything less than total control is considered total failure.

Unfortunately, no human being has ever maintained absolute control over his or her behaviors across time and situations. Rather than being in either absolute control or dyscontrol, most of us find that, at any moment, our behavioral management falls somewhere on a continuum between these two extremes. Our ability to exert behavioral control is affected by many internal and external variables. Thus, encouraging an individual to accept beliefs that hold oneself totally responsible for maintaining absolute behavioral control is an unrealistic, and possibly dangerous, goal.

The Twelve Steps model, as applied to sex offenders, advocates beliefs that appear contradictory and which may pose a countertherapeutic double-bind. At the same time that the goal of absolute behavioral control is advanced, the premise that "addicts are powerless over their behavior" (p. 12) is espoused (Carnes, 1983). Thus, although sexual addicts are encouraged to seek perfection, they are informed that they are powerless to attain that goal. However, this tenet is doubtlessly appealing to the sexually aggressive client who would like to convince the court, his therapist, friends, and victims that he was powerless to refrain from the abuse.

The dilemma of demanding that a powerless offender maintain behavioral perfection is supposedly resolved by "ask[ing] addicts to rely totally on their Higher Power for their recovery" (Carnes, 1983, p. 151). Although reliance on a higher power is a noble goal that may benefit a select group of people, countless sex offenders have purportedly discovered religious dedication in prison, only to find that total reliance on religion was not a very good idea. Total reliance on a higher power neglects the time proven adage, "God helps those who help themselves." One might equally well propose, that for some offenders, the pattern of "being forgiven" and "sinning anew" could be considered a phase of their relapse process. Thus, although Carnes provides an excellent depiction of the way sex offenders view the world, the Twelve Steps model cannot be considered appropriate as an initial intervention with sexual aggressors.

RP offers a more realistic approach to enhancing maintenance of behavioral change. Contrary to the Twelve Steps model, RP proposes that individuals are always found somewhere along a continuum of behavioral control. Rather than frightening participants into maintaining abstinence through the use of doom-saying slogans, RP provides individuals with specific skills that may be employed to enhance self-control in problematical situations. In addition, rather than offering a single approach that is applied uniformly to all, RP offers a wide range of therapeutic activities that may be instituted prescriptively to meet the unique behavioral assets and deficits of each individual.

Rather than postulating dichotomous states of control and dyscontrol without any intermediary stages, RP proposes that relapse is a process that occurs over time. A central tenet of this model holds that abstaining offenders make many decisions, with options influenced by internal and external factors, that lead them closer to, or further away from, high-risk situations under which relapse is likely to occur. Therefore, clients may gain enhanced behavioral control by developing awareness of choices (the seemingly unimportant decisions), that signify they are on the road to relapse. Clients learn that the probability of relapse may be diminished by anticipating high-risk situations. They discover that a progression of precursors, ultimately leading to relapse, exists. By identifying risk factors occurring early in the relapse process and employing coping responses developed during treatment, clients decrease the likelihood of recidivism.

RP differentiates between two different usages of the term, "relapse" (Marlatt & Gordon, 1985). Relapse, as a noun, refers to a terminal state about which little may be done. In this usage, relapse represents "a slip back into a former state, especially illness, after a period of improvement" (Webster's New World Dictionary, 1971). This definition of "relapse" corresponds to the dichotomous view espoused by treatment models such as Alcoholics Anonymous. Either one has maintained total abstinence and is improved, or one has lost control, failed, relapsed. In contrast to its meaning as a noun, relapse has far different significance as a verb. In this usage, relapse denotes an active process that occurs over time. Instead of representing a black-and-white dichotomy of abstinence–relapse, the process definition of relapse encompasses a continuum of behaviors ranging between abstinence and relapse. In defining relapse as an active process, one permits room for small errors in self-management to occur. Recognizing that clients frequently experience relatively minor setbacks in self-control that do not yield the severe consequences of total relapse, RP refers to minor setbacks as "lapses." Since the first lapse need not signify total failure (e.g., buying pornography represents a less severe violation of abstinence than raping), clients have the opportunity to exert influence over the negative aftereffects of a lapse and perform "damage control," rather than concluding that the "ship has sunk."

Therapeutic Control Versus Therapeutic Cure

Historically, many treatment programs for sexual aggressors operated exclusively within institutions (e.g., prisons or maximum security state hospitals). The premise of such programs adhered to the best tradition of a central tenet of the medical model: Treatment enables cure. Within this context, if the disorder is sufficiently severe, therapeutic intervention might necessitate hospitalization. But regardless of the location in which treatment occurs, the central assumption of the medical model remains the same: Effective treatment cures, eradicates disorder, eliminates concern. In many disorders, the medical model functions quite well. Bacteria causing diseases can be annihilated, ruptured appendices removed, weak hearts and lungs replaced. However, in regard to sex offenders, it is the treatment programs adhering to the medical model concept of cure that have been removed and replaced, not the disorder they attempted to address.

For some disorders, within our current state of technology, cure is not possible. Although epilepsy cannot be cured, control of the seizure disorder is possible through medication. If medication is not provided, the likelihood of seizures recurring is quite high. Therefore, epileptics are humanely provided medication to control their disorder.

Sexual aggressors cannot be cured. To permit offenders (and anyone treating them) to have hope of complete, irreversible eradication of their disorder is to establish an expectation that assures failure. No living being has ever maintained total control over his or her behaviors across time and situations. Encouraging offenders to pursue the unrealistic goal of behavioral perfection, thereby ensuring a sense of personal inadequacy when lapses in self-management are encountered, may be tantamount to aiding and abetting their reoffending.

Treatment programs often fail to prepare clients for lapses (i.e., a return to the moods, fantasies, and thoughts encountered during the relapse process). This neglect appears to have two sources: a belief that treatment can cure sex offenders (which appeals to narcissistic mental health providers who enjoy the power inherent in their ability to "cure"), and a fear that predicting recurrence of lapses licenses the offender to have them freely.

Therapists who believe that discussing the likelihood of lapses will encourage their occurrence should not permit their children to participate in fire drills at school or to learn about the existence of child abusers. Obviously, instructing people about how to identify and deal with risky situations can prepare them to avert disastrous experiences.

The dire prognosis for affecting cure may lead one to conclude that any attempt to treat sexual aggressors is misguided. However, just as medication can control, but not cure, epilepsy, specialized treatment interventions for sexual offenders can empower them to gain enhanced control over their disorder. Given the potential efficacy of specialized therapy, any decision not to conduct adequate treatment and supervision of sexual aggressors may be considered utter disregard for the safety of a society of potential victims.

CONCLUSION

No therapeutic intervention can promise that sexual offenders will not victimize again. Initial outcome data derived from application of RP demonstrate that this approach represents an effective method for decreasing recidivism, particularly with pedophiles. The model may be less applicable to rapists, although additional data may demonstrate this early conclusion to have been premature.

REFERENCES

Abel, G. G., Becker, J. V., Mittelman, M., Cunningham-Rathner, J., Rouleau, J. L., & Murphy, W. D. (1987). Self-reported crimes of nonincarcerated paraphiliacs. *Journal of Interpersonal Violence, 2,* 3–25.

Amir, M. (1971). *Patterns of forcible rape.* Chicago: University of Chicago Press.

Brecher, E. M. (1978). *Treatment programs for sex offenders* Washington, DC: U.S. Government Printing Office.

Bureau of Justice Statistics Special Report. (1985, February). *Examining recidivism.* Washington, DC: U.S. Department of Justice.

Carnes, P. (1983). *The sexual addiction.* Minneapolis: CompCare Publications.

Condiotte, M. M., & Lichtenstein, E. (1981). Self-efficacy and relapse in smoking cessation programs. *Journal of Consulting and Clinical Psychology, 49,* 648–658.

Cornu, F. (1973). *Catamnestic studies on castrated sex delinquents from a forensic-psychiatric viewpoint.* Basel, Switzerland: Karger.

Freeman-Longo, R., & Wall, R. (1986). Changing a lifetime of sexual crime. *Psychology Today, 20,* 58–62.

Frisbie, L. V. (1969). *Another look at sex offenders in California.* Sacramento, CA: California Department of Mental Health.

Furby, L., Weinrott, M. R., & Blackshaw, L. (1989). Sex offender recidivism: A review. *Psychological Bulletin, 105,* 3–30.

Groth, A. N., & Burgess, A. W. (1977). Rape: A sexual deviation. *American Journal of Orthopsychiatry, 47,* 400–406.

Guthman, D. H. (1980). MDSO Law: The assumptions challenged. *Criminal Justice Journal, 4,* 75–83.

Hildebran, D. D., & Pithers, W. D. (1989). Enhancing offender empathy for sexual abuse victims. In D. R. Laws (Ed.), *Relapse prevention with sex offenders.* New York: Guilford Press.

Jacks, W. L. (1962). *Sex offenders released on parole.* Harrisburg, PA: Pennsylvania Board of Parole.

Langeluddeke, A. (1963). *Castration of sex criminals.* Berlin: DeGruyter.

Laws, D. R., & Osborn, C. A. (1983). How to build and operate a behavioral laboratory to evaluate and treat sexual deviance. In J. G. Greer & I. R. Stuart (Eds.), *The sexual aggressor: Current perspectives on treatment.* New York: Van Nostrand Reinhold.

MacDonald, R. K., & Pithers, W. D. (1989). Self-monitoring to identify high-risk situations. In D. R. Laws (Ed.), *Relapse prevention with sex offenders.* New York: Guilford.

Marlatt, G. A. (1982). Relapse prevention: A self-control program for the treatment of addictive behaviors. In R. B. Stuart (Ed.), *Adherence, compliance, and generalization in behavioral medicine.* New York: Brunner/Mazel.

Marlatt, G. A., & Gordon, J. R. (1980). Determinants of relapse: Implications for maintenance of change. In P. O. Davidson & S. M. Davidson (Eds.), *Behavioral medicine: Changing health lifestyles.* New York: Brunner/Mazel.

Marlatt, G. A., & Gordon, J. R. (1985). *Relapse prevention.* New York: Guilford.

Marshall, W. L. & Barbaree, H. E. (1988). The long-term evaluation of a behavioral treatment program for child molesters. *Behavior, Research, and Therapy, 26,* 499–511.

McCrady, B. S., Dean, L., Dubrueil, E., & Swanson, S. (1985). The problem drinkers' project: A programmatic application of social-learning-based treatment. In G. A. Marlatt & J. R. Gordon (Eds.), *Relapse prevention.* New York: Guilford.

Mohr, Turner, & Jerry (1964). *Pedophilia and exhibitionism: A handbook.* Toronto: University of Toronto Press.

Pithers, W. D. (1982). *Vermont treatment program for sexual aggressors.* Waterbury, VT: Vermont Department of Corrections.

Pithers, W. D., Beal, L. S., Armstrong, J., & Petty, J. (1989). Identification of risk factors through record review and clinical interview. In D. R. Laws (Ed.), *Relapse prevention with sex offenders.* New York: Guilford.

Pithers, W. D., Buell, M. M., Kashima, K., Cumming, G. F., & Beal, L. S. (1987, May). *Precursors to relapse of sexual offenders.* Paper presented at a meeting of the Association for the Advancement of Behavior Therapy for Sexual Abusers, Newport, OR.

Pithers, W. D., Kashima, K. M., Cumming, G. F., & Beal, L. S. (1988). Relapse prevention: A method of enhancing maintenance of change in sex offenders. In A. C. Salter (Ed.), *Treating child sex offenders and victims: A practical guide.* Newbury Park, CA: Sage.

Pithers, W. D., Marques, J. K., Gibat, C. C., & Marlatt, G. A. (1983). Relapse prevention with sexual aggressives: A self-control model of treatment and maintenance of change. In J. G. Greer & I. R. Stuart (Eds.), *The sexual aggressor: Current perspectives on treatment.* New York: Van Nostrand Reinhold.

Pithers, W. D., Martin, G. R., & Cumming, G. F. (1989). Vermont treatment program for sexual aggressors. In D. R. Laws (Ed.), *Relapse prevention with sex offenders.* New York: Guilford.

Quinsey, V. L., & Marshall W. (1983). Procedures for reducing inappropriate sexual arousal: An evaluation review. In J. G. Greer & I. R. Stuart (Eds.), *The sexual aggressor: Current perspectives on treatment.* New York: Van Nostrand Reinhold.

Radzinowicz, L. (1957). *Sexual offenses.* London: Macmillan.

Rosen, R. C., & Fracher, J. C. (1983). Tension-reduction training in the treatment of compulsive sex offenders. In J. G. Greer & I. R. Stuart (Eds.), *The sexual aggressor: Current perspectives on treatment.* New York: Van Nostrand Reinhold.

Rosenberg, J. (1989). *Fuel on the fire.* Syracuse, NY: Safer Society Press.

Shiffman, S., Read, L., Maltese, J., Rapkin, D., & Jarvik, M. E. (1985). Preventing relapse in ex-smokers: A self-management approach. In G. A. Marlatt & J. R. Gordon (Eds.), *Relapse prevention.* New York: Guilford.

Sternberg, B. (1985). Relapse in weight control: Definitions, processes, and prevention strategies. In G. A. Marlatt & J. R. Gordon (Eds.), *Relapse prevention.* New York: Guilford.

Sturgeon, V. H., & J. Taylor. (1980). Report of a five-year follow-up study of mentally disordered sex offenders released from Atascadero State Hospital in 1973. *Criminal Justice Journal, 4,* 31–63.

Sturup, G. K. (1953). Treatment of sexual offenders in the Herstedvester, Denmark: The rapists. *Acta Psychiatrica Scandinavica, 44.*

William D. Murphy
Mary R. Haynes
I. Jacqueline Page
Department of Psychiatry, University of Tennessee, Memphis

Brecher (1978), in a survey of treatment programs for sexual offenders, identified only one treatment program for adolescent offenders, while Knopp (1985, 1986) identified close to 300 specialized programs for the adolescent sexual offender. The explosion in treatment programs seems to be spurred by three interrelated factors: (1) Adolescents are responsible for a significant proportion of sexual offenses; (2) A realization that many identified adult sexual offenders began their offending in adolescence, and (3) A feeling that intervention early would be preventive and therefore reduce the number of future victims. In the remainder of this introductory section, we will provide a clinical and working definition for the adolescent sex offender, review the data related to the scope of the problem and provide some general overview of the nature of the offenses in this group. Following this, we will review the current clinical knowledge regarding the adolescent sex offender and his family. The final sections of this chapter will focus on clinical approaches to assessment, treatment and recidivism.

DEFINITION

Because the legal definition of a sexual offense varies from state to state, we will adopt the clinical definition of Ryan, Lane, Davis, and Isaac (1987). They define the juvenile sex offender as a youth, from puberty to legal age of majority, who commits any sexual act with a person of any age, against the victim's will, without consent or in an aggressive or threatening manner. This definition is meant to include both hands-on offenses (child molestation and rape) and hands-off (exhibitionism, voyeurism, and obscene phone calls). Not covered but also to be included in this chapter are other "victimless" paraphilic behaviors, such as transvestism and fetishism, although there is limited literature regarding adolescents' engagement in these behaviors. In addition, this chapter will focus only on the male offender, since little is known about the adolescent female offender.

Even with the foregoing definition, there are often questions of whether an adolescent's sexual behavior constitutes a sexual offense and/or is indicative of sexual problems (Groth & Loredo, 1981). Clinically, the following factors should be considered when determining whether a sexual behavior constitutes a sexual offense or whether a specific sexual behavior is problematical.

1. Age differences of at least 5 years between the victim and offender.
2. Use of verbal or physical force or a weapon.
3. Power differences betweeen the offender and victim (e.g., older siblings made responsible for younger siblings).
4. Developmental differences between the offender and victim (e.g., taking advantage of a mentally retarded peer).
5. Difference in emotional stability (e.g., taking advantage of a peer with clear emotional disturbances).
6. Compulsive nature of the behavior (e.g., adolescent who is obsessed with female underwear).

It is recognized that in many of these situations, the adolescent's behavior may not constitute an offense in the legal sense. However, because in a number of these situations consent may not be given freely or there may be impairments in the ability of the other person to give consent, one should assess the situations carefully. Victim characteristics that would suggest impairment of the victim's ability to give informed consent (i.e., age, mental retardation, psychosis, etc.) should alert the clinician to the possibility of sexual abuse.

SCOPE OF THE PROBLEM

There were a number of earlier studies of juvenile offenders seen in Juvenile Court clinics (Atcheson & Williams, 1954; Doshay, 1943; Maclay, 1960; Markey, 1950; McCord, McCord, & Verden, 1962; Shoor, Speed, & Bertelt, 1960). Little attention seemed to be paid to this information. This was partly due to the tendency of early investigations to present a rather favorable outcome for these offenders (Doshay, 1943) or due to a cultural milieu that may have regarded such behavior as normal adolescent curiosity. For example, as will be reviewed later, Doshay found a very low recidivism rate in his population, and Markey's (1950) comment that "The judgement of the court should, however, depend more on the total meaning of the act as it might affect the adolescent's personality development than on the act itself or the effect on the community's neurotic emotion" (p. 719) reflects some of the early interpretation and failure to look at the impact of abuse on the victim.

However, more recently, official arrest records, victims' surveys, and reports from adult offenders have suggested that juveniles are responsible for a large number of offenses (Davis & Leitenberg, 1987; Knopp, 1982). For example, the Unified Crime Reports (U. S. Department of Justice, 1977–1980), based on official arrest statistics, indicated that 20% of arrests for sexual offenses are of individuals under age 18. The National Crime Survey (Brown, Flanagan, & McLeod, 1984), based on random samples of adults, indicated that 22.6% of sexual offenders who committed forcible rapes were between the ages of 12 and 20. Ageton (1983), in a representative sample of 863 adolescents, found that 4% admitted to committing a sexual assault the previous year. However, the definition used for sexual assault was very broad and included the use of "verbal persuasion," which would not meet the definition of sexual offenses used in this chapter (Davis & Leitenberg, 1987).

Court data from St. Paul, Minnesota (cited in Knopp, 1982) indicated that 43% of arrests for sexual offenses were adolescents. Juveniles accounted for 24% of all rapes and 59% of all other sexual offenses. Similarly, 1983 data from California indicated that juveniles accounted for 2,575, or 24% of all felony sexual offenses, with 1,000 of these arrests being for forcible rape. Forty-five hundred juveniles were arrested for misdemeanor sexual offenses (State of California, 1986). Thomas (1982) reported that 46.8% of child victims referred to the Children's Hospital's National Medical Center Program for Sexual Abuse were abused by juveniles. Finkelhor (1979), in a survey of college students, found that 34% of women and 39% of men had been involved prior to adulthood with a sexual partner who was at least 5 years older than them and was between the ages of 10 and 19. There is also fairly clear evidence that the offense that brings adolescents to the attention of clinicians is not their first offense (Becker, Cunningham-Rathner, & Kaplan, 1986; Becker, Kaplan, Cunningham-Rathner, & Kavoussi, 1986; Deisher, Wenet, Paperny, Clark, & Fehrenbach, 1982; Fehrenbach, Smith, Monastersky, & Deisher, 1986). For example, Deisher et al. (1982) found that 57% of their sample of 83 had multiple offenses while

Fehrenbach et al. (1986), in a sample of 297 cases, found that 57.1% had committed at least one other offense.

There is also evidence that many adult offenders' first offenses were in adolescence. Longo and McFadin (1981) found among a group of incarcerated rapists and child molesters that 37% had a history of exhibitionism, 45% had a history of voyeurism, and 62% had a history of both beginning in adolescence. The mean age of onset was 16 for exhibitionism and 13 for voyeurism. A number of these offenders also had even earlier onsets of other paraphilias, such as fetishism and transvestism. Longo and Groth (1983), in a study of 231 adult sexual offenders, present similar data with 35% of a group of rapists and child molesters progressing from less serious offenses to their current offenses, and again many of these started in adolescence. Groth, Longo, and McFadin (1982) found in a group of 83 rapists and 54 child molesters that the modal age of onset of the behavior was 16. Abel and his associates (Abel et al., 1984; Becker & Abel, 1985), in a group of offenders seen in a research study where confidentiality was guaranteed, found that 42% of the adults reported an onset of their paraphilic arousal pattern by age 15 and 57% by age 19. For the group who molested young boys, 74% reported arousal to young boys by age 19.

The above data probably underestimate the extent of adolescent sex offenses, given the common finding of a difference between official statistics and actual victimization and the difficulties obtaining accurate self-reports from offenders. However, even with these limitations, it seems clear that adolescent offenders comprise a large proportion of arrested offenders. Furthermore, data from child victims (Thomas, 1982) suggest that close to 50% report that they were victimized by adolescents. It is also clear that many adult offenders begin their offending in adolescence and many times first offenses are hands-off offenses such as exhibitionism and voyeurism. However, it must be acknowledged that not all adolescent offenders continue their offense pattern into adulthood. Our understanding of the development of compulsive sexual behaviors would be improved by the study of adults who did and did not continue their offending pattern.

CHARACTERISTICS OF THE OFFENSE

Most of the data related to adolescent sexual offenders' offense characteristics have been well reviewed by Davis and Leitenberg (1987) and will only be summarized here. In general, except for hands-off offenses, the majority of victims of adolescent sexual offenders tended to be young children (Deisher et al., 1982; Fehrenbach et al., 1986; Wasserman & Kappel, 1985) with different studies reporting between 36% to 66% (Davis & Leitenberg, 1987) of victims of adolescent offenders being younger children. In looking at all offenses, the majority of victims were female, although when only looking at offenses that involve children, studies find that anywhere between 26% to 63% of victims are male (Deisher et al., 1982; Fehrenbach et al., 1986; Shoor et al., 1966; Van Ness, 1984; Wasserman & Kappel, 1985). It also appears that like adult offenders, most victims were known to their offenders (Thomas, 1982; Wasserman & Kappel, 1985). In incarcerated samples, however, 45% to 48% of the victims were unknown to the offender (Groth, 1977; Van Ness, 1984). It is also clear that the majority of offenders, or at least those reported in the literature, are male. The most common sexual behavior reported, at least in outpatient samples, appears to be fondling (59% of the Fehrenbach et al., 1986 study), but penetration was found in 60% of subjects in the Wasserman and Kappel study, which included subjects identified both through social services and the Vermont Department of Corrections.

These data suggest that the majority of victims of the adolescent offender are female, although when only child victims are considered the proportion of males is higher. The type of offense and the degree of coercion seems to vary from study to study, depending on whether one is reporting on an outpatient sample or an incarcerated sample. The incarcerated samples use more force and are involved in more serious offenses.

CLINICAL CHARACTERISTICS

Clinical descriptions of the adolescent sexual offender have focused on the following areas: (1) general psychological or psychiatric disturbance, (2) social competence, (3) family dysfunction, (4) the offender as past victim, (5) sexual knowledge/experience, (6) intellectual/neurological deficits, (7) generalized delinquency, (8) sex-offender-specific variables, such as deviant sexual arousal patterns and the use of cognitive distortions, to justify the offense.

Psychiatric and Psychological Disturbance

Adolescent offenders, like adult offenders, have been described as experiencing a variety of psychological disturbances. Adolescent offenders are described clinically as young men who feel powerless and confused regarding their sexual role (Ryan et al., 1987), lack self-esteem, have drug and alcohol problems (Mio, Nanjundappa, Verleur, & de Rios, 1986; Van Ness, 1984). However, as we will see throughout the remainder of this section, many of the descriptions used and many of the deficits and problems proposed are quite consistent with adolescents with general behavioral disorders or adolescents displaying delinquent behaviors. In addition, there are few studies in the literature that use standardized assessment approaches, with reliable and valid instruments, and who use appropriate control groups.

Lewis, Shanok, and Pincus (1981) found no differences between sexually assaultive adolescents and other violent juvenile offenders in terms of the presence of psychotic symptoms, depression, major and minor neurological disturbances, and learning disabilities. Both groups, which were committed to a secure unit for violent offenders, showed high levels of emotional disturbance but did not differ from each other quantitatively or qualitatively on this dimension. Saunders, Awad, and White (1986) found less emotional disturbance in courtship disorders (obscene phone calls, exhibitionism, and toucherism (rubbing up against females) than either sexual assaulters or pedophilic offenders. Kavoussi, Kaplan, and Becker (1988), using structured psychiatric interviews, found that 19% of the subjects displayed no psychiatric disorders and that the most frequent diagnosis was conduct disorder (48%). Other diagnoses included some type of substance abuse (18%), adjustment disorder (6%), attention deficit disorder (6%), and social phobia (2%). No control data for a nonsexual offense outpatient population were provided; therefore, whether the data differ for general adolescent psychiatric populations is unknown. However, the type of offense seemed to be related to diagnostic category with 75% of the rapists meeting the DSM-III criteria for conduct disorder, while this was true for only 25% of the nonrapist sexual offenders.

When standardized instruments are used, there is evidence of a good deal of heterogeneity in this population. Using the SCL–90 and the revised Behavioral Checklist, Blaske, Borduin, Henggeler, and Mann (in press) found that sexual offenders were significantly more ruminative and paranoid than violent offenders and both sexual offenders and violent nonsexual offenders scored significantly higher than nondelinquents or nonviolent delinquents on these scales. Sexual offenders also reported more anxiety than any of the other offender groups. Smith, Monastersky, and Deisher (1987) studied the MMPI profiles of 262 adolescent offenders. Using cluster analyses, they identified four profile types, although it should be recognized that the mean MMPI profiles tended to be within normal limits. Among the four groups, two were basically normal profiles with one of these suggesting shyness. There were two profiles considered abnormal, with one describing a group that was narcissistic and attention seeking, and one characterized by impulsive acting out, poor control, and poor judgment.

The study of psychological disturbance in adolescent sex offenders very much parallels the results from years of such studies with adult offenders (see Levin & Stava, 1987, for a review). Results suggest that both adolescent offenders and adult offenders show a variety of psychological disturbances varying from the normal to the severely disturbed. It is clear that there is no one type of ancillary pathology that clearly describes this group.

Social Competence

Social competence is one of the most frequently cited deficits in the adolescent offender. Van Ness (1984), using the unpublished Inventory of Anger Communication Scale, reported that 63% of 27 rapists displayed poor anger control skills, compared with 26% of 27 delinquents. Fehrenbach et al. (1986) based on clinical judgment, found that 65% of the subjects were socially isolated. However, such isolation may depend on the type of offense. Saunders et al. (1986) found that 60% to 72% of sexual assaulters and pedophilic offenders respectively were socially isolated; only 32% of a group of courtship disorders showed such deficits. Kavoussi et al. (1988) found that only 5.2% of their population met DSM-III criteria for a social phobia, while 10.3% showed some symptoms of social phobias.

Blaske et al. (in press) reported one of the few studies using a standardized measure of peer interactions (Missouri Peer Relationship Inventory). Teacher ratings showed no differences between the sexual offenders and other groups while mothers' ratings suggested that the sexual offender group scored significantly lower than the nondelinquent group on an emotional bonding subscale but did not differ from the violent and nonviolent delinquent groups. On an aggressive subscale, the violent offenders scored higher than all other groups who were similar. While anyone who has worked with adolescent sex offenders realizes that some subsets show significant skills deficits, it is not clear that this is true for all offenders and similar observations have been made with adult offenders (Segal & Marshall, 1985; Stermac & Quinsey, 1986). Furthermore, except for the Van Ness study (1984), there is no indication that adolescent sexual offenders show any difference in social competence, compared with other delinquents or psychiatric populations.

Family Dysfunction

Family dysfunction is often viewed as having a major etiological significance in the development of adolescent offender patterns. Again, clinical descriptions of offenders support a variety of family dysfunction, including psychopathology, alcoholism (Mio et al., 1986), and physical abuse from the parents of offenders (Lewis, Shanok, & Pincus, 1981), and a high prevalence of marital violence, at least in some groups of offenders (Saunders et al., 1986). However, these family disturbances do not appear to be specific to adolescent sexual offenders, but are also seen in other delinquent populations (Lewis, Shanok, & Balla, 1981; Lewis, Shanok, & Pincus, 1981).

The use of standardized assessment approaches, such as the Family Adaptation and Cohesion Scale (FACES) suggest that adolescents and their mothers do not perceive more family dysfunction than a nondelinquent control group (Blaske et al., in press). Recent data from our program also using the FACES (Qualls, Stein, & Murphy, 1989) found a good deal of heterogeneity among the adolescent offenders in their perceptions of family dysfunction. This data suggest that, although a number of offenders reported very dysfunctional family systems, there was no one type of family dysfunction that predominated and a number of offenders did perceive that their family was not dysfunctional.

Again, it appears that family dysfunction is present in some percentage of adolescent offenders' families but it is not clear that this dysfunction differs from other types of offenders or nonoffenders. It also seems, given the limited data, that at this point there is no one type of family dysfunction that can be related to adolescent sexual offending.

Offender as Victim

The role of being victimized (both physically and sexually) in the development of sex offense patterns among adolescents has received a significant amount of attention in the literature (Ryan et al., 1987) and in clinical practice. However, depending on the sample, the rates of admitted abuse tend to vary considerably.

For example, Lewis, Shanok, and Pincus (1981), in their sample of violent offenders, found that 76.5% of sexual offenders had been physically abused and 78% had witnessed physical abuse. Very similar percentages were observed in violent nonsexual delinquents (75.5% and 78.6% respectively). Both groups had higher rates than less violent delinquents and Lewis, Shanok, and Balla (1981) reported that approximately 29% of less violent delinquents experienced abuse and 20% had observed abuse. Van Ness (1984) reported very similar data in an incarcerated sample with approximately 41% experiencing interfamily violence versus 15% with nonviolent delinquents, Ryan et al. (1987), reporting on data from 559 subjects, found that approximately 40% of subjects had been physically abused. In an outpatient sample of 22 incest offenders, Becker et al. (1986b) found a rate of physical abuse of 13.6% while Becker et al. (1986a), in a larger mixed group of offenders ($N = 67$), found that approximately 16% had been physically abused. Fehrenbach et al. (1986) reports an overall rate of 23% for their outpatient sample of 305 subjects. Saunders et al. (1986) found that sexual assaulters ($N = 14$) and pedophilic offenders ($N = 17$) reported higher rates of marital violence in their families (30% and 50% respectively) versus only 6% of the courtship disorders ($N = 20$).

Sexual abuse estimates for this population also vary considerably. Ryan et al. (1987) reported 33%; Fehrenbach et al. (1986), 19%, Becker et al. (1986b), 23%; Becker et al. (1986a), 17%; and Gomes-Schwartz (1984), 38%. Longo (1982), in a group of adolescents committed to an adult program, reported the highest rate of 47%. Fehrenbach et al. (1986) also found that sexual abuse rates were higher among subjects who engaged in hands-on offenses (20% to 22%), versus those engaged in hands-off offenses (7.5%).

It is recognized that these abuse rates may be underestimates, since adolescents may find it difficult to admit being victims of abuse, because of the perceived stigma attached to being abused, which may be intensified when the abuse is by the same sex. In addition, much of the data appear to have been collected during initial evaluations and higher rates might be seen after therapeutic relationships have been established. However, with these limitations, a few tentative conclusions can be drawn. Current data would suggest that physical abuse may be correlated more with violence in general than sexual abuse per se. The role of sexual abuse in the development of the adolescent sex offender is less clear. Although probably underestimates, reported rates do seem higher than the 1 in 8 to 1 in 10 reported for nonclinical samples (Finkelhor, 1986). Theories on the role victimization plays in the development of sexual offending vary from analytical concepts, such as identification with the aggressor, to more social learning theories, such as modeling or learned helplessness (Laws & Marshall, in press; Ryan et al., 1987). It is clear that not all offenders are sexual abuse victims and not all sexual abuse victims become offenders. The interaction of being abused with other factors that may lead to offending, such as family dysfunction, learning disabilities, social skills, and so on, should be priorities for future investigations.

Sexual Knowledge/Experience

Sexual knowledge, or experience, has been linked to sexual abuse in the literature. One approach taken is that some sexually deviant acts should be considered exploratory and part of normal adolescent development and not necessarily signs of a set deviant arousal pattern (Markey, 1950). The second approach is that the sex offender lacks adequate sexual knowledge, is inhibited sexually, and instilling positive sexual attitudes and behaviors becomes the basis for some treatment programs (Seabloom, 1980, 1981).

There are little data on the first issue, that is, the extent to which participation in paraphilic behavior occurs as part of normal adolescent development. Surveys of "normal adolescents" and college students do suggest that various forms of coercive sexual behavior, including date rape, occur frequently (Koss & Dinero, 1989; Murphy, Coleman, & Haynes, 1986). Behaviors that impact on others, such as date rape or coercive sexual interactions in the date situation, are not acceptable, even if they are frequent. However, the frequency of such behavior may suggest that intervention needs to be directed at cultural factors that support such behaviors rather than individual pathology.

The second issue (i.e., lack of sexual knowledge, inadequate heterosexual skills or inhibited sexual feelings) also has not been investigated extensively. Becker et al. (1986a) found that their samples gained most of their sexual knowledge from peers, personal experience, or siblings, which probably does not differ from normal populations. They also reported that 82% of their subjects had engaged in nongenital sexual behavior with consenting partners and 58% had engaged in genital behaviors. Very similar data are presented by Groth (1977), Longo (1982), Becker et al. (1986b), and McCord et al. (1962). In the majority of these studies, it appears that nondeviant consensual experiences occurred prior to the occurence of deviant sexual behaviors.

Again, although clinically one sees adolescent offenders who are extremely inhibited sexually and lack sexual knowledge and experience, this does not seem to characterize all offenders and many have engaged in nondeviant mutually consenting sexual behaviors. Currently, there are no controlled studies comparing adolescent sex offenders with other delinquents or nondelinquents in terms of sexual attitudes, sexual experiences, or engagement in paraphilic behaviors in general. It does appear, however, given the large number of offenders who report nondeviant sexual behaviors, that the idea that sexual acting out in adolescents is exploratory behavior probably does not apply to a large number of offenders.

Intellectual/Neurological Deficits

As with adult offenders (Berlin, 1983; Langevin et al., in press; Murphy & Schwarz, 1990) intellectual deficits or neurological deficits have been proposed as having etiological significance in certain groups of sex offenders. As reviewed by Davis and Leitenberg (1987), school problems are common in this group, although it is not clear whether these problems are related to intellectual deficits, learning disabilities, or conduct problems. It also is not clear that school problems experienced by adolescent offenders are any different or any more frequent than those experienced by nonsexual delinquents or by adolescents experiencing emotional difficulties. Lewis, Shanok, and Pincus (1981) found abnormal EEGs or grand mal seizures in 23.3% of their sample of violent adolescent sex offenders with the group showing an average Full Scale IQ of 83 and clear deficits in reading and math performance. However, this group did not differ from the violent nonsexual offenders, although both groups differed significantly than the nonviolent delinquent groups (Lewis, Shanok, & Balla, 1981). In an outpatient sample, Tarter, Hegedus, Alterman, and Katz-Garris (1983) found few differences between sexual offenders, violent offenders, and nonviolent offenders on extensive neuropsychological and psychoeducational assessments.

As with many adolescent clinical populations, some subset will display significant learning and associated neurological problems, or mental retardation that needs to be addressed as part of treatment. However, there are little data to support that such deficits are related to sex-offending behavior per se.

Generalized Delinquency

Are adolescent sexual offenses just another behavior displayed by a group of general delinquents or does sexual offending represent a specific problem to be addressed separately? Since Doshay's (1943) original description of his population, it is clear that there are groups of adolescent sex offenders who show a variety of delinquent behaviors and there are groups in which delinquency appears to be limited to sexual offending. The frequency of nonsexual delinquent behavior varies from study to study. Lewis, Shanok, and Pincus, (1981) and Van Ness (1984) found high rates of deliquency and violent behavior in their incarcerated sample, although rates did not differ significantly from violent delinquents. Fehrenbach et al. (1986) found that 44% of their sample seen for outpatient evaluation had committed nonsexual crimes, while Becker et al. (1986b) found that 50% of their incest group had been arrested for nonsexual offenses while only 28.4% of their larger group had been arrested for nonsexual offenses (Becker et al., 1986a). Saunders et al. (1986) found that the number of delinquent acts and school suspensions were higher among the sexual assaultors and pedophilic group than the courtship disorders. This issue will be addressed further in the section on typologies.

Sex-offender-specific Variables

The review to this point has focused on general psychosocial variables and the results of studies to date very much parallel the adult literature (Langevin, 1983; Levin & Stava, 1987; Murphy & Stalgaitis, 1987). The tentative data suggest that sexual offenders are heterogeneous in terms of psychopathology, social skills deficits, and sexual inhibitions. When appropriate control groups are employed, there are few empirical differences between sexual offenders and other offenders or other clinical samples except possibly in being victimized themselves. Therefore, the relevance of these general psychosocial variables to sexual offending is unclear.

In addition to a focus on general psychosocial variables, the literature on the adult sex offender has focused on other variables that are thought to be theoretically relevant to sexual offending. Two variables frequently mentioned in the literature are sexual interest patterns (Murphy, Haynes, & Worley, in press) and cognitive distortions (the justifications offenders use for the offense; Murphy, 1990). Unfortunately, in the area of cognitive distortions, there are little empirical data either in the adult literature or in the adolescent literature (Murphy, in press; Ryan et al., 1987).

However, in the assessment of sexual interest, there is a very large literature. A recent summary of this literature for rapists and child molesters (Murphy, Haynes, & Worley, 1991) indicates that the psychophysiological assessment of sexual arousal through the use of erection measurement has consistently separated adult sexual offenders from nonoffenders, although these data are more consistent with offenders against children than for rapists of adult women. Apparently, because of ethical concerns (National Adolescent Perpetrator Network, 1988), this procedure has not been used frequently with the adolescent population. Knopp (1985) found that only about 14% adolescent sex offender programs employed psychophysiological assessment, while approximately 31% of adult programs applied such assessment.

We could locate only two unpublished papers describing erection responses in adolescent offenders. Murphy, Haynes, and Stalgaitis

(1985) compared two groups of adolescent offenders against children; one group with a history of nonsexual delinquent behavior ($n = 8$) and a second group with no history of nonsexual delinquent behavior ($n = 7$). Results suggested that groups did not differ in their sexual responding to material depicting children, but that the delinquent group showed more responding to sexual cues involving aggression than the nondelinquent group. Becker, Stein, Kaplan, and Cunningham-Rathner, (1988), in a sample of 70 adolescent child molesters (31 against young boys, 39 against young girls) studied sexual responding to audiotaped descriptions of sexual interactions with young girls or boys that varied in coercion. Scenes that described consenting relationships with peers were also used. Significant correlations were found between erection responses and number of victims the subjects had molested for those who molested young males but not for those who molested young females.

At the present time, there are too little data to discuss the reliability or validity of these measures in adolescent populations. Psychophysiological assessment of sexual arousal in adult populations has been one of the few measures to separate offenders from nonoffenders and has improved our theoretical understanding of sex offending in adults. That suggests that this assessment method merits further investigation with adolescents.

TYPOLOGIES

Because of the heterogeneity seen in adolescent offenders, there have been various typologies proposed in an attempt to organize the disparate information.

As noted, one of the first attempts to subdivide adolescent offenders was Doshay's (1943) description of what was labeled a primary group that displayed little nonsexual delinquent behavior and a mixed group that showed both sexual and nonsexual delinquent behaviors. Doshay's follow-up data indicated that the mixed group had higher rates of recidivism, especially for nonsexual offenses. A number of investigators have attempted to subdivide offenders on the nature of the offense rather than delinquency per se. We have already reviewed many of the findings of Saunders et al. (1986) in which a number of differences emerged between sexual assaulters and pedophiles as compared to courtship disorders. Similarly, Fehrenbach et al. (1986) have reported a number of differences between hands-on and hands-off offenders. Hands-off offenders were more likely to be repetitive than hands-on offenders and more likely to select female victims. Hands-on offenders, on the other hand, were more likely to have been sexually abused themselves. Within a group of adolescent child molesters, Shoor et al. (1966) defined the aggressive molesters (violence and sexuality seemed to be clearly linked) and the passive child molester, who was more sexually immature and more confused about sexual orientation. Shoor et al. proposed that the aggressive offender should be confined where the passive offender may be more amenable to treatment, although no supporting data are provided. Although there are no data to support the Shoor et al. classification of child molesters, it is interesting that Murphy et al. (1985) found that the more delinquent child molesters showed more penile tumescence responses to aggressive material than less delinquent child molesters.

Other investigations have tried to subdivide offenders on type of psychological disturbances shown. Such a distinction is implied in the Smith et al. (1987) study of MMPI profiles in adolescent offenders where basically four types were presented: (1) the normal profile, (2) the normal profile with suggestions of shyness, (3) the narcissistic, attention-seeking profile, and (4) the acting-out, impulsive profile. These profiles were developed from cluster-analysis procedures and each cluster was associated with unique two-point MMPI codes. There were few findings that related history to the general cluster but specific two-point profiles within each cluster did have some relationships to offense history. For example, rape was more frequent among subjects with abnormal F or 7–8 profiles, while hands-off offenders were more frequent among normal profile types. There were also certain two-point codes associated with those who molested younger children versus those who offended against peers and differences between those who chose male versus female victims. Atcheson and Williams (1954) also describe three groups of offenders: (1) emotionally disturbed, (2) mentally defective, (3) normal adolescents whose behavior was based on curiosity. The relationship of this grouping to other factors, however, was not presented.

A classification system that is widely used has been described by O'Brien (1985). The following six groups are proposed: (1) naïve experimenters, (2) undersocialized child exploiters, (3) sexual aggressors, (4) sexual compulsives, (5) disturbed impulsives, and (6) peer-group-influenced offenders. This system has significant face validity for those who work with adolescent offenders and allows classification across a number of potentially relevant variables such as victim's age, hands-on versus hands-off offenses, degree of psychopathology, degree of general delinquency and the degree of aggression used in the offense. However, to date, there are no data available in terms of reliability of the system nor data in terms of validity.

It should be recognized that classification systems may have different values for different uses. For example, some systems may be very useful in predicting recidivism, such as the delinquent versus nondelinquent classification system, while other systems may be useful for treatment planning, such as those that focus on types of psychological disturbance. Within the adolescent area and to some extent within the adult area, it is likely that there will be no one classification system developed that will be appropriate for all uses. It does seem important, however, that research continue with attempts to organize the heterogeneity seen in this population. It is unlikely that our understanding of the adolescent sex offender will increase if we continue to treat them as one homogeneous group.

CLINICAL APPROACHES TO ASSESSMENT

To this point, we have attempted to review the relevant literature regarding the adolescent sex offender. The next two sections will attempt to translate this knowledge (albeit limited) to actual clinical practice. What is to be presented is based on the authors' interpretation of the literature and their clinical experience with this population. It needs to be clearly indicated that the clinical approaches to be described have not been empirically verified and therefore should be applied cautiously. Other approaches to assessment have been described in the literature (Bengis, 1986; Breer, 1987; Groth & Loredo, 1981), which overlap at least partly what is described here.

In approaching assessment of the adolescent sex offender, it is important to determine for what reason assessment is being done and also to determine which referral questions cannot be answered with current knowledge. There are three interrelated assessment questions that seem appropriate for the mental health clinician or researcher. The first two are the degree of dangerousness, either in terms of violence and/or recidivism, and based on degree of dangerousness, the most appropriate treatment environment. The third question is what are the treatment needs and what variables need to be monitored to determine treatment success. There is another question that is many times asked by attorneys, judges, probation officers, and even families and that question is either directly "Did he do it?" or more indirectly, "Does he fit the profile of a sex offender?" At the present time, there is no mental health assessment approach that allows one to determine if an individual has committed a specific sexual offense, apart from the offender admitting to the offense, nor is there at the present time any one profile that characterizes sex offenders. Guilt or innocence is a legal question that can be determined only by adequate police and/or child protective service investigations. Mental health professionals need to be wary of providing assessments to answer guilt or innocence questions and need to educate other professionals about our limitations.

A second issue to be considered prior to discussing specific assessment approaches is the sources from which assessment data are collected. Because offenders and their families do not always provide accurate information, adequate assessment requires multiple sources of information. In addition to assessment of the offender and his family, adequate assessment will involve, where appropriate, collection of school reports, victim statements, child protective service reports, juvenile court records, probation reports, information from past treatment facilities, and reports from the victims's therapist (Murphy & Stalgaitis, 1987; National Adolescent Perpetrator Network, 1988).

Dangerousness and Type of Treatment Facility

In general, except for hands-off offenses that may have high recidivism but probably less victim impact, the higher the chance of recidivism, the more likely one would recommend a more secure treatment facility. Similarly, the more violent the current offense and/or past offense, the more likely one would recommend a secure treatment facility. Monastersky and Smith (1985) presented an extensive checklist that allows classification of offenders into high-risk, medium-risk, or low-risk. This checklist seems to take into account both issues related to recidivism and violence. Validation studies by Smith and Monastersky (1986) did not find this scale highly predictive of recidivism. However, many of the offenders followed up in the study had received treatment and recidivism rates were generally low, making it difficult to allow any significant comparison.

Although from a research standpoint we do not have validated methods for deciding risk, the clinician is still faced with the problem of making recommendations. These recommendations must consider the treatment needs of the offender but more importantly must protect society. Mental health professionals may overpredict dangerousness and have been criticized for the overuse of inpatient/residential facilities for adolescents (Weithorn, 1988). However, the adolescent sexual offender is not the "typical adolescent behavioral problem." Adolescent sexual offenders have committed a crime, a crime which has harmed others. Therefore, it is our bias that until better data are available, the overprediction of dangerousness is more acceptable than underprediction that places members of the community in danger. Table 13.1 outlines issues that we weigh in making decisions regarding outpatient-versus-inpatient treatment in a more secure environment. These factors are not

TABLE 13.1
Factors to Consider in Determining Outpatient versus Secure
Treatment

1. Offender and family level of denial
2. Degree of violence in the offense
3. Use of a weapon in the offense
4. Ritualistic nature of the abuse
5. Compulsive nature of the offending pattern
6. Degree of generalized delinquency and/or generalized aggression
7. Degree of substance abuse
8. Degree of psychopathology
9. Availability of family support system
10. History of failure in other sex offender programs

meant to be a checklist but rather are areas that need to be weighed for the clinician who is faced with making decisions regarding adolescent offenders.

Many offenders and their families will be showing some level of denial during initial evaluation. However, when the clinician assesses that the denial is extremely well ingrained and will not change easily, it is very difficult to provide outpatient treatment since it is very difficult to monitor the offender while they are in the community. At times when the denial is not as well ingrained, we will accept an offender into outpatient treatment for a limited period of time, such as 4 to 6 weeks, to determine if group pressure will lead the offender to become more honest. If, after that period of time, the offender is still denying their offense, then we may recommend more secure treatment. Very similar comments apply to the adolescent who has no social support system or the adolescent whose family is extremely dysfunctional. Without a system to monitor the patient's behavior, to ensure that they are not placing themselves in high-risk situations, one has no way of adequately protecting the community.

Violent offenses, those involving weapons, ritualistic abuse (including satanic components), and extremely compulsive sexual behavior, generally need to be treated in a secure facility. It has also been our clinical experience that adolescents with general nonsexual delinquency, generalized aggressive behavior and substance abuse disorders are difficult to maintain in a community treatment program. Although such individuals may not reoffend sexually while in the outpatient program, their other inappropriate behaviors often continue. Similarly, adolescents who are psychotic or suicidal may need inpatient treatment to stabilize their psychiatric difficulties. Offenders who have failed in other outpatient sex offender programs and reoffend while in treatment should probably not be treated in another outpatient environment. Past behavior would indicate difficulties maintaining patients in such programs.

Case Example 1

Robert was a 15-year-old male referred by juvenile court for evaluation to our outpatient sex offender clinic. Robert had been accused of molesting three boys between the ages of 7 and 9. The victims' reports indicated that abuse had involved fondling as well as the insertion of objects into the boys' rectums and drawing a symbol on one of the boys' abdomen. Robert had no history of previous delinquent behavior, no history of past treatment, no history of drug abuse, and generally no school problems except a possible learning disability. The patient was very controlling of his mother, who was very overprotective of the patient. When interviewed, the mother reported that she did not know whether Robert had committed the offenses. However, she was monitoring the behavior and had moved in with her own mother so that Robert could be supervised at all times. When interviewed, Robert totally denied the offense, showed little empathy for the boys, reported that the boys were lying, and made statements that they would be punished by God for their behavior.

In this case, a decision was made to hospitalize the client. This decision was made based on the nature of the offense, which suggested a possible sadistic component, the fact that there were three victims, raising questions about the compulsive nature of his behavior, and his well-ingrained denial. If, on the other hand, this case had been limited to fondling and if there had only been one victim, the decision might have been made to treat Robert as an outpatient, even given the family dysfunction and his denial.

Assessment for Treatment Planning

In the adolescent sex offender treatment program at the University of Tennessee at Memphis, we have developed an assessment battery that attempts to address areas proposed to be relevant to the adolescent sex offender, both in terms of general treatment needs and sex-offender-specific needs. The battery is geared toward assessing areas thought to be in need of intervention and is geared to developing a baseline assessment that can be repeated throughout treatment. The standardized battery also was designed, where possible, to use instruments that can also be applied to adults so that these two groups can be contrasted. The standardized battery provides an ongoing data set for research. Areas assessed and methods used to assess each area are included in Table 13.2. Similar areas for assessment have been outlined by others (Becker & Abel, 1985; Bengis, 1986; Monastersky & Smith, 1985; National Adolescent Perpetrator Network, 1988). There is some clinical agree-

TABLE 13.2
Assessment of The Adolescent Offender

Area	Method
Social history	Clinical interview[1]
Sexual history (deviant and nondeviant, including attitudes and knowledge)	Clinical interview
	Multiphasic Sex Inventory[2]
	Burt Scales, [2,3]
Drug abuse	Clinical interview
Psychopathology/personality	Clinical interview
	MMPI
	Millon Adolescent Personality Inventory
Intelligence	Standard IQ test
Denial	Clinical interview
	Multiphasic Sex Inventory
Empathy	Clinical interview
Risk factors/Sexual abuse cycle/Cognitive distortions	Clinical interview
	Clinical interview
	Multiphasic Sex Inventory
Social competence	Clinical interview
	Adolescent Problems Inventory
	Interpersonal Behavior Survey
Family functioning	Clinical interview
	FACES
Sexual arousal pattern	Clinical interview
	Multiphasic Sex Inventory
	Psychophysiological assessment of sexual arousal

[1]Clinical interview refers to information gained through interview with the offender, his family, and all other collateral information collected.
[2]Considered experimental in the adolescent population.
[3]A series of attitudinal scales developed by Martha Burt (1980), which include Rape Myth Acceptance, Sex Role Stereotyping, Sexual Conservatism, Adversarial Sexual Beliefs, and Acceptance of Violence (mainly against women).

ment on what needs to be assessed in adolescents, although less agreement on which specific instruments to use (National Adolescent Perpetrator Network, 1988).

The social and sexual histories collected need to be quite detailed. Social and family histories in adolescent offenders are in general no different from that usually collected in a clinical situation with adolescents except a more detailed exploration of history of sexual abuse in the offender's immediate and extended family should be conducted (Monastersky & Smith, 1985). As with any good adolescent social history, one needs to assess clearly: (1) complications during pregnancy and birth, (2) developmental issues including reaching developmental milestones, (3) peer and sibling relationships, (4) school performance, (5) family relationships, (6) drug and alcohol abuse, (7) general impulsivity, (8) adolescent self-esteem, (9) social skills, (10) past medical and psychiatric treatment, and (11) past delinquent behavior.

The sexual history needs to explore (1) where the offender learned about sex, (2) normal sexual experiences, (3) denial concerning the current offense, (4) histories of sexual abuse, (5) questions regarding deviant or paraphilic sexual experiences (with specific questions asked about all possible paraphilias), (6) masturbatory history, (7) types of fantasies used during masturbation as a sign of deviant arousal patterns, (8) attitudes toward sexuality, (9) empathy toward victims, and (10) remorse or guilt regarding the offense. Very detailed questions need to be asked about each of the deviant behaviors, including frequency, duration, aggression used, the offender's feelings preceding and after the abuse, and questions regarding the types of distortions used to justify the behavior (Monastersky & Smith, 1985). From the interview, the clinician is attempting to determine normal sexual experiences, the extent and compulsiveness of the abusive behavior, the justifications used, degree of empathy and guilt, and factors that may place the offender at increased risk to abuse, such as anger, rejection, boredom, being around small children, and so on.

It should be recognized that in most instances this information will not be collected in one interview and often much of the information will not be revealed until after a trusting relationship is established. Offenders and their families will present during initial evaluation in a variety of ways, which can range from being resentful, hostile and angry, to being frightened and confused, to occasionally being open and honest. Families' presentation may dictate the interview style from being rather firm, setting clear limits for the hostile, resistant family, to being supportive of the family feeling overwhelmed by what is happening. The interviewer needs to be fairly comfortable in eliciting sexual information, especially since it may involve rather unusual or violent behaviors.

General screening of personality functioning, psychopathology, and intellectual functioning is recommended because of its possible importance in treatment, not because adolescent offenders will show some specific type of pathology or some specific intellectual deficit. Clinically, if adolescents are psychotic, severely depressed, extremely manipulative, or narcissistic, they may need specific treatments and the adolescent's general personality style may dictate needs for more treatment structure. Adolescents who are intellectually deficient or have significant learning disabilities may require more concrete interventions and many of the homework assignments used in treatment programs may not be appropriate.

Similarly, assessment of social competence and family functioning, although not necessarily deficits in all offenders, need to be addressed similarly to most adolescent populations. The Interpersonal Behavior Survey (Mauger & Adkinson, 1980) has the advantage of assessing a wide variety of social skills under the general heading of assertiveness skills, aggression, and relationship variables, with each of these being assessed by a number of subtests. The Adolescent Problems Inventory (Freedman, Rosenthal, Donahoe, Schlundt, & McFall, 1978), on the other hand, requires adolescents to give verbal responses to a number of problem situations, which allows more direct behavioral assessment in a role-playing situation.

Instruments such as the Burt scales (Burt, 1980), the Multiphasic Sex Inventory (Nichols & Molinder, 1984), and psychophysiological assessment of sexual arousal, although used frequently with adults, are considered experimental at this time in adolescent populations. The Burt scales allow assessment of the offenders' attitudes toward women and violence and such factors have shown a relationship to coercive sexual behavior in other populations (Murphy et al., 1986). The Multiphasic Sex Inventory measures a number of variables thought to be relevant to sexual offenses. These include scales tapping sexual knowledge, normal sexual interests and drives, sexual obsessions, specific paraphilic scales, specific questions regarding a variety of sexual dysfunctions, scales measuring distortions, justifications, and motivation for sex offender treatment.

The psychophysiological assessment of sexual arousal may be somewhat controversial in the adolescent population, but our clinical experience with approximately 150 adolescent offenders suggested that it is well tolerated and can provide valuable information for treatment planning. In our program, the general assessment involves three components: (1) Measuring responses to slides depicting males and females between the ages of 5 and 35; (2) Measuring responses to audiotapes that describe sexual relations with children which vary in level of aggression (Abel, Becker, Murphy, & Flanagan, 1981); and (3) audiotapes describing either nonsexual aggression, sexual aggression or mutual sexual interactions with adults (Abel, Blanchard, Becker, & Djenderedjian, 1978). Our clinical experience has been that some adolescent offenders show no response to such material at probably about the same percentage as adult offenders seen in our program. In such cases, it is probably impossible to interpret the data in adolescents, since no response may only reflect suppression. Some (although not as frequently as supposed) seem to respond rather indiscriminately to any material presented. Indiscriminant responding may represent generalized sexual arousal rather than specific sexual deviant arousal. In general, the data are not interpreted unless there is some clear discrimination between categories. Among adolescents who molest children (the majority of our population) some do seem to show deviant sexual attraction to children similar to seen in adult child molesters. In addition, it appears clinically that more of the adolescents display responding to aggressive material than do our adult child molesters. However, the adolescents seen in our program (which includes an inpatient component) tend to have fairly extensive nonsexual, delinquent and aggressive histories, which is not true of our adult population who are all outpatients.

The major purpose of this assessment approach is treatment planning and evaluation of effectiveness. For example, offenders who show a set deviant arousal pattern would receive behavioral treatment to reduce arousal and arousal would be periodically evaluated throughout treatment. Similarly, those showing family dysfunction would receive specific family therapy and/or parent training and assessment will be repeated to determine the effectiveness of such treatment. The preceding standardized assessment approach also has the advantage of providing a consistent data set for each offender, therefore facilitating clinical research.

CLINICAL APPROACHES TO TREATMENT

As noted earlier, there has been an explosion of treatment programs for adolescent sex offenders in the past 10 years. It will be impossible to review all such programs, so we will briefly give appropriate references to a variety of treatment programs, and from this try to distill what seem to be overall treatment strategies in such programs and give what appear to be the core elements that are specific to sex offender treatment programs. Finally, we will review in slightly more detail the implementation of these components in our own program at the University of Tennessee. It should again be clearly recognized that to date none of these approaches has been adequately validated in the adolescent sexual offender population and at this point are based almost solely on clinical experiences.

Treatment of the adolescent offender is complex and involves the cooperation of multiple agencies and may involve multiple treatment components. A variety of treatment programs have been described

(Becker & Abel, 1985; Breer, 1987; Groth, Hobson, Lucey, & St. Pierre, 1981; Heinz, Gargaro, & Kelly, 1987; Lane & Zamora, 1984; Loss & Ross, 1984; Margolin, 1983, 1984; Monastersky & Smith, 1985: Seabloom, 1981; Smets & Cebula, 1987). Details of nine various programs have been provided by Knopp (1982) and recommendations for components have been made by the National Adolescent Perpetrator Network, Offenders (1988). Even though there are a variety of treatment programs, operating with a number of theoretical orientations, they seem to share certain underlying philosophical beliefs (Knopp, 1982; Loss & Ross, 1984; National Adolescent Perpetrator Network, 1988) that can be summarized in part as follows:

1. Traditional mental health interventions have not been effective with this population and treatment needs to be specific to the sexual offending behavior.
2. Sexual offenses are a crime and the offender should be held legally accountable for his behavior.
3. Sex offender treatment requires the cooperation and coordination between various agencies such as mental health professionals, child protective services, and the juvenile court.
4. Groups specifically for sex offenders are the most appropriate treatment modality.
5. The primary reason for treating the sex offender is to reduce victimization, therefore ensuring the safety of the community is the primary concern of the treatment provider.
6. Sex offenders cannot be "cured," sex offenses are a lifelong problem, and the purpose of treatment is to provide the adolescent with skills for controlling this behavior. This is not to imply that sex offending is an addiction, but that, given current knowledge, we assume that it is a chronic disorder that will require lifelong coping.

These general issues have led to certain differences in the therapeutic relationship maintained in sex offender programs versus the general clinical situation. Because treatment is thought to involve the coordination of a variety of agencies and protection of society is a primary concern, many programs require complete waiver of all confidentiality. This is thought necessary so that not only can reoffenses be reported but patterns of behaviors that are thought to be antecedents to reoffending can be shared with other agencies to prevent offenses from recurring. Many programs also feel strongly that offenders should be court-ordered for treatment and that all sexual offenders whose behavior is criminal should be adjudicated (Loss & Ross, 1984). Also, as implied, most programs use group as the primary treatment modality with some feeling that this is the only appropriate modality (National Adolescent Perpetrator Network, 1988). Since most programs adopt a "no cure" philosophy, most use, formally or informally, some variant of the relapse prevention model (Pithers, Marques, Gibat, & Marlatt, 1983). Also, because of what is seen as the chronic nature of these problems, there have been strong recommendations that states and/or communities develop continua of care (Bengis, 1986) that operate under the same treatment philosophy and that aftercare and strict probation monitoring be included as part of treatment.

Although programs vary from being very narrowly focused (Smets & Cebula, 1987) to being very comprehensive in services delivered (Heinz et al., 1987), there seem to be issues that are considered sex-offender-specific that are addressed in most programs. These are summarized in Table 13.3.

However, most programs also address general issues with family dysfunction being a major component. In addition, programs addressing the issues listed in Table 13.3 also focus on drug and alcohol abuse, the adolescent's self-esteem, depression and anxiety, and/or academic deficits. Family approaches with the adolescent can at times be different from family therapy in a typical mental health facility since the family is often mandated into treatment, may be denying that an offense has occurred, and can be fairly resistant to the offender being held accountable for his behavior. Also, in many instances there are extensive histories of sexual abuse throughout the immediate and extended family and the victim of is often a family member, creating complicated dynamics within the family (see Monastersky & Smith, 1985), for more details of family-based treatment).

In an attempt to present slightly more detail on how the issues in Table 13.3 are addressed within a treatment program, a somewhat more detailed description of the program at the University of Tennessee at Memphis will be provided. Other detailed program descriptions can be found in Knopp (1982), O'Brien (1985), and Heinz et al. (1987).

TABLE 13.3
Treatment Issues

Denial
Cognitive distortions, victim empathy
Victimization issues
Antecedents, risk factors, sexual abuse cycle
Increasing social competency/coping skills
Sex education (attitudes toward sexuality)
Reducing deviant arousal

The sex offender program at the University of Tennessee at Memphis operates outpatient and inpatient programs through a private psychiatric hospital (Midsouth Hospital of Memphis). In the outpatient program, offenders are seen for 1.5 hours in group sessions held each week and once a month are seen in a group with families. When appropriate, offenders are seen in individual and family therapy, and specific behavioral treatments, such as techniques designed to reduce deviant arousal, are employed when appropriate. In the inpatient program, which is more highly structured, offenders participate daily in a sex-offender-specific group. They also are seen in individial therapy at least five times every 2 weeks, and family therapy once every 2 weeks, and in a parent-support group weekly. Where deviant arousal is present, offenders also receive specific behavioral intervention approximately three times a week. The program is also in the process of adding a series of structured skills training modules in areas such as social skills, assertiveness training, anger management skills, and sex education.

In both programs, patients are expected to continue the treatment outside the therapy situation and the program makes use of extensive homework assignments. Patients complete daily self-monitoring records, which require them to record positive and negative events, record the risk factors that they have experienced during the day, record all sexual fantasies, and specify progress on treatment goals. In addition, all patients have an extensive treatment contract, which outlines areas they must address for treatment to be considered complete. These include such factors as detailing all of their sexual behavior both deviant and nondeviant, all of their aggressive and delinquent behaviors, all the violence they have seen within their families, their risk factors, their cognitive distortions, specifying how they would deal with these in the future. They are required to complete each component of the contract in writing and present it to the group.

The treatment techniques used to address each of the areas listed in Table 13.3 vary. Many of the techniques, especially those that address issues such as anger management, skills training, and sex education can be easily adapted from similar programs for adolescents not involved in sexual offenses. The major difference is that in each instance the skills being taught are discussed in terms of their sex offense pattern. That is, when one is dealing with anger management skills, these skills are presented in the context of the adolescent's risk factors and as a method of "breaking" the chain of behaviors that might lead to reoffending. Other issues to be described below are somewhat more specific to sex offender programs.

Offender denial seems best dealt with in group meetings. When new offenders are introduced, group members introduce themselves, giving details of their sexual offense, which sets a clear expectation to the new offender that honesty is expected. Confrontation from peers seems to be a much more effective technique than confrontation from therapists. In addition, the offender can be confronted with police reports, victims' statements, and at times with the results of their psychophysiological assessment to encourage more honest reporting (Abel, Cunningham-Rathner, Becker, & McHugh, 1983).

In our program, we tend to address victim empathy issues in the context of cognitive distortions. We have proposed elsewhere (Murphy, 1990) that the offender's use of distortions, minimizations, and justifications is the major means they use to block empathy. Distortions are confronted continuously in group and occur frequently when the offender is asked to describe in detail their sexual offense. Many offenders will describe very young victims as seducing them and use phrases such as "I just fondled" or "I only did it once." The group is taught to recognize such distortions and cognitive restructuring techniques are used to help the offender change their thinking pattern. In addition, most programs use a variety of victim education material, including readings and films, to educate the offenders about the true impact of sexual victimization.

Addressing the offender's own victimization at times also increases victim empathy as the offenders begin to recall their own feelings when they were abused. For the adolescent male who has been abused by a male, issues around homosexual orientation many times arise. In many instances, the adolescent offender, when sexually victimized, responded with an erection, only further increasing his confusion and increasing self-blame. Generally such confusion is approached by attempting to educate the offender regarding the differences between physiological arousal and psychological arousal. Also, other group members sharing similar experiences tend to make the adolescent feel less isolated and less abnormal.

Most programs, including our own, spend a good deal of time addressing risk factors (Pithers et al., 1983), or in some programs, the sexual abuse cycle (Ryan et al., 1987). In general, these both refer to the chain of behaviors, emotions, and cognitions that seem to precede the actual sexually abusive act. We usually begin approaching this issue by asking the offender to "walk through" one of their sexual abuse incidents. They are asked to describe in detail what was happening during the week of the abuse, on the day of the abuse, and the hour preceding the abuse. They are asked to describe specific behaviors they were engaging in, feelings prior to, during and after the abuse, and what they were thinking prior to, during and after the abuse. In addition, they are asked to describe family and sibling relationships, school functioning, peer relationships, and drug usage during the time when the abuse was occurring. As the offender "mentally walks through" their abuse, the patient, therapist, and other group members begin to identify possible factors that increase the offender's chance of acting out. As this list is refined, treatment then progresses to the offender proposing methods of interrupting the chain, proposing alternative behaviors they could engage in, and to begin developing new skills for dealing with factors such as anger, depression, and rejection, that might be related to their sexual abuse cycle.

Although behavioral procedures to reduce deviant sexual arousal are applied frequently to adult offenders (Laws & Osborn, 1983), these have been applied less often, or at least described less often, with adolescent populations. Within our program, we commonly use self-administered covert sensitization and verbal satiation (Laws & Osborn, 1983) for offenders who show deviant arousal patterns. Figure 13.1 represents changes in the erection response of an adolescent child molester during the course of verbal satiation. This procedure requires the offender to verbalize into a tape recorder for 30 minutes his deviant sexual fantasies and deviant sexual behavior. Figure 13.1 depicts the actual erection responses during the adolescent's verbalizations blocked into trials of four sessions. As one can see, there was a reduction in arousal to these fantasies. Although procedures such as electrical aversion can probably not be used with adolescent offenders, more cognitive procedures such as covert sensitization and verbal satiation seem highly appropriate for this population, and adolescents are probably no more resistant to these procedures than are adult offenders.

The foregoing comments may sound as if the treatment of adolescent sexual offenders is like driving a European racing car across a flat, dry road on a spring day. To the contrary, treating the adolescent offender is many times more like driving a subcompact with poor tires through icy, curving mountain roads. That is, treatment does not proceed in a straight line; there are hills and valleys. The adolescent offender and his family are many times resistant and hostile, and the offender himself has many times experienced significant pain and abandonment in his own life. Clinical treatment of the adolescent offender requires more than the application of a few techniques. Perseverance and creativity of the clinician in adapting specific techniques for specific offenders is still needed.

Recidivism

The question most often asked, and the one for which there is little data, is "does it work?" Data have been presented suggesting a fairly high rate of offending during adolescence among adult offenders, and that most adolescents when apprehended the first time have committed other

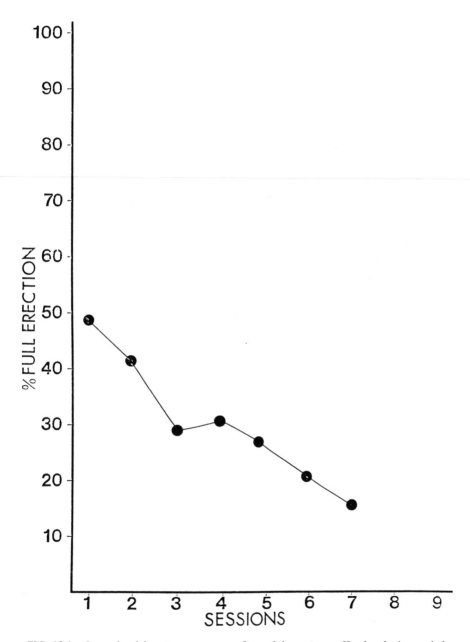

FIG. 13.1.   In-session laboratory measures of an adolescent sex offender during verbal satiation. Treatment blocked in four session trials.

sexual offenses. However, this does not give us any notion of reoffense rates among adolescents once they are identified as an offender.

Early data by Doshay (1943) present a fairly favorable picture for outcome in this group. Doshay's follow-up was a minimum of 6 years and was based on a fairly extensive review of a variety of official records. Of the primary group (that is, the group with no other delinquent behavior) only 2 of 108 reoffended as adolescents and none as adults reoffended sexually. Of the mixed group (148), 14 reoffended sexually during adolescence and 10 during adulthood. However, rates for non-sexual offenses were fairly high in the mixed group. Similarly, Smith and Monastersky (1986), in a follow-up of 112 juvenile offenders, many of whom have been treated although the type of treatment was not specified, found reoffense rates of 34.8% for nonsexual reoffending and 14.3% for sexual reoffending. Specific treatment programs have also presented recidivism data from patients they have been able to follow. Heinz et al. (1987) reported a reoffense rate of 7.1% in 21 juvenile in their program who were from Hennepin County where they could be followed closely. Smets and Cebula (1987) reported one reoffense in 21 boys who were in their program in the first 3 years of operation, although apparently only 7 had actually completed treatment and the length they were followed was not specified. Lane and Zamora (1984) report 2 offenses out of 16 very serious offenders released from their program. Follow-up time was apparently one year or less.

Overall, these very limited data do not suggest a high level of sexual reoffending in adolescent offenders, at least when arrest records are used. The true recidivism rate is probably much higher than this, since official data generally underpredict actual reoffense rates. It also appears that there is a relatively high rate of nonsexual offending, although these rates do not seem higher than one would expect in a general delinquent population and may in fact be somewhat lower. However, the data are difficult to interpret, given that there are no comparisons with offenders who have been identified but untreated, although subjects in the Doshay study seemed to have received little treatment. The treatment appeared to be mainly the induction of guilt by the court process. Treatment outcome studies with the adolescent offender (also with the adult offender) have been extremely difficult to accomplish. Because of the nature of the problem, it has been extremely difficult to have no treatment control groups. Also, the major outcome variable of interest, reoffense rates, is extremely difficult to collect. However, without adequate outcome studies, it is at times very difficult to justify to legislators and insurance companies who pay for treatment why such treatment should be required. Outcome studies in this area probably will have to be creative, using quasi-experimental designs rather than traditional group outcome studies. Studies that look at naturally occurring groups who do and do not receive treatment, although flawed for a number of reasons, may be one of the more viable approaches in the initial stages of outcome research in this area. For an excellent review of the problem in this area, the reader is referred to Furby, Weinrott, and Blackshaw (1989).

CONCLUSIONS

Within this chapter, we have attempted to summarize the current knowledge regarding adolescent sex offenders and their offenses, and attempted to review how such information has been translated into clinical practice. At the current time, our data base for this population is rather limited. It appears that it is time to move beyond the descriptive data that predominate in the literature and to begin testing with better validated instruments, the hypotheses that have been generated from the descriptive literature. It seems clear that the adolescent offender is responsible for a large number of sex offenses in our society and only through the adequate understanding of this population can effective treatment strategies be developed to prevent continued sexual abuse. Also, the study of the adolescent sex offender may provide a significant amount of information on the development of sex-offending patterns, which may in the long run assist in developing primary prevention programs.

ACKNOWLEDGMENT

Preparation of this chapter was supported in part by the Department of Mental Health/Mental Retardation Research Contract ID–89–3242B to the Department of Psychiatry. The authors wish to thank The MidSouth Hospital for continued support of our program and express appreciation to Donna Townsend for secretarial assistance.

REFERENCES

Abel, G. G., Becker, J. V., Cunningham-Rathner, J., Rouleau, J., Kaplan, M., Reich, J. (1984). *The treatment of child molesters: A manual.* (Available from G. G. Abel, Emory University, Atlanta).
Abel, G. G., Becker, J. V., Murphy, W. D., & Flanagan, B. (1981). Identifying dangerous child molesters. In R. B. Stuart (Ed.), *Violent behavior: Special*

learning approaches to prediction, management, and treatment (pp. 116–137). New York: Brunner/Mazel.

Abel, G. G., Blanchard, E. B., Becker, J. V., & Djenderedjian, A. (1978). Differentiating sexual aggressives with penile measures. *Criminal Justice and Behavior, 5*, 315–332.

Abel, G. G., Cunningham-Rather, J., Becker, J. V., & McHugh, J. (1983, December). *Motivating sex offenders for treatment with feedback of their psychophysiologic assessment*. Paper presented at the World Congress of Behavior Therapy, Washington.

Ageton, S. S. (1983). *Sexual assault among adolescents*. Lexington, MA: Lexington Books.

Atcheson, J. D., & Williams, D. C. (1954). A study of juvenile sex offenders. *American Journal of Psychiatry, 11*, 366–370.

Becker, J. V., & Abel, G. G. (1985). Methodological and ethical issues in evaluating and treating adolescent sexual offenders. In E. M. Otey & G. D. Ryan (Eds.), *Adolescent sex offenders: Issues in research and treatment* (DHHS Pub. No. ADM–85–1396, pp. 109–129). Rockville, MD: U. S. Department of Health and Human Services.

Becker, J. V., Cunningham-Rathner, J., & Kaplan, M. S. (1986). Adolescent sexual offenders: Demographics, criminal and sexual histories, and recommendations for reducing future offenders. Special Issue: The prediction and control of violent behavior: II. *Journal of Interpersonal Violence, 1*, 431–445.

Becker, J. V., Kaplan, M. S., Cunningham-Rathner, J., & Kavoussi, R. (1986). Characteristics of adolescent incest sexual perpetrators: Preliminary findings. *Journal of Family Violence, 1*, 85–97.

Becker, J. V., Stein, R., Kaplan, M., & Cunningham-Rathner, J. (1988, November). *Follow-up study of adolescent sex offenders seen at an outpatient treatment clinic*. Paper presented at the 22nd annual convention of the Association for the Advancement of Behavior Therapy, New York.

Bengis, S. M. (1986). *A comparative service-delivery system with a continuum of care for adolescent sexual offenders*. Syracuse, NY: Safer Society.

Berlin, F. S. (1983). Sex offenders: A biomedical perspective and a status report on biomedical treatment. In J. G. Greer & I. R. Stuart (Eds.), *The sexual aggressor: Current perspectives on treatment* (pp. 83–123). New York: Van Nostrand Reinhold.

Blaske, D. M., Borduin, C. M., Henggeler, S. W., & Mann, B. J. (in press). Individual, family, and peer characteristics of adolescent violent offenders and sexual offenders. *Developmental Psychology*.

Brecher, E. M. (1978). *Treatment programs for sex offenders*. Washington, DC: National Institute of Law Enforcement and Criminal Justice.

Breer, W. (1987). *The adolescent molester*. Springfield, IL: Charles C. Thomas.

Brown, E. J., Flanagan, T. J., & McLeod, M. (Eds.). (1984). *Sourcebook of criminal justice statistics—1983*. Washington, DC: Bureau of Justice Statistics.

Burt, M. R. (1980). Cultural myths and supports for rape. *Journal of Personality and Social Psychology, 38*, 217–230.

Davis, G. E., & Leitenberg, H. (1987). Adolescent sex offenders. *Psychological Bulletin, 101*, 417–427.

Deisher, R. W., Wenet, G. A., Paperny, D. M., Clark, T. F., & Fehrenbach, P. A. (1982). Adolescent sexual offense behavior: The role of the physician. *Journal of Adolescent Health Care, 2,* 279–286.

Doshay, L. J. (1943). *The boy sex offender and his later career.* Montclair, NJ: Patterson Smith.

Fehrenbach, P. A., Smith, W., Monastersky, C., & Deisher, R. W. (1986). Adolescent sexual offenders: Offender and offense characteristics. *American Journal of Orthopsychiatry, 56,* 225–233.

Finkelhor, D. (1979). What's wrong with sex between adults and children? *American Journal of Orthopsychiatry, 49,* 692–697.

Finkelhor, D. (Ed.). (1986). *A sourcebook on child sexual abuse.* Beverly Hills, CA: Sage.

Freedman, B. J., Rosenthal, L., Donahoe, C. P., Jr., Schlundt, D. G., & McFall, R. M. (1978). A social–behavioral analysis of skill deficits in delinquent and nondelinquent adolescent boys. *Journal of Consulting and Clinical Psychology, 46,* 1448–1462.

Furby, L., Weinrott, M. R., & Blackshaw, L. (1989). Sex offender recidivism: A review. *Psychological Bulletin, 105,* 3–30.

Gomes-Schwartz, B. (1984). Juvenile sexual offenders. In *Sexually exploited children: Service and research project.* Washington, DC: U. S. Department of Justice.

Groth, A. N. (1977). The adolescent sexual offender and his prey. *Journal of Offender Therapy and Comparative Criminology, 21,* 249–254.

Groth, A. N., Hobson, W. F., Lucey, K. P., & St. Pierre, J. (1981). Juvenile sexual offender: Guidelines for treatment. *International Journal of Offender Therapy and Comparative Criminology, 25,* 265–275.

Groth, A. N., Longo, R. E., & McFadin, J. B. (1982). Undetected recidivis among rapists and child molesters. *Crime and Delinquency, 28,* 450–458.

Groth, A. N., & Loredo, C. M. (1981). Juvenile sexual offenders: Guidelines for assessment. *International Journal of Offender Therapy and Comparative Criminology, 25,* 31–39.

Heinz, J. W., Gargaro, S., & Kelly, K. G. (1987). *A motel residential juvenile sex-offender treatment program: The Hennepin County Home School.* Syracuse, NY: Safer Society.

Kavoussi, R. J., Kaplan, M., & Becker, J. V. (1988). Psychiatric diagnoses in adolescent sex offenders. *Journal of the American Academy of Child and Adolescent Psychiatry, 27,* 241–243.

Knopp, F. H. (1982). *Remedial intervention in adolescent sex offenses: Nine program descriptions.* Syracuse, NY: Safer Society.

Knopp, F. H. (1985). Recent developments in the treatment of adolescent sex offenders. In E. M. Otey & G. D. Ryan (Eds.), *Adolescent sex offenders: Issues in research and treatment* (DHHS Pub. No. ADM-85–1396, pp. 1–108). Rockville, MD: U. S. Department of Health and Human Services.

Knopp, F. H. (1986, February). *Preliminary report on 1985 nationwide survey of U. S. juvenile and adult sex-offender treatment programs and providers.* Paper presented at the National Institute of Mental Health Meeting on the Assessment and Treatment of Sex Offenders, Tampa, FL.

Koss, M. P., & Dinero, T. E. (1989). Discriminant analysis of risk factors for sexual victimization among a national sample of college women. *Journal of Consulting and Clinical Psychology, 57,* 242–250.

Lane, S., & Zamora, P. (1984). A method for treating the adolescent sex offender. In R. A. Mathias, P. DeMuro, & R. S. Allinson (Eds.), *Violent juvenile offenders: An anthology* (pp. 347–363). San Francisco: National Council on Crime and Delinquency.

Langevin, R. (1983). *Sexual strands: Understanding and treating sexual anomalies in men.* Hillsdale, NJ: Lawrence Erlbaum Associates.

Langevin, R., Hucker, S., Wortzman, G., Bain, J., Handy, L., Chambers, J., & Wright, S. (in press). Neuropsychological impairment in pedophiles. *Canadian Journal of Behavioral Science.*

Laws, D. R., & Marshall, W. L. (1990). A conditioning theory of the etiology and maintenance of deviant sexual preference and behavior. In W. L. Marshall, D. R. Laws, & H. E. Barbaree (Eds.), *Handbook of sexual assault: Issues, theories and treatment of the offender* (pp. 209–229). New York: Plenum.

Laws, D. R., & Osborn, C. A. (1983). How to build and operate a behavioral laboratory to evaluate and treat sexual deviance. In J. G. Greer & I. R. Stuart (Eds.), *The sexual aggressor: Current perspectives on treatment* (pp. 293–335). New York: Van Nostrand Reinhold.

Levin, S. M., & Stava, L. (1987). Personality characteristics of sex offenders: A review. *Archives of Sexual Behavior, 16,* 57–79.

Lewis, D. O., Shanok, S. S., & Balla, D. A. (1981). Parents of delinquents. In D. O. Lewis (Ed.), *Vulnerabilities to delinquency* (pp. 265–292). Jamaica, NY: Spectrum.

Lewis, D. O., Shanok, S. S., & Pincus, J. H. (1981). Juvenile male sexual assaulters: Psychiatric, neurological, psychoeducational, and abuse factors. In D. O. Lewis (Ed.), *Vulnerabilities to delinquency* (pp. 89–105). Jamaica, NY: Spectrum.

Longo, R. E. (1982). Sexual learning and experience among adolescent sexual offenders. *International Journal of Offender Therapy and Comparative Criminology, 26,* 235–241.

Longo, R. E., & Groth, A. N. (1983). Juvenile sex offenses in the histories of adult rapists and child molesters. *International Journal of Offender Therapy and Comparative Criminology, 27,* 150–155.

Longo, R. E., & McFadin, B. (1981, December). Sexually inappropriate behavior: Development of the sexual offender. *Law and Order,* pp. 21–23.

Loss, P., & Ross, J. E. (1984, August). *Accountability in sex offender treatment.* Paper presented at the ninth annual National Conference of the American Probation and Parole Association, and the 45th annual New England Conference on Crime and Delinquency, Boston.

Maclay, D. T. (1960). Boys who commit sexual misdemeanors. *British Medical Journal, 11,* 186–190.

Margolin, L. (1983). A treatment model for the adolescent sex offender. *Journal of Offender Counseling, Services and Rehabilitation, 8,* 1–12.

Margolin, L. (1984). Group therapy as a means of learning about the sexually assaultive adolescent. *International Journal of Offender Therapy and Comparative Criminology, 28,* 65–72.

Markey, O. B. (1950). A study of aggressive sex misbehavior in adolescents brought to Juvenile Court. *American Journal of Orthopsychiatry, 20,* 719–731.

Mauger, P. A., & Adkinson, D. R. (1980). *Interpersonal Behavior Survey (IBS) Manual.* Los Angeles: Western Psychological Services.

McCord, W., McCord, J., & Verden, P. (1962). Family relationships and sexual deviance in lower-class adolescents. *International Journal of Social Psychiatry, 8,* 165–179.

Mio, J. S., Nanjundappa, G., Verleur, D. E., & de Rios, M. D. (1986). Drug abuse and the adolescent sex offender: A preliminary analysis. Special Issue: Drug dependency and the family. *Journal of Psychoactive Drugs, 18,* 65–72.

Monastersky, C., & Smith, W. (1985). Juvenile sexual offenders: A family systems paradigm. In E. M. Otey & G. D. Ryan (Eds.), *Adolescent sex offenders: Issues in research and treatment* (DHHS Pub. No. ADM–85–1396, pp. 164–183). Rockville, MD: U. S. Department of Health and Human Services.

Murphy, W. D. (1990). Assessment and modification of cognitive distortions in sex offenders. In W. L. Marshall, D. R. Laws, & H. E. Barbaree (Eds.), *Handbook of sexual assault: Issues, theories, and treatment of the offender* (pp. 331–342). New York: Plenum Press.

Murphy, W. D., Coleman, E. M., & Haynes, M. R. (1986). Factors related to coercive sexual behavior in a nonclinical sample of males. *Violence and Victims, 1,* 255–278.

Murphy, W. D., Haynes, M. R., & Stalgaitis, S. J. (1985, November). *Penile tumescence assessment with the adolescent sexual offender against children: Type of stimulus, instructional set and delinquent histories.* Paper presented at the 19th annual convention of the Association for the Advancement of Behavior Therapy, Houston.

Murphy, W. D., Haynes, M. R., & Worley, P. J. (1991). Assessment of adult sexual interest. In C. Hollin & K. Howells (Eds.), *Clinical approaches to sex offenders and their victims* (pp. 77–92). Sussex, England: Wiley.

Murphy, W. D., & Schwarz, E. D. (1990). The major psychiatric disorder of adults: Paraphilias. In A. Stoudemire (Ed.), *Clinical psychiatry for medical students* (pp. 365–379). Philadelphia: J. B. Lippincott.

Murphy, W. D., & Stalgaitis, S. J. (1987). Assessment and treatment considerations for sexual offenders against children: Behavioral and social learning approaches. In J. R. McNamara & M. A. Appel (Eds.), *Critical issues, developments, and trends in professional psychology* (Vol. 3, pp. 177–210). New York: Praeger.

National Adolescent Perpetrator Network. (1988). Preliminary Report from the National Task Force and Juvenile Sexual Offending. *Juvenile and Family Court Journal, 39,* 5–67.

Nichols, H. R., & Molinder, L. (1984). *Multiphasic Sex Inventory.* Tacoma, WA: Authors.

O'Brien, M. (1985). Adolescent sexual offenders: An outpatient program's perspective on research directions. In E. M. Otey & G. D. Ryan (Eds.), *Adolescent sex offenders: Issues in research and treatment* (DHHS Pub. No. ADM–85–1396, pp. 147–163). Rockville, MD: U. S. Department of Health and Human Services.

Pithers, W. D., Marques, J. K., Gibat, C. C., & Marlatt, G. A. (1983). Relapse prevention with sexual aggressives: As self-control model of treatment and maintenance of change. In J. G. Greer & I. R. Stuart (Eds.), *The sexual aggressor: Current perspectives on treatment* (pp. 214–239). New York: Van Nostrand Reinhold.

Qualls, R. C., Stein, R. A., & Murphy, W. D. (1989, February). *The family dynamics of adolescent sexual offenders.* Paper presented at the annual convention of the Tennessee Association of Marriage and Family Therapists, Memphis.

Ryan, G., Lane, S., Davis, J., & Isaac, C. (1987). Juvenile sex offenders: Development and correlation. Special Issue: Child abuse and neglect. *Child Abuse and Neglect, 11,* 385–395.

Saunders, E., Awad, G. A., & White, G. (1986). Male adolescent sexual offenders: The offender and the offense. Special Issue: Canadian Academy of Child Psychiatry: A Canadian perspective. *Canadian Journal of Psychiatry, 31,* 542–549.

Seabloom, W. L. (1980, June). *Enrichment experiences and family issues in the treatment of sexually disoriented adolescent males.* Paper presented at the International Symposium on Family Sexuality, Minneapolis.

Seabloom, W. L. (1981, June). *Beyond pathology: The economy of early intervention and enrichment treatment modalities for adolescent sexual behavior disorders.* Paper presented at the fifth World Congress of Sexology, Jerusalem.

Segal, Z. V., & Marshall, W. L. (1985). Heterosexual social skills in a population of rapists and child molesters. *Journal of Consulting and Clinical Psychology, 53,* 55–63.

Shoor, M., Speed, M. H., & Bertelt, C. (1966). Syndrome of the adolescent child molester. *American Journal of Psychiatry, 122,* 783–789.

Smets, A. C., & Cebula, C. M. (1987). A group treatment program for adolescent sex offenders: Five steps toward resolution. *Child Abuse and Neglect, 11,* 247–254.

Smith, W. R., & Monastersky, C. (1986). Assessing juvenile sexual offenders' risk for reoffending. *Criminal Justice and Behavior, 13,* 115–140.

Smith, W. R., Monastersky, C., & Deisher, R. M. (1987). MMPI-based personality types among juvenile sexual offenders. *Journal of Clinical Psychology, 43,* 422–430.

State of California Department of Youth Authority. (1986). *Sex offender task force report, January 1986.* Sacramento, CA: Author.

Stermac, L. E., & Quinsey, V. L. (1986). Social competence among rapists. *Behavioral Assessment, 8,* 171–185.

Tarter, R. E., Hegedus, A. M., Alterman, A. I., & Katz-Garris, L. (1983). Cognitive capacities of juvenile, violent, nonviolent, and sexual offenders. *Journal of Nervous and Mental Disease, 171,* 564–567.

Thomas, J. N. (1982). Juvenile sex offender: Physician and parent communication. *Pediatric Annals, 11,* 807–812.

U. S. Department of Justice, Federal Bureau of Investigation. (1977–1980). *Uniform Crime Reports.* Washington, DC: U. S. Government Printing Office.

Van Ness, S. R. (1984). Rape as instrumental violence: A study of youth offenders. *Journal of Offender Counseling, Services, and Rehabilitation, 9,* 161–170.
Wasserman, J., & Kappel, S. (1985). *Adolescent sex offenders in Vermont.* Burlington: Vermont Department of Health.
Weithorn, L. A. (1988). Mental hospitalization of troublesome youth: An analysis of skyrocketing admission rates. *Stanford Law Review, 40,* 773–838.

14

The Child Sexual Abuse Victim as an Adult

Julie A. Lipovsky
Dean G. Kilpatrick
Crime Victims Research and Treatment Center, Department of Psychiatry and Behavioral Sciences, Medical University of South Carolina

In recent years, both clinical and research literature have increased their attention on studying the effects of child sexual abuse (CSA). This chapter will confine its scope to the abuse victim as an adult. Primary emphasis will be placed on the psychosocial effects of CSA on the functioning of adults, conceptual frameworks for understanding such effects, and the assessment and treatment of adults who experienced sexual abuse in childhood. An attempt will be made to address issues relevant to both women and men; however, as will be discussed, much of what we know about the effects of CSA on adults comes from studies of adult women. Therefore, unless specifically mentioned, the information presented will relate to female victims of CSA.

The list of commonly cited problems of adults with a history of CSA is extensive and includes depression, fear and anxiety, dissociative symptoms, Post-traumatic Stress Disorder, suicidal ideation/behavior, substance abuse, relationship difficulties, sexual dysfunction, increased risk of subsequent victimization, and criminal behavior (Browne & Finkelhor, 1986). This chapter will examine each of these effects. Each section will include a description of clinical observations regarding these effects, a thorough review of empirical evidence documenting the associations between these effects and a history of CSA, and a critical examination of theoretical explanations of how these effects develop. Finally, issues related to the assessment and treatment of adults who were victimized as children will be addressed, and suggestions for future research will be presented.

Before discussing the specific effects of CSA on adults, it is important to address several methodological issues that affect the quality of studies examining the abuse victim as an adult. Three primary issues are (1) sampling, (2) screening, and (3) measurement.

While case studies or clinical observations (e.g., Lukianowicz, 1972; Forward & Buck, 1978) are valuable in identifying specific issues related to the experiences and psychological difficulties of abuse victims, the generalizability of their information is limited by their lack of comparison groups, lack of standardized measurement of potential abuse effects, and unrepresentativeness of victim samples. More systematic studies have yielded results that have generally, but not always, supported clinical observations (e.g., Bagley & Ramsay, 1986; Briere & Runtz, 1988a, 1988b; Saunders, Villeponteaux, Kilpatrick, & Veronen, 1987). However, problems related to the lack of standardized measurement and unrepresentativeness of samples continue to affect both the degree to which results relate specifically to CSA and to which results may be generalized to the general population of abuse victims. Empirical studies of college student and community samples that include comparison groups of nonabused adults have the most promise in identifying issues relevant to the more general population of abuse victims. Studies using this approach allow for assessment of individuals who have not been identified a priori on the basis of specific characteristics (such as abuse history or as treatment seekers) and the presence of a comparison group protects against threats to the validity of results.

This chapter will review information gained from clinical, convenience, college student, and community samples. Clinical samples may reflect individuals seeking treatment specifically for problems associated with CSA (e.g., Kelly, MacDonald, & Waterman, 1987; Tsai, Feldman-Summers, & Edgar, 1979), or they may include individuals presenting for treatment for problems in general who are subsequently identified either at intake or during the course of treatment as having been victimized in childhood (e.g., Briere, Evans, Runtz, & Wall, 1988; Briere & Runtz, 1986, 1988b; Carmen, Rieker, & Mills, 1984). Convenience samples are groups of individuals who share a common characteristic, such as having been incarcerated for a criminal offense; they are subsequently studied in relation to abuse experiences (e.g., Burgess, Hazelwood, Rokous, Hartman, & Burgess, 1988; Silbert & Pines, 1981). However, there is no way to determine the representativeness of a convenience sample. College student samples are just that. Finally, community samples may be of two types. The first is a sample of individuals in the general population recruited through advertisements (e.g., Courtois, 1979; Nelson, 1981). The second type is recruited by using more sophisticated methods of sampling, such as stratified sampling, or random digit dialing telephone sampling, used to obtain a sample that maximally approximates the population as a whole (e.g., Murphy et al., 1988; Peters, 1988; Saunders et al., 1987; Stein, Golding, Siegel, Burnam, & Sorenson, 1988). These types of sampling procedures will yield different groups of individuals, in that the samples selected will vary with respect to their representativeness to the population of interest. It is important to keep issues of sampling in mind when evaluating the merit of a particular study.

A second methodological issue that has not been addressed widely in the literature is related to screening for abuse histories. Many published reports do not identify their method of screening for abuse experiences. Clinical reports generally present information gathered from victims who identified themselves as such either at the onset or during the course of psychological treatment. However, not all victims identify themselves as such, and the use of questions specific to abuse experiences tends to increase the identification of victims (Briere & Runtz, 1988b; Lipovsky, 1989; Saunders, Kilpatrick, Resnick, & Tidwell, 1989). Several empirical studies (e.g., Stein et al., 1988; Siegel, Sorenson, Golding, Burnam, & Stein, 1987) use broad, single-question screening approaches, which tend to yield low rates of disclosure of victimization histories (Best, Kilpatrick, Kramer, & McNeill-Harkins, 1990; Lipovsky, 1989; Saunders et al., 1987). Assessment approaches that use questions regarding specific sexual behaviors in evaluating victimization history are the most sound methodologically (e.g., Best et al., 1990; Koss, 1987; Murphy et al., 1988; Saunders et al., 1987).

A third methodological consideration is that of measurement of abuse effects. Many of the studies in this area do not use standardized measures for assessing the psychosocial difficulties of adult abuse victims. Measures of effects have included global estimates of trauma (e.g., Russell, 1986), measures specific to the effects of victimization (e.g., Briere & Runtz, 1988b), standardized measures developed for assessment of symptoms in general practice (e.g., Murphy et al., 1988) and psychiatric interview schedules (e.g., Peters, 1988; Saunders et al., 1987; Stein et al., 1988). Different measurement techniques yield results that are difficult to compare across studies, and the psychometric properties of the measures will affect the validity of results.

These three methodological issues have significant impact on the identification of victims of abuse, the degree to which effects may be attributed specifically to abuse experience, the generalizability of results, and the validity of observed effects. Readers should take into account these methodological characteristics of the study in evaluating scientific merit and in interpreting results as indicative of characteristics of the abuse victim as an adult (see Table 14.1).

TABLE 14.1

Methodological Characteristics of Research on Adults with a History of Child Sexual Abuse

Study	Sample	Screening procedures	Measurement of effects	Comparisons made
Briere & Runtz (1988a)	college students	modification of Finkelhor's questionnaire assessing CSA experiences	standardized measure of general symptomatology with norms	victims versus nonvictims (women only)
Briere & Runtz (1988b)	treatment seekers (in crisis)	unclear as to how behaviorally specific questions were	author-developed standardized measure of crisis-specific symptoms + history of traumata, suicidal behavior, hospitalizations	victims versus nonvictims (women only)
Murphy et al. (1988)	random community random digit dialing	behaviorally specific questions involving unwanted sexual experiences	standardized measures of general symptomatology with norms + trauma-specific standardized measure	victims of child abuse versus abuse during adolescence versus adult sexual assault versus multiple assault versus nonvictims (women only)
Peters (1988)	random community random digit dialing	behaviorally specific questions involving unwanted sexual behavior	standardized measures of general symptomatology	contact abuse versus non-contact abuse versus nonvictims (women only)
Russell, Schurman, & Trocki (1988)	random community probability sample	extensive behaviorally specific interview	global measures of impact/outcome—unstandardized and subjective	Afro-American and Caucasian victims versus nonvictims (women only)
Stein et al. (1988)	random community two-stage probability sample	single question involving force or pressure for sexual contact	standardized measures of psychiatric diagnosis	Hispanic versus non-Hispanic white, male and female victims versus nonvictims

TABLE 14.1
(Continued)

Study	Sample	Screening procedures	Measurement of effects	Comparisons made
Briere et al. (1988)	treatment seekers (in crisis)	unclear as to how behaviorally specific questions were	author-developed standardized measure of crisis-specific symptoms + history of suicidal behavior	male and female victims versus nonvictims
Bryer, Nelson, Miller, & Krol (1987)	consecutive admissions to psychiatric hospital	single question regarding pressure or force for sexual contact	standardized measures of general symptomatology	victims of sexual abuse only versus sexual + physical abuse versus nonvictims; intrafamilial versus extrafamilial
Saunders et al. (1987)	random community random digit dialing	behaviorally-specific questions involving unwanted sexual experiences	standardized measure of psychiatric diagnoses	childhood rape versus molestation versus noncontact sexual abuse versus nonvictims (women only)
Bagley & Ramsay (1986)	random community	modification of Finkelhor's questionnaire assessing CSA experiences	standardized measures of general symptomatology	abused versus nonabused women
Briere & Runtz (1986)	treatment seekers (in crisis)	unclear as to how behaviorally specific questions were	history of suicide attempts	abused versus nonabused women
Fromuth (1986)	college students	unclear as to how behaviorally specific questions were extensive	standardized measures of symptomatology	abused versus nonabused women

Study	Sample	Identification method	Measures	Comparison groups
Russell (1986)	random community probability sample	behaviorally specific interview	global measures of impact/outcome; unstandardized	Afro-American versus white victims versus nonvictims (women only)
Carmen et al. (1984)	psychiatric inpatients	chart review	chart review and observations on unit	male and female abused versus nonabused
Sedney & Brooks (1984)	college students	developed own questionnaire	author-developed questionnaire; unstandardized	abused versus nonabused
Fritz, Stoll, & Wagner (1981)	college students	developed own questionnaire regarding all sexual contacts in childhood	author-developed questionnaire regarding adult sexual adjustment	male and female abuse victims with versus without problems with adult sexuality
Nelson (1981)	community volunteer sample (no randomization)	through advertising, personal contacts, personal references	author-developed questionnaire regarding effects of abuse; unstandardized	no control group
Courtois (1979)	community/treatment seeker volunteer sample (no randomization)	through advertising, identification by therapists	interview utilizing global ratings of adjustment	no control group
Tsai et al. (1979)	treatment seekers, volunteers from community (no randomization)	through advertising	standardized measures of symptomatology; unstandardized measures of psychosexual functioning	clincial group of abuse victims versus nonclinical group of abuse victims versus controls

435

DEPRESSION

Depression is the most common symptom noted in clinical reports on adults who were sexually victimized in childhood (Browne & Finkelhor, 1986). Clinical descriptions of adult women who were victimized as children often indicate a high incidence of depression (Blake-White & Kline, 1985; Goodman & Nowak-Scibelli, 1985; Gordy, 1983; Herman, 1981; Herman & Schatzow, 1984; Jehu, 1988; Lindberg & Distad, 1985; Tsai & Wagner, 1978), and presentation of depression in male victims of CSA appears to be common (Johanek, 1988; Kelly et al., 1987). Associated features of depression, including feelings of helplessness (Agosta & Loring, 1988; Donaldson & Gardner, 1985), negative self-concept and/ or poor self-esteem (Gelinas, 1988; Steele & Alexander, 1981), significant self-blame (Goodman & Nowak-Scibelli, 1985; Jehu, 1988), and guilt feelings (Haller & Alter-Reid, 1986; Herman & Schatzow, 1984) also have been noted in clinical populations.

The results of empirical studies of clinical samples have been mixed regarding the association between depression and a history of CSA. Meiselman (1978) found that incest victims presented to treatment with a higher number of psychosocial complaints, but there was no statistically significant differences in the percentage of victims (35%) and nonvictims (23%) receiving a diagnosis of depressive neurosis at intake. Similarly, several additional studies of clinical populations found no differences between victims and nonvictims on symptoms of depression (Briere & Runtz, 1988b; Carmen et al., 1984). In contrast, there have been reports that confirm the clinical observation of high levels of depression in adults with a history of CSA. Briere et al. (1988) studied an outpatient sample and found that both male and female victims reported significantly greater levels of depression than their nonabused counterparts. Beck and van der Kolk (1987) found a greater incidence of a history of depressive symptoms in chronically hospitalized, psychotic, female incest victims than a comparable group of nonvictims; however, these groups did not differ with respect to current diagnosis of depression. Further research, examining both depressive symptomatology and depressive diagnoses and looking at both current and lifetime incidence is necessary to clarify the relationships between depression and a history of CSA in clinical populations.

In general, empirical studies of nonclinical samples have supported the clinical observation that victims of CSA have significant problems with depression (Bagley & Ramsay, 1986; Briere & Runtz, 1988a; Sedney & Brooks, 1984). Adult survivors have also been found to have decreased self-concept (Alexander & Lupfer, 1987) or poor self-esteem

(Bagley & Ramsay, 1986) when compared with adults without a victimization history. Several community studies of adults who were abused as children have assessed specific psychiatric diagnoses using criteria outlines in the Diagnostic and Statistical Manual (DSM-III; American Psychiatric Association, 1980). Peters (1988), using the Schedule for Affective Disorders—Lifetime version (SADS; Endicott & Spitzer, 1979), examined the impact of contact (i.e., involved "intentional and unambiguous sexual behavior of a physical . . . nature") and noncontact (i.e., verbal solicitation of a sexual nature) abuse in comparison to nonvictims. The prevalence of major depressive episodes diagnosed since age 18 was significantly greater in victims of contact abuse (85%) than in victims of noncontact abuse (59%) or nonvictims (66%). Victims of contact abuse reported a greater total number of major depressive episodes than victims of noncontact abuse or nonvictims; however, there were no significant differences noted on the Beck Depression Inventory (BDI; Beck, Rial, & Rickels, 1974) regarding current depressed mood. These results suggest that the impact of abuse in terms of depressive symptomatology may relate to the degree of intrusiveness of the sexual behavior and that self-report measures such as the BDI may not be sensitive to differences between abused and nonabused individuals.

A second community study (Saunders et al., 1987) similarly addressed differences in the impact of CSA based upon the degree of sexual contact involved in the abuse. Using the Diagnostic Interview Schedule (DIS; Robins, Helzer, Croughan, & Ratcliff, 1981) the authors found that female victims of a rape or molestation in childhood had higher lifetime prevalence of major depressive episodes than their counterparts without abuse histories. Victims of noncontact abuse were not significantly different from nonvictims in terms of lifetime prevalence of major depressive episodes. Victims of childhood rape had a 75% greater risk and victims of molestation had a 65% greater risk than nonvictims for having a lifetime prevalence of major depression. With respect to current difficulties, victims of childhood molestation and victims of noncontact sexual abuse in childhood were three times more likely to have a major depressive episode at the time of the interview than were nonvictims. These results provide mixed support for the notion that the increased sexual intrusiveness of the abuse related to increased problems with depression. While contact abuse was associated with a greater lifetime prevalence of major depression, less intrusive types of abuse were associated with current major depression. Thus, the relationship between the extent of sexual contact and subsequent depression may be complex and is deserving of further study.

Results of a third community study (Stein et al., 1988) that also used the DIS to assess DSM-III diagnoses provide information about the relationship between demographic variables and the psychosocial effects of CSA. In general, victims of CSA had a higher prevalence of major depressive disorder than did nonvictims (18.6% vs. 4.7%, respectively). Female victims and Hispanic victims had higher lifetime rates of major depression than their nonabused counterparts; however, there were no significant differences between abused and nonabused non-Hispanic whites or abused and nonabused men for rates of lifetime major depression. The same pattern of results was reported for current major depression. A multivariate logistic regression model that examined the influence of adult sexual victimization, both adult and child sexual assault, gender, age, ethnicity and education on the rates of psychiatric disorder, yielded results indicating that CSA continued to be associated with both lifetime and current incidence of major depressive disorder even after the effects of demographic variables were controlled for. This suggests that CSA places an individual at significant risk for developing depression, regardless of demographic characteristics.

A number of theoretical approaches may be useful in attempting to explain the depression seen in adults with a history of CSA. As Paykel (1974) has noted, depression usually occurs following one of three environmental events: (1) interpersonal losses, (2) threatening events, or (3) blows to self-esteem. Few would deny that CSA can include any or all of these events.

Historically, the psychoanalytic perspective has implicated loss and ambivalence in the etiology of depression (Freud, 1917/1950). This view may be useful in understanding the depression of adult victims. Abuse victims experience many losses in their lives that may affect the development of depression (Goodman & Nowak-Scibelli, 1985). The betrayal inherent in abuse perpetrated by a trusted adult reflects a loss of significant proportion, and may result in a type of grief reaction (Finkelhor & Browne, 1985). In cases of intrafamilial abuse, victims are deprived of a caring, nurturing relationship with one or both of their parents. Furthermore, dynamics within a family in which sexual abuse occurs that cast the victim in a parental role and social isolation of the child and family reflect the loss of appropriate childhood experiences.

A second theoretical perspective that may account for depression in abuse victims is the learned helplessness model (Gold, 1986; Seligman, 1971). This view suggests that depression occurs as a result of exposure to unpredictable, unavoidable aversive stimulation from which there is no possibility of escape. The power inequality inherent in an adult–child relationship characterizes the CSA experience and leaves the child with strong feelings of helplessness, being unable to avoid, escape, control, or stop the abuse from occurring (Finkelhor & Browne, 1985; Summit, 1983). These experiences may alter individuals' beliefs regarding their ability to control themselves in other situations, and victims often feel that they are powerless to affect the world around them (McCann, Pearlman, Sakheim, & Abrahamson, 1988). In general, the sense of powerlessness may have the effect of decreasing the individual's sense of self-efficacy as well as limiting his or her ability to cope with stressors (Finkelhor, 1988). The beliefs related to a lack of control over self and situations, poor sense of self-efficacy, and compromised coping abilities are viewed as pervasive and as contributing to the depressive experience of victims (Jehu, 1988).

The sense of helplessness may be a function of entrapment strategies utilized by the offender to gain the victim's cooperation and secrecy (e.g., Sgroi & Bunk, 1988) and/or may relate to victims' inability to control their own physiological responses to the inappropriate sexual stimulation (Jehu, 1988). Victims often experience guilt and feelings of self-blame engendered by their participation and possible physical pleasure obtained during the abuse (Fritz, Stoll, & Wagner, 1981; Haller & Alter-Reid, 1986; Sgroi & Bunk 1988; Tsai & Wagner, 1978). Often there is a significant degree of self-blame associated with the fact that they complied with the demands of the offender and did not disclose the abuse. The secrecy involved in maintaining the abuse can be a source of self-blaming cognitions (Jehu, 1988). In addition, the offender may have placed the blame for the abuse on the victim at the time of the abuse. The self-blame of the victim can mirror this as well as societal blaming of victim that is found in history, fiction, and the like (Herman, 1981).

A second dynamic that appears to relate to self-blaming and guilt is that of stigmatization (Finkelhor & Browne, 1985). This refers to the child's feeling that he or she is somehow different and "bad" because of the abuse. The offender might make statements that reinforce the child's view that he or she is bad and which negatively impact the child's self-esteem. Such experiences may result in negative cognitions about the self (Briere & Runtz, 1988b) and contribute to depression. In addition, a sense of inadequacy in the victim is often fostered through the dynamics within the family of origin. Adults may expect things from child victims that are unrealistic or inappropriate (as is, for example, the sexual behavior) and may enact other behaviors that place the child in a parental role. Such expectations may be beyond the child's developmental capabilities and may result in negative feelings about the self (Sgroi & Bunk, 1988). McCann et al. (1988) described a cognitive schema of esteem based upon the individuals' belief in their own worth as well as their sense of their own and others' goodness/badness. Disruptions in this schema result in a significant degree of negative self-evaluation which is likely to contribute to depression.

Finally, the cognitive theory of depression proposed by Beck (1976) is also applicable to adults who were victimized in childhood. Victims are not immune to the myths concerning sexual abuse that permeate our society. They very often feel that they must have done something wrong within the abuse situation, or that the abuse was punishment for having done something wrong. In addition, because CSA is often a frightening and confusing experience that may have been responded to by disbelief from parents or professionals, victims may feel worthless and ashamed. If societal and family reactions to the abuse are rejecting or punitive, the victim might adopt many negative self-statements that can facilitate depression (Kilpatrick, Veronen, & Resick, 1982).

FEAR AND ANXIETY

High levels of fear and anxiety have been reported to be common in clinical samples of both men (Johanek, 1988) and women (Blake-White & Kline, 1985; Donaldson & Gardner, 1985; Sgroi & Bunk, 1988) who were sexually victimized as children. However, some clinical observations suggest that victims may not have greater problems with anxiety than nonvictims (Carmen et al., 1984; Meiselman, 1978). For example, Meiselman (1978) found that 16% of her incest group presented with anxiety, compared with 24% of the comparison group. Furthermore, essentially equal percentages of the two groups were diagnosed as having an anxiety neurosis. In contrast, Briere and Runtz (1988b) found that victims seeking treatment had more anxiety-related problems than nonvictims presenting for treatment. A significantly higher percentage of victims than nonvictims reported anxiety attacks (53.7% vs. 27.9%), nightmares (53.7% vs. 23.3%), fear of men (47.8% vs. 15.1%), and scored higher on the Tension subscale of the Crisis Symptom Checklist (CSC; Briere & Runtz, 1988b). Similarly, Briere et al. (1988) found that both male and female victims tended to report higher levels of anxiety than their nonabused counterparts. In their study of a college student sample, Sedney and Brooks (1984) found that victims of intrafamilial sexual abuse, but not victims of extrafamilial abuse, were more likely to report nervousness and anxiety than were nonvictims.

Mixed findings for greater fear and anxiety in victims, compared with nonvictims, were obtained by Murphy et al. (1988) in a study of a community sample of adult women. Victims did not score higher than nonvictims on the Modified Fear Survey, a measure of specific fears. Victims of sexual assault in childhood or adolescence did score higher than nonvictims on the anxiety subscale of the Symptom Checklist 90–Revised (SCL90R; Derogatis, 1977). These results suggest that victims may not be at greater risk than nonvictims for the development of long-term specific fears, but rather, may experience heightened levels of generalized anxiety when compared with nonvictims.

Stein et al. (1988) found that CSA victims had a significantly higher lifetime prevalence of anxiety disorders than nonvictims (29.2% vs. 10.9%). There were no significant differences between victimized and nonvictimized men in their lifetime prevalence of anxiety disorders. However, victimized women, Hispanics, and non-Hispanic whites were more likely to have a lifetime diagnosis of anxiety disorder than were their nonabused counterparts. Victims in general, and most specifically, female, Hispanic, and non-Hispanic white victims had greater prevalence of phobia than their nonabused counterparts. In terms of current diagnosis, victims were more likely than nonvictims to have an anxiety or panic disorder. Women and non-Hispanic white victims were more likely than their nonabused counterparts to have a current anxiety disorder; however, there were no differences between victimized and nonvictimized males or Hispanics in their current prevalence of anxiety disorder. These results suggest that victims are at risk for developing a variety of anxiety-related problems, including specific phobias, but that there may be ethnic and gender differences in the risk for development of anxiety disorders.

Saunders et al. (1987) found that victims of contact abuse had a higher prevalence of a variety of anxiety disorders than nonvictims. Rape victims had a six-times greater risk of having a lifetime diagnosis of obsessive compulsive disorder, a five-times greater risk of agoraphobia, and a four-times greater risk of social phobia than did nonvictims. Molestation victims had a 4.5 times greater risk than nonvictims for ever having a diagnosis of obsessive compulsive disorder. Current diagnoses showed similar patterns, with victims of childhood rape being more likely to have a current diagnosis of agoraphobia (16 time greater risk), panic disorder (5 times greater risk), obsessive compulsive disorder (4.5 times greater risk), and social phobia (4 times greater risk). Molestation victims were more likely than nonvictims to have an obsessive compulsive disorder at the time of the interview.

The etiology of anxiety difficulties in child victims has been discussed in terms of a classical conditioning model (e.g., Briere & Runtz, 1988b). Obviously, an abusive experience may represent a situation that is out of the victim's control, that is perceived as a threat to physical and psychological safety, and that is frightening. Often the abusive behaviors are painful to the child. When subjected to such a situation, it is reasonable to assume that the abuse victim would respond by experiencing high levels of fear and anxiety. This experience can be conceptualized as a classical conditioning situation in which the entrapment, helplessness, pain, and/or threat of physical harm are unconditioned stimuli (UCSs) that evoke unconditioned responses (UCRs) of fear and anxiety. Stimuli associated with these abuse-induced UCSs acquire the capacity to evoke fear and anxiety as well. Thus, conditioned stimuli (CSs), such as persons (e.g., men), situations (e.g., nighttime), or events (e.g., physical contact) present at the time of the abuse acquire the capacity to produce conditioned responses (CRs) of fear and anxiety through their association with abuse-induced fear and anxiety. Some stimuli that are present in all abuse situations, such as characteristics of the offender and cues associated with the abusive behavior are likely to be CSs for many abuse victims. Other stimuli may be more idiosyncratic to each specific case of abuse, and these stimuli should be CSs only in those cases in which they are involved. Thus, if one wished to predict the types of situations or cues most likely to produce fear and anxiety for a particular abuse victim, it would be necessary to obtain a detailed description of the stimuli present in the abusive situation. The proposed classical conditioning model predicts that a victim's observed fears are related to the particular circumstances of the abuse situation. Classical conditioning literature also suggests that fear and anxiety responses can generalize to other stimuli similar to CSs present during the abuse. Thus, the anxiety response elicited by a male offender might generalize to other men (see Kilpatrick et al., 1982, for a more thorough discussion of classically conditioned fear and anxiety responses in adult victims of rape).

DISSOCIATION

The process of dissociation has been hypothesized to be associated with the experience of trauma (Putnam, 1985). One such trauma clearly is CSA. Victim's use of denial to ward off negative feelings such as powerlessness, fear, depression, or anger may lead to amnestic and/or dissociative experiences (Agosta & Loring, 1988; Blake-White & Kline, 1985). For example, Lindberg & Distad (1985) studied 17 women with a history of sexual abuse and found that 35% of them had dissociative reactions, amnestic episodes, or numbing of body parts.

Child sexual abuse is one type of trauma that is frequently described as producing an extreme form of dissociation; that of multiple personality disorder (Bliss, 1980; Bowman, Blix & Coons, 1985; Coons, 1986). Although there is not a direct one-to-one relationship between CSA and multiple personality disorder, estimates of a history of CSA range from 25% (Bliss, 1980) to 85% (Coons & Milstein, 1986) in clinical samples of patients with multiple personality disorder.

Dissociation has received little focus in empirical studies of the effects of CSA. Briere (1988; Briere & Runtz, 1988a, 1988b) assessed symptoms of dissociation in studies of long-term effects of childhood sexual victimization in both nonclinical and clinical samples. These studies found that victims of CSA were more likely to report problems related to dissociation, including "spacing out," derealization, and out-of-body experiences, than were nonvictims. In the clinical sample, dissociation was associated with abuse that involved sexual intercourse (Briere, 1988). In the nonclinical sample, dissociation was found to be associated with the age of the oldest abuser, parental incest, and duration of abuse (Briere & Runtz, 1988a). This latter study found that dissociation was highly predictive of abuse history. The results of these studies support the notion that dissociation is a potential outcome of CSA. Further study is necessary to document both the occurrence of dissociation and factors that may relate to its etiology.

The dissociation seen in victims of CSA can be seen as an extreme form of denial or avoidance. It has been described as a mechanism of escape or protection from negative feelings associated with the abuse (Blake-White & Kline, 1985; Briere, 1988; Goodman & Nowak-Scibelli, 1985; Sgroi & Bunk, 1988). This mechanism may be adaptive for coping with the discomfort of the abuse. However, in many victims, this coping response persists and becomes a generalized automatic response to any anxiety producing or noxious event (Briere, 1988; Sgroi & Bunk, 1988). What may result then are amnestic periods or situations in which the individual misinterprets events because they were dissociated from reality. These events can be very frightening to the individual and may contribute to further experiences of anxiety.

PTSD

A potential effect of CSA that has received increased attention in the past several years is Post-traumatic Stress Disorder (PTSD) in victims of CSA. PTSD is a psychiatric disorder classified among anxiety disorders and characterized by symptoms of intrusive re-experiencing of the traumatic event and avoidance. Victims of CSA often vacillate between phases of intrusive thinking and denial (Cole & Barney, 1987), and it has been observed that women who experienced CSA have symptom patterns that fit the diagnosis of PTSD (Blake-White & Kline, 1985). In particular, flashbacks (a form of re-experiencing) have been noted in adult victims of CSA (Agosta & Loring, 1988; Deighton & McPeek, 1985), often occurring during sexual closeness (Donaldson & Gardner, 1985).

Two clinical reports (Donaldson & Gardner, 1985; Lindberg & Distad, 1985) found high rates of PTSD in their samples of adult victims. Donaldson and Gardner (1985) noted that 25 of the 26 cases they studied met the DSM-III diagnostic criteria for PTSD. Victims had an average of 6.9 symptoms of PTSD, and also had many associated features of psychopathology, including fears, depression, sexual issues, difficulties with trust, and low self-confidence. Similarly, Lindberg and Distad (1985) reported that all 17 female incest victims that they studied met diagnostic criteria for PTSD. These authors suggested that the initial response to trauma in these women had been a phase of repression that helped them survive emotionally. Following this phase, however, victims experienced intrusive thinking and reexperiencing symptoms.

In the only empirical study investigating PTSD in a community sample of adults with a victimization history, Saunders et al. (1987) found that victims of childhood rape or molestation were more likely than noncontact abuse victims to have PTSD. Victims of childhood rape had a lifetime prevalence of 64.1% for PTSD, compared with 33.3% of victims of molestation and 11.4% of victims of noncontact abuse. At the time of the interview, 17.9% of child rape victims, compared with 8.8% of victims of molestation and 5.7% of victims of noncontact abuse, met DSM-III criteria for PTSD.

Donaldson and Gardner (1985) cite the theoretical formulation of PTSD put forth by Horowitz (1976) in explaining the PTSD seen in victims of CSA. In general, if individuals are unable to complete the cognitive and affective processing of traumatic events, they will push memories of such experiences out of their awareness in order to defend again dysphoric and anxious feelings. This use of avoidance and denial is often unsuccessful, however, as memories tend to have a "push" to consciousness in order for adequate processing to occur. Therefore, the pattern seen in individuals following trauma is alternation between avoidance/denial and intrusive/re-experiencing phases. Donaldson and Gardner suggest further that victims of CSA experience a numbing of affect as a result of chronic avoidance of overwhelming feelings.

Several authors (e.g., Briere & Runtz, 1988b; Finkelhor, 1988) have noted that many problems seen in adults with abuse histories, such as suicidality, substance abuse, revictimization, sexual problems, and self-blame, do not conform well with the diagnosis of PTSD. Finkelhor (1988) suggests that PTSD largely focuses on the affective experience, avoidance, and re-experiencing observed following trauma and does not take into account the cognitive changes that are often outcomes of CSA. He notes that the theoretical underpinnings of a PTSD model emphasize the influence of "overwhelming trauma" on subsequent functioning and argues that CSA often is not characterized by physical or emotional trauma. He suggests further that the alterations in the victim's cognitive framework that result from the abuse are not addressed in the PTSD model. Finkelhor argues that PTSD is not an adequate model for the effects of CSA because it does not describe the functioning of all victims or the central problems of most victims. He suggests that PTSD should be distinguished from sexual abuse trauma and proposes an alternative model, which he contends provides a more complete understanding of the traumatic effects of CSA. This model identifies four traumagenic dynamics of abuse, including: (1) traumatic sexualization; (2) betrayal, (3) stigmatization; and, (4) powerlessness (Finkelhor & Browne, 1985). Each of these dynamics is hypothesized to relate to specific problems noted commonly in victims of sexual abuse. Further research should address Finkelhor's theoretical concerns by examining more closely the association among CSA, symptoms of PTSD, and effects predicted by the model.

ANGER

Victims of CSA often experience a significant degree of anger toward others. Clinical observations have been made of victims' anger related to their mother's lack of protection and their father's exploitation and lack of accountability (Haller & Alter-Reid, 1986). Briere and Runtz (1988b) found that victims of CSA had greater trouble controlling their tempers and reported higher levels of anger than did nonabused women in their clinical sample. Herman (1981) found that women commonly directed their anger at other women rather than at men. This observation is consistent with that of Tsai and Wagner (1978), also investigating a clinical sample, who noted that many victims expressed considerable anger toward their mother for not protecting them or, in cases of incest, for colluding with the father. Thus, persistent anger toward women in general may be a function of the sense of betrayal that victims have in relation to their mother's lack of protection of them in childhood. There may be differences between males and females in terms of how they express their anger, with male victims being more likely to be outwardly aggressive and female victims more likely to turn their anger inward in self-destructive ways (Carmen et al., 1984).

It appears intuitively obvious that victims of CSA would experience anger toward others and the world. The abuse situation has taught the victim that at least some people behave in harmful ways and, when the offender was a previously trusted individual, the victim learns that trust can be illusory. Having been betrayed may influence the victim to feel bitterness, anger, and resentment not only toward the offender who perpetrated direct harm to them, but also to those, like their mothers, who through lack of protection, may have indirectly perpetrated harm. These negative feelings appear to generalize to others and may be a mechanism of self-protection from future betrayals (Finkelhor, 1988). Furthermore, the victim may continually feel angry toward the offender whose behavior undermined their sense of power and control, and may generalize their anger to others who reinforce their powerlessness. Finally, stigmatization within the abuse situation may lead victims to be angry at offenders for being responsible for "ruining" them. Disruption of the esteem schemata may result in a victim's developing the perspective that people are inherently bad and interested in harming others (McCann et al., 1988). These dynamics together or separately may lead the victim to a chronic experience of rage (Briere & Runtz, 1988b). However, anger in victims of CSA has been understudied, particularly in methodologically sound investigations using general population samples.

SUBSTANCE ABUSE

Several clinical reports (Blake-White & Kline, 1985; Herman, 1981; Johanek, 1988; Sgroi & Bunk, 1988) describe abuse victims as having difficulties related to the abuse of substances. In addition, mention has been made (Gordy, 1983) that many victims report that one or both of their parents had significant problems associated with substance abuse. However, Meiselman (1978) found no difference between victims of incest and a comparison group in their rates of alcohol addiction.

The results of empirical studies that assessed substance abuse in clinical samples of victims of CSA have been mixed. Carmen et al. (1984) found no differences in the percentages of abused and nonabused psychiatric inpatients in their history of abuse of alcohol or drugs. Furthermore, victimized and nonvictimized patients did not differ in their substance abuse at the time of admission. In contrast, Briere and Runtz (1988b) found that a higher percentage of abused than non-abused women reported a history of drug addiction (20.9% vs. 2.3%) and history of alcoholism (26.9% vs. 10.5%) in their clinical sample.

Similarly mixed results have been obtained from nonclinical samples. Sedney and Brooks (1984) found no differences between abused and nonabused women in terms of their drug or alcohol abuse in a college student population. In contrast, Peters (1988), examining a community sample, found that victims of contact abuse were more likely than victims of noncontact abuse or nonvictims to have definite alcohol abuse or probable drug abuse. Similarly, Stein et al. (1988) found that victims of CSA were significantly more likely than nonvictims to have met DSM-III criteria for substance use or alcohol abuse/dependence sometime during their lifetimes. Male victims were significantly more likely than their nonabused counterparts to have met criteria for a substance use disorder (55.4% vs. 26.7%, respectively) or for drug abuse/dependence (44.9% vs. 7.8%, respectively). Female victims were more likely than nonabused females to have met criteria for alcohol abuse/dependence (20.8% vs. 4.1%) or drug abuse/dependence (13.7% vs. 3.1%). Hispanic victims were more likely than nonabused Hispanics to have had a lifetime diagnosis of substance abuse disorder (32.7% vs. 16.8%) or drug abuse/dependence (27.6% vs. 3.3%). Finally, non-Hispanic white victims were more likely than their nonabused counterparts to have met criteria for drug abuse/dependence at some point in their lifetime (24.5% versus 9.2%). The only difference noted for current substance use, was that male victims were more likely than male nonvictims to have a current DSM-III diagnosis of drug abuse/dependence (17.6% vs. 3.3%).

As Kilpatrick et al. (1989) have noted, substance use and abuse can be viewed as antecedents, correlates, or consequences of victimization. Clearly, substance use could be an antecedent to or correlate with victimization of an adolescent in that it might increase risk of victimization in the following ways. First, a drug or alcohol-intoxicated individual might engage in high risk-taking behavior due to reduced inhibition associated with intoxication. Second, an intoxicated adolescent might be less able to detect cues signaling danger than a similar individual who was not intoxicated. Third, an intoxicated person might emit behavioral cues signaling vulnerability and thus be singled out for attack. Fourth, an intoxicated person might be less able to resist an attack successfully due to cognitive and motor impairments.

With respect to substance use/abuse as a consequence of victimization, there are two possible ways in which victimization might be expected to increase rates of alcohol/drug consumption. First, given the extremely stressful nature of a CSA experience, it is reasonable to assume that at least some victims turn to alcohol or drug use as a form of self-medication for such stress or to blot out intrusive images of the CSA experience. Second, as has been discussed previously, CSA stigmatizes its victims, sometimes resulting in their becoming involved with a delinquent peer group. As has been noted by Elliot, Huizinga, and Ageton (1985), there is a strong link between delinquency and substance abuse behavior during adolescence.

REVICTIMIZATION

An experience of sexual abuse in childhood apears to leave many victims at risk for a subsequent sexual assault (Agosta & Loring, 1988; Browne & Finkelhor, 1986; Goodman & Nowak-Scibelli, 1985). While there have been reports that do not find this (e.g., Briere & Runtz, 1988b), several empirical studies support this clinical observation (Alexander & Lupfer, 1987; Briere, 1988; Fromuth, 1986; Russell, 1986). In addition, victims have been found to be more likely to be a victim of crime or victim of an accident than nonvictims (Sedney & Brooks, 1984). Siegel et al. (1987) found that about half of the victims in their community study reported more than a single assault. Furthermore, victims of CSA were more than eight times likely to be victimized in adulthood than were nonvictims of CSA. Briere (1988) examined characteristics of CSA that relate to a variety of outcomes, including a history of sexual assault in adulthood. His results suggest that abuse characterized by a long duration, multiple perpetrators, concomitant physical abuse, and having bizarre features was associated with revictimization in adulthood.

It is not surprising that studies have found that multiple sexual assault is associated with greater trauma than is a single assault (e.g., Russell, 1986). Murphy et al. (1988), investigating a community sample, found that victims of assault in both childhood and adulthood reported higher scores on the depression, anxiety, hostility, interpersonal sensitivity, somatization, and obsessive compulsive subscales of the SCL90R. Victims of multiple assault were similar to victims of a single assault in either childhood or adolescence on the phobic anxiety and paranoid ideation subscales, and similar to adolescent victims on the psychoticism subscale. These results suggest that victims of multiple assault have a high level of generalized distress, which affects all areas of functioning.

Adult survivors also have been noted to become involved in abusive marital relationships (Briere & Runtz, 1988b; Jehu, 1988; Russell, 1986; Tsai & Wagner, 1978). Within Herman's (1981) sample, 27.5% of the women with abuse histories were battered, and more than half of these women were raped within the marriage as well. Briere and Runtz (1988b) found in their clinical sample that almost half (48.9%) of abuse victims had been battered as an adult compared to 17.6% of nonvictims.

Each of the four traumagenic effects of abuse that Finkelhor and Browne (1985) have discussed appears to have the potential to contribute to victims' vulnerability to subsequent assaults. The dynamic of traumatic sexualization may foster feelings of anxiety in relation to sexual interactions. Thus, an adult with an abuse history may reject sexual advances because they are frightening which, in turn, may lead to sexual violence on the part of the victim's partner (Russell, 1986). Russell also suggests that the dynamic of betrayal results in an impaired ability to judge the trustworthiness of others and thus, the victim may become involved with people who take advantage of him or her. Consistent with this view is that of McCann et al. (1988) who describe the cognitive schemata of safety as being a belief in one's own ability to protect oneself and a belief in the degree to which others are dangerous. Multiple victimization likely disrupts the safety schemata that may result in a belief that they are unable to protect themselves and that others are dangerous. Furthermore, multiple victimizations are likely to deepen a victim's mistrust of others and increases his or her social isolation (Herman, 1981).

The third dynamic, that of powerlessness, may foster the adult's self-definition of victim and he or she may then expect to be treated as such (Russell, 1986). In addition, a compromised sense of self-efficacy may be manifested as a lack of assertiveness, leaving the victim unable to take self-protective actions. Stigmatization as well may be a factor in victims' vulnerability. Stigmatization involves a negative view of the self and feelings of worthlessness. A victim who experiences this effect may feel unworthy of positive, mutual relationships and may have the view that they deserve to be treated in abusive ways (McCann et al., 1988; Russell, 1986).

Adult abusive experiences within intimate relationships may be a function of faulty learning in addition to being directly related to the traumagenic dynamics of victimization. Victims may have experienced caring and nurturance from the same persons who perpetrated the abuse. In this way, they may have developed an attachment to exploitive love objects early in life. Thus, they subsequently may become involved intimately with partners who similarly treat them both with caring and exploitation (Steele & Alexander, 1981). Herman (1981) discusses the need of abuse victims for caring and nurturing relationships. It may be that victims seek relationships to obtain a feeling of being cared for without attending to negative aspects of relationships. They may tolerate abuse if it is interspersed with warmth and caring.

RELATIONSHIP DIFFICULTIES

Perhaps because CSA is an interpersonal phenomenon, some of the most striking difficulties of adults who were victimized are associated with their interpersonal relationships (Tsai & Wagner, 1978; Van Buskirk & Cole, 1983). Such difficulties tend to occur in all types of relationships, including marital and other intimate relationships, parental, and friendships (Deighton & McPeek, 1985).

In Russell's (1986) community sample, only 12% of women with an abuse history reported that the abuse had a negative impact on their relationships with others. Interestingly, some women noted positive effects on their relationships, indicating that they felt they were more assertive, more independent, and had positive relationships with men as a result of the abuse. Thus, not all women report negative effects of abuse on their interpersonal relationships.

Jehu (1988) reported on a sample of women seen for treatment of abuse-related difficulties and noted that many of these women had significant difficulties in their interpersonal relationships. All of the married women reported discord, oppression, or abuse within their marital relationship. Ninety percent noted relationship problems with men and 49% had problems in relationships with women. Seventy-eight percent of the women reported significant mistrust of others, 88% felt different from others, and 62% indicated that they were isolated or alienated from interpersonal relationships. Many of these problems appeared to relate to a lack of communication skills and assertiveness. This sample of women were treatment seekers and no comparison group was available. Therefore, the findings should be viewed with caution, as they may not reflect abuse-specific relationship problems.

There is a relative paucity of empirical work utilizing comparison groups of nonvictims in assessing relationship difficulties associated with CSA. A study with a clinical sample (Briere & Runtz, 1988b) did not support the view that victims had greater relationship difficulties than nonvictims. While victims were somewhat more likely than nonvictims to report social isolation, this difference was not significant. In addition, equal percentages of victims and nonvictims reported problems related to loneliness. In contrast, the results of two community studies suggest that victims may experience problems in their interpersonal relationships. Bagley and Ramsey (1986) found an increased frequency of divorce and poorer marital satisfaction in abuse victims, compared with nonvictims. Murphy et al. (1988) found that victims of sexual abuse in adolescence scored higher than nonvictims on the Interpersonal Sensitivity subscale of the Symptom Checklist 90–Revised (SCL90R; Derogatis, 1977), suggesting that victims experience significantly more problems related to feelings of personal inadequacy in relation to others, marked discomfort in interpersonal situations, self-consciousness, general uneasiness, and negative expectancies with respect to interpersonal interactions than do nonvictims. Further research in this area is warranted in order to understand better the adult interpersonal experiences of victims of CSA.

The development of problems in the interpersonal arena appears to be a logical result of the betrayal that occurs as a result of experiencing harm at the hands of a trusted adult (Finkelhor & Browne, 1985). Early experiences of betrayal subsequently affect the victim's ability to trust others (Blake-White & Kline, 1985; Deighton & McPeek, 1985; Donaldson & Gardner, 1985; Haller & Alter-Reid, 1986; Herman, 1981; Lindberg & Distad, 1985; McCann et al., 1988; Steele & Alexander, 1981). A consequence of betrayal is that victims often expect to be treated poorly by others (Herman, 1981). Thus, they tend to remain guarded emotionally and limit the degree to which they reveal information about themselves (Van Buskirk & Cole, 1983). Clinical observations (Haller & Alter-Reid, 1986) suggest that victims tend to create a "protective shield" around themselves and interact with others on relatively superficial levels. In this way, the individual attempts to avoid the discomfort of anyone becoming too close and hurting them again which, in turn, has the effect of exacerbating their social isolation.

Stigmatization and the sense of oneself as different, bad, dirty, or unworthy may also interfere with adult survivors' ability to become intimate with other persons for fear that they will be rejected or hurt (Finkelhor & Browne, 1985; Haller & Alter-Reid, 1986; Herman, 1981; McCann et al., 1988). In particular, victims often fear that they will be rejected if others know about the abuse (Sgroi & Bunk, 1988). In reaction to such fears, victims may isolate themselves from others and subsequently feel alienated from people because of their abuse experiences (Agosta & Loring, 1988; Blake-White & Kline, 1985; Haller & Alter-Reid, 1986; Lindberg & Distad, 1985; Steele & Alexander, 1981; Tsai & Wagner, 1978). This, in turn, may help to maintain their victim status (Deighton & McPeek, 1985).

Due to the fact that CSA generally occurs in secret, victims often maintain secretiveness and guardedness within their relationships. Maintaining secrecy about the abuse or other aspects of one's life can be a mechanism for fostering a sense of control, but it also can act as a barrier to intimacy (Sgroi & Bunk, 1988). Secrecy may relate to negative feelings related to stigmatization and tends to contribute to social isolation (Herman, 1981).

Several authors suggest that faulty learning in the family of origin is responsible for the interpersonal problems of adults who experienced intrafamilial sexual abuse. Gelinas (1988) notes that a victim learns that relationships take rather than give. Victims learn to expect that the environment will not meet their needs or be supportive because their experiences in childhood were that their needs were subordinated to those of the offender and the rest of the family (Steele & Alexander, 1981). As a function of learning these patterns of relating to others, the individual does not learn to be assertive. Anger and resentment may be experienced toward others for not meeting their needs even though it may be that they become involved with others who are not capable of having a mutually satisfying relationship (Gelinas, 1988).

Child victims of abuse within the family learn that nurturance and protection from adult caretakers are not predictable (Sgroi & Bunk, 1988). The lack of predictability of positive relational interactions may result in a great deal of uncertainty regarding what to expect from relationships. In addition, victims may become confused about relationships with adult role models and how adults interact with each other and with children and this likely affects their future adult relationships (Bagley & Ramsay, 1986).

Compromised interpersonal functioning in many female victims may also occur in their role as mother. Victims often have fears of being like their own mother and develop unrealistic expectations about themselves in an effort to be very different from their mother (Herman, 1981). While victims are often fearful of being unable to protect their own children from sexual abuse (Herman, 1981), they may be at increased risk of their own children being victimized because they are often able to function in an incest-tolerant manner (Gelinas, 1988). If the child of a victim is victimized, the adult's pain may resurface along with memories of his or her own abusive experiences. A common response to this is to use denial mechanisms that were used when she was victimized. The individual may become paralyzed, avoid the child's pain, or experience painful recollections of her own abuse (Herman, 1981). Issues related to effects on parenting have not been explored in male victims, but are deserving of future study.

CRIMINAL BEHAVIOR/VICTIMIZATION OF OTHERS

A number of reports suggest that individuals with a history of CSA may be prone to becoming involved in criminal behavior such as prostitution (James & Myerding, 1977; Silbert & Pines, 1981), or in sexual offending (Becker, Cunningham-Rathner, & Kaplan, 1987; Groth, 1979). Jehu (1988) found that 70% of a clinical sample had physically abused their children at some time in the past.

Empirical work that has been done in this area has relied primarily on information gathered from convenience samples of individuals who had already been identified through their involvement in some type of criminal activity. Several studies suggest that about one-third of sex offenders have a history of CSA (Becker et al., 1987; Groth, 1979; Seghorn, Prentky, & Boucher, 1987). The incidence of sexual assault in childhood has been found to be much higher for incarcerated child molesters than for rapists (Groth, 1979; Seghorn et al., 1987). Rapists with a history of CSA were more likely than child molesters to have been victimized by someone within the family. This might suggest that there are different patterns of abuse associated with these two types of sex offenders. Seghorn et al. (1987) found that sexual victimization did not occur in isolation in the histories of these men. Additional indexes of family pathology were noted in the family backgrounds of both molesters and rapists who were victimized as children. Victimized molesters were more likely than nonvictimized molesters to have had a father with a criminal and/or substance abuse history, parents with psychiatric histories, sexual deviance within the family that did not involve them (e.g., father sexually abused a sibling), and a higher incidence of child neglect. Rapists who were victimized in childhood were more likely to have been neglected, physically abused, and to have been in a family in which there was sexual deviance not involving them, than were nonvictimized rapists. Thus, it appears that the etiology of criminal sexual behavior is a function of a combination of factors rather than an experience of CSA alone. There are significant methodological problems with studies that examine abuse histories in incarcerated offenders. It is likely that these individuals do not accurately reflect the general characteristics of the sex offender. Offenders whose criminal behavior goes undetected may be very different from those who are detected, prosecuted, and subsequently incarcerated. Therefore, we suggest caution in generalizing the results of the studies described here in to the general population of offenders.

The development of criminal behavior in victims of CSA appears to be a function of both abuse experiences and factors within the family of origin. The stigmatization dynamic (Finkelhor & Browne, 1985) may be a factor, as victims may view themselves as bad and may act out some of these negative feelings. Traumatic sexualization (Finkelhor & Browne, 1985) may relate to sexual deviance in adulthood, as sex and aggression become linked through faulty learning processes. An individual's sense of powerlessness that has been shaped by the CSA experience may lead them to seek inappropriate mechanisms for gaining control over others as a defense against such powerlessness. Burgess et al. (1988) suggest that sexual deviance may be a form of re-enactment of the rapist's own victimization experience.

Prostitution may relate to a combination of abuse and chaotic family functioning (Steele & Alexander, 1981). It may be less a function of a history of CSA but may be more of a direct consequence of running away from an abusive, chaotic family environment (Silbert & Pines, 1981).

SEXUAL DYSFUNCTION

Sexual dysfunctions including difficulties developing sexual intimacy (Haller & Alter-Reid, 1986), lack of sexual response (Donaldson & Gardner, 1985; Tsai & Wagner, 1978), lack of enjoyment of sex (Herman, 1981; Tsai & Wagner, 1978), sexual dissatisfaction (Van Buskirk & Cole, 1983), difficulties differentiating between sex and affection (Gordy, 1983; Tsai & Wagner, 1978), and flashbacks to the molestation (Donaldson & Gardner, 1985; Herman, 1981; Tsai & Wagner, 1978) have been noted in clinical samples. These are common presenting complaints among adult women with CSA histories. For example, at least one sexual dysfunction was reported in 78% of Jehu's (1988) clinical sample. These included sexual phobias or aversions (58%), sexual dissatisfaction (58%), impaired sexual motivation (56%), impaired sexual arousal (49%), and impaired orgasm (45%).

Several empirical studies of clinical samples have found that victims of CSA are more likely to report sexual difficulties than are nonvictims (Briere & Runtz, 1988b; Meiselman, 1978). In Meiselman's (1978) clinical study, 24% of victims of incest presented with sexual problems, compared with only 8% of nonvictims. Briere and Runtz (1988b) found that victims were almost three times as likely to report sexual problems than were nonvictims. In a clinical sample, sexual problems have been found to be associated with longer duration, concomitant physical abuse, bizarre sexual abuse, and multiple perpetrators (Briere, 1988).

Comparing victims who sought treatment with those who did not, Tsai et al. (1979) found that the clinical group had more significant sexual problems that did the nonclinical group. The clinical group had a lower percentage of orgasms during intercourse, more sexual partners, were less responsive and were less satisfied with current sexual relations than the nonclinical and comparison groups.

In general, studies of nonclinical samples yield findings inconsistent with those obtained from clinical samples with regard to sexual difficulties in adults victimized as children. Fromuth (1986) found no evidence of sexual problems or sexual avoidance in victims, compared with nonvictims. In addition, victims did not score differently than nonvictims on a measure of sexual self-esteem. In Russell's (1986) community study, only about 14% of victims reported a negative impact on sexuality. In contrast, Saunders et al. (1987) found that 66.7% of victims of childhood rape and 63.2% of molestation victims, compared with 44.2% of nonvictims, had a lifetime history of having met DSM-III criteria for a sexual disorder. In addition, molestation victims (but not victims of childhood rape) had a two times greater risk than nonvictims to have a sexual disorder at the time of the interview. Racial factors may impact on the development of sexual difficulties, as Stein et al. (1988) found that Hispanic victims reported greater loss of sexual interest than white victims.

It appears that a small percentage of female incest victims develop a homosexual orientation (Herman, 1981; Meiselman, 1978). In contrast, about 45% of male college students who had been victimized by an older male were involved in homosexual activity at the time of the interview and overall, these males were more than four times more likely to be currently engaged in homosexual activity than nonvictims (Finkelhor, 1984).

Two studies of college students provide mixed evidence for sexual adjustment problems in male victims. Finkelhor (1984) found that male victims had lower levels of sexual self-esteem than their nonabused counterparts. In contrast, Fritz et al. (1981) found only 10% of male victims reporting problems with adult sexual adjustment as compared with 23% of the female victims. In addition, males were more likely to express neutral or positive feelings about their childhood sexual experiences than were women. Positive coercion was associated with adult sexual maladjustment in women, suggesting that compliance in the absence of physical force or threats may contribute to guilt related to sexual interactions in adulthood. However, this association was not found for men. The authors suggest that differences in the sexual socialization process may account for sex differences in the effects of early victimization on adult sexual adjustment. They hypothesize that males may view early sexual experiences as initiation, whereas females may experience such events as violation. The difference in interpretation of early sexual experiences may differently affect subsequent sexual adjustment.

Problems related to sexual functioning may relate to classical conditioning of noxious events to sexual behavior (Briere & Runtz, 1988b). A variety of mood states, including dysphoria, feelings of guilt, low self-esteem, or fear and anxiety may become associated with sexual behavior (Jehu, 1988). This view is consistent with the notion of the traumatic sexualization dynamic in CSA (Finkelhor & Browne, 1985). Child sexual abuse involves a distortion, delay, inhibition, or perversion of normal pleasure associated with sexual activity (Steele & Alexander, 1981) such that the victim is unable to benefit as an adult from sexual involvement. In addition, lack of responsiveness may be a function of coping mechanisms used during the abuse. Victims may numb their responsiveness during the abuse in order to minimize their physiological response. It may be that this becomes a long-term adaptation.

SUICIDALITY/SELF-DESTRUCTIVE BEHAVIOR

Self-destructive behaviors, including suicidal ideation and behavior (Blake-White & Kline, 1985; Sgroi & Bunk, 1988) are common presenting problems in victims of CSA (Gordy, 1983; Haller & Alter-Reid, 1986). With Herman's (1981) sample of women in treatment, 38% of the victims had made at least one suicide attempt. Lindberg and Distad (1985) found that 23.5% of their clinical sample had made at least one suicide attempt. An additional 23.5% reported suicidal ideation. These percentages may not, however, be different from those of nonabused treatment seekers, as Meiselman (1978) found no difference in the percentage of victims (20%) and nonvictims (18%) presenting for treatment with suicidal thoughts.

Studies that include comparison groups do suggest that victims have a significant likelihood of behaving in self-destructive ways. In a sample of adults presenting to a crisis clinic, Briere (1984) found that 51% of CSA victims had made at least one suicide attempt, compared with 34% of nonvictims. In a similar study, 54.9% of victims, compared with 22.6% of nonvictims had at least one suicide attempt (Briere & Runtz, 1986). Briere and Runtz (1988b) also found that victims of CSA were more likely than nonvictims to indicate a history of suicide attempts (50.7% vs. 33.7%, respectively). Briere et al. (1988) found no differences between male and female abuse victims in terms of their suicidality. Abuse victims were about twice as likely as nonabused individuals to have made a suicide attempt in the past regardless of whether they were male or female.

Bryer et al. (1987) studied an inpatient psychiatric sample and found that patients with suicidal behavior or ideation were more than three times as likely to be victims of CSA than were subjects without these symptoms. Similarly, Briere and Runtz (1986) noted that individuals presenting with suicidal ideation were more likely to report a history of CSA (35.6%) than were nonsuicidal intakes (22.6%). They found that the age of the first suicide attempt was also associated with CSA. Of women who had made a first suicide attempt prior to the age of 13, 92.9% were victims. Eighty-seven percent of women who made their first suicide attempt during adolescence were victims of CSA. These findings are particularly striking, and suggest that clinicians working with suicidal patients, particularly those less than 18 years old, should be alert to the possibility of a CSA history.

Research with nonclinical samples has also supported the clinical observation that victims of CSA are likely to become self-destructive. Sedney and Brooks (1984) studied a sample of college students and found that victims were more than two times as likely to have made a suicide attempt or to have had thoughts of hurting themselves than were nonvictims. Within a community sample (Peters, 1988), victims of contact or noncontact abuse were approximately three times more likely to have made a suicide attempt than nonvictims.

Investigating a community sample, Saunders et al. (1987) found that victims of childhood rape or molestation were more likely than nonvictims to have had suicidal ideation or to have made a suicide attempt at some time in their life. The results indicated a lifetime prevalence of suicide attempt in 15.8% of molestation victims and 17.9% of victims of childhood rape. These percentages were about three times greater than the prevalence for nonvictims. In addition, approximately one-third of the molestation and rape victims reported suicidal ideation at some point during their lives, compared with 19.6% of nonvictims. These results are consistent with those obtained from clinical samples and support the conclusion that victims of CSA are significantly at risk for developing self-destructive behaviors.

It appears that more severe forms of abuse may be related to the development of self-destructive behavior in victims of CSA. Briere and Runtz (1986) found that the number of suicide attempts and current suicidality were significantly correlated with compound abuse (physical and sexual abuse together) and the number of perpetrators. In addition, the number of suicide attempts was also associated with abuse involving intercourse. Similarly, Briere (1988) examined abuse-related factors that might be associated with self-mutilation and substance abuse in a clinical sample. Canonical correlations indicated that longer duration of abuse, concomitant physical abuse, bizarre sexual abuse, and multiple perpetrators were associated with alcohol/drug use and suicidality. Furthermore, abuse involving intercourse was associated with suicidality.

Explanations of the self-destructiveness of adults with abuse histories focus primarily on issues related to poor self-esteem and self-blame (Briere & Runtz, 1986, 1988b; McCann et al., 1988). The lost self-esteem observed in many victims suggests that they see themselves as unworthy, undeserving of life, and ineffective in coping with stress. Furthermore, the high degree of self-blame that many victims experience in relation to their victimization may lead some victims to believe that they should punish themselves for their involvement (Briere & Runtz, 1986; Jehu, 1988).

A second dynamic that may be associated with self-destructiveness is powerlessness (Briere & Runtz, 1986, 1988b). The individual may experience himself or herself as powerless to cope with situations with which they are confronted and they may actually have a limited repertoire of coping strategies. Thus, self-destructive behaviors may be a maladaptive coping mechanism by which the individual hopes to escape or avoid dysphoric feelings and emotional pain (Blake-White & Kline, 1985; Briere & Runtz, 1986). Alternatively, they may perceive that they have no other mechanism for communicating their pain (Briere & Runtz, 1986).

MALE VICTIMS

While the literature regarding female survivors of CSA is extensive, there is relatively little empirical research that has directly investigated the long-term effects of CSA in males. In addition, the knowledge we have of male victims may not be reflective of male victims in general, as it has been noted that abuse of males is severely underreported (e.g., Finkelhor, 1984; Johanek, 1988). Several factors may combine to limit the disclosure of victimization of males and may affect the development of psychosocial problems in male victims. There appear to be significant cultural biases against males as victims in that there may be the expectation that males are self-reliant and should be capable or preventing abuse from occurring (Finkelhor, 1984; Johanek, 1988). Furthermore, Johanek (1988) suggests that males may have a sexual response to the abuse, which may foster a strong sense of self-blame in male victims. The stigma of homosexuality may be a factor in males' tendency to keep their abuse secret (Finkelhor, 1984; Johanek, 1988), although one report suggests that males may be more likely to be abused by an older female than a male (Fritz et al., 1981). Because of these limits to disclosure in male victims, we caution the reader in interpreting the findings that we will present. It is imperative that future research on the effects of victimization include both male and female victims in order to broaden our understanding of the similarities and differences in the responses of males and females to a victimization experience.

Johanek (1988) has observed that alcoholism and homosexual concerns are common in his clinical experiences with male victims. Furthermore, male victims have particular difficulties in settings that entail close contact with other men. Kelly et al. (1987), who assessed 16 nonabusing men who were sexually abused in childhood, indicated that these men reported a significant number of problems that parallel those discussed in relation to female victims, including emotional reactions (e.g., depression and anxiety), negative self-perceptions, self-destructive behavior, dissociation, interpersonal problems, effects on sexuality, and problems associated with social functioning. For the most part, many of these problems were attributed by these men to their abuse experiences. Almost all of these men waited for a significant length of time to disclose their abusive experiences. Common difficulties that were reported in these men were dissatisfaction with sexual relationships (67%), feelings of isolation (88%), and depression (88%). In addition, most of the men indicated that they had experienced confusion about their sexual identity at some point in their life. This sample was highly selective, as it included a small number of men who presented for treatment and who were not involved in sexual aggression toward others. Furthermore, the lack of a comparison group precludes strong statements regarding the effects of CSA on males.

In contrast to these reports, a number of studies have found that male victims evaluate their early sexual experiences less negatively than females (Finkelhor, 1984; Fritz et al., 1981). In addition, the particular effects on males may be different from those on females according to several reports. Carmen et al. (1984) observed in an inpatient sample that abused males were more abusive toward others, more frequently were involved in criminal behavior, and were less depressed or suicidal than were nonabused males or abused females.

The most common outcome that has been studied in relation to male victims has been violent or criminal behavior (Groth, 1979; Seghorn et al., 1987). Burgess et al. (1988) found 56.1% of a convenience sample of serial rapists studied had been sexually abused and 19.5% more had witnessed at least one sexually disturbing event. More than half of the abuse experiences involved force or exploitation and often there were multiple occurrences with the same abuser. The authors caution that not all rapists have been sexually abused as children and sexual abuse does not in and of itself explain sexual aggression. Family pathology, including physical abuse and neglect, often combines with sexual abuse in the history of rapists. Moreover, samples of sex offenders studied to date cannot be presumed to be representative.

There have only been two empirical studies that have included a large number of male victims in comparison with nonvictims and female victims. Briere et al. (1988) compared male and female victims who were seeking treatment and found no sex differences in the problems victims reported. Both male and female victims reported significantly more problems related to dissociation, anxiety, depression, anger, sleep disturbance, and what the authors termed, "Post Sexual Abuse Trauma-hypothesized," than their nonabused counterparts. However, males had somewhat less severe abuse than females, leading the authors to conclude that either there are effects of abuse regardless of its severity or that males actually have more traumagenic effects from abuse than females. They further suggest that male problems may be qualitatively different from those of females and that additional domains of psychosocial functioning should be investigated in this regard.

Stein et al. (1988), investigating a community sample, found that male abuse victims, compared with male nonvictims, had higher rates of drug abuse/dependence, substance abuse/dependence and a higher probability of having a psychiatric diagnosis at some point in their lives. Male abuse victims were more likely to have a current mental disorder and drug abuse/dependence at the time of the interview than did nonvictimized men. These results suggest that the problems male victims experience center around acting out behaviors. In addition, men appeared to experience fewer psychiatric difficulties than did females.

Theoretical perspectives on the limits to disclosure of male victimization presented here may also be relevant to the understanding of the effects of sexual victimization on males. The cultural biases against males as victims and the stigmatization of homosexuality that may be associated with the victimization experience may have significant effects on the male victim's view of himself. Men may be more likely than women to defend against feelings of vulnerability through the use of acting out behaviors, such as aggression and substance abuse. In addition, whether the offender was male or female may have differential effects on the way in which a male victim views himself and others. When the offender is a male, the victim may fear that the experience has marked him as a homosexual (Burgess et al., 1988; Finkelhor, 1984; Johanek, 1988). In addition, men may then be viewed as dangerous, which may subsequently affect the victim's self-image as a male. If the offender is a woman, the boy must shift his ideas about sexual aggression to include the idea that women can be aggressive. Such an experience may create some dissonance between personal experience and societal views of women as sexually passive, vulnerable and in need of protection (Burgess et al., 1988). This set of dynamics likely will have implications for the male victim's interpersonal relationships with women.

ETHNIC DIFFERENCES

Recently, research has begun to address the impact of ethnicity on mediating the effects of CSA. Stein et al. (1988) found differing patterns of psychiatric diagnoses in Hispanic and non-Hispanic white victims in comparison with their nonabused counterparts. Hispanic victims had higher rates of having any lifetime DSM-III diagnosis and, in particular, had higher lifetime rates of drug abuse/dependence, affective disorder, major depression, anxiety, phobia, and dysthymia relative to nonabused Hispanics. Non-Hispanic white victims were more likely than their nonabused counterparts to have any lifetime DSM–III–diagnosis, drug abuse/dependence, anxiety, and antisocial personality disorders. At the time of the interview, abused Hispanics had higher rates than nonabused Hispanics of having any current diagnosis, as well as higher rates of affective disorder and major depression. The only difference between non-Hispanic victims and nonvictims was that the former had a higher current prevalence of anxiety disorders. The authors suggest that ethnicity may exacerbate effects of CSA or, conversely, that abuse experience may compound problems associated with lower socioeconomic status.

Russell (1986) found differences among ethnic groups in relation to the degree of trauma experienced by women post-CSA. Trauma was greatest in Latin female victims followed by Afro-American, Asian, and White victims. Russell et al. (1988) reported that more Afro-American victims rated their experiences as extremely upsetting than did Whites. Furthermore, Afro-American incest victims were more likely to have reported "worst" outcome (in terms of negative life events) than either White victims or Afro-American nonvictims. The abuse experiences of Afro-American women were reported as being more severe than those of White women in that they included more force/violence, began at a later age, were more likely to be perpetrated by someone other than their biological father, and were more likely to be abused by a stepfather than white victims. Russell comes to similar conclusions as Stein et al., suggesting that the trauma of incest might be compounded by racial inequalities. However, most existing studies have not controlled for the possible effects of socioeconomic class factors that generally are confounded with racial status.

EFFECTS OF DISCLOSURE

An area that has been largely overlooked in empirical research has been the impact of disclosure and the response to disclosure on the functioning of adults who were victimized in childhood (Browne & Finkelhor, 1986; Steele & Alexander, 1981). Events following disclosure, such as the response of others, changes in the family, and/or removal of the child to foster care, likely impact on the degree to which CSA is traumatic (Sgroi & Bunk, 1988). Others may respond to disclosure by expressing shock, disbelief, and denial. In addition, disclosure of intrafamilial sexual abuse disrupts the equilibrium of the family, making it especially difficult for the child's mother to cope with her experience of betrayal by a family member whom she trusts (Herman, 1981). In particular, offenders often deny that they have abused the child in an effort to save themselves, which, in cases of father–child abuse, places the mother in the position of having to choose between her husband and her child. Furthermore, the threats that offenders use to elicit the child's cooperation and secrecy may have accurately predicted the outcome of disclosure, reinforcing the victim's perception of the offender as a powerful individual.

In addition to denial within the family, many professionals deny that abuse occurs or seek to find alternative explanations for the child's report of abuse (e.g., suggesting that somebody, usually the mother, has coached the child to make the report), which further compounds the emotional distress of the child victim. Furthermore, should a professional evaluate the child and conclude that they were not abused, the child may be placed back into an abusive situation. Thus, the child might need to cope not only with an environment of disbelief, but also with being at risk for further abuse by the offender. In contrast, if a professional's evaluation confirms abuse, the child may be removed from the home. This process may have its own traumagenic effects, as it may communicate to the children that they are being punished for the abuse which, in effect, reinforces the stigmatization and betrayal experienced directly from the abuse. In addition, removal of the child increases the chances of the parental dyad uniting against the child (Herman, 1981). Finally, the effects of multiple interviews and experiences with the criminal justice system may impact on the child and are only beginning to be addressed in the literature (Goodman, 1984; Runyan, Everson, Edelsohn, Hunter, & Coulter, 1988).

A child who discloses abuse deserves reassurance and support. In addition, the mother in an incestuous family, and both parents if the abuse is perpetrated by a nonparental figure, require a great deal of support and information in order to cope effectively with the reality of their child's victimization. Unfortunately, support may not be provided to a victim or their family, and the effects of disclosure may exacerbate those that are directly related to the abuse experience.

Wyatt and Mickey (1988) examined features of disclosure in relation to the effects of CSA in an empirical study of a community sample. Their findings suggest that the response to disclosure is important to the child's perception of the experience. Support of significant others validates that the abuse occurred, that it was traumatic, and that it was not the child's fault. In contrast, lack of support may lead to self-blame and negative perceptions about not only the self, but also about trusted others. Thus, in clinical work with an adult survivor of abuse it is essential to understand the events that followed disclosure, as they may have either reinforced or counteracted the traumagenic effects of the abuse (Powell, 1988).

Empirical research is necessary to understand better the relationship between specific responses to disclosure and subsequent psychosocial functioning. Furthermore, research should address the impact of perpetrator's acknowledgment of his or her behavior on the functioning of the child victim. It seems likely that the negative effects of CSA may be mediated if the offender acknowledges his or her behavior, takes responsibility for the behavior, and clarifies to the child that the abuse was not the child's fault. Current treatment strategies that focus on the entire family in cases of intrafamilial abuse facilitate positive interactions between an acknowledging perpetrator and the child victim. It would be helpful to assess whether such strategies do in fact attenuate long-term reactions of victims of CSA.

ASSESSMENT AND TREATMENT

The assessment of adults who were victimized in childhood is a two-pronged process. Assessment should focus on the sexual abuse experience as well as the effects of the abuse on psychosocial functioning. Assessment of abuse experiences is most crucial to research on victimization in that adequate screening for abuse maximizes the extent to which findings may be generalized to other samples of victims. In addition, adequate assessment of victimization is necessary in clinical practice in order to ensure that the etiology of a client's difficulties is identified accurately.

While in many cases clients will present for treatment because of problems that they view as related to CSA, research suggests that many victims do not identify themselves as such without explicit questioning (e.g., Briere & Runtz, 1988b; Saunders et al., 1989). There are many reasons why victims may be reluctant to disclose their abuse experiences and both clinicians and researchers must be aware of these in order to maximize their ability to detect CSA in their clients and research participants.

The literature on sexual assault in adulthood provides some assistance in understanding the reluctance of victims to disclose their experiences as well as offering suggestions for assessment of such experiences (Lipovsky, 1989). Kilpatrick (1983) discussed several reasons why victims of sexual assault do not disclose their victimization. First, victims often have significant fears about the type of response that will follow disclosure. They may fear retribution, lack of belief, or that the recipient of the information may blame them for the crime. If the individual has disclosed their experience previously, either to family members, friends, or police, the response that they received at that time may affect their willingness to disclose to additional people. A second reason for a lack of disclosure of victimization experiences is that victims often do not perceive their psychological or social difficulties to be associated with their sexual victimization. Third, clinicians often do not ask about sexual victimization. Finally, victims may not identify their experience as a victimization. Each of these reasons is relevant to the reluctance of victims of CSA to disclose their experiences.

In order for clinicians to facilitate the disclosure of CSA they must be aware of these reasons for nondisclosure. To offset victim fears of negative responses, clinicians must maintain a nonjudgmental, supportive stance when dealing with their clients in order to prevent unnecessary negative effects of disclosure. In addition, it is important that clinicians ask routine questions about CSA during intake evaluations (Bagley & Ramsay, 1986; Herman, 1981). In asking about abuse, a clinician can convey the nonjudgmental, supportive stance by preceding questions with a statement that conveys an interest in the individual's life experience, awareness that victimization may relate to problems that would be expected in anyone with that experience, and awareness of the difficulties of disclosure. Use of such an introduction may help to put a client somewhat at ease about discussing victimization experiences.

In addition to assessment of CSA history, it is important in both research and clinical work to assess the particular psychosocial difficulties experiences by adults victimized in childhood. The DIS (Robins et al., 1981) has been employed in several studies (e.g., Saunders et al., 1987; Stein et al., 1988) and has been very useful in identifying the prevalence of DSM-III diagnoses in abuse victims. This interview schedule is also useful in clinical work with victims, as it covers the spectrum of DSM-III disorders.

The SCL90 (Derogatis, 1977) or the revised version (SCL90R) have been used in several studies of the effects of CSA. Fromuth (1986) found relatively small relationships between SCL90 subscale scores and a history of CSA. In contrast, two studies (Bryer et al., 1987; Murphy et al., 1988) found significant relationships between different types of abuse and the subscales of the SCL90R. Bryer et al. (1987) found that victims of concomitant physical and sexual abuse scored higher on all subscales of the SCL90R than did victims of either physical or sexual abuse alone. In addition, all victim groups scored higher than the nonvictim comparison group on this measure. A discriminant function analysis indicated that the obsessive–compulsive subscale, combined with the general severity index and the positive symptom distress index, correctly classified 72.7% of their subjects. Murphy et al. (1988) found that victims of multiple assaults scored higher than victims of abuse in childhood, adolescence or adulthood, and nonvictims on all subscales of the SCL90R with the exception of the phobic anxiety and paranoid ideation scales (no differences found between victim groups), and psychoticism (similar to adolescent and adult victims). Adolescent victims scored high-

er than nonvictims on the obsessive–compulsive, interpersonal sensitivity, anxiety, hostility, and paranoid ideation subscales. Victims of abuse
in childhood scored higher than nonvictims on the anxiety subscale. All
of the victim groups scored higher than nonvictims on the positive
symptom total, with multiple victims scoring higher than victims of
abuse in childhood who scored higher than victims of abuse in adolescence. The results of these latter two studies suggest that the SCL90R is a
useful tool for the measurement of distress in victim samples or in
individual clients who have abuse histories.

In addition to assessing current problems, it is essential that clinicians
inquire about initial effects of the abuse, disclosure and the impact of
disclosure, victimization history subsequent to the abuse, and history of
sexually transmitted diseases (Powell, 1988) in order to understand the
client's individual experiences. Furthermore, it is important to assess
whether or not the client has been involved in treatment prior to the
current presentation and whether or not any previous treatment addressed issues related to the CSA. Finally, the expectations of the client
for treatment and the goals that he or she has must be explored in order
to ensure that they have a realistic view of what therapeutic intervention
can offer.

There are quite a few reports of specific suggestions for treatment in
the literature (e.g., Blake-White & Kline, 1985; Donaldson & Gardner,
1985; Faria & Belohlavek, 1984; Goodman & Nowak-Scibelli, 1985;
Jehu, 1988; Lindberg & Distad, 1985). However, to date, there have
been no systematic outcome studies evaluating the effectiveness of extant approaches to the treatment of CSA effects in adult survivors. This
is an area of research that has not been tapped but is important to the
understanding of therapeutic factors that may help to alleviate some of
the psychological and social effects associated with the experience of
CSA.

There appear to be some commonalities amongst reports of treatment strategies used with adults who have been sexually abused in
childhood. First and foremost, both researchers and clinicians working
in this area emphasize that treatment must be victimization-focused
(Blake-White & Kline, 1985; Briere & Runtz, 1988b; Donaldson &
Gardner, 1985) rather than focusing on presenting problems as if they
were unrelated to the client's abusive experiences. This process is facilitated by encouraging victims to disclose and discuss their victimization
experiences in order to learn to manage the feelings associated with
their memories of the experience (Bagley & Ramsay, 1986; Blake-White
& Kline 1985; Faria & Belohlavek, 1984; Gordy, 1983; McCann et al.,
1988; Sgroi & Bunk, 1988; Tsai & Wagner, 1978). Treatment is often
difficult due to the extreme avoidance and denial that victims have in

reference to thoughts and feelings about the abuse (Lindberg & Distad, 1985). Time limited therapy is encouraged by a number of authors (Goodman & Nowak-Scibelli, 1985; Herman & Schatzow, 1984; Sgroi & Bunk, 1988; Tsai & Wagner, 1978) in order to counteract the tendency for victims to attempt to avoid through delaying disclosure and exploration of their abuse experiences. Stringent time limits help to maintain a focus on treatment goals.

The goal in treatment is for the victim to be able to integrate their memories such that recalling events from childhood is not an experience of such emotional distress that it overwhelms them and interferes with adaptive functioning. Integration is a process by which the individual connects his or her past experiences with present behavioral patterns and relationships (Bagley & Ramsay, 1986; Blake-White & Kline, 1985; Cole & Barney, 1987; Sgroi & Bunk, 1988). In addition, it involves exploring current feelings about the abuse and its impact on current functioning (Goodman & Nowak-Scibelli, 1985). In order to work toward the goal of integrating abusive experiences, victims must repeatedly go through the process of exploring their memories, releasing feelings, and reviewing their thoughts and beliefs about the abuse, the offender, significant others, and themselves (Donaldson & Gardner, 1985; Jehu, 1988). Repetition of the exploration process leads to a decrease in intrusive thoughts and distress associated with memories of the abuse (Briere & Runtz, 1988b).

The process of repeated disclosure and exploration, occurring in safe, supportive environment can work to counteract avoidance and denial, and allows the victim to experience thoughts and feelings without automatically denying them or dissociating from them (Donaldson & Gardner, 1985; McCann et al., 1988; Sgroi & Bunk, 1988). The individual needs to be able to tolerate exposure to memories of their abusive experiences in order to explore and ultimately integrate them in an adaptive manner. It is important that the therapist assist each victim in finding the "therapeutic window" (Cole & Barney, 1987), which is the psychological area between being overwhelmed by thoughts or feelings and being overly cut off from feelings. The most successful treatment likely occurs at this juncture in which the victim is at a moderate level of distress so that they are motivated by their discomfort but not prevented by overwhelming affect from exploring dicomforting memories.

It is important that treatment provide clients a framework for helping them to understand that their symptoms may be a logical outcome of their abuse experiences (Briere & Runtz, 1988b; Donaldson & Gardner, 1985; Jehu, 1988). For example, giving victims information about PTSD or the traumagenic effects (Finkelhor & Browne, 1985) of abuse may help them to understand the etiology of their symptoms.

A number of reports in the literature emphasize the need for therapeutic focus on the cognitive distortions that victims have about themselves, the abuse, other people, and the world in general (Briere & Runtz, 1988b; Cole & Barney, 1987; Faria & Belohlavek, 1984; Jehu, 1988; Jehu, Klassen, & Gazan, 1986). Cognitive–behavioral therapy focuses on the relationship between thoughts and feelings. It involves recognizing distorted cognitions, becoming aware of more accurate or healthier beliefs, and substituting these more adaptive beliefs for distorted thinking (Jehu et al., 1986). Treatment involves providing the individual with information, analyzing the logic of specific thoughts, helping him or her to decatastrophize and become more flexible in their thinking, to distance oneself from the feelings aroused by thoughts (Jehu, 1988), and to reinterpret self-damaging beliefs (Cole & Barney, 1987).

In addition to more general strategies for treatment, it is important that therapeutic interventions address specific difficulties presented by individual victims (Meiselman, 1978). Thus, a particular individual's difficulties might necessitate treatment focusing on issues related to trust (Bagley & Ramsay, 1986; Sgroi & Bunk, 1988), the appropriate expression of anger (Agosta & Loring, 1988; Faria & Belohlavek, 1984; Gordy, 1983), building self-esteem (Faria & Belohlavek, 1984; Lindberg & Distad, 1985), increasing social support through networking (Faria & Belohlavek, 1984), developing more effective social skills (Sgroi & Bunk, 1988), reducing sexual difficulties (Meiselman, 1978), and/or increasing assertiveness (Goodman & Nowak-Scibelli, 1985). In addition, treatment should involve the identification of risk factors for further victimization (Goodman & Nowak-Scibelli, 1985).

Family therapy can be an important therapeutic approach for treatment of relational issues that have the basis in the functioning of the victim's family of origin (Gelinas, 1988), particularly when the abuse occurred within the family. The focus of family therapy should be on the interpersonal relationship difficulties and should include exploration of each family member's role within the family as well as in relation to the abuse (Deighton & McPeek, 1985). It is important to support all family members, including the offender. It is possible to keep the perpetrator accountable without scapegoating him or her (Gelinas, 1988; Goodman & Nowak-Scibelli, 1985). That is, while perpetrators are continually viewed as being responsible for their sexual offenses, exploration of factors in their lives that may have contributed to the abuse is also a focus of treatment.

It is possible to complete therapeutic work on family of origin issues in individual therapy with the adult victim of intrafamilial CSA. Such work may address the emotional cutoff of the victim from his or her family of origin and should include education regarding generational issues in the etiology of incest (Deighton & McPeek, 1985). That is, focus will be on dysfunctional relationship patterns within the family of origin that contributed to the development of the sexual abuse. Examination of factors that may have led to the singling out of the client as victim within the family of origin may help to facilitate a more objective view of the client in relation to his or her family (Deighton & McPeek, 1985). It is important that relationships between the victim and his or her family be rebalanced so that the client no longer functions in the role of victim or parental child (Goodman & Nowak-Scibelli, 1985). In particular, issues related to the mother–child relationship, such as the client's experience of their mother's lack of protection, must be addressed in such work (Gold, 1986).

In some situations, it may be important to include therapeutic work with victim's partner (Deighton & McPeek, 1985). In particular, if the victim has difficulty with issues of trust or intimacy, or if he or she is sexually dysfunctional, it may be of value to include the partner. Such work should involve educating the partner to common victim reactions so as to provide a framework for understanding their partner's difficulties. In addition, the victim's partner may have his or her own emotional difficulties, which interact with those of the victim. Finally, if the relationship is abusive, it is imperative that the partner be included in treatment if one of the goals is to maintain the relationship.

Much has been written about the utility of group therapy with adults who were victimized in childhood. Therapeutic work in a group setting helps each victim to see that they are not the only person to have experienced CSA. Group work counteracts the social isolation many victims experience that is a function of secrecy (Bagley & Ramsay, 1986; Deighton & McPeek, 1985). Therapy groups provide support and the opportunity for identifying with others (Donaldson & Gardner, 1985; Gordy, 1983; Van Buskirk & Cole, 1983), as well as facilitating the provision of feedback regarding victims' interpersonal styles and for disconfirming distorted cognitions (Agosta & Loring, 1988).

Many of the group treatments that have been described in the literature carefully screen potential participants (Cole & Barney, 1987; Gordy, 1983; Herman & Schatzow, 1984). It appears that most of the reports are based upon groups of relatively high-functioning individuals who are not in current or chronic crisis (Cole & Barney, 1987; Goodman & Nowak-Scibelli, 1985), who have a social support system and who do not have recent or current substance abuse (Cole & Barney, 1987). In general, one of the requirements of group participation is that group members be involved in an individual therapy relationship (Cole &

Barney, 1987; Goodman & Nowak-Scibelli, 1985; Gordy, 1983; Herman & Schatzow, 1984).

A variety of creative techniques have reportedly been used in treatment of the adult who has an abuse history. Techniques that have been described include using photographs of the victim as a child to facilitate exploration of feelings engendered by the abuse in childhood (Cole & Barney, 1987), journal/letter writing, bibliotherapy, exercise and diet adjustment, hypnosis, gestalt techniques (Faria & Belohlavek, 1984), wilderness therapy and self-defense training (Agosta & Loring, 1988).

Several reports provide suggestions for therapists working with adults who have experienced CSA. It is imperative that the therapist support and believe the client's report and not ascribe the abuse experience to fantasy (Bagley & Ramsay, 1986; Meiselman, 1978). In addition, as victims often have an impaired ability to trust others the therapist must not expect the victimized client to trust them or the therapeutic process. It is important, however, that the therapist behave in a trustworthy manner (Sgroi & Bunk, 1988). The therapist must respect loyalty issues of the client, who may continue to have positive feelings toward the offender and may have difficulty progressing in therapy because of these feelings (Gelinas, 1988; Goodman & Nowak-Scibelli, 1985). The goals of treatment should be identified and defined by the client, but the therapist must ensure that these goals are realistic and attainable (Sgroi & Bunk, 1988). Furthermore, it is important to allow the client to move at their own pace, as proceeding too quickly might be overwhelming and ultimately damaging to the process of healing (Agosta & Loring, 1988).

SUMMARY AND CONCLUSIONS

This chapter has identified the broad range of problems noted in adults with a victimization history. The literature in this area indicates that CSA is a significant public health problem. Clearly, victims present with a wide variety of psychosocial difficulties; however, further research is necessary to understand better the relationship between abuse experiences and specific problems. It should be kept in mind that much of this research is based upon women, the majority of whom did not disclose their abuse or receive treatment for its effects. With greater societal awareness and somewhat greater acceptance of the fact that sexual abuse does occur, it may be that there is an increase in the disclosure of abuse while the victim is a child. Interventions with child victims relatively soon after disclosure are increasingly common, and there has been a growth of resources designed specifically for the child victim and his or her family, as well as for the adult survivor of sexual abuse. It will be interesting to follow the literature on the effects of CSA as therapeutic interventions with children are used more commonly. Hopefully, these interventions will have a preventive effect in attenuating or eradicating the possible lifelong problems of victims of sexual abuse.

In the meantime, there are still questions left unanswered by the extant research. One area of interest is in determining the comorbidity of psychosocial difficulties. That is, is there a subset of victims that has diffuse problems with adjustment that are manifested by coexisting symptoms or syndromes, or do victims develop specific difficulties that directly relate to aspects of the abuse, to family dynamics, or to events following disclosure of the abuse? Research on this issue would help to clarify the relationships among effects seen in adults abused in childhood.

A second set of issues relates to the specific problem areas found to be common to the functioning of victims. Research has attempted to uncover associations between characteristics of the abuse and later symptomatology; however, relationships between specific abuse-related factors and specific psychosocial difficulties have not consistently been found. It may be, as Briere (1988) has observed, that CSA is itself traumatic but it becomes more destructive in the presence of specific factors. Further research should address this issue using representative community samples of victims.

A third area that has been largely unexplored is the impact of disclosure and the aftermath of disclosure on the functioning of the abuse victim. Most of the research does not examine these factors in relation to psychosocial adjustment, which makes it difficult to determine the degree to which symptoms relate to the abuse itself or to the consequences of disclosure. Characteristic aftereffects of disclosure, such as removal of the child victim or separation of an offending parent in cases of intrafamilial abuse, have been understudied and should be a focus of future research.

Finally, several theoretical perspectives have been put forth (Briere & Runtz, 1988b; Finkelhor & Browne, 1985; McCann et al., 1988), but they require systematic testing. While each of these positions attempts to explain the etiology of psychosocial difficulties of victims, they have not, as yet, been investigated in empirical studies. In order to understand more fully the development of specific difficulties in adults victimized in childhood, empirical research should seek to evaluate proferred theoretical explanations of the etiology of abuse-related psychological and social problems.

REFERENCES

Agosta, C., & Loring, M. (1988). Understanding and treating the adult retrospective victim of child sexual abuse. In S. M. Sgroi (Ed.), *Vulnerable populations: Evaluation and treatment of sexually abused children and adult survivors* (Vol. 1, pp. 115–135). Lexington, MA: Lexington Books.

Alexander, P. C., & Lupfer, S. L. (1987). Family characteristics and long-term consequences associated with sexual abuse. *Archives of Sexual Behavior, 16,* 235–245.

American Psychiatric Association. (1980). *Diagnostic and statistical manual of mental disorders* (3rd ed.). Washington, DC: Author.

Bagley, C., & Ramsay, R. (1986). Sexual abuse in childhood: Psychosocial outcomes and implications for social work practice. *Journal of Social Work and Human Sexuality, 4,* 33–47.

Beck, A. T. (1976). *Cognitive therapy and the emotional disorders.* New York: International Universities Press.

Beck, A. T., Rial, W. Y., & Rickels, K. (1974). Short form of the Beck Depression Inventory: Cross-validation. *Psychological Reports, 34,* 1184–1186.

Beck, J. D., & van der Kolk, B. (1987). Reports of childhood incest and current behavior of chronically hospitalized psychotic women. *American Journal of Psychiatry, 144,* 1474–1476.

Becker, J. V., Cunningham-Rathner, J., & Kaplan, M. S. (1987). Adolescent sexual offenders: Demographics, criminal and sexual histories, and recommendations for reducing future offenses. *Journal of Interpersonal Violence, 1,* 431–445.

Best, C. B., & Kilpatrick, D. G., Kramer, T. L., & McNeill-Harkins, K. (1990, unpublished). Methodological issues in the screening and assessment of rape victims. *Journal of Interpersonal Violence.*

Blake-White, J., & Kline, C. M. (1985). Treating the dissociative process in adult victims of childhood incest. *Social Casework: Journal of Contemporary Social Work, 65,* 394–402.

Bliss, E. L. (1980). Multiple personalities: A report of 14 cases with implications for schizophrenia and hysteria. *Archives of General Psychiatry, 37,* 1388–1397.

Bowman, E. S., Blix, S., & Coons, P. M. (1985). Multiple personality in adolescence: Relationship to incestual experiences. *Journal of the American Academy of Child Psychiatry, 24,* 109–114.

Briere, J. (1984). *The effects of childhood sexual abuse on later psychological functioning: Defining a "post-sexual-abuse syndrome."* Paper presented to the third national conference on Sexual Victimization of Children, Washington, DC.

Briere, J. (1988). The long-term clinical correlates of childhood sexual victimization. In R. A. Prentky & V. L. Quinsey (Eds.), *Annals of the New York Academy of Sciences, 528,* 327–334.

Briere, J., Evans, D., Runtz, M., & Wall, T. (1988). Symptomatology in men who were molested as children: A comparison study. *American Journal of Orthopsychiatry, 58,* 457–461.

Briere, J., & Runtz, M. (1986). Suicidal thoughts and behaviours in former sexual abuse victims. *Canadian Journal of Behavioural Sciences, 18,* 413–423.

Briere, J., & Runtz, M. (1988a). Symptomatology associated with childhood sexual victimization in a non-clinical adult sample. *Child Abuse and Neglect, 12,* 51–59.

Briere, J., & Runtz, M. (1988b). Post sexual abuse trauma. In G. E. Wyatt & G. J. Powell (Eds.), *Lasting effects of child sexual abuse* (pp. 85–99). Newberry Park, CA: Sage.

Browne, A., & Finkelhor, D. (1986). Impact of child sexual abuse: A review of the research. *Psychological Bulletin, 99,* 66–77.

Bryer, J. B., Nelson, B. A., Miller, J. B., & Krol, P. A. (1987). Childhood sexual and physical abuse as factors in adult psychiatric illness. *American Journal of Psychiatry, 144,* 1426–1430.

Burgess, A. W., Hazelwood, R. R., Rokous, F. E., Hartman, C. R., & Burgess, A. G. (1988). Serial rapists and their victims: Reenactment and repetition. In R. A. Prentky & V. L. Quinsey (Eds.), *Annals of the New York Academy of Sciences, 528,* 277–295.

Carmen, E. H., Rieker, P. P., & Mills, T. (1984). Victims of violence and psychiatric illness. *American Journal of Psychiatry, 141,* 378–383.

Cole, C. H., & Barney, E. E. (1987). Safeguards and the therapeutic window: A group treatment strategy for adult incest survivors. *American Journal of Orthopsychiatry, 57,* 601–609.

Coons, P. M. (1986). Child abuse and multiple personality disorder: Review of the literature and suggestions for treatment. *Child Abuse and Neglect, 10,* 455–462.

Coons, P. M., & Milstein, V. (1986). Psychosexual disturbances in multiple personality: Characteristics, etiology, and treatment. *Journal of Clinical Psychiatry, 47,* 106–110.

Courtois, C. A. (1979). The incest experience and its aftermath. *Victimology: An International Journal, 4,* 337–347.

Deighton, J., & McPeek, P. (1985). Group treatment: Adult victims of childhood sexual abuse. *Social Casework: Journal of Contemporary Social Work, 66,* 403–410.

Derogatis, L. R. (1977). *SCL–90: Administration, scoring, and procedure manual–I for the R (revised) version.* Baltimore: Johns Hopkins University School of Medicine.

Donaldson, M. A., & Gardner, R. (1985). Diagnosis and treatment of traumatic stress among women and childhood incest. In C. R. Figley (Ed.), *Trauma and its wake* (pp. 356–377). New York: Brunner/Mazel.

Elliot, D. S., Huizinga, D., & Ageton, S. S. (1985). *Explaining delinquency and drug use.* Beverly Hills, CA: Sage.

Endicott, J., & Spitzer, R. L. (1979). Use of the Research Diagnostic Criteria and the Schedule for Affective Disorders and Schizophrenia to study affective disorders. *American Journal of Psychiatry, 136,* 52–56.

Faria, G., & Belohlavek, N. (1984). Treating female adult survivors of childhood incest. *Social Casework, 65,* 465–471.

Finkelhor, D. (1984). *Child sexual abuse: New theory and research.* New York: Free Press.

Finkelhor, D. (1988). The trauma of child sexual abuse: Two models. In G. E. Wyatt & G. J. Powell (Eds.), *Lasting effects of child sexual abuse* (pp. 61–82). Newberry Park, CA: Sage.

Finkelhor, D., & Browne, A. (1985). The traumatic impact of child sexual abuse: A conceptualization. *American Journal of Orthopsychiatry, 55,* 530–541.

Forward, S., & Buck, C. (1978). *Betrayal of innocence: Incest and its devastation.* New York: Penguin Books.

Freud, S. (1917/1950). Mourning and melancholia. In *Collected papers* (Vol. 4). London: Hogarth Press and the Institute of Psychoanalysis.

Fritz, G. S., Stoll, K., & Wagner, N. N. (1981). A comparison of males and females who were sexually molested as children. *Journal of Sex and Marital Therapy, 7,* 54–59.

Fromuth, M. E. (1986). The relationship of childhood sexual abuse with later psychological and sexual adjustment in a sample of college women. *Child Abuse and Neglect, 10,* 5–15.

Gelinas, D. J. (1988). Family therapy: Characteristic family constellation and basic therapeutic stance. In S. M. Sgroi (Ed.), *Vulnerable populations: Evaluation and treatment of sexually abused children and adult survivors* (Vol. 1, pp. 25–49). Lexington, MA: Lexington Books.

Gold, E. R. (1986). Long-term effects of sexual victimization in childhood: An attributional approach. *Journal of Consulting and Clinical Psychology, 54,* 471–475.

Goodman, B., & Nowak-Scibelli, D. (1985). Group treatment for women incestuously abused as children. *International Journal of Group Psychotherapy, 35,* 531–544.

Goodman, G. S. (1984). The child witness: Conclusions and future directions for research and legal practice. *Journal of Social Issues, 40,* 157–175.

Gordy, P. L. (1983). Group work that supports adult victims of childhood incest. *Social Casework: Journal of Contemporary Social Work, 64,* 300–307.

Groth, A. N. (1979). Sexual trauma in the life histories of rapists and child molesters. *Victimology, 4,* 10–16.

Haller, O. L., & Alter-Reid, K. (1986). Secretiveness and guardedness: A comparison of two incest-survivor samples. *American Journal of Psychotherapy, 40,* 554–563.

Herman, J. L. (1981). *Father–daughter incest.* Cambridge, MA: Harvard University Press.

Herman, J., & Schatzow, E. (1984). Time-limited group therapy for women with a history of incest. *International Journal of Group Psychotherapy, 34,* 605–616.

Horowitz, M. J. (1976). *Stress response syndromes.* New York: Jason Aronson.

James, J., Myerding, J. (1977). Early sexual experience and prostitution. *American Journal of Psychiatry, 134,* 1382–1385.

Jehu, D. (1988). *Beyond sexual abuse: Therapy with women who were childhood victims.* New York: Wiley.

Jehu, D., Klassen, C., & Gazan, M. (1986). Cognitive restructuring of distorted beliefs associated with childhood sexual abuse. *Journal of Social Work and Human Sexuality, 4,* 49–69.

Johanek, M. F. (1988). Treatment of male victims of child sexual abuse in military service. In S. M. Sgroi (Ed.), *Vulnerable populations: Evaluation and treatment of sexually abused children and adult survivors* (Vol. 1, pp. 103–113). Lexington, MA: Lexington Books.

Kelly, R. J., MacDonald, V. M., & Waterman, J. M. (1987). *Psychological symptomatology in adult male victims of child sexual abuse: A preliminary report.* Paper presented at the joint conference of the American Psychological Association, Division 12, and the Hawaii Psychological Association, Honolulu.

Kilpatrick, D. G. (1983). Rape victims: Detection, assessment and treatment. *Clinical Psychologist, 36,* 92–95.

Kilpatrick, D. G., Best, C. L., Amick, A. E., Saunders, B. E., Sturgis, E. T., & Veronen, L. J. (1989). *Risk factors for substance abuse: A longitudinal study.* National Institute of Drug Abuse grant No. 1R01–DA05220.

Kilpatrick, D. G., Veronen, L. J., & Resick, P. A. (1982). Psychological sequelae to rape: Assessment and treatment strategies. In D. M. Doleys, R. L. Meredith, & A. R. Ciminero (Eds.), *Behavioral medicine: Assessment and treatment strategies* (pp. 473–497). New York: Plenum Press.

Koss, M. P. (1987). *Rape incidence and prevalence: A review and assessment of the data.* Presented at the NIMH-sponsored State of the Art Workshop on Sexual Assault, Charleston, SC.

Lindberg, F. H., & Distad, L. J. (1985). Post traumatic stress disorders in women who experienced childhood incest. *Child Abuse and Neglect, 9,* 329–334.

Lipovsky, J. A. (1989). *Clinical assessment of Crime Related-Post Traumatic Stress Disorder.* Presented at the midwinter meeting of the Society for Personality Assessment, New York.

Lukianowicz, N. (1972). Incest. *British Journal of Psychiatry, 120,* 301–313.

McCann, L., Pearlman, L. A., Sakheim, D. K., & Abrahamson, D. J. (1988). Assessment and treatment of the adult survivor of childhood sexual abuse within a schema framework. In S. M. Sgroi (Ed.), *Vulnerable populations: Evaluation and treatment of sexually abused children and adult survivors* (Vol. 1, pp. 77–101). Lexington, MA: Lexington Books.

Meiselman, K. C. (1978). *Incest.* New York: Jossey-Bass.

Murphy, S. M., Kilpatrick, D. G., Amick-McMullan, A., Veronen, L. J., Paduhovich, J., Best, C. L., Villeponteaux, L. A., & Saunders, B. E. (1988). Current psychological functioning of child sexual assault survivors: A community study. *Journal of Interpersonal Violence, 3,* 55–79.

Nelson, J. A. (1981). The impact of incest: Factors in self-evaluation. In L. L. Constantine & F. M. Martinson (Eds.), *Children and sex* (pp. 163–174). Boston: Little, Brown.

Paykel, E. S. (1974). Recent life events and clinical depression. In E. K. Gunderson & R. H. Babe (Eds.), *Life stress and illness.* Springfield, IL: Thomas.

Peters, S. D. (1988). Child sexual abuse and later psychological problems. In G. E. Wyatt & G. J. Powell (Eds.), *Lasting effects of child sexual abuse.* Newberry Park, CA: Sage.

Powell, G. J. (1988). Child sexual abuse research: The implications for clinical practice. In G. E. Wyatt & G. J. Powell (Eds.), *Lasting effects of child sexual abuse* (pp. 271–281) Newberry Park, CA: Sage.

Putnam, F. F. (1985). Dissociation as a response to extreme trauma. In R. P. Kluft (Ed.), *Childhood antecedents of multiple personality* (pp. 65–97). Washington, DC: American Psychiatric Association.

Robins, L. N., Helzer, J. E., Croughan, J., & Ratcliff, K. S. (1981). National Institute of Mental Health diagnostic interview schedule. *Archives of General Psychiatry, 848,* 381–389.

Runyan, D. K., Everson, M. D., Edelsohn, G. A., Hunter, W. M., & Coulter, M. L. (1988). Impact of legal intervention on sexually abused children. *Journal of Pediatrics, 113,* 647–653.

Russell, D. E. H. (1986). *The secret trauma: Incest in the lives of girls and women.* New York: Basic Books.

Russell, D. E. H., Schurman, R. A., & Trocki, K. (1988). The long-term effects of incestuous abuse: A comparison of Afro-American and White American victims. In G. E. Wyatt & G. J. Powell (Eds.), *Lasting effects of child sexual abuse* (pp. 119–134). Newberry Park, CA: Sage.

Saunders, B. E., Kilpatrick, D. G., Resnick, H. S., & Tidwell, R. P. (1989). Brief screening for lifetime history or criminal victimization at mental health intake: A preliminary study. *Journal of Interpersonal Violence, 4,* 267–277.

Saunders, B. E., Villeponteaux, L. A., Kilpatrick, D. G., & Veronen, L. J. (1987). *Childhood sexual assault as a risk factor in mental health.* Presentation at Social Work '87, the annual meeting of the National Association of Social Workers, New Orleans.

Sedney, M. A., & Brooks, B. (1984). Factors associated with a history of childhood sexual experience in a nonclinical female population. *Journal of the American Academy of Child Psychiatry, 23,* 215–218.

Seghorn, T. K., Prentky, R. A., & Boucher, R. J. (1987). Childhood sexual abuse in the lives of sexually aggressive offenders. *Journal of American Academy of Child and Adolescent Psychiatry, 26,* 262–267.

Seligman, M. E. P. (1971). Phobias and preparedness. *Behavior Therapy, 2,* 307–321.

Sgroi, S. M., & Bunk. B. S. (1988). A clinical approach to adult survivors of child sexual abuse. In S. M. Sgroi (Ed.), *Vulnerable populations: Evaluation and treatment of sexually abused children and adult survivors.* (Vol. 1, pp. 137–186). Lexington, MA: Lexington Books.

Siegel, J. M., Sorenson, S. B., Golding, J. M., Burnam, M. A., & Stein, J. A. (1987). The prevalence of childhood sexual assault: The Los Angeles Epidemiologic Catchment Area project. *American Journal of Epidemiology, 126,* 1141–1153.

Silbert , M. H., & Pines, A. M. (1981). Sexual child abuse as an antecedent to prostitution. *Child Abuse and Neglect, 5,* 407–411.

Steele, B. F., & Alexander, H. (1981). In P. B. Mrazek & C. H. Kempe (Eds.), *Sexually abused children and their families.* New York: Pergamon Press.

Stein, J. A., Golding, J. M., Siegel, J. M., Burnam, M. A., & Sorenson, S. B. (1988). Long-term psychological sequelae of child sexual abuse: The Los Angeles Epidemiologic Catchment area study. In G. E. Wyatt & G. J. Powell (Ed.), *Lasting effects of child sexual abuse* (pp. 135–154). Newberry Park, CA: Sage.

Summit, R. C. (1983). The child sexual abuse accommodation syndrome. *Child Abuse and Neglect, 7,* 177–193.

Tsazi, M., Feldman-Summers, S., & Edgar, M. (1979). Childhood molestation: Variables related to differential impacts on psychosexual functioning in adult women. *Journal of Abnormal Psychology, 58,* 407–417.

Tsai, M., & Wagner, N. N. (1978). Therapy groups for women sexually molested as children. *Archives of Sexual Behavior, 7,* 417–427.

Van Buskirk, S. S., & Cole, C. F. (1983). Characteristics of eight women seeking therapy for the effects of incest. *Psychotherapy: Theory, Research and Practice, 20,* 503–514.

Wyatt, G. E., & Mickey, M. R. (1988). The support by parents and others as it mediates the effects of child sexual abuse: An exploratory study. In G. E. Wyatt & G. J. Powell (Eds.), *Lasting effects of child sexual abuse* (pp. 211–226). Newberry Park, CA: Sage.

The Primary Prevention of Child Sexual Abuse

William O'Donohue
Northern Illinois University
James H. Geer
Louisiana State University
Ann Elliott
Northern Illinois University

In this chapter we will review research and discuss conceptual issues relating to the primary prevention of child sexual abuse. Preventative interventions are usefully grouped into three distinct types: Primary prevention is an attempt to reduce the incidence of new cases of a problem; secondary prevention attempts to detect problems early so that their magnitude may be limited through intervention; and tertiary prevention attempts to reduce the long-term consequences of a problem that has already progressed beyond its early stages. Some authors believe that tertiary prevention is a misnomer because it is equivalent to traditional therapeutic intervention, which does not attempt to intervene before problems occur (Cowen, 1983).

Preventing new cases of child sexual abuse is a highly desirable goal. First and most obviously, it is most desirable to spare the children and the families (and even the perpetrators) all the negative consequences that are associated with sexual abuse (Browne & Finkelhor, 1986). This is important because the sequelae of sexual abuse can be severe and lifelong. Second, Finkelhor (1986) has suggested that, because most cases of child sexual abuse go undetected, traditional therapy will be able to address only a small percentage of children who have been abused. Third, even given the opportunity to intervene with a child who has been sexually abused, there is a paucity of evidence suggesting that extant therapies are effective (O'Donohue & Elliott, 1990). Although it has been more than 100 years since Freud (1896/1957) discussed the psychological problems and therapy for child sexual abuse, to date there have been no properly controlled outcome studies demonstrating that we can effectively intervene with this type of case. Finally, primary prevention is desirable because it has the potential of having a positive impact on other associated problems (e.g., male sexual aggression, family violence, and quality of family life).

Preventative interventions aimed at child sexual abuse are well under way. In fact, Finkelhor (1986) has called it "one of the great social experiments of the decade" (p. 254). A recent national survey conducted by the National Committee for the Prevention of Child Abuse indicated that more than 25% of all public schools provide some sort of sexual abuse prevention program (Daro, Duerr, & LeProhn, 1986). Recently the California General Assembly has mandated that all schoolchildren participate in sexual abuse prevention programs. However, it is not clear whether these efforts have been based solely on good intentions and plausibility arguments or whether there have been well-conducted outcome studies to show that primary prevention programs actually prevent children from being abused, and that these have no costs (e.g., negative effects on children) that preclude their implementation. We turn now to a review of the prevention outcome literature.

ARE CHILD SEXUAL ABUSE PREVENTION PROGRAMS WORTHWHILE?

Potential Benefits

In order to evaluate the effectiveness of sexual abuse prevention programs, we must ultimately assess the question, "What is the evidence that current sexual abuse prevention programs actually reduce the number of incidents of child sexual abuse?". Unfortunately, the empirical literature is unable to provide evidence concerning this important question. No study has been conducted that has an adequate design to address this question. That is, we have no information that children who have completed prevention programs actually are sexually abused at a lower frequency.

A second means, although more indirect, of assessing the effectiveness of sexual abuse prevention programs is to address the related question, "Do prevention programs lead to changes in related factors (e.g., in presumably relevant knowledge and skills) that are assumed to reflect a child's ability to protect himself or herself?". Three important subsidiary questions arise: (1) Do prevention programs actually lead to knowledge gains in children?; (2) Do prevention programs lead to appropriate skill acquisition in children?; and (3) Do children apply skills/knowledge correctly in the real-life situations? These questions are of critical importance because most prevention programs are based on the implicit presupposition that increasing what are presumed to be relevant knowledge and self-protection skills will reduce the child's susceptibility for sexual abuse. The empirical evidence concerning each of these questions will be presented. Next, we will discuss the important distinction between statistically significant versus practically/clinically significant results.

Do prevention programs actually lead to knowledge gains in children? Most empirical studies have addressed this question and have reported statistically significant increases in knowledge from pretesting to posttesting (e.g., Binder & McNiel, 1987; Downer, 1984; Plummer, 1984). Results also suggest that children who have participated in prevention training generally have statistically greater increases in sexual abuse prevention knowledge, compared with nonintervention control subjects (e.g., Conte, Rosen, Saperstein, & Shermack, 1985; Harvey, Forehand, Brown, & Holmes, 1988; Kolko, Moser, Litz, & Hughes, 1987; Saslawsky & Wurtele, 1986). Older children have generally demonstrated statistically greater overall knowledge following training (Conte et al., 1985; Saslawsky & Wurtele, 1986; Wurtele, Saslawsky, Miller, Marrs, & Britcher, 1986), and regardless of age, children appear to have greater difficulty learning and retaining abstract concepts than more concrete concepts (Conte et al., 1985). Unfortunately, no specific examples of concrete and abstract concepts were provided.

Although significant increases in knowledge are commonly reported immediately following treatment, the results are less clear during follow-up assessments. For example, although 4–7-year-old children demonstrated significant increases in knowledge and skills immediately posttreatment, only the 6- and 7-year-old children maintained these gains at the 2-month follow-up assessment (Miltenberger & Thiesse-Duffy, 1988). Plummer (1984) found that only certain prevention concepts were not maintained at a 2- and 8-month follow-up (i.e., whether promises should ever be broken, whether abusers can be "people I know," and whether children would blame themselves if abuse were to occur). These authors reported that children's knowledge at the time of follow-up assessment was greater than that prior to training, but that a substantial amount of knowledge had been lost in the 8 months since the completion of training. It is an open and important empirical question if further losses would be found in longer follow-up periods, which, of course are more relevant. In a study of children ages 3–5, Borkin and Frank (1986) found that only 4% of the 3-year-olds and 43% of the 4- and 5-year olds correctly responded to the follow-up prevention assessment 4 to 6 weeks later. Saslawsky and Wurtele (1986) report that posttreatment gains in knowledge were maintained at the 3-month fol-

TABLE 15.1
Studies of Prevention Outcome

	Saslawsky & Wurtele (1985)	Wurtele, Saslawsky, Miller, Marrs, & Britcher (1986)	Poche, Brouwer, & Swearingen (1981)
Design used	Solomon 4-group design.	Posttest-only control group design.	Multiple baseline design across subjects.
Subject characteristics	26 Kindergarten—1st graders. 41 5–6th graders. Ages 5–7 & 10–12.	Grades K–1, 5–6. 36 girls, 35 boys. Rural, lower-middle class.	3 preschool children, 1 female, 2 males. Chosen since they readily agreed to accompnay an adult in another study.
Therapist characteristics	Female graduate student. No further information provided.	Female graduate and undergraduate students blind to treatment conditions.	2 adult trainers. Suspects were selected to resemble molestors in that area (male, age 20–35. Black & white).
Dependent variables	Personal Safety Questionnaire. "What if" Situations Test.	Personal Safety Questionnaire—group-administered. "What if" Situation Test—individually administered.	Analogue measure of self-protection. Verbal statements (appropriate, inappropriate, no vocalization). Child's movements (goes with suspect, stays near, goes away from suspect).
Intervention	Film "Touch" shown (models "saying no," yelling for help, getting away, & telling someone until you are believed). 15-minute discussion following.	Film condition vs. Behavior Skills Training Program (BST). vs. Combined group condition vs. No Treatment Control condition. One one-hour training session in school setting with group presentation. Film condition—Film "Touch" that models "saying no," yelling for help, getting away and telling someone. Discussion of film. BST—self-protective skills taught by instruction, modeling, rehearsal, social reinforcement, shaping & feedback. Combined group condition—film, discussion and BST. No treatment control condition—self-concept & personal values discussion.	Training included modeling, behavior rehearsal, and social reinforcement. 15-minute sessions in different locations on & around school grounds. Trained with modeling, behavioral rehearsal, & social reinforcement to resist 3 types of lures. Training completed in 5–6 sessions (90 minutes per child).

Behavior vs. knowledge assessed.	Knowledge & behavioral responses for hypothetical situations.	Assessed knowledge & skills.	Behavior.
Control groups used?	YES. Compared with group who participated in a self-concept and personal values discussion.	YES. Group participated in discussion of self-concept & personal values.	N/A
Random assignment?	YES	YES	Not randomly selected.
Evaluate negative effects of program?	NO	NO	NO
Do they assess which components work?	NO	Comparison across studies. Does not assess within condition components.	NO
Parental involvement?	NO	NO	NO
Is administration of program standardized (conform to protocol?)	YES. It is a filmed production.	No information provided.	No information provided.
Assess previous exposure to prevention program?	NO	No information provided.	No information provided.
No initial measurement sensitization control group	YES. Sensitization effect was not found.	No information provided.	N/A
Follow-up/generalization	3 months. Knowledge was maintained. Other films may not be effective.	3 month follow-up. Follow-up data unavailable for control condition.	All children responded correctly to all three types of lures posttraining. 12-week follow-up.
Authors' conclusions	Film led to statistically significant increases in knowledge of sexual abuse and enhanced personal safety skills compared to controls. Older children achieved higher scores than younger children. Program may help to increase disclosures. Pretesting may not always be necessary to achieve reliable results.	Groups of children can learn appropriate self-protective responses. Older children achieve greater knowledge & skill level. BST alone & in combination with film significantly increased knowledge compared with controls. Some support for BST superiority for enhancing personal safety skills.	Training resulted in substantial improvement in self-protective skills. Skills generalized to novel suspects & locations. Booster sessions may be useful. Children did not respond differentially to types of lures. It is not necessary to provide rationale to obtain good results.

TABLE 15.1
(Continued)

	Fryer, Kraizer, & Miyoshi (1987a)	Poche, Yoder, & Miltenberger (1988)	Binder & McNiel (1987)
Design used	Pretest–posttest control group design.	Posttest-only control group design.	One group pretest–posttest design.
Subject characteristics	48 children. Grades K, 1, 2. Inner city school setting.	74 children. 29 Kindergarten, 45 1st grade. 33 girls, 41 boys. Age 5–7. 19 black, 55 white. Low, middle, & upper middle income.	46 boys, 42 girls. Ages 5–12. 60 parents, 12 teachers. Public elementary school from mixed socioeconomic background.
Therapist characteristics	Characteristics of training leaders not reported. Research assistants were trained in social work or child development and had experience with this age group. Social worker observed videotape for resulting negative effects.	Police officer dressed in street clothes served as trainer. Adults in video appeared similar to convicted kidnappers & molesters (black & white, ages 20–30, dressed casually). Observers were blind to experimental conditions.	Research assistants. No further details reported.
Dependent variables	Simulated stranger abduction test with pass/fail criteria. Peabody Picture Vocabulary Test. Harter Perceived Competence Scale. Children Need to Know Knowledge-Attitude Test.	Verbal and motor responses rated on 4-point scale.	Parent, child, and teacher questionnaires assessing knowledge of coping strategies & self-defense, and level of emotional distress (symptoms & behavioral change).
Intervention	Children Need to Know Personal Safety Training Program vs. delayed training control condition. 20 minute presentations for 8 days. Role-play-based instruction clarifying misconceptions about personal safety and establishing concrete rules and criteria for application of these rules.	Videotape with behavioral rehearsal, videotape only, a standard safety program & no training. Training conducted in classrooms. Posttraining conducted outdoors on a sidewalk near school. Follow-up took place outside near child's home. 20 minute video portraying possible abduction scene with child actor "saying no" and running to the teacher. Interactive video program.	Child Assault Prevention Project. Children, parents, & teachers received separate 2-hour workshop according to the Child Assault Prevention Project in this school-based program. Children taught through role play and guided discussion. Parents taught to identify myths and learned the content of the program.
Behavior vs. knowledge assessed	Behavior.	Behavior.	
Control groups used?	YES. Delayed training with no instruction.	YES. No training control group.	NO

482

Random assignment?	YES	YES	NO
Evaluate negative effects of program?	YES	NO	YES
Do they assess which components work?	NO	YES—Videotape Plus Rehearsal scores significantly higher than Videotape only condition scores, which were significantly higher than Standard or Control condition. No significant difference between Standard and No Training Group.	NO
Parental involvement?	NO	YES—arranged time when child would be outside near home.	YES. Rated children's behavior problems and emotional responses.
Is administration of program standardized (conform to protocol?)	YES. Videotaped and observed.	Videotape is standardized.	No information provided.
Assess previous exposure to prevention program?	No information provided.	No information provided.	YES
No initial measurement sensitization control group	No information provided.	No information provided.	No information provided.
Follow-up/generalization	See Fryer, Kraizer, & Miyoshi (1987b) for six-month follow-up report. Generalization—YES. This is a real life situation of material presented during training.	Follow-up one month post-training for 9 children who both ran away & verbally refused in post-training. Children maintained responses for a month with different setting & different abductor.	2–4 week posttest.
Authors' conclusions	Experimental group demonstrated clinically and statistically significant improvement compared to control group (47% control, & 21% experimental group accompanied stranger in simulation task). Traditional instrumentation with written or verbal responses are not helpful in assessing children's reaction to actual stranger's request.	Most children (age 5–7) who receive standard safety presentation from police are not prepared to respond safely. 20 minute video more effective than hour live presentation. Video plus behavioral rehearsal most effective. Better to teach a descriptive verbal criterion response that occasions a specific escape response. Self-protective skills can be taught without giving a rationale.	Program increases knowledge of coping with abuse. Children reported greater willingness to tell parents if ever abused. Parents and teachers did not generally notice negative emotional reactions. Program increased parents' confidence in their children's knowledge and self-protection abilities.

TABLE 15.1
(Continued)

	Kleemeier, Webb, Hazzard, & Pohl (1988)	Harvey, Forehand, Brown, & Holmes (1988)	Kolko, Moser, Litz, & Hughes (1987)
Design used	Pretest–posttest control group design.	Pretest–posttest control group design.	Pretest–posttest control group design.
Subject characteristics	45 female 3rd & 4th grade teachers. Mean age 41. Mean years of teaching experience 12.5.	71 kindergarten children. Age 5–6.6. Mixed ethnic group. Rural, low & lower-middle class.	349 children, 355 parents, 15 teachers. 3rd & 4th graders.
Therapist characteristics	Two psychologists with expertise in child sexual abuse. Child protective service workers.	College-educated, experienced child worker was blind to the experimental conditions conducted pre-, post-, and follow-up evaluations. Two college educated experienced experimenters conducted interventions.	3 adult community volunteers who participated in two 1½-hour training sessions.
Dependent variables	Teacher knowledge scale Teacher opinion scale Teacher vignette measure Teacher prevention behavior measure Workshop evaluation.	Ten picture presentations with questions assess differentiation between good & abusive touches. Five questions assess general knowledge about coping with abuse. Direct and Generalization test assess application of knowledge to specific situations.	Structured pre- and posttest questionnaires reflecting 4 domains of program impact (knowledge, personal opinions, planned/previous actions). Parent/teacher questionnaire.
Intervention	Teacher training vs teacher control condition. 6-hour training workshop including didactic presentations, videotapes, experimental exercises, role play, group discussion, and question & answer period with a child protective service worker.	Behavioral based program of skills training utilizing instruction, modeling, rehearsal & social reinforcement. Three ½ hour sessions in consecutive days in groups of 20 children at the school in both conditions.	Red Flag/Green Flag Program plus film vs. control group. Staff training, parent inservice & classroom training. Prevention included discussion, coloring book session, and viewing "Better Safe than Sorry Film." Three two-hour sessions.
Behavior vs. knowledge assessed	Knowledge and anticipated behavior.	Behavior and knowledge.	Knowledge and verbal skill.
Control groups used?	YES. Nontrained teachers.	YES. Read stories and viewed a film unrelated to sexual abuse.	YES. No training control group.

484

Random assignment?	YES (though demographic & experiential differences were observed between training & control groups).	YES	Not random selection but random assignment.
Evaluate negative effects of program?	NO	NO	NO
Do they assess which components work?	NO	NO	NO
Parental involvement?	NO	NO	YES. Provided information concerning the impact of the program on their children as well as their own knowledge about abuse.
Is administration of program standardized (conform protocol?)	No information provided.	No information provided.	No information provided.
Assess previous exposure to prevention program?	YES. 72% had at least one hour of prior sexual abuse education.	No information provided.	No information provided.
No initial measurement sensitization control group	No information provided.	No information provided.	No information provided.
Follow-up/generalization	6-week follow-up. Generalization limited since no male teachers were included in the study.	Three-week posttest. Seven-week follow-up. Assessed whether children could apply knowledge to scenarios that had not been presented during the training program.	At follow-up, only 2 children & 2 parent-report measures differentiated the two conditions.
Authors' conclusions	Outcome measures for sexual abuse training programs are presented. Clear changes in knowledge, opinion & anticipated behavior were observed in trained but not control teachers.	Intervention vs. control group demonstrated statistically significant greater knowledge of abuse prevention & performed better when asked to report how they would handle hypothetical scenes. Children as young as kindergarten can be taught skills to prevent abuse.	Experimental group had more knowledge about good/bad touch and parents reported being more willing to use prevention strategies. Longer exposure to a given program may be needed. Parent-training programs should be used with child programs and schools should offer booster sessions or follow-up training. Prevention program should be viewed with cautious optimism.

TABLE 15.1
(Continued)

	Conte, Rosen, Saperstein, & Shermack	Fryer, Kraizer, & Miyoshi (1987b)	Plummer (1984)
Design used	Pretest–posttest control group design.	Follow-up study of Fryer et al. (1987a). Quasi-experimental design employing two comparison groups randomly assigned.	One group pretest–posttest design. Preliminary study.
Subject characteristics	Ages 4–5 and 6–10. 24 boys, 16 girls. Primarily Caucasian.	30/44 experimental and control group children from Fryer et al. (1987a) study. Grades K, 1, 2 in an inner city school setting.	5th graders. 112 children participated in some aspect. 69 students in Prevention Program. Not randomly selected.
Therapist characteristics	Deputy trained in Sexual Abuse Prevention provided training. 4 second-year graduate students conducted assessment interviews. All but one was blind to treatment conditions.	Not reported but assumed to be similar to that of Fryer et al. (1987a).	Authors. No further information provided.
Dependent variables	Questionnaire assessing knowledge. # of correct responses assessed for abstract and explicit questions.	Simulated stranger abduction test with pass/fail criteria.	Questionnaire evaluating changes in group scores on knowledge, attitude and skills measures.
Intervention	One-hour training session on three consecutive days in groups with 20 children in a day-care setting. Teaches personal safety awareness, assertiveness training, practical self-protection skills, saying "NO" and "telling someone."	Children Need to Know Personal Safety Training Program. 20-minute presentation for 8 days. Role-play-based instruction clarifying misconceptions about personal safety and establishing concrete rules and criteria for application of these rules.	Teaches "touch continuum," definition of terms, facts about the problem, attitude, and skills to stop or prevent abuse. 3-day curriculum using visual aids, discussion, roleplay, coloring sheet, and film (no more secrets).
Behavior vs. knowledge assessed	Knowledge.	Behavior.	Knowledge & verbal skill.
Control groups used?	YES. Wait-list control group.	This is follow-up data of both the experimental & control group.	NO

486

Random assignment?	YES	Randomly assigned in original study.	Selection not random.
Evaluate negative effects of program?	NO	YES	NO
Do they assess which components work?	NO	NO	NO
Parental involvement?	NO	NO	NO
Is administration of program standardized (conform protocol?)	YES—They found that training was not conforming to training model.	YES. Videotaped and observed.	They report it is standardized but method of monitoring and assessing this are not reported.
Assess previous exposure to prevention program?	No information provided.	No information provided.	No information provided.
No initial measurement sensitization control group	No information provided.	No information provided.	YES
Follow-up/generalization	Posttest one week after training.	This follow-up report suggested that six months after program participation, retention of skills was total. Previously trained children seemed no less prepared than children who had just participated. Generalization—YES. This is a real-life simulation of material presented during training.	2-month and 8-month. Within 8 months & sometimes even 2, these concepts are forgotten by many 5th graders. Only one school & one grade level.
Authors' conclusions	Training should be monitored to ensure it conforms to model. Treatment group demonstrated statistically greater increases in knowledge than control group. Explicit concepts seem less difficult to learn than abstract concepts. Only 50% of concepts presented were actually learned by posttest.	In the absence of intervention, future safety based upon a single passed simulation cannot be assumed. A small percentage of children may not profit even from repeated exposure to prevention programming and individual attention may be needed.	Kids have little knowledge about what sexual abuse is, & unconfident of what to do if confronted. May give kids a false sense of security. Only 3 hours can significantly increase group learning. Training needed for acquaintance abuse, when to disobey adults & break promises, distinguishing sexual from physical abuse & emphasis that victim is not to blame.

TABLE 15.1
(Continued)

	Wall (1983)	Berrick (1988)	Borkin & Frank (1986)
Design used	One shot case study. Pilot project.	One group pretest–posttest design.	One-shot case study. Pilot project.
Subject characteristics	Kindergarten–5th grade. All classes.	116 parents of preschool children of various economic backgrounds in California. 19% attrition leaving 94 in final sample. 97% women, 31% single mothers, 30% black.	Preschool children (Ages 3, 4, 5). 100 children from one day-care center and three nursery schools.
Therapist characteristics	3 adults unknown to kids from Child Assault/Abuse Prevention Program team. No other information reported.	Not reported.	Two adults. Further information not reported.
Dependent variables	Student surveys, parent participant surveys, general parent survey, classroom teacher survey.	Interview schedule designed for the study to assess parent's perceptions of the prevalence of abuse, indicators of abuse, & services to report abuse.	Incorrect or correct recall of prevention "rules." Coloring book activity assesses retention of learned material.
Intervention	Child Assault/Abuse Prevention Program (CAPP) Single episode class presentation. Right to be "safe, strong & free." Teaches assertiveness & reporting abuse. 1 hour session for grade K–1. 2 hour session for grade 2–5. Observed role plays & guided group discussion. 1:1 discussions with staff optional. 1 hour workshop to parents & teacher to teach them content and how to deal with sexual abuse.	Parents' meetings providing education concerning the prevalence of abuse, indicators of abuse, and possible responses to abuse. Pretest interviews with parents in the schools. Posttest by telephone two to three weeks after child presentation.	The play "Bubbylonian Encounter." Puppet show teaching "rules of what children should do if inappropriate touching occurs. Indicates this can happen from strangers or someone you know well. Coloring book activity used to aid recall, assess, and reinforce material learned in puppet show.
Behavior vs. knowledge assessed	Knowledge.	Knowledge and assumptions of how they would act.	Knowledge.
Control groups used?	NO	NO	NO

488

Random assignment?	NO	NO. Participation was voluntary.	NO
Evaluate negative effects of program?	Collected teachers' opinions.	NO	NO
Do they assess which components work?	NO	NO	NO
Parental involvement?	YES. Parent workshop provided information about sexual abuse and parents completed survey regarding opinions about the program.	YES. Participated in workshop focused on raising standards of awareness. Information was provided on detection, intervention, reporting of abuse, and parenting skills.	YES. Parents completed brief evaluation of the program. Teacher/parent information session included discussion, detection, and reporting of abuse.
Is administration of program standardized (conform to protocol?)	No information provided.	No information provided.	No information provided.
Assess previous exposure to prevention program?	No information provided	No information provided.	No information provided.
No initial measurement sensitization control group	No information provided.	No information provided.	NO
Follow-up/generalization	NO	Posttest by telephone two to three weeks after child's presentation. Assessed across socioeconomic backgrounds but only in California.	4–6 weeks follow-up assessing retention of knowledge. Generalization not assessed.
Author's conclusions	CAPP is effective in raising awareness using short-term methods. Principal reported an increase in reports of abuse. Context & process seemed appropriate for this age level.	Parent education meetings appear to have little affect upon (1) parents' knowledge of the prevalence of sexual abuse, (2) indicators of abuse, or (3) parents' appropriate response to disclosures. Negligible effect of parent education as it is presently delivered. Few parents attended meetings, and those who did, learned very little.	3, 4, 5 year olds could attend to the puppet show but only 4 & 5 year olds remembered the "rules" 4–6 weeks later.

TABLE 15.1
(Continued)

	Garbarino (1987)	Wurtele & Miller-Perrin (1987)	Downer (1984)
Design used	One-shot case study.	One-group pretest-posttest design.	Quasi-experimental, time series design.
Subject characteristics	2nd, 4th, & 6th graders. Mixed but primarily middle class, well-educated. 36 boys, 37 girls.	26 kindergarten children. Lower-middle class. Predominantly white.	70 experimental children. 15 control subjects. 9–10-year-olds.
Therapist characteristics	Female undergraduate for girls. Male undergraduate and author for boys.	Trained undergraduates.	Trained evaluators.
Dependent variables	Self-reported fear responses	Fear Assessment Thermometer Scale. Parent Perception Questionnaire. Items from Eyberg Child Behavior Questionnaire. Global ratings.	Multiple Choice Knowledge Questionnaire and 20-minute interview.
Intervention	Comic book distributed at school. Optional reading.	Behavior Skills Training Program. Single session. Fifty-minute group presentation in school. Personal safety skills taught by instruction, modeling, rehearsal, social reinforcement, shaping and feedback.	"Talking about Touching" prevention program. Skills of discrimination, self-reliance, & assertion taught and discussed. Provides concrete ways to avoid/stop abuse, & provides a channel for reporting abuse. Also utilizes puppets, role-play & incomplete stories.
Behavior vs. knowledge assessed	Assessed comprehension of comic and fear or worry.	Assessed only negative side effects such as fear.	Knowledge.
Control groups used?	NO	NO	YES. Nontrained children.

Random assignment?	NO	NO	Not reported.
Evaluate negative effects of program?	YES, assesses worry or fear.	YES	NO
Do they assess which components work?	NO	NO	NO
Parental involvement?	NO	YES. Rated behavior problems in children and the negative effects of participation in the program.	NO
Is administration of program standardized (conform to protocol?)	NO	No information provided.	No information provided.
Assess previous exposure to prevention program?	Asked about whether anyone had ever spoken to them about sexual abuse before.	No information provided.	No information provided.
No initial measurement sensitization control group	No information provided.	No information provided.	No information provided.
Follow-up/generalization	NO	1-week.	3-week posttest.
Author's conclusions	Fear responses: 4th grade boys and girls: 50%. 2nd grade: boys 17%, girls 35%. 6th grade: boys 17%, girls 30%. It is important to assess long-term costs and benefits of such approaches.	Prevention programs can be implemented effectively in schools without harming children.	Significant differences between pre- & posttest and control vs. experimental group on safety knowledge, problem-solving ability & assertiveness skills. Assertiveness needs greater emphasis in prevention programs.

TABLE 15.1
(Continued)

	Miltenberger & Thiesse-Duffy (1988)	Miller-Perrin & Wurtele (1986)	Johnson (1987)
Design used	Multiple baseline across subjects.	Case study.	Case study.
Subject characteristics	24 children. 4–7 years old. Middle to upper class.	44 parents of children K–1, 5–6 who participated in prevention program. Rural, lower-middle class.	Grades K–6. Rural communities.
Therapist characteristics	Parents of children. Research assistant and experimenter. No further details reported.	Not applicable. Parents were mailed questionnaires.	Undergraduate theater and social work students.
Dependent variables	Picture discrimination task. Verbal scenario response task. Role-play procedure.	Parent Perception Questionnaire to assess harmful effects of participation in prevention program.	Questions and follow-up discussion only. No outcome measure.
Intervention	3 experimental conditions: Red Flag/Green Flag (RF/GF) prevention book with parents *vs.* (RF/GF) prevention plus instructions with parents, *vs.* 1:1 behavioral skills training with research assistant. Parents teach prevention using RF/GF book. This emphasizes saying no, getting away, & telling someone. 1:1 instruction in the home with research assistant, instructions, rehearsal, modeling, praise, & feedback used.	Not applicable. No training implemented. This study assesses parental perception of harmfulness of previous prevention program. See Wurtele, Saslawsky, Miller, Marre, & Britcher (1986) for review of prevention program used with children.	Children observe 40-minute play "Bubylonian Encounters." Teacher training program for identifying and supporting abused children.
Behavior vs. knowledge assessed	Knowledge & skills.	Assesses behavioral side-effects.	Neither.
Control groups used?	Compares three prevention conditions listed above.	NO	NO

492

Random assignment?	Parents not randomly selected but randomly assigned to conditions.	N/A	NO
Evaluate negative effects of program?	YES. Parent report identified no lasting effects.	YES	NO
Do they assess which components work?	YES	Assess specific aspects of side-effects.	NO
Parental involvement?	YES. Parents teach personal safety skills to their children. Also evaluate the negative effects of the program.	YES. Completed questionnaires to assess harmful effects of participation in prevention program.	NO. Invited to observe the play, however.
Is administration of program standardized (conform to protocol?)	No information provided.	N/A	No information provided.
Assess previous exposure to prevention program?	No information provided.	N/A	No information provided.
No initial measurement sensitization control group	No information provided.	N/A	No information provided.
Follow-up/generalization	2-month follow-up. Real-life probe. Child approached by assistant when alone in yard, store, etc. Study concerns only abuse by strangers.	Parents receive 1-week questionnaire postprevention training.	One-week follow-up discussion.
Authors' conclusions	RF/GF was not effective from untrained parents. Behavioral skills training program involving active rehearsal & reinforcement are necessary to acquire targeted skills. Maintenance of gains seen only in 6–7 yr. olds. No lasting side-effects or symptoms seen.	Relatively few negative changes in behavior observed by parents. Sexual abuse prevention programs can be effectively implemented in schools w/o harming children or disrupting the family system.	A successful prevention program depends on community acceptance, training for local teachers and follow-up discussion.

TABLE 15.1
(Continued)

	Stillwell, Lutzker, & Greene (1988)	Hazzard, Kleemeier, & Webb (1990)	Pohl & Hazzard (in press)
Design used	Single-subject design. Multiple baseline across behaviors. 3 replications.	Multiple treatment comparisons. No treatment or placebo control groups.	Descriptive examination of participants' subjective reactions to prevention curriculum.
Subject characteristics	4 preschool children. Ages 3–4. 3 female, 1 male. 3 white, 1 Hispanic. Chosen due to availability.	558 children from 11 schools. 54% 3rd grade. 46% 4th grade.	526 3rd and 4th graders. 50% female, 50% male.
Therapist characteristics	Graduate student observer.	8 lead teachers (similar to assistant principals). 16 regular classroom teachers. Most had previous education and experience in abuse and neglect situations. Not randomly selected—all volunteer.	Female mental health professional with expertise in child sexual abuse. Research assistant.
Dependent variables	Assess verbal responses to yes/no questions and behavioral demonstrations of target behavior.	Knowledge scale (What I know about touching), behavior analogue of prevention skills to a randomly selected group, subjective rating measure with 3 post-only questions, teacher feedback form.	Teacher questionnaire about the reaction of students to the classroom presentations. Parent questionnaire (posttest) What would you do? Structured interview following videotape measure given to randomly selected kids at posttest and follow-up. Silent question box.
Intervention	The Sexual Abuse Prevention Program for Preschoolers. Six sessions. 15–30-minute group presentation at a preschool program setting. Taught to identify different types of touch, saying "NO" and to tell others.	An adaptation of the Feeling Yes, Feeling No program. 3 one-hour sessions with 15-minute video, group discussions and role play. 3 conditions: regular classroom teacher, lead teacher, and child abuse expert consultants.	3 one-hour sessions using curriculum from the Feeling Yes, Feeling No Program. Includes video of potential abuse situation, roleplay, discussion, structured exercises, Spiderman comic book. Concepts taught included: your body belongs to you, how to recognize potentially dangerous situations, saying no and leaving, and telling adults.
Behavior vs. knowledge assessed	Assessed knowledge acquisition and behavioral demonstration.	Assessed knowledge gains and skills through a behavioral analogue measure.	Assessed subjective, emotional, and behavioral reactions to prevention curriculum.
Control groups used?	NO	NO	NO

Random assignment?	NO	NO	Randomly selected children from each classroom were interviewed.
Evaluate negative effects of program?	NO	Subjective rating measure. Children reported the degree to which they felt safe or worried.	Parents reported that children felt more safe and less worried after the program. Randomly chosen children were also interviewed about their reactions to the program. Teacher ratings obtained as well.
Do they assess which components work?	NO	NO	NO
Parental involvement?	NO	NO	YES. Evaluated behavioral and emotional effects of the program on their children.
Is administration of program standardized (conform to protocol?)	Reliability checked and lesson material read directly from prepared plans.	Videotape is standard across groups. Teachers receive detailed written curriculum but program may still vary.	No information provided.
Assess previous exposure to prevention program?	No information provided.	No information provided.	Questioned parents whether they had discussed personal safety issues with their children prior to this program. (74% said yes but provided little information about what was taught). Also questioned children during pretest.
No initial measurement sensitization control group	No information provided.	No information provided.	No information provided.
Follow-up/generalization	2- and 4-week follow-up.	No follow-up reported. Generalization may be limited since all teachers were volunteers. Also, teacher training was extensive (including observational learning) so results may not be found with less intensive training.	NO
Authors' conclusions	Verbal responses do not necessarily reflect the occurrence of actual behavioral responses when placed in a testing situation.	No significant difference in the impact of prevention programs presented by teacher vs. expert consultants. Equal knowledge and skills gains obtained in all 3 conditions.	This study examines participant reactions to the Hazzard et al. (1988) study. Conclusions: 90% of students felt more safe and less worried. Less than 5% of parents noted behavior indicative of anxiety. 69% felt program had a good overall effect and 31% thought it had no effect. 89% of teachers felt children had positive feelings about the program. Negative reactions were rare but a few children were embarrassed and had bad memories triggered.

TABLE 15.1
(Continued)

	Hazzard, Webb, Kleemeier, Angert, & Pohl Study I (in press)	Hazzard, Webb, Kleemeier, Angert, & Pohl Study II (in press)	Woods & Dean (1985)
Design used	Quasi-experimental nonequivalent control group design.	One-year follow-up, booster session compared to no booster session.	Prestest–posttest control group design.
Subject characteristics	399 children from 3rd & 4th grades. (286 treatment & 113 delayed treatment control).	103 4th and 5th graders previously used in Hazzard et al. (1988) study. 56% female, 44% male. Sample did not differ from original group in sex, grade or racial distribution.	4500 3rd thru 5th graders in East Tennessee.
Therapist characteristics	Female mental health professional with expertise in child sexual abuse. Research assistant.	Trained mental health professionals.	Not reported.
Dependent variables	What I know about Touching Scale (pre, post, and follow-up). State-Trait Anxiety Inventory for children (pre, post, and follow-up). Parent Questionnaire (posttest). What would you do? Videotape measure given to randomly selected kids at posttest and follow-up. Disclosure data and demographic information.	What I Know about Touching Knowledge Scale. "What Would You do?" video vignettes.	Questionnaire concerning knowledge about personal safety.
Intervention	3 one hour sessions using curriculum from the Feeling Yes, Feeling No Program. Includes video of potential abuse situation, roleplay, discussion, structured exercises, Spiderman comic book. Concepts taught include: your body belongs to you, how to recognize potentially dangerous situations, saying no and leaving, and telling adults.	A single 1-hour session booster shot intervention using video "Yes you can say no," group discussion, crossword puzzle reviewing concepts from original "Feeling Yes Feeling No" program, definition of sexual abuse, use of prevention skills, and concept that sexual abuse is never the child's fault.	Three-week personal safety instruction using Talking and Touching curriculum (this is a structured and active program in which skills are practiced). Group two was given safety edition of Spiderman comic book to read (this involved reading and was less directive and less structured). Two other groups learned solely by information shared by groups who received curriculum or comic book. 5 treatment conditions (talk about touching curriculum, Safety edition of Spiderman comic book, 2 groups to assess the amount of information shared by each group receiving personal safety information, 1 control group).
Behavior vs. knowledge assessed	Knowledge of prevention material and what to do in a potentially dangerous situation	Knowledge assessed through scaled inventory and video vignettes assess what	Knowledge.

Control groups used?	T.E.S. Delayed training control.		
Random assignment?	Not randomly chosen (volunteered) but matched and then randomly assigned.	Not randomly selected but randomly assigned to groups.	YES
Evaluate negative effects of program?	Parents reported that children felt more safe and less worried after the program. Randomly chosen children were also interviewed about their reactions to the program. Teacher ratings.	YES. Positive and negative reactions to unsafe scenes were assessed through interviewing the child.	¾ of children reported that they were not frightened or worried by any of the personal safety instructions.
Do they assess which components work?	NO	NO	Conducted an item analysis of each question in their questionnaire pre- and post-test to determine which concepts were learned and which were not.
Parental involvement?	Yes. Asked to evaluate negative effects of the program on their children.	NO	NO
Is administration of program standardized? (Conform to protocol?)	No information provided.	Video is standardized but other components are not.	No information provided.
Assess previous exposure to prevention program?	Questioned parents whether they had discussed personal safety issues with their children prior to this program. (74% said yes but provided little information about what was taught). Also questioned children during pretest.	YES. In previous study.	No information provided.
No initial measurement sensitization control group?	NO	NO	No information provided.
Follow-up/Generalization	6-week and 1-year follow-up (reported in Hazzard et al., Study 2).	This is a 1-year follow-up of the Hazzard et al. (1988) study. This study does not assess whether children actually can use increased knowledge and safety discrimination skills to prevent future abuse.	No follow-up reported.
Authors' conclusions	Treatment group had significantly greater knowledge and better discrimination between safe and unsafe situations on video measure. However, scores on prevention skills did not differ from controls at posttesting or at 6-week follow-up. No difference in treatment and control group on self-reported anxiety or parent's report of negative emotional/behavioral consequences. 3rd graders had significantly less knowledge than 4th graders during each testing.	Elementary children slightly increased their knowledge, and retained safety discrimination and prevention skills over a one year period. There were no declines in knowledge on any individual knowledge items. The booster shot did not affect children's knowledge or prevention skills scores. Children reported more angry and sad feelings after the booster shot.	Students who participated in personal safety class learned more than those reading the Spiderman comic. The information-sharing group assigned to the curriculum had significant increase in posttest knowledge. Little sharing of information detected with comic book group.

TABLE 15.1
(Continued)

	Nibert, Cooper, Ford, & Fitch (in press)	Nelson (1985)	Wurtele, Marrs, & Miller-Perrin, (1987)
Design used	Pretest–posttest control group design. Control group for only one site, however.	Post-test only control group design.	Random, matched, pre–post comparison of two treatments.
Subject characteristics	Site 1 contained 33 preschoolers. 15 girls, 18 boys. Ages 3–5. White middle class. Site 2 contained 83 children: 43 girls, 40 boys. Ages 4–5. Low-income Head Start class. 98% black. 42 control group children in site 2.	5th & 6th graders from 16 elementary schools. 330 in lecture/discussion group, 350 in video condition, 211 controls.	12 boys, 14 girls. Kindergarten. Lower to middle class. White.
Therapist characteristics	Two-member research team. No further information provided.	Trained adults in male/female teams. Videotaped presentation also.	Female graduate student led training. 8 male & female graduates & undergraduates, blind to experimental conditions conducted assessments.
Dependent variables	Verbal responses and choice of picture depicting behavior options.	Student knowledge form (criterion-referenced achievement test). 4 scales to assess attitude (self-acceptance, autonomy, internal & external control). Teacher feedback form.	Personal Safety Questionnaire. "What If" Situations Test.
Intervention	Child Assault Prevention (CAP) Project Preschool Model. CAP training. 3 days of 20-minute sessions. Training in assertiveness, physical resistance techniques, physically moving away from the situation, self-defense yells, and telling a trusted adult. Also included informal postworkshop discussions to review and bolster understanding.	You're in Charge Program. School presentation providing factual information through discussion and role play. 3 experimental conditions: lecture/discussion vs. videotaped presentation (mediated videotaped discussion) vs. control condition.	Participant modeling program (PM). Symbolic modeling program (SM). PM—taught self-protective skills through instruction, modeling, rehearsal, social reinforcement, shaping, and feedback. SM—same information as in PM but observe experimenter modeling behavior rather than actively rehearsing skills.
Behavior vs. knowledge assessed.	Knowledge was assessed through verbal responses and through having the child select the picture card that depicted the best response.	Knowledge.	Behavior and knowledge.
Control groups used?	YES. Delayed training control (only at site 2).	YES. Nontraining control.	NO

498

Random assignment?	NO. Existing classes were used. Randomly assigned at Site 2. Site 1 classes not randomly selected.	Not reported.	YES
Evaluate negative effects of program?	NO	NO	NO
Do they assess which components work?	NO	Questioned teachers on most important component but no experimental analysis.	Comparison of Participant & Symbolic modeling.
Parental involvement?	NO	NO	NO
Is administration of program standardized? (Conform to protocol?)	Yes, researchers strictly followed a script and gave only predetermined answers to avoid influencing the child's responding. Identical stories were used across children.	Videotape consistent across groups. Training guidelines were provided for presentations and roleplay.	YES
Assess previous exposure to prevention program?	All children from both sites had been previously exposed to abuse prevention information in classroom activities focusing on stranger avoidance.	No information provided.	No information provided.
No initial measurement sensitization control group	NO. However, control group also demonstrated statistically significant pretest-posttest improvement. This is attributed to pretesting and the reactive nature of the testing procedure.	No information provided.	No information provided.
Follow-up/Generalization	No significant differences were observed between middle and lower income families at pre- or posttest.	NO	6-week follow-up for PM group only.
Authors' conclusions	Many children know basic prevention concepts, especially for strangers, prior to training. Three to five year old children are able to recognize and verbally recommend basic prevention strategies in program-specific situations. Appropriate uses of physical responses as a defensive strategy should be contrasted with the unnecessary use of aggression and violence.	Both experimental conditions superior to control group. Video condition statistically better but of little practical value. Attitude measures correlate with knowledge. Program is effective regardless of socioeconomic level.	PM & SM are equally effective in increasing knowledge. Evidence for greater efficacy of PM for learning personal safety skills. This supports the inclusion of active rehearsal in prevention programs for young children.

TABLE 15.1
(Continued)

	Swan, Press, & Briggs (1985)	Wolfe, MacPherson, Blount, & Wolfe (1986)
Design used	Posttest only, control group design. Controls for sensitization by testing.	Quasi-experimental (posttest only) treatment-control group design.
Subject characteristics	30 boys, 33 girls. Grade 2–5, age 8–11. Catholic, urban school. 56 parents of children grade 1–6 who viewed the film. 225 mental health professionals and parents who viewed the film.	214 4th graders, 76 5th graders. Age 9–12. 143 boys, 147 girls. Middle & lower income.
Therapist characteristics	Adult professional actors from a children's theatrical company. Characteristics of discussion leader not reported.	7 medical students who consulted with child abuse specialists.
Dependent variables	Videotaped vignettes to assess ability to discriminate among positive, negative, and "forced sexual" touches. Pencil-and-paper test to determine recognition that (1) family members can abuse, (2) identification of appropriate self-protective responses, (3) general response to the play.	7-item true/false questionnaire.
Intervention	30 minute live performance of the play "Bubbylonian Encounter." Discussion following. Experimental conditions: pre-test–posttest condition vs. posttest-only condition.	Two 5-minute skits simulating physical & sexual abuse (both by a family member) and one hour discussion concerning description of possible misdeeds, child's feelings, possible actions, responsibility for threat & importance of telling right away. Conditions: Skit/discussion vs. control.

Category	Study 1	Study 2
Behavior vs. knowledge assessed	Knowledge. No participation required.	Knowledge.
Control groups used?	YES	YES. Delayed treatment control.
Random assignment?	YES	YES
Evaluate negative effects of program.	YES. 5% of parents thought it upset their children.	NO
Do they assess which components work?	NO	NO
Parental involvement?	YES. They rated their response to the play and reported whether negative effects were observed in their children.	NO
Is administration of program standardized (conform to protocol)	No information provided.	No information provided.
Assess previous exposure to prevention program?	No information provided.	No information provided.
No initial measurement sensitization control group	YES. No evidence that familiarity with vignettes promoted learning.	No information provided.
Follow-up/generalization	NO. Reported that training generalized to recognition that violent intrafamilial sexual abuse can occur, though only gentle familial abuse was presented.	Posttest 3–5 days after training.
Authors' conclusions	Children do learn to report abuse and learn that sexual touch can occur within the family. Reactions to the play were generally positive by children, parents, and mental health professionals. Age was unrelated to number of correct responses. No evidence suggesting that parents and kids will not be receptive to sexual abuse prevention education.	Brief exposure to inexpensive education program can lead to increase in knowledge of possible actions to take in event of potential or actual abuse. Children's belief that they might not be believed may discourage future disclosures, however.

501

low-up for children in grades kindergarten, one, five, and six. Overall, the results of these studies suggest that additional booster training sessions may be necessary to maintain long-term knowledge gains. The question as to the utility of that knowledge is an unresolved issue.

Does participation in prevention programs lead to acquisition of self-protection skills in children? Although it is necessary for a child to have knowledge concerning effective prevention responses and strategies, knowledge is not sufficient if the child lacks the skills to apply this knowledge successfully. It is unclear what method is most effective in teaching children these skills. Wurtele et al. (1986) advocated the use of a behavioral skills training package in which modeling, rehearsal, and feedback are used. This perspective is based upon Bandura's (1977) assertion that skill-enhancing approaches that emphasize actual performance should be more effective than approaches emphasizing symbolic modeling. A study by Wurtele, Marrs, and Miller-Perrin (1987) lends some empirical support to this notion. They found that participant modeling and symbolic modeling are equally effective in increasing knowledge concerning sexual abuse. However, there was evidence for greater efficacy of participant modeling for learning personal safety skills. The results of this study support the inclusion of active rehearsal in prevention programs for young children.

Skills training is an important component of many prevention programs. Many studies assess skill acquisition by asking children to anticipate how they will respond if an abusive situation arises (e.g., Berrick, 1988; Kleemeier, Webb, Hazzard, & Pohl, 1988; Saslawsky & Wurtele, 1986). Other studies require children to demonstrate verbally and behaviorally their responses in role-playing procedures (Miltenberger & Thiesse-Duffy, 1988). Some evidence suggests that children significantly increased abuse prevention skills as measured immediately postintervention and that these gains were maintained at follow-up sessions conducted 3 to 7 weeks (Harvey et al., 1988), and 3 months following training (Saslawsky & Wurtele, 1986). Miltenberger and Thiesse-Duffy (1988) found that gains were maintained at a 2-month follow-up in the 6–7 year-old children, but not in the 4–5-year-olds. Stilwell, Lutzker, and Greene (1988), however, found no improvements in behavioral scores despite statistically significant improvements in verbal responses. This study points to the importance of assessing actual skills in addition to verbal report because verbal responses do not necessarily reflect actual behavioral responses. Moreover, it should be noted that the index of skills acquisition and maintenance in these studies was based on an analog measure and there are well-known problems with the ecological validity of these measures (Bernstein & Nietzel, 1973).

Finally, even if children do possess the knowledge and skills that are necessary to prevent sexual abuse from occurring, what evidence exists that children will apply these in a real-life situation? The majority of research studies have failed to address this question. Simulated *in vivo* assessment procedures have been used in several studies to evaluate the effectiveness of various prevention programs. Fryer, Kraizer, and Miyoshi (1987a) found that 79% of the children who had completed training refused to accompany a stranger, compared with 53% of the children who had not received training. In a 6-month follow-up study, Fryer, Kraizer, and Miyoshi (1987b) found that retention of skills was total and that previously trained children were no less prepared to accompany a stranger than children who had just participated in the prevention program.

In a study employing a multiple baseline design across subjects, Poche, Brouwer, and Swearingen (1981) found that three preschool children successfully avoided lures from confederates posing as potential abusers following training and that the skills generalized to novel suspects and locations. During the 12-week follow-up assessment of two of the children, only one of them correctly performed the prevention skills. The second child performed the correct verbal response but failed to leave the vicinity of the suspect. Poche, Yoder, and Miltenberger (1988) found that children who had participated in a videotape program with behavioral rehearsal agreed to accompany a stranger with reduced frequency, compared with those who participated in a standard safety program. Three-fourths of the control children who had no training at all agreed to accompany the stranger.

The results of these studies have important implications. They suggest that some children can in fact acquire knowledge and skills and appropriately apply them in some situations. However, the results do not warrant great optimism in terms of the effectiveness of prevention programs. Although some children increase their ability and actually resist stranger solicitation after participation in sexual abuse prevention programs, Fryer et al. (1987a) found that 21% of those children who had participated in training did in fact agree to accompany the stranger. Poche et al. (1988) found that even in the most effective of three treatment conditions (videotape plus rehearsal), 25% of these children failed to resist a stranger successfully.

This brings us to the critical distinction between statistical and clinical significance. Although statistically significant results have been reported in many studies, few researchers have specified the extent to which the results were clinically or practically significant. A study by Conte et al. (1985) demonstrates the importance of this distinction. The author reports a statistically significant increase in knowledge from pretesting (28%) to posttesting (50%) between experimental and control subjects.

Yet, Conte correctly questions the clinical significance of these results in which children failed to learn 50% of the prevention concepts by posttesting. Similarly, although significantly more children refused to accompany a stranger after participating in the training program, Fryer et al. (1987b) concluded that some children failed the simulated task despite repeated training. He concludes that a small percentage of children may not profit even from repeated exposure to prevention programs and additional individual attention may be needed. Thus, it seems reasonable to question how much confidence we are willing to place in studies reporting statistically significant improvements and conclude that this provides practical evidence that prevention programs are effective in preventing abuse.

Unfortunately, most follow-up studies fail to assess the number of both successful and nonsuccessful attempted molestations following prevention training. Kolko et al. (1987) compared children who had participated in the Red Flag/Green Flag prevention (see Table 15.1) with no-training control subjects. In months following the training, children in each condition were equally likely to experience some form of inappropriate sexual touching. All of the children in the control group and the majority in the experimental group indicated that they had reported the abuse to an adult and this was confirmed by the parents. This finding must be interpreted with caution, due to the small number of children who reported being touched inappropriately. At 6-month follow-up, 20 children in the experimental conditions reported having been touched inappropriately since training, whereas no children in the control group reported abuse. This result may reflect differences in likelihood to report rather than actual differences in abusive experiences.

In summary, several conclusions can be drawn from this review of the empirical literature. First, there does not appear to be any evidence at this time that sexual abuse prevention programs actually reduce the incidence of abuse. There is evidence, however, that some prevention programs can lead to increases in knowledge and skills plausibly related to self-protection and that some children can in fact apply this knowledge and skill in a simulated seduction scene. What this line of research does not tell us, however, is the extent to which these prevention techniques are effective in a real-life situation. It is also uncertain whether the knowledge or skills that are presented in prevention programs are either necessary or sufficient to prevent, or at least reduce, the incidence of sexual abuse. An appeal is made to face validity of targeted information, rather than to actual knowledge that possession of this information is actually sufficient to prevent abuse. There is also little information concerning what percentage of children have the opportunity to use the prevention strategies, whether they do in fact use these, and what factors contribute to the actual success or failure of the child's resistance to abuse.

Potential Costs

There are several additional key questions that must be addressed to evaluate comprehensively the net utility of prevention programs. Although prevention programs may have the potential to be highly beneficial, several limitations in the empirical literature caution against the widespread application of these programs until more data are gathered. In other words, the assumption that "something is better than nothing" may not be warranted.

One issue of primary concern is the extent to which prevention programs lead to negative behavioral or emotional effects in children. Several empirical studies have directly addressed this question (Miller-Perrin & Wurtele, 1986; Pohl & Hazzard, in press; Wurtele, & Miller-Perrin, 1987), while other studies (e.g., Binder & McNiel, 1987; Garbarino, 1987; Miltenberger & Thiesse-Duffy, 1988; Swan, Press, & Briggs, 1985; Woods & Dean, 1985) have included brief evaluative components in their assessment. In general, the studies report that negative effects are minimal. However, some studies have indicated that some children experience adverse reactions following prevention programs. For example, in the study by Pohl and Hazzard (in press), less than 5% of the parents noted behavioral problems such as problems with sleeping or fear of men. Teachers reported that negative reactions were rare, although they did observe that some children demonstrated embarrassment about the body, and bad memories were apparently triggered for a few children. Miller-Perrin and Wurtele (1986) reported that the parents of younger children were more likely than parents of older children to indicate that their children experienced sleeping problems, fear of strangers, and changes in eating habits. The authors conclude that only 7% of the parents noted any of the negative side-effects listed here, and none of the parents reported that the prevention program had a net negative effect on their child. Garbarino (1987) found that a minimum of 17% of boys and girls in the second, fourth, and sixth grade reported that Spiderman comics (see Table 15.1) made them feel worried or frightened.

Although there may be an insignificant number of children who are negatively affected by prevention programs, this does not mean that no children are adversely affected. Even if only a limited number of children view the experience as negative, professionals need to be aware of this and have some plan of action concerning how to best detect and intervene with these children, or to modify the prevention programs to reduce these iatrogenic effects further. One problem with this line of research is that studies generally provide only minimal, if any, assessment of negative effects as reported by parents and teachers and these generally do not involve long-term follow-up. Another difficulty is that baseline assessment is frequently omitted, thus preventing the possibility of ruling out alternative explanations, such as premorbid difficulties that could also account for the results.

Sexual abuse prevention programs could possibly lead to negative effects upon children's relationships with adults. Anecdotal reports suggest that children may have difficulty distinguishing between obedience toward one's parents and teachers, and the right to refuse unreasonable requests. One issue that should be of great concern to prevention programmers is the possibility that children are often not capable of distinguishing appropriate from inappropriate touching. A child may have difficulty distinguishing what makes a physical examination from a physician different than being fondled by a parent. An important area of future study concerns the possible misapplication of skills and false accusations that are likely to occur. Since accusations of sexual abuse of children can carry strong legal sanctions and social stigmatization, researchers must assess whether there is an increase in unfounded accusations of abuse. It is important to determine the extent to which prevention programs increase disclosures and reporting of abuse, but it is also very important to evaluate the extent to which these skills have been misapplied.

Because most prevention programs encourage the disclosure of abuse, an observed increase in disclosures following a prevention program does not necessarily mean that it has failed to reduce the incidence of abuse. According to Finkelhor and Strapko (1987), a study by Beland (1986) found that schools that had implemented prevention programs doubled the amount of disclosures 1 year following the programs but no increases were observed in control schools, according to reports by principals, guidance counselors, and nurses. However, 35% of the schools with prevention programs did not receive any disclosures, and the average rate of disclosures in experimental schools was only two per year. According to an exit interview with the principal, Wall (1983) reported that the presentation elicited increased reports of assaults on children. However, in the absence of a control group or pretraining/posttraining evaluation, little confidence can be placed in this statement. Wall also reports that information concerning the accuracy of the reports was not available.

No studies to date have examined whether participation in a prevention program produces any negative interactions between children and their peers. One concern, however, is that prevention programs may have some lasting effects on children's later views concerning sexuality. Hazzard (1990) cautions that prevention programs should not give the children the impression that all sexual touches are negative. Plummer (1984) found that, prior to training, 15.9% of the children in her study reported that touching between people is never good. Unfortunately, 10% of the children still endorsed this even after the prevention program. Finkelhor and Strapko (1987) also suggest that children may draw implications about sexuality based on these programs and may feel guilty or confused if they have already had sexual experiences with peers (e.g., playing doctor). Long-term follow-up studies are required to assess the effects of sexual abuse prevention programs on adult sexual functioning.

Similarly, there is currently no empirical literature concerning the effects that sexual abuse prevention may have on children who have been previously abused. Empirical evidence is needed to determine how prevention programs affect these children and ways to decrease the likelihood of causing additional stress. This is a particularly relevant concern because it is plausible to assume that children simply cannot prevent all forms of sexual abuse. Children cannot prevent sudden abuse, such as being flashed by a stranger on the street, or being grabbed without warning. Even adults cannot be expected to learn sufficient skills to prevent all incidences of their own sexual abuse. At best adults can take precautions that decrease the likelihood of their victimization. The same applies for children. Thus, it might be important for prevention programs to give the message that even if children graduate from this program and are still abused, they are not responsible for this abuse and that their responsibility has in no way increased as a result of participation in the program.

An indirect potentially negative effect of prevention programs is that a false sense of security may arise in parents, professionals, and the children themselves. Several authors have cautioned against this (Plummer, 1984; Miller-Perrin & Wurtele, 1988). Binder and McNiel (1987) found that children reported feeling safer and more confident in their ability to protect themselves after training. However, these programs do not provide all children with the knowledge or skills to avoid an abusive situation successfully. Some children may lack the knowledge or skills to protect themselves, and others may simply be unable to defend themselves against an adult. It is also unclear whether prevention training actually provides children with the skills to avoid abuse when the situation is ambiguous, or threats, bribes, or other types of coercion are used. Once a child has completed a prevention program, some parents may overestimate the degree to which their children are now competent to protect themselves. This could potentially result in decreased communication between parents and their children concerning sexual abuse (although one study, Binder and McNiel, 1987, noted a significant increase in the amount that parents reported talking to their children about abuse after the program). However, in the absence of clear evidence that prevention programs do provide children with the knowledge and skills necessary to prevent abuse, despite a sense of security, children may continue to be at risk for victimization.

At present, there are no empirical studies assessing the effects of prevention programs on children who are abused by a family member or acquaintance. Relatively little emphasis in the literature has been placed on helping children protect themselves from someone they know. Do these programs protect children from abusive family situations and should there be a distinction drawn between how to protect yourself from a stranger, versus an acquaintance or family member? One might reasonably ask whether the strategy of "saying no, yelling for help, getting away, and telling someone until you are believed" would work as effectively with a child's father as it might with a stranger.

This brings up a related issue concerning the skills that children are taught in prevention programs. One potential cost of teaching children assertiveness and self-protection skills such as kicking someone, saying "no," and running away (Child Assault and Prevention Project, 1983; Binder & McNiel, 1987) is that this might lead to increased aggressiveness on the part of the perpetrator. Whereas sexual abuse involving physical violence is considered relatively rare (Finkelhor, 1982), one very serious potential implication of teaching children physical self-defensive maneuvers is that this may increase children's likelihood of being physically abused when the perpetrator is trying to overcome the child's defenses and gain cooperation. Physical defensiveness may not be desired, especially since most children are not physically capable of actually protecting themselves from an adult. It should be noted, however, that the use of physical skills, such as kicking, is not advocated by many programs.

Another potential negative effect of sexual abuse prevention programs concerns the parent's reactions to their child's participation. Many parents may feel uncomfortable and embarrassed with the topic of sexual abuse. Parents may become increasingly protective and possibly increase the child's anxiety concerning abuse.

Problematical Assumptions of Sexual Abuse Prevention Programs

One assumption that underlies all prevention programs is the belief that the potential benefits outweigh both the costs of participating and the costs of not participating. Although researchers have begun to assess negative effects resulting from such programs, there continues to be the view that prevention training is, on balance, beneficial until proven otherwise. As previously discussed, both benefits and costs exist and there is no definitive answer to this question. The problem arises when it is assumed that prevention programs are beneficial, when in fact it remains an open empirical question worthy of future research. It is also important to ask whether there are any costs that are sufficient to preclude the use of prevention programs.

It is often assumed that educating children in prevention strategies is of primary importance for a reduction of abuse to occur. Although this is one method, greater emphasis is generally placed upon the child's role in prevention, rather than upon other strategies, such as societal changes or greater emphasis concerning perpetrators. Although a combination of approaches may lead to the greatest reduction in actual abuse, it is crucial that children should not be placed in the ultimate position of responsibility to prevent abuse. Interventions aimed at modifying problematical aspects of adult sexuality and related matters (such as advertisements that promote a view of children as sex objects) should also be considered worthy targets for prevention programs.

Perhaps the most misleading assumption concerns the belief that children need to be trained to avoid sexual abuse from a stranger. Although many researchers seem to recognize that children are more frequently abused by a family member or acquaintance than by a stranger (Conte & Berliner, 1981) programs continue to place greater emphasis on prevention of abuse by a stranger. Despite a trend in prevention programs to address the issue of intrafamilial abuse, several of the studies continue to focus primarily, if not exclusively, on abuse by a stranger. As has been indicated, it is possible that different prevention strategies would be effective in protecting a child from a family member or acquaintance as opposed to a stranger. This does not mean that prevention strategies for stranger abuse should be eliminated from prevention programs. Rather, perhaps a proportional amount of time and emphasis should be allotted to teaching children how to cope with abuse that does not come from a stranger.

An early assumption in the literature was that children have the ability to distinguish what is, from what is not abuse. Programs with this assumption sometimes encouraged children to "trust their feeling" and assumed that children could prevent abuse by immediately and confidently knowing the difference between good touching and bad touching. There was also a tendency to believe that the abuse was always a bad experience for the children, when in fact sometimes it may feel good. For many children the experience may be confusing, and the progression from nurturance or playfulness to sexual abuse may be ambiguous and difficult to discriminate. Many sexual abuse prevention programs seem to have the implicit assumption that the modus operandi (i.e., the typical way of abusing a child) occurs quickly and would be obvious to the child. Conte et al. (1988) interviewed 20 perpetrators in an effort to gather preliminary information concerning the strategies that perpetrators used to identify, recruit, and maintain the child's compliance. He found that some offenders offered material enticements, and the majority engaged the child in some type of relationship prior to initiating sexual contact. Offenders also reported using adult authority and efforts to isolate the child, and the majority reported that they had not threatened the children. They also reported efforts to desensitize the children through the development of a relationship and a gradual progression from nonsexual to sexual touching. Due to the recognition that children may in fact have difficulty distinguishing an abusive from a nonabusive situation, there has been a trend away from teaching children to trust their feelings. Rather, increased emphasis has been placed upon teaching children concrete skills and decision rules to distinguish an abusive from a nonabusive experience (Wurtele et al., 1986, 1987). However, in general, future prevention programs need to be based on a more secure and complete understanding of the varieties of ways that abusers approach children. We need to have a much more thorough understanding of what the child may face when confronted with a potential abuser.

Another assumption is that schools are the appropriate place to teach children about sexual abuse. Due to the fact that schools reach the greatest amount of children and that programs can be implemented at a relatively low cost, there has been a natural tendency to implement programs in such settings. Other settings that have been suggested include the home, church, and day-care centers. However, many parents do not want their children to participate in prevention programs in the school and are unwilling to sign consent forms. Parents may have numerous reasons for not wanting their children to participate. Some parents may feel that the proper setting for discussing sex education and abuse prevention should be in the home. Parents may feel that sexual content is appropriately discussed in religious and moral terms and therefore public schools are inappropriate settings for such discussions.

However, a study by Finkelhor (1983) reported that only 29% of parents surveyed had talked to their children about sexual abuse directly, and an additional 31% of the parents reported that they had indirectly discussed the topic. Upon further questioning, however, the authors reported being skeptical of the quality of the instruction and the usefulness of the information. They reported that many of the conversations were primarily extensions of discussions about kidnaping and that discussions rarely included the fact that family members or friends could be abusers. However, it appears that prevention programs should assess what parents have been telling and will be telling their children about sexual abuse and sexual abuse prevention to avoid potentially contradictory and confusing messages.

In summary, many sexual abuse prevention programs appear to have many problematical assumptions. These include the assumption that the benefits of prevention programs outweigh the costs, that the child has the ability both to recognize and prevent the abuse from occurring, and that schools are the appropriate place to teach children about sexual abuse. Each of these awaits empirical verification or disconfirmation. The implicit assumption that primary emphasis needs to be placed on teaching children to resist solicitation from a stranger is particularly distressing, given the empirical evidence that abusers are generally known to the victim (Conte & Berliner, 1981). On the brighter side, recent trends in the literature suggest that these assumptions are now being questioned and that future prevention programs may be designed to address the limitations of earlier prevention programs.

CONCLUSIONS AND RECOMMENDATIONS

In order to prevent child sexual abuse effectively, empirical evidence is needed concerning the knowledge and skills that are both necessary and sufficient to prevent sexual victimization. Additional information is needed concerning the most effective methods of conveying this information to children in a manner that is developmentally appropriate and presents minimum risks for leading to negative emotional and behavioral reactions. We also need to improve our ability to identify high-risk children and methods of protecting them that are not stigmatizing. Furthermore it is important to determine ways to increase the likelihood that the children will successfully apply these skills in the real-life setting. Although *in vivo* assessments provide useful information, they may not represent actual strategies that offenders utilize in soliciting a victim (threats, bribes, etc.).

Because evidence suggests that the majority of sexual abuse is committed by a family member or someone familiar to the child, we propose that prevention programs need to place greater emphasis upon determining effective prevention strategies for situations in which an acquaintance is the offender. Additional empirical evidence is also needed to determine what strategies are most effective in warding off abuse by a stranger.

Future research should attempt to elucidate what prevention concepts were and were not useful for children who were actually approached by an offender after the training. Further clarification of the processes involved in children who are in fact abused despite participation in prevention training would be highly valuable. It will be of critical importance to improve assessment and be able to recognize and take the appropriate actions for children who have not benefited from training, or who experienced negative reactions as a result of it.

Given inevitable cost considerations, it may be useful to target high-risk children or to target these children and their families for more intensive primary prevention programs. Although admittedly the state of knowledge regarding what factors are risk factors is tentative and incomplete, Finkelhor and Baron (1986) suggest that the following factors increased a child's risk of being sexually abused: being female, being preadolescent, living apart from a natural father, having a mother who is employed outside the home, having a mother who is disabled or ill, witnessing conflict between parents, having a poor relationship with one parent, and living with a stepfather.

Preventative efforts with children have focused exclusively on the child as a potential victim. It is also appropriate for primary prevention programs to target the participants' current and future potential as abusers. This is particularly important for older children. Groth, Longo, and McFadin (1982) found that approximately 50% of 500 adult sexual offenders attempted or committed their first sexual offense by the age of 16. Thus, a more comprehensive primary prevention program with children should contain a component that attempts to decrease children's (especially high-risk groups, such as boys) potential to be abusers.

In Fig. 15.1 we present a depiction of what we call "The Child Sexual Abuse Prevention Network." This is an attempt to illustrate in a more complete manner the various points of intervention that a more comprehensive attempt at primary prevention would need to address. Although traditional programs aimed at teaching children skills to avoid or escape abuse should be a useful part of prevention, it appears that currently it is not a part of a more comprehensive effort. We suggest a consideration of a multifactorial approach, which does not place such a heavy responsibility on children but rather also focuses on changes that adults can make to have a positive impact on this problem.

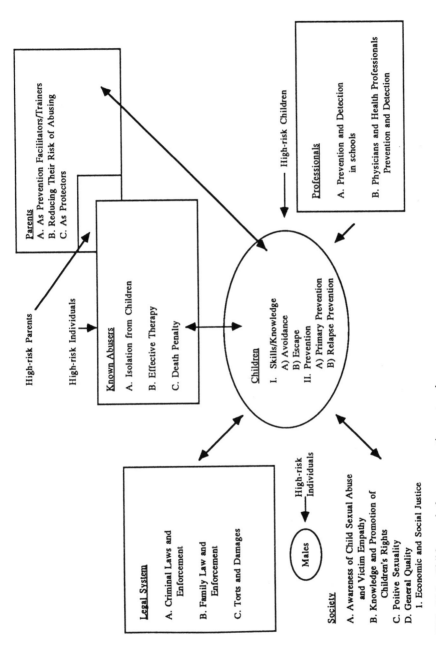

Parents
A. As Prevention Facilitators/Trainers
B. Reducing Their Risk of Abusing
C. As Protectors

Professionals
A. Prevention and Detection
   in schools
B. Physicians and Health Professionals
   Prevention and Detection

High-risk Children

High-risk Parents

High-risk Individuals

Known Abusers
A. Isolation from Children
B. Effective Therapy
C. Death Penalty

Children
I. Skills/Knowledge
    A) Avoidance
    B) Escape
II. Prevention
    A) Primary Prevention
    B) Relapse Prevention

Legal System
A. Criminal Laws and
   Enforcement
B. Family Law and
   Enforcement
C. Torts and Damages

High-risk
Individuals

Males

Society
A. Awareness of Child Sexual Abuse
   and Victim Empathy
B. Knowledge and Promotion of
   Children's Rights
C. Poitive Sexuality
D. General Quality
   1. Economic and Social Justice

FIG. 15.1   Child sexual abuse prevention network.

513

First, general societal changes should be considered. Would more general dissemination of information regarding child sexual abuse and empathy for the victim have a positive impact on preventing abuse? Are there general myths in society that this is a rare problem, perpetrated only by "dirty old men in parks," and victimizing only seductive "naughty" girls? If so, such myths need to be criticized and replaced. Would a more general delineation, appreciation, and promotion of children's rights have a positive impact? Would the promotion of a more positive, less exploitative and aggressive sexuality (especially for males) decrease incidences of child sexual abuse? Finally, would increases in the general quality of life in a society such as increases in economic and social justice contrive to reduce further incidents of child sexual abuse?

Linked to such societal changes, although more circumscribed, are preventative measures that may be taken in the legal system. What changes need to be made in criminal law and enforcement to reduce incidents of sexual abuse? Can changes in family law and in allied agencies, such as child protective services, reduce future incidences of child sexual abuse? Finally, would enabling children or their guardians to sue for civil damages have any impact as a general deterent?

The manner in which various professionals view and treat children and sexual abuse might also potentially impact primary preventative efforts. Should the detection of child sexual abuse be a more integral part of professional training? Should various professionals more routinely screen for this problem?

Should parents have an increased role in child sexual abuse preventative efforts? Would a prevention program aimed at high-risk parents be worthwhile? Should all parents receive increased training aimed at improving their abilities to protect and guide their children in this area?

Finally, should changes be made in the way known perpetrators are treated so that future incidences of child sexual abuse are decreased? Are perpetrators routinely receiving effective therapy? Are they being effectively isolated from children until requisite gains in therapy are made? If there are some child molesters who are incurable, what measures should be taken—life sentences? The death penalty?

Therefore, although we believe that the primary prevention of the sexual abuse of children is a praiseworthy goal, caution must be exercised in regard to current preventative efforts. Prevention programs aimed at teaching children relevant skills and knowledge are being adopted on a wide-scale basis despite the lack of evidence that these programs actually prevent sexual abuse. The (unintended) negative effects of these programs are unknown. Moreover, other plausible points of intervention are being virtually ignored and as a consequence too much of the burden of prevention is falling primarily on children.

REFERENCES

Bandura, A. (1977). *Social learning theory.* Englewood Cliffs, NJ: Prentice-Hall.

Beland, K. (1986). *Prevention of child sexual victimization: A school-based statewide prevention model.* Seattle: Committee for Children.

Bernstein, D. A., & Nietzel, M. T. (1973). Procedural variation in behavioral avoidance tests. *Journal of Consulting and Clinical Psychology, 41,* 165–174.

Berrick, J. D. (1988). Parental involvement in child abuse prevention training: What do they learn? *Child Abuse and Neglect, 12,* 543–553.

Binder, R. L., & McNiel, D. E. (1987). Evaluation of a school-based sexual abuse prevention program: Cognitive and emotional effects. *Child Abuse and Neglect, 11,* 497–506.

Borkin, J., & Frank, L. (1986). Sexual abuse prevention for pre-schoolers: A pilot program. *Child Welfare, LXV(1),* 75–82.

Browne, A., & Finkelhor, D. (1986). Impact of child sexual abuse: A review of the research. *Psychological Bulletin, 99,* 66–77.

Child Assault and Prevention Project. (1983). Strategies for Free Children. CAPP, Columbus, OH.

Conte, J. R., & Berliner, L. (1981). Sexual abuse of children: Implications for practice. *Social Casework, 62,* 601–606.

Conte, J., Rosen, C., Saperstein, L. (1986). An analysis of programs to prevent the sexual victimization of children. *Journal of Primary Prevention, 6(3),* 141–155.

Conte, J., Rosen, C., Saperstein, L., & Shermack, R. (1985). An evaluation of a program to prevent the sexual victimization of young children. *Child Abuse and Neglect, 9,* 319–328.

Cowen, E. L. (1983). Primary prevention in mental health: Past, present and future. In R. Felner, L. Moritsugu, & S. Farber (Eds.), *Preventive psychology: Theory, research and practice* (pp. 11–25). New York: Pergamon.

Daro, D., Duerr, J., & LeProhn, N. (1986). *Child assault prevention instruction: What works with preschoolers.* Chicago: National Committee for the Prevention of Child Abuse.

Downer, A. (1984). *Evaluation of Talking About Touching.* Seattle: Committee for Children.

Finkelhor, D. (1982). Sexual abuse: A sociological perspective. *Child Abuse and Neglect, 6,* 95–102.

Finkelhor, D. (1983, August). *What parents tell their children about child sexual abuse.* Paper prepared for the meeting of the American Psychological Association, Anaheim, CA.

Finkelhor, D. (1986). Prevention: A review of programs and research. In D. Finkelhor (Ed.), *A sourcebook on child sexual abuse* (pp. 224–254). Beverly Hills, CA: Sage.

Finkelhor, D. (1986). *A sourcebook on child sexual abuse.* Beverly Hills, CA: Sage.

Finkelhor, D., & Baron, L. (1986). High-risk children. In D. Finkelhor (Ed.), *A sourcebook on child sexual abuse* (pp. 60–88). Beverly Hills, CA: Sage.

Finkelhor, D., & Strapko, N. (1987). Sexual abuse prevention education: A review of evaluation studies. In D. Willis, E. Holder, & M. Rosenberg (Eds.), *Child abuse prevention.* New York: Wiley.

Freud, S. (1896/1957). *The aetiology of hysteria.* Standard Edition. London: Hogarth Press.

Fryer, G. E., Kraizer, S. K., & Miyoshi, T. (1987a). Measuring children's retention of skills to resist stranger abduction: use of the simulation technique. *Child Abuse and Neglect, 11,* 181–185.

Fryer, G. E., Kraizer, S. K., & Miyoshi, T. (1987b). Measuring actual reduction of risk to child abuse: A new approach. *Child Abuse and Neglect, 11,* 173–179.

Garbarino, J. (1987). Children's response to a sexual abuse prevention program: A study of the spiderman comic. *Child Abuse and Neglect, 11,* 143–148.

Groth, A. N., Longo, R. E., & McFadin, J. B. (1982). Undetected recidivism among rapists and child molesters. *Crime and Delinquency, 22,* 212–225.

Harvey, P., Forehand, R., Brown, C., & Holmes, T. (1988). The prevention of sexual abuse: Examination of the effectiveness of a program with kindergarten-age children. *Behavior Therapy, 19,* 429–435.

Hazzard, A. (1990). Child sexual abuse prevention. In R. Ammerman, & M. Hersen (Eds.), *Treatment of family violence—A source book.* New York: Wiley.

Hazzard, A., Kleemeier, C., & Webb, C. (1990). Teacher versus expert presentations of sexual abuse prevention programs. *Journal of Interpersonal Violence, 5,* 23–36.

Kleemeier, C., Webb, C., Hazzard, A., & Pohl, J. (1988). Child sexual abuse prevention: Evaluation of a teacher training model. *Child Abuse and Neglect, 12,* 555–561.

Kolko, D. J. (1988). Educational programs to promote awareness and prevention of child sexual victimization: A review and methodological critique. *Clinical Psychology Review, 8,* 195–209.

Kolko, D. J., Moser, J., Litz, J., & Hughes, J. (1987). Promoting awareness and prevention of child sexual victimization using the red flag/green flag program: An evaluation with follow-up. *Journal of Family Violence, 2*(1), 11–35.

Miller-Perrin, C. L., & Wurtele, S. K. (1986). *Harmful effects of school-based sexual abuse prevention programs? Reassure the parents.* Paper presented at the annual convention of the American Psychological Association, Washington, DC.

Miller-Perrin, C. L., & Wurtele, S. K. (1988). The child sexual abuse prevention movement: A critical analysis of primary and secondary approaches. *Clinical Psychology Review, 8,* 313–329.

Miltenberger, R. G., & Thiesse-Duffy, E. (1988). Evaluation of home-based programs for teaching personal safety skills to children. *Journal of Applied Behavior Analysis, 21,* 81–87.

Nelson, D. E. (1985). *An evaluation of the student outcomes and instructional characteristics of the "You're in Charge" program.* Unpublished manuscript, Utah State Office of Education, Salt Lake City.

Nibert, D., Cooper. S., Ford, J., & Fitch, L. K. (in press). An examination of young children's ability to learn abuse prevention strategies. *Response to the victimization of women and children, the Journal of the Center for Women's Policy Studies.*

O'Donohue, W. T., & Elliott, A. N. (1990). *The treatment of the sexually abused child: A review and treatment model.* Manuscript submitted for publication.

Plummer, C. (1984). *Preventing sexual abuse: What in-school programs teach children.* Kalamazoo, MI.

Poche, C., Brouwer, R., & Swearingen, M. (1981). Teaching self-protection to young children. *Journal of Applied Behavior Analysis, 14*(2), 169–176.

Poche, C., Yoder, P., & Miltenberger, R. (1988). Teaching self-protection to children using television techniques. *Journal of Applied Behavior Analysis, 21*(3), 253–261.

Pohl, J., & Hazzard, A. (in press). Reactions of children, parents, and teachers to child sexual abuse prevention programs. *Education.*

Saslawsky, D. A., & Wurtele, S. K. (1986). Educating children about sexual abuse: Implications for pediatric intervention and possible prevention. *Journal of Pediatric Psychology, 11*(2), 235–245.

Stilwell, S. L., Lutzker, J. R., & Greene, B. F. (1988). Evaluation of a sexual abuse prevention program for preschoolers. *Journal of Family Violence, 13*(4), 269–281.

Swan, H. L., Press, A. N., & Briggs, S. L. (1985). Child sexual abuse prevention: Does it work? *Child Welfare, LXIV*(4), 395–405.

Wall, H. R. (1983). *Child assault/abuse prevention project pilot program evaluation.* Mount Diablo Unified School District. 1936 Carlotta Drive, Concord, CA 94519 (1983).

Wolfe, D. A., MacPherson, T., Blount, R. L., Wolfe, V. (1986). Evaluation of a brief intervention for educating school children in awareness of physical and sexual abuse. *Child Abuse and Neglect, 10*(1), 85–92.

Woods, S. C., & Dean, K. S. (1985). *Evaluating sexual abuse prevention strategies.* Paper presented at the seventh National Conference on Child Abuse and Neglect, November 12, Chicago.

Wurtele, S., & Miller-Perrin, C. (1987). An evaluation of side effects associated with participation in a child sexual abuse prevention program. *Journal of School Health, 57*, 228–231.

Wurtele, S., Marrs, S., & Miller-Perrin, C. (1987). Practice makes perfect? The role of participant modeling in sexual abuse prevention programs. *Journal of Consulting and Clinical Psychology, 55*(4), 599–602.

Wurtele, S., Saslawsky, D., Miller, C., Marrs, S., & Britcher, J. (1986). Teaching personal safety skills for potential prevention of sexual abuse: A comparison of treatments. *Journal of Consulting and Clinical Psychology, 54*(5), 688–692.

Author Index

Subject Index